SECOND EDITION

D0225106

Earth Ethics

Introductory Readings on Animal Rights and Environmental Ethics

Edited by

JAMES P. STERBA

University of Notre Dame

PRENTICE HALL
UPPER SADDLE RIVER, NEW JERSEY 07458

Library of Congress Cataloging-in-Publication Data

Earth ethics: introductory readings on animal rights and
  environmental ethics / edited by James P. Sterba. —2nd ed.
      p.   cm.
    Includes bibliographical references and index.
    ISBN 0-13-014827-X
    1. Environmental ethics.   2. Animal rights.   I. Sterba, James P.
  GE42.E18   2000
  179'.1—dc21   99-33762

Editorial director: *Charlyce Jones Owen*
Acquisitions editor: *Karita France*
Editorial/production supervision: *Edie Riker*
Buyer: *Tricia Kenny*
Cover director: *Jayne Conte*
Cover Photo: *Ken Aerni/Stock Photography*
Marketing manager: *Ilse Wolfe*
Editorial assistant: *Jennifer Ackerman*

This book was set in 10/12 Bembo by East End Publishing Services, Inc.,
and was printed and bound by RR Donnelly & Sons Company. The cover was
printed by Phoenix Color Corp.

© 2000, 1995 by Prentice-Hall, Inc.
Upper Saddle River, New Jersey 07458

All rights reserved. No part of this book may be
reproduced, in any form or by any means,
without permission in writing from the publisher.

Printed in the United States of America

10   9   8   7   6   5   4   3   2   1

ISBN   0-13-014827-X

Prentice-Hall International (UK) Limited, *London*
Prentice-Hall of Australia Pty. Limited, *Sydney*
Prentice-Hall Canada Inc., *Toronto*
Prentice-Hall Hispanoamericana, S.A., *Mexico*
Prentice-Hall of India Private Limited, *New Delhi*
Prentice-Hall of Japan, Inc., *Tokyo*
Pearson Education Asia Pte. Ltd., *Singapore*
Editora Prentice-Hall do Brasil, Ltda., *Rio de Janeiro*

To all my nonhuman friends,
past and present

CONTENTS

PREFACE

Earth Ethics contains up-to-date readings reflecting opposing views on issues of both animal rights/animal liberation and environmental ethics. The anthology is large enough, but not too large, to cover in one semester, and the readings are interconnected and ordered for the pedagogically best presentation. One doesn't have to "slash and burn" through a larger anthology to determine what readings can be covered in a one semester course. All the readings have been class tested for accessibility. In addition, its introduction makes the arguments of the readings clearer and provides useful critical comment.

The second edition has been revised and updated throughout with seventeen new readings, including new challenges to ethical vegetarianism and environmental holism and new sections on Environmental Racism and on Western and non-Western Religious and Cultural Perspectives.

In putting together and revising this anthology, I have benefited from the advice and help of many people. Special thanks go to Eugene Hargrove, Max Oelschlaeger, Holmes Rolston III, Mark Sagoff, George Sessions, Laurence Simon, Karen Warren, and Laura Westra. Thanks also go to Karita France at Prentice Hall, Edie Riker of East End Publishing Services, and my wife and fellow philosopher, Janet Kourany. I would also like to thank Jennifer Welchman of University of Maryland, Baltimore Campus for the helpful review.

J.P.S.

ACKNOWLEDGMENTS

Selection 1. Reprinted from *Science*, Vol.155 (1967) by permission of the American Association for the Advancement of Science.

Selection 2. Reprinted from *Between the Species* by permission.

Selection 3. Reprinted from *Animal Liberation*, Revised Edition, by permission of Peter Singer.

Selection 4. Reprinted from *Animal Sacrifices* by permission of Temple University Press.

Selection 5. Reprinted from *Animal Liberation*, Revised Edition by permission of Peter Singer.

Selection 6. Reprinted from *Animal Sacrifices* by permission of Tom Regan and Peter Singer.

Selection 7. Reprinted from *Ethics* by permission of the University of Chicago Press and the author.

Selection 8. Printed here for the first time by permission of the author.

Selection 9. Reprinted from *Encounter* (London, February, 1972) by permission of the D.S. Stewart estate.

Selection 10. Reprinted from *Environmental Ethics* by permission of Paul Taylor.

Selection 11. Printed from *Problems of International Justice* by permission of Bernard Rollin.

Selection 12. From *Toward Unity Among Environmentalists* by Bryan Norton, Copyright (c) 1991 by Oxford University Press, Inc. Reprinted by permission.

Selection 13. Reprinted from *Eugene Hargrove: Foundations of Wildlife Protection Attitudes*. Inquiry 1987, Vol, 30, Nos 1-2, pp. 18-25, by permission of Scandinavian University Press.

Selection 14. Exerpted from *A Sand County almanac: And Sketches Here and There* by Aldo Leopold. Copyright 1949, 1977 by Oxford University Press, Inc. and from "Some Fundamentals of Conservation in the Southwest," *Environmental Ethics* (1979) by permission of Nina Leopold Bradley.

Selection 15. Reprinted from *Deep Ecology*, by permission of Gibbs Smith Publisher.

Selection 16. Reprinted from *Environmental History* with permission.

Selection 17. Reprinted from *Environmental Philosophy* edited by Elliot and Gare by permission of Mary Anne Warren.

Selection 18. Reprinted from *Environmental Ethics* by permission of James P. Sterba.

Selection 19. Reprinted from *Ecofeminism* by permission of Temple University Press.

Selection 20. Reprinted from *Environmental Ethics* by permission of Karen Warren.

Selection 21. Reprinted from Zimmerman et al., *Environmental Philosophy: From Animal Rights to Radical Ecology*, (c) 1993 pp.354-373 by permission of Prentice Hall, Upper Saddle River, NJ.

Selection 22. Reprinted from *Environment* Vol. 36 by permission of Heldref Publications.

Selection 23. Reprinted from *Environmental Ethics* by permission of the authors.

Selection 24. Reprinted from *Earth's Insights* by permission of the University of California Press.

Selection 25. Reprinted from *Buddhist Perspectives on the Ecocrisis* by permission of the Buddhist Publication Society

Selection 26. Reprinted from *Religion and environmental Crisis* by permission of the editor.

Selection 27. Reprinted from *Sustaining the Earth*, 3rd ed. by permission of Brooks/Cole Publishing.

Selection 28. Reprinted from *Science*, Vol. 260 (1993) by permission of the American Association for the Advancement of Science.

Selection 30. Reprinted from *BioScience* Vol. 35, No. 11. By permisson.

Selection 31. Reprinted from *Losing Strands in the Web of Life* by permission of the Worldwatch Institute.

Selection 33. Reprinted with permission from *Earth First: The Radical Environmental Journal* XI (1990) by permission.

Selection 34. Reprinted by permission of *The Progressive*, 409 East Main Street, Madison, WI 53703

Selection 35. Reprinted from *Earth Day Wall Street Action Handbook* by permission of Chaia Heller.

Selection 36. Reprinted from *Environmental Ethics* by permission of Eugene Hargrove.

Selection 37. Reprinted from *Atlantic Monthly* by permission of the author.

Selection 38. Reprinted from *Atlantic Monthly* by permission of the authors.

Selection 39. Reprinted from *Atlantic Monthly* by permission of the author.

Selection 40. Reprinted from *Ecological Economics* (1998) by permission of Elsevier Science.

I
INTRODUCTION

Each day on this planet, 35,000 people die of starvation; 26,000 of them are children, yet enough food is raised each year to feed not only the current human population of 5.2 billion but also the population of 6.1 billion expected by the year 2000.

Each day, 57 million tons of topsoil are lost to erosion. In the past 100 years, one-third of the topsoil on American farms has been stripped from the land.

Each day, there are 70 square miles more of desert. Already, one-third of the world's cropland is threatened by desertification.

Each day, there are 116 square miles less tropical forest—an area larger than Maine or Indiana.

Each day, between 10–100 species of life become extinct. Three-fourths of the 9,000 known bird species in the world are declining in numbers or are threatened with extinction.

Each day, at least 1.5 million tons of hazardous waste will be "disposed of" by being released into our air, water, and land, and Americans will throw away enough garbage to fill the Superdome in New Orleans two times.

Each day, 14 million chickens and 300,000 cows, pigs, and sheep are slaughtered in the United States alone, and 64 percent of the total U.S. grain crop is fed to livestock.[1]

These are just some of the environmental problems that we face each day. The question is what should we be doing about them? This anthology has been created to help you acquire some of the knowledge that you will need to answer this question from a moral perspective. The central question of earth ethics is: What does morality require with respect to the particular environmental problems that we face? To answer this question, you should first know what it means to take a moral approach to any practical problem.

THE ESSENTIAL FEATURES OF A MORAL APPROACH
TO PRACTICAL PROBLEMS

To begin with, a moral approach to practical problems must be distinguished from various nonmoral approaches. Nonmoral approaches to practical problems include the *legal approach* (what the law requires with respect to this practical problem), the *group-* or *self-interest* approach (what the group- or self-interest is of each of the parties affected by this problem), and the *scientific approach* (how this practical problem can best be accounted for or understood). To call these approaches nonmoral, of course, does not imply that they are immoral. All that is implied is that the requirements of these approaches may or may not accord with the requirements of morality.

What, then, essentially characterizes a moral approach to practical problems? I suggest that there are two essential features to such an approach:

1. The approach is prescriptive, that is, it issues in prescriptions, such as "do this" and "don't do that."
2. The approach's prescriptions are acceptable from the standpoint of everyone affected by them.

The first feature distinguishes a moral approach from scientific approach because a scientific approach is not prescriptive. The second feature distinguishes a moral approach from both a legal approach and a group- or self-interest approach because the prescriptions that accord best with the law or serve the interest of particular groups or individuals may not be acceptable from the standpoint of everyone affected by them.

Here the notion of "acceptable" means "ought to be accepted" or "is reasonable to accept" and not simply "could be accepted." Understood in this way, certain prescriptions may be acceptable even though they are not actually accepted by everyone affected by them. For example, a particular welfare program may be acceptable even though many people oppose it because it involves an increased tax burden. Likewise, certain prescriptions may be unacceptable even though they have been accepted by everyone affected by them. For example, it may be that most women have been socialized to accept prescriptions requiring them to fill certain social roles even though these prescriptions are unacceptable because they impose second-class status on them.

ALTERNATIVE MORAL APPROACHES
TO PRACTICAL PROBLEMS

Using the two essential features of a moral approach to practical problems, let us consider three principal alternative moral approaches to practical problems: a *utilitarian approach*, an *Aristotelian approach*, and a *Kantian approach*.[2] The basic principle of a utilitarian approach is

Do those actions that maximize the net utility or satisfaction of everyone affected by them.

A utilitarian approach qualifies as a moral approach because it is prescriptive and because it can be argued that its prescriptions are acceptable from the standpoint of everyone affected by them since they take the utility or satisfaction of all those individuals equally into account.

To illustrate, let's consider how this approach applies to the question of whether individual A should aid individual B when A's choice would have the following consequences:

	Individual A's Choice	
	Aid	*Don't Aid*
Net utility to A	4 units	8$^1/_2$ units
Net utility to B	2 units	-2 units
Total utility	6 units	6$^1/_2$ units

Given that these are all the consequences that are relevant to individual A's choice, a utilitarian approach favors A's not aiding B. Note that in this case, the choice favored by a utilitarian approach does not conflict with the self-interest of A, although it does conflict with the self-interest of B.

But are such calculations of utility possible? Admittedly, they can be difficult to make, but even large-scale calculations of utility seem to serve as a basis for public discussion. Once President Reagan, addressing a group of African-American business leaders, asked whether African-Americans were better off because of the Great Society programs, and although many disagreed with the answer he gave, no one found his question unanswerable.[3] Thus faced with the exigencies of measuring utility, a utilitarian approach simply counsels that we do our best to determine what maximizes net utility and act on the result.

The second approach to be considered is an Aristotelian approach. Its basic principle is

Do those actions that would further one's proper development.

This approach also qualifies as a moral approach because it is prescriptive and because it can be argued that its prescriptions are acceptable from the standpoint of everyone affected by them.

There are, however, different versions of this approach. According to some versions, each individual can determine his or her proper development through the use of reason. Other versions disagree. For example, many religious traditions rely on revelation as a guide to proper development. However, although an Aristotelian approach can take different forms, I want to focus on what is probably its philosophically most interesting form. That form specifies proper development in terms of virtuous activity and understands virtuous activity to preclude intentionally doing evil that good may come of it. In this form, an Aristotelian approach conflicts most radically with a utilitarian approach, which requires intentionally doing evil whenever a *greater* good would come of it.

The third approach to be considered is a Kantian approach. This approach has its origins in seventeenth- and eighteenth-century social contract theories, which tended to rely on actual contracts to specify moral requirements. However, actual contracts may or may not have been made, and, even if they were made, they may or may not have been moral or fair. This led Immanuel Kant to resort to hypothetical contracts to ground moral requirements. A difficulty with this approach is in determining under what conditions a hypothetical contract is fair and moral. Currently, the most favored Kantian approach, developed by John Rawls, is specified by the following basic principle

Do those actions that would unanimously be agreed to from the standpoint of individuals behind an imaginary veil of ignorance.[4]

This imaginary veil extends to most particular facts about individuals-anything that would bias choice or stand in the way of a unanimous agreement. Accordingly, the imaginary veil of ignorance would mask the knowledge of an individual's native or social assets, but not the knowledge of such general information as would be contained in political, social, economic, psychological, or biological theories. A Kantian approach qualifies as a moral approach because it is prescriptive and because it can be argued that its prescriptions would be acceptable from the standpoint of everyone affected by them since they would be agreed to from the standpoint of everyone affected by them from behind an imaginary veil of ignorance.

To illustrate the approach, let's return to the example of individual A and individual B used earlier. The choice facing individual A was the following:

	Individual A's Choice	
	Aid	*Don't Aid*
Net utility to A	4 units	8½ units
Net utility to B	2 units	-2 units
Total utility	6 units	6½ units

Given that these are all the consequences relevant to individual A's choice, a Kantian approach favors aid because from the standpoint of individuals behind an imaginary veil of ignorance one would have to consider that one might turn out to be individual B, and in that case, it would not be in one's interest to be so disadvantaged for the greater benefit of individual A. This resolution conflicts with the resolution favored by a utilitarian approach and the self-interest of A, but not with the self-interest of B.

ASSESSING ALTERNATIVE
MORAL APPROACHES

Needless to say, each of these moral approaches has its strengths and weaknesses. The main strength of a utilitarian approach is that once the relevant utilities are determined, there is an effective decision-making procedure that can be used to resolve all practical problems. After determining the relevant utilities, all that remains is to total the net utilities and choose the alternative with the highest net utility. The basic weakness of this approach, however, is that it does not give sufficient weight to the distribution of utility among the relevant parties. For example, consider a community whose members are equally divided between Those Privileged and Those Subordinated facing the following alternatives:

	Alternative A	*Alternative B*
Net utility to Those Privileged	5½ trillion units	4 trillion units
Net utility to Those Subordinated	1 trillion units	2 trillion units
Total utility	6½ trillion units	6 trillion units

Given that these are all the relevant utilities, a utilitarian approach favors Alternative A even though Alternative B provides a higher minimum payoff. And if the utility values for two alternatives were

	Alternative A	*Alternative B*
Net utility to Those Privileged	4 trillion	5 trillion
Net utility to Those Subordinated	2 trillion	1 trillion
Total utility	6 trillion	6 trillion

a utilitarian approach would be indifferent between the alternatives, despite the fact that Alternative A provides a higher minimum payoff. In this way, a utilitarian approach fails to take into account the distribution of utility among the relevant parties. All that matters for this approach is maximizing total utility, and the distribution of utility among the affected parties is taken into account only insofar as it contributes toward the attainment of that goal.

By contrast, the main strength of an Aristotelian approach in the form we are considering is that it limits the means that can be chosen in pursuit of good consequences. In particular, it absolutely prohibits intentionally doing evil that good may come of it. However, although some limit on the means available for the pursuit of good consequences seems desirable, the main weakness of this version of an Aristotelian approach is that the limit it imposes is too strong. Indeed, exceptions to this limit would seem to be justified whenever the evil to be done is

1. Trivial (e.g., stepping on someone's foot to get out of a crowded subway).
2. Easily repairable (e.g., lying to a temporarily depressed friend to keep her from committing suicide).
3. Sufficiently outweighed by the consequences of the action (e.g., shooting 1 of 200 civilian hostages to prevent in the only way possible the execution of all 200).

Still another weakness of this approach is that it lacks an effective decision-making procedure for resolving practical problems. Beyond imposing limits on the means that can be employed in the pursuit of good consequences, the advocates of this approach have not agreed on criteria for selecting among the available alternatives.

The main strength of a Kantian approach is that like an Aristotelian approach, it seeks to limit the means available for the pursuit of good consequences. However, unlike the version of the Aristotelian approach we considered, a Kantian approach does not impose an absolute limit on intentionally doing evil that good may come of it. Behind the veil of ignorance, it would surely be agreed that if the evil were trivial, easily repairable, or sufficiently outweighed by the consequences, there would be an adequate justification for permitting it. On the other hand, it would appear that the main weakness of a Kantian approach is that although it provides an effective decision-making procedure for resolving some practical problems, such as the problem of how to distribute income and wealth and the problem of distant peoples and future generations, it will not work for the problems of animal rights and environmental justice. For how are we to imagine animals and plants choosing behind the veil of ignorance?

But while it may be difficult, if not impossible, to imagine ourselves being animals and plants, it does seem possible to formulate a Kantian approach more generally so as to allow for the possibility that the interests of nonhuman could count. So formulated, the basic principle of a Kantian approach would be

Do those actions that are acceptable (i.e., ought to be accepted) from the standpoint of all those affected by them.

Given this formulation, actions would be acceptable from the standpoint of nonhumans if *human* advocates of the interests of nonhumans, acting reasonably, accepted such actions, just as actions would be acceptable from the standpoint of nonrational humans if human advocates of the interests of nonrational humans, acting reasonably, accepted such actions.

Yet while it is possible to formulate a Kantian approach to practical problems in a way that allows for possibility that the interests of nonhumans count, the questions to be considered are: Should they count? Should some count but not others? To what degree should they count, if any such count at all? In fact, most of the debate within earth ethics, whether it is focused on animal liberation/rights or more broadly on our obligations to the environment (environmental ethics), has been directed at just these questions.

JUDEO-CHRISTIAN PERSPECTIVES

If we look to Judeo-Christian sources to answer questions about who is to count, Lynn White Jr. argues (Selection 1) that we are apt to find an extreme anthropocentrism. In fact, White calls Christianity the "most anthropocentric religion the world has seen." By destroying pagan animism, he claims, Christianity made it possible to exploit nature with indifference as to the fate of natural objects. The Genesis creation story was also interpreted as giving humans the right to dominate nature. White argues that the only way we are going to avoid an ecological crisis is to give up this widely held interpretation of Christianity in favor of St. Francis's view that all living creatures are equal.

In Selection 2, Andrew Linzey is also critical of the general attitude of Christians toward nature, but he argues that the central Christian message of God's love embraces all of nature. Linzey points out that within a historically short period of time, 50 to 100 years, Christians came to change their view about slavery, and he thinks that the same could happen with regard to the view that Christians currently have of nature.

ANIMAL LIBERATION AND ANIMAL RIGHTS

Relatively recently, those raising questions about the moral status of nonhuman animals began to attract widespread public attention. Beginning with the 1973 publication of Peter Singer's article, "Animal Liberation," in the *New York Review of Books*, followed by the publication two years later of his book of the same title, people have become increasingly concerned with two of the most serious forms of animal exploitation: factory farming and animal experimentation.

In factory farming, millions of animals are raised in such a way that their short lives are dominated by pain and suffering. Veal calves are put in narrow stalls and tethered with a chain so that they cannot turn around, lie down comfortably, or groom themselves. They are fed a totally liquid diet to promote rapid weight gain, and they are given no water because thirsty animals eat more than those who drink water. Animal experimentation is also a big business, involving 60 to 100 million animals a year. Two experiments alone—the rabbit-blinding Draize eye test and the LD50 toxicity test designed to find the lethal dose for 50 percent of a sample of animals—cause the deaths of more than 5 million animals per year in the United States alone. The practices of factory farming and animal experimentation are discussed in detail in Selections 3 and 4.

In Selection 5, Peter Singer argues for the liberation of animals on utilitarian grounds by comparing the bias against animals, which he calls "speciesism," with biases against blacks and women. According to Singer, the grounds we have for opposing racism and sexism are also grounds for opposing speciesism because all forms of discrimination run counter to the principle of equal consideration. Racists violate this principle by giving greater weight to the interests of members of their own race in cases of conflict; sexists violate this principle by giving greater weight to the interests of members of their own sex in cases of conflict; and speciesists violate this principle by giving greater weight to the interests of members of their own species in cases of conflict.

Animals have interests, Singer maintains, because they have a capacity for suffering and enjoyment. According to the principle of equal consideration, there is no justification for regarding the pain animals feel as less important than the same amount of pain (or pleasure) humans feel. As for the practical requirements of this view, Singer contends that we cannot go astray if we give the same respect to the lives of animals that we give to the lives of humans at a similar mental level. In the end, Singer thinks, this will require us to make radical changes in our diet, the farming methods we use, experimental procedures in many fields of science, our approach to wildlife and to hunting, trapping and the wearing of furs, and areas of entertainment like circuses, rodeos and zoos.

Critics of Singer have argued that utilitarianism does not ultimately support a strong case for animal liberation for several reasons. First of all, by Singer's own omission, it is permissible to eat farm animals, typically cattle and sheep, that are reared and killed without suffering. Second, Singer's objection to the suffering inflicted on animals in factory farms can be overcome by reforming the practices used on such farms rather than by requiring us to become vegetarians. Third, a radical turn to vegetarianism would probably result in the elimination of most farm animals as we know them because they certainly cannot survive in the wild. This would also seriously disrupt and/or eliminate many industries and social practices, resulting in significant disutility.

Responding to these criticisms in an article in the *New York Review of Books*, Singer makes two points. First, he claims that adopting vegetarianism would improve people's general health, eliminate Third World poverty, and create new and beneficial industries and social practices. Second, Singer claims that in political campaigning, opposition to the current techniques of factory farming is not taken seriously unless one is also a committed vegetarian. According to Singer, only vegetarians can silence that invariable objection to reforming our treatment of animals: But don't you eat them?

Nevertheless, Singer's response turns on the political effectiveness of being a vegetarian and the effects vegetarianism would have on human welfare rather than its direct impact on animal welfare. However, it is in terms of its direct impact on animal welfare that the case for animal liberation must ultimately be made.

Another difficulty with Singer's view concerns whether in calculating what maximizes overall utility, qualitative differences between human and animal interests might not always lead us to favor human over animal interests. If that were the case, then, even though in theory nonhuman animals would count, they would not count in practice because their interests would always be outweighed by human interests.

To avoid this difficulty, Tom Regan, in Selection 6, adopts a different approach to defending animal liberation. According to Regan, what is fundamentally wrong with our treatment of nonhuman animals is that it implies that they are simply resources for our use. Regan begins by considering how the moral status of animals has been understood by people who deny that animals have rights.

Regan first considers the view that all of our duties toward animals are indirect, ultimately grounded in duties to other human beings. This view holds that animals do not have an independent moral status. Regan argues that this view cannot be supported on the grounds that animals feel no pain or that only human pain matters. Nor can this view be supported, Regan argues, on the basis of contractarianism because contractarianism is inadequate even in accounting for the moral status of human beings.

Regan next considers the view that we do have direct duties toward animals but that these duties do not support animal rights. According to this view, animals do have an independent moral status, but that status falls short of having rights. On one interpretation of this view, we have direct duties to be kind and not cruel to animals but nothing more. Regan argues, however, that this interpretation does not suffice for an account of right action. On another interpretation of this view, our duties toward animals are simply a consequence of what maximizes overall utility. But, as noted previously, Regan believes that the aggregative requirement of utilitarianism will lead us to act unjustly and at least sometimes ignore animal rights. The correct grounding for our duties to animals and their rights against us, Regan argues, is their inherent value, which they possess, equally with ourselves as experiencing subjects of life. Because animals, who are experiencing subjects of life, are entitled to equal respect, Regan argues that we should totally abolish the use of animals in science, end commerical animal agriculture and eliminate both commerical and sport hunting and trapping. To those who might concede that animals have inherent value but to a lesser degree than humans, Regan argues that this view would only be defensible if similarly deficient humans were also seen as having less inherent value—a stance Regan feels his opponents are not willing to take.

One obvious difficulty with Regan's view is its absolutist character. According to Regan, it is always wrong to sacrifice a few animals, or even just one animal, to save the lives of countless others, even if this were the only way to develop a general cure for cancer, for example. However, it is difficult to see why such absolutism is needed to ground animal rights, for surely it is possible to reject utilitarianism without endorsing absolutism. In fact, this is just the way we earlier interpreted a Kantian approach to practical problems.

Another difficulty with Regan's view is that it is not clear why only *experiencing* subjects of life have inherent value and not all subjects of life. This particular challenge to Regan's view is taken up by Paul Taylor in Selection 10.

In Selection 7, Dale Jamieson argues that Regan's view faces another difficulty. Regan wants to recognize a duty to render assistance, but not a duty to protect animals from their predators. Jameson argues, however, that Regan has no defensible basis for drawing this distinction and that the most plausible revisions of his theory lead him back in the direction of utilitarianism. But utilitarianism itself of the sort endorsed by Singer also has the difficulty explaining why we do not have a duty to protect animals from their predators if doing so would maximize utility.[5]

Kathryn George, in Selection 8, argues that the ethical vegetarianism endorsed by Singer and Regan is partial to adult males and to people living in developed countries rather than to those living in developing or underdeveloped countries. This is because for people not living in developed countries, ethical vegetarianism is so burdensome that they are exempt from its requirements. But if most people are exempt from the requirements of ethical vegetarianism, in what sense is it an ideal? George argues that it is not. She further argues that the way diets are supplemented in developed countries by fortifying foods so as to make it easier to be a vegetarian are not part of a sustainable food production. So they cannot serve as a way of making vegetarianism morally required for more people. What is morally required, according to George, is semi-vegetarianism, with moderate continued food fortification and preservation.

Desmond Stewart's short story, in Selection 9, suggests that the ways we currently treat animals are far from moral, unless we are willing to concede the "morality" of more powerful beings doing to us what we currently are doing to other animals. In Stewart's short story, invading Troogs acquire a taste for eating human flesh, hunting human animals, and raising human pets. The implication of the story is that what the Troogs are doing is wrong, but then how can it be wrong given that it closely parallels what we are doing to other animals? (In the story the Troogs even acquire their new practices by imitating us!)

It is important to note that the force of Stewart's argument by analogy does not depend on there actually being an invasion of Trooglike creatures. The argument has the form: If what we are doing to animals is justified, then what the Troogs are depicted as doing to humans *would be* justified as well, or if what the Troogs are depicted as doing to humans *would not be justified*, then what we are doing to animals is not justified. This is a powerful argument that can only be undercut if there are relevant differences between ourselves and other animals that would justify our treatment of them, and the absence of relevant differences between ourselves and Trooglike creatures that would justify their treatment of us.

RESPECT FOR NATURE

In Selection 10, Paul W. Taylor presents the following argument:

(1) Humans are members of the earth's community of life.
(2) All living things are related to one another in an order of interdependence.
(3) Each organism is a teleological center of life.
(4) The assertion of human superiority is groundless.
(5) Therefore, we should recognize the equal inherent worth of every living being.

Given the general acceptability of the premises (1–3), Taylor devotes most of his time to arguing for (4) on the grounds that we have no nonquestion-begging reason for maintaining human superiority in the sense that it would justify our domination of other living beings.

The main difficulty with Taylor's argument concerns how we are to weigh human welfare against the welfare of other living beings once we grant that human beings are not superior to other species. In a later book that develops the argument of this essay, Taylor distinguishes between basic and nonbasic interests of living beings, but because he doesn't hold that the basic interests always have priority over nonbasic interests, it is difficult to know how decisions are to be made when there is conflict between human and nonhuman interests.

In opposition to Taylor, Bernard E. Rollin, in Selection 11, argues that only sentient beings have independent moral status. According to Rollin, the grounds for that status is that what we do to such beings matters to them. But while denying that other living things such as forests, plants, and ecosystems have any independent moral status, Rollin contends that they still have instrumental value which in some cases is enormous. For that reason, he thinks that the argument against their destruction can be extremely strong.

But why should we agree with Rollin that the fact that what we do to sentient beings matters to them supports the view that sentient beings have independent moral status, and not agree with Taylor that the fact that each individual organism is a teleological center of life, pursuing its own good in its own way, supports the view that all living things have independent moral status? Of course, we wouldn't need to answer this question if the instrumental value of nonsentient living beings were so great that in valuing them instrumentally, we would be required to treat them just as if they had independent moral status. But how can we expect that this coincidence of interest will always obtain?

In Selection 12, Bryan Norton begins by helpfully distinguishing between three generations of environmental problems that have been recognized over the past century. The first generation of problems concerns wise use of resources and protection of spectacular natural monuments. The second generation of problems focuses on pollution and destruction of natural environments through thoughtless land development.

The third and current generation of environmental problems concerns the possibility of cataclysmic loss due to ozone depletion, the greenhouse effect, and acid rain. A distinctive feature of this third generation of environmental problems is that their costs impact most significantly on future generations.

Norton goes on to argue that all the environmental problems that we face can be adequately dealt with from an anthropocentric or human-centered perspective provided that we take future generations of humans into account. To take future generations into account, Norton proposes to employ a Rawlsian veil of ignorance between generations of humans. Norton argues that humans, choosing in imagined ignorance of the generation to which they belong, would choose to impose the appropriate constraints on the use of resources to avoid cataclysmic loss to future generations.

But who would actually lose if we continue to destroy our natural environment? If we continue our destructive practices, different humans will be born then if we were to restrain those practices. (Any significant change in our social practices will impact on who will be conceived and born in the future.) And most of those who would be born, if we were to continue our destructive practices, could not claim to be thereby made worse off, because if we had restrained our destructive practices, they would not have been born at all!

Why then should we restrain our destructive practices? Norton's answer is that such restraint would benefit the *class* of future human beings, and he thinks this proposed justification involves a rejection of individualism. But we could also say that such restraint will benefit individual future human beings more than any alternative action open to us since we would be providing future human individuals not only with life, but with, as far as it is possible to us, a good life. So interpreted, our actions need not involve a rejection of individualism. Of course, it is still possible to criticize such an anthropocentric approach for failing to ascribe any intrinsic value to nonhuman living beings.

In Selection 13, Eugene Hargrove argues that the interest of landscape artists and naturalists in wildlife has primarily been directed at species rather than at individual members of those species. He further argues that this way of valuing wildlife is anthropocentric, but it need not limit us to valuing wildlife only instrumentally. Just as we can find anthropocentric but (aesthetic) intrinsic value in works of art, both in the art objects themselves and in our experience of them, so Hargrove contends we can also find anthropocentric but aesthetic intrinsic value in wildlife, particularly in species and ecosystems and in our experience of them. Hargrove thinks that valuing wildlife in these ways is sufficient to justify protecting it. Accordingly, he denies that we need to postulate that wildlife has nonanthropocentric value in order to justify its protection.

While Hargrove may be right that recognizing the (aesthetic) intrinsic value in wildlife will go a long way toward justifying its protection, there does appear to be another sense of intrinsic value that we employ in human ethics that may also have application to wildlife. It is the way we intrinsically value individual human beings. Thus, we say that individual human beings are intrinsically valuable in the sense that their good ought to constrain the ways that we can use them. It is this sense of value that Kantians are referring to when they claim that people should never be used as means only, and it differs from valuing things aesthetically. Given this different sense of intrinsic value, why can't we ascribe value of this sort to nonhuman living beings on the grounds that they are either experiencing subjects of life or sentient beings or have a good of their own? Moreover, if wildlife have intrinsic value of this sort, it would be nonanthropocentric in the sense that it is grounded directly in the good of wildlife and not in the good of humans.

THE LAND ETHIC/DEEP ECOLOGY

It turns out that much of the contemporary work in earth ethics is traceable to Aldo Leopold's attempt to defend a nonanthropocentric environmental ethic in *The Sand County Almanac*. In Selection 14, Leopold argues that "A thing is right when it tends to preserve the integrity, stability and beauty of the biotic community. It is wrong when it tends otherwise." In Leopold's view, adherence to this "land ethic" results in a change of human self-perception; we will cease to see ourselves as conquerors or as members of a superior species on the planet, but rather see ourselves as plain members and participating citizens of the land community. To achieve this new perception, we will need to "think like a mountain." Thinking like a mountain may involve seeing all living beings as part of one organism, as Leopold suggests in an earlier article, excerpted here, or it may involve seeing all living beings as part of a biotic community, as Leopold proposes in the selection from *The Sand County Almanac*. In either case, it involves thinking about all living beings in a holistic manner as members of species and parts of ecosystems.

Deep ecology is a more recent environmental philosophy which sees itself as a development of Leopold's land ethic. The term "deep ecology" was coined in 1974 by Arne Naess, a Norwegian philosopher, to contrast with the notion of shallow ecology, which includes all superficial, short-term reform approaches to solving such environmental problems as pollution and resource depletion. Deep ecology requires an intensive questioning of the values and lifestyles that originally led to our serious environmental problems. According to Bill Devall and George Sessions, in Selection 15, deep ecology advocates two ultimate norms: self-realization and biocentric equality. These two norms, however, are closely interconnected since the identification with nature required by the norm of self-realization leads naturally to the respect for nature required by the norm of biocentric equality; the good of each individual becomes identical with the good of the whole.

In Selection 16, Donald Worster points out that early models of ecology such as those endorsed by Aldo Leopold, George Sessions, and Bill Devall supported a view of ecosystems as stable and harmonious. For many environmentalists, this view implies that we should maintain or return ecosytems in just such a state. However, Worster claims that in more recent decades a more chaotic model of nature has prevailed in ecology. He wonders what implications this change in the prevailing model of ecology will have for the environmentalist's concern for nature.

RECONCILIATION AND DEFENSE

Can the gap between individualists and holists be bridged? Mary Ann Warren thinks that it can. In Selection 17, Warren argues that the gap can be bridged provided individualists and holists are each willing to make certain concessions. Specifically, animal liberationists must allow that human beings have stronger rights than the rights nonhuman animals have, and defenders of a land ethic or deep ecology must allow that although nonsentient living things do have intrinsic value, they do not have rights. Given these concessions, Warren claims that the lesser rights of nonhuman animals and the absence of rights in nonsentient living beings would permit them to be sacrificed for the good of the whole, whereas the stronger rights of human beings would prohibit similarly sacrificing them for the good of the whole. This, Warren thinks, would represent an acceptable bridging of the gap between individualists and holists.

In Selection 18, I note that biocentrists, whether they are individuals or holists, are criticized (1) for failing to state their view in such a way that it is not biased in favor of the human species, (2) for following Aldo Leopold and basing their view on an ecology that regards ecosystems as tending toward stability and harmony—an ecology that is now widely challenged, (3) for failing to reasonably distinguish the life that they claim has intrinsic value from the animate and inanimate things that they claim lack intrinsic value. In this selection, I show how biocentrism can meet these three criticisms by developing a set of environmental principles that (1) are clearly not biased in favor of human species, (2) can adjust to changes in ecological science and (3) can reasonably distinguish what has intrinsic value from what doesn't.

ECOLOGICAL FEMINISM

Ecological feminism raises an important challenge to the mainstream earth ethics that we have so far considered. The challenge is that mainstream earth ethics has failed to recognize that the domination of nature is rooted in the domination of women, or at least has failed to recognize that both these forms of domination are interconnected.

In Selection 19, Marti Kheel argues that throughout Western civilization, there have been two controlling images of nature: the image of nature as a (threatening) Beast and the image of nature as mindless matter. Behind both images, Kheel claims, lies a single theme—the notion of nature as *other* conceived in opposition to a *masculine* autonomous self. In the image of nature as a Beast, nature is to be conquered by force. In the image of nature as mindless matter, nature is to be dominated by reason.

By contrast, Kheel claims, much of mainstream earth ethics (which she calls "nature ethics") has been conceived not to dominate nature but to protect it by constraining aggressive or self-interested human conduct toward nature. But why are humans conceived to be aggressive and self-interested in the first place? Isn't this a conception, Kheel suggests, of how men, not women, are in patriarchal society? According to Kheel, even deep ecology or ecophilosophy, which seeks to transform consciousness toward all of life to discover our identity with all life, has its problems. For example, she criticizes Leopold, an intellectual founder of the view, for glorifying the killing of animals for sport.

Kheel suggests that a better way of viewing nature is as a community of living beings with instincts, desires, and interests of their own. In accord with this image, Kheel claims that we need to see and experience nature firsthand and what we are doing to it (e.g., factory farming) and then we will know better what to do. According to Kheel, "We should not kill, eat, torture and exploit animals because they do not want to be so treated, and we know that. If we listen we can hear them."

In Selection 20, Karen Warren claims that at least within the dominant Western culture, the following argument is sanctioned

(1) Women are identified with nature and the realm of the physical; men are identified with the "human" and the realm of the mental. (For example, naturist language describes women as cows, foxes, chicks, serpents, bitches, beavers, old bats, pussycats, cats, bird-brains, harebrains. Sexist language feminizes and sexualizes Nature: Nature is raped, mastered, conquered, controlled, mined. Her "secrets" are "penetrated" and her "womb" is put into the services of the "man

of science." "Virgin timber" is felled, cut down. "Fertile soil" is tilled and land that lies "fallow" is "barren," useless.)

(2) Whatever is identified with nature and the realm of the physical is inferior to whatever is identified with the "human" and the realm of the mental; or, conversely, the latter is superior to the former.

(3) Thus, women are inferior to men; or, conversely, men are superior to women.

(4) For any X and Y, if X is superior to Y, then X is justified in subordinating Y.

(5) Thus, men are justified in subordinating women.

Warren points out that there is a "logic of domination" to this argument. It begins with a *claim of difference*. It then moves from a claim of difference to a *claim of superiority* and then from a claim of superiority to a *claim of subordination or domination*. Warren contends that this same logic of domination is common to all forms of domination and so is used to support, for example, racism, classism, ageism as well as sexism and naturism (Warren's term for the domination of nature). If Warren is correct, it follows that if one is against any one of these forms of domination, one should be against them all.

SOCIAL ECOLOGY AND ENVIRONMENTAL RACISM

According to Murray Bookchin, in Selection 21, what is distinctive about social ecology is its recognition that nearly all our present environmental problems are rooted in a deep-seated social problem, specifically in the hierarchical and class structure of our societies. If we are to solve these environmental problems, Bookchin contends, we must restructure our societies without hierarchies and without classes. Bookchin is also critical of certain trends that he perceives in deep ecology and in ecological feminism. He criticizes deep ecologists for attempting to reduce our ecological crisis to a cultural rather than a social problem that can be solved simply by changing our thinking and identifying with nature. He also criticizes ecological feminists for contending that

> all the evils in the world stem from a monolithic "patriarchy"... or that hierarchy will wither away once women or putative "female values" replace "male supremacy" and its "male values."[6]

In response, it could be argued that ridding society of its hierarchical and class structure will surely require a change in our thinking, and maybe a change in which we identify more with nature, and surely if we are ever successful in ridding society of its deep-seated patriarchy, we will also rid society of many other forms of domination as well.

Although the problem of environmental racism has been with us for some time, attention only began to focus on the problem with the protest of a hazardous waste landfill in a predominantly African-American community in 1982, the publication of a U.S. Accounting Office report on race and hazardous wastes in 1983, and a similar report issued by the United Church of Christ in 1987. A subsequent more extensive report by the *National Law Journal* appeared in 1992, and in February 1994 President Clinton issued an executive order requiring that environmental justice with respect to minority and low-income populations be addressed.

But what would be a fair allocation of the environmental risks to health and well-being? In Selection 22, Robert Bullard proposes that

> Every individual has a right to be protected from environmental degradation.

This seems like a reasonable principle, but what does it require? Bullard says that it requires nondiscrimination, but how should nondiscrimination be understood here? Bullard goes on to propose two helpful concrete specifications. The first is that the burden of proof be shifted to those who would impose environmental risks upon others to prove that their activities are nondiscriminatory. The second is that it does not suffice that those who impose environmental risks have no intention of discriminating. Whatever their intentions, their actions would still be discriminatory if they imposed unfair burdens on anyone. Yet when are burdens unfair here?

One way to specify a fair allocation of the burdens with respect to environmental policies is the following:

A *Principle of Allocating Risks by Production:* One's share of the environmental risks to health and well-being should be proportionate to the amount of pollution and contaminates one produces.

According to this principle, the more pollution and contaminates one produces, the more risks to health and well-being one should have to bear. The main difficulty with this principle is that production is often driven by consumption—what consumers want or are willing and able to buy. So to impose risks to health and well-being primarily on producers does not attack the problem at its source with the preference of consumers. A more appropriate principle would seem to be the following:

A *Principle of Allocating Risks by Consumption:* One's share of the risks to health and well-being should be in proportion to the amount of resources one consumes.

According to this principle, those who consume more should bear a greater risk. This would mean, for example, that waste disposal sites should be located, other things being equal, in or near rich white communities rather than in or near poor minority communities. Moreover, if rich white communities were required to shoulder their fair share of the risks to health and well-being, they would most likely push for less production of pollutants and contaminates overall so as to reduce the size of their own share of the risk to health and well-being. Clearly, this should have beneficial consequences for everyone.

NON-WESTERN RELIGIOUS AND CULTURAL PERSPECTIVES

If we think we have a defensible earth ethics, we must determine to what degree it can be supported or challenged by non-Western religious and cultural perspectives. This is because justification for any view is comparable, and any defensible earth ethics must be able to draw support or answer challenges from alternative perspectives. The readings in this section discuss what can be learned from native American, African, Australian, Buddhist, and Taoist perspectives with respect to the task of formulating a defensible earth ethics.

In Selection 23, Annie L. Booth and Harvey M. Jacobs argue that despite the significant diversity among native American cultures, native Americans tended to preserve the biological integrity within natural communities for a significant period of historical time. They had such a strong identity with the particular land where they lived that they felt a certain kinship with it. Although native Americans killed animals in large numbers, rarely were species endangered or exterminated. Reciprocity and balance were required from both humans and other living beings. Booth and Jacobs note that certain elements of the views of native American cultures can be found in the contemporary views of deep ecology, ecological feminism, and bioregionalism which stresses the need to become intimately aware of particular places.

In Selection 24, J. Baird Callicott discusses both the relationship of African and Australian cultures to the natural world. He points out that indigenous religions in Africa tended to be both monotheistic and anthropocentric, but he argues that the effect of these religions on wild animals may have been moderated due to the fact that they had a longer evolutionary time to evolve defenses against the human population.

By contrast with other indigenous groups, Callicott notes that there is an amazing unity in the culture of Australian aboriginals. He argues that Australian totemism, by requiring the protection of certain "increase sites," provided sanctuaries in which wild species could thrive that are analogous to our game preserves. He also points out similiarities between the views of Australian aboriginals and the views of both Aldo Leopold and bioregionalists.

In Selection 25, Lily de Silva claims that Buddhism is primarily concerned with the problem of human suffering and so does not directly address the concerns of environmental ethics. Nevertheless, de Silva thinks it is possible to infer what would be required by a Buddhist environmental ethics from other requirements of Buddhism. Thus, Buddhism requires us all to adopt a simple moderate lifestyle, and so impose the least possible burden on the environment. Buddhism also requires us to prevent injury to all living beings as much as possible, which is a central requirement of any nonanthropocentric environmental ethics. The Buddhist belief that fellow humans, or even one's own relatives, may be reborn as animals provides yet another reason to be kind and sympathetic toward animals; in sum, Buddhism requires that we interact with nature as much as possible, like the bee that harms neither the fragrance nor the beauty of the flower in gathering its nectar.

According to Po-Keung Ip in Selection 26, Taoism can provide the metaphysical foundation for an environmental ethics. In Taoism, Tao is the ultimate reality of nature. It has two cosmic principles—Ying and Yang—which explain the rhythmic processes of the natural world. In Taoism, everything is to be treated on an equal footing as "ontologically equal," which opens up the possibility of ascribing values to nonhumans regardless of their usefulness to human beings. Challenging the traditional interpretation of the Taoist doctrine of "wu wei" as inaction, Po-Keung argues that it should be interpreted as acting in accord with nature, which he argues is Taoism's basic recommendation for an environmental ethics.

PRACTICAL APPLICATIONS

The remaining selections of this anthology are focused on a variety of practical problems to which the views discussed in previous selections need to be applied. In Selection 27, G. Tyler Miller seeks to determine what is the scientific consensus with respect to global warming, and what, if anything, should be done about it. In Selection 28, Gary Taubes considers the current backlash against the dominant view that we have a serious problem of ozone depletion and shows that much of it stems from work published by supporters of Lyndon LaRouche, an extreme politician currently serving 15 years in jail for conspiracy to evade taxes. Selection 29 is the International Convention on Climate Change agreed to at the United Nations Rio Conference.

In Selection 30, Holmes Rolston III argues that species and not just individual members of species have intrinsic value and deserve respect in their own right and not just insofar as they serve human welfare. John Tuxill, in Selection 31, reviews the various unilateral and multilateral efforts that have been made to promote biodiversity conservation and the various problems they have faced. Selection 32 is the International Convention on Biological Diversity agreed to at the United Nations Rio Conference, which President Clinton said the United States would honor.

Paul Watson, one of the founding members of Greenpeace, was expelled from the organization in 1977 because of his radical tactics. He subsequently founded the Sea Shepherd Society. In Selection 33, Watson chronicles the actions taken by the sea shepherds to block illegal drift netting in the North Pacific. Each year, the incidental kill of drift nettings is one million sea birds, a quarter of a million marine mammals such as dolphins, seals and sea lions, and hundreds of million tons of fish and squid. In an effort to eliminate this killing, sea shepherds have engaged in violence against property but never against life, human or otherwise.

In Selection 34, Dave Foreman sketches the political agenda of Earth First!, a radical environmental action group that he helped start up and he goes on to describe some of the recent activities of the group. In Selection 35, Chaia Heller stresses the connection between the domination of nature and the domination of women and rallies ecological feminists and others for a disruptive protest on Wall Street which took place on Earth Day April 21, 1990. In Selection 36, Eugene Hargrove, the founding editor of *Environmental Ethics*, argues against the violent strategies of some radical environment groups, like Earth First!, on the grounds that they are not only unnecessary but also counterproductive.

Mark Sagoff, in Selection 37, argues that neither those who believe that an expanding world economy will use up natural resources nor those who see no reason, environmental or otherwise, to limit economic growth have it right. Sagoff argues against the first group that there are virtually no physical limits to economic growth and against the second group that there are still moral, religious, and cultural reasons to be opposed to it.

Explicitly writing against Sagoff's view, Paul R. Ehrlich, Gretchen C. Daily, and others in Selection 38 argue that moral, religious, and cultural constraints on economic growth are not enough and that we are facing physical limits to economic growth which are not reflected in current prices. They compare our current practice of driving species to extinction to popping the rivets out of a plane that your children must fly in.

In Selection 40, William Rees argues for a truly "ecological" economics which sees humans as secondary producers and recognizes that all economic production actually requires the consumption of a vast quantity of available energy and material first produced by nature. For example, Rees claims that the ecological footprint of the City of Vancouver is 12 times the geographical area of its home territory. He argues that we are becoming increasingly indebted to nature rather than becoming more independent of it.

As it turns out, most of the practical application selections in this anthology are written from a human-centered or anthropocentric standpoint. While they may call for radical changes in the way we are dealing with environmental problems, the justification for those changes is given in terms of the good of human beings, usually including the good of present and future generations of human beings. At the same time, some of the practical application selections and most of the theoretical selections that preceded them are written from an explicitly nonanthropocentric standpoint.

Do these differences in standpoint make a difference in practice? They may not make a difference in practice if that there are moral constraints on even an anthropocentric perspective that would require us to recognize the intrinsic value of nonhuman living beings whenever the basic needs of humans are not at stake. Another way in which these differences in perspective may not matter in practice is if it turned out that there was a happy coincidence between what is for the overall good of present generations of humans and what is for the overall good of all other living beings, or at least a coincidence between what is for the overall good of present and *future* generations of humans and what is for the overall good of all other present and future living beings.[7] No doubt, with respect to some environmental problems, like global warming and ozone depletion, the coincidence of interest is there, but with respect to other environmental problems, like endangered species, it may not be. In cases of conflict, obviously, it will be important to determine whether an anthropocentric perspective must be constrained in certain ways or rejected in its entirety for a nonanthropocentric perspective. Hence, at least in cases of conflict, we can see the practical relevance of our previous theoretical selections. It may also be the case that even where there is a practical coincidence between anthropocentric and nonanthropocentric perspectives, we will still need the motivation that *both* perspectives can provide to motivate the radical practical changes that must be made. So even where there is no conflict, the practical relevance of our previous theoretical selections will still remain.

Working through the selections in this anthology will not always be an easy task. Some articles will be clear on the first reading, whereas others will require closer scrutiny. You should also make sure you give each selection a fair hearing, because although some will accord with your current views, others will not. It is important that you evaluate these latter with an open mind, allowing for the possibility that after sufficient reflection you may come to view them as the most morally defensible. Indeed, to approach the selections of this anthology in any other way would surely undermine the grounds you have for thinking you are a moral person given that morality requires just the sort of open-minded investigation of environmental problems that this anthology makes possible.

NOTES

1. Daniel Chiras, *Lessons from Nature* (Washington, D.C., 1992); Donella Meadows, *Global Citizen* (Washington, D.C., 1991); Lester Brown et al. *State of the World* (New York, 1993); Peter Singer, *Animal Liberation* (New York, 1990); *Priorities for the Nineties* (Santa Cruz, Calif., 1991), p. 5.
2. Obviously, other moral approaches to practical problems could be distinguished, but I think the three I will be considering reflect the range of possible approaches that are relevant to the resolution of most of the practical problems we face.
3. In fact, the debate as to whether African-Americans are better off now because of the programs of the Great Society has also taken a more scholarly turn. See Charles Murray, *Losing Ground* (New York: Basic Books, 1984), and Christopher Jencks, "How Poor Are the Poor?" *New York Review of Books*, May 9, 1985.
4. For further elaboration, see my book, *The Demands of Justice* (Notre Dame, Ind.: University of Notre Dame Press, 1980), especially Chapter 2.
5. For an argument that supports this conclusion, see S.F. Sapontzis, *Morals, Reason, and Animals* (Philadelphia: Temple University Press, 1987).
6. Murray Bookchin, *The Ecology of Freedom* (New York, 1991), p. xxv.
7. Of course, what is for the overall good of human beings, present and future, or what is for the overall good of all living beings, present and future, may not be for the good of particular human beings, present or future, or particular living beings, present or future.

1

⚐ *The Historical Roots* ⚑ *of Our Ecological Crisis*

LYNN WHITE, JR.

Lynn White, Jr. was president of Mills College and then taught at University of California at Los Angeles where he founded and directed the Center for Medieval and Renaissance Studies.

A conversation with Aldous Huxley not infrequently put one at the receiving end of an unforgettable monologue. About a year before his lamented death he was discoursing on a favorite topic: Man's unnatural treatment of nature and its sad results. To illustrate his point he told how, during the previous summer, he had returned to a little valley in England where he had spent many happy months as a child. Once it had been composed of delightful grassy glades; now it was becoming overgrown with unsightly brush because the rabbits that formerly kept such growth under control had largely succumbed to a disease, myxomatosis, that was deliberately introduced by the local farmers to reduce the rabbits' destruction of crops. Being something of a Philistine, I could be silent no longer, even in the interests of great rhetoric. I interrupted to point out that the rabbit itself had been brought as a domestic animal to England in 1176, presumably to improve the protein diet of the peasantry.

All forms of life modify their contexts. The most spectacular and benign instance is doubtless the coral polyp. By serving its own ends, it has created a vast undersea world favorable to thousands of other kinds of animals and plants. Ever since man became a numerous species he has affected his environment notably. The hypothesis that his fire-drive method of hunting created the world's great grasslands and helped to exterminate the monster mammals of the Pleistocene from much of the globe is plausible, if not proved. For 6 millennia at least, the banks of the lower Nile have been a human artifact rather than the swampy African jungle which nature, apart from man, would have made it. The Aswan Dam, flooding 5000 square miles, is only the latest stage in a long process. In many regions terracing or irrigation, overgrazing, the cutting of forests by Romans to build ships to fight Carthaginians or by Crusaders to solve the logistics problems of their expeditions, have profoundly changed some ecologies. Observation that the French landscape falls into two basic types, the open fields of the north and the *bocage* of the south and west, inspired Marc Bloch to undertake his classic study of medieval agricultural methods. Quite unintentionally, changes in human ways often affect nonhuman nature. It has been noted, for example, that the advent of the automobile eliminated huge flocks of sparrows that once fed on the horse manure littering every street.

The history of ecologic change is still so rudimentary that we know little about what really happened, or what the results were. The extinction of the European aurochs as late as 1627 would seem to have been a simple case of overenthusiastic hunting. On more intricate matters it often is impossible to find solid information. For a thousand years or more the Frisians and Hollanders have been pushing back the North Sea, and the process is culminating in our own time in the reclamation of the Zuider Zee. What, if any, species of animals, birds, fish, shore life, or plants have died out in the process? In their epic combat with Neptune, have the Netherlanders overlooked ecological values in such a way that the quality of human life in the Netherlands has suffered? I cannot discover that the questions have ever been asked, much less answered.

People, then, have often been a dynamic element in their own environment, but in the present state of historical scholarship we usually do not know exactly when, where, or with what effects man-induced changes came. As we enter the last third of the 20th century, however, concern for the problem of ecologic backlash is mounting feverishly. Natural science, conceived as the effort to understand the nature of things, had flourished in several eras and among several peoples. Similarly there had been an age-old accumulation of technological skills, sometimes growing rapidly, sometimes slowly. But it was not until about four generations ago that Western Europe and North America arranged a marriage between science and technology, a union of the theoretical and the empirical approaches to our natural environment. The emergence in widespread practice of the Baconian creed that scientific knowledge means technological power over nature can scarcely be dated before about 1850, save in the chemical industries, where it is anticipated in the 18th century. Its acceptance as a normal pattern of action may mark the greatest event in human history since the invention of agriculture, and perhaps in nonhuman terrestrial history as well.

Almost at once the new situation forced the crystallization of the novel concept of ecology; indeed, the word *ecology* first appeared in the English language in 1873. Today, less than a century later, the impact of our race upon the environment has so increased in force that it has changed in essence. When the first cannons were fired, in the early 14th century, they affected ecology by sending workers scrambling to the forests and mountains for more potash, sulfur, iron ore, and charcoal, with some resulting erosion and deforestation. Hydrogen bombs are of a different order: a war fought with them might alter the genetics of all life on this planet. By 1285 London had a smog problem arising from the burning of soft coal, but our present combustion of fossil fuels threatens to change the chemistry of the globe's atmosphere as a whole, with consequences which we are only beginning to guess. With the population explosion, the carcinoma of planless urbanism, the now geological deposits of sewage and garbage, surely no creature other than man has ever managed to foul its nest in such short order.

There are many calls to action, but specific proposals, however worthy as individual items, seem too partial, palliative, negative: ban the bomb, tear down the billboards, give the Hindus contraceptives and tell them to eat their sacred cows. The simplest solution to any suspect change is, of course, to stop it, or, better yet, to revert to a romanticized past: make those ugly gasoline stations look like Anne Hathaway's cottage or (in the Far West) like ghost-town saloons. The "wilderness area" mentality invariably advocates deep-freezing an ecology, whether San Gimignano or the High Sierra, as it was before the first Kleenex was dropped. But neither atavism nor prettification will cope with the ecologic crisis of our time.

What shall we do? No one yet knows. Unless we think about fundamentals, our specific measures may produce new backlashes more serious than those they are designed to remedy.

As a beginning we should try to clarify our thinking by looking, in some historical depth, at the presuppositions that underlie modern technology and science. Science was traditionally aristocratic, speculative, intellectual in intent; technology was lower-class, empirical, action-oriented. The quite sudden fusion of these two, towards the middle of the 19th century, is surely related to the slightly prior and contemporary democratic revolutions which, by reducing social barriers, tended to assert a functional unity of brain and hand. Our ecologic crisis is the product of an emerging, entirely novel, democratic culture. The issue is whether a democratized world can survive its own implications. Presumably we cannot, unless we rethink our axioms.

THE WESTERN TRADITIONS
OF TECHNOLOGY AND SCIENCE

One thing is so certain that it seems stupid to verbalize it: both modern technology and modern science are distinctively *Occidental*. Our technology has absorbed elements from all over the world, notably from China; yet everywhere today, whether in Japan or in Nigeria, successful technology is Western. Our science is the heir to all the sciences of the past, especially perhaps to the work of the great Islamic scientists of the Middle Ages, who so often outdid the ancient Greeks in skill and perspicacity: al-Rāzī in medicine, for example; or ibn-al-Haytham in optics; or Omar Khayyám in mathematics. Indeed, not a few works of such geniuses seem to have vanished in the original Arabic and to survive only in medieval Latin translations that helped to lay the foundations for later Western developments. Today, around the globe, all significant science is Western in style and method, whatever the pigmentation or language of the scientists.

A second pair of facts is less well recognized because they result from quite recent historical scholarship. The leadership of the West, both in technology and in science, is far older than the so-called Scientific Revolution of the 17th century or the so-called Industrial Revolution of the 18th century. These terms are in fact outmoded and obscure the true nature of what they try to describe—significant stages in two long and separate developments. By A.D. 1000 at the latest—and perhaps, feebly, as much as 200 years earlier—the West began to apply water power to industrial processes other than milling grain. This was followed in the late 12th century by the harnessing of wind power. From simple beginnings, but with remarkable consistency of style, the West rapidly expanded its skills in the development of power machinery, labor-saving devices, and automation. Those who doubt should contemplate that most monumental achievement in the history of automation: the weight-driven mechanical clock, which appeared in two forms in the early 14th century. Not in craftsmanship but in basic technological capacity, the Latin West of the later Middle Ages far outstripped its elaborate, sophisticated, and esthetically magnificent sister cultures, Byzantium and Islam. In 1444 a great Greek ecclesiastic, Bessarion, who had gone to Italy, wrote a letter to a prince in Greece. He is amazed by the superiority of Western ships, arms, textiles, glass. But above all he is astonished by the spectacle of waterwheels sawing timbers and pumping the bellows to blast furnaces. Clearly, he had seen nothing of the sort in the Near East.

By the end of the 15th century the technological superiority of Europe was such that its small, mutually hostile nations could spill out over all the rest of the world, conquering, looting, and colonizing. The symbol of this technological superiority is the fact that Portugal, one of the weakest states of the Occident, was able to become, and to remain for a century, mistress of the East Indies. And we must remember that the technology of Vasco da Gama and Albuquerque was built by pure empiricism, drawing remarkably little support or inspiration from science.

In the present-day vernacular of understanding, modern science is supposed to have begun in 1543, when both Copernicus and Vesalius published their great works. It is no derogation of their accomplishments, however, to point out that such structures as the *Fabrica* and the *De revolutionibus* do not appear overnight. The distinctive Western tradition of science, in fact, began in the late 11th century with a massive movement of translation of Arabic and Greek scientific works into Latin. A few notable books—Theophrastus, for example—escaped the West's avid new appetite for science, but within less than 200 years, effectively the entire corpus of Greek and Muslim science was available in Latin, and was being eagerly read and criticized in the new European universities. Out of criticism arose new observation, speculation, and increasing distrust of ancient authorities. By the late 13th century Europe had seized global scientific leadership from the faltering hands of Islam. It would be as absurd to deny the profound originality of Newton, Galileo, or Copernicus as to deny that of the 14th century scholastic scientists like Buridan or Oresme on whose work they built. Before the 11th century, science scarcely existed in the Latin West, even in Roman times. From the 11th century onward, the scientific sector of Occidental culture has increased in a steady crescendo.

Since both our technological and our scientific movements got their start, acquired their character, and achieved world dominance in the Middle Ages, it would seem that we cannot understand their nature or their present impact upon ecology without examining fundamental medieval assumptions and developments.

MEDIEVAL VIEW OF MAN AND NATURE

Until recently, agriculture has been the chief occupation even in "advanced" societies; hence, any change in methods of tillage has much importance. Early plows, drawn by two oxen, did not normally turn the sod but merely scratched it. Thus, cross-plowing was needed and fields tended to be squarish. In the fairly light soils and semi-arid climates of the Near East and Mediterranean, this worked well. But such a plow was inappropriate to the wet climate and often sticky soils of northern Europe. By the latter part of the 7th century after Christ, however, following obscure beginnings, certain northern peasants were using an entirely new kind of plow, equipped with a vertical knife to cut the line of the furrow, a horizontal share to slice under the sod, and a moldboard to turn it over. The friction of this plow with the soil was so great that it normally required not two but eight oxen. It attacked the land with such violence that cross-plowing was not needed, and fields tended to be shaped in long strips.

In the days of the scratch-plow, fields were distributed generally in units capable of supporting a single family. Subsistence farming was the presupposition. But no peasant owned eight oxen: to use the new and more efficient plow, peasants pooled their oxen to form large plow-teams, originally receiving (it would appear) plowed strips in proportion to their contribution. Thus, distribution of land was based no longer on the needs of a family but, rather, on the capacity of a power machine to till the earth. Man's relation to the soil was profoundly changed. Formerly man had been part of nature; now he was the exploiter of nature. Nowhere else in the world did farmers develop any analogous agricultural implement. Is it coincidence that modern technology, with its ruthlessness toward nature, has so largely been produced by descendants of these peasants of northern Europe?

This same exploitive attitude appears slightly before A.D. 830 in Western illustrated calendars. In older calendars the months were shown as passive personifications. The new Frankish calendars, which set the style for the Middle Ages, are very different: they show men coercing the world around them—plowing, harvesting, chopping trees, butchering pigs. Man and nature are two things, and man is master.

These novelties seem to be in harmony with larger intellectual patterns. What people do about their ecology depends on what they think about themselves in relation to things around them. Human ecology is deeply conditioned by beliefs about our nature and destiny—that is, by religion. To Western eyes this is very evident in, say, India or Ceylon. It is equally true of ourselves and of our medieval ancestors.

The victory of Christianity over paganism was the greatest psychic revolution in the history of our culture. It has become fashionable today to say that, for better or worse, we live in "the post-Christian age." Certainly the forms of our thinking and language have largely ceased to be Christian, but to my eye the substance often remains amazingly akin to that of the past. Our daily habits of action, for example, are dominated by an implicit faith in perpetual progress which was unknown either to Greco-Roman antiquity or to the Orient. It is rooted in, and is indefensible apart from, Judeo-Christian teleology. The fact that Communists share it merely helps to show what can be demonstrated on many other grounds: that Marxism, like Islam, is a Judeo-Christian heresy. We continue today to live, as we have lived for about 1700 years, very largely in a context of Christian axioms.

What did Christianity tell people about their relations with the environment?

While many of the world's mythologies provide stories of creation, Greco-Roman mythology was singularly incoherent in this respect. Like Aristotle, the intellectuals of the ancient West denied that the visible world had had a beginning. Indeed, the idea of a beginning was impossible in the framework of their cyclical notion of time. In sharp contrast, Christianity inherited from Judaism not only a concept of time as non-repetitive and linear but also a striking story of creation. By gradual stages a loving and all-powerful God had created light and darkness, the heavenly bodies, and earth and all its plants, animals, birds, and fishes. Finally, God had created Adam and, as an afterthought, Eve to keep man from being lonely. Man named all the animals, thus establishing his dominance over them. God planned all of this explicitly for man's benefit and rule: no item in the physical creation had any purpose save to serve man's purposes. And, although man's body is made of clay, he is not simply part of nature: he is made in God's image.

Especially in its Western form, Christianity is the most anthropocentric religion the world has seen. As early as the 2nd century both Tertullian and St. Irenaeus of Lyons were insisting that when God shaped Adam he was foreshadowing the image of the incarnate Christ, the Second Adam. Man shares, in great measure, God's transcendence of nature. Christianity, in absolute contrast to ancient paganism and Asia's religions (except, perhaps, Zoroastrianism), not only established a dualism of man and nature but also insisted that it is God's will that man exploit nature for his proper ends.

At the level of the common people this worked out in an interesting way. In Antiquity every tree, every spring, every stream, every hill had its own *genius loci,* its guardian spirit. These spirits were accessible to men, but were very unlike men; centaurs, fauns, and mermaids show their ambivalence. Before one cut a tree, mined a mountain, or dammed a brook, it was important to placate the spirit in charge of that particular situation, and to keep it placated. By destroying pagan animism, Christianity made it possible to exploit nature in a mood of indifference to the feelings of natural objects.

It is often said that for animism the Church substituted the cult of saints. True; but the cult of saints is functionally quite different from animism. The saint is not *in* natural objects; he may have special shrines, but his citizenship is in heaven. Moreover, a saint is entirely a man; he can be approached in human terms. In addition to saints, Christianity of course also had angels and demons inherited from Judaism and perhaps, at one remove, from Zoroastrianism. But these were all as mobile as the saints themselves. The spirits *in* natural objects, which formerly had protected nature from man, evaporated. Man's effective monopoly on spirit in this world was confirmed, and the old inhibitions to the exploitation of nature crumbled.

When one speaks in such sweeping terms, a note of caution is in order. Christianity is a complex faith, and its consequences differ in differing contexts. What I have said may well apply to the medieval West, where in fact technology made spectacular advances. But the Greek East, a highly civilized realm of equal Christian devotion, seems to have produced no marked technological innovation after the late 7th century, when Greek fire was invented. The key to the contrast may perhaps be found in a difference in the tonality of piety and thought which students of comparative theology find between the Greek and the Latin Churches. The Greeks believed that sin was intellectual blindness, and that salvation was found in illumination, orthodoxy—that is, clear thinking. The Latins, on the other hand, felt that sin was moral evil, and that salvation was to be found in right conduct. Eastern theology has been intellectualist. Western theology has been voluntarist. The Greek saint contemplates; the Western saint acts. The implications of Christianity for the conquest of nature would emerge more easily in the Western atmosphere.

The Christian dogma of creation, which is found in the first clause of all the Creeds, has another meaning for our comprehension of today's ecologic crisis. By revelation, God had given man the Bible, the Book of Scripture. But since God had made nature, nature also must reveal the divine mentality. The religious study of nature for the better understanding of God was known as natural theology. In the early Church, and always in the Greek East, nature was conceived primarily as a symbolic system through which God speaks to men: the ant is a sermon to sluggards; rising flames are the symbol of the soul's aspiration. This view of nature was essentially artistic rather than scientific. While Byzantium preserved and copied great numbers of ancient Greek scientific texts, science as we conceive it could scarcely flourish in such an ambiance.

However, in the Latin West by the early 13th century natural theology was following a very different bent. It was ceasing to be the decoding of the physical symbols of God's communication with man and was becoming the effort to understand God's mind by discovering how his creation operates. The rainbow was no longer simply a symbol of hope first sent to Noah after the Deluge: Robert Grosseteste, Friar Roger Bacon, and Theodoric of Freiberg produced startlingly sophisticated work on the optics of the rainbow, but they did it as a venture in religious understanding. From the 13th century onward, up to and including Leibnitz and Newton, every major scientist, in effect, explained his motivations in religious terms. Indeed if Galileo had not been so expert an amateur theologian he would have got into far less trouble: the professionals resented his intrusion. And Newton seems to have regarded himself more as a theologian than as a scientist. It was not until the late 18th century that the hypothesis of God became unnecessary to many scientists.

It is often hard for the historian to judge, when men explain why they are doing what they want to do, whether they are offering real reasons or merely culturally acceptable reasons. The consistency with which scientists during the long formative centuries of Western science said that the task and the reward of the scientist was "to think God's thoughts after him" leads one to believe that this was their real motivation. If so, then modern Western science was cast in a matrix of Christian theology. The dynamism of religious devotion, shaped by the Judeo-Christian dogma of creation, gave it impetus.

AN ALTERNATIVE CHRISTIAN VIEW

We would seem to be headed toward conclusions unpalatable to many Christians. Since both *science* and *technology* are blessed words in our contemporary vocabulary, some may be happy at the notions, first, that, viewed historically, modern science is an extrapolation of natural theology and, second, that modern technology is at least partly to be explained as an Occidental, voluntarist realization of the Christian dogma of man's transcendence of and rightful mastery over nature. But, as we now recognize, somewhat over a century ago science and technology—hitherto quite separate activities—joined to give mankind powers which, to judge by many of the ecologic effects, are out of control. If so, Christianity bears a huge burden of guilt.

I personally doubt that disastrous ecologic backlash can be avoided simply by applying to our problems more science and more technology. Our science and technology have grown out of Christian attitudes toward man's relation to nature which are almost universally held not only by Christians and neo-Christians but also by those who fondly regard themselves as post-Christians. Despite Copernicus, all the cosmos rotates around our little globe. Despite Darwin, we are *not,* in our hearts, part of the natural process. We are superior to nature, contemptuous of it, willing to use it for our slightest whim. The newly elected Governor of California, like myself a churchman but less troubled than I, spoke for the Christian tradition when he said (as is alleged), "when you've seen one redwood tree, you've seen them all." To a Christian a tree can be no more than a physical fact. The whole concept of the sacred grove is alien to Christianity and to the ethos of the West. For nearly 2 millennia Christian missionaries have been chopping down sacred groves, which are idolatrous because they assume spirit in nature.

What we do about ecology depends on our ideas of the man–nature relationship. More science and more technology are not going to get us out of the present ecologic crisis until we find a new religion, or rethink our old one. The beatniks, who are the basic revolutionaries of our time, show a sound instinct in their affinity for Zen Buddhism, which conceives of the man–nature relationship as very nearly the mirror image of the Christian view. Zen, however, is as deeply conditioned by Asian history as Christianity is by the experience of the West, and I am dubious of its viability among us.

Possibly we should ponder the greatest radical in Christian history since Christ: St. Francis of Assisi. The prime miracle of St. Francis is the fact that he did not end at the stake, as many of his left-wing followers did. He was so clearly heretical that a General of the Franciscan Order, St. Bonaventura, a great and perceptive Christian, tried to suppress the early accounts of Franciscanism. The key to an understanding of Francis is his belief in the virtue of humility—not merely for the individual but for man as a species. Francis tried to depose man from his monarchy over creation and set up a democracy of all God's creatures. With him the ant is no longer simply a homily for the lazy, flames a sign of the thrust of the soul toward union with God; now they are Brother Ant and Sister Fire, praising the Creator in their own ways as Brother Man does in his.

Later commentators have said that Francis preached to the birds as a rebuke to men who would not listen. The records do not read so: he urged the little birds to praise God, and in spiritual ecstasy they flapped their wings and chirped rejoicing. Legends of saints, especially the Irish saints, had long told of their dealings with animals but always, I believe, to show their human dominance over creatures. With Francis it is different. The land around Gubbio in the Apennines was being ravaged by a fierce wolf. St. Francis, says the legend, talked to the wolf and persuaded him of the error of his ways. The wolf repented, died in the odor of sanctity, and was buried in consecrated ground.

What Sir Steven Runciman calls the "Franciscan doctrine of the animal soul" was quickly stamped out. Quite possibly it was in part inspired, consciously or unconsciously, by the belief in reincarnation held by the Cathar heretics who at that time teemed in Italy and southern France, and who presumably had got it originally from India. It is significant that at just the same moment, about 1200, traces of metempsychosis are found also in western Judaism, in the Provençal *Cabbala*. But Francis held neither to transmigration of souls nor to pantheism. His view of nature and of man rested on a unique sort of pan-psychism of all things animate and inanimate, designed for the glorification of their transcendent Creator, who, in the ultimate gesture of cosmic humility, assumed flesh, lay helpless in a manger, and hung dying on a scaffold.

I am not suggesting that many contemporary Americans who are concerned about our ecologic crisis will be either able or willing to counsel with wolves or exhort birds. However, the present increasing disruption of the global environment is the product of a dynamic technology and science which were originating in the Western medieval world against which St. Francis was rebelling in so original a way. Their growth cannot be understood historically apart from distinctive attitudes toward nature which are deeply grounded in Christian dogma. The fact that most people do not think of these attitudes as Christian is irrelevant. No new set of basic values has been accepted in our society to displace those of Christianity. Hence we shall continue to have a worsening ecologic crisis until we reject the Christian axiom that nature has no reason for existence save to serve man.

The greatest spiritual revolutionary in Western history, St. Francis, proposed what he thought was an alternative Christian view of nature and man's relation to it: he tried to substitute the idea of the equality of all creatures, including man, for the idea of man's limitless rule of creation. He failed. Both our present science and our present technology are so tinctured with orthodox Christian arrogance toward nature that no solution for our ecologic crisis can be expected from them alone. Since the roots of our trouble are so largely religious, the remedy must also be essentially religious, whether we call it that or not. We must rethink and refeel our nature and destiny. The profoundly religious, but heretical, sense of the primitive Franciscans for the spiritual autonomy of all parts of nature may point a direction. I propose Francis as a patron saint for ecologists.

2

⚘ *For God So Loved the World* ⚘

ANDREW LINZEY

Andrew Linzey is Chaplain and Director of Studies at the Center for the Study of Theology, University of Essex and the author of Christianity and the Rights of Animals.

Imagine a scene. The date is the 18th of April, 1499. The time is sometime in the afternoon. The place is the Abbey of Josaphat, near Chartres. Within this Abbey a trial is taking place. It is a criminal prosecution before the Bailiff of the Abbey. The defendant is charged with having killed an infant. The verdict is announced. The defendant is found guilty. The sentence of the ecclesiastical court is that the defendant should be hanged. Mercifully, unlike other defendants, the fate is only death and not torture or mangulation. And the defendant was hanged by its neck at a public hanging that day in the market square. The defendant, however, was not a human being, but a pig.

What is the point of recounting this grisly, surely altogether extraordinary episode from the 15th century, you may ask? The answer is this: grisly it certainly was, extraordinary it certainly was not. From the 9th to the 19th century we have over 200 written accounts of the criminal prosecution and capital punishment of animals. These trials of animals, pigs, dogs, wolves, locusts, rats, termites, cows, horses and doves inflicted great and terrible suffering. And the important thing to appreciate is that these trials were mainly or wholly religious in character. They drew their inspiration from Christian doctrine, based on a silly biblical fundamentalism—a fundamentalism I'm distressed to say is still with us in some quarters of the Church today. In particular it was St. Thomas Aquinas in his *Summa Theologiae* who held that some animals were satellites of Satan: "instigated by the powers of hell and proper to be cursed." St. Thomas added: "the anathema then is not to be pronounced against the animals as such, but should be hurled inferentially at the devil who makes use of irrational creatures to our detriment."

Armed with this awful dictum (however originally qualified by St. Thomas) Christians have spent more than 10 centuries anathematizing, cursing and reviling the animal world. The echoes of this violence are found today in our very language. The word 'animal' is a term of abuse, not to mention "brute," "beast," or "bestial." How we have libelled the animal world. For myself I cannot but be bemused by the reference in the marriage service of the *Book of Common Prayer* to "brute beasts which hath no understanding." Who are these brute beasts? Most higher mammals seem to know more about life-long monogamy than many human beings.

This low, negative, even hating, attitude towards animals, regarding them as a source of evil, or as instruments of the devil, or regarding them as beings without any moral status, has, sad to say, been the dominant view within Christendom for the largest part of its history. In the 9th century, Pope Stephen IV prepared great quantities of holy water with which to anathematize hordes of locusts. In the 19th century, Pope Pius IX forbade the opening of an animal protection office in Rome on the grounds that humans had duties to other humans, but none to animals. For a clear run of at least 10 centuries the dominant ecclesiastical voice did not even regard animals as worthy of moral concern. We do well to remember that Catholic textbooks still regard animals as morally without status, save when they are deemed human property. Worse than that, they have been frequently classified as things without rights, to be used—as St. Thomas himself wrote—"in any way whatever." If Jesus can weep over Jerusalem we have more than good reason to weep over the sins of Mother Church.

It seems to me that there is no use pretending that all has been well with the Church either in the past, or even now in the present. The very community which should be the cradle of the Gospel of God's Love for the world has only been too good at justifying violence and legitimizing hatred towards the world. Those like myself who have the temerity to preach to Christian and non-Christian alike, must be quite clear that the record of Christianity has been, and still is, on this issue as on many others, in many respects shameful and second rate. Christians are simply too good at forgetting how awful they have been. The fact is that Christians have had enormous difficulties in believing their own Gospel.

And what is this Gospel? It is nothing less than the conviction and experience that God loves the whole world. What we see in Jesus is the revelation of an inclusive, all-embracing, generous Loving. A Loving that washes the feet of the world. A Loving that heals individuals from oppression—physical and spiritual. A Loving that takes sides with the poor, vulnerable, diseased, hated, despised, and outcasts of his day. A Loving that is summed up in his absolute commitment to love at all costs even in extreme suffering and death. As that distinguished former Dean of Salisbury, Sydney Evans, once wrote: "What Jesus did on the Cross was to demonstrate the truth of what he had taught: he showed a quality of love—such that the worst that evil could do to such love was to give such love ever fresh opportunities for loving."

The world we live in is desperate for love. The whole world needs to be loved. When I was young I used to mock the notion of "Gentle Jesus, meek and mild." How wrong I was! For there is great power in humility, strength in gentleness, wisdom in forbearance. We need to listen again to Father Zossima's advice in Dostoyevsky's *The Brothers Karamazov*:

Brothers, be not afraid of men's sins. Love man even in his sin, for that already bears the semblance of divine love and is the highest love on earth. Love all God's creation, the whole of it and every grain of sand. Love every leaf, every ray of God's light! Love the animals, love the plants, love everything. And if you love everything you will perceive the divine mystery in things. And once you have perceived it, you will begin to comprehend it ceaselessly more and more every day. And you will at last come to love the whole world with an abiding, universal love.

Not all Christians have been happy with this Gospel. While God's love is free, generous and unlimited, we Christians have only been too good at placing limits on Divine Love. St. Thomas Aquinas was a great scholar and saint, but even he believed quite erroneously that God did not love animals for their own sakes, but only in so far as they were of use to human beings. We Christians have at various times made of this Revelation of Unlimited Love its precise opposite. We have conceived of this Revelation in exclusive terms, exclusive of one group or race: those who were non-Jews, those who are not women, those who are not coloured, and so on. Not all Christians have seen how the love of God gives each individual human being a unique and equal value. But at least we can say that these issues have been on the agenda of the Churches. Not so with other suffering non-human creatures. What has not been seen is that the love of God is inclusive not only of humans *but also all creatures.* It took Christians many years to realize that we cannot love God and keep humans as slaves. It has taken even longer for Christians to realize that we cannot love God and regard women as second class humans. Now is the time for Christians to realize that we cannot love God and hate his non-human creatures. Christians are people who need to be liberated by the Gospel they preach. Christians cannot love God and be free to hate.

For people, like myself, who are concerned for justice in our dealings with animals there are three things we must learn.

The first is that we must not hate even those who hate animals. "Do not be afraid of men's sins," writes Dostoyevsky. People who work for justice for animals are often disappointed, angry, unhappy people, and more often than not with just cause. It is incredible that we should treat God's creatures with so little love and respect; incredible that we should despoil animal life for fun and amusement; incredible that we should wantonly slaughter; incredible that we should make wild animals captive for entertainment; incredible that we should inflict suffering and pain on farm and laboratory animals. It is spiritually infantile that we should continue to look upon the world as "made for us" and animals simply as means to human ends, as resources, as tools, as machines, indeed simply as things. And yet we must not hate those who hate God's world. By doing so we simply push them further into their own abyss and spiritual darkness. All of us need to be loved, all of us need interior resources to go on loving. And all this is very, very hard especially when we see creatures treated so cruelly that their cause cries to heaven for justice. But we have one real and lasting weapon at our disposal: 'Soul-force.' As Dostoyevsky writes: "Loving humility is a terrible force, the strongest of all . . . (with it we shall) conquer the world." So I don't want to hate anybody, even vivisectors, butchers, trappers, factory farmers and bullfighters. On the contrary I want to love them so much that they will not find time, or have the inclination, to hunt, and kill, and destroy and maim God's good creatures. I refuse to give those who exploit animals another good reason for not believing in a God of love.

Secondly, we must not hate, even the Church. I know that this is very difficult, not least of all because the Church has a lamentable record on animals and, what is more, is still a party to animal cruelty. I say now, and have said privately in the past, to the Church Commissioners that the time has come when in the name of God most loving they must stop allowing factory farming (and also hunting) on their owned lands. Christians, even Church Commissioners, must be signs of the Gospel for which all creatures long. I know that the Church is not always very lovable to say the least. But I also say to you that we shall not advance the cause of animals by hating the Church. On the contrary we must love it so much that it repents of its theological foolishness, its far too frequent humanist arrogance and its complicity in sins against animals. But I say to you that hatred is too great a burden to bear.

I want to give you one example that should give us hope. If we go back in history 200 years or so, we will find intelligent, respectable, conscientious Christians for whom slavery was not a moral issue. If pressed some might have defended slavery as 'progress' as many thought it was. Some might even have taken the view of William Henry Holcombe writing in 1860 that slavery was a natural means of "the Christianization of the dark races." The quite staggering fact to grapple with is that this very same community which in some ways provided the major ideological impetus for the defence of slavery came within an historically short period, 100, perhaps only 50, years to change its mind. The same tradition which helped keep slavery alive was the same community that became by and large determined to end it. So successful has this change been that within this congregation today we shall have difficulty in finding one slave trader, even one individual Christian who thought that the practice was anything other than inimical to the moral demands of the Christian faith. In short, while it is true that Christian churches have been and frequently are awful on the subject of animals, it is just possible, even plausible that given say 50 or 100 years we shall witness among this same community amazing shifts of consciousness as we have witnessed on other moral issues, no less complex or controversial. Christian Churches then have been agents of oppression—that is commonplace—but they can also be agents of liberation.

We do well in this context to remember and honour all those courageous Christians: saints, and seers, theologians and poets, mystics and writers who have championed the cause of animals. The list must include almost two thirds of those canonized saints East and West, not only St. Francis but also St. Martin, Richard of Chichester, Chrysostom, Isaac the Syrian, Bonaventure, and countless others. Poets also like Rosetti, Browning, Carlyle, Longfellow, Hardy, Cowper, and the many others who have led the way in sensitivity to the animal world. And if we are to be grateful for these luminaries, then one name especially must be mentioned, namely Arthur Broome. Few people appreciate that it was this Anglican priest who founded the first animal welfare society in the world, the RSPCA, in 1824. Fewer people appreciate that this Society was the result of Christian inspiration and vision. Even fewer appreciate that this Society was founded specifically on "Christian Faith and Christian Principles." Broome's work was immensely sacrificial. He served the Society as its first secretary; he gave up his London living to work full-time for the Society, he suffered imprisonment for the Society's debts, and finally died in obscurity. The animal movement today would be nowhere if it was not for this one man's courage and Christian faith. Long may his name be honoured among those who work for the cause of animals.

And there are just one or two hints today that Christians are again waking up to the idea that God's creation must not be reviled, anathematized, and treated as evil as in the past.

"[P]reoccupation with humanity will seem distinctly parochial . . . our theology . . . has been distorted by being too man-centered. We need to maintain the value, the preciousness of the human by maintaining the value, the preciousness of the non-human also." These words are not mine. They come from no less a person than the Archbishop of Canterbury, Robert Runcie, speaking in April of this year. He went on:

"For our concept of God forbids the idea of a cheap creation, of a throwaway universe in which everything is expendable save human existence. The whole universe is a work of love. And nothing which is made in love is cheap. The value, the worth of natural things is not found in Man's view of himself but in the goodness of God who made all things good and precious in his sight. . . ." As Barbara Ward used to say, "We have only one earth. Is it not worth our love?" These words may have cost our Archbishop more than we imagine. Let us congratulate him on his testimony and take heart.

The third thing we must learn is that we must not hate one another. It is no use people like me in the animal rights movement—complaining about animal abusers and the churches for their lack of love and compassion—when we so often show so little love and compassion to one another. I can give personal testimony here. I spent 4 years on the ruling council of one of the largest animal welfare societies in this country and 10 or more years later I am still trying to heal the wounds I suffered. The animal movement is the place where we can find as much if not more sin than anywhere else. Jealously, rivalry, misquotation, guile, stupidity, and, worst of all, self-righteousness. We must not fall into this last trap especially. None of us is pure when it comes to animals. We are all involved in animal abuse either through the food we eat, the products we buy, or the taxes we pay. There is no pure land on earth. A clean conscience is a figment of the imagination. I spend some of my time counselling students who suffer from unrelieved feelings of guilt—often inculcated by the Churches—I have no desire to make anyone feel guilty. Guilt is a redundant emotion.

Christians in the animal movement have a unique opportunity. St. Paul speaks of the creation as in a state of childbirth awaiting a new age. Together we have vision of a new age, a new world. A world at peace, a world in which we have begun to make peace with creation. A world in which the Love of God is claimed and championed and through whose Spirit new world possibilities are constantly being opened up for us. What a difference it would make if Christians began to practice the Gospel of Love they preach. At the very least what we need to do is to encourage and inspire people to live free of injury to animals. All of us, in addition to whatever social vision we may have, need a programme of personal disengagement from injury to animal life.

Let me be personal for a moment. I haven't always been an advocate of animal rights. By no means. When I was young I used to enjoy controlling animals and making them captive. I used to enjoy fishing. I used to eat animals. I had no problems about eating veal. My entry into the animal rights movement coincided with my entry into a slaughterhouse when I was 16 years old. The questions that it raised in my mind have been with me ever since. Recently, during my speaking tour of the United States, I visited another slaughterhouse in the State of Massachusetts. As I stood watching a young pig being slaughtered—"stuck" as they say in the US—I asked myself this question: "What has changed in 26 years when animals are still treated as things?" And soon I had my answer: the owner of the slaughterhouse, despite the fact that I had asked permission in the usual way, turfed me out. I'm not used to being turfed out of places. It was a new experience and a valuable one. For I learnt this one thing: What is changing is that many people, even those intensely involved in the exploitation of animals, many people are not so sure as they once were that what they are doing is right. People are beginning to have a conscience even in the most unlikely places.

When I became intellectually convinced of the case for animal rights, I first thought it one of those important but comparatively minor questions in Christian ethics. I don't think that today. On the contrary, I think the question of how we treat animals one of the BIG questions confronting all humanity: if God loves and cares for this world, shall we learn to live at peace with one another and with this world? In short: Are we to hate the world or are we to love it? "We must love one another or die," wrote W. H. Auden. The truth we also have to learn is this: We must love the world, or we shall perish with it.

3

⊿ *Down on the Factory Farm* ⊿

PETER SINGER

Peter Singer is the Ira W. DeCamp Professor of Bioethics at Princeton University. His many writings in ethics include Animal Liberation *from which this selection is taken,* Practical Ethics *and* In Defense of Animals.

For most human beings, especially those in modern urban and suburban communities, the most direct form of contact with non-human animals is at mealtime: we eat them. This simple fact is the key to our attitudes to other animals, and also the key to what each one of us can do about changing these attitudes. The use and abuse of animals raised for food far exceeds, in sheer numbers of animals affected, any other kind of mistreatment. Over 100 million cows, pigs, and sheep are raised and slaughtered in the United States alone each year; and for poultry the figure is a staggering 5 billion. (That means that about eight thousand birds—mostly chickens—will have been slaughtered in the time it takes you to read this page.) It is here, on our dinner table and in our neighborhood supermarket or butcher's shop, that we are brought into direct touch with the most extensive exploitation of other species that has ever existed.

In general, we are ignorant of the abuse of living creatures that lies behind the food we eat. Buying food in a store or restaurant is the culmination of a long process, of which all but the end product is delicately screened from our eyes. We buy our meat and poultry in neat plastic packages. It hardly bleeds. There is no reason to associate this package with a living, breathing, walking, suffering animal. The very words we use conceal its origins: we eat beef, not bull, steer, or cow, and pork, not pig—although for some reason we seem to find it easier to face the true nature of a leg of lamb. The term "meat" is itself deceptive. It originally meant any solid food, not necessarily the flesh of animals. This usage still lingers in an expression like "nut meat," which seems to imply a substitute for "flesh meat" but actually has an equally good claim to be called "meat" in its own right. By using the more general "meat" we avoid facing the fact that what we are eating is really flesh.

These verbal disguises are merely the top layer of a much deeper ignorance of the origin of our food. Consider the images conjured up by the word "farm": a house; a barn; a flock of hens, overseen by a strutting rooster, scratching around the farm-yard; a herd of cows being brought in from the fields for milking; and perhaps a sow rooting around in the orchard with a litter of squealing piglets running excitedly behind her.

Very few farms were ever as idyllic as that traditional image would have us believe. Yet we still think of a farm as a pleasant place, far removed from our own industrial, profit-conscious city life. Of those few who think about the lives of animals on farms, not many know much about modern methods of animal raising. Some people wonder whether animals are slaughtered painlessly, and anyone who has followed a truckload of cattle on the road will probably know that farm animals are transported in extremely crowded conditions; but not many suspect that transportation and slaughter are anything more than the brief and inevitable conclusion of a life of ease and contentment, a life that contains the natural pleasures of animal existence without the hardships that wild animals must endure in their struggle for survival.

These comfortable assumptions bear little relation to the realities of modern farming. For a start, farming is no longer controlled by simple country folk. During the last fifty years, large corporations and assembly-line methods of production have turned agriculture into agribusiness. The process began when big companies gained control of poultry production, once the preserve of the farmer's wife. Today, fifty large corporations virtually control all poultry production in the United States. In the field of egg production, where fifty years ago a big producer might have had three thousand laying hens, today many producers have more than 500,000 layers, and the largest have over 10 million. The remaining small producers have had to adopt the methods of the giants or else go out of business. Companies that had no connection with agriculture have become farmers on a huge scale in order to gain tax concessions or to diversify profits. Greyhound Corporation now produces turkeys, and your roast beef may have come from John Hancock Mutual Life Insurance or from one of a dozen oil companies that have invested in cattle feeding, building feedlots that hold 100,000 or more cattle.

The big corporations and those who must compete with them are not concerned with a sense of harmony among plants, animals, and nature. Farming is competitive and the methods adopted are those that cut costs and increase production. So farming is now "factory farming." Animals are treated like machines that convert low-priced fodder into high-priced flesh, and any innovation will be used if it results in a cheaper "conversion ratio." Most of this chapter is simply a description of these methods, and of what they mean for the animals to whom they are applied. The aim is to demonstrate that under these methods animals lead miserable lives from birth to slaughter. Once again, however, my point is not that the people who do these things to the animals are cruel and wicked. On the contrary, the attitudes of the consumers and the producers are not fundamentally different. The farming methods I am about to describe are merely the logical application of the attitudes and prejudices that are discussed elsewhere in this book. Once we place nonhuman animals outside our sphere of moral consideration and treat them as things we use to satisfy our own desires, the outcome is predictable.

The first animal to be removed from the relatively natural conditions of the traditional farm was the chicken. Human beings use chickens in two ways: for their flesh and for their eggs. There are now standard mass-production techniques for obtaining both of these products.

Promoters of agribusiness consider the rise of the chicken industry to be one of the great success stories of farming. At the end of World War II chicken for the table was still relatively rare. It came mainly from small independent farmers or from the unwanted males produced by egg-laying flocks. Today in the United States, 102 million broilers—as table chickens are called—are slaughtered each week after being reared in highly automated factorylike plants that belong to the large corporations that control production. Eight of these corporations account for over 50 percent of the 5.3 billion birds killed annually in the U.S.

The essential step in turning chickens from farmyard birds into manufactured items was confining them indoors. A producer of broilers gets a load of 10,000, 50,000, or more day-old chicks from the hatcheries, and puts them into a long, windowless shed— usually on the floor, although some producers use tiers of cages in order to get more birds into the same size shed. Inside the shed, every aspect of the birds' environment is controlled to make them grow faster on less feed. Food and water are fed automatically from hoppers suspended from the roof. The lighting is adjusted according to advice from agricultural researchers: for instance, there may be bright light twenty-four hours a day for the first week or two, to encourage the chicks to gain weight quickly; then the lights may be dimmed slightly and made to go off and on every two hours, in the belief that the chickens are readier to eat after a period of sleep; finally there comes a point, around six weeks of age, when the birds have grown so much that they are becoming crowded, and the lights will then be made very dim at all times. The point of this dim lighting is to reduce the aggression caused by crowding.

Broiler chickens are killed when they are seven weeks old (the natural lifespan of a chicken is about seven years). At the end of this brief period, the birds weigh between four and five pounds; yet they still may have as little as half a square foot of space per chicken—or less than the area of a sheet of standard typing paper. (In metric terms, this is 450 square centimeters for a hen weighing more than two kilos.) Under these conditions, when there is normal lighting, the stress of crowding and the absence of natural outlets for the birds' energies lead to outbreaks of fighting, with birds pecking at each other's feathers and sometimes killing and eating one another. Very dim lighting has been found to reduce such behavior and so the birds are likely to live out their last weeks in near-darkness.

Feather-pecking and cannibalism are, in the broiler producer's language, "vices." They are not natural vices, however; they are the result of the stress and crowding to which modern broiler producers subject their birds. Chickens are highly social animals, and in the farmyard they develop a hierarchy, sometimes called a "pecking order." Every bird yields, at the food trough or elsewhere, to those who are higher in the pecking order, and takes precedence over those who are below. There may be a few confrontations before the order is established, but more often than not a show of force, rather that actual physical contact, is enough. As Konrad Lorenz, a renowned observer of animal behavior, wrote in the days when flocks were still small:

Do animals thus know each other among themselves? They certainly do. . . . Every poultry farmer knows that. . . . there exists a very definite order, in which each bird is afraid of those that are above her in rank. After some few disputes, which need not necessarily come to blows, each bird knows which of the others she has to fear and which must show respect to her. Not only physical strength, but also personal courage, energy, and even the self-assurance of every individual bird are decisive in the maintenance of the pecking order.

Other studies have shown that a flock of up to ninety chickens can maintain a stable social order, each bird knowing its place; but 80,000 birds crowded together in a single shed is obviously a different matter. The birds cannot establish a social order, and as a result they fight frequently with each other. Quite apart from the inability of the individual bird to recognize so many other birds, the mere fact of extreme crowding probably contributes to irritability and excitability in chickens, as it does in human beings and other animals. This is something that farmers have long known:

> Feather-pecking and cannibalism easily become serious vices among birds kept under intensive conditions. They mean lower productivity and lost profits. Birds become bored and peck at some outstanding part of another bird's plumage. . . . While idleness and boredom are predisposing causes of the vices, cramped, stuffy and overheated housing are contributory causes.

Farmers must stop "vices" since they cost money; but, although they may know that overcrowding is the root cause, they cannot do anything about this, since in the competitive state of the industry, eliminating overcrowding could mean eliminating one's profit margin at the same time. Costs for the building, for the automatic feeding equipment, for the fuel used to heat and ventilate the building, and for the labor would remain the same, but with fewer birds per shed to sell, income would be reduced. So farmers direct their efforts to reducing the consequences of the stress that costs them money. The unnatural way in which the birds are kept causes the vices, but to control them the poultry farmer must make the conditions still more unnatural. Very dim lighting is one way of doing this. A more drastic step, though one now very widely used in the industry, is "debeaking."

First started in San Diego in the 1940s, debeaking used to be performed with a blowtorch. The farmer would burn away the upper beaks of the chickens so that they were unable to pick at each other's feathers. A modified soldering iron soon replaced this crude technique, and today specially designed guillotinelike devices with hot blades are the preferred instrument. The infant chick's beak is inserted into the instrument, and the hot blade cuts off the end of it. The procedure is carried out very quickly, about fifteen birds a minute. Such haste means that the temperature and sharpness of the blade can vary, resulting in sloppy cutting and serious injury to the bird:

> An excessively hot blade causes blisters in the mouth. A cold or dull blade may cause the development of a fleshy, bulblike growth on the end of the mandible. Such growths are very sensitive.

Joseph Mauldin, a University of Georgia extension poultry scientist, reported on his field observations at a conference on poultry health:

> There are many cases of burned nostrils and severe mutilations due to incorrect procedures which unquestionably influence acute and chronic pain, feeding behavior and production factors. I have evaluated beak trimming quality for private broiler companies and most are content to achieve 70% falling into properly trimmed categories. . . . Replacement pullets have their beaks trimmed by crews who are paid for quantity rather than quality work.

Even when the operation is done correctly, it is a mistake to think of it as a painless procedure, like cutting toenails. As an expert British government committee under zoologist Professor F. W. Rogers Brambell found some years ago:

Between the horn and the bone is a thin layer of highly sensitive soft tissue, resembling the "quick" of the human nail. The hot knife used in debeaking cuts through this complex of horn, bone and sensitive tissue, causing severe pain.

Moreover the damage done to the bird by debeaking is long term: chickens mutilated in this way eat less and lose weight for several weeks. The most likely explanation for this is that the injured beak continues to cause pain. J. Breward and M. J. Gentle, researchers at the British Agricultural and Food Research Council's Poultry Research Centre, investigated the beak stumps of debeaked hens and found that the damaged nerves grew again, turning in on themselves to form a mass of intertwining nerve fibers, called a neuroma. These neuromas have been shown in humans with amputated stumps to cause both acute and chronic pain. Breward and Gentle found that this is probably also the case in the neuromas formed by debeaking.

"A hen," Samuel Butler once wrote, "is only an egg's way of making another egg." Butler, no doubt, thought he was being funny; but when Fred C. Haley, president of a Georgia poultry firm that controls the lives of 225,000 laying hens, describes the hen as "an egg producing machine" his words have more serious implications. To emphasize his businesslike attitude, Haley adds, "The object of producing eggs is to make money. When we forget this objective, we have forgotten what it is all about."

Nor is this only an American attitude. A British farming magazine has told its readers:

> The modern layer is, after all, only a very efficient converting machine, changing the raw material—feedingstuffs—into the finished product—the egg—less, of course, maintenance requirements.

The idea that the layer is an efficient way to turn feed into eggs is common in the industry trade journals, particularly in advertisements. As may be anticipated, its consequences for the laying hens are not good.

Laying hens go through many of the same procedures as broilers, but there are some differences. Like broilers, layers have to be debeaked, to prevent the cannibalism that would otherwise occur in their crowded conditions; but because they live much longer than broilers, they often go through this operation twice. So we find poultry specialist Dick Wells, head of Britain's National Institute of Poultry Husbandry, recommending debeaking "sometime between 5 and 10 days of age," because there is less stress on the chicks at this time than if the operation is done earlier, and in addition "it is a good way of decreasing the risk of early mortality." When the hens are moved from the growing house to the laying facility between twelve and eighteen weeks of age they are often debeaked again.

The sufferings of laying chickens begin early in life. The newly hatched chicks are sorted into males and females by a "chick-puller." Since the male chicks have no commercial value, they are discarded. Some companies gas the little birds, but often they are dumped alive into a plastic sack and allowed to suffocate under the weight of other chicks dumped on top of them. Others are ground up, while still alive, to be turned into feed for their sisters. At least 160 million birds are gassed, suffocated, or die this way every year in the United States alone. Just how many suffer each particular fate is impossible to tell, because no records are kept: the growers think of getting rid of male chicks as we think of putting out the trash.

The economic demand that labor costs be kept to an absolute minimum means that laying hens get no more individual attention than broilers. Alan Hainsworth, owner of a poultry farm in upstate New York, told an inquiring local reporter that four hours a day was all he needed for the care of his 36,000 laying hens, while his wife looked after the 20,000 pullets: "It takes her about 15 minutes a day. All she checks is their automatic feeders, water cups and any deaths during the night."

This kind of care does not ensure a happy flock, though, as the reporter's description shows:

> Walk into the pullet house and the reaction is immediate—complete pandemonium. The squawking is loud and intense as some 20,000 birds shove to the farthest side of their cages in fear of the human intruders.

Julius Goldman's Egg City, fifty miles northwest of Los Angeles, was one of the first million-plus layer units. Already in 1970, when the *National Geographic Magazine* did an enthusiastic survey of what were then still relatively novel farming methods, it consisted of two million hens divided into block-long buildings containing 90,000 hens each, five birds to a sixteen-by-eighteen-inch cage. Ben Shames, Egg City's executive vice-president, explained to their reporter the methods used to look after so many birds:

> We keep track of the food eaten and the eggs collected in 2 rows of cages among the 110 rows in each building. When production drops to the uneconomic point, all 90,000 birds are sold to processors for potpies or chicken soup. It doesn't pay to keep track of every row in the house, let alone individual hens; with 2 million birds on hand you have to rely on statistical samplings.

In most egg factories the cages are stacked in tiers, with food and water troughs running along the rows filled automatically from a central supply. The cages have sloping wire floors. The slope—usually a gradient of one in five—makes it more difficult for the birds to stand comfortably, but it causes the eggs to roll to the front of the cage where they can easily be collected by hand or, in the more modern plants, carried by conveyor belt to a packing plant.

Since the first edition of this book was published, the conditions under which hens are housed in modern intensive farming have been the subject of numerous studies, both by scientific and governmental committees. In 1981 the British House of Commons Agriculture Committee issued a report on animal welfare in which it said "we have seen for ourselves battery cages, both experimental and commercial, and we greatly dislike what we saw." The committee recommended that the British government should take the initiative in having battery cages phased out within five years. Still more telling, however, was a study conducted at the Houghton Poultry Research Station in Britain on the space required by hens for various activities. This study found that the typical hen at rest physically occupies an area of 637 square centimeters, but if a bird is to be able to turn around at ease, she would need a space of 1,681 square centimeters if kept in a single cage. In a five-bird cage, the study concluded that the size of the cage should allow room at the front for all birds, and therefore needed to be not less than 106.5 centimeters long and 41 centimeters deep, giving each bird 873 square centimeters (approximately 42 by 16 inches). The 48 square inches noted above in the *Poultry Tribune* article, when five birds are in the standard twelve-by-twenty-inch cages, converts to just 300 square centimeters. With only four birds in such cages, each bird has 375 square centimeters.

Although the British government has taken no action on the recommendation to take the initiative in phasing out cages, change is possible. In 1981 Switzerland began a ten-year phase-out of battery cages. By 1987 birds in cages had to have a minimum of 500 square centimeters; and on the first day of 1992, traditional cages will be outlawed and all laying hens will have access to protected, soft-floored nesting boxes. In the Netherlands, conventional battery cages will become illegal in 1994, and hens will have a minimum space allowance of 1,000 square centimeters, as well as access to nesting and scratching areas. More far-reaching still, however, is a Swedish law passed in July 1988 that requires the abolition of cages for hens over the next ten years and states that cows, pigs, and animals raised for their furs must be kept "in as natural an environment as possible."

The rest of Europe is still debating the future of the battery cage. In 1986 the ministers of agriculture of the European Community countries set the minimum space allowance for laying hens at 450 square centimeters. Now it has been decided that this minimum will not become a legal requirement until 1995. Dr. Mandy Hill, deputy director of the British Ministry of Agriculture's Gleadthorpe experimental farm, has estimated that 6.5 million birds in Britain will need to be rehoused, indicating that this many birds at present have less than this ridiculously low minimum. But since the total British laying flock is around 50 million, and approximately 90 percent of these are kept in cages, this also shows that the new minimum will do no more than write into the law the very high stocking densities that most egg producers are already using. Only a minority who squeeze their birds even more tightly than is standard in the industry will have to change. Meanwhile in 1987 the European Parliament recommended that battery cages be phased out in the European Community within ten years. But the European Parliament only has advisory powers, and Europeans anxious to see the end of the cages have nothing to celebrate yet.

The United States, however, lags far behind Europe in even beginning to tackle this problem. The European Community minimum standard of 450 square centimeters is equivalent to seventy square inches per hen; in the United States, United Egg Producers has recommended forty-eight square inches as a U.S. standard. But the space allowed to birds on farms is often still less. At the Hainsworth farm in Mt. Morris, New York, four hens were squeezed into cages twelve inches by twelve inches—36 square inches per bird—and the reporter added: "Some hold five birds when Hainsworth has more birds than room." The truth is that whatever official or semiofficial recommendations there may be, one never knows how many hens are packed into cages unless one goes and looks. In Australia, where a government "Code of Practice" suggests that there should be no more than four hens in an eighteen-by-eighteen-inch cage, an unannounced visit to one farm in the state of Victoria in 1988 revealed seven birds in one cage that size, and five or six in many others. Yet the Department of Agriculture in the state of Victoria refused to prosecute the producer. Seven birds in a cage eighteen inches square have just 289 square centimeters, or forty-six square inches. At these stocking rates a single sheet of typing paper represents the living space for two hens, and the birds are virtually sitting on top of each other.

Of all the forms of intensive farming now practiced, the veal industry ranks as the most morally repugnant. The essence of veal raising is the feeding of a high-protein food to confined, anemic calves in a manner that will produce a tender, pale-colored flesh that will be served to the patrons of expensive restaurants. Fortunately this industry does not compare in size with poultry, beef, or pig production; nevertheless it is worth our attention became it represents an extreme, both in the degree of exploitation to which it subjects the animals and in its absurd inefficiency as a method of providing people with nourishment.

Veal is the flesh of a young calf. The term was originally reserved for calves killed before they had been weaned from their mothers. The flesh of these very young animals was paler and more tender than that of a calf who had begun to eat grass; but there was not much of it, since calves begin to eat grass when they are a few weeks old and still very small. The small amount available came from the unwanted male calves produced by the dairy industry. A day or two after being born they were trucked to market where, hungry and frightened by the strange surroundings and the absence of their mothers, they were sold for immediate delivery to the slaughterhouse.

Then in the 1950s veal producers in Holland found a way to keep the calf alive longer without the flesh becoming red or less tender. The trick depends on keeping the calf in highly unnatural conditions. If calves were left to grow up outside they would romp around the fields, developing muscles that would toughen their flesh and burning up calories that the producer must replace with costly feed. At the same time they would eat grass, and their flesh would lose the pale color that the flesh of newborn calves has. So the specialist veal producers take their calves straight from the auction ring to a confinement unit. Here, in a converted barn or specially built shed, they have rows of wooden stalls, each 1 foot 10 inches wide by 4 feet 6 inches long. It has a slatted wooden floor, raised above the concrete floor of the shed. The calves are tethered by a chain around the neck to prevent them from turning in their stalls when they are small. (The chain may be removed when the calves grow too big to turn around in such narrow stalls.) The stall has no straw or other bedding, since the calves might eat it, spoiling the paleness of their flesh. They leave their stalls only to be taken out to slaughter. They are fed a totally liquid diet, based on nonfat milk powder with vitamins, minerals, and growth-promoting drugs added. Thus the calves live for the next sixteen weeks. The beauty of the system, from the producers' point of view, is that at this age the veal calf may weigh as much as four hundred pounds, instead of the ninety-odd pounds that newborn calves weigh; and since veal fetches a premium price, rearing veal calves in this manner is a profitable occupation.

This method of raising calves was introduced to the United States in 1962 by Provimi, Inc., a feed manufacturer based in Watertown, Wisconsin. Its name comes from the "proteins, vitamins, and minerals" of which its feeds are composed—ingredients that, one might think, could be put to better use than veal raising. Provimi, according to its own boast, created this "new and complete concept in veal raising" and it is still by far the largest company in the business, controlling 50 to 75 percent of the domestic market. Its interest in promoting veal production lies in developing a market for its feed. Describing what it considered "optimum veal production," Provimi's now defunct newssheet, *The Stall Street Journal,* gives us an insight into the nature of the industry, which in the United States and some European countries has remained essentially unchanged since its introduction:

> The dual aims of veal production are firstly, to produce a calf of the greatest weight in the shortest possible time and secondly, to keep its meat as light colored as possible to fulfill the consumer's requirement. All at a profit commensurate to the risk and investment involved.

The young calves sorely miss their mothers. They also miss something to suck on. The urge to suck is strong in a baby calf, as it is in a baby human. These calves have no teat to suck on, nor do they have any substitute. From their first day in confinement—which may well be only the third or fourth day of their lives—they drink from a plastic bucket. Attempts have been made to feed calves through artificial teats, but the task of keeping the teats clean and sterile is apparently not worth the producer's trouble. It is common to see calves frantically trying to suck some part of their stalls, although there is usually nothing suitable; and if you offer a veal calf your finger you will find that he immediately begins to suck on it, as human babies suck their thumbs.

Later the calf develops a need to ruminate—that is, to take in roughage and chew the cud. But roughage is strictly forbidden because it contains iron and will darken the flesh, so, again, the calf may resort to vain attempts to chew the sides of his stall. Digestive disorders, including stomach ulcers, are common in veal calves. So is chronic diarrhea. To quote the Bristol study once again:

> The calves are deprived of dry feed. This completely distorts the normal development of the rumen and encourages the development of hair balls which may also lead to chronic indigestion.

As if this were not enough, the calf is deliberately kept anemic. Provimi's *Stall Street Journal* explains why:

> Color of veal is one of the primary factors involved in obtaining "top-dollar" returns from the fancy veal markets. . . . "Light color" veal is a premium item much in demand at better clubs, hotels and restaurants. "Light color" or pink veal is partly associated with the amount of iron in the muscle of the calves.

So Provimi's feeds, like those of other manufacturers of veal feeds, are deliberately kept low in iron. A normal calf would obtain iron from grass and other forms of roughage, but since veal calves are not allowed this, they become anemic. Pale pink flesh is in fact anemic flesh. The demand for flesh of this color is a matter of snob appeal. The color does not affect the taste and it certainly does not make the flesh more nourishing—it just means that it lacks iron.

The anemia is, of course, controlled. Without any iron at all the calves would drop dead. With a normal intake their flesh will not fetch as much per pound. So a balance is struck which keeps the flesh pale and the calves—or most of them—on their feet long enough for them to reach market weight.

The anemic calf's insatiable craving for iron is one of the reasons the producer is anxious to prevent him turning around in his stall. Although calves, like pigs, normally prefer not to go near their own urine or manure, urine does contain some iron. The desire for iron is strong enough to overcome the natural repugnance, and the anemic calves will lick the slats that are saturated with urine.

To make animals grow quickly they must take in as much food as possible, and they must use up as little of this food as possible in their daily life. To see that the veal calf takes in as much as possible, most calves are given no water. Their only source of liquid is their food—the rich milk replacer based on powdered milk and added fat. Since the buildings in which they are housed are kept warm, the thirsty animals take in more of their food than they would do if they could drink water. A common result of this overeating is that the calves break out in a sweat, rather like, it has been said, an executive who has had too much to eat too quickly. In sweating, the calf loses moisture, which makes him thirsty, so that he overeats again next time. By most standards this process is an unhealthy one, but by the standards of the veal producer aiming at producing the heaviest calf in the shortest possible time, the long-term health of the animal is irrelevant, so long as he survives to be taken to market; and so Provimi advises that sweating is a sign that "the calf is healthy and growing at capacity."

The one bright spot in this sorry tale is that the conditions created by the veal crates are so appalling for animal welfare that British government regulations now require that a calf must be able to turn around without difficulty, must be fed a daily diet containing "sufficient iron to maintain it in full health and vigour," and must receive enough fiber to allow normal development of the rumen. These are minimal welfare requirements, and still fall well short of satisfying the needs of calves; but they are violated by almost all the veal units in the United States and by many in Europe.

If the reader will recall that this whole laborious, wasteful, and painful process of veal raising exists for the sole purpose of pandering to people who insist on pale, soft veal, no further comment should be needed.

4

⋈ The Use of Animals in Science ⋈

SIDNEY GENDIN

Sidney Gendin teaches philosophy at Eastern Michigan University. He has contributed numerous papers to professional journals in moral, political, and social philosophy.

Although each year only about 5 percent of all animal deaths at the hands of human beings result from the use of animals in science, the number killed—in the neighborhood of 500 million—is not inconsiderable.[1] If we are to make an intelligent judgment about the ethics and scientific wisdom of permitting this many animals to be used in scientific settings, we must begin to inform ourselves at least about the broad contours of their use: for what purposes they are used, under what conditions, and with what legal protection, for example. . . .

CATEGORIES AND NUMBERS

Product Testing

Animals are routinely used to test the safety of consumer products. Acute and chronic toxicity tests are carried out on animals to establish toxic effects of low or high doses of such items as insecticides, pesticides, antifreeze, brake fluids, bleaches, Christmas tree sprays, silver and brass polish, oven cleaners, deodorants, skin fresheners, bubble baths, freckle creams, eye makeup, crayons, inks, suntan lotions, nail polish, zipper lubricants, paints, food dyes, chemical solvents, and floor cleaners. The test animals may be force-fed these products or have them rubbed or injected into their skin or dropped into their eyes. . . .

Behavioral Research

Behavioral research using animals may or may not involve pain. In many cases the experiments are the classic learning experiments in which mice or rats are required to run through mazes, move levers, or perform some comparable task. These may involve reward and punishment for success and failure. If the animal does not move the proper lever or does not move it quickly enough, it may not be fed or it may receive a small shock. Other psychological experiments typically performed on larger animals (usually primates) differ. For example, chimpanzees may be taken from their mothers, and a soft chimplike toy may serve as a surrogate mother. The baby chimps may experience different discomforts, while the scientist observes their degree of reliance on the mother-substitute.

Instructional Purposes

Animals are used for study in the classroom. High school students learning some elementary anatomy frequently dissect frogs. The frogs are often dead, but sometimes the students themselves must first deliver the *coup de grace.* High school students, and particularly college students, are not limited to frogs. Mice, rats, hamsters, guinea pigs, and cats are used to teach students, the majority of whom have no plans to become biologists, the elementary facts of anatomy by way of "hands-on" learning. . . .

In Vivo Tests

Animals are used whole and alive in so-called *in vivo* tests in the pharmaceutical industry. New drugs and vaccines are routinely tested on animals for their efficacy and safety before they are made available to humans.

Emergency Medicine

Animals are used in emergency medical situations. For example, primates have been killed and their organs have been immediately transplanted into humans to serve as very short-term support until satisfactory donors arrive. . . .

Long-Term Medical Research

Animals are used in long-term medical research, including research on cancer, AIDS, and herpes.

Biological Research

Animals are used in "pure" biological research. Frequently investigators have no particular medical aims in mind but, rather, are trying to advance scientific knowledge. It is commonplace knowledge in science that some of the most important medical advances have come about serendipitously in the course of pure research.

A statistical tabulation of the number of animals used for scientific purposes in any country can at best be only a good estimate. Despite claims to the contrary, nobody is keeping very close count. What is counted, in the United Kingdom for example, are the number of animals used in experiments that are funded by government agencies and, to a lesser extent, the number of animals used by pharmaceutical companies. In the United States, the convention is to estimate the number of animals used for such purposes at about 70 to 90 million per year. Some estimates, however, are as low as 15 million per year. Yet there are a few persons who claim that the best estimate is 120 million per year.[2] . . .

BEHIND THE STATISTICS

Besides statistics, the details of some uses of animals need our attention. The Draize test, an eye irritancy test, will concern us first. Then, in turn, we will examine some specific uses of animals—and the controversies they have inspired—in behavioral research, drug testing, and cancer research. Our aim is not to resolve but to better understand the ethical and scientific divisions these uses engender.

The Draize Test[3]

In the cosmetics industry, one of the more commonly used methods to screen products for their safety is the Draize test, named after its inventor, John Draize, who developed the method in 1944. The test consists of placing rabbits in stocks that immobilize their heads and then dropping the substance to be tested into one eye, using the other eye as a control. The testing takes place over several days and may lead to opacity of the cornea, hemorrhage, ulceration, blindness, and nearly always to considerable irritation and pain. Indeed, the pain is sometimes so great that rabbits have been known to break their backs in efforts to free themselves from the stocks. Rabbits are particularly well suited for this experiment because their tear ducts are too inefficient to wipe away or dilute the product being tested.

In the United States, retail cosmetics sales amount to about $10 billion per year and there are approximately 24,000 different cosmetics containing about 8,000 ingredients. . . . Indeed, there are hundreds of small firms, such as the by-now well known Beauty Without Cruelty, that produce lines of cosmetics, toiletries, and clothing that are neither tested on animals nor made from animal parts.

Behavioral Research

Although behavioral research is not the exclusive domain of psychologists, and although psychologists sometimes report their findings in nonpsychological journals, we shall limit the survey to what appears in psychology journals because that is the area in dispute.[4]

In a 1975 paper in the *Journal of Abnormal Psychology,* researchers reported investigations of the facial expressions and social responsiveness of blind monkeys. First, the eyes of five macaque monkeys were removed prior to the 19th day of life. The young monkeys were then separated from their mothers, who were placed in separate cages. Upon the mothers' uttering calls of alarm, the time required for the monkeys to contact their mothers' cages was measured. These interactions were compared with those of young monkeys who were not blinded. The researchers concluded that all the usual facial expressions of sighted monkeys are also observed in blinded ones.

Cats are often used in brain lesion experiments. Several such experiments are reported in the *Journal of Comparative and Physiological Psychology* in 1977. A team of researchers from the Department of Psychology of the University of Iowa offered this report:

Because an abnormal grooming behavior that is mediated by the superior colliculi is elicited from cats with pontile lesions, an ablation study of the structures was conducted to specify quantitatively the changes in grooming behavior. Cats that underwent the surgical procedure except for the lesion and cats with lesions of the auditory and visual cortices served as control groups.

The researchers found that "grooming behavior in cats with pontile or tectal lesions [was] deficient in removing tapes stuck on their fur."

Experiments at Harvard University utilized squirrel monkeys trained to press a lever under fixed-interval schedules of food or electric shock presentation. The purpose was to compare hose biting induced by these two methods of scheduling. The monkeys were strapped in restraining chairs and a bite hose was mounted in front of them. Shocks were administered to the monkeys' tails and the frequency, duration, and pressure of biting were measured. The responses were compared with those induced by food presentations in various sophisticated ways. The animals were also studied under a range of doses of amphetamines. Various findings were duly reported in the *Journal of Experimental Analysis of Behavior,* vol. 27, 1977.

At the Veteran's Administration Hospital, Perry Point, Maryland, dogs were placed in an experimental chamber and restrained on a table. They had to press a response panel to escape electric shock. Later their bladders were removed and ureters were externalized so that urine samples could be taken without storage in the now missing bladders. After surgery, the "animals were subjected to lengthy experience with various aversive schedules." In fact, they were subjected to 140 sessions of unavoidable shock with an intensity of 8.0 mA. The sessions lasted five hours per day, five days per week. Tranquilizers were administered, and the researchers concluded that "chlorpromazine consistently reduced avoidance response rates in dogs, producing consequent increases in shock rate." They also discovered that heart rate and urinary volume "showed no consistent pattern of results in response to drug administration."

Drs. Steven Maier and Martin Seligman did "learned helplessness" studies on 150 dogs over a four-year period in which inescapable shock was studied. These responses were compared with responses in cats, rats, primates, and other species. It was noted that when response is totally debilitated and nothing can be done to escape pain, then "the learned helplessness effect seems rather general among species that learn." Elsewhere it is argued that learned helplessness serves as a laboratory model of depression in humans. The effects of uncontrollable events influence a person's self-concept, assertiveness, aggressiveness, and even spatial localization. It is argued that to the extent that a person's depression makes him deficient in these various traits "the learned helplessness model is confirmed or disconfirmed."

Behavioral research on animals remains one of the most controversial areas even within the psychology community itself. . . .

Drug Testing

Drug testing is a central part of medical research, and the former use of the drug thalidomide highlights most dramatically the grave problems encountered in this area. Thalidomide was introduced to treat morning sickness in pregnant women and tested on a wide range of animal species before being made available to humans. Its use by pregnant women caused severe abnormalities in newborn babies. . . .

As the thalidomide tragedy illustrates, there is an inherent difficulty in trying to predict adverse reactions to humans from studies in experimental animals. One simply cannot automatically extrapolate information from animal studies that yields either necessary or sufficient conditions concerning their safety for humans. In other words, drugs that are harmless or positively beneficial to other species of animals sometimes prove highly dangerous to us. Penicillin is an interesting example of a drug that is fatal to guinea pigs even in very low doses. Other drugs useful to humans that are deadly to many animals include epinephrine, salicylates, insulin, cortisone, and meclizine. Drugs are not only dose-specific but species specific. Species specificity is a function of differences in absorption, metabolism, excretion, gestation periods and a host of other common biological functions.

A second problem inherent in toxicity testing of drugs on animals is that the animals cannot describe their experiences, including the aches and pains that are sometimes the side effects of drugs. For example, they cannot inform us of headache, giddiness, and feelings of nausea. Finally, animal tests are nearly all short term, and some chemicals may take the length of a human life time to produce their delayed effects. . . .

Cancer Research

The most feared of all diseases is cancer, and for that reason I shall focus the medical discussion exclusively on animal cancer research, but to a great extent the following remarks are generalizable throughout the entire area of medicine.

The infectious and nutritive-based diseases that ravaged the people of previous centuries are now in decline. It is generally conceded that progress made against infectious diseases owes most to personal hygiene and community-wide sanitation, the concern for these factors having been inspired by the discovery of germs. The foundation of nutritional science was the discovery of vitamins, and their role in health owes almost nothing to animal experimentation.[5] In any case, the decrease of these diseases has meant the rise of deaths attributable to other causes. Today, about one in three deaths in middle age is due to cancer. There are of course many kinds of cancers and these tend to affect specific parts of the body: the breast, lung, lymph glands, pancreas, esophagus, rectum, and stomach are the principal areas. Over the last 30 years or so, the incidence of cancer of the rectum and stomach has declined but most of the other cancers have increased. The greatest increase is in lung cancer. In England there was a 136 percent increase from 1951 to 1975. Yet even as far back as 1914 epidemiology successfully identified the causes of a variety of cancers. About 85 percent of them are environmentally induced: excessive exposure to sunlight (skin cancers), smoking cigarettes (lung cancer), smoking pipes (lip and tongue cancers), industrial pollution (a range of blood, lung and other cancers), and carcinogenic food additives (a similar wide range). Smoking accounts for 40 percent of cancers in men. Meat consumption has been found to be associated with cancer of the colon, and breast cancers are related to dietary fats. Asbestos, vinyl chloride, and benzene are examples of industrial carcinogens. X-rays used to counter cancer (radiation therapy) and anticancer drugs are ironically also implicated in the production of cancers.

How was all this discovered? Not by animal experimentation but mainly by studies in epidemiology. Accordingly, many see a bitter irony in the experimental production of cancers in animals. In the vast majority of cases, they claim, the tested substances are already known to be carcinogenic to humans. . . .

Moreover, critics allege that animal-based research, despite public relations to the contrary, tends to be unproductive. The favorite cancer research animal is the mouse. Since 1955 the National Cancer Institute (NCI) has screened about half a million chemicals on mice in its search for a useful drug against cancer. NCI does not just test chemicals on mice to see if they are effective; it also uses these chemicals to induce cancers in the animals. But most mouse cancers are sarcomas (cancers arising in the bone, connective tissue or muscle), while most human cancers are carcinomas (cancers arising in membranes). Thus, although the screening has had some good results, critics claim that none of the drugs discovered as a result of it are as effective or useful as the ten major anticancer drugs discovered before the screening began.

ALTERNATIVES

Those critical of the use of animals in science do not argue that we ought to forgo science. Rather, they insist that we must explore alternatives. What are these alternatives and what are their possibilities? Here, briefly, is a list of the major ones:

1. Mathematical and computer modeling of anatomy-physiology relationships.
2. The use of lower organisms, such as bacteria and fungi, for tests of mutagenicity.
3. The development of more sophisticated *in vitro* techniques, including the use of subcellular fractions, short-term cellular systems (cell suspensions, tissue biopsies, whole organ perfusion), and tissue cultures (the maintenance of living cells in a nutritive medium for 24 hours or longer).
4. More reliance on human studies, including epidemiology, postmarketing surveillance, and the carefully regulated use of human volunteers.

I shall discuss only the first three of these because it is in these areas that scientists who use animals in medical research have been the most skeptical. . . .

Models

Computer simulations are often mentioned as a better model for scientific purposes than any animal. Although this claim may be a bit of hyperbole, the fact is that for many purposes they are as good, and future dependency on them can only result in their becoming much better. In particular, where physiological systems are well understood and definable in mathematical terms, good programs are already available. (In the ensuing discussion, a number of examples will be offered.) Some complex systems are poorly understood and therefore programs don't exist in these areas. Of course, in such cases, critics claim that relying on animals as models cannot be much better. But unlike the programs, the animals are already available.

It is important to understand that when mathematicians speak of computer models, they do not mean tiny replicas of large things. Mathematicians construct systems that they hope will mirror biological systems. Although the mathematical details are intricate, we can at least say this: These systems consist of equations into which biological data are input and analyses of data are output. Perhaps an example will elucidate. It is from a report by Dr. Alan Brady of the Bowman Gray School of Medicine, Winston-Salem.

According to Brady, the glucose tolerance test is an example of something that may be simulated by a computer in a way that actually facilitates research. The computer model offers researchers the opportunity to explore situations that are not practical or ethical with animal experiments. Computer simulation also organizes material more systematically than animal experiments do and thus is better suited for teaching physiology students. A computer user first enters starting and stopping times for glucose infusion, the rate of glucose utilization, and the initial insulin concentration, then data on blood pressure and certain rate constants. The programmed algorithms manipulate the figures to generate the simulated results. Plainly, glucose tolerance can be calculated more quickly, for a vaster array of "animals," and over a range of values far more inclusive than would occur in real life. As an added benefit, Brady points out that computer simulations in physiology are much cheaper than animal experiments because costs are pretty much limited to initial outlay for program development. . . .

Opponents of animal experiments who cry out for greater reliance upon computer simulations frequently exaggerate what is currently available, but those who are content simply to insist upon the current limitations perhaps reveal their own biases as well as a failure of the imagination. . . .

Some anatomy departments have begun interesting experiments in simulation. They have found that they can teach dissection and a host of other important surgical techniques to medical students using pseudoanimals. These can bleed, blink, cough, vomit, simulate gas exchange, and even "die" when necessary. Recently, Dr. Charles Short, Chief of Anesthesiology at Cornell Veterinary College, developed a dog mannequin called Resusci-Dog. It responds to a broad range of techniques necessary for practicing and refining "hands-on" cardiopulmonary skills. For example, if a student applies excessive pressure while doing cardiac massage, a certain signal bleeps; if pressure is misplaced, there is a different bleep; and a white light indicates proper massage. Typically, veterinary students induce heart attacks in real dogs and only then begin to practice their resuscitation skills. Death may show they have done the massage poorly. Resusci-Dog has a femoral pulse, and it can also be used for practice in certain syringe injections.

The Use of Lower Organisms

The best known of all tests on lower organisms as a replacement for animal tests is the Ames test, developed by Dr. Bruce Ames at the University of California at Berkeley. Although the Ames test actually discovers mutations-causing substances (mutagenicity), Ames believes it also screens for cancer-causing substances (carcinogenicity). This idea is based on the view that most carcinogenic substances are also mutagenic. Ames takes the suspected cancer-producing substance and puts it into a nutrient medium in which a strain of *Salmonella* bacteria is growing. If the tested substance really is mutagenic, then the *Salmonella* will develop the indicated mutations. About 80 percent of the carcinogens tested this way have resulted in mutation. When substances known not to be carcinogens are tested this way, only about 10 percent of them result in mutations. This corroborates the very close association of carcinogenicity and mutagenicity and makes the Ames test an excellent way of screening presumptive cancer-producing agents.[6] The Ames test, however, is not quite what some critics of animal-based tests claim it is. The medium in which the *Salmonella* grow is actually treated with a rat liver preparation first. Some liver preparation or other is needed at this point in the development of the test, but it need not be rat liver. In fact, Ames has used human liver obtained from autopsies, and his preference for rat liver is dictated by convenience. Nevertheless, the humane killing of a rat to induce mutagenic changes in *Salmonella* is much preferred by many opponents of animal tests to inducing cancers in rats themselves. The test is now fairly standard in about 3,000 laboratories.

Another interesting use for bacteria is in tests of water pollution. The standard procedure is to immerse fish in different concentrations of the effluent to be tested and observe what concentration kills 50 percent—one more variation of the LD-50 test. But Beckman Instruments company uses a strain of luminescent bacteria as the bioassay organism. The light–producing metabolism of the bacteria is six times more sensitive to toxicants than are fish, and the test takes half an hour in contrast to the 96–hour test used for fish.

Finally, work has begun in utilizing plants both for synthesis of useful drugs and as the subjects of *in vivo* research. Indeed, recent progress has been so significant that it has been argued that "there are sufficient numbers of bioassay techniques described in the current literature so that almost any biological activity of interest can be studied without utilizing intact animals." The National Cancer Institute has now screened over 40,000 species of plants for *in vivo* antitumor activity and has identified many that are highly active antitumor agents. Of course, their safety is first screened on animals before they are allowed to be included in clinical trials on humans. But Dr. Robert Sharpe has argued that plants themselves can have cancer induced into them. In particular, he claims, there is research supporting the replacement of mice by potatoes in traditional tests of leukemia. Although NCI has been doing plant tumor research for 25 years, it remains a fairly exotic frontier.

Tissue Cultures

Tissue culture research requires keeping cells alive outside a total organism. Animal cells have been cultured in laboratories since the 1920s. In the early days, the possibility of bacterial contamination imposed immense limitations on the use of tissue cultures. Today, antibiotics have removed those restrictions and tissue culture is available in nearly all research institutes in the world.

A tissue cell is typically cultivated in a medium such as a salt solution supplemented by various plasmas and serums to make the environment as natural as possible. The establishment of cell lines out of tissue cultures is essential for modern virology. Most viruses grow nicely in these media, enabling biochemists to observe all their changes. This, of course, is exactly what is needed for clinical diagnosis of viral disease. The best–known commercial application of virology is the production of vaccines for the polio virus, originally grown in kidney cells of monkeys but now normally grown in human cells. Rabies vaccines also are now grown in human diploid-cell cultures rather than in live animals.

Cell cultures are important in cancer research. For example, we can study the effect of certain hormones on tumor cells in cultures that have been obtained by the surgical removal of a cancerous breast. If the hormone inhibits the growth of the cells, this would be a promising sign for therapy. Another promising piece of research involves putting known cancer cells into a fertilized hen's egg. This causes the embryo to put outgrowths of cells toward the cancer cells, and the extent of the growth is related to the malignancy of the tumor. Some researchers maintain that the standard practice of introducing cancer cells into live animals to observe the development of the malignancy is not as sensible, since tumor development in animals is far slower than in fertilized eggs. . . . [7]

Advances are being made. For example, the liver is the main site of drug metabolism, and it is possible to incubate a drug with a liver preparation before putting it into a tissue culture. Some recent work has been successful in testing for a drug's carcinogenic activity. Hence the reliance on living creatures with livers may be overcome. In fact, it is the opinion of Dr. Philip Hanawalt, biology professor at Stanford University, that that day has already arrived. Hanawalt maintains that studies utilizing only cultured cells can elucidate the differences in how mouse cancers and human cancers originate. "New experimental techniques such as the analysis of cloned DNA from one cell to another, and the use of hybrid cells are particularly powerful and now render obsolete many approaches that have utilized animals to study mechanisms of carcinogenesis."

NOTES

1. This is an estimate of the number of animals killed for scientific purposes throughout the world. No figures are released by either the U.S.S.R. or China. Estimates for the United States range as low as 15 million to as high as 200 million. Conventional estimates are approximately 70 to 120 million. Among nations releasing data, Japan ranks second, with 19 million. My own estimate assumes that figures for the U.S.S.R. and China are comparable to those for the United States.

2. For a "traditional" estimate of 70 million, see Scientists Center for Animal Welfare (SCAW) *Newsletter* (June and October, 1984), p. 2. For 100 million, see B. E. Rollin, *Animal Rights and Human Morality* (Buffalo: Prometheus Books, 1981), p. 91. For 200 million, see R. Ryder, *Victims of Science* (London: National Anti-Vivisection Society, 1983), p. 24. Ryder only reports this estimate, he does not endorse it. He suggests 120 million. For the low estimate of 15 million, see Perrie Adams, "The Need to Conduct Scientific Investigations," address to the American Psychological Association, 1984.

3. The Draize test is one of the two major commercial tests that have aroused the ire of animal welfare and animal rights groups. The other is the LD-50 test. LD stands for lethal dose. In this test, animals are force-fed a dose of a substance that is being screened for toxicity. The amount of the dose is gradually increased to the point at which 50 percent of the test animals succumb. Further details may be gleaned from the aforementioned books by Rollin and Ryder.

4. More details of all five cases reported under Behavioral Research, including author citations, can be found in Jeff Diner, *Physical and Mental Suffering of Experimental Animals* (Washington, D.C.: Animal Welfare Institute, 1979). Diner's survey of over 200 experiments covers just the years 1973–1978.

5. Among dozens of skeptics and their publications concerning medicine's role in reducing infectious diseases are Rick Carlson, *The End of Medicine* (New York: Wiley, 1975), James Giles, *Medical Ethics* (Cambridge: Schenkman, 1983), and Victor Fuchs, *Who Shall Live?* (New York: Basic Books, 1975).

6. Bruce Ames is the author of over 140 articles on the subject of mutagenicity. I am indebted to him for having sent me a considerable number of these. Among the more recent are "A New Salmonella Tester Strain, TA97, for the Detection of Frameshift Mutagens: A Run of Cytosines as a Mutational Hot-Spot," *Mutation Research* (no. 94, 1982), pp. 315–330; "Revised Methods for the Salmonella Mutagenicity Test," *Mutation Research* (no. 113, 1983), pp. 173–215; and "A New Salmonella Tester Strain (TA 102) with A:T Base Pairs at the Site of Mutation Detects Oxidative Mutagens," *Proceedings of the National Academy of Science, USA* (no. 79, 1982), pp. 7445–7449.

7. The claim these researchers are making is not necessarily true of brain cancer but it is true of the far more common cancers of the breast and the lung.

5

⚏ *All Animals Are Equal* ⚏

PETER SINGER

"Animal Liberation" may sound more like a parody of other liberation movements than a serious objective. The idea of "The Rights of Animals" actually was once used to parody the case for women's rights. When Mary Wollstonecraft, a forerunner of today's feminists, published her *Vindication of the Rights of Woman* in 1792, her views were widely regarded as absurd, and before long an anonymous publication appeared entitled *A Vindication of the Rights of Brutes.* The author of this satirical work (now known to have been Thomas Taylor, a distinguished Cambridge philosopher) tried to refute Mary Wollstonecraft's arguments by showing that they could be carried one stage further. If the argument for equality was sound when applied to women, why should it not be applied to dogs, cats, and horses? The reasoning seemed to hold for these "brutes" too; yet to hold that brutes had rights was manifestly absurd. Therefore the reasoning by which this conclusion had been reached must be unsound, and if unsound when applied to brutes, it must also be unsound when applied to women, since the very same arguments had been used in each case.

In order to explain the basis of the case for the equality of animals, it will be helpful to start with an examination of the case for the equality of women. Let us assume that we wish to defend the case for women's rights against the attack by Thomas Taylor. How should we reply?

One way in which we might reply is by saying that the case for equality between men and women cannot validly be extended to nonhuman animals. Women have a right to vote, for instance, because they are just as capable of making rational decisions about the future as men are; dogs, on the other hand, are incapable of understanding the significance of voting, so they cannot have the right to vote. There are many other obvious ways in which men and women resemble each other closely, while humans and animals differ greatly. So, it might be said, men and women are similar beings and should have similar rights, while humans and nonhumans are different and should not have equal rights.

The reasoning behind this reply to Taylor's analogy is correct up to a point, but it does not go far enough. There are obviously important differences between humans and other animals, and these differences must give rise to some differences in the rights that each have. Recognizing this evident fact, however, is no barrier to the case for extending the basic principle of equality to nonhuman animals. The differences that exist between men and women are equally undeniable, and the supporters of Women's Liberation are aware that these differences may give rise to different rights. Many feminists hold that women have the right to an abortion on request. It does not follow that since these same feminists are campaigning for equality between men and women they must support the right of men to have abortions too. Since a man cannot have an abortion, it is meaningless to talk of his right to have one. Since dogs can't vote, it is meaningless to talk of their right to vote. There is no reason why either Women's Liberation or Animal Liberation should get involved in such nonsense. The extension of the basic principle of equality from one group to another does not imply that we must treat both groups in exactly the same way, or grant exactly the same rights to both groups. Whether we should do so will depend on the nature of the members of the two groups. The basic principle of equality does not require equal or identical *treatment;* it requires equal consideration. Equal consideration for different beings may lead to different treatment and different rights.

So there is a different way of replying to Taylor's attempt to parody the case for women's rights, a way that does not deny the obvious differences between human beings and nonhumans but goes more deeply into the question of equality and concludes by finding nothing absurd in the idea that the basic principle of equality applies to so-called brutes. At this point such a conclusion may appear odd; but if we examine more deeply the basis on which our opposition to discrimination on grounds of race or sex ultimately rests, we will see that we would be on shaky ground if we were to demand equality for blacks, women, and other groups of oppressed humans while denying equal consideration to nonhumans. To make this clear we need to see, first, exactly why racism and sexism are wrong. When we say that all human beings, whatever their race, creed, or sex, are equal, what is it that we are asserting? Those who wish to defend hierarchical, inegalitarian societies have often pointed out that by whatever test we choose it simply is not true that all humans are equal. Like it or not we must face the fact that humans come in different shapes and sizes; they come with different moral capacities, different intellectual abilities, different amounts of benevolent feeling and sensitivity to the needs of others, different abilities to communicate effectively, and different capacities to experience pleasure and pain. In short, if the demand for equality were based on the actual equality of all human beings, we would have to stop demanding equality.

Still, one might cling to the view that the demand for equality among human beings is based on the actual equality of the different races and sexes. Although, it may be said, humans differ as individuals, there are no differences between the races and sexes as such. From the mere fact that a person is black or a woman we cannot infer anything about that person's intellectual or moral capacities. This, it may be said, is why racism and sexism are wrong. The white racist claims that whites are superior to blacks, but this is false; although there are differences among individuals, some blacks are superior to some whites in all of the capacities and abilities that could conceivably be relevant. The opponent of sexism would say the same: a person's sex is no guide to his or her abilities, and this is why it is unjustifiable to discriminate on the basis of sex.

The existence of individual variations that cut across the lines of race or sex, however, provides us with no defense at all against a more sophisticated opponent of equality, one who proposes that, say, the interests of all those with IQ scores below 100 be given less consideration than the interests of those with ratings over 100. Perhaps those scoring below the mark would, in this society, be made the slaves of those scoring higher. Would a hierarchical society of this sort really be so much better than one based on race or sex? I think not. But if we tie the moral principle of equality to the factual equality of the different races or sexes, taken as a whole, our opposition to racism and sexism does not provide us with any basis for objecting to this kind of inegalitarianism.

There is a second important reason why we ought not to base our opposition to racism and sexism on any kind of factual equality, even the limited kind that asserts that variations in capacities and abilities are spread evenly among the different races and between the sexes: we can have no absolute guarantee that these capacities and abilities really are distributed evenly, without regard to race or sex, among human beings. So far as actual abilities are concerned there do seem to be certain measurable differences both among races and between sexes. These differences do not, of course, appear in every case, but only when averages are taken. More important still, we do not yet know how many of these differences are really due to the different genetic endowments of the different races and sexes, and how many are due to poor schools, poor housing, and other factors that are the result of past and continuing discrimination. Perhaps all of the important differences will eventually prove to be environmental rather than genetic. Anyone opposed to racism and sexism will certainly hope that this will be so, for it will make the task of ending discrimination a lot easier; nevertheless, it would be dangerous to rest the case against racism and sexism on the belief that all significant differences are environmental in origin. The opponent of, say, racism who takes this line will be unable to avoid conceding that if differences in ability did after all prove to have some genetic connection with race, racism would in some way be defensible.

Fortunately there is no need to pin the case for equality to one particular outcome of a scientific investigation. The appropriate response to those who claim to have found evidence of genetically based differences in ability among the races or between the sexes is not to stick to the belief that the genetic explanation must be wrong, whatever evidence to the contrary may turn up; instead we should make it quite clear that the claim to equality does not depend on intelligence, moral capacity, physical strength, or similar matters of fact. Equality is a moral idea, not an assertion of fact. There is no logically compelling reason for assuming that a factual difference in ability between two people justifies any difference in the amount of consideration we give to their needs and interests. *The principle of the equality of human beings is not a description of an alleged actual equality among humans: it is a prescription of how we should treat human beings.*

Jeremy Bentham, the founder of the reforming utilitarian school of moral philosophy, incorporated the essential basis of moral equality into his system of ethics by means of the formula: "Each to count for one and none for more than one." In other words, the interests of every being affected by an action are to be taken into account and given the same weight as the like interests of any other being. A later utilitarian, Henry Sidgwick, put the point in this way: "The good of any one individual is of no more importance, from the point of view (if I may say so) of the Universe, than the good of any other." More recently the leading figures in contemporary moral philosophy have shown a great deal of agreement in specifying as a fundamental presupposition of their moral theories some similar requirement that works to give everyone's interests equal consideration—although these writers generally cannot agree on how this requirement is best formulated.

It is an implication of this principle of equality that our concern for others and our readiness to consider their interest ought not to depend on what they are like or on what abilities they may possess. Precisely what our concern or consideration requires us to do may vary according to the characteristics of those affected by what we do: concern for the well-being of children growing up in America would require that we teach them to read; concern for the well-being of pigs may require no more than that we leave them with other pigs in a place where there is adequate food and room to run freely. But the basic element—the taking into account of the interests of the being, whatever those interests may be—must, according to the principle of equality, be extended to all beings, black or white, masculine or feminine, human or nonhuman.

Thomas Jefferson, who was responsible for writing the principle of the equality of men into the American Declaration of Independence, saw this point. It led him to oppose slavery even though he was unable to free himself fully from his slaveholding background. He wrote in a letter to the author of a book that emphasized the notable intellectual achievements of Negroes in order to refute the then common view that they had limited intellectual capacities:

> Be assured that no person living wishes more sincerely than I do, to see a complete refutation of the doubts I myself have entertained and expressed on the grade of understanding alloted to them by nature, and to find that they are on a par with ourselves . . . but whatever be their degree of talent it is no measure of their rights. Because Sir Isaac Newton was superior to others in understanding, he was not therefore lord of the property or persons of others.

Similarly, when in the 1850s the call for women's rights was raised in the United States, a remarkable black feminist named Sojourner Truth made the same point in more robust terms at a feminist convention:

> They talk about this thing in the head; what do they call it? ["Intellect," whispered someone nearby.] That's it. What's that got to do with women's rights or Negroes' rights? If my cup won't hold but a pint and yours holds a quart, wouldn't you be mean not to let me have my little half-measure full?

It is on this basis that the case against racism and the case against sexism must both ultimately rest; and it is in accordance with this principle that the attitude that we may call "speciesism," by analogy with racism, must also be condemned. Speciesism—the word is not an attractive one, but I can think of no better term—is a prejudice or attitude of bias in favor of the interests of members of one's own species and against those of members of other species. It should be obvious that the fundamental objections to racism and sexism made by Thomas Jefferson and Sojourner Truth apply equally to speciesism. If possessing a higher degree of intelligence does not entitle one human to use another for his or her own ends, how can it entitle humans to exploit nonhumans for the same purpose?

Many philosophers and other writers have proposed the principle of equal consideration of interests, in some form or other, as a basic moral principle; but not many of them have recognized that this principle applies to members of other species as well as to our own. Jeremy Bentham was one of the few who did realize this. In a forward-looking passage written at a time when black slaves had been freed by the French but in the British dominions were still being treated in the way we now treat animals, Bentham wrote:

The day *may* come when the rest of the animal creation may acquire those rights which never could have been withholden from them but by the hand of tyranny. The French have already discovered that the blackness of the skin is no reason why a human being should be abandoned without redress to the caprice of a tormentor. It may one day come to be recognized that the number of the legs, the villosity of the skin, or the termination of the *os sacrum* are reasons equally insufficient for abandoning a sensitive being to the same fate. What else is it that should trace the insuperable line? Is it the faculty of reason, or perhaps the faculty of discourse? But a full-grown horse or dog is beyond comparison a more rational, as well as a more conversable animal, than an infant of a day or a week or even a month, old. But suppose they were otherwise, what would it avail? The question is not, Can they *reason?* nor Can they *talk?* but, Can they *suffer?*

In this passage Bentham points to the capacity for suffering as the vital characteristic that gives a being the right to equal consideration. The capacity for suffering—or more strictly, for suffering and/or enjoyment or happiness—is not just another characteristic like the capacity for language or higher mathematics. Bentham is not saying that those who try to mark "the insuperable line" that determines whether the interests of a being should be considered happen to have chosen the wrong characteristic. By saying that we must consider the interests of all beings with the capacity for suffering or enjoyment Bentham does not arbitrarily exclude from consideration any interests at all—as those who draw the line with reference to the possession of reason or language do. The capacity for suffering and enjoyment is a *prerequisite for having interests at all,* a condition that must be satisfied before we can speak of interests in a meaningful way. It would be nonsense to say that it was not in the interests of a stone to be kicked along the road by a schoolboy. A stone does not have interests because it cannot suffer. Nothing that we can do to it could possibly make any difference to its welfare. The capacity for suffering and enjoyment is, however, not only necessary, but also sufficient for us to say that a being has interests—at an absolute minimum, an interest in not suffering. A mouse, for example, does have an interest in not being kicked along the road, because it will suffer if it is.

Although Bentham speaks of "rights" in the passage I have quoted, the argument is really about equality rather than about rights. Indeed, in a different passage, Bentham famously described "natural rights" as "nonsense" and "natural and imprescriptable rights" as "nonsense upon stilts." He talked of moral rights as a shorthand way of referring to protections that people and animals morally ought to have; but the real weight of the moral argument does not rest on the assertion of the existence of the right, for this in turn has to be justified on the basis of the possibilities for suffering and happiness. In this way we can argue for equality for animals without getting embroiled in philosophical controversies about the ultimate nature of rights.

In misguided attempts to refute the arguments of this book, some philosophers have gone to much trouble developing arguments to show that animals do not have rights. They have claimed that to have rights a being must be autonomous, or must be a member of a community, or must have the ability to respect the rights of others, or must possess a sense of justice. These claims are irrelevant to the case for Animal Liberation. The language of rights is a convenient political shorthand. It is even more valuable in the era of thirty-second TV news clips than it was in Bentham's day; but in the argument for a radical change in our attitude to animals, it is in no way necessary.

If a being suffers there can be no moral justification for refusing to take that suffering into consideration. No matter what the nature of the being, the principle of equality requires that its suffering be counted equally with the like suffering—insofar as rough comparisons can be made—of any other being. If a being is not capable of suffering, or of experiencing enjoyment or happiness, there is nothing to be taken into account. So the limit of sentience (using the term as a convenient if not strictly accurate shorthand for the capacity to suffer and/or experience enjoyment) is the only defensible boundary of concern for the interests of others. To mark this boundary by some other characteristic like intelligence or rationality would be to mark it in an arbitrary manner. Why not choose some other characteristic, like skin color?

Racists violate the principle of equality by giving greater weight to the interests of members of their own race when there is a clash between their interests and the interests of those of another race. Sexists violate the principle of equality by favoring the interests of their own sex. Similarly, speciesists allow the interests of their own species to override the greater interests of members of other species. The pattern is identical in each case.

Most human beings are speciesists. The following chapters show that ordinary human beings—not a few exceptionally cruel or heartless humans, but the overwhelming majority of humans—take an active part in, acquiesce in, and allow their taxes to pay for practices that require the sacrifice of the most important interests of members of other species in order to promote the most trivial interests of our own species.

There is, however, one general defense of the practices to be described in the next two chapters that needs to be disposed of before we discuss the practices themselves. It is a defense which, if true, would allow us to do anything at all to nonhumans for the slightest reason, or for no reason at all, without incurring any justifiable reproach. This defense claims that we are never guilty of neglecting the interests of other animals for one breathtakingly simple reason: they have no interests. Nonhuman animals have no interests, according to this view, because they are not capable of suffering. By this is not meant merely that they are not capable of suffering in all the ways that human beings are—for instance, that a calf is not capable of suffering from the knowledge that it will be killed in six months time. That modest claim is, no doubt, true; but it does not clear humans of the charge of speciesism, since it allows that animals may suffer in other ways—for instance, by being given electric shocks, or being kept in small, cramped cages. The defense I am about to discuss is the much more sweeping, although correspondingly less plausible, claim that animals are incapable of suffering in any way at all; that they are, in fact, unconscious automata, possessing neither thoughts nor feelings nor a mental life of any kind.

Although, as we shall see in a later chapter, the view that animals are automata was proposed by the seventeenth-century French philosopher René Descartes, to most people, then and now, it is obvious that if, for example, we stick a sharp knife into the stomach of an unanesthetized dog, the dog will feel pain. That this is so is assumed by the laws in most civilized countries that prohibit wanton cruelty to animals. Readers whose common sense tells them that animals do suffer may prefer to skip the remainder of this section, moving straight on to page 63, since the pages in between do nothing but refute a position that they do not hold. Implausible as it is, though, for the sake of completeness this skeptical position must be discussed.

Do animals other than humans feel pain? How do we know? Well, how do we know if anyone, human or nonhuman, feels pain? We know that we ourselves can feel pain. We know this from the direct experience of pain that we have when, for instance, somebody presses a lighted cigarette against the back of our hand. But how do we know that anyone else feels pain? We cannot directly experience anyone else's pain, whether that "anyone" is our best friend or a stray dog. Pain is a state of consciousness, a "mental event," and as such it can never be observed. Behavior like writhing, screaming, or drawing one's hand away from the lighted cigarette is not pain itself; nor are the recordings a neurologist might make of activity within the brain observations of pain itself. Pain is something that we feel, and we can only infer that others are feeling it from various external indications.

In theory, we *could* always be mistaken when we assume that other human beings feel pain. It is conceivable that one of our close friends is really a cleverly constructed robot, controlled by a brilliant scientist so as to give all the signs of feeling pain, but really no more sensitive than any other machine. We can never know, with absolute certainty, that this is not the case. But while this might present a puzzle for philosophers, none of us has the slightest real doubt that our close friends feel pain just as we do. This is an inference, but a perfectly reasonable one, based on observations of their behavior in situations in which we would feel pain, and on the fact that we have every reason to assume that our friends are beings like us, with nervous systems like ours that can be assumed to function as ours do and to produce similar feelings in similar circumstances.

If it is justifiable to assume that other human beings feel pain as we do, is there any reason why a similar inference should be unjustifiable in the case of other animals?

Nearly all the external signs that lead us to infer pain in other humans can be seen in other species, especially the species most closely related to us—the species of mammals and birds. The behavioral signs include writhing, facial contortions, moaning, yelping or other forms of calling, attempts to avoid the source of pain, appearance of fear at the prospect of its repetition, and so on. In addition, we know that these animals have nervous systems very like ours, which respond physiologically as ours do when the animal is in circumstances in which we would feel pain: an initial rise of blood pressure, dilated pupils, perspiration, an increased pulse rate, and, if the stimulus continues, a fall in blood pressure. Although human beings have a more developed cerebral cortex than other animals, this part of the brain is concerned with thinking functions rather than with basic impulses, emotions, and feelings. These impulses, emotions, and feelings are located in the diencephalon, which is well developed in many other species of animals, especially mammals and birds.

We also know that the nervous systems of other animals were not artificially constructed—as a robot might be artificially constructed—to mimic the pain behavior of humans. The nervous systems of animals evolved as our own did, and in fact the evolutionary history of human beings and other animals, especially mammals, did not diverge until the central features of our nervous systems were already in existence. A capacity to feel pain obviously enhances a species' prospects of survival, since it causes members of the species to avoid sources of injury. It is surely unreasonable to suppose that nervous systems that are virtually identical physiologically, have a common origin and a common evolutionary function, and result in similar forms of behavior in similar circumstances should actually operate in an entirely different manner on the level of subjective feelings.

It has long been accepted as sound policy in science to search for the simplest possible explanation of whatever it is we are trying to explain. Occasionally it has been claimed that it is for this reason "unscientific" to explain the behavior of animals by theories that refer to the animal's conscious feelings, desires, and so on—the idea being that if the behavior in question can be explained without invoking consciousness or feelings, that will be the simpler theory. Yet we can now see that such explanations, when assessed with respect to the actual behavior of both human and nonhuman animals, are actually far more complex than rival explanations. For we know from our own experience that explanations of our own behavior that did not refer to consciousness and the feeling of pain would be incomplete; and it is simpler to assume that the similar behavior of animals with similar nervous systems is to be explained in the same way than to try to invent some other explanation for the behavior of nonhuman animals as well as an explanation for the divergence between humans and nonhumans in this respect.

The overwhelming majority of scientists who have addressed themselves to this question agree. Lord Brain, one of the most eminent neurologists of our time, has said:

> I personally can see no reason for conceding mind to my fellow men and denying it to animals. . . . I at least cannot doubt that the interests and activities of animals are correlated with awareness and feeling in the same way as my own, and which may be, for aught I know, just as vivid.

The author of a book on pain writes:

> Every particle of factual evidence supports the contention that the higher mammalian vertebrates experience pain sensations at least as acute as our own. To say that they feel less because they are lower animals is an absurdity; it can easily be shown that many of their senses are far more acute than ours—visual acuity in certain birds, hearing in most wild animals, and touch in others; these animals depend more than we do today on the sharpest possible awareness of a hostile environment. Apart from the complexity of the cerebral cortex (which does not directly perceive pain) their nervous systems are almost identical to ours and their reactions to pain remarkably similar, though lacking (so far as we know) the philosophical and moral overtones. The emotional element is all too evident, mainly in the form of fear and anger.

In Britain, three separate expert government committees on matters relating to animals have accepted the conclusion that animals feel pain. After noting the obvious behavioral evidence for this view, the members of the Committee on Cruelty to Wild Animals, set up in 1951, said:

> . . . we believe that the physiological, and more particularly the anatomical, evidence fully justifies and reinforces the commonsense belief that animals feel pain.

And after discussing the evolutionary value of pain the committee's report concluded that pain is "of clear-cut biological usefulness" and this is "a third type of evidence that animals feel pain." The committee members then went on to consider forms of suffering other than mere physical pain and added that they were "satisfied that animals do suffer from acute fear and terror." Subsequent reports by British government committees on experiments on animals and on the welfare of animals under intensive farming methods agreed with this view, concluding that animals are capable of suffering both from straightforward physical injuries and from fear, anxiety, stress, and so on. Finally, within the last decade, the publication of scientific studies with titles such as *Animal Thought, Animal Thinking,* and *Animal Suffering: The Science of Animal Welfare* have made it plain that conscious awareness in nonhuman animals is now generally accepted as a serious subject for investigation.

That might well be thought enough to settle the matter; but one more objection needs to be considered. Human beings in pain, after all, have one behavioral sign that nonhuman animals do not have: a developed language. Other animals may communicate with each other, but not, it seems, in the complicated way we do. Some philosophers, including Descartes, have thought it important that while humans can tell each other about their experience of pain in great detail, other animals cannot. (Interestingly, this once neat dividing line between humans and other species has now been threatened by the discovery that chimpanzees can be taught a language.) But as Bentham pointed out long ago, the ability to use language is not relevant to the question of how a being ought to be treated—unless that ability can be linked to the capacity to suffer, so that the absence of a language casts doubt on the existence of this capacity.

This link may be attempted in two ways. First, there is a hazy line of philosophical thought, deriving perhaps from some doctrines associated with the influential philosopher Ludwig Wittgenstein, which maintains that we cannot meaningfully attribute states of consciousness to beings without language. This position seems to me very implausible. Language may be necessary for abstract thought, at some level anyway; but states like pain are more primitive, and have nothing to do with language.

The second and more easily understood way of linking language and the existence of pain is to say that the best evidence we can have that other creatures are in pain is that they tell us that they are. This is a distinct line of argument, for it is denying not that non-language-users conceivably *could* suffer, but only that we could ever have sufficient reason to *believe* that they are suffering. Still, this line of argument fails too. As Jane Goodall has pointed out in her study of chimpanzees, *In the Shadow of Man,* when it comes to the expression of feelings and emotions language is less important than nonlinguistic modes of communication such as a cheering pat on the back, an exuberant embrace, a clasp of the hands, and so on. The basic signals we use to convey pain, fear, anger, love, joy, surprise, sexual arousal, and many other emotional states are not specific to our own species. The statement "I am in pain" may be one piece of evidence for the conclusion that the speaker is in pain, but it is not the only possible evidence, and since people sometimes tell lies, not even the best possible evidence.

Even if there were stronger grounds for refusing to attribute pain to those who do not have a language, the consequences of this refusal might lead us to reject the conclusion. Human infants and young children are unable to use language. Are we to deny that a year-old child can suffer? If not, language cannot be crucial. Of course, most parents understand the responses of their children better than they understand the responses of other animals; but this is just a fact about the relatively greater knowledge that we have of our own species and the greater contact we have with infants as compared to animals. Those who have studied the behavior of other animals and those who have animals as companions soon learn to understand their responses as well as we understand those of an infant, and sometimes better.

So to conclude: there are no good reasons, scientific or philosophical, for denying that animals feel pain. If we do not doubt that other humans feel pain we should not doubt that other animals do so too.

Animals can feel pain. As we saw earlier, there can be no moral justification for regarding the pain (or pleasure) that animals feel as less important than the same amount of pain (or pleasure) felt by humans. But what practical consequences follow from this conclusion? To prevent misunderstanding I shall spell out what I mean a little more fully.

If I give a horse a hard slap across its rump with my open hand, the horse may start, but it presumably feels little pain. Its skin is thick enough to protect it against a mere slap. If I slap a baby in the same way, however, the baby will cry and presumably feel pain, for its skin is more sensitive. So it is worse to slap a baby than a horse, if both slaps are administered with equal force. But there must be some kind of blow—I don't know exactly what it would be, but perhaps a blow with a heavy stick—that would cause the horse as much pain as we cause a baby by slapping it with our hand. That is what I mean by "the same amount of pain," and if we consider it wrong to inflict that much pain on a baby for no good reason then we must, unless we are speciesists, consider it equally wrong to inflict the same amount of pain on a horse for no good reason.

Other differences between humans and animals cause other complications. Normal adult human beings have mental capacities that will, in certain circumstances, lead them to suffer more than animals would in the same circumstances. If, for instance, we decided to perform extremely painful or lethal scientific experiments on normal adult humans, kidnapped at random from public parks for this purpose, adults who enjoy strolling in parks would become fearful that they would be kidnapped. The resultant terror would be a form of suffering additional to the pain of the experiment. The same experiments performed on nonhuman animals would cause less suffering since the animals would not have the anticipatory dread of being kidnapped and experimented upon. This does not mean, of course, that it would be *right* to perform the experiment on animals, but only that there is a reason, which is *not* speciesist, for preferring to use animals rather than normal adult human beings, if the experiment is to be done at all. It should be noted, however, that this same argument gives us a reason for preferring to use human infants—orphans perhaps—or severely retarded human beings for experiments, rather than adults, since infants and retarded humans would also have no idea of what was going to happen to them. So far as this argument is concerned nonhuman animals and infants and retarded humans are in the same category; and if we use this argument to justify experiments on nonhuman animals we have to ask ourselves whether we are also prepared to allow experiments on human infants and retarded adults; and if we make a distinction between animals and these humans, on what basis can we do it other than a bare-faced—and morally indefensible—preference for members of our own species?

There are many matters in which the superior mental powers of normal adult humans make a difference: anticipation, more detailed memory, greater knowledge of what is happening, and so on. Yet these differences do not all point to greater suffering on the part of the normal human being. Sometimes animals may suffer more because of their more limited understanding. If, for instance, we are taking prisoners in wartime we can explain to them that although they must submit to capture, search, and confinement, they will not otherwise be harmed and will be set free at the conclusion of hostilities. If we capture wild animals, however, we cannot explain that we are not threatening their lives. A wild animal cannot distinguish an attempt to overpower and confine from an attempt to kill; the one causes as much terror as the other.

It may be objected that comparisons of the sufferings of different species are impossible to make and that for this reason when the interests of animals and humans clash the principle of equality gives no guidance. It is probably true that comparisons of suffering between members of different species cannot be made precisely, but precision is not essential. Even if we were to prevent the infliction of suffering on animals only when it is quite certain that the interests of humans will not be affected to anything like the extent that animals are affected, we would be forced to make radical changes in our treatment of animals that would involve our diet, the farming methods we use, experimental procedures in many fields of science, our approach to wildlife and to hunting, trapping and the wearing of furs, and areas of entertainment like circuses, rodeos, and zoos. As a result, a vast amount of suffering would be avoided.

So far I have said a lot about inflicting suffering on animals, but nothing about killing them. This omission has been deliberate. The application of the principle of equality to the infliction of suffering is, in theory at least, fairly straightforward. Pain and suffering are in themselves bad and should be prevented or minimized, irrespective of the race, sex, or species of the being that suffers. How bad a pain is depends on how intense it is and how long it lasts, but pains of the same intensity and duration are equally bad, whether felt by humans or animals.

The wrongness of killing a being is more complicated. I have kept, and shall continue to keep, the question of killing in the background because in the present state of human tyranny over other species the more simple, straightforward principle of equal consideration of pain or pleasure is a sufficient basis for identifying and protesting against all the major abuses of animals that human beings practice. Nevertheless, it is necessary to say something about killing.

Just as most human beings are speciesists in their readiness to cause pain to animals when they would not cause a similar pain to humans for the same reason, so most human beings are speciesists in their readiness to kill other animals when they would not kill human beings. We need to proceed more cautiously here, however, because people hold widely differing views about when it is legitimate to kill humans, as the continuing debates over abortion and euthanasia attest. Nor have moral philosophers been able to agree on exactly what it is that makes it wrong to kill human beings, and under what circumstances killing a human being may be justifiable.

Let us consider first the view that it is always wrong to take an innocent human life. We may call this the "sanctity of life" view. People who take this view oppose abortion and euthanasia. They do not usually, however, oppose the killing of nonhuman animals—so perhaps it would be more accurate to describe this view as the "sanctity of *human* life" view. The belief that human life, and only human life, is sacrosanct is a form of speciesism. To see this, consider the following example.

Assume that, as sometimes happens, an infant has been born with massive and irreparable brain damage. The damage is so severe that the infant can never be any more than a "human vegetable," unable to talk, recognize other people, act independently of others, or develop a sense of self-awareness. The parents of the infant, realizing that they cannot hope for any improvement in their child's condition and being in any case unwilling to spend, or ask the state to spend, the thousands of dollars that would be needed annually for proper care of the infant, ask the doctor to kill the infant painlessly.

Should the doctor do what the parents ask? Legally, the doctor should not, and in this respect the law reflects the sanctity of life view. The life of every human being is sacred. Yet people who would say this about the infant do not object to the killing of nonhuman animals. How can they justify their different judgments? Adult chimpanzees, dogs, pigs, and members of many other species far surpass the brain-damaged infant in their ability to relate to others, act independently, be self-aware, and any other capacity that could reasonably be said to give value to life. With the most intensive care possible, some severely retarded infants can never achieve the intelligence level of a dog. Nor can we appeal to the concern of the infant's parents, since they themselves, in this imaginary example (and in some actual cases) do not want the infant kept alive. The only thing that distinguishes the infant from the animal, in the eyes of those who claim it has a "right to life," is that it is, biologically, a member of the species Homo sapiens, whereas chimpanzees, dogs, and pigs are not. But to use *this* difference as the basis for granting a right to life to the infant and not to the other animals is, of course, pure speciesism. It is exactly the kind of arbitrary difference that the most crude and overt kind of racist uses in attempting to justify racial discrimination.

This does not mean that to avoid speciesism we must hold that it is as wrong to kill a dog as it is to kill a human being in full possession of his or her faculties. The only position that is irredeemably speciesist is the one that tries to make the boundary of the right to life run exactly parallel to the boundary of our own species. Those who hold the sanctity of life view do this, because while distinguishing sharply between human beings and other animals they allow no distinctions to be made within our own species, objecting to the killing of the severely retarded and the hopelessly senile as strongly as they object to the killing of normal adults.

To avoid speciesism we must allow that beings who are similar in all relevant respects have a similar right to life—and mere membership in our own biological species cannot be a morally relevant criterion for this right. Within these limits we could still hold, for instance, that it is worse to kill a normal adult human, with a capacity for self-awareness and the ability to plan for the future and have meaningful relations with others, than it is to kill a mouse, which presumably does not share all of these characteristics; or we might appeal to the close family and other personal ties that humans have but mice do not have to the same degree; or we might think that it is the consequences for other humans, who will be put in fear for their own lives, that makes the crucial difference; or we might think it is some combination of these factors, or other factors altogether.

Whatever criteria we choose, however, we will have to admit that they do not follow precisely the boundary of our own species. We may legitimately hold that there are some features of certain beings that make their lives more valuable than those of other beings; but there will surely be some nonhuman animals whose lives, by any standards, are more valuable than the lives of some humans. A chimpanzee, dog, or pig, for instance, will have a higher degree of self-awareness and a greater capacity for meaningful relations with others than a severely retarded infant or someone in a state of advanced senility. So if we base the right to life on these characteristics we must grant these animals a right to life as good as, or better than, such retarded or senile humans.

This argument cuts both ways. It could be taken as showing that chimpanzees, dogs, and pigs, along with some other species, have a right to life and we commit a grave moral offense whenever we kill them, even when they are old and suffering and our intention is to put them out of their misery. Alternatively one could take the argument as showing that the severely retarded and hopelessly senile have no right to life and may be killed for quite trivial reasons, as we now kill animals.

Since the main concern of this book is with ethical questions having to do with animals and not with the morality of euthanasia I shall not attempt to settle this issue finally. I think it is reasonably clear, though, that while both of the positions just described avoid speciesism, neither is satisfactory. What we need is some middle position that would avoid speciesism but would not make the lives of the retarded and senile as cheap as the lives of pigs and dogs now are, or make the lives of pigs and dogs so sacrosanct that we think it wrong to put them out of hopeless misery. What we must do is bring nonhuman animals within our sphere of moral concern and cease to treat their lives as expendable for whatever trivial purposes we may have. At the same time, once we realize that the fact that a being is a member of our own species is not in itself enough to make it always wrong to kill that being, we may come to reconsider our policy of preserving human lives at all costs, even when there is no prospect of a meaningful life or of existence without terrible pain.

I conclude, then, that a rejection of speciesism does not imply that all lives are of equal worth. While self-awareness, the capacity to think ahead and have hopes and aspirations for the future, the capacity for meaningful relations with others and so on are

not relevant to the question of inflicting pain—since pain is pain, whatever other capacities, beyond the capacity to feel pain, the being may have—these capacities are relevant
to the question of taking life. It is not arbitrary to hold that the life of a self-aware being,
capable of abstract thought, of planning for the future, of complex acts of communication, and so on, is more valuable than the life of a being without these capacities. To
see the difference between the issues of inflicting pain and taking life, consider how we
would choose within our own species. If we had to choose to save the life of a normal
human being or an intellectually disabled human being, we would probably choose to
save the life of a normal human being; but if we had to choose between preventing pain
in the normal human being or the intellectually disabled one—imagine that both have
received painful but superficial injuries, and we only have enough painkiller for one
of them—it is not nearly so clear how we ought to choose. The same is true when we
consider other species. The evil of pain is, in itself, unaffected by the other characteristics of the being who feels the pain; the value of life is affected by these other
characteristics. To give just one reason for this difference, to take the life of a being who
has been hoping, planning, and working for some future goal is to deprive that being
of the fulfillment of all those efforts; to take the life of a being with a mental capacity
below the level needed to grasp that one is a being with a future—much less make plans
for the future—cannot involve this particular kind of loss.

Normally this will mean that if we have to choose between the life of a human
being and the life of another animal we should choose to save the life of the human;
but there may be special cases in which the reverse holds true, because the human being
in question does not have the capacities of a normal human being. So this view is not
speciesist, although it may appear to be at first glance. The preference, in normal cases,
for saving a human life over the life of an animal when a choice *has* to be made is a
preference based on the characteristics that normal humans have, and not on the mere
fact that they are members of our own species. This is why when we consider members of our own species who lack the characteristics of normal humans we can no longer
say that their lives are always to be preferred to those of other animals. This issue comes
up in a practical way in the following chapter. In general, though, the question of when
it is wrong to kill (painlessly) an animal is one to which we need give no precise answer.
As long as we remember that we should give the same respect to the lives of animals
as we give to the lives of those humans at a similar mental level, we shall not go far
wrong.

In any case, the conclusions that are argued for in this book flow from the principle of minimizing suffering alone. The idea that it is also wrong to kill animals painlessly
gives some of these conclusions additional support that is welcome but strictly unnecessary. Interestingly enough, this is true even of the conclusion that we ought to become
vegetarians, a conclusion that in the popular mind is generally based on some kind of
absolute prohibition on killing.

The reader may already have thought of some objections to the position I have
taken in this chapter. What, for instance, do I propose to do about animals who may
cause harm to human beings? Should we try to stop animals from killing each other?
How do we know that plants cannot feel pain, and if they can, must we starve? To avoid
interrupting the flow of the main argument I have chosen to discuss these and other
objections in a separate chapter, and readers who are impatient to have their objections
answered may look ahead.

The next two chapters explore two examples of speciesism in practice. I have limited myself to two examples so that I would have space for a reasonably thorough

discussion, although this limit means that the book contains no discussion at all of other practices that exist only because we do not take seriously the interests of other animals—practices like hunting, whether for sport or for furs; farming minks, foxes, and other animals for their fur; capturing wild animals (often after shooting their mothers) and imprisoning them in small cages for humans to stare at; tormenting animals to make them learn tricks for circuses and tormenting them to make them entertain the audiences at rodeos; slaughtering whales with explosive harpoons, under the guise of scientific research; drowning over 100,000 dolphins annually in nets set by tuna fishing boats; shooting three million kangaroos every year in the Australian outback to turn them into skins and pet food; and generally ignoring the interests of wild animals as we extend our empire of concrete and pollution over the surface of the globe.

I shall have nothing, or virtually nothing, to say about these things, because as I indicated in the preface to this edition, this book is not a compendium of all the nasty things we do to animals. Instead I have chosen two central illustrations of speciesism in practice. They are not isolated examples of sadism, but practices that involve, in one case, tens of millions of animals, and in the other, billions of animals every year. Nor can we pretend that we have nothing to do with these practices. One of them—experimentation on animals—is promoted by the government we elect and is largely paid for out of the taxes we pay. The other—rearing animals for food—is possible only because most people buy and eat the products of this practice. That is why I have chosen to discuss these particular forms of speciesism. They are at its heart. They cause more suffering to a greater number of animals than anything else that human beings do. To stop them we must change the policies of our government, and we must change our own lives, to the extent of changing our diet. If these officially promoted and almost universally accepted forms of speciesism can be abolished, abolition of the other speciesist practices cannot be far behind.

6

⋈ *The Case for Animal Rights* ⋈

TOM REGAN

Tom Regan is Professor of Philosophy at North Carolina State University. His most well known books are The Case for Animal Rights *and* All that Dwell Therein.

I regard myself as an advocate of animal rights—as a part of the animal rights movement. That movement, as I conceive it, is committed to a number of goals, including:

- the total abolition of the use of animals in science;
- the total dissolution of commercial animal agriculture;
- the total elimination of commercial and sport hunting and trapping.

There are, I know, people who profess to believe in animal rights but do not avow these goals. Factory farming, they say, is wrong—it violates animals' rights—but traditional animal agriculture is all right. Toxicity tests of cosmetics on animals violates their rights, but important medical research—cancer research, for example—does not. The clubbing of baby seals is abhorrent, but not the harvesting of adult seals. I used to think I understood this reasoning. Not any more. You don't change unjust institutions by tidying them up.

What's wrong—fundamentally wrong—with the way animals are treated isn't the details that vary from case to case. It's the whole system. The forlornness of the veal calf is pathetic, heart wrenching; the pulsing pain of the chimp with electrodes planted deep in her brain is repulsive; the slow, torturous death of the raccoon caught in the leg-hold trap is agonizing. But what is wrong isn't the pain, isn't the suffering, isn't the deprivation. These compound what's wrong. Sometimes—often—they make it much, much worse. But they are not the fundamental wrong.

The fundamental wrong is the system that allows us to view animals as *our resources,* here for *us*—to be eaten, or surgically manipulated, or exploited for sport or money. Once we accept this view of animals—as our resources—the rest is as predictable as it is regrettable. Why worry about their loneliness, their pain, their death? Since animals exist for us, to benefit us in one way or another, what harms them really doesn't matter—or matters only if it starts to bother us, makes us feel a trifle uneasy when we eat our veal escalope, for example. So, yes, let us get veal calves out of solitary confinement, give them more space, a little straw, a few companions. But let us keep our veal escalope.

But a little straw, more space and a few companions won't eliminate—won't even touch—the basic wrong that attaches to our viewing and treating these animals as our resources. A veal calf killed to be eaten after living in close confinement is viewed and treated in this way: but so, too, is another who is raised (as they say) "more humanely." To right the wrong of our treatment of farm animals requires more than making rearing methods "more humane"; it requires the total dissolution of commercial animal agriculture.

How we do this, whether we do it or, as in the case of animals in science, whether and how we abolish their use—these are to a large extent political questions. People must change their beliefs before they change their habits. Enough people, especially those elected to public office, must believe in change—must want it—before we will have laws that protect the rights of animals. This process of change is very complicated, very demanding, very exhausting, calling for the efforts of many hands in education, publicity, political organization and activity, down to the licking of envelopes and stamps. As a trained and practising philosopher, the sort of contribution I can make is limited but, I like to think, important. The currency of philosophy is ideas—their meaning and rational foundation—not the nuts and bolts of the legislative process, say, or the mechanics of community organization. That's what I have been exploring over the past ten years or so in my essays and talks and, most recently, in my book, *The Case for Animal Rights.* I believe the major conclusions I reach in the book are true because they are supported by the weight of the best arguments. I believe the idea of animal rights has reason, not just emotion, on its side.

In the space I have at my disposal here I can only sketch, in the barest outline, some of the main features of the book. Its main themes—and we should not be surprised by this—involve asking and answering deep, foundational moral questions about what morality is, how it should be understood and what is the best moral theory, all considered. I hope I can convey something of the shape I think this theory takes. The attempt to do this will be (to use a word a friendly critic once used to describe my work) cerebral, perhaps too cerebral. But this is misleading. My feelings about how animals are sometimes treated run just as deep and just as strong as those of my more volatile compatriots. Philosophers do—to use the jargon of the day—have a right side to their brains. If it's the left side we contribute (or mainly should), that's because what talents we have reside there.

How to proceed? We begin by asking how the moral status of animals has been understood by thinkers who deny that animals have rights. Then we test the mettle of their ideas by seeing how well they stand up under the heat of fair criticism. If we start our thinking in this way, we soon find that some people believe that we have no duties directly to animals, that we owe nothing to them, that we can do nothing that wrongs them. Rather, we can do wrong acts that involve animals, and so we have duties regarding them, though none to them. Such views may be called indirect duty views. By way of illustration: suppose your neighbour kicks your dog. Then your neighbour has done something wrong. But not to your dog. The wrong that has been done is a wrong to you. After all, it is wrong to upset people, and your neighbour's kicking your dog upsets you. So you are the one who is wronged, not your dog. Or again: by kicking your dog your neighbour damages your property. And since it is wrong to damage another person's property, your neighbour has done something wrong—to you, of course, not to your dog. Your neighbour no more wrongs your dog than your car would be wronged if the windshield were smashed. Your neighbour's duties involving your dog are indirect duties to you. More generally, all of our duties regarding animals are indirect duties to one another—to humanity.

How could someone try to justify such a view? Someone might say that your dog doesn't feel anything and so isn't hurt by your neighbour's kick, doesn't care about the pain since none is felt, is as unaware of anything as is your windshield. Someone might say this, but no rational person will, since, among other considerations, such a view will commit anyone who holds it to the position that no human being feels pain either—that human beings also don't care about what happens to them. A second possibility is that though both humans and your dog are hurt when kicked, it is only human pain that matters. But, again, no rational person can believe this. Pain is pain wherever it occurs. If your neighbour's causing you pain is wrong because of the pain that is caused, we cannot rationally ignore or dismiss the moral relevance of the pain that your dog feels.

Philosophers who hold indirect duty views—and many still do—have come to understand that they must avoid the two defects just noted: that is, both the view that animals don't feel anything as well as the idea that only human pain can be morally relevant. Among such thinkers the sort of view now favoured is one or other form of what is called *contractarianism*.

Here, very crudely, is the root idea: morality consists of a set of rules that individuals voluntarily agree to abide by, as we do when we sign a contract (hence the name contractarianism). Those who understand and accept the terms of the contract are covered directly; they have rights created and recognized by, and protected in, the contract. And these contractors can also have protection spelled out for others who, though they lack the ability to understand morality and so cannot sign the contract themselves, are loved or cherished by those who can. Thus young children, for example, are unable to sign contracts and lack rights. But they are protected by the contract none the less because of the sentimental interests of others, most notably their parents. So we have, then, duties involving these children, duties regarding them, but no duties to them. Our duties in their case are indirect duties to other human beings, usually their parents.

As for animals, since they cannot understand contracts, they obviously cannot sign; and since they cannot sign, they have no rights. Like children, however, some animals are the objects of the sentimental interest of others. You, for example, love your dog or cat. So those animals that enough people care about (companion animals, whales, baby seals, the American bald eagle), though they lack rights themselves, will be protected because of the sentimental interests of people. I have, then, according to contractarianism, no duty directly to your dog or any other animal, not even the duty not to cause them pain or suffering; my duty not to hurt them is a duty I have to those people who care about what happens to them. As for other animals, where no or little sentimental interest is present—in the case of farm animals, for example, or laboratory rats—what duties we have grow weaker and weaker, perhaps to vanishing point. The pain and death they endure, though real, are not wrong if no one cares about them.

When it comes to the moral status of animals, contractarianism could be a hard view to refute if it were an adequate theoretical approach to the moral status of human beings. It is not adequate in this latter respect, however, which makes the question of its adequacy in the former case, regarding animals, utterly moot. For consider: morality, according to the (crude) contractarian position before us, consists of rules that people agree to abide by. What people? Well, enough to make a difference—enough, that is, *collectively* to have the power to enforce the rules that are drawn up in the contract. That is very well and good for the signatories but not so good for anyone who is not asked to sign. And there is nothing in contractarianism of the sort we are discussing that guarantees or requires that everyone will have a chance to participate equally in framing the rules of morality. The result is that this approach to ethics could sanction the most blatant forms of social, economic, moral and political injustice, ranging from a repressive caste system to systematic racial or sexual discrimination. Might, according to this theory, does make right. Let those who are the victims of injustice suffer as they will. It matters not so long as no one else—no contractor, or too few of them—cares about it. Such a theory takes one's moral breath away . . . as if, for example, there would be nothing wrong with apartheid in South Africa if few white South Africans were upset by it. A theory with so little to recommend it at the level of the ethics of our treatment of our fellow humans cannot have anything more to recommend it when it comes to the ethics of how we treat our fellow animals.

The version of contractarianism just examined is, as I have noted, a crude variety, and in fairness to those of a contractarian persuasion it must be noted that much more refined, subtle and ingenious varieties are possible. For example, John Rawls, in his *A Theory of Justice,* sets forth a version of contractarianism that forces contractors to ignore the accidental features of being a human being—for example, whether one is white or black, male or female, a genius or of modest intellect. Only by ignoring such features, Rawls believes, can we ensure that the principles of justice that contractors would agree upon are not based on bias or prejudice. Despite the improvement a view such as Rawls's represents over the cruder forms of contractarianism, it remains deficient: it systematically denies that we have direct duties to those human beings who do not have a sense of justice—young children, for instance, and many mentally retarded humans. And yet it seems reasonably certain that, were we to torture a young child or a retarded elder, we would be doing something that wronged him or her, not something that would be wrong if (and only if) other humans with a sense of justice were upset. And since this is true in the case of these humans, we cannot rationally deny the same in the case of animals.

Indirect duty views, then, including the best among them, fail to command our rational assent. Whatever ethical theory we should accept rationally, therefore, it must at least recognize that we have some duties directly to animals, just as we have some duties directly to each other. The next two theories I'll sketch attempt to meet this requirement.

The first I call the cruelty-kindness view. Simply stated, this says that we have a direct duty to be kind to animals and a direct duty not to be cruel to them. Despite the familiar, reassuring ring of these ideas, I do not believe that this view offers an adequate theory. To make this clearer, consider kindness. A kind person acts from a certain kind of motive—compassion or concern, for example. And that is a virtue. But there is no guarantee that a kind act is a right act. If I am a generous racist, for example, I will be inclined to act kindly towards members of my own race, favouring their interests above those of others. My kindness would be real and, so far as it goes, good. But I trust it is too obvious to require argument that my kind acts may not be above moral reproach—may, in fact, be positively wrong because rooted in injustice. So kindness, notwithstanding its status as a virtue to be encouraged, simply will not carry the weight of a theory of right action.

Cruelty fares no better. People or their acts are cruel if they display either a lack of sympathy for or, worse, the presence of enjoyment in another's suffering. Cruelty in all its guises is a bad thing, a tragic human failing. But just as a person's being motivated by kindness does not guarantee that he or she does what is right, so the absence of cruelty does not ensure that he or she avoids doing what is wrong. Many people who perform abortions, for example, are not cruel, sadistic people. But that fact alone does not settle the terribly difficult question of the morality of abortion. The case is no different when we examine the ethics of our treatment of animals. So, yes, let us be for kindness and against cruelty. But let us not suppose that being for the one and against the other answers questions about moral right and wrong.

Some people think that the theory we are looking for is utilitarianism. A utilitarian accepts two moral principles. The first is that of equality: everyone's interests count, and similar interests must be counted as having similar weight or importance. White or black, American or Iranian, human or animal—everyone's pain or frustration matters, and matters just as much as the equivalent pain or frustration of anyone else. The second principle a utilitarian accepts is that of utility: do the act that will bring about the best balance between satisfaction and frustration for everyone affected by the outcome.

As a utilitarian, then, here is how I am to approach the task of deciding what I morally ought to do: I must ask who will be affected if I choose to do one thing rather than another, how much each individual will be affected, and where the best results are most likely to lie—which option, in other words, is most likely to bring about the best results, the best balance between satisfaction and frustration. That option, whatever it may be, is the one I ought to choose. That is where my moral duty lies.

The great appeal of utilitarianism rests with its uncompromising *egalitarianism*: everyone's interests count and count as much as the like interests of everyone else. The kind of odious discrimination that some forms of contractarianism can justify—discrimination based on race or sex, for example—seems disallowed in principle by utilitarianism, as is speciesism, systematic discrimination based on species membership.

The equality we find in utilitarianism, however, is not the sort an advocate of animal or human rights should have in mind. Utilitarianism has no room for the equal moral rights of different individuals because it has no room for their equal inherent value or worth. What has value for the utilitarian is the satisfaction of an individual's interests, not the individual whose interests they are. A universe in which you satisfy your desire for water, food and warmth is, other things being equal, better than a universe in which these desires are frustrated. And the same is true in the case of an animal with similar desires. But neither you nor the animal has any value in your own right. Only your feelings do.

Here is an analogy to help make the philosophical point clearer: a cup contains different liquids, sometimes sweet, sometimes bitter, sometimes a mix of the two. What has value are the liquids: the sweeter the better, the bitterer the worse. The cup, the container, has no value. It is what goes into it, not what they go into, that has value. For the utilitarian you and I are like the cup; we have no value as individuals and thus no equal value. What has value is what goes into us, what we serve as receptacles for; our feelings of satisfaction have positive value, our feelings of frustration negative value.

Serious problems arise for utilitarianism when we remind ourselves that it enjoins us to bring about the best consequences. What does this mean? It doesn't mean the best consequences for me alone, or for my family or friends, or any other person taken individually. No, what we must do is, roughly, as follows: we must add up (somehow!) the separate satisfactions and frustrations of everyone likely to be affected by our choice, the satisfactions in one column, the frustrations in the other. We must total each column for each of the options before us. That is what it means to say the theory is aggregative. And then we must choose that option which is most likely to bring about the best balance of totalled satisfactions over totalled frustrations. Whatever act would lead to this outcome is the one we ought morally to perform—it is where our moral duty lies. And that act quite clearly might not be the same one that would bring about the best results for me personally, or for my family or friends, or for a lab animal. The best aggregated consequences for everyone concerned are not necessarily the best for each individual.

That utilitarianism is an aggregative theory—different individuals' satisfactions or frustrations are added, or summed, or totalled—is the key objection to this theory. My Aunt Bea is old, inactive, a cranky, sour person, though not physically ill. She prefers to go on living. She is also rather rich. I could make a fortune if I could get my hands on her money, money she intends to give me in any event, after she dies, but which she refuses to give me now. In order to avoid a huge tax bite, I plan to donate a handsome sum of my profits to a local children's hospital. Many, many children will benefit from my generosity, and much joy will be brought to their parents, relatives and friends. If I don't get the money rather soon, all these ambitions will come to naught. The once-in-a-lifetime opportunity to make a real killing will be gone. Why, then, not kill my Aunt Bea? Of course I *might* get caught. But I'm no fool and, besides, her doctor can be counted on to co-operate (he has an eye for the same investment and I happen to know a good deal about his shady past). The deed can be done . . . professionally, shall we say. There is *very* little chance of getting caught. And as for my conscience being guiltridden, I am a resourceful sort of fellow and will take more than sufficient comfort—as I lie on the beach at Acapulco—in contemplating the joy and health I have brought to so many others.

Suppose Aunt Bea is killed and the rest of the story comes out as told. Would I have done anything wrong? Anything immoral? One would have thought that I had. Not according to utilitarianism. Since what I have done has brought about the best balance between totalled satisfaction and frustration for all those affected by the outcome, my action is not wrong. Indeed, in killing Aunt Bea the physician and I did what duty required.

This same kind of argument can be repeated in all sorts of cases, illustrating, time after time, how the utilitarian's position leads to results that impartial people find morally callous. It *is* wrong to kill my Aunt Bea in the name of bringing about the best results for others. A good end does not justify an evil means. Any adequate moral theory will have to explain why this is so. Utilitarianism fails in this respect and so cannot be the theory we seek.

What to do? Where to begin anew? The place to begin, I think, is with the utilitarian's view of the value of the individual—or, rather, lack of value. In its place, suppose we consider that you and I, for example, do have value as individuals—what we'll call *inherent value*. To say we have such value is to say that we are something more than, something different from, mere receptacles. Moreover, to ensure that we do not pave the way for such injustices as slavery or sexual discrimination, we must believe that all who have inherent value have it equally, regardless of their sex, race, religion, birthplace and so on. Similarly to be discarded as irrelevant are one's talents or skills, intelligence and wealth, personality or pathology, whether one is loved and admired or despised and loathed. The genius and the retarded child, the prince and the pauper, the brain surgeon and the fruit vendor, Mother Teresa and the most unscrupulous used-car salesman—all have inherent value, all possess it equally, and all have an equal right to be treated with respect, to be treated in ways that do not reduce them to the status of things, as if they existed as resources for others. My value as an individual is independent of my usefulness to you. Yours is not dependent on your usefulness to me. For either of us to treat the other in ways that fail to show respect for the other's independent value is to act immorally, to violate the individual's rights.

Some of the rational virtues of this view—what I call the rights view—should be evident. Unlike (crude) contractarianism, for example, the rights view *in principle* denies the moral tolerability of any and all forms of racial, sexual or social discrimination; and unlike utilitarianism, this view *in principle* denies that we can justify good results by using evil means that violate an individual's rights—denies, for example, that it could be moral to kill my Aunt Bea to harvest beneficial consequences for others. That would be to sanction the disrespectful treatment of the individual in the name of the social good, something the rights view will not—categorically will not—ever allow.

The rights view, I believe, is rationally the most satisfactory moral theory. It surpasses all other theories in the degree to which it illuminates and explains the foundation of our duties to one another—the domain of human morality. On this score it has the best reasons, the best arguments, on its side. Of course, if it were possible to show that only human beings are included within its scope, then a person like myself, who believes in animal rights, would be obliged to look elsewhere.

But attempts to limit its scope to humans only can be shown to be rationally defective. Animals, it is true, lack many of the abilities humans possess. They can't read, do higher mathematics, build a bookcase or make *baba ghanoush*. Neither can many human beings, however, and yet we don't (and shouldn't) say that they (these humans) therefore have less inherent value, less of a right to be treated with respect, than do others. It is the *similarities* between those human beings who most clearly, most non-controversially have such value (the people reading this, for example), not our differences, that matter most. And the really crucial, the basic similarity is simply this: we are each of us the experiencing subject of a life, a conscious creature having an individual welfare that has importance to us whatever our usefulness to others. We want and prefer things, believe and feel things, recall and expect things. And all these dimensions of our life, including our pleasure and pain, our enjoyment and suffering, our satisfaction and frustration, our continued existence or our untimely death—all make a difference to the quality of our life as lived, as experienced, by us as individuals. As the same is true of those animals that concern us (the ones that are eaten and trapped, for example), they too must be viewed as the experiencing subjects of a life, with inherent value of their own.

Some there are who resist the idea that animals have inherent value. "Only humans have such value," they profess. How might this narrow view be defended? Shall we say that only humans have the requisite intelligence, or autonomy, or reason? But there are many, many humans who fail to meet these standards and yet are reasonably viewed as having value above and beyond their usefulness to others. Shall we claim that only humans belong to the right species, the species *Homo sapiens?* But this is blatant speciesism. Will it be said, then, that all—and only—humans have immortal souls? Then our opponents have their work cut out for them. I am myself not ill-disposed to the proposition that there are immortal souls. Personally, I profoundly hope I have one. But I would not want to rest my position on a controversial ethical issue on the even more controversial question about who or what has an immortal soul. That is to dig one's hole deeper, not to climb out. Rationally, it is better to resolve moral issues without making more controversial assumptions than are needed. The question of who has inherent value is such a question, one that is resolved more rationally without the introduction of the idea of immortal souls than by its use.

Well, perhaps some will say that animals have some inherent value, only less than we have. Once again, however, attempts to defend this view can be shown to lack rational justification. What could be the basis of our having more inherent value than animals? Their lack of reason, or autonomy, or intellect? Only if we are willing to make the same judgment in the case of humans who are similarly deficient. But it is not true that such humans—the retarded child, for example, or the mentally deranged—have less inherent value than you or I. Neither, then, can we rationally sustain the view that animals like them in being the experiencing subjects of a life have less inherent value. *All* who have inherent value have it *equally,* whether they be human animals or not.

Inherent value, then, belongs equally to those who are the experiencing subjects of a life. Whether it belongs to others—to rocks and rivers, trees and glaciers, for example—we do not know and may never know. But neither do we need to know, if we are to make the case for animal rights. We do not need to know, for example, how many people are eligible to vote in the next presidential election before we can know whether I am. Similarly, we do not need to know how many individuals have inherent value before we can know that some do. When it comes to the case for animal rights, then, what we need to know is whether the animals that, in our culture, are routinely eaten, hunted and used in our laboratories, for example, are like us in being subjects of a life. And we do know this. We do know that many—literally, billions and billions—of these animals are the subjects of a life in the sense explained and so have inherent value if we do. And since, in order to arrive at the best theory of our duties to one another, we must recognize our equal inherent value as individuals, reason—not sentiment, not emotion—reason compels us to recognize the equal inherent value of these animals and, with this, their equal right to be treated with respect.

That, *very* roughly, is the shape and feel of the case for animal rights. Most of the details of the supporting argument are missing. They are to be found in the book to which I alluded earlier. Here, the details go begging, and I must, in closing, limit myself to four final points.

The first is how the theory that underlies the case for animal rights shows that the animal rights movement is a part of, not antagonistic to, the human rights movement. The theory that rationally grounds the rights of animals also grounds the rights of humans. Thus those involved in the animal rights movement are partners in the struggle to secure respect for human rights—the rights of women, for example, or minorities, or workers. The animal rights movement is cut from the same moral cloth as these.

Second, having set out the broad outlines of the rights view, I can now say why its implications for farming and science, among other fields, are both clear and uncompromising. In the case of the use of animals in science, the rights view is categorically abolitionist. Lab animals are not our tasters; we are not their kings. Because these animals are treated routinely, systematically as if their value were reducible to their usefulness to others, they are routinely, systematically treated with a lack of respect, and thus are their rights routinely, systematically violated. This is just as true when they are used in trivial, duplicative, unnecessary or unwise research as it is when they are used in studies that hold out real promise of human benefits. We can't justify harming or killing a human being (my Aunt Bea, for example) just for these sorts of reason. Neither can we do so even in the case of so lowly a creature as a laboratory rat. It is not just refinement or reduction that is called for, not just larger, cleaner cages, not just more generous use of anaesthetic or the elimination of multiple surgery, not just tidying up the system. It is complete replacement. The best we can do when it comes to using animals in science is—not to use them. That is where our duty lies, according to the rights view.

As for commercial animal agriculture, the rights view takes a similar abolitionist position. The fundamental moral wrong here is not that animals are kept in stressful close confinement or in isolation, or that their pain and suffering, their needs and preferences are ignored or discounted. All these *are* wrong, of course, but they are not the fundamental wrong. They are symptoms and effects of the deeper, systematic wrong that allows these animals to be viewed and treated as lacking independent value, as resources for us—as, indeed, a renewable resource. Giving farm animals more space, more natural environments, more companions does not right the fundamental wrong, any more than giving lab animals more anaesthesia or bigger, cleaner cages would right the fundamental wrong in their case. Nothing less than the total dissolution of commercial animal agriculture will do this, just as, for similar reasons I won't develop at length here, morality requires nothing less than the total elimination of hunting and trapping for commercial and sporting ends. The rights views' implications, then, as I have said, are clear and uncompromising.

My last two points are about philosophy, my profession. It is, most obviously, no substitute for political action. The words I have written here and in other places by themselves don't change a thing. It is what we do with the thoughts that the words express—our acts, our deeds—that changes things. All that philosophy can do, and all I have attempted, is to offer a vision of what our deeds should aim at. And the why. But not the how.

Finally, I am reminded of my thoughtful critic, the one I mentioned earlier, who chastised me for being too cerebral. Well, cerebral I have been: indirect duty views, utilitarianism, contractarianism—hardly the stuff deep passions are made of. I am also reminded, however, of the image another friend once set before me—the image of the ballerina as expressive of disciplined passion. Long hours of sweat and toil, of loneliness and practice, of doubt and fatigue: those are the discipline of her craft. But the passion is there too, the fierce drive to excel, to speak through her body, to do it right, to pierce our minds. That is the image of philosophy I would leave with you, not "too cerebral" but *disciplined passion*. Of the discipline enough has been seen. As for the passion: there are times, and these not infrequent, when tears come to my eyes when I see, or read, or hear of the wretched plight of animals in the hands of humans. Their pain, their suffering, their loneliness, their innocence, their death. Anger. Rage. Pity. Sorrow. Disgust. The whole creation groans under the weight of the evil we humans visit upon these mute, powerless creatures. It *is* our hearts, not just our heads, that call for an end to it all, that demand of us that we overcome, for them, the habits and forces behind their systematic oppression. All great movements, it is written, go through three stages: ridicule, discussion, adoption. It is the realization of this third stage, adoption, that requires both our passion and our discipline, our hearts and our heads. The fate of animals is in our hands. God grant we are equal to the task.

7

A Critique of Regan's Theory of Rights

DALE JAMIESON*

Dale Jamieson is Henry R. Luce Professor in Human Dimensions of Global Change at Carleton College. He is the editor of Reflecting on Nature: Readings in Environmental Philosophy, *and* Readings on Animal Cognition.

In *The Case for Animal Rights,* Tom Regan seeks to develop a moral theory that is a dramatic alternative to utilitarian theories, and then to apply it to some practical problems concerning our treatment of animals.[1] The range of Regan's book is enormous: it includes thorough and subtle discussion of the foundation and nature of rights, as well as eloquent passages telling us what we must do to respect them. Even the reader who is uninterested in the question of animal rights will find much that is stimulating and provocative. In the wake of Regan's achievement, the facile dismissal of animal rights may finally be seen as the prejudice that it is.

Still, despite his impressive accomplishments, Regan has failed to develop a compelling and dramatic alternative to utilitarian theories. In this essay I present an overview of Regan's theory, then . . . I argue that Regan's theory has serious problems and that the most plausible revisions would lead Regan back in the direction of utilitarianism.

AN OVERVIEW

A familiar objection to utilitarianism is this: utilitarianism regards individuals as valuable only insofar as they contribute to making the world a better place; when individuals cease to so contribute, either by being unhappy themselves or by causing others misery, it is not wrong to kill them. But this conclusion is unacceptable.[2]

* Many people have helped write this paper. I thank Robert Elliot, Susan Finsen, Lori Gruen, Betsy Israel, James W. Nickel, Peter Singer, and an anonymous referee for their comments on an earlier draft. I am especially grateful to Nancy (Ann) Davis for her comments on several different drafts and for many helpful discussions concerning the issues addressed in this paper.

Regan's positive theory begins from this familiar objection. He charges that utilitarianism views individuals as "mere receptacles" for value. Regan espouses instead what he calls the "Postulate of Inherent Value": individuals have value that is logically independent of the value of their experiences and of their value to others. Inherent value is, so to speak, the value of the receptacle rather than the value of what the receptacle contains. According to Regan, when the Postulate of Inherent Value is conjoined with some other plausible assumptions, it logically implies his theory of rights.

Regan argues in the following way. Everything with inherent value must have equal inherent value, since the alternative would lead to a "perfectionist" theory of justice, one which sanctions differential treatment of individuals on the basis of the degree to which they exemplify various virtues. According to Regan, perfectionist theories of justice have morally pernicious consequences and, hence, are unacceptable. Since both moral agents and "patients"—those individuals, like infants and most animals, who can be benefited or harmed but are not responsible for their actions—are "subjects of a life," they are of equal inherent value. Next Regan introduces the Respect Principle, which "rests on" the Postulate of Inherent Value. It states that we must treat those individuals who have inherent value in ways that respect their inherent value. According to Regan, the Respect Principle requires not only that we refrain from treating others in ways forbidden by this principle but also that we come to their defense when they are threatened by moral agents. Regan takes the Respect Principle to imply the Harm Principle. This principle tells us that we must not harm either moral agents or patients, since to harm them is to treat them in ways which do not respect their inherent value. Regan goes on to argue that these principles generate basic rights: creatures who have inherent value have basic rights. It is not merely that it would be wrong for us to treat others in ways that are forbidden by these principles but, rather, that to do so would be unjust. . . .

In such an ambitious book there is much that deserves reflection and discussion. In what follows I will consider only the duty to render assistance, ...

DUTIES OF ASSISTANCE

According to Regan, duties of assistance are grounded in the Respect Principle. They are "unacquired" duties; they do not rest on promises, contracts, or other special relationships. He writes: "The respect principle, as a principle of justice, requires more than that we not harm some so that optimific results may be produced for all affected by the outcome; it also imposes the prima facie duty to assist those who are victims of injustice at the hands of others" (p. 249). Creatures are victims of injustice when their rights are violated. Though both moral agents and patients can be victims of injustice, only moral agents can commit injustices, for only they can violate rights.[3] This provides Regan with the basis of an important distinction: although we are required to assist those who are victims of injustice, we are not required to help those in need who are not victims of injustice.[4]

Limiting the duty to render assistance in this way permits Regan to avoid one common objection to the idea that animals have rights. It is sometimes said that if animals have rights, then we have duties to protect them from their predators. Many people find this conclusion absurd and hold that animals do not have rights. But, according to Regan, we (typically) have no duties to protect animals from their predators, for predators are not moral agents and therefore cannot commit injustices. He writes: "In claiming that we have a prima facie duty to assist those animals *whose rights are violated,* therefore, we are not claiming that we have a duty to assist the sheep against the attack of the wolf, since the wolf neither can nor does violate anyone's rights" (p. 285). There are serious difficulties with circumscribing the duty to assist in the way that Regan does. These difficulties can be illuminated by considering some hypothetical cases.

Suppose that I am hiking across the slope of a mountain. Somewhat ahead of me, on a trail below, is a man I do not know. Also somewhat ahead of me, but on a trail above, is a woman I do not know. In the five cases which I will describe, a boulder is set in motion. As a result, the man will be killed unless I warn him. In Case 1 the woman intentionally pushes the boulder down the mountain toward the man. In Case 2 the woman takes a step, inadvertently causing the boulder to roll. In Case 3 the woman sneezes, and the boulder rolls toward the man as a result. In Case 4 there is a wolf on the trail above instead of the woman. While stalking her prey, the wolf causes a boulder to roll down the mountain toward the man. In Case 5 the boulder is set in motion by a landslide.

On the basis of what Regan says, we would have to conclude that, in Cases 4 and 5, I do not have a duty of justice to warn the man. On Regan's view neither wolves nor landslides can violate rights since they are not agents, and for this reason we do not have a duty of justice to aid their victims.

It is less clear what Regan would say about Cases 1–3. Regan believes that only agents can violate rights, but he says little about the circumstances in which an agent-caused harm constitutes rights violation. There seem to be three different positions that he could take.

The first position is that only in Case 1 is there a rights violation. The ground for this claim might be the view that agents only commit injustices when what they bring about is the intended result of an action which they perform.

A second position is that in both Cases 1 and 2 there are rights violations, but not in Cases 3–5. The ground for this claim might be the view that any action performed by an agent can be an injustice, even if the consequence is not intended, or the action is not intentional under the description in which it constitutes an injustice.

Finally it could be claimed that Cases 1–3 are all examples of injustices. The ground for this view might be that any harm caused by an agent can be an injustice, even if no action is involved in bringing about the harm.

There are difficulties with all three positions. None provides a satisfactory ground for distinguishing cases in which we are required to provide assistance from those in which we are not required to provide assistance.

It seems arbitrary to suppose that we are required to warn the man when the woman intentionally pushes the boulder, but not when she inadvertently causes it to roll in his direction. It seems just as arbitrary to hold that we are required to warn the man when the woman inadvertently sets the boulder in motion, but not when the boulder is set in motion by her sneeze. And if it is granted that we ought to warn the man in all three of these cases, what plausible reason could be given for supposing that we do not have a duty to warn him in Cases 4 and 5? All five cases are alike in important respects. We can even suppose that the boulder describes the same trajectory and travels at the same velocity in all five cases and that only the causes of its being in motion are different. The man will be killed unless he is warned; only I am in a position to warn him; and the costs of my warning him are very low. It is thus natural to suppose that what I ought to do is the same in all five cases. I believe that I ought to warn the man, but if I believed otherwise about Cases 4 and 5 I think I would believe otherwise about the other cases as well. The different origins of the threats in these cases do not seem relevant to determining my duty.[5]

The following example may help make this clear. Suppose that I see a boulder headed straight for the man. On the trail above is a woman walking her dog. I am unsure whether the woman intentionally pushed the boulder at the man, whether it began rolling because she slipped and dislodged it, whether her dog caused the boulder to roll, or whether the boulder was set in motion by a geological tremor. Despite my uncertainties about what set the boulder in motion, I should have no uncertainties about my duty: I ought to warn the man.

Still, it might be claimed that some limit (short of maximal utility) must be set on the duty to assist, otherwise too great a burden would be placed on people who are in the wrong place at the wrong time with the right resources. Limiting the duty to provide assistance to victims of injustice is one way of setting the limit.

Even if we accept the need to limit duties to assist, there are reasons to resist Regan's way of doing it. We might instead limit the duty to assist to those cases in which it is obvious that the costs of providing assistance would be very low and the benefits would be very great. The reason for setting the limit in this way might be our concern to protect the freedom of moral agents to pursue their own ends in a world which is very "needy."[6] Regan's approach, however, leads to the conclusion that in cases in which rights are threatened we may have duties to assist even when the costs would be great and the benefits small, while in cases in which rights are not threatened we may have no duties to assist even though the costs would be small and the benefits great. For example, I may have a duty to help prevent a thief from stealing your toothbrush while you are camping at the top of Long's Peak, even if this means that I must miss a rare performance of Mahler's Sixth Symphony; yet I may not have a duty to make a phone call which would save one hundred children from a collapsing circus tent. . . .

In this section I have argued that Regan's own views concerning duties of assistance are inadequate and incomplete. They are incomplete in that he does not tell us under what conditions we have duties to assist those who are threatened by agents. They are inadequate in that, contrary to Regan, we sometimes have duties to assist those in distress even if they are not threatened by agents. . . . It appears that Regan faces a dilemma: either rest with an inadequate account of duties to assist or move to a more consequentialist account of when we have such duties. Neither horn is attractive for someone who seeks a dramatic alternative to utilitarian moral theory.

Notes

1. Tom Regan, *The Case for Animal Rights* (Berkeley: University of California Press, 1983). All parenthetical page references are to this book.
2. For a version of this objection, see Richard Henson, "Utilitarianism and the Wrongness of Killing," *Philosophical Review* 80 (1971): 320–37. For a reply, see my "Utilitarianism and the Morality of Killing," *Philosophical Studies* 45 (1984): 209–21.
3. For present purposes I do not challenge Regan's claim that only moral agents can violate rights. It can be maintained, however, that moral patients can also violate rights, though we do not hold them responsible for such violations.
4. For the purposes of this paper "X has a duty to do (or not to do) A," "X ought to do (or not to do) A," "X is required to do (or not to do) A," and "X must do (or not do) A" are usually taken to be equivalent. Finer distinctions can and should be drawn, but they are not necessary for present purposes.
5. A more general argument for a similar conclusion is given by Nancy Davis, "The Priority of Avoiding Harm," in *Killing and Letting Die,* ed. Bonnie Steinbock (Upper Saddle River, N.J.: Prentice Hall, 1980), pp. 172–216. See also Thomas Nagel, *The View from Nowhere* (New York: Oxford University Press, 1986), p. 178.
6. This approach is suggested by some remarks of Bernard Williams in sec. 5 of his "Critique of Utilitarianism," in J. J. C. Smart and Bernard Williams, *Utilitarianism: For and Against* (Cambridge: Cambridge University Press, 1973); and by Thomas Nagel in the third of his Tanner Lectures, "The Limits of Objectivity," in *The Tanner Lectures on Human Values,* ed. Sterling M. McMurrin (Salt Lake City: University of Utah Press, 1980). See also Joel Feinberg, *Harm to Others,* vol. 1 of *The Moral Limits of the Criminal Law* (New York: Oxford University Press, 1984), chap. 4.

8

⚞ Ethical Vegetarianism ⚟
Is Unfair to Women and Children

KATHRYN PAXTON GEORGE

Kathryn Paxton George is Professor of Philosophy at the University of Idaho and is the author of Animal, Vegetable, or Woman: A Feminist Critique of Ethical Vegetarianism.

Vegetarianism has been promoted by a variety of authorities as both humanitarian and healthful. Not only should people avoid harming animals by eating them, but we can also avoid the harmful effects of high-fat diets by avoiding meat, eggs, and dairy products. The claim that vegetarian diets are healthful is separate from the claim that such diets are morally required, but these ideas do influence one another. I am going to suggest here that the apparent safety and benefits of vegetarian diets for adult males has led some philosophers, especially Peter Singer and Tom Regan, to assume that the adult male body is considered the normal *human* body. Assuming facts about this male human norm, they derive a general moral rule demanding ethical vegetarianism for everyone regardless of age, sex, or environment. I will refer to these arguments as the "Regan–Singer arguments." I will show that their assumption about the male norm is mistaken, and their call for ethical vegetarianism results in ageism, sexism, and classism. The Regan–Singer arguments for ethical vegetarianism rely on the *Principle of Equality*, but as I will show, if all animals are equal, women and children become less equal than men. That logical outcome will show that their arguments are incoherent and fail. Finally, the standard against which risk is presumed to be measured is arbitrarily assumed to be the adult male body.

First, let's review the moral claims. Singer, Regan, and virtually all other philosophers defending the moral status of animals claim that animals are the moral equals of humans and that we may not kill them for food. According to Peter Singer (1975, 1990), we may not use their products unless we could be sure that these products are obtained under painless conditions. Singer's utilitarian position would permit some people to eat animals or their products if they have a strong welfare-interest (say, for reasons of ill health), but these would be *exceptional cases*. Singer's reasons are apparently similar to those offered by Tom Regan (1983). Regan's rights position allows certain people to consume meat as exceptional cases based on what he calls the *Liberty Principle*:

> Provided that all those involved are treated with respect, and assuming that no special considerations obtain, any innocent individual has the right to act to avoid being made worse-off even if doing so harms other innocents (1983, p. 333).

Being made to starve or suffer a significant decline in health and vigor would make a person worse-off, and Regan accedes that if some humans have a strong welfare-interest in consuming meat or animal products, this would excuse them from a duty to be vegetarians. But Regan clearly thinks most people do not fall into such a category. He briefly discusses protein complementation and then dismisses the argument from nutrition:

> Certain animo acids are essential for our health. Meat isn't. We cannot, therefore, defend meat-eating on the grounds that we will ruin our health if we don't eat it or even that we will run a very serious risk of doing so if we abstain (1983, p. 337).

Traditional moral theories used by Regan and singer assume the moral equality of persons regardless of age, sex, race, and so forth. This assumption is called the *Principle of Equality*. Without the Principle of Equality, Tom Regan and Peter Singer cannot begin to make an argument for the rights and welfare of animals. Rights-holders deserve equal treatment, and the rules generated by the moral system should be impartial and nondiscriminatory concerning aspects about the rights-holders that they cannot change by choice. No particular group of people should bear a very much greater burden than others in attempting to keep the moral rule. That can mean that society should eliminate moral, social, or legal constraints that will cause people to suffer an increased burden in their attempts to function in society, at least as far as possible. For example, the Principle of Equality is the underlying reason that our society provides ramps and elevators for those who cannot use stairs. And because we subscribe to the Principle of Equality, we believe it is wrong to punish criminal offenders of one race more harshly than those of another. Nondiscrimination is the attempt by fair-minded people to affirm the equal worth of each member of the moral community. No single group can simply assume that its own practices are the only right ones, or even the best ones. If the rule prescribing ethical vegetarian diets is truly impartial, it should not require greater or very much greater burdens for some groups because of aspects about themselves that cannot be changed and that are thought to be neutral to the interests served by the rule.

Having set out a brief exposition of the foundations for ethical vegetarianism, I will now present a critical examination of this proposed moral rule. My claim is that the rule is partial to adult males and that, probably unwittingly, no one has noticed that the rule systematically imposes greater burdens on women and children. Second, the rule unfairly penalizes people who live in certain kinds of economic and environmental circumstances. My critique takes three tacks: (1) Regan and Singer (probably unwittingly) assume that there is no significant difference in the nutritional needs of males, females, children, and the elderly. To make their moral arguments, these scholars rely on conclusions drawn from nutritional studies done on adult males in industrialized countries. In addition, they do not consider studies citing the limitations of such diets for other age groups and for many women. Instead, the male body is assumed to be the norm for all. Women, children, and others are referred to in the scientific literature as "nutritionally vulnerable" with respect to certain vitamins and minerals such as iron, calcium, vitamin D, and zinc. All current arguments for ethical vegetarianism treat such nutritional vulnerability as an *exception* rather than as a norm. But, the very fact that the majority is regarded as a mere exception suggests that the ideal is skewed in favor of a group in power. A hidden assumption in the moral argument is that *being less vulnerable is good*, simply because one is *stronger*, and *being vulnerable is bad* or, at least not as good, because one is *weaker*. But that is a bald argument for power rather than for justice or moral virtue. So, the traditional moral theories fail on grounds of arbitrariness; i.e., the mere imposition of power through acceptance of a false belief. And, the theories become incoherent for their failure to treat all members of the moral community impartially. (2) The requirement of ethical vegetarianism is also inconsistent and classist because it presupposes a society largely structured on wealth generated from unsustainable environmental, agricultural, and industrial practices. But most people in the world live in ethnic, cultural, economic, and environmental circumstances where this supposed ethical ideal poses much more serious health risks than it does for people in the United States, Europe, and other rich countries. But being richer does not automatically make people more moral. (3) Attempts to correct inequities by requiring supplementation for women and children exacerbate rather than resolve the problem of unfairness.

The first criticism will show that Regan-Singer become incoherent because they cannot consistently apply the Principle of Equality. Neither Singer nor Regan consider the different nutritional needs of adults versus infants and children and men versus women, although these differences are well documented in the medical and nutrition literature. Infants and young children have higher energy, vitamin, and mineral needs than adults do because they are continuously growing and adding new tissue to their bodies. Nationally recognized nutrition authority, Dr. Johanna T. Dwyer of Tufts University Schools of Medicine and Nutrition writes:

> Vegetarianism in children deserves special attention because diets that sustain adults in good health are not necessarily appropriate for infants, young children, or adolescents (1993b, p. 171).

Phyllis B. Acosta of Florida State University's Department of Nutrition and Food Science states her concerns in stronger terms:

> Eating practices that promote health in the adult may have detrimental effects on growth and health status of the infant and young child (1988, p. 872).

Adolescents also need diets that are dense in nutrients per kilocalorie because they undergo the pubertal growth spurt. "Sex differences in nutrient needs become especially pronounced during adolescence" (Dwyer 1993a, p. 258). The onset of menstruation in females increases their iron needs, and the need for protein increases because the body size is increasing rapidly (Dwyer 1993a). Because bone mass is being accumulated, calcium needs remain higher until about age 25. The recommended daily allowances (RDAs) are "considerably higher for adolescents than they are for younger children or adults, especially if they are expressed on a nutrients-per-calorie basis" (Dwyer 1993a, p. 257). Pregnant adult women have greater protein, calcium, iron, vitamin C, vitamin D, vitamin E, thiamin, riboflavin, niacin, vitamin B-6, folate, vitamin B-12, phosphorus, magnesium, zinc, selenium, and iodide needs than adult males, and breastfeeding women have requirements that are higher still for almost all of these nutrients (National Research Council 1989). People over age 50 have different requirements for several nutrients as reflected in the RDAs (National Research Council 1989; Munro et al. 1987).

In pregnant women, "certain dietary practices that restrict or prohibit the consumption of an important source of nutrients, such as avoidance of all animal foods or of vitamin D-fortified milk, increase the risk of inadequate nutrient intake" (Institute of Medicine 1990, p. 18). Pregnant vegan women may be at greater nutritional risk for "inadequate weight gain, low protein intake, inadequate iron intake with resulting anemias, low calcium, zinc, and vitamin B-12 intakes, and in some instances low vitamin D, zinc and iodide intakes" (Dwyer 1991, pp. 75-76). Because the health of a fetus depends upon the health of the individual woman carrying it, these factors may pose a fetal risk as well. In some cases, nutritional deficiency in a woman at the time of conception can seriously impair fetal development or the health of a breast-feeding child (e.g., folic acid deficiency; vitamin B-12 deficiency) (Institute of Medicine 1990).

Women and children are more likely to suffer iron deficiency than adult males even in industrialized societies. Only a few years ago, marginal iron levels in women were not regarded with much alarm by physicians and nutritionists. Recently, however, it has been found that iron plays a vital role in childhood development and maintenance of the central nervous system, organ function, and immune function (Dallman 1989). Researchers usually categorize their test subjects as "normal," "iron deficient," or "iron deficient anemic," where iron deficiency is a state preceding anemia. In a review of 45 studies, Hercberg and Galan (1989) note that iron deficiency has "effects on skeletal muscle, cardiac muscle, brain tissue, liver tissue, gastrointestinal tractus [sic], body temperature relation, [and] DNA synthesis [because] iron participates in a wide variety of biochemical processes. . . . The key liabilities of tissue iron deficiency, even at a mild degree relate to decrease in intellectual performance, and in physical capacity during exercise, alteration of temperature regulation, [and] immune function" (p. 63; see also Dallman 1989; Parks and Wharton 1989; Scrimshaw 1991). Moreover, the effects of diets without adequate available sources of iron in infancy and young childhood cannot be compensated for by later improvements and/or later supplementation, and "maternal mortality, prenatal and perinatal infant death and prematurity are significantly increased" for iron deficiency in pregnancy (Scrimshaw 1991, p. 50; see also Dallman 1989; Oski 1993; Walter et al. 1989).

Women are particularly sensitive to iron deficiency because of periodic blood loss at menses and during pregnancy (Scrimshaw 1991; Hercberg and Galan 1992). Because iron carries oxygen to body cells, anemia causes reduction in capacity to perform work, reduction in mental acuity, greater vulnerability to other kinds of illnesses, and a variety of other symptoms. A significant number of women become iron deficient during pregnancy even when they eat iron-rich foods including meat (Bothwell et al. 1989), and nutritionists have expressed concern that because vegetarian diets restrict nutrient sources further, vegetarian diets may not provide adequate iron (Dwyer 1991). Although pregnant "vegan women [in the U.S.] can meet increased needs for most nutrients during pregnancy by diet alone . . . iron needs rise so much after the second trimester that supplements are usually needed since plant sources of iron are less bioavailable than heme iron" (Dwyer and Loew 1994, p. 91). The point about supplements is important because these are more commonly available in industrialized environments.

Vegans reject dairy products and that significantly reduces sources of calcium. Most of the concern centers on bone health among women and children. Continued inadequacy of calcium in the diet is thought to be a major contributing factor to osteoporosis (Dawson–Hughes 1991; Matkovic et al. 1979; Rodysill 1987), and milk is still recommended as the best source of calcium: "The calcium in milk and milk products is well-absorbed, whereas that in most plant sources is either poorly or negligibly available" (Allen 1986, p. 7). Osteoporosis is a major concern for post-menopausal women because it causes bone loss and fractures, particularly of the hip, forearm, and vertebrae. Women are at much greater risk for this disease than men. Although men are not completely exempt, their generally denser skeletons and testosterone levels prevent its occurrence until quite late in life (Johns Hopkins Medical Institutions 1994a, b).

But the time to preventing osteoporosis appears to be in childhood and adolescence. Peak bone mass is built then and the better it is built, the more bone there will be. Then, when bone loss begins it will take a longer time to reach a stage of severe depletion. Young women have already built almost all of their bone by about age 17 with some new bone formation perhaps continuing into the twenties (Dawson–Hughes 1991). By age 30 many women begin to lose bone (Rodysill 1987). In women "over the first several years after menopause, the skeleton undergoes a period of accelerated mineral loss in the process of adapting to declining concentrations of estrogen. After this period of adjustment, the rate of bone loss declines and remains fairly constant" (Dawson–Hughes 1991).

The nutritional evidence suggests that the best candidates for vegetarianism and veganism are young, adult, healthy males living in industrialized cultures. Males have generally larger skeletons and so have a lower risk of osteoporosis in late middle and old age. Adult males have higher iron levels than females and are at much less risk of anemia in adolescence and adulthood because they do not have periodic blood loss with menstruation and childbirth. They do not have protein, vitamin, or mineral stresses from feeding a rapidly growing fetus or a nursing infant, nor are they unduly stressed by their own growth requirements, as most of their growth is accomplished.

Do these facts mean that women and children in the United States cannot be healthy vegetarians? No, it does not. Dwyer (1991) and Dwyer and Loew (1994) maintain that all risks for vegans in the United States can be overcome with a well-planned and well-supplemented diet. What does "well-planned" mean? Here I quote more fully the context of Dwyer's (1991) statement:

> For those who wish to progress to a vegan diet that includes no animal foods whatsoever, additional care in dietary planning is needed. In addition to iron and zinc, unplanned vegan diets are often low in kilocalories, calcium, and are always low in vitamin B-12 and vitamin D unless supplementary sources of these vitamins are provided, since plant foods contain no known sources of these vitamins. The assistance of a registered dietitian is helpful, since a good deal of skill in planning and familiarity with unconventional food sources is needed by omnivores who wish to alter their dietary intakes in this way. Certainly, if the individual in question is an infant, child, pregnant or lactating woman, over 65 years of age, recovering from an illness, or a chronic sufferer of a disease, dietetic consultation is highly advisable in order to incorporate these additional considerations into dietary planning and to avoid or circumvent adverse nutritional consequences. Several good articles are available to guide counseling efforts for vulnerable groups . . . (pp. 82–83).

Ethical vegetarianism does not pose insurmountable risk of harm in industrialized societies. But if the harms can be overcome only by imposing a significantly greater burden on some groups while granting health benefits to others, then the standard against which the risk is measured must surely be unfair. Moralists like Regan and Singer claim that anyone can be an ethical vegetarian with no extra special burden. Their norm identifies physical strength in maintaining health on a particular diet as *morally good*. But morality is a matter of *will* and *choice*, not physical strength. Women and children are treated as outliers, exceptions, and "vulnerable groups," who do not fit expected norms. However, scientifically, there is no ideal "human" body, but only real men, women, and children.

What kind of response might Regan or Singer make to my criticisms? It is really no use attacking the facts. They are too well substantiated. To be fair, those defending vegetarianism from traditional moral theories would say that anyone who needs to eat milk, eggs, or meat should not be required to abstain. But Singer and Regan assume or argue that these people will be *exceptional cases*. That is, their bodily needs fall outside the usual or expected norm. Regan's (1983) animal rights position allows certain people to consume meat as exceptional cases (p. 333). He says that any humans having a strong welfare-interest in consuming meat or animal producs would be *excused* from a duty to be vegetarians. People who live in an environment where vegetables and grains cannot be grown (such as the arctic) would be excused. Regan clearly thinks most persons do not or would not (ideally) fall into such a category, and he does not notice that his exceptions are granted along gender and age lines. If all human beings had a male physiology, then the argument that Regan and Singer make for ethical vegetarianism would be valid. But because humans have many different physiologies roughly identifiable by age groups and sex, that premise is false and their arguments are invalid. Women, children, and others who do not fit these norms are excused whenever they have different requirements. But they are excused because they are "vulnerable," i.e., *weaker*.

Here is the core of my objection: Who are these others that traditionalists like Regan and Singer think may be excused? They are the vast majority of the *world's* population. And, if women, infants and children, the elderly, and people who live almost everywhere else besides western societies are *routinely* excused for doing what would normally be considered wrong, in practice this relegates them to a *moral underclass* of beings who, because of their natures or cultures, are not capable of being fully moral. They are *physiologically* barred from "doing the right thing" because they are not "being the right thing." The structure of this ethical thinking degrades the reality and human worth of these groups of people who do not fit.

After considering the nutritional facts, Regan or Singer might answer that the vegetarian ideal is not a moral ideal for women, children, and others who would be exempt because of the burden of risk. It is simply an ideal for males, one among a plurality of ideals. There are several problems with this reply, however. First, women and children are being exempted or excused because of their vulnerability, that is to say, their supposed physical weakness. But this so-called weakness is weakness *only* in comparison with an arbitrarily established standard of strength, one peculiar ability of the male body. But men and women have a variety of different kinds of strengths and weaknesses. In this case the Regan-Singer standard favors males in a world where males have the most social and political power as well. Second, positing a plurality of ideals tied to physical differences implies a kind of essential male nature and an essential female nature that is divisive of the implementation of the Principle of Equality. Morality should focus on what one can will and choose rather than on aspects of the self that one cannot change.

My second general criticism of the Regan-Singer arguments is that they assume a social standard largely structured on wealth generated from unsustainable environmental, agricultural, and industrial practices. Women, children, and people who live in other cultures and environments should conform their ethical behavior as if they have the same kind of bodies as adult males living in wealthy countries. Making judgments about whether other people can reasonable choose to be vegetarians and excusing the others is quite unfair. From a white middle-class college professor's perspective, American or Western society may appear quite homogeneous. The education level is high, food is available in great variety, is plentiful and fortified; the unemployed have Food Stamps; supplements seem readily available. These are conditions of great wealth by world standards, and they make vegetarianism reasonably safe. But, setting aside conditions outside the United States, a significant number of Americans do not have access to adequate food or nutritional information, and they are defined by their economic class. For example, many inner city residents cannot buy vegetables—there is no supermarket nearby (Kozol 1988). Shall we simply excuse them then? But there really is something quite arrogant about excusing all of these people from attaining the ideal; it supposes the richer are better. They are not. They are just luckier.

Ethical vegetarians might respond to these criticisms in still another way. In industrialized societies supplements are readily available and they are effective. Women and children should use them to minimize their risk minimal (Varner 1994). Essentially, this is a "separate but equal" or "special rights" argument. Women and men have separate but "equal" needs. Thus, ethical vegetarianism would not denigrate the moral equality of women (or children) because their requirements are "separate but equally valid."

This counter argument is flawed for two reasons. First, even if risks for vegetarians were equalized, burdens would not be. Western adult male vegetarians have many fewer burdens to bear, while women and child vegetarians must work harder to be "equal" simply because of their age or sex. Adult males rarely suffer anemia; they do not lose iron through periodic menstruation; they do not carry fetuses in their bodies or nurse infants; their growth is completed and they almost always have larger skeletons than females and so have a much lower incidence of osteoporosis. Supplements are expensive, some are best prescribed by a physician to avoid overdose, they are usually not covered by insurance, and they may increase a vegetarian woman's personal and psychological worries (Herbert and Subak-Sharpe 1990; Ossell 1993).

Second, the arbitrary adult male norm remains. Even if it is not too risky for a middle-class infant, child, adolescent, pregnant, lactating, perimenopausal, post-menopausal female, or elderly person to be an ethical vegetarian, that judgment will surely be made from a biased perspective—one that assesses the risk from the standpoint of the supposed male norm. Women, children, and seniors are being told to fix, mend, or correct their imperfect bodies as necessary (by supplementation, fortified foods, or eating in special ways) to meet a vegetarian ideal that is much less burdensome for adult men. A moral demand that these groups use supplementation again negates the life and value of those who do not fit a norm based on the male body (cf. Tuana 1993).

Regan or Singer might also make a third sort of response to my criticisms: Many nutritionists believe that obligatory vegans—that is vegetarians by circumstance of not having meat or dairy available—in "developing" countries have a poor health status attributable to "environmental factors (such as lack of medical care, vaccination, education, and sanitation) rather than solely to diet" (Dwyer and Loew 1994, p. 88). That is, if we could improve those background conditions to a level similar to the United States, then supplemented vegan diets would constitute little risk in those places, too. We might conclude that the risks would then be equalized (although burdens would not be equalized) among the sexes and ages, at least in theory.

My response is that the fundamental problem of bias would still remain, but even if we set that problem aside, the program comes at a cost to humans and animals. Vegan and vegetarian diets are lower in risk in Western nations when individuals have access to education, medical care, and sufficient resources to buy proper foods and supplements. Most importantly, these diets pose less risk in our culture largely because much of our food is fortified. We tend to think of our food as "naturally" protecting us. And it does! A diet consisting of the worst junk food is unlikely to result in pellagra or beriberi in the United States because virtually all flours are vitamin B fortified. Vitamin D is added to milk and is perhaps the single most important factor in the reduction of the incidence of rickets in children and osteomalacia in women and adolescents (Sanders and Reddy 1994).

In many parts of the world, beriberi, pellagra, rickets, scurvy, kwashikor, megaloblastic anemia, and iron deficiency are still endemic (Scrimshaw 1990), although the incidence has declined this century and the severity of the affected is usually less marked. Our food system protects us against these diseases, but that protection depends on food preservation, transportation, fortification, variety and plenty—a system that also includes some unsustainable agricultural and environmental practices inconsistent with environmental goals. The industrialized food system has alleviated human suffering on one hand and caused environmental damage on the other. Exporting safe vegan or vegetarian diets to the rest of the developing world would require exporting our food system with even more fortification of cereals and other foods, greater processing of foods such as egg substitutes, calcium-fortified soy products, and so forth. Fortification and food processing presuppose a complex industrialized food system, with research biochemistry, food processing plants, mines to produce supplements, quality control bureaucracies, food preservation techniques, refrigeration, shipping, and perhaps even chemical-dependent agriculture. A sophisticated research scientific and industrial complex with vitamin and mineral factories able to synthesize supplements without using animal products would be needed. For that, research biochemistry and chemistry labs are necessary, mines for extraction of raw materials, and a network of universities to train scientists, and so forth. All of these aspects of our food systems have environmental consequences, many or most of which are at odds with environmental goals. Environmental goals aim at reduction of some industrialized food production, but if one wishes to simultaneously encourage vegetarian diets, then a return to whole foods and unsupplemented or less supplemented diets may be necessary. Downscaling industrialized food production may mean that cereals and infant formulas may not be iron-fortified, milk may not have vitamin D added (if dairy is consumed), soy milk may not be calcium-fortified, and vitamin B-12 may be unavailable for vegans. Very likely, human suffering would increase. Such circumstances would place even greater burdens on women, children, and others unless diets are adjusted to personal physiology and consumption of animal flesh and animal products continues in moderation.

De-industrialization of agriculture and the scientific food production process suggests that at least some animal agriculture and fishing should be maintained to assure that infants, children, adolescents, the elderly, pregnant and lactating women have good sources of iron, zinc, and vitamin B-12 (meat/flesh of animals), calcium and B-12 (dairy), vitamin D (eggs and fatty fish). And as I have said, even an industrialized food system places discriminatory burdens on these groups, despite mitigation by supplementation. While we should, of course, encourage the worldwide availability of health care and good nutrition, the concomitant requirement of ethical vegetarianism may defeat environmental sustainability. The best course seems to be a middle ground such as semi-vegetarianism with moderate continued food fortification and preservation. A strict moral censure of meat eating will be hard-pressed to escape the exploitation of the earth, of nonindustrialized cultures, and of the animals it seeks to spare. It is more likely to preserve class distinctions and discrimination than to dissipate them. Nutritional education, medical care, and dietary supplements should, of course, be made available to those who want and need them. Agreeing to these facts and values does not, however, commit us to the ethical vegetarian ideal. It would, at most, commit us to improving conditions for all human and nonhuman animals depending on ecosystem impacts and cultural conditions.

Finally, *individuals* should not consider themselves responsible for being vegetarians or non-vegetarians per se. Moral decisions about what to eat should be made in social, political, and temporal contexts. In my view eating groups constitute contexts. For example, most people around the world eat as members of families where women are the primary food preparers for relatives of mixed ages and sexes. Preparing different meals for adult males due to ethical considerations would very likely burden women disproportionately. Therefore, eating in the context of such families should permit semi-vegetarian meals for all. For example, are you eating at home with your children? If so, eat semi-vegetarian. Are you living at home with an aging parent? Eat semi-vegetarian. On the other hand, if an adult, healthy male between the ages of 20 and 50 is out of town (not eating with young children), catching a dinner alone in a restaurant, he should eat vegetarian. If one were an adult woman in the same situation, things are less clear. Is she pregnant or could she become pregnant, nursing a child, at risk for anemia or osteoporosis, etc.? If so, then she may choose to eat semi-vegetarian or not, depending upon her own health circumstances and the availability of fortified food in her culture. If she is alone and does not have these burdens or risks, then in a culture such as ours she should eat vegetarian. The context of with whom, where, and when one is eating is the most important factor in a day-to-day decision about what it is right to eat.

REFERENCES

Acosta, Phyllis B. 1988. Availability of essential amino acids and nitrogen in vegan diets. *American Journal of Clinical Nutrition* 48: 868-74.

Allen, Lindsay H. 1986. Calcium and osteoporosis. *Nutrition Today* 21 (May/June): 6-10.

Bothwell, T.H., R.D. Baynes, B.J. MacFarlane, and A.P. MacPhail. 1989. Nutritional iron requirements and food iron absorption. *Journal of Internal Medicine* 226: 357-65.

Dallman, Peter R. 1989. Iron deficiency: Does it matter? *Journal of Internal Medicine* 226: 5 (November): 367-72.

Dawson-Hughes, Bess. 1991. Calcium supplementation and bone loss: A review of controlled clinical trials. *American Journal of Clinical Nutrition* 54 (supplement): 274S-80S.

Dwyer, Johanna T. 1988. Health aspects of vegetarian diets. *American Journal of Clinical Nutrition* 48: 712-38.

―――. 1991. Nutritional consequences of vegetarianism. *Annual Reviews in Nutrition* 11: 61-9.

―――. 1993a. Nutrition and the adolescent. In Robert M. Suskind and Leslie Lewinter-Suskind, *Textbook of Pediatric Nutrition*, 2nd ed., 257-64. New York: Raven Press.

―――. 1993b. Vegetarianism in children. In Patricia M. Queen and Carol E. Lang, eds., *Handbook of Pediatric Nutrition*, 171-86. Gaithersburg, MD: Aspen Publishers.

―――, and Franklin M. Loew. 1994. Nutritional risks of vegan diets to women and children: Are they preventable? *Journal of Agricultural and Environmental Ethics* 7:1 87-109.

Freeland-Graves, Jeanne. 1988. Mineral adequacy of vegetarian diets. *American Journal of Clinical Nutrition* 48: 859-62.

George, Kathryn Paxton. 2000. *Animal, Vegetable, or Woman? A Feminist Critique of Ethical Vegetarianism.* Ithaca, NY: SUNY Press, forthcoming.

Gussow, Joan Dye. 1994. Ecology and vegetarian considerations: Does environmental responsibility demand the elimination of livestock? *American Journal of Clinical Nuturition* 59 (supplement): 1110S-1116S.

Hercberg, Serge, and Pilar Galan. 1989. Biochemical effects of iron deprivation. *Acta Paediatrica Scandinavica* 361 (supplement): 63-70.

Herbert, Victor, and Genell J. Subak-Sharpe, eds. 1990. *The Mount Sinai School of Medicine Complete Book of Nutrition.* New York: St. Martin's Press.

Institute of Medicine. 1991. *Nutrition during Lactation.* Subcommittee on Nutrition during Lactation, Committee on Nutritional Status during Pregnancy and Lactation, Food and Nutrition Board, National Academy of Sciences. Washington, DC: National Academy Press.

———. 1990. *Nutrition during Pregnancy.* Subcommittee on Nutritional Status and Weight Gain during Pregnancy, Subcommittee on Dietary Intakes and Nutrient Supplements during Pregnancy, Committee on Nutritional Status during Pregnancy and Lactation, Food and Nutrition Board, National Academy of Sciences. Washington, DC: National Academy Press.

Johns Hopkins Medical Institutions. 1994a. Calcium: Maximizing its benefit. *The Johns Hopkins Medical Letter: Health after 50* 5:12 (February): 4-5.

———. 1994b. Osteoporosis: No sex discrimination. *Johns Hopkins Medical Letter: Health after 50* 6:1 (March): 3.

Kozol, Jonathan. 1988. *Rachel and Her Children: Homeless Families in America.* New York: Crown.

Lappé, Frances Moore. 1971. *Diet for a Small Planet.* New York: Ballantine.

———. 1982. *Diet for a Small Planet* 10th ed. New York: Ballantine.

Lewis, Stephen. 1994. An opinion on the global impact of meat consumption. *American Journal of Clinical Nutrition* 59 (supplement): 1099S-1102S.

Matkovic, Velimir K., K. Kostial, I. Simonovic, R. Buzina, A. Broderac, and B. E. C. Nordin. 1979. Bone status and fracture rates in two regions of Yugoslavia. *American Journal of Clinical Nutrition* 32: 540-49.

Munro, Hamish N., Paulo M. Suter, and Robert M. Russell. 1987. Nutritional requirements of the elderly. *Annual Review of Nutrition* 7: 23-49.

National Research Council. 1989. *Recommended Dietary Allowances* 10th ed. Subcommittee on the Tenth Edition of the RDAs, Food and Nutrition Board, Commission on Life Sciences. Washington, DC: National Academy Press.

Oski, Frank A. 1993. Current concepts: Iron deficiency in infancy and childhood. *New England Journal of Medicine* 329(3): 190-93.

Ossell, Joanne. 1993. *Food Analyst Plus: A Complete Nutritional Analysis Software.* CD-ROM Hopkins, MN: Hopkins Technology.

Parks, Y. A., and B. A. Wharton. 1989. Iron deficiency and the brain. *Acta Paediatrica Scandinavica* 361 (supplement): 71-77.

Regan, Tom. 1983. *The Case for Animal Rights.* Berkeley: University of California Press.

Rodysill, Kirk J. 1987. Postmenopausal osteoporosis: Intervention and prophylaxis: A review. *Journal of Chronic Diseases* 40(8): 743-60.

Sanders, T. A. B., and Sheela Reddy. 1994. Vegetarian diets and children. *American Journal of Clinical Nutrition* 59 (supplement): S1176-S1181.

Scrimshaw, Nevin S. 1991. Iron deficiency. *Scientific American* (October): 46-52.

Singer, Peter. 1975. *Animal Liberation.* New York: Avon.

———. 1990. *Animal Liberation* 2nd ed. New York: Random House.

Truesdell, Delores D., E. N. Whitney, and P. B. Acosta. 1984. Nutrients in vegetarian foods. *Journal of the American Dietetic Association* 84: 28-35.

Tuana, Nancy. 1993. *The Less Noble Sex: Scientific, Religious, and Philosophical Conceptions of Woman's Nature.* Bloomington: Indiana University Press.

Varner, Gary. 1994. In defense of the vegan ideal. *Journal of Agricultural and Environmental Ethics* 7(1): 29-40.

Walter, T., I. De Andraca, P. Chadud, and C. G. Perales. 1989. Iron deficiency anemia: Adverse effects on infant psychomotor development. *Pediatrics* 84: 7-17.

9

⊿ *The Limits of Trooghaft* ⊾

DESMOND STEWART

Desmond Stewart is a novelist and short-story writer. His fiction includes the trilogy A
Sequence of Roles.

The Troogs took one century to master the planet, then another three to restock it with
men, its once dominant but now conquered species. Being hierarchical in temper, the
Troogs segregated *homo insipiens* into four castes between which there was no traffic
except that of bloodshed. The four castes derived from the Troog experience of human
beings.

   The planet's new masters had an intermittent sense of the absurd; Troog laughter
could shake a forest. Young Troogs first captured some surviving children, then tamed
them as "housemen," though to their new pets the draughty Troog structures seemed
far from house-like. Pet-keeping spread. Whole zoos of children were reared on a bean
diet. For housemen, Troogs preferred children with brown or yellow skins, finding them
neater and cleaner than others; this preference soon settled into an arbitrary custom.
Themselves hermaphrodite, the Troogs were fascinated by the spectacle of marital cou-
plings. Once their pets reached adolescence, they were put in cages whose nesting boxes
had glass walls. Troogs would gaze in by the hour. Captivity—and this was an important discovery—did not inhibit the little creatures from breeding, nor, as was feared, did
the sense of being watched turn the nursing females to deeds of violence. Cannibalism was rare. Breeders, by selecting partners, could soon produce strains with certain
comical features, such as cone-shaped breasts or cushion-shaped rumps.

   The practice of keeping pets was fought by senior Troogs; the conservative disap-
proved of innovations while the fastidious found it objectionable when bean-fed humans
passed malodorous wind. After the innovation became too general to suppress, the Troog

elders hedged the practice with laws. No pet should be kept alive if it fell sick, and since bronchitis was endemic, pets had short lives. The young Troogs recognised the wisdom behind this rule for they too dislike the sound of coughing. But in some cases they tried to save an invalid favourite from the lethal chamber, or would surrender it only after assurances that the sick were happier dead.

Adaptability had enabled the Troogs to survive their travels through time and space; it helped them to a catholic approach to the food provided by the planet, different as this was from their previous nourishment. Within two generations they had become compulsive carnivores. The realisation, derived from pet-keeping, that captive men could breed, led to the establishment of batteries of capons, the second and largest human caste. Capons were naturally preferred when young, since their bones were supple; at this time they fetched, as "eat-alls," the highest price for the lowest weight. Those kept alive after childhood were lodged in small cages maintained at a steady 22 degrees; the cage floors were composed of rolling bars through which the filth fell into a sluice. Capons were not permitted to see the sky or smell unfiltered air. Experience proved that a warm pink glow kept them docile and conduced to weight-gain. Females were in general preferred to males and the eradication of the tongue (sold as a separate delicacy) quietened the batteries.

The third category—the ferocious hound-men—were treated even by the Troogs with a certain caution; the barracks in which they were kennelled were built as far as possible from the batteries lest the black predators escape, break in and massacre hundreds. Bred for speed, obedience and ruthlessness, they were underfed. Unleashed they sped like greyhounds. Their unreliable tempers doomed the few surreptitious efforts to employ them as pets. One night they kept their quarters keening in rhythmic sound; next day, they slumped in yellow-eyed sulks, stirring only to lunge at each other or at their keepers' tentacles. None were kept alive after the age of thirty. Those injured in the chase were slaughtered on the spot and minced for the mess bowl.

Paradoxically, the swift hound-men depended for survival on the quarry they despised and hunted: the fourth human caste, the caste most hedged with laws.

The persistence, long into the first Troog period, of lone nomadic rebels, men and women who resisted from remote valleys and caves, had perplexed the planet's rulers. Then they made an advantage out of the setback. The wits and endurance of the defeated showed that the Troogs had suppressed a menace of some mettle. This was a compliment and Troogs, like the gods of fable, found praise enjoyable. They decided to preserve a caste of the uncorralled. This fourth caste, known as quarry-men or game, were protected within limits and seasons. It was forbidden, for example, to hunt pre-adolescents or pregnant females. All members of the caste enjoyed a respite during eight months of each year. Only at the five-yearly Nova Feast—the joyous commemoration of the greatest escape in Troog history—were all rules abandoned: then the demand for protein became overpowering.

Quarry-men excited more interest in their masters than the three other castes put together. On one level, gluttonous Troogs found their flesh more appetising than that of capons. On another, academically minded Troogs studied their behavior-patterns. Moralising Troogs extolled their courage against hopeless odds to a Troog generation inclined to be complacent about its power. The ruins which spiked the planet were testimony to the rudimentary but numerous civilisations which, over ten millennia, men had produced, from the time when they first cultivated grains and domesticated animals till their final achievement of an environment without vegetation (except under glass) and with only synthetic protein. Men, it was true, had never reached the stage where they could rely on the telepathy that served the Troogs. But this was no reason to despise them. Originally Troogs, too, had conversed through sound hitting a tympanum; they had retained a hieroglyphic system deep into their journey through time; indeed, their final abandonment of what men called writing (and the Troogs "incising") had been an indirect tribute to men: telepathic waves were harder to decipher than symbols. It moved antiquarian Troogs to see that some men still frequented the ruined repositories of written knowledge; and though men never repaired these ancient libraries, this did not argue that they had lost the constructional talents of forbears who had built skyscrapers and pyramids. It showed shrewd sense. To repair old buildings or build new ones would attract the hound-men. Safety lay in dispersal. Libraries were a place of danger for a quarry-man, known to the contemptuous hound-men as a "book-roach." The courageous passion for the little volumes in which great men had compressed their wisdom was admired by Troogs. In their death throes quarry-men often clutched these talismans.

It was through a library that, in the fifth Troog century, the first attempt was made to communicate between the species, the conquerors and the conquered.

Curiosity was a characteristic shared by both species. Quarry-men still debated what the Troogs were and where they had come from. The first generation had known them as Extra-Terrestrials, when Terra, man's planet, was still the normative centre. Just as the natives of central America had welcomed the Spaniards as gods till the stake gave the notion of the godlike a satanic quality, millions of the superstitious had identified the Troogs with angels. But Doomsday was simply Troog's Day. The planet continued spinning, the sun gave out its heat and the empty oceans rolled against their shores. Living on an earth no longer theirs, quarry-men gazed at the glittering laser beams and reflected light which made the Troog-Halls and speculated about their tenants. A tradition declared that the first space vehicles had glowed with strange pictures. The Troogs, it was correctly deduced, had originally conversed by means analogous to language but had discarded speech in order to remain opaque, untappable. This encouraged some would-be rebels. They saw in precaution signs of caution and in caution proof of fallibility. A counter-attack might one day be possible, through science or magic. Some cynics pretended to find the Troogs a blessing. They quoted a long-dead writer who had believed it was better for a man to die on his feet when not too old. This was now the common human lot. Few quarry-men lived past thirty and the diseases of the past, such as cardiac failure and carcinoma, were all but unknown. But most men dreamed simply of a longer and easier existence.

The first human to be approached by a Troog was a short, stocky youth who had survived his 'teens thanks to strong legs, a good wind and the discovery of a cellar underneath one of the world's largest libraries. Because of his enthusiasm for a poet of that name, this book-roach was known to his group as "Blake." He had also studied other idealists such as the Egyptian Akhenaten and the Russian Tolstoy. These inspired him to speculate along the most hazardous paths, in the direction, for example, of the precipice-question: might not the Troogs have something akin to human consciousness, or even conscience? If so, might man perhaps address his conqueror? Against the backspace of an insentient universe one consciousness should greet another. His friends, his woman, laughed at the notion. They had seen what the Troogs had done to their species. Some men were bred to have protuberant eyes or elongated necks; others were kept in kennels on insufficient rations, and then, at the time of the Nova Feast or in the year's open season, unleashed through urban ruins or surrounding savannah to howl after their quarry—those related by blood and experience to Blake and his fellows. "I shall never trust a Troog," said his woman's brother, "even if he gives me a gold safe-conduct."

One Troog, as much an exception among his species as Blake among his, read this hopeful brain. It was still the closed season and some four months before the quinquennial Nova Feast. Quarry-men still relaxed in safety; the hounds sang or sulked; the Troogs had yet to prepare the lights and sounds for their tumultuous celebrations. Each morning Blake climbed to the Library. It was a long, rubbish-encumbered place with aisles still occupied by books, once arranged according to subject, but now higgledy-piggledy in dust and dereliction, thrown down by earthquake or scattered in the hunt. Each aisle had its attendant bust—Plato, Shakespeare, Darwin, Marx—testifying to a regretted time when men, divided by nationality, class or colour, suffered only from their fellows.

In the corner watched by Shakespeare, Blake had his reading place. He had restored the shelves to some order; he had dusted the table. This May morning a Troog's fading odour made him tremble. A new object stood on his table; a large rusty typewriter of the most ancient model. In it was a sheet of paper.

Blake bent to read.

Are you ready to communicate question.

Blake typed the single word: *yes*.

He did not linger but retreated in mental confusion to the unintellectual huddle round babies and potatoes which was his cellar. He half feared that he had begun to go mad, or that some acquaintance was playing him a trick. But few of his group read and no man could duplicate the distinctive Troog smell.

The days that followed constituted a continual seance between "his" Troog and himself. Blake contributed little to the dialogue. His Troog seemed anxious for a listener but little interested in what that listener thought. Blake was an earphone, an admiring confessor. Try as he feebly did, he got no response when he tried to evoke his woman, his children.

"Trooghaft, you are right," wrote the unseen communicator, attested each time by his no longer frightening scent, "was noble once." Blake had made no such suggestion. "The quality of being a Troog was unfrictional as space and as tolerant as time. It has become—almost human."

Then next morning: "To copy the habits of lower creatures is to sink below them. What is natural to carnivores is unnatural to us. We never ate flesh before the Nova; nor on our journey. We adopted the practice from reading the minds of lower creatures, then copying them. Our corruption shows in new diseases; earlier than in the past, older Troogs decompose. It shows in our characters. We quarrel like our quarry. Our forms are not apt for ingesting so much protein. Protein is what alcohol was to humans. It maddens; it corrupts. Protein, not earth's climate, is paling our. . . ."

Here there was a day's gap before the typewriter produced, next morning, the word *complexion*. And after it, *metaphor*. Blake had learnt that the old Troog hieroglyphs were followed by determinants, symbols showing, for example, whether the concept *rule* meant tyranny or order. Complexion could only be used metaphorically of faceless and largely gaseous creatures.

To one direct question Blake obtained a direct answer: "How," he had typed, "did you first turn against the idea of eating us?"

"My first insight flashed at our last Nova Feast. Like everyone, I had been programmed to revel. Stench of flesh filled every Troog-Hall. Amid the spurt of music, the ancient greetings with which we flare still, the coruscations, I passed a meat-shop where lights pirouetted. I looked. I saw. Hanging from iron hooks—each pierced a foot-palm—were twenty she-capons, what you call women. Each neck was surrounded by a ruffle to hide the knife-cut; a tomato shut each anus. I suddenly shuddered. Nearby, on a slab of marble, smiled a row of jellied heads. Someone had dressed their sugar-hair in the manner of your Roman empresses: 'Flavian Heads.' A mass of piled up, tong-curled hair in front, behind a bun encoiled by a marzipan fillet. I lowered myself and saw as though for the first time great blocks of neutral-looking matter: 'Pate of Burst Liver.' The owner of the shop was glad to explain. They hold the woman down, then stuff nutriment through a V-shaped funnel. The merchant was pleased by my close attention. He displayed his Sucking Capons and Little Loves, as they call the reproductive organs which half of you split creatures wear outside your bodies."

"Was this," I asked in sudden repugnance, "Trooghaft?"

Encouraged by evidence of soul, Blake brought to the Troog's notice, from the miscellaneous volumes on the shelves, quotations from his favourite writers and narrative accounts of such actions as the death of Socrates, the crucifixion of Jesus and the murder of Che Guevara. Now in the mornings he found books and encyclopaedias open on his table as well as typed pages. Sometimes Blake fancied that there was more than one Troog smell; so perhaps his Troog was converting others.

Each evening Blake told Janine, his partner, of his exploits. She was at first sceptical, then half-persuaded. This year she was not pregnant and therefore could be hunted. For love of her children, the dangers of the Nova season weighed on her spirits. Only her daughter was Blake's; her son had been sired by Blake's friend, a fast-runner who had sprained his ankle and fallen easy victim to the hounds two years before. As the Nova Feast approached, the majority of the quarry-men in the city began to leave for the mountains. Not that valleys and caves were secure; but the mountains were vast and the valleys remote one from another. The hound-men preferred to hunt in the cities; concentrations of people made their game easier.

Blake refused to join them. Out of loyalty Janine stayed with him.

"I shall build," the Troog had written, "a bridge between Trooghaft and Humanity. The universe calls me to revive true Trooghaft. My Troog-Hall shall become a sanctuary, not a shed of butchers."

Blake asked: "Are you powerful? Can you make other Troogs follow your example?"

The Troog answered: "I can at least do as your Akhenaten did."

Blake flushed at the mention of his hero. Then added: "But Akhenaten's experiment lasted briefly. Men relapsed. May not Troogs do likewise?" He longed for reassurance that his Troog was more than a moral dilettante.

Instead of an answer came a statement:

"We can never be equals with *homo insipiens*. But we can accept our two species as unequal productions of one universe. Men are small, but that does not mean they cannot suffer. Not one tongueless woman moves, upside-down, towards the throat-knife, without trembling. I have seen this. I felt pity, *metaphor*. Our young Troogs argue that fear gives flesh a quivering tenderness. I reject such arguments. Why should a complex, if lowly, life—birth, youth, growth to awareness—be sacrificed for one mealtime's pleasure?"

Although Blake recognised that his Troog was soliloquising, the arguments pleased him. Convinced of their sincerity, Blake decided to trust his Troog and remain where he was, not hide or run as on previous occasions. There was a sewer leading from his refuge whose remembered stench was horrible. He would stay in the cellar. On the first day of the Nova Feast he climbed as usual to his corner of the library. But today there was no paper in the typewriter. Instead, books and encyclopaedias had been pulled from the shelves and left open; they had nothing to do with poetry or the philosophers and the stench was not that of his Troog. Sudden unease seized him. Janine was alone with the children, her brother having left to join the others in the mountains. He returned to his cellar and, as his fear already predicted, found the children alone, wailing in one corner. The elder, the boy, told the doleful tale. Two hound-men had broken in and their mother had fled down the disused sewer.

Blake searched the sewer. It was empty. His one hope, as he too hid there, lay in his Troog's intervention. But neither the next day nor the day after, when he stole to the library, watching every shadow lest it turn to a hound-man, was there any message. This silence was atoned for on the third morning.

"If we still had a written language, I should publish a volume of confessions." The message was remote, almost unrelated to Blake's anguish. He read, "A few fat-fumes blow away a resolution. It was thus, the evening of the Nova Feast's beginning. Three Troog friends, *metaphor,* came to my Hall where no flesh was burning, where instead I was pondering these puny creatures to whom we cause such suffering. 'You cannot exile yourself from your group; Trooghaft is what Troogs do together.' I resisted such blandishments. The lights and sounds of the Nova were enough. I felt no craving for protein. Their laughter at this caused the laser beams to buckle and the lights to quiver. There entered four black hound-men dragging a quarry-female, filthy from the chase, her hands bound behind her. I was impassive. Housemen staggered under a great cauldron; they fetched logs. They placed the cauldron on a tripod and filled it with water; the logs were under it."

Blake shook as he read. This was the moment for his Troog to incarnate pity and save his woman.

"They now unbound and stripped the female, then set her in the water. It was cold and covered her skin with pimples.

"Again laughter, again the trembling lights and the buckling lasers.

"We, too, have been reading, brother. We have studied one of their ways of cooking. *Place the lobster*—their name for a long extinct sea-thing—*in warm water. Bring the water gently to the boil. The lobster will be lulled to sleep, not knowing it is to be killed. Most experts account this the humane way of treating lobster.*

"The logs under the cauldron gave a pleasant aroma as they started to splutter. The female was not lulled. She tried to clamber out: perhaps a reflex action. The hound-men placed an iron mesh over the cauldron."

Blake saw what he could not bear to see, heard the unhearable. The Troog's confession was humble.

"The scent was so persuasive. 'Try this piece,' they flashed, 'it is so tender. It will harden your scruples.' I hesitated. Outside came the noise of young Troogs whirling in the joy of satiety. A Nova Feast comes only once in five years. I dipped my hand, *metaphor"*—(even now the Troog's pedantry was present)—"in the cauldron. If one must eat protein, it is better to do so in a civilised fashion. And as for the humanity, *metaphor,* of eating protein—I should write Trooghaft—if we ate no capons, who would bother to feed them? If we hunted no quarry, who would make the game-laws or keep the hound-men? At least now they live, as we do, for a season. And while they live, they are healthy. I must stop. My stomach, *metaphor,* sits heavy as a mountain."

As Blake turned in horror from the ancient typewriter, up from his line of retreat, keening their happiest music, their white teeth flashing, loped three lithe and ruthless hound-men. All around was the squid-like odour of their master.

10

⚘ *The Ethics of Respect* ⚘ *for Nature*

PAUL W. TAYLOR

Paul Taylor is Professor Emeritus of Philosophy at Brooklyn College, City University of New York. He is the author of Normative Discourse, Principles of Ethics: An Introduction, *and* Respect for Nature.

HUMAN-CENTERED AND LIFE-CENTERED SYSTEMS OF ENVIRONMENTAL ETHICS

In this paper I show how the taking of a certain ultimate moral attitude toward nature, which I call "respect for nature," has a central place in the foundations of a life-centered system of environmental ethics. I hold that a set of moral norms (both standards of character and rules of conduct) governing human treatment of the natural world is a rationally grounded set if and only if, first, commitment to those norms is a practical entailment of adopting the attitude of respect for nature as an ultimate moral attitude, and second, the adopting of that attitude on the part of all rational agents can itself be justified. When the basic characteristics of the attitude of respect for nature are made clear, it will be seen that a life-centered system of environmental ethics need not be holistic or organicist in its conception of the kinds of entities that are deemed the appropriate objects of moral concern and consideration. Nor does such a system require that the concepts of ecological homeostasis, equilibrium, and integrity provide us with normative principles from which could be derived (with the addition of factual knowledge) our obligations with regard to natural ecosystems. The "balance of nature" is not itself a moral norm, however important may be the role it plays in our general outlook on the natural world that underlies the attitude of respect for nature. I argue that finally it is the good (well-being, welfare) of individual organisms considered as entities having inherent worth, that determines our moral relations with the Earth's wild communities of life.

In designating the theory to be set forth as life-centered, I intend to contrast it with all anthropocentric views. According to the latter, human actions affecting the natural environment and its nonhuman inhabitants are right (or wrong) by either of two criteria: they have consequences which are favorable (or unfavorable) to human well-being, or they are consistent (or inconsistent) with the system of norms that protect and implement human rights. From this human-centered standpoint it is to humans and only to humans that all duties are ultimately owed. We may have responsibilities *with regard* to the natural ecosystems and biotic communities of our planet; but these responsibilities are in every case based on the contingent fact that our treatment of those ecosystems and communities of life can further the realization of human values and/or human rights. We have no obligation to promote or protect the good of nonhuman living things, independently of this contingent fact.

A life-centered system of environmental ethics is opposed to human-centered ones precisely on this point. From the perspective of a life-centered theory, we have prima facie moral obligations that are owed to wild plants and animals themselves as members of the Earth's biotic community. We are morally bound (other things being equal) to protect or promote their good for *their* sake. Our duties to respect the integrity of natural ecosystems, to preserve endangered species, and to avoid environmental pollution stem from the fact that these are ways in which we can help make it possible for wild species populations to achieve and maintain a healthy existence in a natural state. Such obligations are due those living things out of recognition of their inherent worth. They are entirely additional to and independent of the obligations we owe to our fellow humans. Although many of the actions that fulfill one set of obligations will also fulfill the other, two different grounds of obligation are involved. Their well-being, as well as human well-being, is something to be realized *as an end in itself.*

If we were to accept a life-centered theory of environmental ethics, a profound reordering of our moral universe would take place. We would begin to look at the whole of the Earth's biosphere in a new light. Our duties with respect to the "world" of nature would be seen as making prima facie claims upon us to be balanced against our duties with respect to the "world" of human civilization. We could no longer simply take the human point of view and consider the effects of our actions exclusively from the perspective of our own good.

THE GOOD OF A BEING AND THE CONCEPT OF INHERENT WORTH

What would justify acceptance of a life-centered system of ethical principles? In order to answer this it is first necessary to make clear the fundamental moral attitude that underlies and makes intelligible the commitment to live by such a system. It is then necessary to examine the considerations that would justify any rational agent's adopting that moral attitude.

Two concepts are essential to the taking of a moral attitude of the sort in question. A being which does not "have" these concepts, that is, which is unable to grasp their meaning and conditions of applicability, cannot be said to have the attitude as part of its moral outlook. These concepts are, first, that of the good (well-being, welfare) of a living thing, and second, the idea of an entity possessing inherent worth. I examine each concept in turn.

(1) Every organism, species population, and community of life has a good of its own which moral agents can intentionally further or damage by their actions. To say that an entity has a good of its own is simply to say that, without reference to any *other*

entity, it can be benefited or harmed. One can act in its overall interest or contrary to its overall interest, and environmental conditions can be good for it (advantageous to it) or bad for it (disadvantageous to it). What is good for an entity is what "does it good" in the sense of enhancing or preserving its life and well-being. What is bad for an entity is something that is detrimental to its life and well-being.[1]

We can think of the good of an individual nonhuman organism as consisting in the full development of its biological powers. Its good is realized to the extent that it is strong and healthy. It possesses whatever capacities it needs for successfully coping with its environment and so preserving its existence throughout the various stages of the normal life cycle of its species. The good of a population or community of such individuals consists in the population or community maintaining itself from generation to generation as a coherent system of genetically and ecologically related organisms whose average good is at an optimum level for the given environment. (Here *average good* means that the degree of realization of the good of *individual organisms* in the population or community is, on average, greater than would be the case under any other ecologically functioning order of interrelations among those species populations in the given ecosystem.)

The idea of a being having a good of its own, as I understand it, does not entail that the being must have interests or take an interest in what affects its life for better or for worse. We can act in a being's interest or contrary to its interest without its being interested in what we are doing to it in the sense of wanting or not wanting us to do it. It may, indeed, be wholly unaware that favorable and unfavorable events are taking place in its life. I take it that trees, for example, have no knowledge or desires or feelings. Yet it is undoubtedly the case that trees can be harmed or benefited by our actions. We can crush their roots by running a bulldozer too close to them. We can see to it that they get adequate nourishment and moisture by fertilizing and watering the soil around them. Thus we can help or hinder them in the realization of their good. It is the good of trees themselves that is thereby affected. We can similarly act so as to further the good of an entire tree population of a certain species (say, all the redwood trees in a California valley) or the good of a whole community of plant life in a given wilderness area, just as we can do harm to such a population or community.

When construed in this way, the concept of a being's good is not coextensive with sentience or the capacity for feeling pain. William Frankena has argued for a general theory of environmental ethics in which the ground of a creature's being worthy of moral consideration is its sentience. I have offered some criticisms of this view elsewhere, but the full refutation of such a position, it seems to me, finally depends on the positive reasons for accepting a life-centered theory of the kind I am defending in this essay.[2]

It should be noted further that I am leaving open the question of whether machines—in particular, those which are not only goal-directed, but also self-regulating—can properly be said to have a good of their own.[3] Since I am concerned only with human treatment of wild organisms, species populations, and communities of life as they occur in our planet's natural ecosystems, it is to those entities alone that the concept "having a good of its own" will here be applied. I am not denying that other living things, whose genetic origin and environmental conditions have been produced, controlled, and manipulated by humans for human ends, do have a good of their own in the same sense as do wild plants and animals. It is not my purpose in this essay, however, to set out or defend the principles that should guide our conduct with regard to their good. It is only insofar as their production and use by humans have good or ill effects upon natural ecosystems and their wild inhabitants that the ethics of respect for nature comes into play.

(2) The second concept essential to the moral attitude of respect for nature is the idea of inherent worth. We take that attitude toward wild living things (individuals, species populations, or whole biotic communities) when and only when we regard them as entities possessing inherent worth. Indeed, it is only because they are conceived in this way that moral agents can think of themselves as having validly binding duties, obligations, and responsibilities that are *owed* to them as their *due*. I am not at this juncture arguing why they *should be* so regarded; I consider it at length below. But so regarding them is a presupposition of our taking the attitude of respect toward them and accordingly understanding ourselves as bearing certain moral relations to them. This can be shown as follows:

What does it mean to regard an entity that has a good of its own as possessing inherent worth? Two general principles are involved: the principle of moral consideration and the principle of intrinsic value.

According to the principle of moral consideration, wild living things are deserving of the concern and consideration of all moral agents simply in virtue of their being members of the Earth's community of life. From the moral point of view their good must be taken into account whenever it is affected for better or worse by the conduct of rational agents. This holds no matter what species the creature belongs to. The good of each is to be accorded some value and so acknowledged as having some weight in the deliberations of all rational agents. Of course, it may be necessary for such agents to act in ways contrary to the good of this or that particular organism or group of organisms in order to further the good of others, including the good of humans. But the principle of moral consideration prescribes that, with respect to each being an entity having its own good, every individual is deserving of consideration.

The principle of intrinsic value states that, regardless of what kind of entity it is in other respects, if it is a member of the Earth's community of life, the realization of its good is something *intrinsically* valuable. This means that its good is prima facie worthy of being preserved or promoted as an end in itself and for the sake of the entity whose good it is. Insofar as we regard any organism, species population, or life community as an entity having inherent worth, we believe that it must never be treated as if it were a mere object or thing whose entire value lies in being instrumental to the good of some other entity. The well-being of each is judged to have value in and of itself.

Combining these two principles, we can now define what it means for a living thing or group of living things to possess inherent worth. To say that it possesses inherent worth is to say that its good is deserving of the concern and consideration of all moral agents, and that the realization of its good has intrinsic value, to be pursued as an end in itself and for the sake of the entity whose good it is.

The duties owed to wild organisms, species populations, and communities of life in the Earth's natural ecosystems are grounded on their inherent worth. When rational, autonomous agents regard such entities as possessing inherent worth, they place intrinsic value on the realization of their good and so hold themselves responsible for performing actions that will have this effect and for refraining from actions having the contrary effect.

THE ATTITUDE OF RESPECT FOR NATURE

Why should moral agents regard wild living things in the natural world as possessing inherent worth? To answer this question we must first take into account the fact that, when rational, autonomous agents subscribe to the principles of moral consideration and intrinsic value and so conceive of wild living things as having that kind of worth, such agents are *adopting a certain ultimate moral attitude toward the natural world*. This is the attitude I call "respect for nature." It parallels the attitude of respect for persons in human ethics. When we adopt the attitude of respect for persons as the proper (fitting, appropriate) attitude to take toward all persons as persons, we consider the fulfillment of the basic interests of each individual to have intrinsic value. We thereby make a moral commitment to live a certain kind of life in relation to other persons. We place ourselves under the direction of a system of standards and rules that we consider validly binding on all moral agents as such.[4]

Similarly, when we adopt the attitude of respect for nature as an ultimate moral attitude we make a commitment to live by certain normative principles. These principles constitute the rules of conduct and standards of character that are to govern our treatment of the natural world. This is, first, an *ultimate* commitment because it is not derived from any higher norm. The attitude of respect for nature is not grounded on some other, more general, or more fundamental attitude. It sets the total framework for our responsibilities toward the natural world. It can be justified, as I show below, but its justification cannot consist in referring to a more general attitude or a more basic normative principle.

Second, the commitment is a *moral* one because it is understood to be a disinterested matter of principle. It is this feature that distinguishes the attitude of respect for nature from the set of feelings and dispositions that comprise the love of nature. The latter stems from one's personal interest in and response to the natural world. Like the affectionate feelings we have toward certain individual human beings, one's love of nature is nothing more than the particular way one feels about the natural environment and its wild inhabitants. And just as our love for an individual person differs from our respect for all persons as such (whether we happen to love them or not), so love of nature differs from respect for nature. Respect for nature is an attitude we believe all moral agents ought to have simply as moral agents, regardless of whether or not they also love nature. Indeed, we have not truly taken the attitude of respect for nature ourselves unless we believe this. To put it in a Kantian way, to adopt the attitude of respect for nature is to take a stance that one wills it to be a universal law for all rational beings. It is to hold that stance categorically, as being validly applicable to every moral agent without exception, irrespective of whatever personal feelings toward nature such an agent might have or might lack.

Although the attitude of respect for nature is in this sense a disinterested and universalizable attitude, anyone who does adopt it has certain steady, more or less permanent dispositions. These dispositions, which are themselves to be considered disinterested and universalizable, comprise three interlocking sets: dispositions to seek certain ends, dispositions to carry on one's practical reasoning and deliberation in a certain way, and dispositions to have certain feelings. We may accordingly analyze the attitude of respect for nature into the following components. (a) The disposition to aim at, and to take steps to bring about, as final and disinterested ends, the promoting and protecting of the good of organisms, species populations, and life communities in natural ecosystems. (These ends are "final" in not being pursued as means to further ends. They are "disinterested" in being independent of the self-interest of the agent.) (b) The disposition to consider actions that tend to realize those ends to be prima facie obligatory *because* they have that tendency. (c) The disposition to experience positive and negative feelings toward states of affairs in the world *because* they are favorable or unfavorable to the good of organisms, species populations, and life communities in natural ecosystems.

The logical connection between the attitude of respect for nature and the duties of a life-centered system of environmental ethics can now be made clear. Insofar as one sincerely takes that attitude and so has the three sets of dispositions, one will at the same time be disposed to comply with certain rules of duty (such as nonmaleficence and non-interference) and with standards of character (such as fairness and benevolence) that determine the obligations and virtues of moral agents with regard to the Earth's wild living things. We can say that the actions one performs and the character traits one develops in fulfilling these moral requirements are the way one *expresses* or *embodies* the attitude in one's conduct and character. In his famous essay, "Justice as Fairness," John Rawls describes the rules of the duties of human morality (such as fidelity, gratitude, honesty, and justice) as "forms of conduct in which recognition of others as persons is manifested."[5] I hold that the rules of duty governing our treatment of the natural world and its inhabitants are forms of conduct in which the attitude of respect for nature is manifested.

THE JUSTIFIABILITY OF THE ATTITUDE OF RESPECT FOR NATURE

I return to the question posed earlier, which has not yet been answered: why *should* moral agents regard wild living things as possessing inherent worth? I now argue that the only way we can answer this question is by showing how adopting the attitude of respect for nature is justified for all moral agents. Let us suppose that we were able to establish that there are good reasons for adopting the attitude, reasons which are inter-subjectively valid for every rational agent. If there are such reasons, they would justify anyone's having the three sets of dispositions mentioned above as constituting what it means to have the attitude. Since these include the disposition to promote or protect the good of wild living things as a disinterested and ultimate end, as well as the disposition to perform actions for the reason that they tend to realize that end, we see that such dispositions commit a person to the principles of moral consideration and intrinsic value. To be disposed to further, as an end in itself, the good of any entity in nature just because it is that kind of entity, is to be disposed to give consideration to *every* such entity and to place intrinsic value on the realization of its good. Insofar as we subscribe to these two principles we regard living things as possessing inherent worth. Subscribing to the principles is what it *means* to so regard them. To justify the attitude of respect for nature, then, is to justify commitment to these principles and thereby to justify regarding wild creatures as possessing inherent worth.

We must keep in mind that inherent worth is not some mysterious sort of objective property belonging to living things that can be discovered by empirical observation or scientific investigation. To ascribe inherent worth to an entity is not to describe it by citing some feature discernible by sense perception or inferable by inductive reasoning. Nor is there a logically necessary connection between the concept of a being having a good of its own and the concept of inherent worth. We do not contradict ourselves by asserting that an entity that has a good of its own lacks inherent worth. In order to show that such an entity "has" inherent worth we must give good reasons for ascribing that kind of value to it (placing that kind of value upon it, conceiving of it to be valuable in that way). Although it is humans (persons, valuers) who must do the valuing, for the ethics of respect for nature, the value so ascribed is not a human value. That is to say, it is not a value derived from considerations regarding human well-being or human rights. It is a value that is ascribed to nonhuman animals and plants themselves, independently of their relationship to what humans judge to be conducive to their own good.

Whatever reasons, then, justify our taking the attitude of respect for nature as defined above are also reasons that show why we *should* regard the living things of the natural world as possessing inherent worth. We saw earlier that, since the attitude is an ultimate one, it cannot be derived from a more fundamental attitude nor shown to be a special case of a more general one. On what sort of grounds, then, can it be established?

The attitude we take toward living things in the natural world depends on the way we look at them, on what kind of beings we conceive them to be, and on how we understand the relations we bear to them. Underlying and supporting our attitude is a certain *belief system* that constitutes a particular world view or outlook on nature and the place of human life in it. To give good reasons for adopting the attitude of respect for nature, then, we must first articulate the belief system which underlies and supports that attitude. If it appears that the belief system is internally coherent and well-ordered, and if, as far as we can now tell, it is consistent with all known scientific truths relevant to our knowledge of the object of the attitude (which in this case includes the whole set of the Earth's natural ecosystems and their communities of life), then there remains the task of indicating why scientifically informed and rational thinkers with a developed capacity of reality awareness can find it acceptable as a way of conceiving of the natural world and our place in it. To the extent we can do this we provide at least a reasonable argument for accepting the belief system and the ultimate moral attitude it supports.

I do not hold that such a belief system can be *proven* to be true, either inductively or deductively. As we shall see, not all of its components can be stated in the form of empirically verifiable propositions. Nor is its internal order governed by purely logical relationships. But the system as a whole, I contend, constitutes a coherent, unified, and rationally acceptable "picture" or "map" of a total world. By examining each of its main components and seeing how they fit together, we obtain a scientifically informed and well-ordered conception of nature and the place of humans in it.

This belief system underlying the attitude of respect for nature I call (for want of a better name) "the biocentric outlook on nature." Since it is not wholly analyzable into empirically confirmable assertions, it should not be thought of as simply a compendium of the biological sciences concerning our planet's ecosystems. It might best be described as a philosophical world view, to distinguish it from a scientific theory or explanatory system. However, one of its major tenets is the great lesson we have learned from the science of ecology: the interdependence of all living things in an organically unified order whose balance and stability are necessary conditions for the realization of the good of its constituent biotic communities.

Before turning to an account of the main components of the biocentric outlook, it is convenient here to set forth the overall structure of my theory of environmental ethics as it has now emerged. The ethics of respect for nature is made up of three basic elements: a belief system, an ultimate moral attitude, and a set of rules of duty and standards of character. These elements are connected with each other in the following manner. The belief system provides a certain outlook on nature which supports and makes intelligible an autonomous agent's adopting, as an ultimate moral attitude, the attitude of respect for nature. It supports and makes intelligible the attitude in the sense that, when an autonomous agent understands its moral relations to the natural world in terms of this outlook, it recognizes the attitude of respect to be the only *suitable* or *fitting* attitude to take toward all wild forms of life in the Earth's biosphere. Living things are now viewed as *the appropriate objects of the attitude of respect* and are accordingly regarded as entities possessing inherent worth. One then places intrinsic value on the promotion and protection of their good. As a consequence of this, one makes a moral commitment to abide by a set of rules of duty and to fulfill (as far as one can by one's own efforts) certain standards of good character. Given one's adoption of the attitude of respect, one makes that moral commitment because one considers those rules and standards to be validly binding on all moral agents. They are seen as embodying forms of conduct and character structures in which the attitude of respect for nature is manifested.

This three-part complex which internally orders the ethics of respect for nature is symmetrical with a theory of human ethics grounded on respect for persons. Such a theory includes, first, a conception of oneself and others as persons, that is, as centers of autonomous choice. Second, there is the attitude of respect for persons as persons. When this is adopted as an ultimate moral attitude it involves the disposition to treat every person as having inherent worth or "human dignity." Every human being, just in virtue of her or his humanity, is understood to be worthy of moral consideration, and intrinsic value is placed on the autonomy and well-being of each. This is what Kant meant by conceiving of persons as ends in themselves. Third, there is an ethical system of duties which are acknowledged to be owed by everyone to everyone. These duties are forms of conduct in which public recognition is given to each individual's inherent worth as a person.

This structural framework for a theory of human ethics is meant to leave open the issue of consequentialism (utilitarianism) versus nonconsequentialism (deontology). That issue concerns the particular kind of system of rules defining the duties of moral agents toward persons. Similarly, I am leaving open in this paper the question of what particular kind of system of rules defines our duties with respect to the natural world.

THE BIOCENTRIC OUTLOOK ON NATURE

The biocentric outlook on nature has four main components. (1) Humans are thought of as members of the Earth's community of life, holding that membership on the same terms as apply to all the nonhuman members. (2) The Earth's natural ecosystems as a totality are seen as a complex web of interconnected elements, with the sound biological functioning of each being dependent on the sound biological functioning of the others. (This is the component referred to above as the great lesson that the science of ecology has taught us.) (3) Each individual organism is conceived of as a teleological center of life, pursuing its own good in its own way. (4) Whether we are concerned with standards of merit or with the concept of inherent worth, the claim that humans by their very nature are superior to other species is a groundless claim and, in the light of elements (1), (2), and (3) above, must be rejected as nothing more than an irrational bias in our own favor. . . .

THE DENIAL OF HUMAN SUPERIORITY

This fourth component of the biocentric outlook on nature is the single most important idea in establishing the justifiability of the attitude of respect for nature. Its central role is due to the special relationship it bears to the first three components of the outlook. This relationship will be brought out after the concept of human superiority is examined and analyzed.[6]

In what sense are humans alleged to be superior to other animals? We are different from them in having certain capacities that they lack. But why should these capacities be a mark of superiority? From what point of view are they judged to be signs of superiority and what sense of superiority is meant? After all, various nonhuman species have capacities that humans lack. There is the speed of a cheetah, the vision of an eagle, the agility of a monkey. Why should not these be taken as signs of *their* superiority over humans?

One answer that comes immediately to mind is that these capacities are not as *valuable* as the human capacities that are claimed to make us superior. Such uniquely human characteristics as rational thought, aesthetic creativity, autonomy and self-determination, and moral freedom, it might be held, have a higher value than the capacities found in other species. Yet we must ask: valuable to whom, and on what grounds?

The human characteristics mentioned are all valuable to humans. They are essential to the preservation and enrichment of our civilization and culture. Clearly it is from the human standpoint that they are being judged to be desirable and good. It is not difficult here to recognize a begging of the question. Humans are claiming human superiority from a strictly human point of view, that is, from a point of view in which the good of humans is taken as the standard of judgment. All we need to do is to look at the capacities of nonhuman animals (or plants, for that matter) from the standpoint of *their* good to find a contrary judgment of superiority. The speed of the cheetah, for example, is a sign of its superiority to humans when considered from the standpoint of the good of its species. If it were as slow a runner as a human, it would not be able to survive. And so for all the other abilities of nonhumans which further their good but which are lacking in humans. In each case the claim to human superiority would be rejected from a nonhuman standpoint.

When superiority assertions are interpreted in this way, they are based on judgments of *merit*. To judge the merits of a person or an organism one must apply grading or ranking standards to it. (As I show below, this distinguishes judgments of merit from judgments of inherent worth.) Empirical investigation then determines whether it has the "good-making properties" (merits) in virtue of which it fulfills the standards being applied. In the case of humans, merits may be either moral or nonmoral. We can judge one person to be better than (superior to) another from the moral point of view by applying certain standards to their character and conduct. Similarly, we can appeal to nonmoral criteria in judging someone to be an excellent piano player, a fair cook, a poor tennis player, and so on. Different social purposes and roles are implicit in the making of such judgments, providing the frame of reference for the choice of standards by which the nonmoral merits of people are determined. Ultimately such purposes and roles stem from a society's way of life as a whole. Now a society's way of life may be thought of as the cultural form given to the realization of human values. Whether moral or nonmoral standards are being applied, then, all judgments of people's merits finally depend on human values. All are made from an exclusively human standpoint.

The question that naturally arises at this juncture is: why should standards that are based on human values be assumed to be the only valid criteria of merit and hence the only true signs of superiority? This question is especially pressing when humans are being judged superior in merit to nonhumans. It is true that a human being may be a better mathematician than a monkey, but the monkey may be a better tree climber than a human being. If we humans value mathematics more than tree climbing, that is because our conception of civilized life makes the development of mathematical ability more desirable than the ability to climb trees. But is it not unreasonable to judge nonhumans by the values of human civilization, rather than by values connected with what it is for a member of *that* species to live a good life? If all living things have a good of their own, it at least makes sense to judge the merits of nonhumans by standards derived from *their* good. To use only standards based on human values is already to commit oneself to holding that humans are superior to nonhumans, which is the point in question.

A further logical flaw arises in connection with the widely held conviction that humans are *morally* superior beings because they possess, while others lack, the capacities of a moral agent (free will, accountability, deliberation, judgment, practical reason). This view rests on a conceptual confusion. As far as moral standards are concerned, only beings that have the capacities of a moral agent can properly be judged to be *either* moral (morally good) *or* immoral (morally deficient). Moral standards are simply not applicable to beings that lack such capacities. Animals and plants cannot therefore be said to be morally inferior in merit to humans. Since the only beings that can have moral merits *or be deficient in such merits* are moral agents, it is conceptually incoherent to judge humans as superior to nonhumans on the ground that humans have moral capacities while nonhumans don't.

Up to this point I have been interpreting the claim that humans are superior to other living things as a grading or ranking judgment regarding their comparative merits. There is, however, another way of understanding the idea of human superiority. According to this interpretation, humans are superior to nonhumans not as regards their merits but as regards their inherent worth. Thus the claim of human superiority is to be understood as asserting that all humans, simply in virtue of their humanity, have *a greater inherent worth* than other living things.

The inherent worth of an entity does not depend on its merits.[7] To consider something as possessing inherent worth, we have seen, is to place intrinsic value on the realization of its good. This is done regardless of whatever particular merits it might have or might lack, as judged by a set of grading or ranking standards. In human affairs, we are all familiar with the principle that one's worth as a person does not vary with one's merits or lack of merits. The same can hold true of animals and plants. To regard such entities as possessing inherent worth entails disregarding their merits and deficiencies, whether they are being judged from a human standpoint or from the standpoint of their own species.

The idea of one entity having more merit than another, and so being superior to it in merit, makes perfectly good sense. Merit is a grading or ranking concept, and judgments of comparative merit are based on the different degrees to which things satisfy a given standard. But what can it mean to talk about one thing being superior to another in inherent worth? In order to get at what is being asserted in such a claim it is helpful first to look at the social origin of the concept of degrees of inherent worth.

The idea that humans can possess different degrees of inherent worth originated in societies having rigid class structures. Before the rise of modern democracies with their egalitarian outlook, one's membership in a hereditary class determined one's social status. People in the upper classes were looked up to, while those in the lower classes were looked down upon. In such a society one's social superiors and social inferiors were clearly defined and easily recognized.

Two aspects of these class-structured societies are especially relevant to the idea of degrees of inherent worth. First, those born into the upper classes were deemed more worthy of respect than those born into the lower orders. Second, the superior worth of upper class people had nothing to do with their merits nor did the inferior worth of those in the lower classes rest on their lack of merits. One's superiority or inferiority entirely derived from a social position one was born into. The modern concept of a meritocracy simply did not apply. One could not advance into a higher class by any sort of moral or nonmoral achievement. Similarly, an aristocrat held his title and all the privileges that went with it just because he was the eldest son of a titled nobleman. Unlike the bestowing of knighthood in contemporary Great Britain, one did not earn membership in the nobility by meritorious conduct.

We who live in modern democracies no longer believe in such hereditary social distinctions. Indeed, we would wholeheartedly condemn them on moral grounds as being fundamentally unjust. We have come to think of class systems as a paradigm of social injustice, it being a central principle of the democratic way of life that among humans there are no superiors and no inferiors. Thus we have rejected the whole conceptual framework in which people are judged to have different degrees of inherent worth. That idea is incompatible with our notion of human equality based on the doctrine that all humans, simply in virtue of their humanity, have the same inherent worth. (The belief in universal human rights is one form that this egalitarianism takes.)

The vast majority of people in modern democracies, however, do not maintain an egalitarian outlook when it comes to comparing human beings with other living things. Most people consider our own species to be superior to all other species and this superiority is understood to be a matter of inherent worth, not merit. There may exist thoroughly vicious and depraved humans who lack all merit. Yet because they are human they are thought to belong to a higher class of entities than any plant or animal. That one is born into the species *Homo sapiens* entitles one to have lordship over those who are one's inferiors, namely, those born into other species. The parallel with hereditary social classes is very close. Implicit in this view is a hierarchical conception of nature according to which an organism has a position of superiority or inferiority in the Earth's community of life simply on the basis of its genetic background. The "lower" orders of life are looked down upon and it is considered perfectly proper that they serve the interests of those belonging to the highest order, namely humans. The intrinsic value we place on the well-being of our fellow humans reflects our recognition of their rightful position as our equals. No such intrinsic value is to be placed on the good of other animals, unless we choose to do so out of fondness or affection for them. But their well-being imposes no moral requirement on us. In this respect there is an absolute difference in moral status between ourselves and them.

This is the structure of concepts and beliefs that people are committed to insofar as they regard humans to be superior in inherent worth to all other species. I now wish to argue that this structure of concepts and beliefs is completely groundless. If we accept the first three components of the biocentric outlook and from that perspective look at the major philosophical traditions which have supported that structure, we find it to be at bottom nothing more than the expression of an irrational bias in our own favor. The philosophical traditions themselves rest on very questionable assumptions or else simply beg the question. I briefly consider three of the main traditions to substantiate the point. These are classical Greek humanism, Cartesian dualism, and the Judeo-Christian concept of the Great Chain of Being.

The inherent superiority of humans over other species was implicit in the Greek definition of man as a rational animal. Our animal nature was identified with "brute" desires that need the order and restraint of reason to rule them (just as reason is the special virtue of those who rule in the ideal state). Rationality was then seen to be the key to our superiority over animals. It enables us to live on a higher plane and endows us with a nobility and worth that other creatures lack. This familiar way of comparing humans with other species is deeply ingrained in our Western philosophical outlook. The point to consider here is that this view does not actually provide an argument *for* human superiority but rather makes explicit the framework of thought that is implicitly used by those who think of humans as inherently superior to nonhumans. The Greeks who held that humans, in virtue of their rational capacities, have a kind of worth greater than that of any nonrational being, never looked at rationality as but one capacity of living things among many others. But when we consider rationality from the standpoint of the first three elements of the ecological outlook, we see that its value lies in its importance for *human* life. Other creatures achieve their species-specific good without the need of rationality, although they often make use of capacities that humans lack. So the humanistic outlook of classical Greek thought does not give us a neutral (nonquestion-begging) ground on which to construct a scale of degrees of inherent worth possessed by different species of living things.

The second tradition, centering on the Cartesian dualism of soul and body, also fails to justify the claim to human superiority. That superiority is supposed to derive from the fact that we have souls while animals do not. Animals are mere automata and lack the divine element that makes us spiritual beings. I won't go into the now famil-iar criticisms of this two-substance view. I only add the point that, even if humans are composed of an immaterial, unextended soul and a material, extended body, this in itself is not a reason to deem them of greater worth than entities that are only bodies. Why is a soul substance a thing that adds value to its possessor? Unless some theological reasoning is offered here (which many, including myself, would find unacceptable on epistemological grounds), no logical connection is evident. An immaterial something which thinks is better than a material something which does not think only if think-ing itself has value, either intrinsically or instrumentally. Now it is intrinsically valuable to humans alone, who value it as an end in itself, and it is instrumentally valuable to those who benefit from it, namely humans.

For animals that neither enjoy thinking for its own sake nor need it for living the kind of life for which they are best adapted, it has no value. Even if "thinking" is broad-ened to include all forms of consciousness, there are still many living things that can do without it and yet live what is for their species a good life. The anthropocentricity under-lying the claim to human superiority runs throughout Cartesian dualism.

A third major source of the idea of human superiority is the Judeo-Christian con-cept of the Great Chain of Being. Humans are superior to animals and plants because their Creator has given them a higher place on the chain. It begins with God at the top, and then moves to the angels, who are lower than God but higher than humans, then to humans, positioned between the angels and the beasts (partaking of the nature of both), and then on down to the lower levels occupied by nonhuman animals, plants, and finally inanimate objects. Humans, being "made in God's image," are inherently superior to animals and plants by virtue of their being closer (in their essential nature) to God.

The metaphysical and epistemological difficulties with this conception of a hier-archy of entities are, in my mind, insuperable. Without entering into this matter here, I only point out that if we are unwilling to accept the metaphysics of traditional Judaism and Christianity, we are again left without good reasons for holding to the claim of inherent human superiority.

The foregoing considerations (and others like them) leave us with but one ground for the assertion that a human being, regardless of merit, is a higher kind of entity than any other living thing. This is the mere fact of the genetic makeup of the species *Homo sapiens*. But this is surely irrational and arbitrary. Why should the arrangement of genes of a certain type be a mark of superior value, especially when this fact about an organ-ism is taken by itself, unrelated to any other aspect of its life? We might just as well refer to any other genetic makeup as a ground of superior value. Clearly we are confronted here with a wholly arbitrary claim that can only be explained as an irrational bias in our own favor.

That the claim is nothing more than a deep-seated prejudice is brought home to us when we look at our relation to other species in the light of the first three elements of the biocentric outlook. Those elements taken conjointly give us a certain overall view of the natural world and of the place of humans in it. When we take this view we come to understand other living things, their environmental conditions, and their ecological relationships in such a way as to awake in us a deep sense of our kinship with them as fellow members of the Earth's community of life. Humans and nonhumans alike are viewed together as integral parts of one unified whole in which all living things are functionally interrelated. Finally, when our awareness focuses on the individual lives of plants and animals, each is seen to share with us the characteristic of being a teleological center of life striving to realize its own good in its own unique way.

As this entire belief system becomes part of the conceptual framework through which we understand and perceive the world, we come to see ourselves as bearing a certain moral relation to nonhuman forms of life. Our ethical role in nature takes on a new significance. We begin to look at other species as we look at ourselves, seeing them as beings which have a good they are striving to realize just as we have a good we are striving to realize. We accordingly develop the disposition to view the world from the standpoint of their good as well as from the standpoint of our own good. Now if the groundlessness of the claim that humans are inherently superior to other species were brought clearly before our minds, we would not remain intellectually neutral toward that claim but would reject it as being fundamentally at variance with our total world outlook. In the absence of any good reasons for holding it, the assertion of human superiority would then appear simply as the expression of an irrational and self-serving prejudice that favors one particular species over several million others.

Rejecting the notion of human superiority entails its positive counterpart: the doctrine of species impartiality. One who accepts that doctrine regards all living things as possessing inherent worth—the *same* inherent worth, since no one species has been shown to be either "higher" or "lower" than any other. Now we saw earlier that, insofar as one thinks of a living thing as possessing inherent worth, one considers it to be the appropriate object of the attitude of respect and believes that attitude to be the only fitting or suitable one for all moral agents to take toward it.

Here, then, is the key to understanding how the attitude of respect is rooted in the biocentric outlook on nature. The basic connection is made through the denial of human superiority. Once we reject the claim that humans are superior either in merit or in worth to other living things, we are ready to adopt the attitude of respect. The denial of human superiority is itself the result of taking the perspective on nature built into the first three elements of the biocentric outlook.

Now the first three elements of the biocentric outlook, it seems clear, would be found acceptable to any rational and scientifically informed thinker who is fully "open" to the reality of the lives of nonhuman organisms. Without denying our distinctively human characteristics, such a thinker can acknowledge the fundamental respects in which we are members of the Earth's community of life and in which the biological conditions necessary for the realization of our human values are inextricably linked with the whole system of nature. In addition, the conception of individual living things as teleological centers of life simply articulates how a scientifically informed thinker comes to understand them as the result of increasingly careful and detailed observations. Thus, the biocentric outlook recommends itself as an acceptable system of concepts and beliefs to anyone who is clear-minded, unbiased, and factually enlightened, and who has a developed capacity of reality awareness with regard to the lives of individual organisms. This, I submit, is as good a reason for making the moral commitment involved in adopting the attitude of respect for nature as any theory of environmental ethics could possibly have.

MORAL RIGHTS AND THE MATTER
OF COMPETING CLAIMS

I have not asserted anywhere in the foregoing account that animals or plants have moral rights. This omission was deliberate. I do not think that the reference class of the concept, bearer of moral rights, should be extended to include nonhuman living things. My reasons for taking this position, however, go beyond the scope of this paper. I believe I have been able to accomplish many of the same ends which those who ascribe rights to animals or plants wish to accomplish. There is no reason, moreover, why plants and animals, including whole species populations and life communities, cannot be accorded *legal* rights under my theory. To grant them legal protection could be interpreted as giving them legal entitlement to be protected, and this, in fact, would be a means by which a society that subscribed to the ethics of respect for nature could give public recognition to their inherent worth.

There remains the problem of competing claims, even when wild plants and animals are not thought of as bearers of moral rights. If we accept the biocentric outlook and accordingly adopt the attitude of respect for nature as our ultimate moral attitude, how do we resolve conflicts that arise from our respect for persons in the domain of human ethics and our respect for nature in the domain of environmental ethics? This is a question that cannot adequately be dealt with here. My main purpose in this paper has been to try to establish a base point from which we can start working toward a solution to the problem. I have shown why we cannot just begin with an initial presumption in favor of the interests of our own species. It is after all within our power as moral beings to place limits on human population and technology with the deliberate intention of sharing the Earth's bounty with other species. That such sharing is an ideal difficult to realize even in an approximate way does not take away its claim to our deepest moral commitment.

NOTES

1. The conceptual links between an entity *having* a good, something being good *for* it, and events doing good *to* it are examined by G. H. Von Wright in *The Varieties of Goodness* (New York: Humanities Press, 1963), chaps. 3 and 5.
2. See W. K. Frankena, "Ethics and the Environment," in K. E. Goodpaster and K. M. Sayre, eds., *Ethics and Problems of the 21st Century* (Notre Dame: University of Notre Dame Press, 1979), pp. 3–20. I critically examine Frankena's views in "Frankena on Environmental Ethics," *Monist,* vol. 64, no. 3 (July 1981) pp. 313–324.
3. In the light of considerations set forth in Daniel Dennett's *Brainstorms: Philosophical Essays on Mind and Psychology* (Montgomery, Vermont: Bradford Books, 1978), it is advisable to leave this question unsettled at this time. When machines are developed that function in the way our brains do, we may well come to deem them proper subjects of moral consideration.
4. I have analyzed the nature of this commitment of human ethics in "On Taking the Moral Point of View," *Midwest Studies in Philosophy,* vol. 3, *Studies in Ethical Theory* (1978), pp. 35–61.
5. John Rawls, "Justice As Fairness," *Philosophical Review* 67 (1958): 183.
6. My criticisms of the dogma of human superiority gain independent support from a carefully reasoned essay by R. and V. Routley showing the many logical weaknesses in arguments for human-centered theories of environmental ethics. R. and V. Routley, "Against the Inevitability of Human Chauvinism," in K. E. Goodpaster and K. M. Sayre, eds., *Ethics and Problems of the 21st Century* (Notre Dame: University of Notre Dame Press, 1979), pp. 36–59.
7. For this way of distinguishing between merit and inherent worth, I am indebted to Gregory Vlastos, "Justice and Equality," in R. Brandt, ed., *Social Justice* (Upper Saddle River, N. J.: Prentice Hall, 1962), pp. 31–72.

11

⚞ Environmental Ethics ⚟ and International Justice

BERNARD E. ROLLIN

Bernard E. Rollin is Professor of Philosophy and Physiology and Biophysics at Colorado State University. His books include Animal Rights and Human Morality *and* The Unheeded Cry.

The past two decades have witnessed a major revolutionary thrust in social moral awareness, one virtually unknown in mainstream Western ethical thinking, although not unrecognized in other cultural traditions; for example, the Navajo, whose descriptive language for nature and animals is suffused with ethical nuances; the Australian Aboriginal people; and the ancient Persians. This thrust is the recognition that nonhuman entities enjoy some moral status as objects of moral concern and deliberation. Although the investigation of the moral status of nonhuman entities has sometimes been subsumed under the global rubric of environmental ethics, such a blanket term does not do adequate justice to the substantial conceptual differences of its components.

THE MORAL STATUS OF NONHUMAN THINGS

As a bare minimum, environmental ethics comprises two fundamentally divergent concerns—namely, concern with individual nonhuman animals as direct objects of moral concern and concern with species, ecosystems, environments, wilderness areas, forests, the biosphere, and other nonsentient natural or even abstract objects as direct objects of moral concern. Usually, although with a number of major exceptions,[1] those who give primacy to animals have tended to deny the moral significance of environments and species as direct objects of moral concern, whereas those who give moral primacy to enviro-ecological concerns tend to deny or at least downplay the moral significance of individual animals.[2] Significant though these differences are, they should not cloud the dramatic nature of this common attempt to break out of a moral tradition that finds loci of value only in human beings and, derivatively, in human institutions.

Because of the revolutionary nature of these attempts, they also remain somewhat undeveloped and embryonic. Writings in this area by and large have tended to focus more on making the case for the attribution of moral status to these entities than in working out detailed answers to particular issues.[3] Thus, in order to assess these thrusts in relation to international justice, one must first attempt to articulate a consensus concerning the basic issue of attributing moral status to nonhumans, an attribution that, prima facie, flies in the face of previous moral tradition. In attempting such an articulation, one cannot hope to capture all approaches to these issues, but rather to glean what appears most defensible when assessed against the tribunal of common moral practice, moral theory attempting to explain that practice, and common moral discourse.

The most plausible strategy in attempting to revise traditional moral theory and practice is to show that the seeds of the new moral notions or extensions of old moral notions are, in fact, already implicit in the old moral machinery developed to deal with other issues. Only when such avenues are exhausted will it make sense to recommend major rebuilding of the machinery, rather than putting it to new uses. The classic examples of such extensions are obviously found in the extension of the moral/legal machinery of Western democracies to cover traditionally disenfranchised groups such as women and minorities. The relatively smooth flow of such applications owes much of its smoothness to the plausibility of a simple argument of the form:

> Our extant moral principles ought to cover all humans.
> Women are humans.
> _____
> ∴ Our extant moral principles ought to cover women.

On the other hand, conceptually radical departures from tradition do not lend themselves to such simple rational reconstruction. Thus, for example, the principles of *favoring* members of traditionally disenfranchised groups at the expense of innocent members of nondisenfranchised groups for the sake of rectifying historically based injustice is viewed as much more morally problematic and ambivalent than simply according rights to these groups. Thus, it would be difficult to construct a simple syllogism in defense of this practice that would garner universal acquiescence with the ease of the one indicated previously.

Thus, one needs to distinguish between moral revolutionary thrusts that are ostensibly paradoxical to common sense and practice because they have been ignored in a wholesale fashion, yet are in fact logical extensions of common morality, and those revolutionary thrusts that are genuinely paradoxical to previous moral thinking and practice because they are not implicit therein. Being genuinely paradoxical does not invalidate a new moral thrust—it does, however, place upon its proponents a substantially greater burden of proof. Those philosophers, like myself, who have argued for a recognition of the moral status of individual animals and the rights and legal status that derive therefrom, have attempted to place ourselves in the first category. We recognize that a society that kills and eats billions of animals, kills millions more in research, and disposes of millions more for relatively frivolous reasons and that relies economically on animal exploitation as a mainstay of social wealth, considers talk of elevating the moral status of animals as impossible and paradoxical. But this does not mean that such an elevation does not follow unrecognized from moral principles we all hold. Indeed, the abolition of slavery or the liberation of women appeared similarly paradoxical and economically impossible, yet gradually both were perceived as morally necessary, in part because both were implicit, albeit unrecognized, in previously acknowledged assumptions.[4]

My own argument for elevating the status of animals has been a relatively straight-forward deduction of unnoticed implications of traditional morality. I have tried to show that no morally relevant grounds for excluding animals from the full application of our moral machinery will stand up to rational scrutiny. Traditional claims that rely on notions such as animals have no souls, are inferior to humans in power or intelligence or evolutionary status, are not moral agents, are not rational, are not possessed of free will, are not capable of language, are not bound by social contract to humans, and so forth, do not serve as justifiable reasons for excluding animals and their interests from the moral arena.

By the same token, morally relevant similarities exist between us and them in the case of the "higher" animals. Animals can suffer, as Jeremy Bentham said; they have interests; what we do to them matters to them; they can feel pain, fear, anxiety, loneliness, pleasure, boredom, and so on. Indeed, the simplicity and power of the argument calling attention to such morally relevant similarities has led Cartesians from Descartes to modern physiologists with a vested interest against attributing moral status to animals to declare that animals are machines with no morally relevant modes of awareness, a point often addressed today against moral claims such as mine. In fact, such claims have become a mainstay of what I have elsewhere called the "common sense of science." Thus, one who argues for an augmented moral status for animals finds it necessary to establish philosophically and scientifically what common sense takes for granted—namely, that animals *are* conscious.[5] Most people whose common sense is intact are not Cartesians and can see that moral talk cannot be withheld from animals and our treatment of them.

In my own work, appealing again to common moral practice, I have stressed our society's quasi-moral, quasi-legal notion of rights as a reflection of our commitment to the moral primacy of the individual, rather than the state. Rights protect what are hypothesized as the fundamental interests of human beings from cavalier encroachment by the common good—such interests as speech, assembly, belief, property, privacy, freedom from torture and so forth. But those animals who are conscious also have fundamental interests arising out of *their* biologically given natures (or *teloi*), the infringement upon which matters greatly to them, and the fulfillment of which is central to their lives. Hence, I deduce the notion of animal rights from our common moral theory and practice and attempt to show that conceptually, at least, it is a deduction from the moral framework of the status quo rather than a major revision therein. Moral concern for individual animals follows from the hitherto ignored presence of morally relevant characteristics, primarily sentience, in animals. As a result, I am comfortable in attributing what Immanuel Kant called "intrinsic value," not merely use value, to animals if we attribute it to people.[6]

The task is far more formidable for those who attempt to make nonsentient natural objects, such as rivers and mountains, or, worse, quasi-abstract entities, such as species and ecosystems, into direct objects of moral concern. Interestingly enough, in direct opposition to the case of animals, such moves appear prima facie plausible to common morality, which has long expressed concern for the value and preservation of some natural objects, while condoning wholesale exploitation of others. In the same way, common practice often showed extreme concern for certain favored kinds of animals, while systematically exploiting others. Thus, many people in the United States strongly oppose scientific research on dogs and cats, but are totally unconcerned about such use of rodents or swine. What is superficially plausible, however, quite unlike the case of animals, turns out to be deeply paradoxical given the machinery of traditional morality.

Many leading environmental ethicists have attempted to do for nonsentient natural objects and abstract objects the same sort of thing I have tried to do for animals—namely, attempted to elevate their status to direct objects of intrinsic value, ends in themselves, which are morally valuable not only because of their relations and utility to sentient beings, but in and of themselves.[7] To my knowledge, none of these theorists has attempted to claim, as I do for animals, that the locus of such value lies in the fact that what we do to these entities matters to them. No one has argued that we can harm rivers, species, or ecosystems in ways that matter to them.

Wherein, then, do these theorists locate the intrinsic value of these entities? This is not at all clear in the writings, but seems to come down to one of the following doubtful moves:

1. Going from the fact that environmental factors are absolutely essential to the well-being or survival of beings that are loci of intrinsic value to the conclusion that environmental factors therefore enjoy a similar or even higher moral status. Such a move is clearly fallacious. Just because I cannot survive without insulin, and I am an object of intrinsic value, it does not follow that insulin is, too. In fact, the insulin is a paradigmatic example of instrumental value.

2. Going from the fact that the environment "creates" all sentient creatures to the fact that its welfare is more important than theirs. This is really a variation on (1) and succumbs to the same sort of criticism, namely, that this reasoning represents a genetic fallacy. The cause of something valuable need not itself be valuable and certainly not necessarily more valuable than its effect—its value must be established independently of its result. The Holocaust may have caused the state of Israel; that does not make the Holocaust more valuable than the state of Israel.

3. Confusing aesthetic or instrumental value for sentient creatures, notably humans, with intrinsic value and underestimating aesthetic value as a category. We shall return to this shortly, for I suspect it is the root confusion in those attempting to give nonsentient nature intrinsic value.

4. Substituting rhetoric for logic at crucial points in the discussions and using a poetic rhetoric (descriptions of natural objects in terms such as "grandeur," "majesty," "novelty," "variety") as an unexplained basis for according them "intrinsic value."

5. Going from the metaphor that infringement on natural objects "matters" to them in the sense that disturbance evokes an adjustment by their self-regulating properties, to the erroneous conclusion that such self-regulation, being analogous to conscious coping in animals, entitles them to direct moral status.

In short, traditional morality and its theory do not offer a viable way to raise the moral status of nonsentient natural objects and abstract objects so that they are direct objects of moral concern on a par with or even higher than sentient creatures. Ordinary morality and moral concern take as their focus the effects of actions on beings who can be helped and harmed, in ways that matter to them, either directly or by implication. If it is immoral to wreck someone's property, it is because it is someone's; if it is immoral to promote the extinction of species, it is because such extinction causes aesthetic or practical harm to humans or to animals or because a species is, in the final analysis, a group of harmable individuals.

There is nothing, of course, to stop environmental ethicists from making a recommendation for a substantial revision of common and traditional morality. But such recommendations are likely to be dismissed or whittled away by a moral version of Occam's razor: Why grant animals rights and acknowledge in animals intrinsic value? Because they are conscious and what we do to them matters to them? Why grant rocks, or trees, or species, or ecosystems rights? Because these objects have great aesthetic value, or are essential to us, or are basic for survival? But these are paradigmatic examples of *instrumental* value. A conceptual confusion for a noble purpose is still a conceptual confusion.

There is nothing to be gained by attempting to elevate the moral status of nonsentient natural objects to that of sentient ones. One can develop a rich environmental ethic by locating the value of nonsentient natural objects in their relation to sentient ones. One can argue for the preservation of habitats because their destruction harms animals; one can argue for preserving ecosystems on the grounds of unforeseen pernicious consequences resulting from their destruction, a claim for which much empirical evidence exists. One can argue for the preservation of animal species as the sum of a group of individuals who would be harmed by its extinction. One can argue for preserving mountains, snail darters, streams, and cockroaches on aesthetic grounds. Too many philosophers forget the moral power of aesthetic claims and tend to see aesthetic reasons as a weak basis for preserving natural objects. Yet the moral imperative not to destroy unique aesthetic objects and even nonunique ones is an onerous one that is well ingrained into common practice—witness the worldwide establishment of national parks, preserves, forests, and wildlife areas.

Rather than attempting to transcend all views of natural objects as instrumental by grafting onto nature a mystical intrinsic value that can be buttressed only by poetic rhetoric, it would be far better to nurture public appreciation of subtle instrumental value, especially aesthetic value. People can learn to appreciate the unique beauty of a desert, or of a fragile ecosystem, or even of a noxious creature like a tick, when they understand the complexity and history therein and can read the story each life form contains. I am reminded of a colleague in parasitology who is loath to destroy worms he has studied upon completing his research because he has aesthetically learned to value their complexity of structure, function, and evolutionary history and role.

It is important to note that the attribution of value to nonsentient natural objects as a relational property arising out of their significance (recognized or not) for sentient beings does not denigrate the value of natural objects. Indeed, this attribution does not even imply that the interests or desires of individual sentient beings always trump concern for nonsentient ones. Our legal system has, for example, valuable and irreplaceable property laws that forbid owners of aesthetic objects, say a collection of Vincent Van Gogh paintings, to destroy them at will, say by adding them to one's funeral pyre. To be sure, this restriction on people's right to dispose of their own property arises out of a recognition of the value of these objects to other humans, but this is surely quite sensible. How else would one justify such a restriction? Nor, as we said earlier, need one limit the value of natural objects to their relationship to humans. Philosophically, one could, for example, sensibly (and commonsensically) argue for preservation of acreage from the golf-course developer because failure to do so would mean the destruction of thousands of sentient creatures' habitats—a major infringement of their interests—while building the golf course would fulfill the rarefied and inessential interests of a few.

Thus, in my view, one would accord moral concern to natural objects in a variety of ways, depending on the sort of object being considered. Moral status for individual animals would arise from their sentience. Moral status of species and their protection from humans would arise from the fact that a species is a collection of morally relevant individuals; moral status also would arise from the fact that humans have an aesthetic concern in not letting a unique and irreplaceable aesthetic object (or group of objects) disappear forever from our *Umwelt* (environment). Concern for wilderness areas, mountains, deserts, and so on would arise from their survival value for sentient animals as well as from their aesthetic value for humans. (Some writers have suggested that this aesthetic value is so great as to be essential to human mental/physical health, a point perfectly compatible with my position.[8])

Nothing in what I have said as yet tells us how to weigh conflicting interests, whether between humans and other sentient creatures or between human desires and environmental protection. How does one weigh the aesthetic concern of those who oppose blasting away part of a cliff against the pragmatic concern of those who wish to build on a cliffside? But the problem of weighing is equally thorny in traditional ethics—witness lifeboat questions or questions concerning the allocation of scarce medical resources. Nor does the intrinsic value approach help in adjudicating such issues. How does one weigh the alleged intrinsic value of a cliffside against the interests of the (intrinsic-value-bearing) homebuilders?

Furthermore, the intrinsic value view can lead to results that are repugnant to common sense and ordinary moral consciousness. Thus, for example, it follows from what has been suggested by one intrinsic value theorist that if a migratory herd of plentiful elk were passing through an area containing an endangered species of moss, it would be not only permissible but obligatory to kill the elk in order to protect the moss because in one case we would lose a species, in another "merely" individuals.[9] In my view, such a case has a less paradoxical resolution. Destruction of the moss does not matter to the moss, whereas elk presumably care about living or being injured. Therefore, one would give prima facie priority to the elk. This might presumably be trumped if, for example, the moss were a substratum from which was extracted an ingredient necessary to stop a raging, lethal epidemic in humans or animals. But such cases—and indeed most cases of conflicting interests—must be decided on the actual occasion. These cases are decided by a careful examination of the facts of the situation. Thus, our suggestion of a basis for environmental ethics does not qualitatively change the situation from that of current ethical deliberation, whereas granting intrinsic value to natural objects would leave us with a "whole new ball game"—and one where we do not know the rules.

In sum, then, the question of environmental ethics in relation to international justice must be analyzed into two discrete components. First are those questions that pertain to direct objects of moral concern—nonhuman animals whose sentience we have good reason to suspect—and that require the application of traditional moral notions to a hitherto ignored domain of moral objects. Second are those questions pertaining to natural objects or abstract natural objects. Although it is nonsensical to attribute intrinsic or direct moral value to these objects, they nonetheless must become (and are indeed becoming) central to our social moral deliberations. This centrality derives from our increasing recognition of the far-reaching and sometimes subtle instrumental value these objects have for humans and animals. Knowing that contamination of remote desert areas by pollutants can destroy unique panoplies of fragile beauty, or that dumping wastes into the ocean can destroy a potential source of antibiotics, or that building a pipeline can have undreamed-of harmful effects goes a long way toward making us think twice about these activities—a far longer way than endowing them with quasi-mystical rhetorical status subject to (and begging for) positivistic torpedoing.

THE ENVIRONMENT AND INTERNATIONAL JUSTICE

How do both of these newly born areas of moral concern relate to issues of international justice? In the case of issues pertaining to moral awareness of the questions involved in the preservation and despoliation of nonsentient natural objects, processes, and abstract objects, the connection becomes increasingly clear as our knowledge increases. The interconnectedness of all things occupying the biosphere, the tenuousness and violability of certain natural objects and events whose permanence and invulnerability were long taken for granted have become dramatically clearer as environmental science has developed and the results of cavalier treatment of nature have become known.

Even those lacking any moral perspective on the instrumental values in nature now ought to have some prudential ones. Thus, even if one does not care about poisoning the air that other people and animals breathe, prudential reason would dictate that one realize that one is also poisoning oneself. Thus, the question of control of the actions of those who would or could harm another or everyone for the sake of selfish interests begins to loom large as our knowledge of environmental impact of individual actions begins to grow. These effects therefore enter into the dialectic of social justice. What constraints can legitimately be placed upon my freedoms in order to protect the environment? What social or individual benefits balance what costs to the environment or to natural objects? How much ought aesthetic values weigh against economic ones? Whole bureaucracies like the Environmental Protection Agency in the United States exist to ponder and regulate such questions in almost all civilized countries, and recent legal thinking has sought ways to codify the importance of natural objects in the law—for example, by granting them legal standing.[10] (Such a granting can and should be based on a realization of their instrumental value, not on intrinsic value; we already have such a precedent in legal standing for ships, cities, and corporations.)

Nevertheless, increased environmental knowledge has driven home a major but often ignored point: Environmental effects do not respect national boundaries. I recall traveling more than twenty years ago to the northernmost regions of eastern Canada that can be reached by road—areas inhabited almost exclusively by Native Americans to whom the benefits accruing from technological progress were manifestly limited. I was appalled to discover that in this land of few roads and fewer amenities, atmospheric pollutants such as sulfur dioxide and hydrogen sulfide reigned supreme—an unwelcome gift from factories hundreds of miles away across the U.S. border. I had no doubt that the respiratory systems of those native people were paying a heavy, and totally unjustified, price for another country's prosperity in which they did not share.

Similar examples abound. When propellant gases released by people in affluent societies (possibly) succeed in tearing a hole in the ozone layer, which hole then has cataclysmic effects on global weather, penetration of noxious rays, and so on, we again see that environmental damage does not respect national boundaries.

In a slightly different vein, one can consider underdeveloped countries struggling to raise the living standards of their populace. To do so, they must exploit and perhaps despoil resources and environments that, from the point of view of a detached observer, ought to be left alone or whose exploitation will or may in some measure ultimately threaten the whole biosphere. The detached observer may well be (and probably is) where he is in virtue of similar despoliation routinely engaged in by his country generations before environmental consciousness had dawned. Is the underdeveloped country to bear a burden of poverty just because its awakening is happening a hundred years late? Or is the new environmental knowledge to count for naught in the face of the need for development?

An excellent example of this point was recently given by an environmental scientist, Michael Mares, in an article in *Science*. Echoing the point we just made, Mares asserts that "broad-scale ecological problems have little to do with national boundaries. In our complex world, where multiple links of commerce, communications, and politics join all countries to a remarkable degree, the suggestion that ecological problems of large magnitude can or should be solved only at a local level is unrealistic. We are all involved in biospheric problems."[11]

Using the case of South America, for which massive extinction of species has been predicted and where wholesale destruction of rain forests has occurred, Mares points out that one cannot look at this situation strictly as South America's problem, but as one caused by global as well as local pressures with global and local consequences. With South American countries in economic difficulties, can one really expect governments there to take a long-run ecological perspective rather than acceding to short-term gain? If other countries in an immediate position to adopt a long-run perspective wish to do so, they must help South America with the requisite expertise as well as with significant financial assistance. . . .

The ultimate example is, of course, the ecological catastrophe of the nuclear winter that is projected to follow nuclear war. Those who would suffer from the effects of such a winter far outnumber the belligerents. Thus, nuclear war becomes a pressing matter not only to those nations with a penchant for annihilating one another, but even to those simple innocents thousands of miles and cultural light years away from the principals who have no notion of the ideological and economic disputes leading to the conflagration and no allegiance to either side.

Yet another striking example of the need for international cooperation and justice in environmental matters comes from the burgeoning area of biotechnology and genetic engineering. For some time, the United States has led in genetic engineering and also in attempts to create rules and guidelines for its regulation. Interest groups have brought suit against projects that might have untoward and unpredictable environmental consequences—for example, the ice nucleation experiments in California that use genetically engineered bacteria to protect crops from frost.[12] Demands for stringent federal regulation of such work have persisted, primarily on the grounds that such activities could wreak havoc with the environment in undreamed-of ways. What is all too often forgotten is that genetic engineering is a problem for international regulation, not merely for national rules. By and large, the technology for doing pioneering work in genetic engineering is relatively inexpensive, compared, for example, to the need for enormous amounts of capital to build particle accelerators. Thus, stringent regulation or even abolition of genetic engineering in a country such as the United States would not alone solve the problem; regulation would merely move genetic engineering into countries less concerned with potential national and global catastrophe. The net effect is that probably riskier, less supervised work would be done under less stringent conditions. Thus, by its very nature, genetic engineering must be controlled internationally if national control is to be effective.

The point about genetic engineering can be made even more strongly when one contemplates its use for military purposes. If there is a real possibility of environmental disaster arising adventitiously out of benign applications of biotechnology, this is a fortiori the case regarding those uses whose avowed purpose is destructive and whose sphere of effect is unpredictable. So much is manifest in the ratification of the Biological Weapons Convention of 1975, widely cited as the world's first disarmament treaty, "since it is the only one that outlaws the production and use of an entire class of weapons of mass destruction."[13] In October 1986, steps were taken to strengthen the verificational procedures of the treaty, but these essentially boil down to merely voluntary compliance, with no system of sanctions or enforcement.

The final example of environmental problems depending for their solution on some system of international justice concerns the extinction of species. Such problems fall into two distinct categories given the argument we have developed, although this distinction has traditionally been ignored. In my view, we must distinguish between threats of extinction involving sentient and nonsentient species. In the case of sentient species, the fact that a species is threatened is trumped by the fact that its members are sentient. First and foremost, the issue involves harming individual, direct objects of moral concern, just as genocide amounts to mass murder, not the elimination of an abstract entity.

Thus, from the point of view of primary loci of moral concern, killing *any* ten Siberian tigers is no different than killing the *last* ten. Our greater horror at the latter stems from invoking the relational value dimension to humans—no human will ever again be able to witness the beauty of these creatures; our world is poorer in the same way that it would be if one destroyed the last ten Van Goghs, not just any ten; the loss of the last ten tigers may lead to other losses of which we are not aware. But we should not lose sight of the fact that the greater harm is to the animals, not to us. For this reason, I will discuss the destruction of sentient species separately, along with cases where individual animals are destroyed and hurt without endangering the species.

This still leaves us with the case of species extinction involving nonsentient species—plants or animals in whom we have no reason to suspect the presence of consciousness. Such extinction is not necessarily an evil. Few (albeit some) bemoaned the eradication of the smallpox virus, and David Baltimore recently remarked that, in his view, all viruses could be eradicated with no loss (save perhaps to intrinsic value theorists).[14] On the other hand, most cases of extinction presumably would be cases of (relational) evil because nonsentient species that do not harm us or other sentient creatures directly or indirectly are at worst neutral, and their loss is both an aesthetic loss for their uniqueness and beauty (the humblest organisms often contain great beauty—in symmetry, adaptation, complexity, or whatever, as my friend the parasitologist discovered), or a loss of a potential tool whose value is not yet detected (as a source of medicine, dye, and so on), or as crucial to the ecosystem in some unrecognized way.

The destruction of myriad species is a major problem. The greatest threat lies in the tropics, where species diversity is both the richest and under the greatest threat. It has been estimated that only one in ten to one in twenty species in the tropics are known to science.[15] A hectare of land in the Peruvian Amazon rain forest contains 41,000 species of insect alone, according to a recent count.[16] A *single tree* contained 43 species of ant. In ten separate hectare plots in Borneo, 700 species of tree were identified, matching the count for all of North America.[17] According to a report in *Science,* "The continued erosion of tropical rain forests—through small-scale slash and burn agriculture at one extreme to massive timber operations at the other—is . . . closing in on perhaps half the world's natural inventory of species. Most biologists agree that the world's rain forests will be all but obliterated at some point in the next century."[18] Furthermore, small parks and preserves could not harbor numbers and varieties of species proportional to their size. Thus, standard conservation compromises do not represent a viable solution to the problem.

Other habitats holding a large diversity of species also are threatened. These include coral reefs, coastal wetlands, such as those in California, and large African lakes. The last have been especially threatened by the attempt to cultivate within them varieties of fish not indigenous to the area. A mere documentation of species unknown to science and possibly threatened would require the life work of twenty-five thousand taxonomists; currently there are a mere fifteen hundred such individuals at work.[19] Standard techniques of conserving representative members of such species in zoos and herbaria or preserving germ plasm in essence represent the proverbial drop in the bucket, although they are of course better than nothing.

Scientists who have devoted a great deal of study to these issues again echo the point cited earlier from Mares: These concerns are not local, but international. Michael Robinson puts the point dramatically: "We are facing 'the enlightenment fallacy.' The fallacy is that if you educate the people of the Third World, the problem will disappear. It won't. The problems are not due to ignorance and stupidity. The problems . . . derive from the poverty of the poor and the greed of the rich."[20] *Science,* in concluding its analysis, asserted that "the problems are those of economics and politics. Inescapably, therefore, the solutions are to be found in those same areas."[21]

Some recognition of this politico-economic dimension of environmental problems has been slowly forthcoming politically. There are, for example, indications that policies of the World Bank, which lends development money to countries, are being restructured to take more cognizance of environmental concerns. The bank has been criticized for funding the Polonoroeste project in Brazil, which would have destroyed large forest areas in Brazil in order to allow mass migration of farmers from impoverished areas, and for funding cattle ranching projects in Africa that promote desertification.[22]

Thus, even a cursory examination of some major environmental issues affecting the nonsentient environment indicates that those problems are insoluble outside of the context of international justice. The question then becomes: What, if any, philosophical basis exists for a system of international justice in this area? History has shown, after all, that attempts to create viable machinery of international justice in any area, ranging from an end to genocide to the prevention of war, have run the gamut from laughable to ineffectual. Self-interest has always trumped justice; the situation among nations, it is often remarked, is essentially the Hobbesian "war of each against all." This historical point again blunts even the pragmatic justification for attributing intrinsic value to the nonsentient environment. After all, widespread recognition in the Western tradition of the intrinsic value of humans has not at all assisted in the development of effective mechanisms to ensure that such value is respected.

Ironically, if we begin with the Hobbesian insight, it actually may be easier to provide a rational (and pragmatically effective) basis for a system of international justice regarding environmental concerns rather than human rights. After all, there is no pragmatic reason for a nation to sacrifice its sovereignty in the international arena regarding matters of human rights. If a given country benefits significantly from oppressing all or some of its citizenry, what positive incentive is there for that nation to respond to other nations' protests, and what incentive is there for other nations to protest? In the latter case, of course, there may be moral or ideological reasons for a nation to protest another's human rights policies, but such concerns usually give way to more pragmatic pressures—for example, if the oppressive country stands in a mutually beneficial trade or defensive relationship with the concerned nation.

In the case of global environmental concerns—destruction of the ozone, pollution of air and water, nuclear winter, dangers arising out of genetic engineering, loss of species—*everyone* loses (or might lose) if these concerns are not addressed. A leit-motif of our discussion has been precisely the global nature of such concerns. We have, in the case of all of the examples cited previously, something closer to what game theorists call a game of cooperation rather than a game of competition. That is, if one nation loses its fight with an environmental problem, or simply does not address it, any other nation could, and in many cases would, be likely to suffer as well. Thus, if the United States, through excessive use of fluorocarbons, weakens the ozone barrier, the results will not be restricted to the United States, but will have global impact.

By the same token, even if a given nation X stands to gain by ignoring environmental despoliation, others may lose and, without a system of regulation, may in turn bear the brunt of Y's or Z's cavalier disregard of other aspects of the environment. Furthermore, there is good reason to believe that the short-run gains accruing to a nation by a disregard of environmental concerns may well be significantly out-weighed in the long run by unforeseen or ignored consequences. Thus, the wholesale conversion of African grasslands into grazing lands for domestic animals not ecologically adapted to such an environment may yield short-term profits, but in the long run lead to desertification, which leaves the land of no use at all. By the same token, cavalier disregard of species loss in the deforestation of the tropics may certainly provide short-term windfall profits, but at the expense of far richer resources. *Time* magazine recounted a number of examples of these riches.

> These threatened ecosystems have already proved a valuable source of medicines, foods and new seed stock for crops. Nine years ago, for example, a strain of perennial, disease-resistant wild maize named *Zea diploperennis* was found in a Mexican mountain forest, growing in three small plots. Crossing domestic corn varieties with this maize produces hardy hybrids that should ultimately be worth billions of dollars to farmers. A great many of the prescription drugs sold in the U.S. are based on unique chemical compounds found in tropical plants. For example, vincristine, originally isolated from the Madagascan periwinkle, is used to treat some human cancers. Scientists are convinced that still undiscovered forest plants could be the source of countless new natural drugs.[23]

The fundamental argument, however, is still the Hobbesian one of rational self-interest. Any country, if utterly unbridled in its pursuit of short-term economic gains, or in its cavalier disregard for the impact of its activities on other nations, can permanently harm the interests of other nations. An irresponsibly genetically engineered microorganism does not respect national boundaries or military power, nor does oceanic or atmospheric pollution. The consequences of lack of control of environmental damage can range from loss of potential benefits—such as loss of new medication derived from plants, or loss of the delight and wonder in seeing a fragile tundra aglow in wildflowers—to positive and serious harm—the dramatic rise in cancers or other diseases produced by environmental despoliation of air, water, or the food chain, or even to a new ice age of or tidal waves resulting from destruction of the ozone. Given modern technology, virtually any nation can damage any or all nations in any number of these ways; hence, a situation ripe for Hobbesian contractualism is reached.

In Hobbesian terms, of course, individuals engaged in a war of each against all are rendered equal by their ultimate vulnerability to harm and death by action on the part of others or combinations of others. Thus, we rationally relinquish our natural tendency toward rapaciousness in recognition of others' similar tendency, and our vulnerability thereto. Unrestricted greed is sacrificed for security and protection from the unrestricted greed of others, and a sovereign who, as it were, builds fences protecting each from all is constituted by each individual surrendering a portion of his or her unbridled autonomy. As we have seen, a precisely analogous situation exists regarding environmental vulnerability, and thus rationality would dictate that each nation surrender some of its autonomy to an international authority in order to protect itself, or the whole world including itself, from major disaster. This is of course especially clear, as we have seen earlier, in matters pertaining to biological warfare, where any nation can effectively annihilate any or all others.

In summary, then, the relevance of a viable mechanism of international justice to environmental ethical concerns is manifest. Indeed, many if not most environmental issues, and certainly the most vexing and important ones, entail major global consequences and thus cannot be restricted to local issues of sovereignty. An environmental ethics is inseparable from a system of international justice, not only in terms of policing global dangers and verifying and monitoring compliance with international agreements, but also in terms of implementing the distributive justice necessary to prevent poor countries from looking only at short-term gains. The rain forests are not only a problem for the countries in which they are found; if other developed nations are to benefit from the continued existence of the rain forests, we must be prepared to pay for that benefit. No country should be expected to bear the full brunt of environmental concerns. Classical economics does not work for ecological and environmental concerns; each unit pursuing its own interest will not enrich the biosphere, but deplete and devastate it. As E. O. Wilson put it in a recent conference on biodiversity, "The time has come to link ecology to economic and human development. . . . What is happening to the rain forests of Madagascar and Brazil will affect us all."[24] In other words, if a tree is felled in a primeval forest and there is no one else around, one should care about it anyway. . . .

Nonetheless, the situation is not hopeless. The case of the Canadian harp seal hunt dramatically illustrates that nations can be motivated by a moral concern that is actually inimical to self-interest. The European Economic Community recently banned the importation of seal products derived from the barbaric Newfoundland hunt. This was done despite the fact that at least some European nations derived economic benefit from the seal hunt and despite the fact that the European public was a major traditional consumer of seal products. This case dramatically illustrates that human consciousness is being increasingly sensitized to the suffering and interests of animals.

Cynics might argue that the seal case derives from the sentiment attached to the furry cuteness of baby seals and the jarring image of their slaughter by clubbing—big eyes and blood on the white snow. Although there is some truth in this claim, it is by no means all. Until recently, moral concern as embodied in the "humane ethic" was highly selective and favored the cute, cuddly, and familiar. Thus, for example, the Animal Welfare Act of 1966 and 1970, the only legal constraint on animal research in the United States, exempted from its very limited purview (it concerned itself only with food, caging, transport, and so on and disavowed concern with the actual content and conduct of research) rats, mice, and farm animals, in fact, 90 percent of the animals used in research. For purposes of the act, a dead dog was defined as an animal, a live mouse was not. Recently, however, things have changed. With the rise of an articulated moral concern for sentient beings by philosophers such as Peter Singer, Tom Regan, Steven Sapontzis,[25] and myself, that concern has captured the social imagination nationally and internationally. New guidelines and laws extend concern even to the more prosaic and unlovely animals, and a new amendment to the Animal Welfare Act in the United States, which I helped to draft, now mandates control of pain, suffering, and distress, which is a direct insult to the ideology of science that treated these as unknowable. Similar thrusts have occurred in other countries; in Germany, a new law bans animal research for military and cosmetic purposes, as does a new Dutch law. By the same token, many countries, such as Britain, Switzerland, and Denmark, have put constraints on confinement agriculture—"factory farming"—even though a price is paid in "efficiency" and cost to the consumer.

We sometimes forget that there is an international dimension even to animal research and factory farming. Unilateral and major constraints on such practices by one country for the sake of moral concern for animals, with other countries not making similar moves, can lead, for example, to an erosion of the legislating country's agricultural economy if the constraints make its products prohibitively more expensive and drastically reduce a market for them. But a universal constraint applicable to all countries would merely put all competitors back at the same starting gate. Public education also can convince consumers to "put their money where their morality is."

In the case of animals in science, a parallel problem arises. Multinational corporations, and even individual researchers, when unable to do a particular kind of experiment in one country will simply go to another. Given that experimenters then are shifting the suffering from one animal to another who is not different morally, this is not a just solution. Here we cannot even use the rationalization we do with humans—"Their culture makes things tolerable to them that are not tolerable to us"—because, as a Dutch colleague of mine said, "All dogs bark in the same language." Thus, scientific research must also be regulated by internationally accepted rules, else the burden of injustice is merely shifted from one innocent animal to another who happens to be living in a different place. For this reason, the European Economic Community member nations are drafting rules designed to govern all member nations, which is a step in the right direction because it would probably be impractical for companies smarting under such rules to move out of Europe altogether to less enlightened countries.

There are many areas of animal abuse where the network of interests and thus the need for rules are obviously international. There are other cases—for example, a horrendous blood sport practiced in a small country—where there are fewer international connections and implications. Nonetheless, the key to stopping all such evils is, in the final analysis, the same. It lies in a widespread philosophical extension of widespread moral notions. Thus, the philosophical basis for a system of international justice that can stop, for example, the slaughter of rhinoceroses for frivolous consumer goods such as ornamental knives and aphrodisiacs (which reduced the black rhino population from 65,000 in 1970 to 4,500 today),[26] or the killing of the snow leopard for fur, lies in the expanded moral vision of many people in diverse nations. Such expanded awareness is contagious and creates a new gestalt on animals that finds expression in legislation, boycotts, embargos, and the like. Such concern is likely to manifest first on a national level, with demands for regulation of research and mandated protection of research animals (including recent demands for housing that respects their telos); legal constraints on agricultural practices that yield efficiency at the expense of animals' suffering; restriction of frivolous and painful testing on animals, such as the LD 50 and Draize tests used in developing cosmetics and the like; tighter controls imposed over zoos, circuses, and rodeos; and so on.

But as I said, animal exploitation does not stop at national boundaries, nor does moral concern for animals. Thus, such abuses as traffic in rare birds where vast shipments of them arrive dead and dying; unregulated transport of all varieties of animals; the murder of porpoises in pursuit of tuna; the slaughter of migrating whales in the Faroe Islands as a sport and "cultural tradition," will—whether happening in any or all countries—be subjected to international pressures for regulation. These inevitably will result in tighter monitoring and restriction of such activities, which in turn will require international cooperation of the sort that is starting to develop in order to control the drug traffic.

It is perhaps not totally utopian to suggest that expanded concern for animals, a concern crossing geopolitical barriers, may lead to expanded concern for other human beings in countries not one's own, in a lovely dialectical reversal of the traditional wisdom preached by St. Thomas Aquinas and Immanuel Kant, suggesting that concern for animals is merely disguised concern for human beings.

NOTES

1. See the chapters in Tom Regan, *All That Dwell Therein* (Berkeley: University of California Press, 1982).
2. See Aldo Leopold, *A Sand County Almanac* (Oxford: Oxford University Press, 1949); J. Baird Callicott, "Animal Liberation: A Triangular Affair," *Environmental Ethics* 2 (1980):311–338; Holmes Rolston III, *Philosophy Gone Wild* (Buffalo, N.Y.: Prometheus Books, 1986).
3. There are exceptions to this generalization—for example, my own work in abolishing multiple use of animals as a standard teaching practice in medical and veterinary schools and my efforts in writing and promoting new legislation on proper care of laboratory animals.
4. See the discussions of this point in Peter Singer, *Animal Liberation* (New York: New York Review of Books, 1975); and B. Rollin, *Animal Rights and Human Morality* (Buffalo, N.Y.: Prometheus Books, 1981).
5. See my "Animal Pain," in M. Fox and L. Mickley (eds.), *Advances in Animal Welfare Science 1985* (The Hague: Martinus Nijhoff, 1985); and my "Animal Consciousness and Scientific Change," *New Ideas in Psychology* 4, no. 2 (1986): 141–152, as well as the replies to the latter by P. K. Feyerabend, H. Rachlin, and T. Leahey in the same issue, p. 153. See also my *Animal Consciousness, Animal Pain, and Scientific Change* (tentative title) (Oxford: Oxford University Press, forthcoming).
6. See my *Animal Rights,* Part I.
7. See the works mentioned in footnotes 1 and 2.
8. This point is made with great rhetorical force in Edward Abbey, *Desert Solitaire* (New York: Ballantine Books, 1971).
9. See Holmes Rolston, "Duties to Endangered Species," *Philosophy Gone Wild.*
10. See the seminal discussion in Christopher Stone, *Should Trees Have Standing? Toward Legal Rights for Natural Objects* (Los Altos, Calif.: William Kaufmann, 1974).
11. Michael Mares, "Conservation in South America: Problems, Consequences, and Solutions." *Science* 233 (1986):734.
12. For a discussion of various ethical issues surrounding genetic engineering, see my "The Frankenstein Thing," in J. W. Evans and A. Hollaender (eds.), *Genetic Engineering of Agricultural Animals* (New York: Plenum, 1986).
13. *Science* 234 (1986):143.
14. *Time,* November 3, 1986, p. 74.
15. *Science* 234 (1986): 149.
16. Ibid.
17. Ibid.
18. Ibid.
19. Ibid., p. 150.
20. Ibid.
21. Ibid.
22. *Science* 234 (1986):813.
23. *Time,* October 13, 1986, p. 80.
24. Ibid.
25. Steven Sapontzis, *Morals, Reason, and Animals* (Philadelphia: Temple University Press, 1987).
26. *Science* 234 (1986):147.

12

⚶ Environmental Problems ⚶ and Future Generations

BRYAN NORTON

Bryan Norton is Professor of Philosophy of Science and Technology at Georgia Institute of Technology. He is the author of Why Preserve Natural Variety? *and* Toward Unity Among Environmentalists.

Environmentalists have not faced a single, unchanging pattern of problems over the past century. As a reactive movement, they have been regularly forced to adapt their policies, and even their ideologies, to changing conditions. For example, Rachel Carson's *Silent Spring* is often seen as a herald of modern environmentalism, a shift away from concerns for wise use of resources and protection of particularly spectacular natural monuments toward the more pervasive and less focused problems of pollution, biological simplification, and regional deterioration due to thoughtless land development. Robert Mitchell has therefore distinguished second-generation environmental problems from the earlier first-generation problems.

Recent headlines have underscored yet another shift in the challenges modern industrial societies pose for environmental protectors. Fears of ozone depletion, of the greenhouse effect, of acid rain, and of an abrupt and cataclysmic loss of biological diversity form an emerging group of problems that bear little relation to first-generation problems. But these more newly recognized environmental problems share a complex of features that distinguish them from second-generation problems as well. In each case a catastrophic effect, resulting from a large number of small but incremental decisions made in the present, would affect mainly future generations. These catastrophic effects would harm large numbers of people over geographically broad areas. While these effects may appear unlikely if the historical record is taken as a base, fear of them nevertheless seems rational because respectable scientific models predict serious consequences that would be irreversible.

These newer problems form a subset of the problems that have been classified by Talbot Page and Ezra Mishan as "zero-infinity dilemmas." Zero-infinity dilemmas are decision situations that represent apparently small risks of cataclysmic effects, such as risks of a serious accident in the production of nuclear power. The newer environmental problems that I am defining share the characteristics of zero-infinity dilemmas, but have an additional distinguishing feature: The heaviest risks involved in the newer environmental problems fall not upon present actors but upon future generations who will not have participated in the decision to incur the risks; nor will they, in most cases, enjoy the benefits of the currently wasteful activities involved. New environmental problems therefore share all of the difficulties involved in other zero-infinity dilemmas and, in addition, raise serious ethical issues of intergenerational equity. The distinctive character of these emerging problems suggests that it will be useful to designate them as "third-generation problems."

In approaching such risks, the Aggregators have often extended the standard benefit-cost approach to decisions involving risk by considering increments of risk as a cost and decrements of risk a benefit. In this manner, economists who accept the standard benefit-cost model can incorporate concerns regarding risks into their decision models because avoidance of risk in the future will have value to decision-makers in the present. Since the decisions we make now must be justified by considerations apparent to us now, rational decision-making must incorporate currently available information and currently accepted ideas about what is valuable. The present-value approach therefore has unquestioned appeal.

Third-generation environmental problems, however, place a heavy burden on certain aspects of the standard analytic approach. Mishan and Page concluded that decisions entailing risks of this magnitude are not susceptible to quantification, and that the decision to accept the risk should rest rather on a reasonable choice between risk acceptance and risk aversion. The argument of Mishan and Page turns mainly on the difficulty of reliably quantifying risk values of events that would entail catastrophic costs. Another feature of third-generation problems that causes difficulties for standard analyses is the long time-latency of the effects in question. The newer problems are extrapolated theoretically according to models that assume that the effects may increase rapidly after decades of minimal effects. For example, the greenhouse effect, a warming of the atmosphere mainly resulting from the consumption of fossil fuels, is projected to cause relatively small changes in temperature in the near future. These early effects would be difficult to discriminate from natural, cyclical changes in climate. Some climatological models predict, however, that the effect will accelerate over time and, by the time the problem is clearly demonstrable, irreversible destabilizations of contexts will occur. These will cause great harm to the next and succeeding generations. It can be argued that losses in biological diversity will have similarly accelerating effects.

Standard resource analyses usually deal with time preference by discounting future benefits and costs. This approach can be quite useful in dealing with relatively short frames of time. Further, economists can cite considerable theoretical and empirical evidence that human decision-makers display a distinct time preference for the present. Discounting the costs and benefits of various policies across time provides an important systematization of this common human practice.

Policy decisions such as those exemplified in newer environmental problems, however, involve effects with time horizons extending far past individual lifetimes and would seem to require understanding of *social,* as well as *individual,* discounting of future effects. As long as risks are felt by the same generation that creates them through incremental choices, the problem of risk assessment and management can plausibly be considered within a consensual model in which risk-aversive activities will have present value to the choice-maker. But when intergenerational times are considered and the risks incurred in the present fall mainly upon future individuals, the model lacks this consensual claim to validity. Whereas consumers are well trained in choosing between their own short- and long-term interests by the school of hard knocks, they must distribute cross-generational risks through altruistic impulses toward the not-yet-born. Therefore, third-generation environmental problems necessarily involve questions regarding the fairness of intergenerational distribution of risk, and it is difficult to see how the standard economic model can adequately conceptualize these essentially ethical considerations.

The contextual approach to environmental management recognizes constraints based in the dynamic interplay between specific actions (such as use of CFCs in aerosols or continued unrestrained use of fossil fuels) and the larger, normally slower-changing context in which those decisions are implemented. According to contextualism, there exists a threshold within which individual decisions to use CFC aerosols or burn fossil fuels will have insignificant impacts on the larger environmental context, which in these cases we can understand as the atmospheric envelope surrounding the earth. The atmosphere has significant resilience and can damp out consequences of the activities in question up to some point; if, however, major and persistent trends over several generations (such as accelerating use of fossil fuels since the onset of the industrial revolution) continue indefinitely, the atmospheric threshold is exceeded, and the autonomous and slow-changing characteristics of the atmosphere can undergo rapid change, such as changes in temperature many times more rapid than those that would normally occur with the advance and recession of the ice ages. According to this reasoning, activities that threaten no thresholds raise no ethical questions—they can be decided freely by individuals on the basis of choice. As scientific models, such as the climatological models now being developed to indicate global warming trends, indicate cross-generational impacts, the contextual approach to environmental management counsels behavioral adjustments, incentives to reverse the trend, mitigative efforts such as massive tree planting, and eventually constraints to avoid rapid destabilization of the large-scale environmental context. . . .

The usefulness of the contextual approach in conceptualizing newer environmental problems can be more specifically illustrated by examining problems in managing national parks in a period of rapid climatological change caused by the greenhouse effect. Linda Brubaker has argued that the effects of climatological change on managed vegetative systems must by discussed with respect to three time scales of variation:

1. Long-term variations (ten thousand to one hundred thousand years) are exemplified by changes from glacial to interglacial climates. Responses of vegetation to climate on this scale involve major changes in the ranges of species and result in evolutionary changes in the genetic composition of the species themselves.
2. Intermediate-term variations (two thousand to five thousand years) represent major changes within glacial and interglacial periods and, on this scale, species respond mainly through behavioral adjustments and perhaps through some evolutionary change.
3. Short-term variations (up to 500 years) may occur within the life-span of single individuals of long-lived species such as trees. Established plants may undergo physiological or morphological changes in response to variations in temperature and these changes may also affect rates of reproduction and establishment of the various species. These latter changes may affect the composition of the vegetative community.

On scale (1), the current interglacial period, the holocene, began about ten thousand years ago and appears to be one of the warmest periods in the past two million years. By examining the fossil record indicating change on scale (1), Brubaker concludes that, historically, plant communities have been transient assemblages, seldom persisting more that two thousand to five thousand years in the fossil record. This evidence leads Brubaker to conclude that

> the ice-age vegetation of North America was markedly different from the present-day vegetation. Most modern forest types did not exist in the past, and many of the most important forest species of today's forests were rare. Thus modern communities should not be thought of as highly coevolved complexes of species bound together by tightly linked and balanced interactions. Modern communities have not had long histories, and the species rather than the community should be the focus when considering the consequences of future environmental change. Historical records show that species can expand rapidly as climate becomes less limiting; they also suggest that species that are rare on the modern landscape have potential for becoming common under changed climates (and vice versa).

Similarly, Brubaker argues that, since variations on the intermediate scale (2) also cause major changes in composition of plant communities, the preservation focus again should be on the total complement of species rather than on attempting to preserve, in a rigid manner, particular complexes of species current today. Brubaker's argument, which may or may not be correct in detail, illustrates in its general pattern the ecological/contextual approach to environmental management. Brubaker recommends, in effect, management in three distinct scales of time.

Her reasoning therefore supports the argument made earlier that total diversity should be the major focus of species preservation efforts, and also represents comparatively good news regarding the future of management to protect biological complexity. If we can stabilize the larger ecological context by reducing extreme trends, and if we act aggressively to protect total diversity of large areas, the creative and productive forces of the future may not be destroyed. Specialist species, even those that are confined by natural forces or by human activities to small preserves, will provide a healthy group of competitors to create new assemblages of species that remain efficient in exploiting and transporting energy.

On the shortest scale of time (3), she concludes: "Decade and century-long climatic variations can affect both species ranges and growth rates," and consequently that "present-day forest stands may have established under different conditions than exist today and thus may not return to current composition following disturbance." Environmental management must be based on a dynamic, contextual criterion of health. There must be, according to environmentalists, a forward-looking but ecologically formulated standard by which to judge the future effects of current activities.

Brubaker's analysis therefore requires a dynamic model in which changes in microhabitats takes place against the backdrop of a constantly changing mosaic of macrohabitats; the macrohabitats, in turn, change also against the backdrop of dynamically changing climate. Brubaker's approach therefore suggests a hierarchy of nested systems changing on different spatial and temporal scales.

While Brubaker cautions that several scenarios for climate change are plausible, that the sensitivities to climate of many species are unknown, and therefore that current projections of vegetative changes are too speculative to dictate management plans at this time, the general approach she suggests provides the beginnings of a means to study the management implications of global climate change. In particular, by tracing patterns of vegetational change on scales (1) and (2), projections of future changes on scale (3) can be modeled simply by assuming that accelerated global climate change caused by the build-up of greenhouse gases will be similar to climatological changes on the longer time scales indicated in the fossil record and in pollen deposits in lake sediments. By modeling changes of vegetation patterns within a hierarchy of nested systems changing according to different scales of time, it is possible to create analogues to the rapid changes in vegetative patterns that will result if rapid global warming occurs. It is in this sense that natural history, as well as human history, can clarify policy issues.

A contextual model of management problems may therefore provide important insights to guide environmental management in the face of rapid atmospheric changes brought about by human-induced (and relatively rapid) changes in concentrations of greenhouse gases in the atmosphere. By extension, similar modeling may prove useful in understanding change brought about by acid deposition, by ozone depletion, and by rapid deforestation in the tropics.

The dust bowl proved that rapid and pervasive changes in human use of land can lead to breakdowns of entire geographical systems; such breakdowns both signal and exacerbate destruction of the complexity and integrity of the land system, destroying the complex pathways by which energy flows through the system. Hierarchy theory, which aspires to model and relate the various temporal scales that constitute ecological complexity, may therefore provide a precise means to explore the thresholds and limits beyond which human-induced changes in larger systems such as the whole atmosphere are likely to result in ecological breakdowns with unacceptable consequences.

While this exploration of the impact of third-generation, environmental problems has been of necessity both sketchy and speculative, perhaps enough has been said to suggest some future applications of contextualism in environmental management. First-generation problems were mainly problems in the use of resources—wastefulness in timber production, rapid depletion of nonrenewable resources, or specific threats to a species or a spectacular natural area. Accordingly, these early problems were understood atomistically, and the analysis of them could be largely aggregative. The shift to second-generation environmental problems such as the overuse of persistent pesticides and the spread of pollution, more generally, forced emphasis on the ecological context, and imposed a systematic view on environmentalists. Individual actions take on normative aspects, mainly insofar as they represent larger trends destabilizing ecological systems. Pesticides were seen to affect whole ecological systems; air pollution affects the atmosphere above cities, resulting in smog and unhealthy air; and dumping industrial and household wastes in a stream was recognized as a threat to whole watersheds. For these problems, aggregative techniques were less adequate and environmentalists since Carson have consistently called for limits on economic behaviors that negatively affect larger systems.

The growing prominence of third-generation problems can be interpreted as another step in this progression. Just as second-generation problems were superimposed on first-generation problems (that did not go away), third-generation problems represent effects of changes in intermediate subsystems, such as the atmosphere over cities or tropical forests, on yet larger systems, such as the global climate system. The progression from first-generation to third-generation problems therefore represents a shift from isolated problems to which an atomistic response is not entirely implausible, toward global problems that can be addressed only by paying close attention to larger and larger, and more and more inclusive systems. As newer environmental problems affect dynamic, autonomous processes in larger and larger spatial and temporal contexts, contextual management will become increasingly necessary to understand and manage the interrelated problems that plague the beleaguered biosphere.

THE VEIL OF INTERTEMPORAL IGNORANCE

Reflecting on the fierce green fire he saw dying in the old she-wolf's eyes, [Aldo] Leopold concluded that we must learn to think like a mountain. Leopold flirted with a literal and moral organicism, but was unsure how much reality to ascribe to the organicist analogy: is the mountain *really* alive and thinking? Is the mountain itself a moral being?

These metaphysical and moral questions had little effect on his management ideas, however, because he never questioned that man will be henceforth "the captain of the adventuring ship" and he believed that all of his management strategies could be justified according to a longsighted and "noble" anthropocentrism. As long as it was coupled with the unquestioned truth that all things are interrelated, Leopold believed anthropocentrism would support the land-use policies he advocated in the Southwest Territories.

Looked at across generations, alteration of the American landscape, especially in the arid and semiarid regions, had been a sad story of progressive deterioration and declining land health. Starving deer, deepening gullies, and the dust bowl were the legacy of just a few generations of land "management" by white settlers. One of the strongest elements of Leopold's land ethic is its sensitivity to cross-generational impacts of land management. Thinking like a mountain is thinking in the mountain's longer and slower-changing frame of time—time measured in generations, not seasons.

These long-term relationships must therefore be modeled in intergenerational time. Contextualism, modeled hierarchically, showed promise to exhibit the dynamic relationships between managed cells and their larger temporal and spatial context. Might it also provide a model for understanding problems in intertemporal morality?

Standard theories of intertemporal ethics, or of "intergenerational equity," always have reached the conclusion that our obligations to proximate generations (our children and their children, for example) differ radically from our obligations to distant generations. In an extreme form such theories state that, while we might have substantial obligations to the next generation—our children—we have *no* obligations whatsoever to the generations that succeed them.

After surveying both utilitarian and justice-based theories of our obligations to the future, John Passmore concludes:

> So whether we approach the problem of obligations to posterity by way of [the utilitarians] Bentham and Sidgwick, [or the rights theorists] Rawls or Golding, we are led to something like the same conclusion: Our obligations are to *immediate* posterity, we ought to try to improve the world so that we shall be able to hand it over to our immediate successors in a better condition [than we found it in], and that is all.

While this theory is given broad support among highly respected philosophers, it conflicts with some strong intuitions of environmentalists. Consider three examples. First, take the case of storage of radioactive wastes materials. Environmentalists have insisted on measures that would store radioactive wastes for the duration, measured in millennia, of their toxicity to humans. Second, consider the reactions of environmentalists to global warming models. If it turns out that severe impacts of global warming are unlikely to be felt for two generations, environmentalists would not stop insisting on remedial activity. As a third example, consider environmentalists' widely held belief that the ongoing *processes of nature,* including ecological and evolutionary processes, have great value. But this obligation does not extend just to the next generation. If events that we set in motion today play themselves out in such a way as to destroy the last autonomously functioning systems a century hence, environmentalists believe we will have done wrong. We will have deprived future generations of their aesthetic and natural scientific heritage.

When moral intuitions conflict with moral principles, we sometimes give up our intuitions, provided that the theoretical arguments are strong. Passmore's argument, in both the utilitarian and rights-bases cases, turns crucially on our inability to project human individual wants and interests into the further future: Since we cannot predict what future consumers will want or need, nor what new resources may become available to them through advancing technology, it is senseless to act to protect resources they may neither want nor need. His reasoning is little more than an application of the individualistic bias of contemporary ethics, a bias he assumes as a premise. If Passmore's argument assumes individualism—that causing the deterioration of an *environmental system* can never be a moral issue—the argument will justifiably be rejected by environmentalists as unpersuasive and question-begging. That systems can be made ill, and that human causes of this illness raise moral issues are, after all, the core ideas of the land ethic!

By reversing the direction of the individualistic argument of Passmore, however, we can accept the environmentalists' intuitively felt obligations to the distant future as valid and can conclude, not as Passmore does, "so much the worse for future generations," but "so much the worse for standard, individualistic ethics." If the exclusive concentration on individual preferences, interests, and rights characteristic of theories of utilitarianism and of justice prohibits recognition of felt obligations to distant generations, then those theories are inadequate, by their essential nature, to deal with second- and third-generation environmental problems.

If . . . we have already placed a value on protecting the creative productivity of biotic systems—as the context that gives meaning to human activity, they carry the value of all human uses and interactions with nature into the indefinite future. Intertemporal contextual thinking therefore presupposes an independent *value* axiom, the Axiom of Future Value: The continuance and thriving of the human species (and its evolutionary successors) is a good thing, and every generation is obliged to do what is necessary to perpetuate that good. The obligation to perpetuate and protect the human species is therefore accepted as a fundamental moral axiom, which exists independently of obligations to individuals. The conservative philosopher Edmund Burke expresses this organicist attitude toward society as "a partnership not only between those who are living, but between those who are living, those who are dead and those who are to be born."

Passmore despairs of understanding our obligations to distant generations because he is looking at the wrong scale. It is true that we cannot criticize the trend toward anthropogenically caused global warming on the basis of harms to specific individuals. If your children, for example, have the foresight to buy land in the northern plains of Canada, your grandchildren may have reason to rejoice at global warming. If, on the other hand, they are stuck with investments in Atlantic City hotels, they may complain. Environmentalists do not wish to argue the intragenerational questions of fairness to individuals, but to argue that current global warming models suggest change that is too rapid to be intergenerationally benign.

The choice to plant wheat or to take the car instead of the bicycle takes on intergenerational implications when a threshold is approached; it raises issues in intertemporal ethics when exemplary of trends that may, given local conditions and the fragility of the larger bioregional system, have serious intergenerational consequences. That threshold is contextual because it depends on local conditions and the fragility of the larger bioregional systems in question. Building on this concept of ecosystem fragility, we can circumscribe a set of environmental problems that have intergenerational implications from those that do not. What we need, in effect, is a moral filter that corresponds to the coarse-grained filter of contextual, hierarchial thinking and that focuses on phenomena in the larger scale of bioregional change, not on particular effects on individuals within that region.

John Rawls, in his infinitely fertile treatise *A Theory of Justice,* suggests such a moral filter, which he calls the "veil of ignorance." Imagine a rational, self-interested individual, Ric, who chooses the general rules for a just society, knowing that he will have to live in that society subsequently. In fact, the veil of ignorance is many veils. By varying Ric's knowledge, we can filter out individually motivated interests based on gender, class, economic status, and so on.

For our present purposes, we can place Ric behind a veil of intergenerational ignorance—he must design a society that he would be willing to live in without knowing the generation in which he is going to live. Now, if Ric accepts Leopold's concern that land use practices and other activities of modern humans, which are distinguished by enormous technological capabilities and growing populations, may alter bioregional systems so rapidly that there will be significant and detrimental impacts on the wellbeing of society, then he would design a society that constrains trends that destabilize larger environmental contexts.

If it turns out that Ric is born into a primitive society, or even European medieval society, the intergenerational constraints may seem minimal; with hindsight and improved scientific monitoring, however, we can say that conformity to these constraints would have protected the countryside in Greece and China, for example, from the disastrous effect of deforestation and erosion, and might have extended the duration of prior civilizations, and padded their fall when the reason was not ecological destruction. Contextualism understands moral obligations to land systems in a historical context and emphasizes that, given our knowledge of ecological fragility and our powerful technological capabilities to alter those systems, a generation such as ours has special obligations. As Ric foresees a society such as our own, which alters nature rapidly and has available frightening models projecting cataclysmic changes in the environmental context, he would expect us to question the moral acceptability of our violent activities. He would choose a society that would struggle to delineate parameters and thresholds, based on the best models of biology, ecology, climatology, and so on. These parameters and thresholds would, in turn, imply constraints on trends in individual behaviors that threaten to accelerate destabilizing changes in a normally slow-changing environing system. From a moral viewpoint, these constraints would represent "fair" treatment of future generations—the treatment a rational, self-interested chooser would insist upon if he did not know which generation he will inhabit.

When environmentalists accept an obligation to future generations, they do not see this as an obligation to any particular individuals; the relationship occurs at the interface of two systems (human economics, demography, and so forth) with geophysical systems. Viewed on that level, environmentalists believe that there are biological and climatological constraints and that these correspond to moral constraints limiting the extent to which any generation could fairly degrade the world's resources. Believing this, it is not surprising that environmentalists also believe that we are morally required to undertake stabilizing actions when projections show that trends in individual behavior threaten a biological or climatological threshold and institute accelerating changes in the environing systems.

These obligations are viewed holistically, organically—they are owed to the future, just as we are indebted to our forefathers, not individually but collectively, for our cultural heritage; these obligations derive from faith in the value of the human struggle, the Axiom of Future Value. Environmentalists do not wish to meddle in the individual affairs of future generations; they want simply to ensure that those individual dealings take place against a livable environmental context.

Environmentalists' moral intuitions that we should limit fossil fuel use to slow the greenhouse effect, for example, are not based on a balancing of winners and losers, but on the belief that we ought not to destabilize the normally slow-changing systems on which our daily activities depend. That belief depends on (1) a factual scientific model that emphasizes the importance of complexity and autonomously functioning natural systems; (2) a concern that rapid, anthropogenic alterations of larger, environing systems such as the atmosphere will threaten the stability of conditions necessary for an orderly society; and (3) a moral commitment not to engage recklessly in activities that perhaps will cause irreversible changes in the normally slow-changing atmospheric system within which all species, including our own, act to maintain their well-being.

We have concerned ourselves mainly with examples of preemptive constraints limiting the physical context in which our society will evolve in the future: Will there still be wildness? Will the climate be sufficiently stable for human and multispecies communities to thrive? Will the future be spared costly clean-ups of our toxic wastes? But for environmentalists it is almost as important to recognize the cultural implications of their emerging worldview. Environmentalists have fully endorsed Muir's idea that we should set aside beautiful natural areas because these are essential to the formation of sound human values. They believe that contact with nature is contact with our past, and embodies wisdom. If the moral future of a given regional lifestyle is to have roots in that region's past and if distant offspring are to be expected to respect the present as a part of their past, they must see past generations as sensitive to the ongoing organism that is our common society and to the larger organism that is nature. The lesson of ecology is that one cannot care for the future of the human race without caring for the future of its context. Destruction of our cultural and natural history accelerates the dynamic of moral change.

If we act as individualists and do not value the systematic context of the human values we pass to the next generation, we will have acted out Passmore's self-fulfilling prophecy. If we pay no heed to the context in which future generations form and question their values, they will indeed live in a different world than we do; we will have contributed nothing to their culture; we will be strangers across only two generations. That is the consequence of acting on Passmore's theoretical arguments—if we pay the future no heed, they will pay us no heed. And if we destroy the natural link in our melting-pot community, the common American experience of "pioneering," we have severed our history. Our offspring will no longer understand our aesthetic sensibilities; our culture will be irrelevant to them. Context gives meaning to all experience; consequently, it is a shared context that allows shared meanings—what we call culture—to survive across generations.

13

☒ The Aesthetics ☒ of Wildlife Preservation

EUGENE HARGROVE

Eugene Hargrove is Professor of Philosophy at North Texas State University. He is editor of the journal Environmental Ethics *and author of* Foundations of Environmental Ethics.

Nature aesthetics evolved directly out of art aesthetics. Two main lines of development were landscape painting and landscape gardening. The parallel developments in these areas may be characterized as follows: In painting, there was a movement from the appreciation of composed paintings representing imaginary places to an appreciation of paintings accurately representing real places and finally to an appreciation of natural landscapes resembling picturesque paintings. In gardening, there was a movement from improved, composed gardens to ones closely resembling natural landscapes and from plants viewed as building material to entities worthy of study and appreciation in a natural, unimproved state. In both cases, the movement was from the ideal to the actual or real, from the general or universal to the particular or individual, and from the artificial to the natural in such a way that aesthetic appreciation became focused on natural objects and living organisms as objects of interest for their own sake.

To a degree, these aesthetic developments also involved wildlife, since wild animals and plants often found their way into landscape paintings, and wild foreign plants routinely found their way into informal and botanical gardens. As noted earlier, naturalists, as part of their professional training, took art lessons, which provided them with the same general aesthetic perceptions of the artists with whom they trained. Moreover, the properties that they used to classify and identify animals and plants were the same secondary properties that were of special interest to artists and poets: colors, textures, shapes, smells, and the like. Nevertheless, there was no comparable movement aesthetically from the ideal to the real and particular, for the species classification system was composed of ideals in a very straightforward Platonic sense—they were *life* forms, to be sure, but *forms* nonetheless.

To illustrate this point, we do not need to reconstruct the wildlife perceptions of the early naturalists, for the contemporary perceptions of a tourist visiting a natural area or even a zoo are quite sufficient. A person who sees a wild animal for the first time will try to discern the properties that are characteristic of the species the animal represents. Because of the great diversity of appearance among animals of each species, the first sighting of a new animal may be misleading. Only after having seen many specimens will the tourist have an adequately generalized conception of what a member of that particular species should look like. The tourist may decide, upon reflection, that the first animal sighted was a good example, an outstanding one, or a poor one. This is an aesthetic judgment made in terms of a generalized, even idealized listing of essential properties for the species in question.

Phenomenologically, this activity is in most respects identical to the account that Locke, for example, gives concerning the creation of abstract ideas. Indeed, that is exactly what the tourist is doing—finding the properties in individual animals which are essential and putting them together as an idea by which animals encountered in the future can be identified and aesthetically evaluated (a good representative, a poor one, and so on). Once the "abstraction" is complete, the tourist's conception of the species is functionally a Platonic form. Any aesthetic judgment concerning a particular animal involves three elements: the perceiver, the object perceived, and the perceiver's conception of the particular species, the form. The animal is treated aesthetically as if it is supposed to "participate" in the perceiver's conception of the species. Individual differences or irregularities are considered "imperfections": The animal in question may be too large, too small, not quite the right color; there may be something unusual about part of its body, for example, peculiarly shaped ears or horns.

This kind of appreciation is very different from all other nature appreciation, which places great value on diversity and uniqueness. A tourist looking at mountains does not expect all mountains to look alike or judge their beauty in terms of a Platonic ideal for all mountains. The observer wants each mountain to be different, to be an individual, to offer something which he or she has not seen before. To be sure, it is eventually possible for the tourist to adopt a similar view with regard to wild animals with which he or she has become familiar so as to savor the unique qualities of each specimen encountered. In terms of the theory of evolution, for example, the observer may come to see each individual as an attempt in the natural history of the species at innovation and change. In terms of ecology, he or she may see each individual as an attempt to adapt to particular natural conditions. However, I submit, the Platonic idea continues in the background as the framework within which this diversity is appreciated in a way that it does not for natural objects such as mountains.

VALUE IN WILDLIFE PRESERVATION

The focus on the species, rather than the individual, in both nature appreciation and nature preservation creates interesting problems concerning the value of wildlife. Two kinds of value must be considered. The first is instrumental value. An entity is instrumentally valuable if its existence or use benefits another entity, usually a human being. The second is intrinsic value. An entity has intrinsic value if it is (1) valuable for its own sake or (2) valuable without regard to its use. These kinds of value may, moreover, be either anthropocentric or nonanthropocentric. An anthropocentric value is basically a human value. It is often customary to assume that all anthropocentric values are also instrumental, that is, valuable because they benefit human beings. It is nevertheless possible for values to be anthropocentric and intrinsic. An art object, for example, is appreciated and preserved in terms of human aesthetic values but is not regarded as being valuable instrumentally. Most environmental ethicists, however, have been critical of anthropocentric values of any kind and have attempted to develop some kind of nonanthropocentric value theory that can be used to establish environmental or ecological value independent of human judgment. It is within this framework—instrumental versus intrinsic and anthropocentric versus nonanthropocentric—that the value of wildlife must be sought.

There is, furthermore, a great deal of confusion caused by the two conflicting meanings of *anthropocentric* used in environmental ethics. As already noted, the word is often used to mean "instrumental" and just as often to mean "human" or "conceived in terms of human consciousness." Nonanthropocentrists, on the one hand, thus frequently call for the recognition, or discovery, of nonanthropocentric value so that natural things will no longer be treated in a purely instrumental manner. Anthropocentrists, on the other hand, who do not wish to treat all natural things instrumentally and define the term in the second sense, respond that even if we attribute nonanthropocentric value to nonhuman animals and natural objects, the values will still be anthropocentric or "human," since they are still values created by human valuers.

Bryan Norton has developed what he calls a weak anthropocentric position, which avoids the metaphysical issues involved in nonanthropocentrism, the search for value independent of the human mind, while also avoiding the perils of strong anthropocentrism, according to which all anthropocentric value is instrumental. In particular, Norton's discussion of societal ideals as the basis for environmental decision making leaves plenty of room for anthropocentric intrinsic value—human values cherished without regard to their instrumental value or use in terms of human interests. This conception of intrinsic value provides the easiest and most straight-forward foundation for nineteenth- and twentieth-century aesthetic interest in wildlife. Although it may eventually be possible to develop a nonanthropocentric conception of intrinsic value that conforms better to current twentieth-century intuitions, such a conception would probably still be in conflict with nineteenth-century intuitions, since aesthetic values at that time were generally thought of as matters of taste.

Viewed as a matter of taste, our aesthetic appreciation of art objects requires anthropocentric intrinsic value of some kind. There are three possibilities: (1) that the anthropocentric intrinsic value is in the object itself, (2) that it is in the aesthetic experience of the object, or (3) that it is in both the experience and the object itself. The third possibility seems to be the one that best fits our basic aesthetic intuitions and practice. Anthropocentrically, it seems to be correct to say that the value is in the object as long as we do not make a metaphysical claim the value exists as a property of the object itself. Such an attribution of value to an object does not rule out the possibility that it may also possess intrinsic value nonanthropocentrically. It only means that humans aesthetically consider the object to be valuable without regard to its use or instrumental value. Whereas an object might be instrumentally valuable as a paperweight, an object intrinsically valued is valuable without regard to such use—that is, its intrinsic value is considered more important than and overrides its instrumental value. (For example, a tool of unusual beauty might be considered too beautiful or "good" to use.) It is also possible for humans to consider the aesthetic contemplation of an art object to be intrinsically valuable. There is nothing wrong with this position either unless it requires that we reject the first position—for example, that we conclude that the art object is merely instrumentally valuable as a trigger for the aesthetic experience. To attribute intrinsic value exclusively to the experience demeans the object of the experience by converting it into something that is merely instrumentally valuable. Likewise, it leads to the equally counterintuitive conclusion that the mind itself is merely instrumental to the creation of the intrinsically valuable experience.

The writings of most nature preservationists in the nineteenth century strongly imply that nature is intrinsically valuable aesthetically in this double sense. In the later part of the century, however, another kind of environmentalism, resource conservation, also developed, which tended to treat nature instrumentally. A forest, for example, in accordance with this view of nature, was primarily valuable as a source of wood for various human purposes, not simply as a place for wild animals to roam or for nature lovers to wander. By the turn of the century, many preservationists, following the conservationists, had come to see the aesthetic value of natural objects as an instrumental trigger for the aesthetic experiences of humans. Yosemite, in this value scheme, is not intrinsically valuable as such but rather is instrumentally valuable insofar as it aids in the creation of aesthetic experiences, position two above.

This conversion of natural objects into aesthetic instruments for the production of aesthetic experiences has created a dilemma for policymakers that would not have occurred had the intrinsic/instrumental distinction been retained for both objects and experiences of them. If the object, viewed instrumentally, is damaged by tourists trying to create aesthetic experiences in their minds by exposing themselves to the object, the object becomes expendable and is consumed by the efforts to create these mental states or feelings. For example, cave formations and prehistoric cave paintings can be damaged and destroyed by fungus that grows using the light required for tourist viewing. When such objects are protected by turning out the lights and discontinuing the tours, they are considered to be of intrinsic value. If the tours are continued until the objects are destroyed and the tours are no longer profitable, the value of the objects is instrumental only, as a trigger for intrinsically valuable aesthetic experiences in humans.

The misguided efforts to establish rights for natural objects in this century is a reaction against this conversion of intrinsic value into instrumental value. The best way to resolve the problem, however, is simply to reinstate the intrinsic/instrumental distinction. Such confusion does not occur with art, since art objects are routinely removed from public viewing whenever such viewing starts to damage them. They are not, as our practice demonstrates, simply instrumental triggers to aesthetic experience. If natural objects are once again treated like art objects, as intrinsically valuable entities, the dilemma of whether or not to consume natural beauty disappears. If the direct generation of intrinsically valuable aesthetic experiences threatens to destroy, damage, or consume the natural object, we take whatever steps are necessary to preserve the object, including limiting or terminating visitation. Usually these experiences can be generated indirectly through the contemplation of artistic or photographic reproductions or through the exercise of the imagination without external aid.

If the value is perceived (anthropocentrically or nonanthropocentrically) as being in the object, as in the case of mountains, one preserves the value by preserving the object. While it is true that natural objects are gradually changing in accordance with the principles of uniformitarianism, there is enough permanence or durability in the objects for long-term preservationist efforts (in human time scales) to make sense. This element of impermanence, moreover, is not unique to objects of natural beauty, for art objects are also subject to deterioration over time. If, however, the value of the nature object is in its *use,* as in the case of trees to be used for lumber and paper pulp, the idea of preserving the trees as individuals is inappropriate. Since in such cases the instrumental value takes precedence over whatever intrinsic value the object may have, the practice is to consume the object and, if possible, take steps to ensure that there will be more objects of the same kind to consume in the future on a regular basis.

When one tries to assess the value of wildlife within the context of nature preservation and conservation, difficulties immediately appear, for the protection of species seems to be a problem of nature preservation, while the protection of the animals making up those species is a conservation problem. Just as the mountains are gradually changing in accordance with the principles of uniformitarian geology, the various forms of life are evolving in accordance with the principles of evolution. In this context, long-term preservation efforts make sense, since specific actions can be taken with a high expectation of success. Provided that human beings cooperate, natural catastrophe is the only major threat. Individual wild animals, by contrast, do not endure long enough in terms of preservationist time scales for any efforts at this level to be of much consequence. Their lives are extremely hazardous: Under natural conditions, they may be killed or eaten at almost any time. The only way to be reasonably sure that any particular animals will have an opportunity to live out a full life span is to remove them from their natural habitat and place them in an artificial environment—such as a zoo or a park—where they are safe from predation and other hazards. Medical care, comparable to that provided for human beings, is also a must.

In terms of the intrinsic/instrumental distinction, there are also serious problems. Species, like mountains, seem to be valuable for their own sake, without regard (primarily) to their use. Unlike mountains, however, which do have some instrumental value, species have none at all. As a concept, a species does not really do anything for its member exemplifications, the environment, or human beings. Indeed, as a concept, it certainly does nothing to cause its exemplifications to be or to continue in existence in any Platonic sense. Yet when we look at individual animals from almost any standpoint, they have both intrinsic and instrumental value, and the instrumental value predominates over the intrinsic. This is the case not only from the standpoint of the hunter and the commercial trapper but also from the standpoint of the naturalist, the environmentalist, the ecologist, and the ordinary person seeking aesthetic experience in nature. In each case, there is something of value beyond the individual that it contributes to instrumentally—income, the ecosystem, the species. To think in terms of the intrinsic value of the animal, one must take the position of an animal liberationist of some kind and start worrying about the welfare, interests, and rights of the individual organism, which is contrary to our basic practice as it has evolved over the past several centuries. By common consent among most of those concerned about wildlife, this last position the only one based on the intrinsic worth of the individual, is the abandonment of proper attitudes toward wildlife in favor of improper sentimentalism. Thus, although the preservation of the species as a life form conforms with the intrinsic value perspective of nature preservation, the preservation of the member animals of the species conforms best with the instrumentalist perspective of nature conservation.

Because the individual animal is valued primarily as a representation of something beyond and distinct from it, the species, we value it in much the same way that we value a reproduction of a painting. However, since we are still much more protective of prints than individual wild animals, perhaps the best analogy is a mass-produced toy, such as a *Star Wars* action figure. The child's interest in the figure is primarily as an exemplification of the design, just as our natural (or cultural) interest in the individual animal is as an exemplification of the species. The child is not interested in preserving the figure for all times, only in using it in various ways in acting out imaginary stories. This use is not necessarily in the best "interest" of the figure, for the child may do things with the figure that eventually cause its head or arm to fall off or completely destroy it—for example, dropping it from a great height, crushing it with a brick, or throwing it in a fire. Likewise, we are interested in using wildlife in ways that are not necessarily in the best interests of the individual animals—hunting them, letting them be eaten by other animals, or letting them starve to death so as to preserve the natural character of the landscape. If the factory stops making *Star Wars* figures or it becomes difficult to obtain them, the child may tend to be more careful during play. If animals belonging to a particular species become rare, more difficult to find or obtain, we may also tend to be more careful in the way we use these particular animals. The analogy seems to break down only in one respect: The animals produce their own replacements in most cases, whereas the figures are produced in a factory. Even this distinction, however, is not absolute, since various species of birds and fish are factory-farm raised and released into the wild to be caught or shot for sport.

ECOLOGY AND EVOLUTION RECONSIDERED

I noted at the beginning of this chapter that the history of ideas out of which an attitude develops may not necessarily have much to do with the justifications that eventually arise to explain it. This is certainly the case with wildlife protection attitudes, which are routinely justified in terms of ecology and evolution even though (1) they developed in terms of a preevolutionary and ecological conception of species as fixed and immutable and (2) were little affected by the new ecological and evolutionary perspectives that replaced that conception. Even today, in fact, the practical influence of the theory of evolution and the science of ecology on our behavior appears to be marginal at best. For example, if we look closely at our own intuitions, we will find, I believe, that we do care more strongly than evolution and ecology really allow. If a species faces extinction, even naturally, it is likely that there will be attempts to preserve the species in some way—for example, in zoos. Even if it is impractical to preserve a large enough population to maintain a healthy gene pool, there will be interest in preserving groups of individuals with an inadequate gene pool. Even if preservation efforts eliminate the natural behavior of the animals, considered by many to be properties of the species, the preservation of individuals lacking natural behavior will still be considered valuable by many people.

Curiously, the history of ideas that shaped our basic intuitions about wildlife protection has been a movement not through a series of incompatible foundations but rather through a series that has sustained a basic set of intuitions. Although the fixed species theory is incompatible with the evolutionary view of species and perhaps with their role in ecological systems, all three of these supported a common view of wildlife as instrumentally valuable entities serving as a means to some greater intrinsically valuable end—maintaining the great chain of being, continuing the natural evolution of species, or preserving the health and natural functioning of various ecosystems. Moving from the fixed species perspective to the evolutionary to the ecological, wildlife has been consistently regarded as something instrumentally valuable in a sense that is independent of the specific value of the individual animals living at any given moment. This instrumentalist approach to wildlife, moreover, has been remarkably compatible with nonenvironmental uses of wildlife. Since wild animals are entities that have instrumental status from the standpoints of both environmentalists and their opponents, wildlife preservation and conservation have been able to coexist with sport and subsistence hunting, even with trapping to a large degree. As long as there are enough of each kind to support the needs of the given ecosystems and the needs of trappers and hunters, on the one hand, and to preserve the life form classifications in such a way that many exemplifications are able to exhibit natural behavior and lead natural lives, on the other, serious problems do not arise. What we end up with is a layering of perspectives that all have a role in producing and justifying our basic ethical beliefs and behavior toward wild animals.

What ties all these perspectives together and reduces the conflict between them is the aesthetic element in both the concern for and the appreciation of wild animals. Aside from subsistence hunting and commercial trapping, human interest in wildlife is fundamentally aesthetic. Although, as I argue, wild animals are not straightforwardly regarded as aesthetic objects analogous to art objects, they are a key ingredient in various kinds of human experiences that are aesthetic in a broad sense. As I have already noted, aesthetic and scientific interests in nature overlap significantly. Scientists and nature lovers frequently have aesthetic experiences through the study of nature—and wildlife is a fundamental element in such study. Sport hunting, like other forms of outdoor recreation, likewise has its aesthetic component. These various perspectives provide additional dimensions, almost a kind of depth. From the standpoint of these perspectives, it is possible to admire wildlife in terms of their evolutionary history, as exemplifications of unique life forms, as worthy opponents and/or trophies, and as fundamental elements in healthy ecosystems—without having to choose between these viewpoints. Given that none of these perspectives allows for the intrinsic value of individual animals to outweigh their instrumental value to something else, thereby nearly closing the door on the animal liberationist, grounding our wildlife intuitions, beliefs, and practices in such (anthropocentric) aesthetic experience seems to be the best approach—one that takes into account not only those intuitions, beliefs, and practices as they are now understood by most people but also the history of ideas that produced them.

14

⟐ The Land Ethic: ⟐
Conservation as a Moral Issue;
Thinking Like a Mountain

ALDO LEOPOLD

Aldo Leopold was Professor of Wildlife Management at the University of Wisconsin from 1933 until his death in 1949. He is the author of A Sand County Almanac.

When god-like Odysseus returned from the wars in Troy, he hanged all on one rope a dozen slave-girls of his household whom he suspected of misbehavior during his absence.

This hanging involved no question of propriety. The girls were property. The disposal of property was then, as now, a matter of expediency, not of right and wrong.

Concepts of right and wrong were not lacking from Odysseus' Greece: witness the fidelity of his wife through the long years before at last his blackprowed galleys clove the wine-dark seas for home. The ethical structure of that day covered wives, but had not yet been extended to human chattels. During the three thousand years which have since elapsed, ethical criteria have been extended to many fields of conduct, with corresponding shrinkages in those judged by expediency only.

THE ETHICAL SEQUENCE

This extension of ethics, so far studied only by philosophers, is actually a process in ecological evolution. Its sequences may be described in ecological as well as in philosophical terms. An ethic, ecologically, is a limitation on freedom of action in the struggle for existence. An ethic, philosophically, is a differentiation of social from anti-social conduct. These are two definitions of one thing. The thing has its origin in the tendency of interdependent individuals or groups to evolve modes of co-operation. The ecologist calls these symbioses. Politics and economics are advanced symbioses in which the original free-for-all competition has been replaced, in part, by co-operative mechanisms with an ethical content.

The complexity of co-operative mechanisms has increased with population density, and with the efficiency of tools. It was simpler, for example, to define the anti-social uses of sticks and stones in the days of the mastodons than of bullets and billboards in the age of motors.

The first ethics dealt with the relation between individuals; the Mosaic Decalogue is an example. Later accretions dealt with the relation between the individual and society. The Golden Rule tries to integrate the individual to society; democracy to integrate social organization to the individual.

There is as yet no ethic dealing with man's relation to land and to the animals and plants which grow upon it. Land, like Odysseus' slave-girls, is still property. The land-relation is still strictly economic, entailing privileges but not obligations.

The extension of ethics to this third element in human environment is, if I read the evidence correctly, an evolutionary possibility and an ecological necessity. It is the third step in a sequence. The first two have already been taken. Individual thinkers since the days of Ezekiel and Isaiah have asserted that the despoliation of land is not only inexpedient but wrong. Society, however, has not yet affirmed their belief. I regard the present conservation movement as the embryo of such an affirmation.

An ethic may be regarded as a mode of guidance for meeting ecological situations so new or intricate, or involving such deferred reactions, that the path of social expediency is not discernible to the average individual. Animal instincts are modes of guidance for the individual in meeting such situations. Ethics are possibly a kind of community instinct in-the-making.

THE COMMUNITY CONCEPT

All ethics so far evolved rest upon a single premise: that the individual is a member of a community of interdependent parts. His instincts prompt him to compete for his place in the community, but his ethics prompt him also to co-operate (perhaps in order that there may be a place to compete for).

The land ethic simply enlarges the boundaries of the community to include soils, waters, plants, and animals, or collectively: the land.

This sounds simple: do we not already sing our love for and obligation to the land of the free and the home of the brave? Yes, but just what and whom do we love? Certainly not the soil, which we are sending helter-skelter downriver. Certainly not the waters, which we assume have no function except to turn turbines, float barges, and carry off sewage. Certainly not the plants, of which we exterminate whole communities without batting an eye. Certainly not the animals, of which we have already extirpated many of the largest and most beautiful species. A land ethic of course cannot prevent the alteration, management, and use of these 'resources,' but it does affirm their right to continued existence, and, at least in spots, their continued existence in a natural state.

In short, a land ethic changes the role of *Homo sapiens* from conqueror of the land-community to plain member and citizen of it. It implies respect for his fellow-members, and also respect for the community as such.

THE LAND PYRAMID

An ethic to supplement and guide the economic relation to land presupposes the existence of some mental image of land as a biotic mechanism. We can be ethical only in relation to something we can see, feel, understand, love, or otherwise have faith in.

The image commonly employed in conservation education is "the balance of nature." For reasons too lengthy to detail here, this figure of speech fails to describe accurately what little we know about the land mechanism. A much truer image is the one employed in ecology: the biotic pyramid. I shall first sketch the pyramid as a symbol of land, and later develop some of its implications in terms of land-use.

Plants absorb energy from the sun. This energy flows through a circuit called the biota, which may be represented by a pyramid consisting of layers. The bottom layer is the soil. A plant layer rests on the soil, an insect layer on the plants, a bird and rodent layer on the insects, and so on up through various animal groups to the apex layer, which consists of the larger carnivores.

The species of a layer are alike not in where they came from, or in what they look like, but rather in what they eat. Each successive layer depends on those below it for food and often for other services, and each in turn furnishes food and services to those above. Proceeding upward, each successive layer decreases in numerical abundance. Thus, for every carnivore there are hundreds of his prey, thousands of their prey, millions of insects, uncountable plants. The pyramidal form of the system reflects this numerical progression from apex to base. Man shares an intermediate layer with the bears, raccoons, and squirrels which eat both meat and vegetables.

The lines of dependency for food and other services are called food chains. Thus soil-oak-deer-Indian is a chain that has now been largely converted to soil-corn-cow-farmer. Each species, including ourselves, is a link in many chains. The deer eats a hundred plants other than oak, and the cow a hundred plants other than corn. Both, then, are links in a hundred chains. The pyramid is a tangle of chains so complex as to seem disorderly, yet the stability of the system proves it to be a highly organized structure. Its functioning depends on the co-operation and competition of its diverse parts.

In the beginning, the pyramid of life was low and squat; the food chains short and simple. Evolution has added layer after layer, link after link. Man is one of thousands of accretions to the height and complexity of the pyramid. Science has given us many doubts, but it has given us at least one certainty: the trend of evolution is to elaborate and diversify the biota.

Land, then, is not merely soil; it is a fountain of energy flowing through a circuit of soils, plants, and animals. Food chains are the living channels which conduct energy upward; death and decay return it to the soil. The circuit is not closed; some energy is dissipated in decay, some is added by absorption from the air, some is stored in soils, peats, and long-lived forests; but it is a sustained circuit, like a slowly augmented revolving fund of life. There is always a net loss by downhill wash, but this is normally small and offset by the decay of rocks. It is deposited in the ocean and, in the course of geological time, raised to form new lands and new pyramids.

The velocity and character of the upward flow of energy depend on the complex structure of the plant and animal community, much as the upward flow of sap in a tree depends on its complex cellular organization. Without this complexity, normal circulation would presumably not occur. Structure means the characteristic numbers, as well as the characteristic kinds and functions, of the component species. This interdependence between the complex structure of the land and its smooth functioning as an energy unit is one of its basic attributes.

When a change occurs in one part of the circuit, many other parts must adjust themselves to it. Change does not necessarily obstruct or divert the flow of energy; evolution is a long series of self-induced changes, the net result of which has been to elaborate the flow mechanism and to lengthen the circuit. Evolutionary changes, however, are usually slow and local. Man's invention of tools has enabled him to make changes of unprecedented violence, rapidity, and scope.

One change is in the composition of floras and faunas. The larger predators are lopped off the apex of the pyramid; food chains, for the first time in history, become shorter rather than longer. Domesticated species from other lands are substituted for wild ones, and wild ones are moved to new habitats. In this world-wide pooling of faunas and floras, some species get out of bounds as pests and diseases, others are extinguished. Such effects are seldom intended or foreseen; they represent unpredicted and often untraceable readjustments in the structure. Agricultural science is largely a race between the emergence of new pests and the emergence of new techniques for their control.

Another change touches the flow of energy through plants and animals and its return to the soil. Fertility is the ability of soil to receive, store, and release energy. Agriculture, by overdrafts on the soil, or by too radical a substitution of domestic for native species in the superstructure, may derange the channels of flow or deplete storage. Soils depleted of their storage or of the organic matter which anchors it, wash away faster than they form. This is erosion.

Waters, like soil, are part of the energy circuit. Industry, by polluting waters or obstructing them with dams, may exclude the plants and animals necessary to keep energy in circulation.

Transportation brings about another basic change: the plants or animals grown in one region are now consumed and returned to the soil in another. Transportation taps the energy stored in rocks, and in the air, and uses it elsewhere; thus we fertilize the garden with nitrogen gleaned by the guano birds from the fishes of seas on the other side of the Equator. Thus the formerly localized and self-contained circuits are pooled on a world-wide scale.

The process of altering the pyramid for human occupation releases stored energy, and this often gives rise, during the pioneering period, to a deceptive exuberance of plant and animal life, both wild and tame. These releases of biotic capital tend to becloud or postpone the penalties of violence.

This thumbnail sketch of land as an energy circuit conveys three basic ideas:

1. That land is not merely soil.
2. That the native plants and animals kept the energy circuit open; others may or may not.
3. That man-made changes are of a different order than evolutionary changes, and have effects more comprehensive than is intended or foreseen.

These ideas, collectively, raise two basic issues: Can the land adjust itself to the new order? Can the desired alterations be accomplished with less violence?

Biotas seem to differ in their capacity to sustain violent conversion. Western Europe, for example, carries a far different pyramid than Caesar found there. Some large animals are lost; swampy forests have become meadows or plowland; many new plants and animals are introduced, some of which escape as pests; the remaining natives are greatly changed in distribution and abundance. Yet the soil is still there and, with the help of imported nutrients, still fertile; the waters flow normally; the new structure seems to function and to persist. There is no visible stoppage or derangement of the circuit.

Western Europe, then, has a resistant biota. Its inner processes are tough, elastic, resistant to strain. No matter how violent the alterations, the pyramid, so far, has developed some new *modus vivendi* which preserves its habitability for man, and for most of the other natives.

Japan seems to present another instance of radical conversion without disorganization.

Most other civilized regions, and some as yet barely touched by civilization, display various stages of disorganization, varying from initial symptoms to advanced wastage. In Asia Minor and North Africa diagnosis is confused by climatic changes, which may have been either the cause or the effect of advanced wastage. In the United States the degree of disorganization varies locally; it is worst in the South-west, the Ozarks, and parts of the South, and least in New England and the North-west. Better land-uses may still arrest it in the less advanced regions. In parts of Mexico, South America, South Africa, and Australia a violent and accelerating wastage is in progress, but I cannot assess the prospects.

This almost world-wide display of disorganization in the land seems to be similar to disease in an animal, except that it never culminates in complete disorganization or death. The land recovers, but at some reduced level of complexity, and with a reduced carrying capacity for people, plants, and animals. Many biotas currently regarded as "lands of opportunity" are in fact already subsisting on exploitative agriculture, i.e., they have already exceeded their sustained carrying capacity. Most of South America is over-populated in this sense.

In arid regions we attempt to offset the process of wastage by reclamation, but it is only too evident that the prospective longevity of reclamation projects is often short. In our own West, the best of them may not last a century.

The combined evidence of history and ecology seems to support one general deduction: the less violent the man-made changes, the greater the probability of successful readjustment in the pyramid. Violence, in turn, varies with human population density; a dense population requires a more violent conversion. In this respect, North America has a better chance for permanence than Europe, if she can contrive to limit her density.

This deduction runs counter to our current philosophy, which assumes that because a small increase in density enriched human life, that an indefinite increase will enrich it indefinitely. Ecology knows of no density relationship that holds for indefinitely wide limits. All gains from density are subject to a law of diminishing returns.

Whatever may be the equation for men and land, it is improbable that we as yet know all its terms. Recent discoveries in mineral and vitamin nutrition reveal unsuspected dependencies in the up-circuit: incredibly minute quantities of certain substances determine the value of soils to plants, of plants to animals. What of the down-circuit? What of the vanishing species, the preservation of which we now regard as an esthetic luxury? They helped build the soil; in what unsuspected ways may they be essential to its maintenance? Professor Weaver proposes that we use prairie flowers to reflocculate the wasting soils of the dust bowl; who knows for what purpose cranes and condors, otters and grizzlies may some day be used?

THE OUTLOOK

It is inconceivable to me that an ethical relation to land can exist without love, respect, and admiration for land, and a high regard for its value. By value, I of course mean something far broader than mere economic value; I mean value in the philosophical sense.

Perhaps the most serious obstacle impeding the evolution of a land ethic is the fact that our educational and economic system is headed away from, rather than toward, an intense consciousness of land. Your true modern is separated from the land by many middlemen, and by innumerable physical gadgets. He has no vital relation to it; to him it is the space between cities on which crops grow. Turn him loose for a day on the land, and if the spot does not happen to be a golf links or a "scenic" area, he is bored stiff. If crops could be raised by hydroponics instead of farming, it would suit him very well. Synthetic substitutes for wood, leather, wool, and other natural land products suit him better than the originals. In short, land is something he has "outgrown."

Almost equally serious as an obstacle to a land ethic is the attitude of the farmer for whom the land is still an adversary, or a taskmaster that keeps him in slavery. Theoretically, the mechanization of farming ought to cut the farmer's chains, but whether it really does is debatable.

One of the requisites for an ecological comprehension of land is an understanding of ecology, and this is by no means co-extensive with "education"; in fact, much higher education seems deliberately to avoid ecological concepts. An understanding of ecology does not necessarily originate in courses bearing ecological labels; it is quite as likely to be labeled geography, botany, agronomy, history, or economics. This is as it should be, but whatever the label, ecological training is scarce.

The case for a land ethic would appear hopeless but for the minority which is in obvious revolt against these "modern" trends.

The "key-log" which must be moved to release the evolutionary process for an ethic is simply this: quit thinking about decent land-use as solely an economic problem. Examine each question in terms of what is ethically and esthetically right, as well as what is economically expedient. A thing is right when it tends to preserve the integrity, stability, and beauty of the biotic community. It is wrong when it tends otherwise.

It of course goes without saying that economic feasibility limits the tether of what can or cannot be done for land. It always has and it always will. The fallacy the economic determinists have tied around our collective neck, and which we now need to cast off, is the belief that economics determines *all* land-use. This is simply not true. An innumerable host of actions and attitudes, comprising perhaps the bulk of all land relations, is determined by the land-users' tastes and predilections, rather than by his purse. The bulk of all land relations hinges on investments of time, forethought, skill, and faith rather than on investments of cash. As a land-user thinketh, so is he.

I have purposely presented the land ethic as a product of social evolution because nothing so important as an ethic is ever "written." Only the most superficial student of history supposes that Moses "wrote" the Decalogue; it evolved in the minds of a thinking community, and Moses wrote a tentative summary of it for a "seminar." I say tentative because evolution never stops.

The evolution of a land ethic is an intellectual as well as emotional process. Conservation is paved with good intentions which prove to be futile, or even dangerous, because they are devoid of critical understanding either of the land, or of economic land-use. I think it is a truism that as the ethical frontier advances from the individual to the community, its intellectual content increases.

The mechanism of operation is the same for any ethic: social approbation for right actions: social disapproval for wrong actions.

By and large, our present problem is one of attitudes and implements. We are remodeling the Alhambra with a steam-shovel, and we are proud of our yardage. We shall hardly relinquish the shovel which after all has many good points, but we are in need of gentler and more objective criteria for its successful use.

CONSERVATION AS A MORAL ISSUE

Thus far we have considered the problem of conservation of land purely as an economic issue. A false front of exclusively economic determinism is so habitual to Americans in discussing public questions that one must speak in the language of compound interest to get a hearing. In my opinion, however, one can not round out a real understanding of the situation in the Southwest without likewise considering its moral aspects.

In past and more outspoken days conservation was put in terms of decency rather than dollars. Who can not feel the moral scorn and contempt for poor craftsmanship in the voice of Ezekiel when he asks: *Seemeth it a small thing unto you to have fed upon good pasture, but ye must tread down with your feet the residue of your pasture? And to have drunk of the clear waters, but ye must foul the residue with your feet?*

In these two sentences may be found an epitome of the moral question involved. Ezekiel seems to scorn waste, pollution, and unnecessary damage as something unworthy—as something damaging not only to the reputation of the waster, but to the self-respect of the craft and the society of which he is a member. We might even draw from his words a broader concept—that the privilege of possessing the earth entails the responsibility of passing it on, the better for our use, not only to immediate posterity, but to the Unknown Future, the nature of which is not given us to know. It is possible that Ezekiel respected the soil, not only as a craftsman respects his material, but as a moral being respects a living thing.

Many of the world's most penetrating minds have regarded our so-called "inanimate nature" as a living thing, and probably many of us who have neither the time nor the ability to reason out conclusions on such matters by logical processes have felt intuitively that there existed between man and the earth a closer and deeper relation than would necessarily follow the mechanistic conception of the earth as our physical provider and abiding place.

Of course, in discussing such matters we are beset on all sides with the pitfalls of language. The very words *living thing* have an inherited and arbitrary meaning derived not from reality, but from human perceptions of human affairs. But we must use them for better or for worse.

A good expression of this conception of an organized animate nature is given by the Russian philosopher Onpensky, who presents the following analogy:

> Were we to observe, from the inside, one cubic centimetre of the human body, knowing nothing of the existence of the entire body and of man himself, then the phenomena going on in this little cube of flesh would seem like elemental phenomena in inanimate nature.

He then states that it is at least not impossible to regard the earth's parts—soil, mountains, rivers, atmosphere, etc.—as organs, or parts of organs, or a coordinated whole, each part with a definite function. And, if we could see this whole, as a whole, through a great period of time, we might perceive not only organs with coordinated functions, but possibly also that process of consumption and replacement which in biology we call the metabolism, or growth. In such a case we would have all the visible attributes of a living thing, which we do not now realize to be such because it is too big, and its life processes too slow. And there would also follow that invisible attribute—a soul, or consciousness—which not only Onpensky, but many philosophers of all ages, ascribe to all living things and aggregations thereof, including the "dead" earth.

There is not much discrepancy, except in language, between this conception of a living earth, and the conception of a dead earth, with enormously slow, intricate, and interrelated functions among its parts, as given us by physics, chemistry, and geology. The essential thing for present purposes is that both admit the interdependent functions of the elements. But "anything indivisible is a living being," says Onpensky. Possibly, in our intuitive perceptions, which may be truer than our science and less impeded by words than our philosophies, we realize the indivisibility of the earth—its soil, mountains, rivers, forests, climate, plants, and animals, and respect it collectively not only as a useful servant but as a living being, vastly less alive than ourselves in degree, but vastly greater than ourselves in time and space—a being that was old when the morning stars sang together, and, when the last of us has been gathered unto his fathers, will still be young.

Philosophy, then, suggests one reason why we can not destroy the earth with moral impunity; namely, that the "dead" earth is an organism possessing a certain kind and degree of life, which we intuitively respect as such. Possibly, to most men of affairs, this reason is too intangible to either accept or reject as a guide to human conduct. But philosophy also offers another and more easily debatable question: was the earth made for man's use, or has man merely the privilege of temporarily possessing an earth made for other and inscrutable purposes? The question of what he can properly do with it must necessarily be affected by this question.

Most religions, insofar as I know, are premised squarely on the assumption that man is the end and purpose of creation, and that not only the dead earth, but all creatures thereon, exist solely for his use. The mechanistic or scientific philosophy does not start with this as a premise, but ends with it as a conclusion and hence may be placed in the same category for the purpose in hand. This high opinion of his own importance in the universe Jeanette Marks stigmatizes as "the great human impertinence." John Muir, in defense of rattlesnakes, protests: ". . . as if nothing that does not obviously make for the benefit of man had any right to exist; as if our ways were God's ways." But the noblest expression of this anthropomorphism is Bryant's "Thanatopsis":

> . . . The hills
> Rock-ribbed and ancient as the sun,—the vales
> Stretching in pensive quietness between;
> The venerable woods—rivers that move
> In majesty, and the complaining brooks
> That make the meadows green, and, poured round all
> Old oceans gray and melancholy waste,—
> *Are but the solemn decorations all*
> *Of the great tomb of man.*

Since most of mankind today profess either one of the anthropomorphic religions or the scientific school of thought which is likewise anthropomorphic, I will not dispute the point. It just occurs to me, however, in answer to the scientists, that God started his show a good many million years before he had any men for audience—a sad waste of both actors and music—and in answer to both, that it is just barely possible that God himself likes to hear birds sing and see flowers grow. But here again we encounter the insufficiency of words as symbols for realities.

Granting that the earth is for man—there is still a question: what man? Did not the cliff dwellers who tilled and irrigated these our valleys think that they were the pinnacle of creation—that these valleys were made for them? Undoubtedly. And then the

Pueblos? Yes. And then the Spaniards? Not only thought so, but said so. And now we Americans? Ours beyond a doubt! (How happy a definition is that one of Hadley's which states, "Truth is that which prevails in the long run"!)

Five races—five cultures—have flourished here. We may truthfully say of our four predecessors that they left the earth alive, undamaged. Is it possibly a proper question for us to consider what the sixth shall say about us? If we are logically anthropomorphic, yes. We and

> . . . all that tread
> The globe are but a handful to the tribes
> That slumber in its bosom. Take the wings
> Of morning; pierce the Barcan wilderness
> Or lose thyself in the continuous woods
> Where rolls the Oregon, and hears no sound
> Save his own dashings—yet the dead are there,
> And millions in those solitudes, since first
> The flight of years began, have laid them down
> In their last sleep.

And so, in time, shall we. And if there be, indeed, a special nobility inherent in the human race—a special cosmic value, distinctive from and superior to all other life—by what token shall it be manifest?

By a society decently respectful of its own and all other life, capable of inhabiting the earth without defiling it? Or by a society like that of John Burrough's potato bug, which exterminated the potato, and thereby exterminated itself? As one or the other shall we be judged in "the derisive silence of eternity."

THINKING LIKE A MOUNTAIN

A deep chesty bawl echoes from rimrock to rimrock, rolls down the mountain, and fades into the far blackness of the night. It is an outburst of wild defiant sorrow, and of contempt for all the adversities of the world.

Every living thing (and perhaps many a dead one as well) pays heed to that call. To the deer it is a reminder of the way of all flesh, to the pine a forecast of midnight scuffles and of blood upon the snow, to the coyote a promise of gleanings to come, to the cowman a threat of red ink at the bank, to the hunter a challenge of fang against bullet. Yet behind these obvious and immediate hopes and fears there lies a deeper meaning, known only to the mountain itself. Only the mountain has lived long enough to listen objectively to the howl of a wolf.

Those unable to decipher the hidden meaning know nevertheless that it is there, for it is felt in all wolf country, and distinguishes that country from all other land. It tingles in the spine of all who hear wolves by night, or who scan their tracks by day. Even without sight or sound of wolf, it is implicit in a hundred small events: the midnight whinny of a pack horse, the rattle of rolling rocks, the bound of a fleeing deer, the way shadows lie under the spruces. Only the ineducable tyro can fail to sense the presence or absence of wolves, or the fact that mountains have a secret opinion about them.

My own conviction on this score dates from the day I saw a wolf die. We were eating lunch on a high rimrock, at the foot of which a turbulent river elbowed its way. We saw what we thought was a doe fording the torrent, her breast awash in white water. When she climbed the bank toward us and shook out her tail, we realized our error:

it was a wolf. A half-dozen others, evidently grown pups, sprang from the willows and all joined in a welcoming melee of wagging tails and playful maulings. What was literally a pile of wolves writhed and tumbled in the center of an open flat at the foot of our rimrock.

In those days we had never heard of passing up a chance to kill a wolf. In a second we were pumping lead into the pack, but with more excitement than accuracy: how to aim a steep downhill shot is always confusing. When our rifles were empty, the old wolf was down, and a pup was dragging a leg into impassable slide-rocks.

We reached the old wolf in time to watch a fierce green fire dying in her eyes. I realized then, and have known ever since, that there was something new to me in those eyes—something known only to her and to the mountain. I was young then, and full of trigger-itch; I thought that because fewer wolves meant more deer, that no wolves would mean hunters' paradise. But after seeing the green fire die, I sensed that neither the wolf nor the mountain agreed with such a view.

Since then I have lived to see state after state extirpate its wolves. I have watched the face of many a newly wolfless mountain, and seen the south-facing slopes wrinkle with a maze of new deer trails. I have seen every edible bush and seedling browsed, first to anaemic desuetude, and then to death. I have seen every edible tree defoliated to the height of a saddlehorn. Such a mountain looks as if someone had given God a new pruning shears, and forbidden Him all other exercise. In the end the starved bones of the hoped for deer herd, dead of its own too much, bleach with the bones of the dead sage, or molder under the high-lined junipers.

I now suspect that just as a deer herd lives in mortal fear of its wolves, so does a mountain live in mortal fear of its deer. And perhaps with better cause, for while a buck pulled down by wolves can be replaced in two or three years, a range pulled down by too many deer may fail of replacement in as many decades.

So also with cows. The cowman who cleans his range of wolves does not realize that he is taking over the wolf's job of trimming the herd to fit the range. He has not learned to think like a mountain. Hence we have dustbowls, and rivers washing the future into the sea.

We all strive for safety, prosperity, comfort, long life, and dullness. The deer strives with his supple legs, the cowman with trap and poison, the statesman with pen, the most of us with machines, votes, and dollars, but it all comes to the same thing: peace in our time. A measure of success in this is all well enough, and perhaps is a requisite to objective thinking, but too much safety seems to yield only danger in the long run. Perhaps this is behind Thoreau's dictum: In wildness is the salvation of the world. Perhaps this is the hidden meaning in the howl of the wolf, long known among mountains, but seldom perceived among men.

15

◁ *Deep Ecology* ▷

BILL DEVALL AND GEORGE SESSIONS

Bill Devall teaches sociology at Humboldt State University and George Sessions teaches philosophy at Sierra College. They co-authored the book Deep Ecology.

The term *deep ecology* was coined by Arne Naess in his 1973 article, "The Shallow and the Deep, Long-Range Ecology Movements." Naess was attempting to describe the deeper, more spiritual approach to Nature exemplified in the writings of Aldo Leopold and Rachel Carson. He thought that this deeper approach resulted from a more sensitive openness to ourselves and nonhuman life around us. The essence of deep ecology is to keep asking more searching questions about human life, society, and Nature as in the Western philosophical tradition of Socrates. As examples of this deep questioning, Naess points out "that we ask why and how, where others do not. For instance, ecology as a science does not ask what kind of a society would be the best for maintaining a particular ecosystem—that is considered a question for value theory, for politics, for ethics." Thus deep ecology goes beyond the so-called factual scientific level to the level of self and Earth wisdom.

Deep ecology goes beyond a limited piecemeal shallow approach to environmental problems and attempts to articulate a comprehensive religious and philosophical worldview. The foundations of deep ecology are the basic intuitions and experiencing of ourselves and Nature which comprise ecological consciousness. Certain outlooks on politics and public policy flow naturally from this consciousness. And in the context of this book, we discuss the minority tradition as the type of community most conducive both to cultivating ecological consciousness and to asking the basic questions of values and ethics addressed in these pages.

Many of these questions are perennial philosophical and religious questions faced by humans in all cultures over the ages. What does it mean to be a unique human individual? How can the individual self maintain and increase its uniqueness while also being an inseparable aspect of the whole system wherein there are no sharp breaks between self and the *other?* An ecological perspective, in this deeper sense, results in what Theodore Roszak calls "an awakening of wholes greater than the sum of their parts. In spirit, the discipline is contemplative and therapeutic."

Ecological consciousness and deep ecology are in sharp contrast with the dominant worldview of technocratic-industrial societies which regards humans as isolated and fundamentally separate from the rest of Nature, as superior to, and in charge of, the rest of creation. But the view of humans as separate and superior to the rest of Nature is only part of larger cultural patterns. For thousands of years, Western culture has become increasingly obsessed with the idea of *dominance:* with dominance of humans over non-human Nature, masculine over the feminine, wealthy and powerful over the poor, with the dominance of the West over non-Western cultures. Deep ecological consciousness allows us to see through these erroneous and dangerous illusions.

For deep ecology, the study of our place in the Earth household includes the study of ourselves as part of the organic whole. Going beyond a narrowly materialist scientific understanding of reality, the spiritual and the material aspects of reality fuse together. While the leading intellectuals of the dominant worldview have tended to view religion as "just superstition," and have looked upon ancient spiritual practice and enlightenment, such as found in Zen Buddhism, as essentially subjective, the search for deep ecological consciousness is the search for a more objective consciousness and state of being through an active deep questioning and meditative process and way of life.

Many people have asked these deeper questions and cultivated ecological consciousness within the context of different spiritual traditions—Christianity, Taoism, Buddhism, and Native American rituals, for example. While differing greatly in other regards, many in these traditions agree with the basic principles of deep ecology.

Warwick Fox, an Australian philosopher, has succinctly expressed the central intuition of deep ecology: "It is the idea that we can make no firm ontological divide in the field of existence: That there is no bifurcation in reality between the human and the non-human realms . . . to the extent that we perceive boundaries, we fall short of deep ecological consciousness."

From this most basic insight or characteristic of deep ecological consciousness, Arne Naess has developed two *ultimate norms* or intuitions which are themselves not derivable from other principles or intuitions. They are arrived at by the deep questioning process and reveal the importance of moving to the philosophical and religious level of wisdom. They cannot be validated, of course, by the methodology of modern science based on its usual mechanistic assumptions and its very narrow definition of data. These ultimate norms are *self-realization* and *biocentric equality.*

SELF-REALIZATION

In keeping with the spiritual traditions of many of the world's religions, the deep ecology norm of self-realization goes beyond the modern Western self which is defined as an isolated ego striving primarily for hedonistic gratification or for a narrow sense of individual salvation in this life or the next. This socially programmed sense of the narrow self or social self dislocates us, and leaves us prey to whatever fad or fashion is prevalent in our society or social reference group. We are thus robbed of beginning the search for our unique spiritual/biological personhood. Spiritual growth, or unfolding, begins when we cease to understand or see ourselves as isolated and narrow competing egos and begin to identify with other humans from our family and friends to, eventually, our species. But the deep ecology sense of self requires a further maturity and growth, an identification which goes beyond humanity to include the nonhuman world. We must see beyond our narrow contemporary cultural assumptions and values, and the conventional wisdom of our time and place, and this is best achieved by the meditative deep questioning process. Only in this way can we hope to attain full mature personhood and uniqueness.

A nurturing nondominating society can help in the "real work" of becoming a whole person. The "real work" can be summarized symbolically as the realization of "self-in-Self" where "Self" stands for organic wholeness. This process of the full unfolding of the self can also be summarized by the phrase, "No one is saved until we are all saved," where the phrase "one" includes not only me, an individual human, but all humans, whales, grizzly bears, whole rain forest ecosystems, mountains and rivers, the tiniest microbes in the soil, and so on.

BIOCENTRIC EQUALITY

The intuition of biocentric equality is that all things in the biosphere have an equal right to live and blossom and to reach their own individual forms of unfolding and self-realization within the larger Self-realization. This basic intuition is that all organisms and entities in the ecosphere, as parts of the interrelated whole, are equal in intrinsic worth. Naess suggests that biocentric equality as an intuition is true in principle, although in the process of living, all species use each other as food, shelter, etc. Mutual predation is a biological fact of life, and many of the world's religions have struggled with the spiritual implications of this. Some animal liberationists who attempt to side-step this problem by advocating vegetarianism are forced to say that the entire plant kingdom including rain forests have no right to their own existence. This evasion flies in the face of the basic intuition of equality. Aldo Leopold expressed this intuition when he said humans are "plain citizens" of the biotic community, not lord and master over all other species.

Biocentric equality is intimately related to the all-inclusive Self-realization in the sense that if we harm the rest of Nature then we are harming ourselves. There are no boundaries and everything is interrelated. But insofar as we perceive things as individual organisms or entities, the insight draws us to respect all human and nonhuman individuals in their own right as parts of the whole without feeling the need to set up hierarchies of species with humans at the top.

The practical implications of this intuition or norm suggest that we should live with minimum rather than maximum impact on other species and on the Earth in general. Thus we see another aspect of our guiding principle: "simple in means, rich in ends." Further practical implications of these norms are discussed at length in chapters seven and eight.

A fuller discussion of the biocentric norm as it unfolds itself in practice begins with the realization that we, as individual humans, and as communities of humans, have vital needs which go beyond such basics as food, water, and shelter to include love, play, creative expression, intimate relationships with a particular landscape (or Nature taken in its entirety) as well as intimate relationships with other humans, and the vital need for spiritual growth, for becoming a mature human being.

Our vital material needs are probably more simple than many realize. In technocratic-industrial societies there is overwhelming propaganda and advertising which encourages false needs and destructive desires designed to foster increased production and consumption of goods. Most of this actually diverts us from facing reality in an objective way and from beginning the "real work" of spiritual growth and maturity.

Many people who do not see themselves as supporters of deep ecology nevertheless recognize an overriding vital human need for a healthy and high-quality natural environment for humans, if not for all life, with minimum intrusion of toxic waste, nuclear radiation from human enterprises, minimum acid rain and smog, and enough free flowing wilderness so humans can get in touch with their sources, the natural rhythms and the flow of time and place.

Drawing from the minority tradition and from the wisdom of many who have offered the insight of interconnectedness, we recognize that deep ecologists can offer suggestions for gaining maturity and encouraging the processes of harmony with Nature, but that there is no grand solution which is guaranteed to save us from ourselves.

The ultimate norms of deep ecology suggest a view of the nature of reality and our place as an individual (many in the one) in the larger scheme of things. They cannot be fully grasped intellectually but are ultimately experiential. We encouraged readers to consider our further discussion of the psychological, social and ecological implications of these norms in later chapters.

As a brief summary of our position thus far, these lists summarize the contrast between the dominant worldview and deep ecology.

Dominant Worldview	Deep Ecology
Dominance over Nature	Harmony with Nature
Natural environment as resource for humans	All nature has intrinsic worth/biospecies equality
Material/economic growth for growing human population	Elegantly simple material needs (material goals serving the larger goal of self-realization)
Belief in ample resource reserves	Earth "supplies" limited
High technological progress and solutions	Appropriate technology; nondominating science
Consumerism	Doing with enough/recycling
National/centralized community	Minority tradition/bioregion

BASIC PRINCIPLES OF DEEP ECOLOGY

In April 1984, during the advent of spring and John Muir's birthday, George Sessions and Arne Naess summarized fifteen years of thinking on the principles of deep ecology while camping in Death Valley, California. In this great and special place, they articulated these principles in a literal, somewhat neutral way, hoping that they would be understood and accepted by persons coming from different philosophical and religious positions.

Readers are encouraged to elaborate their own versions of deep ecology, clarify key concepts and think through the consequences of acting from these principles.

Basic Principles

1. The well-being and flourishing of human and nonhuman Life on Earth have value in themselves (synonyms: intrinsic value, inherent value). These values are independent of the usefulness of the nonhuman world for human purposes.

2. Richness and diversity of life forms contribute to the realization of these values and are also values in themselves.
3. Humans have no right to reduce this richness and diversity except to satisfy *vital* needs.
4. The flourishing of human life and cultures is compatible with a substantial decrease of the human population. The flourishing of nonhuman life requires such a decrease.
5. Present human interference with the nonhuman world is excessive, and the situation is rapidly worsening.
6. Policies must therefore be changed. These policies affect basic economic, technological, and ideological structures. The resulting state of affairs will be deeply different from the present.
7. The ideological change is mainly that of appreciating *life quality* (dwelling in situations of inherent value) rather than adhering to an increasingly higher standard of living. There will be a profound awareness of the difference between big and great.
8. Those who subscribe to the foregoing points have an obligation directly or indirectly to try to implement the necessary changes.

NAESS AND SESSIONS PROVIDE COMMENTS ON THE BASIC PRINCIPLES

RE (1). This formulation refers to the biosphere, or more accurately, to the ecosphere as a whole. This includes individuals, species, populations, habitat, as well as human and nonhuman cultures. From our current knowledge of all-pervasive intimate relationships, this implies a fundamental deep concern and respect. Ecological processes of the planet should, on the whole, remain intact. "The world environment should remain 'natural'" (Gary Snyder).

The term "life" is used here in a more comprehensive nontechnical way to refer also to what biologists classify as "nonliving"; rivers (watersheds), landscapes, ecosystems. For supporters of deep ecology, slogans such as "Let the river live" illustrate this broader usage so common in most cultures.

Inherent value as used in (1) is common in deep ecology literature. ("The presence of inherent value in a natural object is independent of any awareness, interest, or appreciation of it by a conscious being.")

RE (2). More technically, this is a formulation concerning diversity and complexity. From an ecological standpoint, complexity and symbiosis are conditions for maximizing diversity. So-called simple, lower, or primitive species of plants and animals contribute essentially to the richness and diversity of life. They have value in themselves and are not merely steps toward the so-called higher or rational life forms. The second principle presupposes that life itself, as a process over evolutionary time, implies an increase of diversity and richness. The refusal to acknowledge that some life forms have greater or lesser intrinsic value than others (see points 1 and 2) runs counter to the formulations of some ecological philosophers and New Age writers.

Complexity, as referred to here, is different from complication. Urban life may be more complicated than life in a natural setting without being more complex in the sense of multifaceted quality.

RE (3). The term "vital need" is left deliberately vague to allow for considerable latitude in judgment. Differences in climate and related factors, together with differences in the structures of societies as they now exist, need to be considered (for some Eskimos, snowmobiles are necessary today to satisfy vital needs).

People in the materially richest countries cannot be expected to reduce their excessive interference with the nonhuman world to a moderate level overnight. The stabilization and reduction of the human population will take time. Interim strategies need to be developed. But this in no way excuses the present complacency—the extreme seriousness of our current situation must first be realized. But the longer we wait the more drastic will be the measures needed. Until deep changes are made, substantial decreases in richness and diversity are liable to occur: the rate of extinction of species will be ten to one hundred times greater than any other period of earth history.

RE (4). The United Nations Fund for Population Activities in their State of World Population Report (1984) said that high human population growth rates (over 2.0 percent annum) in many developing countries "were diminishing the quality of life for many millions of people." During the decade 1974–1984, the world population grew by nearly 800 million—more than the size of India. "And we will be adding about one Bangladesh (population 93 million) per annum between now and the year 2000."

The report noted that "The growth rate of the human population has declined for the first time in human history. But at the same time, the number of people being added to the human population is bigger than at any time in history because the population base is larger."

Most of the nations in the developing world (including India and China) have as their official government policy the goal of reducing the rate of human population increase, but there are debates over the types of measures to take (contraception, abortion, etc.) consistent with human rights and feasibility.

The report concludes that if all governments set specific population targets as public policy to help alleviate poverty and advance the quality of life, the current situation could be improved.

As many ecologists have pointed out, it is also absolutely crucial to curb population growth in the so-called developed (i.e., overdeveloped) industrial societies. Given the tremendous rate of consumption and waste production of individuals in these societies, they represent a much greater threat and impact on the biosphere per capita than individuals in Second and Third World countries.

RE (5). This formulation is mild. For a realistic assessment of the situation, see the unabbreviated version of the I.U.C.N.'s *World Conservation Strategy*. There are other works to be highly recommended, such as Gerald Barney's *Global 2000 Report to the President of the United States.*

The slogan of "noninterference" does not imply that humans should not modify some ecosystems as do other species. Humans have modified the earth and will probably continue to do so. At issue is the nature and extent of such interference.

The fight to preserve and extend areas of wilderness or near-wilderness should continue and should focus on the general ecological functions of these areas (one such function: large wilderness areas are required in the biosphere to allow for continued evolutionary speciation of animals and plants). Most present designated wilderness areas and game preserves are not large enough to allow for such speciation.

RE (6). Economic growth as conceived and implemented today by the industrial states is incompatible with (1)–(5). There is only a faint resemblance between ideal sustainable forms of economic growth and present policies of the industrial societies. And "sustainable" still means "sustainable in relation to humans."

Present ideology tends to value things because they are scarce and because they have a commodity value. There is prestige in vast consumption and waste (to mention only several relevant factors).

Whereas "self-determination," "local community," and "think globally, act locally," will remain key terms in the ecology of human societies, nevertheless the implementation of deep changes requires increasingly global action—action across borders.

Governments in Third World countries (with the exception of Costa Rica and a few others) are uninterested in deep ecological issues. When the governments of industrial societies try to promote ecological measures through Third World governments, practically nothing is accomplished (e.g., with problems of desertification). Given this situation, support for global action through nongovernmental international organizations becomes increasingly important. Many of these organizations are able to act globally "from grassroots to grassroots," thus avoiding negative governmental interference.

Cultural diversity today requires advanced technology, that is, techniques that advance the basic goals of each culture. So-called soft, intermediate, and alternative technologies are steps in this direction.

RE (7). Some economists criticize the term "quality of life" because it is supposed to be vague. But on closer inspection, what they consider to be vague is actually the nonquantitative nature of the term. One cannot quantify adequately what is important for the quality of life as discussed here, and there is no need to do so.

RE (8). There is ample room for different opinions about priorities: what should be done first, what next? What is most urgent? What is clearly necessary as opposed to what is highly desirable but not absolutely pressing?

Interview with Arne Naess

The following excerpts are from an interview with Arne Naess conducted at the Zen Center of Los Angeles in April 1982. It was originally published as an interview in *Ten Directions*. In the interview, Naess further discusses the major perspective of deep ecology. We include it at the conclusion of this chapter so that the reader can gain further information in preparation for reading the remaining chapters.

"The essence of deep ecology is to ask deeper questions. The adjective 'deep' stresses that we ask why and how, where others do not. For instance, ecology as a science does not ask what kind of a society would be the best for maintaining a particular ecosystem—that is considered a question for value theory, for politics, for ethics. As long as ecologists keep narrowly to their science, they do not ask such questions. What we need today is a tremendous expansion of ecological thinking in what I call ecosophy. *Sophy* comes from the Greek term *sophia,* 'wisdom,' which relates to ethics, norms, rules, and practice. Ecosophy, or deep ecology, then, involves a shift from science to wisdom.

"For example, we need to ask questions like, Why do we think that economic growth and high levels of consumption are so important? The conventional answer would be to point to the economic consequences of not having economic growth. But in deep ecology, we ask whether the present society fulfills basic human needs like love and security and access to nature, and, in so doing, we question our society's underlying assumptions. We ask which society, which education, which form of religion, is beneficial for all life on the planet as a whole, and then we ask further what we need to do in order to make the necessary changes. We are not limited to a scientific approach; we have an obligation to verbalize a total view.

"Of course, total views may differ. Buddhism, for example, provides a fitting background or context for deep ecology, certain Christian groups have formed platforms of action in favor of deep ecology, and I myself have worked out my own philosophy, which I call ecosophy. In general, however, people do not question deeply enough to explicate or make clear a total view. If they did, most would agree with saving the planet from the destruction that's in progress. A total view, such as deep ecology, can provide a single motivating force for all the activities and movements aimed at saving the planet from human exploitation and domination.

". . . It's easier for deep ecologists than for others because we have certain fundamental values, a fundamental view of what's meaningful in life, what's worth maintaining, which makes it completely clear that we're opposed to further development for the sake of increased domination and an increased standard of living. The material standard of living should be drastically reduced and the quality of life, in the sense of basic satisfaction in the depths of one's heart or soul, should be maintained or increased. This view is intuitive, as are all important views, in the sense that it can't be proven. As Aristotle said, it shows a lack of education to try to prove everything, because you have to have a starting point. You can't prove the methodology of science, you can't prove logic, because logic presupposes fundamental premises.

"All the sciences are fragmentary and incomplete in relation to basic rules and norms, so it's very shallow to think that science can solve our problems. Without basic norms, there is no science.

". . . People can then oppose nuclear power without having to read thick books and without knowing the myriad facts that are used in newspapers and periodicals. And they must also find others who feel the same and form circles of friends who give one another confidence and support in living in a way that the majority find ridiculous, naive, stupid and simplistic. But in order to do that, one must already have enough self-confidence to follow one's intuition—a quality very much lacking in broad sections of the populace. Most people follow the trends and advertisements and become philosophical and ethical cripples.

"There is a basic intuition in deep ecology that we have no right to destroy other living beings without sufficient reason. Another norm is that, with maturity, human beings will experience joy when other life forms experience joy and sorrow when other life forms experience sorrow. Not only will we feel sad when our brother or a dog or a cat feels sad, but we will grieve when living beings, including landscapes, are destroyed. In our civilization, we have vast means of destruction at our disposal but extremely little maturity in our feelings. Only a very narrow range of feelings have interested most human beings until now.

"For deep ecology, there is a core democracy in the biosphere. . . . In deep ecology, we have the goal not only of stabilizing human population but also of reducing it to a sustainable minimum without revolution or dictatorship. I should think we must have no more than 100 million people if we are to have the variety of cultures we had one hundred years ago. Because we need the conservation of human cultures, just as we need the conservation of animal species.

". . . Self-realization is the realization of the potentialities of life. Organisms that differ from each other in three ways give us less diversity than organisms that differ from each other in one hundred ways. Therefore, the self-realization we experience when we identify with the universe is heightened by an increase in the number of ways in which individuals, societies, and even species and life forms realize themselves. The greater the diversity, then, the greater the self-realization. This seeming duality between individuals and the totality is encompassed by what I call the Self and the Chinese call the Tao. Most people in deep ecology have had the feeling—usually, but not always, in nature—that they are connected with something greater than their ego, greater than their name, their family, their special attributes as an individual—a feeling that is often called oceanic because many have it on the ocean. Without that identification, one is not easily drawn to become involved in deep ecology. . . .

". . . Insofar as these deep feelings are religious, deep ecology has a religious component, and those people who have done the most to make societies aware of the destructive way in which we live in relation to natural settings have had such religious feelings. Rachel Carson, for example, says that we _cannot_ do what we do, we have no religious or ethical justification for behaving as we do toward nature. . . . She is saying that we are simply not permitted to behave in that way. Some will say that nature is not man's property, it's the property of God; others will say it in other ways. The main point is that deep ecology has a religious component, fundamental intuitions that everyone must cultivate if he or she is to have a life based on values and not function like a computer.

". . . To maximize self-realization—and I don't mean self as ego but self in a broader sense—we need maximum diversity and maximum symbiosis. . . . Diversity, then, is a fundamental norm and a common delight. As deep ecologists, we take a natural delight in diversity, as long as it does not include crude, intrusive forms, like Nazi culture, that are destructive to others."

16

⩕ *The Ecology of Order* ⩔ *and Chaos*

DONALD WORSTER

Donald Worster is Professor of Environmental History at the University of Kansas.

The science of ecology has had a popular impact unlike that of any other academic field of research. Consider the extraordinary ubiquity of the word itself: it has appeared in the most everyday places and the most astonishing, on day-glo T-shirts, in corporate advertising, and on bridge abutments. It has changed the language of politics and philosophy—springing up in a number of countries are political groups that are self-identified as "Ecology Parties."Yet who ever proposed forming a political party named after comparative linguistics or advanced paleontology? On several continents we have a philosophical movement termed "Deep Ecology," but nowhere has anyone announced a movement for "Deep Entomology" or "Deep Polish Literature." Why has this funny little word, ecology, coined by an obscure 19th-century German scientist, acquired so powerful a cultural resonance, so widespread a following?

Behind the persistent enthusiasm for ecology, I believe, lies the hope that this science can offer a great deal more than a pile of data. It is supposed to offer a pathway to a kind of moral enlightenment that we can call, for the purposes of simplicity, "conservation."The expectation did not originate with the public but first appeared among eminent scientists within the field. For instance, in his 1935 book *Deserts on the March,* the noted University of Oklahoma, and later Yale, botanist Paul Sears urged Americans to take ecology seriously, promoting it in their universities and making it part of their governing process. "In Great Britain," he pointed out,

> the ecologists are being consulted at every step in planning the proper utilization of those parts of the Empire not yet settled, thus . . . ending the era of haphazard

exploitation. There are hopeful, but all too few signs that our own national government realizes the part which ecology must play in a permanent program.[1]

Sears recommended that the United States hire a few thousand ecologists at the county level to advise citizens on questions of land use and thereby bring an end to environmental degradation; such a brigade, he thought, would put the whole nation on a biologically and economically sustainable basis.

In a 1947 addendum to his text, Sears added that ecologists, acting in the public interest, would instill in the American mind that "body of knowledge," that "point of view, which peculiarly implies all that is meant by conservation."[2] In other words, by the time of the 1930s and 40s, ecology was being hailed as a much needed guide to a future motivated by an ethic of conservation. And conservation for Sears meant restoring the biological order, maintaining the health of the land and thereby the well-being of the nation, pursuing by both moral and technical means a lasting equilibrium with nature.

While we have not taken to heart all of Sears's suggestions—have not yet put any ecologists on county payrolls, with an office next door to the tax collector and sheriff—we have taken a surprisingly long step in his direction. Every day in some part of the nation, an ecologist is at work writing an environmental impact report or monitoring a human disturbance of the landscape or testifying at a hearing.

Twelve years ago I published a history, going back to the 18th century, of this scientific discipline and its ideas about nature.[3] The conclusions in that book still strike me as being, on the whole, sensible and valid: that this science has come to be a major influence on our perception of nature in modern times; that its ideas, on the other hand, have been reflections of ourselves as much as objective apprehensions of nature; that scientific analysis cannot take the place of moral reasoning; that science, including the science of ecology, promotes, at least in some of its manifestations, a few of our darker ambitions toward nature and therefore itself needs to be morally examined and critiqued from time to time. Ecology, I argued, should never be taken as an all-wise, always trustworthy guide. We must be willing to challenge this authority, and indeed challenge the authority of science in general; not be quick to scorn or vilify or behead, but simply, now and then, to question.

During the period since my book was published, there has accumulated a considerable body of new thinking and new research in ecology. In this essay I mean to survey some of that recent thinking, contrasting it with its predecessors, and to raise a few of the same questions I did before. Part of my argument will be that Paul Sears would be astonished, and perhaps dismayed, to hear the kind of advice that ecological experts have to give these days. Less and less do they offer, or even promise to offer, what he would consider to be a program of moral enlightenment—of "conservation" in the sense of a restored equilibrium between humans and nature.

There is a clear reason for that outcome, I will argue, and it has to do with drastic changes in the ideas that ecologists hold about the structure and function of the natural world. In Sears's day ecology was basically a study of equilibrium, harmony, and order; it had been so from its beginnings. Today, however, in many circles of scientific research, it has become a study of disturbance, disharmony, and chaos, and coincidentally or not, conservation is often not even a remote concern.

At the time *Deserts on the March* appeared in print, and through the time of its second and even third edition, the dominant name in the field of American ecology was that of Frederic L. Clements, who more than any other individual introduced scientific ecology into our national academic life. He called his approach "dynamic ecology," meaning it was concerned with change and evolution in the landscape. At its heart Clements's ecology dealt with the process of vegetational succession—the sequence of plant communities that appear on a piece of soil, newly made or disturbed, beginning with the first pioneer communities that invade and get a foothold.[4] Here is how I have defined the essence of the Clementsian paradigm:

> Change upon change became the inescapable principle of Clements's science. Yet he also insisted stubbornly and vigorously on the notion that the natural landscape must eventually reach a vaguely final climax stage. Nature's course, he contended, is not an aimless wandering to and fro but a steady flow toward stability that can be exactly plotted by the scientist.[5]

Most interestingly, Clements referred to that final climax stage as a "superorganism," implying that the assemblage of plants had achieved the close integration of parts, the self-organizing capability, of a single animal or plant. In some unique sense, it had become a live, coherent thing, not a mere collection of atomistic individuals, and exercised some control over the nonliving world around it, as organisms do.

Until well after World War II Clements's climax theory dominated ecological thought in this country.[6] Pick up almost any textbook in the field written forty, or even thirty, years ago, and you will likely find mention of the climax. It was this theory that Paul Sears had studied and took to be the core lesson of ecology that his county ecologists should teach their fellow citizens: that nature tends toward a climax state and that, as far as practicable, they should learn to respect and preserve it. Sears wrote that the chief work of the scientist ought to be to show "the unbalance which man has produced on this continent" and to lead people back to some approximation of nature's original health and stability.[7]

But then, beginning in the 1940s, while Clements and his ideas were still in the ascendent, a few scientists began trying to speak a new vocabulary. Words like "energy flow," "trophic levels," and "ecosystem" appeared in the leading journals, and they indicated a view of nature shaped more by physics than botany. Within another decade or two nature came to be widely seen as a flow of energy and nutrients through a physical or thermodynamic system. The early figures prominent in shaping this new view included C. Juday, Raymond Lindeman, and G. Evelyn Hutchinson. But perhaps its most influential exponent was Eugene P. Odum, hailing from North Carolina and Georgia, discovering in his southern saltwater marshes, tidal estuaries, and abandoned cotton fields the animating, pulsating force of the sun, the global flux of energy. In 1953 Odum published the first edition of his famous textbook, *The Fundamentals of Ecology*.[8] In 1966 he became president of the Ecological Society of America.

By now anyone in the United States who regularly reads a newspaper or magazine has come to know at least a few of Odum's ideas, for they furnish the main themes in our popular understanding of ecology, beginning with the sovereign idea of the ecosystem. Odum defined the ecosystem as "any unit that includes all of the organisms (i.e., the 'community') in a given area interacting with the physical environment so that a flow of energy leads to clearly defined trophic structure, biotic diversity, and material cycles (i.e., exchange of materials between living and nonliving parts) within the system."[9] The whole earth, he argued, is organized into an interlocking series of such "ecosystems," ranging in size from a small pond to so vast an expanse as the Brazilian rainforest.

What all those ecosystems have in common is a "strategy of development," a kind of game plan that gives nature an overall direction. That strategy is, in Odum's words, "directed toward achieving as large and diverse an organic structure as is possible within the limits set by the available energy input and the prevailing physical conditions of existence."[10] Every single ecosystem, he believed, is either moving toward or has already achieved that goal. It is a clear, coherent, and easily observable strategy; and it ends in the happy state of order.

Nature's strategy, Odum added, leads finally to a world of mutualism and cooperation among the organisms inhabiting an area. From an early stage of competing against one another, they evolve toward a more symbiotic relationship. They learn, as it were, to work together to control their surrounding environment, making it more and more suitable as a habitat, until at last they have the power to protect themselves from its stressful cycles of drought and flood, winter and summer, cold and heat. Odum called that point "homeostasis." To achieve it, the living components of an ecosystem must evolve a structure of interrelatedness and cooperation that can, to some extent, manage the physical world—manage it for maximum efficiency and mutual benefit.

I have described this set of ideas as a break from the past, but that is misleading. Odum may have used different terms than Clements, may even have had a radically different vision of nature at times; but he did not repudiate Clements's notion that nature moves toward order and harmony. In the place of the theory of the "climax" stage he put the theory of the "mature ecosystem." His nature may have appeared more as an automated factory than as a Clementsian super-organism, but like its predecessor it tends toward order.

The theory of the ecosystem presented a very clear set of standards as to what constituted order and disorder, which Odum set forth in the form of a "tabular model of ecological succession." When the ecosystem reaches its end point of homeostasis, his table shows, it expends less energy on increasing production and more on furnishing protection from external vicissitudes: that is, the biomass in an area reaches a steady level, neither increasing nor decreasing, and the emphasis in the system is on keeping it that way—on maintaining a kind of no-growth economy. Then the little, aggressive, weedy organisms common at an early stage in development (the r-selected species) give way to larger, steadier creatures (K-selected species), who may have less potential for fast growth and explosive reproduction but also better talents at surviving in dense settlements and keeping the place on an even keel.[11] At that point there is supposed to be more diversity in the community—i.e., a greater array of species. And there is less loss of nutrients to the outside; nitrogen, phosphorous, and calcium all stay in circulation within the ecosystem rather than leaking out. Those are some of the key indicators of ecological order, all of them susceptible to precise measurement. The suggestion was implicit but clear that if one interfered too much with nature's strategy of development, the effects might be costly: a serious loss of nutrients, a decline in species diversity, an end to biomass stability. In short, the ecosystem would be damaged.

The most likely source of that damage was no mystery to Odum: it was human beings trying to force up the production of useful commodities and stupidly risking the destruction of their life support system.

> Man has generally been preoccupied with obtaining as much "production" from the landscape as possible, by developing and maintaining early successional types of ecosystems, usually monocultures. But, of course, man does not live by food and fiber alone; he also needs a balanced CO_2-O_2 atmosphere, the climatic buffer provided by oceans and masses of vegetation, and clean (that is, unproductive) water for cultural and industrial uses. Many essential life-cycle resources, not to mention recreational and esthetic needs, are best provided man by the less "productive"

landscapes. In other words, the landscape is not just a supply depot but is also the *oikos*—the home—in which we must live.[12]

Odum's view of nature as a series of balanced ecosystems, achieved or in the making, led him to take a strong stand in favor of preserving the landscape in as nearly natural a condition as possible. He suggested the need for substantial restraint on human activity—for environmental planning "on a rational and scientific basis." For him as for Paul Sears, ecology must be taught to the public and made the foundation of education, economics, and politics; America and other countries must be "ecologized."

Of course not every one who adopted the ecosystem approach to ecology ended up where Odum did. Quite the contrary, many found the ecosystem idea a wonderful instrument for promoting global technocracy. Experts familiar with the ecosystem and skilled in its manipulation, it was hoped in some quarters, could manage the entire planet for improved efficiency. "Governing" all of nature with the aid of rational science was the dream of these ecosystem technocrats.[13] But technocratic management was not the chief lesson, I believe, the public learned in Professor Odum's classroom; most came away devoted, as he was, to preserving large parts of nature in an unmanaged state and sure that they had been given a strong scientific rationale, as well as knowledge base, to do it. We must defend the world's endangered ecosystems, they insisted. We must safeguard the integrity of the Greater Yellowstone ecosystem, the Chesapeake Bay ecosystem, the Serengeti ecosystem. We must protect species diversity, biomass stability, and calcium recycling. We must make the world safe for K-species.[14]

That was the rallying cry of environmentalists and ecologists alike in the 1960s and early 1970s, when it seemed that the great coming struggle would be between what was left of pristine nature, delicately balanced in Odum's beautifully rational ecosystems, and a human race bent on mindless, greedy destruction. A decade or two later the situation has changed considerably. There are still environmental threats around, to be sure, and they are more dangerous than ever. The newspapers inform of us of continuing disasters like the massive 1989 oil spill in Alaska's Prince William Sound, and reporters persist in using words like "ecosystem" and "balance" and "fragility" to describe such disasters. So do many scientists, who continue to acknowledge their theoretical indebtedness to Odum. For instance, in a recent British poll, 447 ecologists out of 645 questioned ranked the "ecosystem" as one of the most important concepts their discipline has contributed to our understanding of the natural world; indeed, "ecosystem" ranked first on their list, drawing more votes than nineteen other leading concepts.[15] But all the same, and despite the persistence of environmental problems, Odum's ecosystem is no longer the main theme in research or teaching in the science. A survey of recent ecology textbooks shows that the concept is not even mentioned in one leading work and has a much diminished place in the others.[16]

Ecology is not the same as it was. A rather drastic change has been going on in this science of late—a radical shifting away from the thinking of Eugene Odum's generation, away from its assumptions of order and predictability, a shifting toward what we might call a new *ecology of chaos*.

In July 1973, the *Journal of the Arnold Arboretum* published an article by two scientists associated with the Massachusetts Audubon Society, William Drury and Ian Nisbet, and it challenged Odum's ecology fundamentally. The title of the article was simply "Succession," indicating that old subject of observed sequences in plant and animal associations. With both Frederic Clements and Eugene Odum, succession had been taken to be the straight and narrow road to equilibrium. Drury and Nisbet disagreed completely with that assumption. Their observations, drawn particularly from

northeastern temperate forests, strongly suggested that the process of ecological succession does not lead anywhere. Change is without any determinable direction and
goes on forever, never reaching a point of stability. They found no evidence of any
progressive development in nature: no progressive increase over time in biomass stabilization, no progressive diversification of species, no progressive movement toward
a greater cohesiveness in plant and animal communities, nor toward a greater success
in regulating the environment. Indeed, they found none of the criteria Odum had
posited for mature ecosystems. The forest, they insisted, no matter what its age, is nothing but an erratic, shifting mosaic of trees and other plants. In their words, "most of
the phenomena of succession should be understood as resulting from the differential
growth, differential survival, and perhaps differential dispersal of species adapted to
grow at different points on stress gradients."[17] In other words, they could see lots of
individual species, each doing its thing, but they could locate no emergent collectiv-
ity, nor any strategy to achieve one.

Prominent among their authorities supporting this view was the nearly forgotten
name of Henry A. Gleason, a taxonomist who, in 1926, had challenged Frederic
Clements and his organismic theory of the climax in an article entitled, "The Individualistic Concept of the Plant Association." Gleason had argued that we live in a world
of constant flux and impermanence, not one tending toward Clements's climaxes. There
is no such thing, he argued, as balance or equilibrium or steady-state. Each and every
plant association is nothing but a temporary gathering of strangers, a clustering of species
unrelated to one another, here for a brief while today, on their way somewhere else
tomorrow. "Each . . . species of plant is a law unto itself," he wrote.[18] We look for cooperation in nature and we find only competition. We look for organized wholes, and
we can discover only loose atoms and fragments. We hope for order and discern only
a mishmash of conjoining species, all seeking their own advantage in utter disregard
of others.

Thanks in part to Drury and Nisbet, this "individualistic" view was reborn in the
mid-1970s and, during the past decade, it became the core idea of what some scientists hailed as a new, revolutionary paradigm in ecology. To promote it, they attacked the
traditional notion of succession; for to reject that notion was to reject the larger idea
that organic nature tends toward order. In 1977 two more biologists, Joseph Connell
and Ralph Slatyer, continued the attack, denying the old claim that an invading community of pioneering species, the first stage in Clements's sequence, works to prepare
the ground for its successors, like a group of Daniel Boones blazing the trail for civilization. The first comers, Connell and Slatyer maintained, manage in most cases to stake
out their claims and successfully defend them; they do not give way to a later, superior
group of colonists. Only when the pioneers die or are damaged by natural disturbances,
thus releasing the resources they have monopolized, can latecomers find a foothold and
get established.[19]

As this assault on the old thinking gathered momentum, the word "disturbance"
began to appear more frequently in the scientific literature and be taken far more seriously. "Disturbance" was not a common subject in Odum's heyday, and it almost never
appeared in combination with the adjective "natural." Now, however, it was as though
scientists were out looking strenuously for signs of disturbance in nature—especially
signs of disturbance that were not caused by humans—and they were finding it everywhere. During the past decade those new ecologists succeeded in leaving little tranquility
in primitive nature. Fire is one of the most common disturbances they noted. So is
wind, especially in the form of violent hurricanes and tornadoes. So are invading populations of microorganisms and pests and predators. And volcanic eruptions. And

invading ice sheets of the Quaternary Period. And devastating droughts like that of the 1930s in the American West. Above all, it is these last sorts of disturbances, caused by the restlessness of climate, that the new generation of ecologists have emphasized. As one of the most influential of them, Professor Margaret Davis of the University of Minnesota, has written: "For the last 50 years or 500 or 1,000—as long as anyone would claim for 'ecological time'—there has never been an interval when temperature was in a steady state with symmetrical fluctuations about a mean. . . . Only on the longest time scale, 100,000 years, is there a tendency toward cyclical variation, and the cycles are asymmetrical, with a mean much different from today."[20]

One of the most provocative and impressive expressions of the new post–Odum ecology is a book of essays edited by S.T.A. Pickett and P.S. White, *The Ecology of Natural Disturbance and Patch Dynamics* (published in 1985). I submit it as symptomatic of much of the thinking going on today in the field. Though the final section of the book does deal with ecosystems, the word has lost much of its former meaning and implications. Two of the authors in fact open their contribution with a complaint that many scientists assume that "homogeneous ecosystems are a reality," when in truth "virtually all naturally occurring and man-disturbed ecosystems are mosaics of environmental conditions." "Historically," they write, "ecologists have been slow to recognize the importance of disturbances and the heterogeneity they generate." The reason for this slowness? "The majority of both theoretical and empirical work has been dominated by an equilibrium perspective."[21] Repudiating that perspective, these authors take us to the tropical forests of South and Central America and to the Everglades of Florida, showing us instability on every hand: a wet, green world of continual disturbance—or as they prefer to say, "of perturbations." Even the grasslands of North America, which inspired Frederic Clements's theory of the climax, appear in this collection as regularly disturbed environments. One paper describes them as a "dynamic, fine-textured mosaic" that is constantly kept in upheaval by the workings of badgers, pocket gophers, and mound-building ants, along with fire, drought, and eroding wind and water.[22] The message in all these papers is consistent: The climax notion is dead, the ecosystem has receded in usefulness, and in their place we have the idea of the lowly "patch." Nature should be regarded as a landscape of patches, big and little, patches of all textures and colors, a patchwork quilt of living things, changing continually through time and space, responding to an unceasing barrage of perturbations. The stitches in that quilt never hold for long.

Now, of course, scientists have known about gophers and winds, the Ice Age and droughts for a considerable time. Yet heretofore they have not let those disruptions spoil their theories of balanced plant and animal associations, and we must ask why that was so. Why did Clements and Odum tend to dismiss such forces as climatic change, at least of the less catastrophic sort, as threats to the order of nature? Why have their successors, on the other hand, tended to put so much emphasis on those same changes, to the point that they often see nothing but instability in the landscape?

One clue comes from the fact that many of these disturbance boosters are not and have never been ecosystem scientists; they received their training in the subfield of population biology and reflect the growing confidence, methodological maturity, and influence of that subfield.[23] When they look at a forest, the population ecologists see only the trees. See them and count them—so many white pines, so many hemlocks, so many maples and birches. They insist that if we know all there is to know about the individual species that constitute a forest, and can measure their lives in precise, quantitative terms, we will know all there is to know about that forest. It has no "emergent" or organismic properties. It is not some whole greater than the sum of its parts, requiring "holistic" understanding. Outfitted with computers that can track the life histories of individual species, chart the rise and fall of populations, they have brought a degree of mathematical precision to ecology that is awesome to contemplate. And what they see when they look at population histories for any patch of land is wildly swinging oscillations. Populations rise and populations fall, like stock market prices, auto sales, and hemlines. We live, they insist, in a non-equilibrium world.[24]

There is another reason for the paradigmatic shift I have been describing, though I suggest it quite tentatively and can offer only sketchy evidence for it. For some scientists, a nature characterized by highly individualistic associations, constant disturbance, and incessant change may be more ideologically satisfying than Odum's ecosystem, with its stress on cooperation, social organization, and environmentalism. A case in point is the very successful popularizer of contemporary ecology, Paul Colinvaux, author of *Why Big Fierce Animals Are Rare* (1978). His chapter on succession begins with these lines: "If the planners really get hold of us so that they can stamp out all individual liberty and do what they like with our land, they might decide that whole counties full of inferior farms should be put back into forest." Clearly, he is not enthusiastic about land-use planning or forest restoration. And he ends that same chapter with these remarkably revealing and self-assured words:

We can now . . . explain all the intriguing, predictable events of plant successions in simple, matter of fact, Darwinian ways. Everything that happens in successions comes about because all the different species go about earning their livings as best they may, each in its own individual manner. What look like community properties are in fact the summed results of all these bits of private enterprise.[25]

Apparently, if this example is any indication, the social Darwinists are back on the scene, and at least some of them are ecologists, and at least some of their opposition to Odum's science may have to do with a revulsion toward its political implications, including its attractiveness for environmentalists. Colinvaux is very clear about the need to get some distance between himself and groups like the Sierra Club.

I am not alone in wondering whether there might be a deeper, half-articulated ideological motive generating the new direction in ecology. The Swedish historian of science, Thomas Söderqvist, in his recent study of ecology's development in his country, concludes that the present generation of evolutionary ecologists

seem to do ecology for fun only, indifferent to practical problems, including the salvation of the nation. They are mathematically and theoretically sophisticated, sitting indoors calculating on computers, rather than traveling out in the wilds. They are individualists, abhorring the idea of large-scale ecosystem projects. Indeed, the transition from ecosystem ecology to evolutionary ecology seems to reflect the generational transition from the politically consciousness generation of the 1960s to the "yuppie" generation of the 1980s.[26]

That may be an exaggerated characterization, and I would not want to apply it to every scientist who has published on patch dynamics or disturbance regimes. But it does draw our attention to an unmistakable attempt by many ecologists to disassociate themselves from reform environmentalism and its criticisms of human impact on nature.

I wish, however, that the emergence of the new post-Odum ecology could be explained so simply in those two ways: as a triumph of reductive population dynamics over holistic consciousness, or as a triumph of social Darwinist or entrepreneurial ideology over a commitment to environmental preservation. There is, it seems, more going on than that, and it is going on all through the natural sciences—biology, astronomy, physics—perhaps going on through all modern technological societies. It is nothing less than the discovery of chaos. Nature, many have begun to believe, is *fundamentally* erratic, discontinuous, and unpredictable. It is full of seemingly random events that elude our models of how things are supposed to work. As a result, the unexpected keeps hitting us in the face. Clouds collect and disperse, rain falls or doesn't fall, disregarding our careful weather predictions, and we cannot explain why. Cars suddenly bunch up on the freeway, and the traffic controllers fly into a frenzy. A man's heart beats regularly year after year, then abruptly begins to skip a beat now and then. A ping pong ball bounces off the table in an unexpected direction. Each little snowflake falling out of the sky turns out to be completely unlike any other. Those are ways in which nature seems, in contrast to all our previous theories and methods, to be chaotic. If the ultimate test of any body of scientific knowledge is its ability to predict events, then all the sciences and pseudo-sciences—physics, chemistry, climatology, economics, ecology—fail the test regularly. They all have been announcing laws, designing models, predicting what an individual atom or person is supposed to do; and now, increasingly, they are beginning to confess that the world never quite behaves the way it is supposed to do.

Making sense of this situation is the task of an altogether new kind of inquiry calling itself the science of chaos. Some say it portends a revolution in thinking equivalent to quantum mechanics or relativity. Like those other 20th-century revolutions, the science of chaos rejects tenets going back as far as the days of Sir Isaac Newton. In fact, what is occurring may be not two or three separate revolutions but a single revolution against all the principles, laws, models, and applications of classical science, the science ushered in by the great Scientific Revolution of the 17th century.[27] For centuries we have assumed that nature, despite a few appearances to the contrary, is a perfectly predictable system of linear, rational order. Give us an adequate number of facts, scientists have said, and we can describe that order in complete detail—can plot the lines along which everything moves and the speed of that movement and the collisions that will occur. Even Darwin's theory of evolution, which in the last century challenged much of the Newtonian worldview, left intact many people's confidence that order would prevail at last in the evolution of life; that out of the tangled history of competitive struggle would come progress, harmony, and stability. Now that traditional assumption may have broken down irretrievably. For whatever reason, whether because empirical data suggests it or because extrascientific cultural trends do—the experience of so much rapid social change in our daily lives—scientists are beginning to focus on what they had long managed to avoid seeing. The world is more complex than we ever imagined, they say, and indeed, some would add, ever can imagine.[28]

Despite the obvious complexity of their subject matter, ecologists have been among the slowest to join the cross-disciplinary science of chaos. I suspect that the influence of Clements and Odum, lingering well into the 1970s, worked against the new perspective, encouraging faith in linear regularities and equilibrium in the interaction of species. Nonetheless, eventually there arrived a day of conversion. In 1974 the Princeton mathematical ecologist Robert May published a paper with the title, "Biological Populations with Nonoverlapping Generations: Stable Points, Stable Cycles, and Chaos."[29] In it he admitted that the mathematical models he and others had constructed were inadequate approximations of the ragged life histories of organisms. They did not fully explain, for example, the aperiodic outbreaks of gypsy moths in eastern hardwood forests or the Canadian lynx cycles in the subarctic. Wildlife populations do not follow some simple Malthusian pattern of increase, saturation, and crash.

More and more ecologists have followed May and begun to try to bring their subject into line with chaotic theory. William Schaefer is one of them; though a student of Robert MacArthur, a leader of the old equilibrium school, he has been lately struck by the same anomaly of unpredictable fluctuations in populations as May and others. Though taught to believe in "the so-called 'Balance of Nature'," he writes, ". . . the idea that populations are at or close to equilibrium," things now are beginning to look very different.[30] He describes himself has having to reach far across the disciplines, to make connections with concepts of chaos in the other natural sciences, in order to free himself from his field's restrictive past.

The entire study of chaos began in 1961, with efforts to simulate weather and climate patterns on a computer at MIT. There, meteorologist Edward Lorenz came up with his now famous "Butterfly Effect," the notion that a butterfly stirring the air today in a Beijing park can transform storm systems next month in New York City. Scientists call this phenomenon "sensitive dependence on initial conditions." What it means is that tiny differences in input can quickly become substantial differences in output. A corollary is that we cannot know, even with all our artificial intelligence apparatus, every one of the tiny differences that have occurred or are occurring at any place or point in time; nor can we know which tiny differences will produce which substantial differences in output. Beyond a short range, say, of two or three days from now, our predictions are not worth the paper they are written on.

The implications of this "Butterfly Effect" for ecology are profound. If a single flap of an insect's wings in China can lead to a torrential downpour in New York, then what might it do to the Greater Yellowstone Ecosystem? What can ecologists possibly know about all the forces impinging on, or about to impinge on, any piece of land? What can they safely ignore and what must they pay attention to? What distant, invisible, minuscule events may even now be happening that will change the organization of plant and animal life in our back yards? This is the predicament, and the challenge, presented by the science of chaos, and it is altering the imagination of ecologists dramatically.

John Muir once declared, "When we try to pick out anything by itself, we find it hitched to everything else in the universe."[31] For him, that was a manifestation of an infinitely wise plan in which everything functioned with perfect harmony. The new ecology of chaos, though impressed like Muir with interdependency, does not share his view of "an infinitely wise plan" that controls and shapes everything into order. There is no plan, today's scientists say, no harmony apparent in the events of nature. If there is order in the universe—and there will no longer be any science if all faith in order vanishes—it is going to be much more difficult to locate and describe than we thought.

For Muir, the clear lesson of cosmic complexity was that humans ought to love and preserve nature just as it is. The lessons of the new ecology, in contrast, are not at all clear. Does it promote, in Ilya Prigogine and Isabelle Stenger's words, "a renewal of nature," a less hierarchical view of life, and a set of "new relations between man and nature and between man and man"?[32] Or does it increase our alienation from the world, our withdrawal into post-modernist doubt and self-consciousness? What is there to love or preserve in a universe of chaos? How are people supposed to behave in such a universe? If such is the kind of place we inhabit, why not go ahead with all our private ambitions, free of any fear that we may be doing special damage? What, after all, does the phrase "environmental damage" mean in a world of so much natural chaos? Does the tradition of environmentalism to which Muir belonged, along with so many other nature writers and ecologists of the past—people like Paul Sears, Eugene Odum, Aldo Leopold, and Rachel Carson—make sense any longer? I have no space here to attempt to answer those questions or to make predictions but only issue a warning that they are too important to be left for scientists alone to answer. Ecology today, no more than in the past, can be assumed to be all-knowing or all-wise or eternally true.

Whether they are true or false, permanent or passingly fashionable, it does seem entirely possible that these changes in scientific thinking toward an emphasis on chaos will not produce any easing of the environmentalist's concern. Though words like ecosystem or climax may fade away and some new vocabulary take their place, the fear of risk and danger will likely become greater than ever. Most of us are intuitively aware, whether we can put our fears into mathematical formulae or not, that the technological power we have accumulated is *destructively* chaotic; not irrationally, we fear it and fear what it can to do us as well as the rest of nature.[33] It may be that we moderns, after absorbing the lessons of today's science, find we cannot love nature quite so easily as Muir did; but it may also be that we have discovered more reason than ever to respect it—to respect its baffling complexity, its inherent unpredictability, its daily turbulence. And to flap our own wings in it a little more gently.

NOTES

1. Paul Sears, *Deserts on the March,* 3rd ed. (Norman: University of Oklahoma Press, 1959), p. 162.
2. Ibid., p. 177.
3. Donald Worster, *Nature's Economy: A History of Ecological Ideas* (New York: Cambridge University Press, 1977).
4. This is the theme in particular of Clements's book *Plant Succession* (Washington: Carnegie Institution, 1916).
5. Worster, p. 210
6. Clements's major rival for influence in the United States was Henry Chandler Cowles of the University of Chicago, whose first paper on ecological succession appeared in 1899. The best study of Cowles's ideas is J. Ronald Engel, *Sacred Sands: The Struggle for Community in the Indiana Dunes* (Middletown, CT: Wesleyan University Press, 1983), pp. 137–59. Engel describes him as having a less deterministic, more pluralistic notion of succession, one that "opened the way to a more creative role for human beings in nature's evolutionary adventure." (p. 150). See also Ronald C. Tobey, *Saving the Prairies: The Life Cycle of the Founding School of American Plant Ecology, 1895–1955* (Berkeley: University of California, 1981).
7. Sears, p. 142.
8. This book was co-authored with his brother Howard T. Odum, and it went through two more editions, the last appearing in 1971.
9. Eugene P. Odum, *Fundamentals of Ecology* (Philadelphia: W.B. Saunders, 1971), p. 8.
10. Odum, "The Strategy of Ecosystem Development," *Science,* 164 (18 April 1969): 266.
11. The terms "K-selection" and "r-selection" came from Robert MacArthur and Edward O. Wilson, *Theory of Island Biogeography* (Princeton: Princeton University Press, 1967). Along with Odum, MacArthur was the leading spokesman during the 1950s and 60s for the view of nature as a series of thermodynamically balanced ecosystems.
12. Odum, "Strategy of Ecosystem Development," p. 266. See also Odum, "Trends Expected in Stressed Ecosystems," *BioScience,* 35 (July/August 1985): 419–422.
13. A book of that title was published by Earl F. Murphy, *Governing Nature* (Chicago: Quadrangle Books, 1967). From time to time, Eugene Odum himself seems to have caught that ambition or leant his support to it, and it was certainly central to the work of his brother, Howard T. Odum. On this theme see Peter J. Taylor, "Technocratic Optimism, H. T. Odum, and the Partial Transformation of Ecological Metaphor after World War II," *Journal of the History of Biology,* 21 (Summer 1988): 213–44.
14. A very influential popularization of Odum's view of nature (though he is never actually referred to in it) is Barry Commoner's *The Closing Circle: Nature, Man, and Technology* (New York: Alfred A. Knopf, 1971). See in particular the discussion of the four "laws" of ecology, pp. 33–46.
15. Communication from Malcolm Cherrett, *Ecology,* 70 (March 1989): 41–42.
16. See Michael Begon, John L. Harper, and Colin R. Townsend, *Ecology: Individuals, Populations, and Communities* (Sunderland, Mass.: Sinauer, 1986). In another textbook, Odum's views are presented critically as the traditional approach: R. J. Putnam and S. D. Wratten, *Principles of Ecology* (Berkeley: University of California Press, 1984). More loyal to the ecosystem model are Paul Ehrlich and Jonathan Roughgarden, *The Science of Ecology* (New York: Macmillan, 1987); and Robert Leo Smith, *Elements of Ecology,* 2nd ed. (New York: Harper & Row, 1986), though the latter admits that he has shifted from an "ecosystem approach" to more of an "evolutionary approach" (p. xiii).

17. William H. Drury and Ian C. T. Nisbet, "Succession," *Journal of the Arnold Arboretum,* 54 (July 1973): 360.
18. H. A. Gleason, "The Individualistic Concept of the Plant Association," *Bulletin of the Torrey Botanical Club,* 53 (1926): 25. A later version of the same article appeared in *American Midland Naturalist,* 21 (1939): 92–110.
19. Joseph H. Connell and Ralph O. Slatyer, "Mechanisms of Succession in Natural Communities and Their Role in Community Stability and Organization," *The American Naturalist,* 111 (November–December 1977): 1119–1144.
20. Margaret Bryan Davis, "Climatic Instability, Time Lags, and Community Disequilibrium," in *Community Ecology,* ed. Jared Diamond and Ted J. Case (New York: Harper & Row, 1986), p. 269.
21. James R. Karr and Kathryn E. Freemark, "Disturbance and Vertebrates: An Integrative Perspective," *The Ecology of Natural Disturbance and Patch Dynamics,* eds., S.T.A. Pickett and P.S. White (Orlando, Fla.: Academic Press, 1985), pp. 154–55. The Odum school of thought is, however, by no means silent. Another recent compilation has been put together in his honor, and many of its authors express a continuing support for his ideas: L. R. Pomeroy and J.J. Alberts, eds., *Concepts of Ecosystem Ecology: A Comparative View* (New York: Springer-Verlag, 1988).
22. Orie L. Loucks, Mary L. Plumb-Mentjes, and Deborah Rogers, "Gap Processes and Large-Scale Disturbances in Sand Prairies," *ibid.,* pp. 72–85.
23. For the rise of population ecology see Sharon E. Kingsland, *Modeling Nature: Episodes in the History of Population Ecology* (Chicago: University of Chicago Press, 1985).
24. An influential exception to this tendency is F. H. Bormann and G. E. Likens, *Pattern and Process in a Forested Ecosystem* (New York: Springer-Verlag, 1979), which proposes in Chap. 6 the model of a "shifting mosaic steady-state." See also P.Yodzis, "The Stability of Real Ecosystems," *Nature,* 289 (19 February 1981): 674–76.
25. Paul Colinvaux, *Why Big Fierce Animals Are Rare: An Ecologist's Perspective* (Princeton: Princeton University Press, 1978), pp. 117, 135.
26. Thomas Söderqvist, *The Ecologists: From Merry Naturalists to Saviours of the Nation. A Sociologically informed narrative survey of the ecologization of Sweden, 1895–1975.* (Stockholm: Almqvist & Wiksell International, 1986), p. 281.
27. This argument is made with great intellectual force by Ilya Prigogine and Isabelle Stengers, *Order Out of Chaos: Man's New Dialogue with Nature* (Boulder: Shambala/New Science Library, 1984). Prigogine won the Nobel Prize in 1977 for his work on the thermodynamics of nonequilibrium systems.
28. An excellent account of the change in thinking is James Gleick, *Chaos: The Making of a New Science* (New York: Viking, 1987). I have drawn on his explanation extensively here. What Gleick does not explore are the striking intellectual parallels between chaotic theory in science and post-modern discourse in literature and philosophy. Post-Modernism is a sensibility that has abandoned the historic search for unity and order in nature, taking an ironic view of existence and debunking all established faiths. According to Todd Gitlin, "Post-Modernism reflects the fact that a new moral structure has not yet been built and our culture has not yet found a language for articulating the new understandings we are trying, haltingly, to live with. It objects to all principles, all commitments, all crusades—in the name of an unconscientious evasion." On the other hand, and more positively, the new sensibility leads to emphasis on democratic coexistence: "a new 'moral ecology'—that in the preservation of the other is a condition for the preservation of the self." Gitlin, "Post-Modernism: The Stenography of Surfaces," *New Perspectives Quarterly,* 6 (Spring 1989): 57, 59.
29. The paper was published in *Science,* 186 (1974): 645–647. See also Robert M. May, "Simple Mathematical Models with Very Complicated Dynamics," *Nature,* 261 (1976): 459–67. Gleick discusses May's work in *Chaos,* pp. 69–80.
30. W. M. Schaeffer, "Chaos in Ecology and Epidemiology," in *Chaos in Biological Systems,* ed., H. Degan, A.V. Holden, and L.F. Olsen (New York: Plenum Press, 1987), p. 233. See also Schaeffer, "Order and Chaos in Ecological Systems," *Ecology,* 66 (February 1985): 93–106.
31. John Muir, *My First Summer in the Sierra* (1911; Boston: Houghton Mifflin, 1944), p. 157.
32. Prigogine and Stengers, pp. 312–13.
33. Much of the alarm that Sears and Odum, among others, expressed has shifted to a global perspective, and the older equilibrium thinking has been taken up by scientists concerned about the geo- and biochemical condition of the planet as a whole and about human threats, particularly from the burning of fossil fuels, to its stability. One of the most influential texts in this new development is James Lovelock's *Gaia: A New Look at Life on Earth* (Oxford: Oxford University Press, 1979). See also Edward Goldsmith, "Gaia: Some Implications for Theoretical Ecology," *The Ecologist,* 18, nos. 2/3 (1988): 64–74.

17

⚞ *The Rights* ⚟
of the Nonhuman World

MARY ANNE WARREN

Mary Ann Warren teaches philosophy at San Francisco State University. She has written a number of well-known articles in ethical theory and most recently the book Moral States.

Western philosophers have typically held that human beings are the only proper objects of human moral concern. Those who speak of *duties* generally hold that we have duties only to human beings (or perhaps to God), and that our apparent duties towards animals, plants and other nonhuman entities in nature are in fact indirect duties to human beings. Those who speak of moral *rights* generally ascribe such rights only to human beings.

This strictly *homocentric* (human-centered) view of morality is currently challenged from two seemingly disparate directions. On the one hand, environmentalists argue that because humanity is only one part of the natural world, an organic species in the total, interdependent, planetary biosystem, it is necessary for consistency to view all of the elements of that system, and not just its human elements, as worthy of moral concern in themselves, and not only because of their usefulness to us. The ecologist Aldo Leopold was one of the first and most influential exponents of the view that not only human beings, but plants, animals and natural habitats, have moral rights. We need, Leopold argued, a new ethical system that will deal with our relationships not only with other human individuals and with human society, but also with the land, and its nonhuman inhabitants. Such a "land ethic" would seek to change "the role of *Homo sapiens* from conqueror of the land community to plain member and citizen of it." It would judge our interaction with the nonhuman world as "right when it tends to preserve the integrity, stability, and beauty of the biotic community," and "wrong when it tends otherwise."

On the other hand, homocentric morality is attacked by the so-called animal liberationists, who have argued, at least as early as the eighteenth century (in the Western tradition), that insofar as (some) nonhuman animals are sentient beings, capable of experiencing pleasure and pain, they are worthy in their own right of our moral concern. On the surface at least, the animal liberationist ethic appears to be quite different from that of ecologists such as Leopold. The land ethic is *wholistic* in its emphasis: it treats the good of the biotic *community* as the ultimate measure of the value of individual organisms or species, and of the rightness or wrongness of human actions. In contrast, the animal–liberationist ethic is largely inspired by the utilitarianism of Jeremy Bentham and John Stuart Mill. The latter tradition is individualist in its moral focus, in that it treats the needs and interests of individual sentient beings as the ultimate basis for conclusions about right and wrong.

These differences in moral perspective predictably result in differences in the emphasis given to specific moral issues. Thus, environmentalists treat the protection of endangered species and habitats as matters for utmost concern, while, unlike many of the animal liberationists, they generally do not object to hunting, fishing or rearing animals for food, so long as these practices do not endanger the survival of certain species or otherwise damage the natural environment. Animal liberationists, on the other hand, regard the inhumane treatment or killing of animals which are raised for meat, used in scientific experimentation and the like, as just as objectionable as the killing or mistreatment of "wild" animals. They oppose such practices not only because they may sometimes lead to environmental damage, but because they cause suffering or death to sentient beings.

Contrasts such as these have led some philosophers to conclude that the theoretical foundations of the Leopoldian land ethic and those of the animal–liberationist movement are fundamentally incompatible, or that there are "intractable practical differences" between them. I shall argue on the contrary, that a harmonious marriage between these two approaches is possible, provided that each side is prepared to make certain compromises. In brief, the animal liberationists must recognize that although animals do have significant moral rights, these rights are not precisely the same as those of human beings; and that part of the difference is that the rights of animals may sometimes be overridden, for example, for environmental or utilitarian reasons, in situations where it would not be morally acceptable to override human rights for similar reasons. For their part, the environmentalists must recognize that while it may be acceptable, as a legal or rhetorical tactic, to speak of the rights of trees or mountains, the logical foundations of such rights are quite different from those of the rights of human and other sentient beings. The issue is of enormous importance for moral philosophy, for it centres upon the theoretical basis for the ascription of moral rights, and hence bears directly upon such disputed cases as the rights of (human) foetuses, children, the comatose, the insane, etc. Another interesting feature is the way in which utilitarians and *deontologists* often seem to exchange sides in the battle—the former insist upon the universal application of the principle that to cause unnecessary pain is wrong, while the latter refuse to apply that principle to other than human beings, unless there are utilitarian reasons for doing so.

In section I, I will examine the primary line of argument presented by the contemporary animal–rights advocates, and suggest that their conclusions must be amended in the way mentioned above. In section II, I will present two arguments for distinguishing between the rights of human beings and those of (most) nonhuman animals. In section III, I will consider the animal liberationists' objection that any such distinction will endanger the rights of certain "nonparadigm" human beings, for example, infants and the mentally incapacitated. In section IV, I will reply to several current objections to the attempt to found basic moral rights upon the sentience, or other psychological capacities, of the entity involved. Finally, in section V, I will examine the moral theory implicit in the land ethic, and argue that it may be formulated and put into practice in a manner which is consistent with the concerns of the animal liberationists.

I. WHY (SOME) ANIMALS HAVE (SOME) MORAL RIGHTS

Peter Singer is the best known contemporary proponent of animal liberation. Singer maintains that all sentient animals, human or otherwise, should be regarded as morally equal; that is, that their interests should be given equal consideration. He argues that sentience, the capacity to have conscious experiences such as pain or pleasure, is "the only defensible boundary of concern for the interests of others." In Bentham's often-quoted words, "the question is not, Can they reason? nor, Can they talk? but Can they suffer?" To suppose that the interests of animals are outside the scope of moral concern is to commit a moral fallacy analogous to sexism or racism, a fallacy which Singer calls *speciesism.* True, women and members of "minority" races are more *intelligent* than (most) animals—and almost certainly no less so than white males—but that is not the point. The point does not concern these complex capabilities at all. For, Singer says, "The claim to equality does not depend on intelligence, moral capacity, physical strength, or similar matters of fact."

As a utilitarian, Singer prefers to avoid speaking of moral *rights,* at least insofar as these are construed as claims which may sometimes override purely utilitarian considerations. There are, however, many other advocates of animal liberation who do maintain that animals have moral rights, rights which place limitations upon the use of utilitarian justifications for killing animals or causing them to suffer. Tom Regan, for example, argues that if all or most human beings have a right to life, then so do at least some animals. Regan points out that unless we hold that animals have a right to life, we may not be able to adequately support many of the conclusions that most animal liberationists think are important, for example, that it is wrong to kill animals painlessly to provide human beings with relatively trivial forms of pleasure.

This disagreement between Singer and Regan demonstrates that there is no single well-defined theory of the moral status of animals which can be identified as *the* animal liberationist position. It is clear, however, that neither philosopher is committed to the claim that the moral status of animals is completely identical to that of humans. Singer points out that his basic principle of equal *consideration* does not imply identical *treatment.* Regan holds only that animals have *some* of the same moral rights as do human beings, not that *all* of their rights are necessarily the same.

Nevertheless, none of the animal liberationists have thus far provided a clear explanation of how and why the moral status of (most) animals differs from that of (most) human beings; and this is a point which must be clarified if their position is to be made fully persuasive. That there is such a difference seems to follow from some very strong moral intuitions which most of us share. A man who shoots squirrels for sport may or may not be acting reprehensibly; but it is difficult to believe that his actions should be placed in *exactly* the same moral category as those of a man who shoots women, or black children, for sport. So too is it doubtful that the Japanese fishermen who slaughtered dolphins because the latter were thought to be depleting the local fish populations were acting quite *as* wrongly as if they had slaughtered an equal number of their human neighbours for the same reason.

Can anything persuasive be said in support of these intuitive judgments? Or are they merely evidence of unreconstructed speciesism? To answer these questions we must consider both certain similarities and certain differences between ourselves and other animals, and then decide which of these are relevant to the assignment of moral rights. To do this we must first ask just what it means to say than an entity possesses a certain moral right.

There are two elements of the concept of a moral right which are crucial for our present purposes. To say that an entity, X, has a moral right to Y (some activity, benefit or satisfaction) is to imply at least the following: (1) that it would be morally wrong for any moral agent to intentionally deprive X or Y without some sufficient justification; (2) that this would be wrong, at least in part, *because of the (actual or potential) harm which it would do to the interests of X.*

On this (partial) definition of a moral right, to ask whether animals have such rights is to ask whether there are some ways of treating them which are morally objectionable because of the harm done to the animals themselves, and not merely because of some *other* undesirable results, such as damaging the environment or undermining the moral character of human beings. As Regan and other animal liberationists have pointed out, the arguments for ascribing at least some moral rights to sentient nonhuman animals are very similar to the arguments for ascribing those same rights to sentient human beings. If we argue that human beings have rights not to be tortured, starved or confined under inhumane conditions, it is usually by appealing to our knowledge that they will suffer in much the same ways that we would under like circumstances. A child must learn that other persons (and animals) can experience, for example, pain, fear or anger, on the one hand; pleasure or satisfaction, on the other, in order to even begin to comprehend why some ways of behaving towards them are morally preferable to others.

If these facts are morally significant in the case of human beings, it is attractive to suppose that they should have similar significance in the case of animals. Everything that we know about the behaviour, biology and neurophysiology of, for instance, nonhuman mammals, indicates that they are capable of experiencing the same basic types of physical suffering and discomfort as we are, and it is reasonable to suppose that their pleasures are equally real and approximately as various. Doubts about the sentience of other animals are no more plausible than doubts about that of other human beings. True, most animals cannot use human language to *report* that they are in pain, but the vocalizations and "body language" through which they *express* pain, and many other psychological states, are similar enough to our own that their significance is generally clear.

But to say this is not yet to establish that animals have moral rights. We need a connecting link between the premise that certain ways of treating animals cause them to suffer, and the conclusion that such actions are *prima facie* morally wrong, that is, wrong unless proven otherwise. One way to make this connection is to hold that it is a *self-evident truth* that the unnecessary infliction of suffering upon any sentient being is wrong. Those who doubt this claim may be accused (perhaps with some justice) of lacking empathy, the ability to "feel with" other sentient beings, to comprehend the reality of their experience. It may be held that it is possible to regard the suffering of animals as morally insignificant only to the extent that one suffers from blindness to "the *ontology* of animal reality," that is, from a failure to grasp the fact that they are centres of conscious experience, as we are.

This argument is inadequate, however, since there may be those who fully comprehend the fact that animals are sentient beings, but who still deny that their pains and pleasures have any direct moral significance. For them, a more persuasive consideration may be that our moral reasoning will gain in clarity and coherence if we recognize that the suffering of a nonhuman being is an evil of the same general sort as that of a human being. For if we do not recognize that suffering is an intrinsic evil, something which ought not to be inflicted deliberately without just cause, then we will not be able to fully understand why treating *human beings* in certain ways is immoral.

Torturing human beings, for example, is not wrong merely because it is illegal (where it is illegal), or merely because it violates some implicit agreement amongst human beings (though it may). Such legalistic or contractualistic reasons leave us in the dark as to why we *ought* to have, and enforce, laws and agreements against torture. The essential reason for regarding torture as wrong is that it *hurts,* and that people greatly prefer to avoid such pain—as do animals. I am not arguing, as does Kant, that cruelty to animals is wrong because it causes cruelty to human beings, a position which con-sequentialists often endorse. The point, rather, is that unless we view the deliberate infliction of needless pain as inherently wrong we will not be able to understand the moral objection to cruelty of *either* kind.

It seems we must conclude, therefore, that sentient nonhuman animals have cer-tain basic moral rights, rights which they share with all beings that are psychologically organized around the pleasure/pain axis. Their capacity for pain gives them the right that pain not be intentionally and needlessly inflicted upon them. Their capacity for pleasure gives them the right not to be prevented from pursuing whatever pleasures and fulfillments are natural to creatures of their kind. Like human rights, the rights of animals may be overridden if there is a morally sufficient reason for doing so. What *counts* as a morally significant reason, however, may be different in the two cases.

II. HUMAN AND ANIMAL RIGHTS COMPARED

There are two dimensions in which we may find differences between the rights of human beings and those of animals. The first involves the *content* of those rights, while the second involves their strength; that is, the strength of the reasons which are required to override them.

Consider, for instance, the right to liberty. The *human* right to liberty precludes imprisonment without due process of law, even if the prison is spacious and the con-ditions of confinement cause no obvious physical suffering. But it is not so obviously wrong to imprison animals, especially when the area to which they are confined pro-vides a fair approximation of the conditions of their natural habitat, and a reasonable opportunity to pursue the satisfactions natural to their kind. Such conditions, which often result in an increased lifespan, and which may exist in wildlife sanctuaries or even well-designed zoos, need not frustrate the needs or interests of animals in any signifi-cant way, and thus do not clearly violate their rights. Similarly treated human beings, on the other hand (e.g., native peoples confined to prison-like reservations), do tend to suffer from their loss of freedom. Human dignity and the fulfillment of the sorts of plans, hopes and desires which appear (thus far) to be uniquely human, require a more extensive freedom of movement than is the case with at least many nonhuman animals. Furthermore, there are aspects of human freedom, such as freedom of thought, free-dom of speech and freedom of political association, which simply do not apply in the case of animals.

Thus, it seems that the human right to freedom is more extensive; that is, it pre-cludes a wider range of specific ways of treating human beings than does the corresponding right on the part of animals. The argument cuts both ways, of course. *Some* animals, for example, great whales and migratory birds, may require at least as much physical freedom as do human beings if they are to pursue the satisfactions natural to their kind, and this fact provides a moral argument against keeping such creatures impris-oned. And even chickens may suffer from the extreme and unnatural confinement to which they are subjected on modern "factory farms." Yet it seems unnecessary to claim for *most* animals a right to a freedom quite as broad as that which we claim for ourselves.

Similar points may be made with respect to the right to life. Animals, it may be argued, lack the cognitive equipment to value their lives in the way that human beings do. Ruth Cigman argues that animals have *no* right to life because death is no misfortune for them. In her view, the death of an animal is not a misfortune, because animals have no desires which are *categorical;* that is which do not "merely presuppose being alive (like the desire to eat when one is hungry), but rather answer the question whether one wants to remain alive." In other words, animals appear to lack the sorts of long-range hopes, plans, ambitions and the like, which give human beings such a powerful interest in continued life. Animals, it seems, take life as it comes and do not specifically desire that it go on. True, squirrels store nuts for the winter and deer run from wolves; but these may be seen as instinctive or conditioned responses to present circumstances, rather than evidence that they value life as such.

These reflections probably help to explain why the death of a sparrow seems less tragic than that of a human being. Human lives, one might say, have greater intrinsic value, because they are worth more *to their possessors.* But this does not demonstrate that no nonhuman animal has *any* right to life. Premature death may be a less *severe* misfortune for sentient nonhuman animals than for human beings, but it is a misfortune nevertheless. In the first place, it is a misfortune in that it deprives them of whatever pleasures the future might have held for them, regardless of whether or not they ever *consciously anticipated* those pleasures. The fact that they are not here afterwards, to *experience* their loss, no more shows that they have not lost anything than it does in the case of humans. In the second place, it is (possibly) a misfortune in that it frustrates whatever future-oriented desires animals *may* have, unbeknownst to us. Even now, in an age in which apes have been taught to use simplified human languages and attempts have been made to communicate with dolphins and whales, we still know very little about the operation of nonhuman minds. We know much too little to assume that nonhuman animals never consciously pursue relatively distant future goals. To the extent that they do, the question of whether such desires provide them with *reasons for living* or merely *presuppose* continued life, has no satisfactory answer, since they cannot contemplate these alternative—or, if they can, we have no way of knowing what their conclusions are. All we know is that the more intelligent and psychologically complex an animal is, the more *likely* it is that it possesses specifically future-oriented desires, which would be frustrated even by *painless* death.

For these reasons, it is premature to conclude from the apparent intellectual inferiority of nonhuman animals that they have no right to life. A more plausible conclusion is that animals do have a right to life but that it is generally somewhat weaker than that of human beings. It is, perhaps, weak enough to enable us to justify killing animals when we have no other ways of achieving such vital goals as feeding or clothing ourselves, or obtaining knowledge which is necessary to save human lives. Weakening their right to life in this way does not render meaningless the assertion that they have such a right. For the point remains that *some* serious justification for the killing of sentient nonhuman animals is always necessary; they may not be killed merely to provide amusement or minor gains in convenience.

If animals' rights to liberty and life are somewhat weaker than those of human beings, may we say the same about their right to *happiness;* that is, their right not to be made to suffer needlessly or to be deprived of the pleasures natural to their kind? If so, it is not immediately clear why. There is little reason to suppose that pain or suffering are any less unpleasant for the higher animals (at least) than they are for us. Our large brains *may* cause us to experience pain more intensely than do most animals, and *probably* cause us to suffer more from the anticipation or remembrance of pain. These facts might tend to suggest that pain is, on the whole, a worse experience for us than for them. But it may also be argued that pain may be *worse* in some respects for non-human animals, who are presumably less able to distract themselves from it by thinking of something else, or to comfort themselves with the knowledge that it is temporary. Brigid Brophy points out that "pain is likely to fill the sheep's whole capacity for experience in a way it seldom does in us, whose intellect and imagination can create breaks for us in the immediacy of our sensations."

The net result of such contrasting considerations is that we cannot possibly claim to know whether pain is, on the whole, worse for us than for animals, or whether their pleasures are any more or any less intense than ours. Thus, while we may justify assigning them a somewhat weaker right to life or liberty, on the grounds that they desire these goods less intensely than we do, we cannot discount their rights to freedom from needlessly inflicted pain or unnatural frustration on the same basis. There may, however, be *other* reasons for regarding all of the moral rights of animals as somewhat less stringent than the corresponding human rights.

A number of philosophers who deny that animals have moral rights point to the fact that nonhuman animals evidently lack the capacity for moral autonomy. Moral autonomy is the ability to act as a moral agent; that is, to act on the basis of an understanding of, and adherence to, moral rules or principles. H.J. McCloskey, for example, holds that "it is the capacity for moral autonomy . . . that is basic to the possibility of possessing a right." McCloskey argues that it is inappropriate to ascribe moral rights to any entity which is not a moral agent, or *potentially* a moral agent, because a right is essentially an entitlement granted to a moral agent, licensing him or her to *act* in certain ways and to *demand* that other moral agents refrain from interference. For this reason, he says, "Where there is no possibility of [morally autonomous] action, potentially or actually . . . and where the being is not a member of a kind which is normally capable of [such] action, we withhold talk of rights."

If moral autonomy—or being *potentially* autonomous, or a member of a kind which is *normally* capable of autonomy—is a necessary condition for having moral rights, then probably no nonhuman animal can qualify. For moral autonomy requires such probably uniquely human traits as "the capacity to be critically self-aware, manipulate concepts, use a sophisticated language, reflect, plan, deliberate, choose, and accept responsibility for acting."

But why, we must ask, should the capacity for autonomy be regarded as a precondition for possessing moral rights? Autonomy is clearly crucial for the *exercise* of many human moral or legal rights, such as the right to vote or to run for public office. It is less clearly relevant, however, to the more basic human rights, such as the right to life or to freedom from unnecessary suffering. The fact that animals, like many human beings, cannot *demand* their moral rights (at least not in the words of any conventional human language) seems irrelevant. For, as Joel Feinberg points out, the interests of non-morally autonomous human beings may be defended by others, for example, in legal proceedings; and it is not clear why the interests of animals might not be represented in a similar fashion.

It is implausible, therefore, to conclude that because animals lack moral autonomy they should be accorded *no moral rights whatsoever.* Nevertheless, it may be argued that the moral autonomy of (most) human beings provides a second reason, in addition to their more extensive interests and desires, for according somewhat *stronger* moral rights to human beings. The fundamental insight behind contractualist theories of morality is that, for morally autonomous beings such as ourselves, there is enormous mutual advantage in the adoption of a moral system designed to protect each of us from the harms that might otherwise be visited upon us by others. Each of us ought to accept and promote such a system because, to the extent that others also accept it, we will all be safer from attack by our fellows, more likely to receive assistance when we need it, and freer to engage in individual as well as cooperative endeavours of all kinds.

Thus, it is the possibility of *reciprocity* which motivates moral agents to extend *full* and *equal* moral rights, in the first instance, only to other moral agents. I respect your rights to life, liberty and the pursuit of happiness in part because you are a sentient being, whose interests have intrinsic moral significance. But I respect them as *fully equal to my own* because I hope and expect that you will do the same for me. Animals, insofar as they lack the degree of rationality necessary for moral autonomy, cannot agree to respect our interests as equal in moral importance to their own, and neither do they expect or demand such respect from us. Of course, domestic animals may expect to be fed, etc. But they do not, and cannot, expect to be treated as moral equals, for they do not understand that moral concept or what it implies. Consequently, it is neither pragmatically feasible nor morally obligatory to extend to them the same *full and equal* rights which we extend to human beings.

Is this a speciesist conclusion? Defenders of a more extreme animal-rights position may point out that this argument, from the lack of moral autonomy, has exactly the same form as that which has been used for thousands of years to rationalize denying equal moral rights to women and members of "inferior" races. Aristotle, for example, argued that women and slaves are naturally subordinate beings, because they lack the capacity for moral autonomy and self-direction; and contemporary versions of this argument, used to support racist or sexist conclusions, are easy to find. Are we simply repeating Aristotle's mistake, in a different context?

The reply to this objection is very simple: animals, unlike women and slaves, really *are* incapable of moral autonomy, at least to the best of our knowledge. Aristotle certainly *ought* to have known that women and slaves are capable of morally autonomous action; their capacity to use moral language alone ought to have alerted him to this likelihood. If comparable evidence exists that (some) nonhuman animals are moral agents we have not yet found it. The fact that some apes (and, possibly, some *cetaceans*) are capable of learning radically simplified human languages, the terms of which refer primarily to objects and events in their immediate environment, in no way demonstrates that they can understand abstract moral concepts, rules or principles, or use this understanding to regulate their own behaviour.

On the other hand, this argument implies that if we *do* discover that certain nonhuman animals are capable of moral autonomy (which is certainly not impossible), then we ought to extend full and equal moral rights to those animals. Furthermore, if we someday encounter extraterrestrial beings, or build robots, *androids* or supercomputers which function as self-aware moral agents, then we must extend full and equal moral rights to these as well. Being a member of the human species is not a necessary condition for the possession of full "human" rights. Whether it is nevertheless a *sufficient* condition is the question to which we now turn.

III. THE MORAL RIGHTS OF NONPARADIGM HUMANS

If we are justified in ascribing somewhat different, and also somewhat stronger, moral rights to human beings than to sentient but non-morally autonomous animals, then what are we to say of the rights of human beings who happen not to be capable of moral autonomy, perhaps not even potentially? Both Singer and Regan have argued that if any of the superior intellectual capacities of normal and mature human beings are used to support a distinction between the moral status of *typical,* or paradigm, human beings, and that of animals, then consistency will require us to place certain "nonparadigm" humans, such as infants, small children and the severely retarded or incurably brain damaged, in the same inferior moral category. Such a result is, of course, highly counterintuitive.

Fortunately, no such conclusion follows from the autonomy argument. There are many reasons for extending strong moral rights to nonparadigm humans; reasons which do not apply to most nonhuman animals. Infants and small children are granted strong moral rights in part because of their *potential* autonomy. But *potential* autonomy, as I have argued elsewhere, is not in itself a sufficient reason for the ascription of full moral rights; if it were, then not only human foetuses (from conception onwards) but even ununited human sperm-egg pairs would have to be regarded as entities with a right to life the equivalent of our own—thus making not only abortion, but any intentional failure to procreate, the moral equivalent of murder. Those who do not find this extreme conclusion acceptable must appeal to reasons other than the *potential* moral autonomy of infants and small children to explain the strength of the latter's moral rights.

One reason for assigning strong moral rights to infants and children is that they possess not just *potential* but *partial* autonomy, and it is not clear how much of it they have at any given moment. The fact that, unlike baby chimpanzees, they are already learning the things which will enable them to *become* morally autonomous, makes it likely that their minds have more subtleties than their speech (or the lack of it) proclaims. Another reason is simply that most of us tend to place a very high value on the lives and well-being of infants. Perhaps we are to some degree "programmed" by nature to love and protect them; perhaps our reasons are somewhat egocentric; or perhaps we value them for their potential. Whatever the explanation, the fact that we do feel this way about them is in itself a valid reason for extending to them stronger moral and legal protections than we extend to nonhuman animals, even those which may have just as well or better-developed psychological capacities. A third, and perhaps the most important, reason is that if we did *not* extend strong moral rights to infants, far too few of them would ever *become* responsible, morally autonomous adults; too many would be treated "like animals" (i.e., in ways that it is generally wrong to treat even animals), and would consequently become socially crippled, antisocial or just very unhappy people. If any part of our moral code is to remain intact, it seems that infants and small children *must* be protected and cared for.

Analogous arguments explain why strong moral rights should also be accorded to other nonparadigm humans. The severely retarded or incurably senile, for instance, may have no potential for moral autonomy, but there are apt to be friends, relatives or other people who care what happens to them. Like children, such individuals may have more mental capacities than are readily apparent. Like children, they are more apt to achieve, or return to moral autonomy if they are valued and well cared for. Furthermore, any one of us may someday become mentally incapacitated to one degree or another, and we would all have reason to be anxious about our own futures if such incapacitation were made the basis for denying strong moral rights.

There are, then, sound reasons for assigning strong moral rights even to human beings who lack the mental capacities which justify the general distinction between human and animal rights. Their rights are based not only on the value which they themselves place upon their lives and well-being, but also on the value which other human beings place upon them.

But is this a valid basis for the assignment of moral rights? Is it consistent with the definition presented earlier, according to which X may be said to have a moral right to Y only if depriving X of Y is *prima facie* wrong *because of the harm done to the interests of X,* and not merely because of any further consequences? Regan argues that we cannot justify the ascription of stronger rights to nonparadigm humans than to nonhuman animals in the way suggested, because "what underlies the ascription of rights to any given X is that X has value independently of anyone's valuing X." After all, we do not speak of expensive paintings or gemstones as having rights, although many people value them and have good reasons for wanting them protected.

There is, however, a crucial difference between a rare painting and a severely retarded or senile human being; the latter not only has (or may have) value for other human beings but *also* has his or her own needs and interests. It may be this which leads us to say that such individuals have intrinsic value. The sentience of nonparadigm humans, like that of sentient nonhuman animals, gives them a place in the sphere of rights holders. So long as the moral rights of all sentient beings are given due recognition, there should be no objection to providing some of them with *additional* protections, on the basis of our interests as well as their own. Some philosophers speak of such additional protections, which are accorded to X on the basis of interests other than X's own, as *conferred* rights, in contrast to *natural* rights, which are entirely based upon the properties of X itself. But such "conferred" rights are not necessarily any weaker or less binding upon moral agents than are "natural" rights. Infants, and most other nonparadigm humans have the *same* basic moral rights that the rest of us do, even though the reasons for ascribing those rights are somewhat different in the two cases.

IV. OTHER OBJECTIONS TO ANIMAL RIGHTS

We have already dealt with the primary objection to assigning *any* moral rights to nonhuman animals; that is, that they lack moral autonomy, and various other psychological capacities which paradigm humans possess. We have also answered the animal liberationists' primary objection to assigning somewhat *weaker,* or less-extensive rights to animals; that is, that this will force us to assign similarly inferior rights to nonparadigm humans. There are two other objections to animal rights which need to be considered. The first is that the claim that animals have a right to life, or other moral rights, has absurd consequences with respect to the natural relationships *among* animals. The second is that to accord rights to animals on the basis of their (differing degrees of) sentience will introduce intolerable difficulties and complexities into our moral reasoning.

Opponents of animal rights often accuse the animal liberationists of ignoring the realities of nature, in which many animals survive only by killing others. Callicott, for example, maintains that whereas environmentally aware persons realize that natural predators are a vital part of the biotic community, those who believe that animals have a right to life are forced to regard all predators as "merciless, wanton, and incorrigible murderers of their fellow creatures." Similarly, Ritchie asks whether, if animals have rights, we are not morally obligated to "protect the weak among them against the strong? Must we not put to death blackbirds and thrushes because they feed on worms, or (if capital punishment offends our humanitarianism) starve them slowly by permanent captivity and vegetarian diet?"

Such a conclusion would of course be ridiculous, as well as wholly inconsistent with the environmental ethic. However, nothing of the sort follows from the claim that animals have moral rights. There are two independently sufficient reasons why it does not. In the first place, nonhuman predators are not moral agents, so it is absurd to think of them as wicked, or as *murdering* their prey. But this is not the most important point. Even if wolves and the like *were* moral agents, their predation would still be morally acceptable, given that they generally kill only to feed themselves, and generally do so without inflicting prolonged or unnecessary suffering. If we have the right to eat animals, in order to avoid starvation, then why shouldn't animals have the right to eat one another, for the same reason?

This conclusion is fully consistent with the lesson taught by the ecologists, that natural predation is essential to the stability of biological communities. Deer need wolves, or other predators, as much as the latter need them; without predation they become too numerous and fall victim to hunger and disease, while their overgrazing damages the entire ecosystem. Too often we have learned (or failed to learn) this lesson the hard way, as when the killing of hawks and other predators produces exploding rodent populations—which must be controlled, often in ways which cause further ecological damage. The control of natural predators may *sometimes* be necessary, for example, when human pressures upon the populations of certain species become so intense that the latter cannot endure continued *natural* predation. (The controversial case of the wolves and caribou in Alaska and Canada may or may not be one of this sort.) But even in such cases it is preferable, from an environmentalist perspective, to reduce human predation enough to leave room for natural predators as well.

Another objection to assigning moral rights to sentient nonhuman animals is that it will not only complicate our own moral system, but introduce seemingly insoluble dilemmas. As Ritchie points out, "Very difficult questions of casuistry will . . . arise because of the difference in grades of sentience." For instance, is it morally worse to kill and eat a dozen oysters (which are at most minimally sentient) or one (much more highly sentient) rabbit? Questions of this kind, considered in isolation from any of the practical circumstances in which they might arise, are virtually unanswerable. But this ought not to surprise us, since similarly abstract questions about the treatment of human beings are often equally unanswerable. (For instance, would it be worse to kill one child or to cause a hundred to suffer from severe malnutrition?)

The reason such questions are so difficult to answer is not just that we lack the skill and knowledge to make such precise comparisons of interpersonal or interspecies utility, but also that these questions are posed in entirely unrealistic terms. Real moral choices rarely depend entirely upon the comparison of two abstract quantities of pain or pleasure deprivation. In deciding whether to eat *molluscs* or mammals (or neither or both) a human society must consider *all* of the predictable consequences of each option, for example, their respective impacts on the *ecology* or the economy, and not merely the individual interests of the animals involved.

Of course, other things being equal, it would be morally preferable to refrain from killing *any* sentient animal. But other things are never equal. Questions about human diet involve not only the rights of individual animals, but also vital environmental and human concerns. On the one hand, as Singer points out, more people could be better fed if food suitable for human consumption were not fed to meat-producing animals. On the other hand, a mass conversion of humanity to vegetarianism would represent "an increase in the efficiency of the conversion of solar energy from plant to human biomass," with the likely result that the human population would continue to expand and, in the process, to cause greater environmental destruction than might occur otherwise. The issue is an enormously complex one, and cannot be solved by any simple appeal to the claim that animals have (or lack) certain moral rights.

In short, the ascription of moral rights to animals does not have the absurd or environmentally damaging consequences that some philosophers have feared. It does not require us to exterminate predatory species, or to lose ourselves in abstruse speculations about the relative degrees of sentience of different sorts of animals. It merely requires us to recognize the interests of animals as having intrinsic moral significance; as demanding some consideration, regardless of whether or not human or environmental concerns are also involved. We must now consider the question of how well the animal rights theory meshes with the environmental ethic, which treats not only animals but plants, rivers and other nonsentient elements of nature as entities which may demand moral consideration.

V. ANIMAL LIBERATION AND THE LAND ETHIC

The fundamental message of Leopold's land ethic, and of the environmentalist movement in general, is that the terrestrial biosphere is an integrated whole, and that humanity is a part of that natural order, wholly dependent upon it and morally responsible for maintaining its integrity. Because of the wholistic nature of biotic systems, it is impossible to determine the value of an organism simply by considering its individual moral rights: we must also consider its relationship to other parts of the system. For this reason, some philosophers have concluded that the theoretical foundations of the environmentalist and animal liberation movements are mutually contradictory. Alastair Gunn states: "Environmentalism seems incompatible with the Western obsession with individualism, which leads us to resolve questions about our treatment of animals by appealing to the essentially atomistic, competitive notion of rights."

As an example of the apparent clash between the land ethic and the ascription of rights to animals, Gunn points to the situation on certain islands off the coast of New Zealand, where feral goats, pigs and cats have had to be exterminated in order to protect indigenous species and habitats, which were threatened by the introduced species. "Considered purely in terms of rights," he says, "it is hard to see how this could be justified. [For,] if the goats, etc., are held to have rights, then we are violating these rights in order perhaps to save or increase a rare species."

I maintain, on the contrary, that the appearance of fundamental contradiction between the land ethic and the claim that sentient nonhuman animals have moral rights is illusory. If we were to hold that the rights of animals are *identical to those of human beings,* then we would indeed be forced to conclude that it is wrong to eliminate harmful introduced species for the good of the indigenous ones or of the ecosystem as a whole—just as wrong as it would be to exterminate all of the human inhabitants of North America who are immigrants, however greatly this might benefit the native Americans and the natural ecology. There is no inconsistency, however, in the view that animals have a significant right to life, but one which is somewhat more easily overridden by certain kinds of utilitarian or environmental considerations than is the human right to life. On this view, it is wrong to kill animals for trivial reasons, but not wrong to do so when there is no other way of achieving a vital goal, such as the preservation of threatened species.

Another apparent point of inconsistency between the land ethic and the animal liberation movement involves the issue of whether sentience is a *necessary,* as well as *sufficient,* condition for the possession of moral rights. Animal liberationists sometimes maintain that it is, and that consequently plants, rivers, mountains and other elements of nature which are not themselves sentient (though they may *contain* sentient life forms) cannot have moral rights. Environmentalists, on the other hand, sometimes argue for the ascription of moral rights to even the nonsentient elements of the biosphere. Does this difference represent a genuine contradiction between the two approaches?

One argument that it does not is that the fact that a particular entity is not accorded moral rights does not imply that there are no sound reasons for protecting it from harm. Human health and survival alone requires that we place a high value on clean air, unpolluted land, water and crops, and on the maintenance of stable and diverse natural ecosystems. Furthermore, there are vital scientific, spiritual, aesthetic and recreational values associated with the conservation of the natural world, values which cannot be dismissed as luxuries which benefit only the affluent portion of humanity. Once we realize how *valuable* nature is, it may seem immaterial whether or not we also wish to speak of its nonsentient elements as possessing moral *rights.*

But there is a deeper issue here than the precise definition of the term "moral rights." The issue is whether trees, rivers and the like ought to be protected *only* because of their value to us (and to other sentient animals), or whether they also have *intrinsic* value. That is, are they to be valued and protected because of what they are, or only because of what they are good for? Most environmentalists think that the natural world is intrinsically valuable, and that it is therefore wrong to wantonly destroy forests, streams, marshes and so on, even where doing so is not *obviously* inconsistent with the welfare of human beings. It is this conviction which finds expression in the claim that even nonsentient elements of nature have moral rights. Critics of the environmental movement, on the other hand, often insist that the value of the nonhuman world is purely instrumental, and that it is only sentimentalists who hold otherwise.

John Passmore, for instance, deplores "the cry . . . for a new morality, a new religion, which would transform man's attitude to nature, which would lead us to believe that it is *intrinsically* wrong to destroy a species, cut down a tree, clear a wilderness." Passmore refers to such a call for a nonhomocentric morality as "mystical rubbish." In his view, nothing in the nonhuman world has *either* intrinsic value or moral rights. He would evidently agree with William F. Baxter, who says that "damage to penguins, or to sugar pines, or geological marvels is, without more, simply irrelevant. . . . Penguins are important [only] because people enjoy seeing them walk about the rocks."

This strictly instrumentalist view of the value of the nonhuman world is rejected by animal liberationists and environmentalists alike. The animal liberationists maintain that the sentience of many nonhuman animals constitutes a sufficient reason for regarding their needs and interests as worthy of our moral concern, and for assigning them certain moral rights. Sentience is, in this sense, a sufficient condition for the possession of intrinsic value. It does not follow from this that it is also a *necessary* condition for having intrinsic value. It may be a necessary condition for having individual moral *rights;* certainly it is necessary for *some* rights, such as the right not to be subjected to unnecessary pain. But there is room to argue that even though mountains and trees are not subject to pleasure or pain, and hence do not have rights of the sort we ascribe to sentient beings, nevertheless they have intrinsic value of another sort, or for another reason.

What sort of intrinsic value might they have? The environmentalists' answer is that they are valuable as organic parts of the natural whole. But this answer is incomplete, in that it does not explain why we ought to value the natural world *as a whole,* except insofar as it serves our own interests to do so. No clear and persuasive answer to this more basic question has yet been given. Perhaps, as Thomas Auxter has suggested, the answer is to be found in a teleological ethic of the same general sort of that of Plato or Aristotle, an ethic which urges us "to seek the highest good, which is generally understood as the most perfect or complete state of affairs possible." This most perfect or complete state of affairs would include "a natural order which encompasses the most developed and diverse types of beings," one in which "every species finds a place . . . and . . . the existence and functioning of any one species is not a threat to the existence and functioning of any other species."

It is not my purpose to endorse this or any other philosophical explanation of why even the nonsentient elements of nature should be regarded as having intrinsic value. I want only to suggest that better answers to this question can and should be developed, and that there is no reason to presume that these answers will consist entirely of "mystical rubbish." Furthermore, I would suggest that the claim that mountains and forests have intrinsic value of *some* sort is intuitively much more plausible than its denial.

One way to test your own intuitions, or unformulated convictions, about this claim is to consider a hypothetical case of the following sort. Suppose that a virulent virus, developed by some unwise researcher, has escaped into the environment and will inevitably extinguish all animal life (ourselves included) within a few weeks. Suppose further that this or some other scientist has developed another virus which, if released, would destroy all plant life as well, but more slowly, such that the effects of the second virus would not be felt until after the last animal was gone. If the second virus were released *secretly,* its release would do no further damage to the well-being of any sentient creature; no one would suffer, even from the knowledge that the plant kingdom is as doomed as we are. Finally, suppose that it is known with certainty that sentient life forms would never re-evolve on the earth (this time from plants), and that no sentient aliens will ever visit the planet. The question is would it be morally preferable, in such a case, *not* to release the second virus, even secretly? If we tend to think that it would be, that it would certainly be better to allow the plants to survive us than to render the earth utterly lifeless (except perhaps for the viruses), then we do not really believe that it is only sentient—let alone only human—beings which have intrinsic value.

This being the case, it is relatively unimportant whether we say that even nonsentient natural entities may have moral *rights,* or whether we say only that, because of their intrinsic value, they ought to be protected, even at some cost to certain human interests. Nevertheless, there is an argument for preferring the latter way of speaking. It is that nonsentient entities, not being subject to pleasure or pain, and lacking any preferences with respect to what happens to them, cannot sensibly be said to have *interests.* The Gulf Stream or the south wind may have value because of their role in the natural order, but if they were to be somehow altered or destroyed, *they* would not experience suffering, or lose anything which it is in *their* interest to have. Thus, "harming" them would not be wrong *in and of itself,* but rather because of the kinds of environmental efforts which the land ethic stresses. In contrast, harm done to a sentient being has moral significance even if it has no further consequences whatsoever.

The position at which we have arrived represents a compromise between those animal liberationists who hold that only sentient beings have *either* intrinsic value or moral rights, and those environmentalists who ascribe *both* intrinsic value and moral rights to even the nonsentient elements of nature. Mountains and trees should be protected not because they have moral rights, but because they are intrinsically—as well as instrumentally—valuable.

So stated, the land ethic is fully compatible with the claim that individual sentient animals have moral rights. Indeed, the two positions are complementary; each helps to remedy some of the apparent defects of the other. The animal liberation theory, for instance, does not in itself explain why we ought to protect not only *individual* animals, but also threatened *species* of plants as well as animals. The land ethic, on the other hand, fails to explain why it is wrong to inflict needless suffering or death even upon domestic animals, which may play little or no role in the maintenance of natural ecosystems, or only a negative role. Practices such as rearing animals in conditions of severe confinement and discomfort, or subjecting them to painful experiments which have no *significant* scientific purpose, are wrong primarily because of the suffering inflicted upon individual sentient beings, and only secondarily because of any social or environmental damage they may incidentally cause.

Thus, it is clear that as we learn to extend our moral concern beyond the boundaries of our own species we shall have to take account of both the rights of individual animals *and* the value of those elements of the natural world which are not themselves sentient. Respecting the interests of creatures who, like ourselves, are subject to pleasure and pain is in no way inconsistent with valuing and protecting the richness, diversity and stability of natural ecosystems. In many cases, such as the commercial slaughter of whales, there are both environmental and humane reasons for altering current practices. In other cases, in which humane and environmental considerations appear to point in opposite directions (e.g., the case of the feral goats on the New Zealand islands) these factors must be weighed against each other, much as the rights of individual human beings must often be weighed against larger social needs. In no case does a concern for the environment preclude *also* considering the rights of individual animals; it may, for instance, be possible to trap and deport the goats alive, rather than killing them.

VI. SUMMARY AND CONCLUSION

I have argued that the environmentalist and animal liberationist perspectives are complementary, rather than essentially competitive or mutually inconsistent approaches towards a nonhomocentric moral theory. The claim that animals have certain moral rights, by virtue of their sentience, does not negate the fact that ecosystems are complexly unified wholes, in which one element generally cannot be damaged without causing repercussions elsewhere in the system. If sentience is a necessary, as well as sufficient, condition for having moral rights, then we cannot ascribe such rights to oceans, mountains and the like; yet we have a moral obligation to protect such natural resources from excessive damage at human hands, both because of their value to us and to future generations, and because they are intrinsically valuable, as elements of the planetary biosystem. It is not necessary to choose between regarding biological communities as unified systems, analogous to organisms, and regarding them as containing many individual sentient creatures, each with its own separate needs and interests; for it is clearly both of these things at once. Only by *combining* the environmentalist and animal rights perspectives can we take account of the full range of moral considerations which ought to guide our interactions with the nonhuman world.

18

⋈ *A Biocentrist Strikes Back* ⋈

JAMES P. STERBA*

James P. Sterba is Professor of Philosophy at the University of Notre Dame. His many books include Morality in Practice, *6th edition,* Feminist Philosophies, *2nd edition,* Justice for Here and Now, *and* Three Challenges to Ethics: Environmentalism, Feminism and Multiculturalism.

I

It is difficult to be a supporter of biocentrism these days with all the criticism that has come its way. First of all, biocentrists are criticized for failing to state their view in such a way that it is not biased in favor of the human species.[1] Second, they are criticized for following Aldo Leopold and basing their view on an ecology that regards ecosystems as tending toward stability and harmony—an ecology that is now widely challenged.[2] Third, biocentrists are criticized for failing to reasonably distinguish the life they claim has intrinsic value from the animate and inanimate things they claim lack intrinsic value.[3] Accordingly, one might think that it would be best, as critics have urged, to abandon biocentrism altogether in favor of a hierarchical or anthropocentric view. In this paper, however, I show that biocentrism can be defended against these three criticisms and, therefore, need not be abandoned. Specifically, I do so by developing a set of environmental principles that (1) are clearly not biased in favor of human

* The author thanks William Aiken, Michael DePaul, Robert Goodland, Dale Jamieson, Val Plumwood, Ernest Partridge, Kenneth Sayre, Laura Westra, and the anonymous reviewers of *Environmental Ethics*, Sara Ebenreck, and Scott Lehmann, for their comments on earlier versions of this paper.

species, (2) can adjust to changes in ecological science and (3) can reasonably distinguish what has intrinsic value from what doesn't. If I am right that biocentrists can adequately defend themselves against their critics, then the ethical demands of life will appear to be much stronger than many environmental philosophers have thought.

According to their critics, biocentrists talk a lot about the equality of species, but when they turn to the practical applications of their view, time and time again, they show their bias in favor of the human species. For example, Arne Naess defends a form of biocentrism that is committed to biospherical egalitarianism—"the equal right of [all living things] to live and bloom."[4] Yet when Naess gets around to discussing the practical applications of his view, he says that biospherical egalitarianism only holds in principle, and he rejects any interpretation of his view suggesting that "human needs should never have priority over non-human needs."[5] Critics see this rejection as indicative of the attempt by biocentrists to have their cake and literally eat it too.

Similarly, Paul Taylor endorses a biocentric outlook on nature with a principle of species impartiality according to which

> . . . every species counts as having the same value in the sense that, regardless of what species a living thing belongs to, it is deemed to be prima facie deserving of equal concern and consideration on the part of moral agents. . . . Species-impartiality . . . means regarding every entity that has a good of its own [humans, animals and plants] as possessing inherent worth—the same inherent worth, since none is superior to another.[6]

Nevertheless, when Taylor gets around to discussing the practical applications of his view, he allows that we can aggress against the basic interests of (wild) animals and plants even to meet nonbasic human needs provided that it is compatible with the attitude of respect for nature and provided that no alternative way of pursuing those nonbasic human needs would involve fewer wrongs.[7] What is difficult to comprehend here is how aggression against the basic needs of nonhumans for the sake of meeting the nonbasic needs of humans can be compatible with the equality of species. The critics of biocentrism claim that it can't.

In earlier work, I too tried to defend biocentrism, particularly, a revision of Taylor's view, against this criticism, but I now think that my defense was wanting, in part, because the environmental principles I proposed were not general enough.[8] As formulated, my principles still made reference to humans. They were not stated in a species-neutral way, and so at least gave the impression of being biased in favor of humans. I now think that I do better.

II

Biocentrists are well known for their commitment to the equality of species. Yet if this commitment is to be defensible, I claim that it needs to be understood by analogy with the equality of humans. Accordingly, just as we claim that humans are equal, and yet justifiably treat them differently, so too we should be able to claim that all species are equal, yet justifiably treat them differently. In human ethics, there are various interpretations that we give to human equality that allow for different treatment of humans. In ethical egoism, everyone is *equally at liberty* to pursue his or her own interests, but in this pursuit we are allowed always to prefer ourselves to others, who are understood to be like opponents in a competitive game. In libertarianism, everyone has an *equal right to liberty;* yet, although this right imposes some limits on the pursuit of self-interest, it is said to allow us to refrain from helping others in severe need. In welfare liberalism, everyone has an *equal right to welfare and to opportunity,* but these rights need not commit us to providing everyone with exactly the same resources. In socialism, everyone has an *equal right to self-development,* and although this right may commit us to providing everyone with something like the same resources, it still sanctions some degree of self-preference. Thus, just as there are various ways to interpret human equality that still allow us to treat humans differently, there can be various justifiable ways to interpret species equality that still allow species to be treated differently.

One could interpret species equality in a very strong sense, analogous to the interpretation of equality found in socialism. However, the kind of species equality that I wish to defend is more akin to the equality found in welfare liberalism or in libertarianism than to the equality found in socialism with respect to the degree of preference that it allows for oneself and the members of one's own species.[9] I maintain that we can justify such preference, in part, on grounds of limited defense. Accordingly, I propose the following two principles, one concerning defense and one concerning nondefense, that apply to all agents who are capable of understanding and acting on them:

> The principle of defense that permits actions in defense of both basic and nonbasic needs against the aggression of others, even if it necessitates killing or harming those others, unless prohibited.[10]

> The principle of nondefense that prohibits defending nonbasic needs against the aggression of others that is undertaken as the only way to meet basic needs, if one can reasonably expect a comparable degree of altruistic forbearance from those others.

The principle of defense allows the members of a species to defend themselves and others from harmful aggression first against their persons and the persons of others to whom they are committed or happen to care about, and second against their justifiably held property and the justifiably held property of others to whom they are committed or happen to care about.

This principle is analogous to the principle of self-defense that applies in human ethics[11] and permits actions in defense of oneself or other human beings against harmful human aggression. In the case of human aggression, however, it is sometimes possible to effectively defend oneself and other human beings by first suffering the aggression and then securing adequate compensation later. Because in the case of nonhuman aggression by the members of other species with which we are familiar, such an approach is unlikely to work, justifying more harmful preventive actions such as killing a rabid dog or swatting a mosquito, potentially carrying disease. There are simply more ways to effectively stop aggressive humans than there are to effectively stop aggressive nonhumans.

Yet, there is a limit to the degree of defense that is justified. Defending nonbasic needs against the aggression of others that is undertaken as the only way to meet basic needs is prohibited if you can reasonably expect a comparable degree of altruistic forbearance from those others. In the case of human ethics, we can see how this type of aggression can be justified when the poor, who have exhausted all the other means that are legitimately available to them, take from the surplus possessions of the rich just what they need to meet their basic needs. Expressed in terms of an ideal of negative liberty endorsed by libertarians, the justification for this aggression is the priority of the liberty of the poor not to be interfered with when taking from the surplus possessions of the rich what they require to meet their basic needs over the liberty of the rich not to be interfered with when using their surplus for luxury purposes.[12] Expressed in terms of an ideal of fairness endorsed by welfare liberals, the justification for this aggression is the right to welfare that the needy have against those with a surplus. Expressed in terms of an ideal of equality endorsed by socialists, the justification for this aggression is the right that everyone has to equal self-development.

The principle of nondefense is simply a species-neutral generalization of this justification for aggression that is found in human ethics. The principle of defense and the principle of nondefense together, therefore, express the grounds of limited defense for preferring oneself and the members of one's own species over other species that is consistent with the equality of species.

A preference for oneself and the members of one's own species, however, can also be on grounds of preservation. Accordingly, we have the following two principles that apply to all agents who are capable of understanding and acting on them:

The principle of (aggression for) preservation that permits aggression when necessary against the basic needs of others for the sake of basic needs unless prohibited.

The principle of nonaggression that prohibits aggression against the basic needs of others either (1) to meet nonbasic needs or (2) even to meet basic needs if one can reasonably expect a comparable degree of altruistic forbearance from those others.

Needs, in general, if not satisfied, lead to lacks or deficiencies with respect to various standards. The basic needs of humans, if not satisfied, lead to lacks or deficiencies with respect to a standard of a decent life. The basic needs of animals and plants, if not satisfied, lead to lacks or deficiencies with respect to a standard of a healthy life.[13] The means necessary for meeting the basic needs of humans can vary widely from society to society. By contrast, the means necessary for meeting the basic needs of particular species of animals and plants are more invariant. Of course, while only some needs can be clearly classified as basic, and others are clearly classified as nonbasic, there still are other needs that are more difficult to classify. Yet, the fact that not every need can be clearly classified as either basic or nonbasic—as is true of a whole range of such dichotomous concepts as moral/immoral, legal/illegal, living/nonliving, human/nonhuman—should not immobilize us from acting at least with respect to clear cases.[14]

In human ethics, there is no principle that is strictly analogous to the principle of (aggression for) preservation. There is a principle of self-preservation in human ethics that permits actions that are necessary for meeting one's own basic needs or the basic needs of other people, even if these actions require failing to meet (through an act of omission) the basic needs of still other people. For example, we can use our resources to feed ourselves and our family, even if doing so necessitates failing to meet the basic needs of people in other countries. However, in general, we don't have a principle that allows us to aggress against (through an act of commission) the basic needs of some people in order to meet our own basic needs or the basic needs of other people to whom we are committed or happen to care about. Actually, the closest we come to permitting aggressing against the basic needs of other people in order to meet our own basic needs or the basic needs of people to whom we are committed or happen to care about is our acceptance of the outcome of life and death struggles in lifeboat cases, where no one has an antecedent right to the available resources. For example, if you had to fight off others in order to secure the last place in a lifeboat for yourself or for a member of your family, we might say that you justifiably aggressed against the basic needs of those whom you fought to meet your own basic needs or the basic needs of the member of your family.[15]

Nevertheless, survival requires a principle of preservation that permits aggressing against the basic needs of at least some other living things whenever doing so is necessary to meet one's own basic needs or the basic needs of others whom one happens to care about. Here there are two possibilities. The first is a principle of preservation that allows one to aggress against the basic needs of anyone to obtain basic needs. The second is the principle of preservation, given above, that allows one to aggress against the basic needs of others to fulfill basic needs, unless (when the principle of nonaggression applies) one can reasonably expect a comparable degree of altruistic forbearance from those others. The first principle does not place any limit on whom one can aggress against to satisfy basic needs, and thus it permits even cannibalism provided that it serves to meet basic needs. In contrast, the second principle (when the principle of nonaggression applies) does place a limit on whom one can aggress against to obtain basic needs by prohibiting aggression against those from whom one can reasonably expect a comparable degree of altruistic forbearance. Moreover, because those from whom one can reasonably expect a comparable degree of altruistic forbearance normally turn out to be members of one's own species, the principle of (aggression for) preservation together with its allied principle of nonaggression sanctions a certain preference for the members of one's own species.[16]

But is this degree of preference for the members of one's own species compatible with the equality of species? Of course, it is theoretically possible to interact with the members of one's own species on the basis of the first principle of preservation considered above—the one that permits even cannibalism as a means for meeting basic needs. In the case of humans, adopting such a principle would clearly reduce the degree of predation of humans on other species, and so would be of some benefit to other species. Yet, implicit nonaggression pacts based on a reasonable expectation of a comparable degree of altruistic forbearance from fellow humans have been enormously beneficial and probably were necessary for the survival of the human species. Thus, it is difficult to see how humans can be justifiably required to forgo such benefits.[17] Moreover, to require humans to extend these benefits to the members of all species would, in effect, be to require humans to be saints, and surely morality is not in the business of requiring anyone to be a saint. Given then that this greater altruism cannot be morally required, the degree of preference for the members of one's own species sanctioned by the principle of (aggression for) preservation together with its allied principle of nonaggression would be morally justified.[18]

Nevertheless, preference for the members of one's own species can go beyond bounds, and the bounds that are compatible with the equality of species are captured by the first requirement of the principle of nonaggression, which prohibits aggressing against basic needs for the sake of nonbasic needs.[19] This requirement is needed to give substance to the claim that the members of all species are equal. One can no more consistently claim that the members of all species are equal, yet aggress against the basic needs of the members of some species whenever doing so serves one's own nonbasic or luxury needs, or the nonbasic or luxury needs of others than we can consistently claim that all humans are equal, yet aggress against the basic needs of some humans whenever doing so serves our nonbasic or luxury needs or the nonbasic or luxury needs of other humans.[20] Consequently, if equality of species is to mean anything, it must be the case that the basic needs of members of species are protected against aggressive actions which only serve to meet nonbasic needs, as demanded by the first requirement of the principle of nonaggression.[21] Another way to put the central claim here is to claim that equality of species rules out domination, where domination means aggressing against the basic needs of the members of some species for the sake of satisfying the nonbasic needs of the members of other species.

Finally, we need one more principle to deal with violations of the above four principles. Accordingly, I propose the principle of rectification, which requires compensation and reparation when the other principles have been violated. Obviously, this principle is somewhat vague, but for those who are willing to abide by the other four principles, it should be possible to remedy this vagueness in practice. Taken altogether, I claim, these five principles constitute a set of environmental principles that are clearly not biased in favor of the human species, and thus provide a defensible interpretation of commitment of biocentrists to the equality of species.

III

Yet, even if biocentrism can be provided with a set of environmental principles that are clearly not biased in favor of the human species, it still needs to be defended against the criticism that it is based on an ecological perspective that is now widely challenged. According to Aldo Leopold, "A thing is right when it tends to preserve the integrity, stability and beauty of the biotic community. It is wrong when it tends otherwise."[22] Leopold's claim has been frequently quoted and endorsed by environmental philosophers. For example, according to J. Baird Callicott, "in the last analysis, the integrity, beauty, and stability of the biotic community is the measure of right and wrong actions affecting the environment."[23] According to Holmes Rolston, "The land ethic rests on the discovery of certain values—integrity, projective creativity, life support, community—already present in ecosystems, and it imposes an obligation to act so as to maintain these."[24] Such environmental ethics is based on the view of natural systems as integrated, stable wholes that are either at, or moving toward, mature equilibrium states.

Recently, however, ecologists have come to challenge this view.[25] The more radical challengers argue that change and disturbance are the norm and that natural environments do not even typically tend toward balanced, stable, and integrated states. On the large scale, this view is evidenced by glacial and climatic changes that show little recurring pattern and ensure that over the long term, natural environments will remain in constant flux. Margaret Davis writes:

> For the last 50 years or 500, or 1,000—as long as anyone would claim for "ecological time"—there has never been an interval when temperature was in a steady state with symmetrical fluctuations about a mean. . . . Only on the longest time scale, 100,000 years, is there a tendency toward cyclical variation, and the cycles are asymmetrical, with a mean much different from today.[26]

On a smaller scale, this view is evidenced by fires, storms, floods, droughts, invasions of exotic species, and many other factors that continually modify natural environments in ways that do not create repeating patterns of return to the same equilibrium states. "Nature," claims Donald Worster, "is fundamentally erratic, discontinuous and unpredictable. It is full of seemingly random events that elude models of how things are supposed to work."[27] Obviously, this "ecology of disequilibrium" contrasts sharply with the "ecology of equilibrium" endorsed by Leopold.

What then are the implications for environmental ethics of these contrasting views of ecology? Clearly, the basic concern of environmental ethics is to determine the prerogatives of and constraints on moral agents in their relationship with other living beings, that is, what moral agents are permitted to do, and what they are not permitted to do with respect to other living beings.[28] Now the environmental principles that I set out above are just such an attempt to determine these prerogatives and constraints. The prerogatives, as captured by the principle of defense and the principle of (aggression for) preservation, specify when moral agents can justifiably pursue their own interests and the interests of those whom they care about. The constraints, as captured by the principle of nondefense and the principle of nonaggression, specify the justifiable constraints on moral agents in their pursuit of their own interests and the interests of those whom they care about. Accordingly, as long as moral agents do not exceed these prerogatives or fail to observe these constraints, they will have behaved morally with respect to other living beings, including individual species, ecosystems, and the whole biotic community.

Of course, these principles do require a specification of the basic needs of living beings. Although establishing such a specification with respect to species and members of species may not be very difficult, it is certainly more difficult to do with respect to ecosystems and the whole biotic community, if it can be done at all. Moreover, it is just here that the difference between the ecology of equilibrium and the ecology of disequilibrium comes into play. Thus, if the ecology of disequilibrium is true, then normally no specific course of development is good for ecosystems or the whole biotic community, and, hence, in many cases, they cannot be benefited or harmed by the actions of moral agents. Hoping to avoid this conclusion, Callicott notes that human-caused perturbations of the environment such as industrial forestry and agriculture, the elimination of large predators, and drift-net fishing are far more frequent, widespread, and regularly occurring than are nonhuman-caused perturbations.[29] Accordingly, he offers a revised maxim for a land ethic: A thing is right when it tends to disturb the biotic community only at normal spatial and temporal scales. It is wrong when it tends otherwise.[30] But if the biotic community does not tend toward any equilibrium, as the ecology of disequilibrium maintains, and Callicott grants this point at least for the sake of argument, then it is difficult to see how normal perturbations can somehow be better for the biotic community than abnormal perturbations. To the contrary, it would seem that the biotic community would just be different under normal perturbations than under abnormal perturbations, not better off.

Nevertheless, even if the ecology of disequilibrium is true, and normally no specific course of development is good for ecosystems or the whole biotic community, it will still be the case that the actions of moral agents can significantly harm or benefit particular species or their members, and thus this possible effect of their actions has to be taken into account in accessing the morality of those actions. By contrast, if the ecology of equilibrium is true, then ecosystems and the whole biotic community can frequently be benefited or harmed by the actions of moral agents. But given that, in many cases, we seem to lack the knowledge of when this benefit or harm obtains, it follows that, in these cases, only the impact we have on particular species or their members can be taken into account in assessing the morality of our actions.[31] Thus, it turns out that irrespective of whether an ecology of disequilibrium or an ecology of equilibrium is true, in many cases, the same considerations would be taken into account in assessing the morality of the actions of moral agents. In time, the debate between these two ecological perspectives may well be resolved, but however it is resolved, it should leave the defensibility, if not the application, of biocentrism unaffected.

IV

Yet, even if their view is unaffected by the debate between the ecology of equilibrium and the ecology of disequilibrium, biocentrists still need to reasonably distinguish the life that they claim has intrinsic value from the animate and inanimate things that they claim lack intrinsic value. In order to do so, it is useful to get clear about what it means to claim that life of a certain sort has intrinsic value which inanimate and some animate things lack.

Here we need to distinguish at least two notions of intrinsic value. According to the first notion of intrinsic value, to say that X has intrinsic value is to say that X is good as an end for some agent Y as opposed to saying that X has instrumental value, which is to say that X is good as a means for some agent Y. According to the second notion of intrinsic value, to say that X has intrinsic value is to say that the good of X ought to constrain the way that others use X in pursuing their own interests.[32] While the first notion of intrinsic value is the more familiar one, it is the second notion of intrinsic value that is more useful in this context. Thus, to say that certain living beings have intrinsic value is to say that the good of those living beings ought to constrain the way that others use them in pursuing their own interests. The actual constraints that are operative in this regard, I claim, are given by the above environmental principles.

Critics of biocentrism, however, can accept this analysis of intrinsic value. What they question is how biocentrists can reasonably distinguish the life they claim has intrinsic value from the animate and inanimate things they claim lack intrinsic value. In particular, these critics claim that biocentrists cannot reasonably distinguish the living things they claim have intrinsic value from machines and from various other kinds of living things, such as hearts and kidneys, which they claim lack intrinsic value. Since critics point out that machines, hearts, and kidneys can all be benefited and harmed, why should they not also have intrinsic value? Of course, if biocentrists were to allow that all these things have intrinsic value that would be the *reducio ad absurdum* of their position. Accordingly, biocentrists need to provide some way of reasonably distinguishing what they claim has intrinsic value from what they claim lacks intrinsic value.

Biocentrists have responded to this challenge in various ways. Paul Taylor claims that in addition to being capable of being benefited or harmed, a being must have a good of its own in order to have intrinsic value.[33] Taylor claims that machines and such living things as hearts and kidneys do not have a good of their own because their good is derived from the good of living beings whose good is not so derived.[34] Laurence Johnson responds in a similar, but more expansive, way, claiming that moral subjects are living systems in a persistent state of low entropy sustained by metabolic processes for accumulating energy whose organic unity and self-identity is maintained in equilibrium by homeostatic feedback processes.[35] Gary Varner takes a different approach, claiming that what characterizes living beings which have intrinsic value is that the capacities of these living beings arose by a process of natural selection.[36] According to Nicholas Agar, who builds on Varner's account, it is having capabilities that arose by natural selection together with having certain representational goals that characterize living beings that have intrinsic value.[37] In my earlier work, I argued that Taylor's account was a reasonable way of distinguishing what has intrinsic value from what doesn't, but now I have my doubts.[38]

The problem with all of these accounts, as I now see it, is that they all involve a derivation of "values" from "facts" in such a way that we can always ask why these "facts" and not others are the grounds for the derivation.[39] Of course, animal liberationists, who hold that only sentient beings have intrinsic value, and most people, who I would say are anthropocentrists and hold that only humans or, more generally, rational beings have intrinsic value, face the same problem. But is there any way out of this problem? I think that there is.

To begin with, we need to recall that the basic concern of environmental ethics is to determine the prerogatives of and constraints on moral agents in their relationship with other living beings. The prerogatives specify the ways that moral agents can justifiably harm other living beings (the principles of defense and preservation) while the constraints specify the ways that moral agents cannot justifiably harm other living beings (the principles of nondefense and nonaggression). Moreover, when moral agents recognize beings as having intrinsic value, they simply recognize that these constraints apply to their interactions with them.

It is important to notice that the constraints specifying ways that moral agents should not harm other living beings are simply requirements that, under certain conditions, moral agents should leave other living beings alone, that is, not interfere with them. They are not requirements that moral agents do anything for other living beings. To generally require that moral agents do something (beneficial) for other living beings (except when rectification is required) is to require much more of them. It entails positive obligations to benefit other living beings, not just negative obligations not to harm them by interfering with them. In general, this would be to demand too much from moral agents, in effect, requiring them to be saints, and, as we have noted before, morality is not in the business of requiring moral agents to be saints. Accordingly, the general obligation of noninterference that moral agents have with respect to other living beings is fixed not so much by the nature of those other living beings (although they must be capable of being benefited and harmed in some nonderivative way), but rather by what constraints or requirements can be reasonably imposed on moral agents. Accordingly, we can see that those who benefit from the obligations that can be reasonably imposed on moral agents must have a certain independence to their lives; they must be able to get along on their own, without the help of others. In other words, they must have a good of their own.[40]

Some living things, such as hearts and kidneys, don't have a good of their own in this sense, and, therefore, they won't benefit from simply being left alone. For example, hearts and kidneys require a certain kind of sustaining environment, and to demand that moral agents provide that kind of environment, when it is contrary to their interest to do so, is to impose a significantly demanding requirement on them. Of course, there is no problem when the heart or kidney is healthy and one's own, because in that case, one would almost surely want to preserve one's own heart or kidney. But when one's heart or kidney is diseased, or not one's own, one is under no positive moral obligation to preserve it as such.[41] That would be to ask too much of moral agents. As a moral agent, one's only general obligation to all living beings is simply not to interfere with them as specified by the principles of nondefense and nonaggression. But it is assumed here that the living beings who are standardly covered by these principles actually will benefit from such noninterference and, hence, that they do not additionally require for their survival positive support from moral agents who have no obligation to provide it.[42] It is such living beings who have intrinsic value; it is such living beings whose good ought to constrain the way that moral agents pursue their own interests.[43]

The same holds true for machines. It is not good for them to be left alone. They too need a sustaining environment. Yet moral agents are not under any positive obligation to provide such an environment. The only obligation moral agents have in this regard is an obligation, under certain conditions, not to interfere with beings who would benefit from such noninterference. To require that moral agents do more would be to require that moral agents do too much, since morality does not require that moral agents do more than can be reasonably expected of them.

Nevertheless, there is a further problem with machines, beyond their need for positive support, that undercuts the very possibility of moral agents having any obligations toward them. It is that, unlike living things, including hearts and kidneys, machines cannot be benefited and harmed except derivatively through their ability to serve the (instrumental) purposes of their creators or owners. Of course, we do say that a car needs an oil change or a fill up. Yet meeting such needs doesn't really benefit the car. Rather it usually benefits the owner of the car who is thereby provided with a more reliable means of transportation. Suppose the owner of the car wants to turn it into a work of modern art by judiciously applying a sledgehammer to it. Is the car thereby harmed? It is not clear that it is. Rather the car now serves the artistic needs of its owner and possibly others, thereby benefiting them in a new way. Moreover, in this new role, the car no longer needs oil changes and fill ups.[44]

Of course, it is possible that machines could be constructed that are so self-sufficient and independent that it would make sense to talk about them as being benefited and harmed in their own right and as having a good of their own. We clearly have already been exposed to such machines in science fiction, the creation of them in real life seems only to be a matter of time. At the moment, however, the machines that we actually deal with cannot be benefited or harmed except derivatively through their ability to serve the purposes of their creators or owners. As a consequence, the moral constraints of the principles of nondefense and nonaggression does not apply to them.

Accordingly, I have specified the class of those who have intrinsic value not primarily in terms of the factual characteristics of those who have it (although they must be capable of being benefited and harmed in a nonderivative sense), but rather in terms of what constraints or requirements can reasonably be imposed on moral agents in this regard.[45] This class is not a derivation of "values" from "facts" or of "ought" from "is" in which one can ask why these facts and not some others support the derivation. Rather it is a derivation of "values" from "values" or of "ought" from "ought" in which the necessity of the derivation can be displayed.

We can more clearly display this derivation as a two-step argument. First, we need a set of premises that limits the requirements of morality:

(1a) The requirements of morality are not among the requirements that it is unreasonable to impose on moral agents.

(2a) It is unreasonable to impose on moral agents a positive obligation to benefit all things capable of being benefited and harmed (which is required to extend intrinsic value to living things, such as hearts and kidneys, and to any machines that qualify).

(3a) A positive obligation to benefit all things capable of being benefited and harmed is not a requirement of morality.

Second, we need a set of premises stating what the requirements of morality are:

(1b) Morality imposes reasonable requirements on moral agents.

(2b) The principles of defense, nondefense, preservation, nonagression, and rectification, unlike the other alternatives, are reasonable to impose on all moral agents.

(3b) The principles of defense, nondefense, preservation, nonaggression, and rectification are requirements of morality.

Because the basic premises of this two-step argument—(1a) and (1b)—are widely accepted as fundamental characterizations of morality, and (1b), in fact, is the contrapositive of (1a), I think that the conclusions (3a) and (3b) can be seen to clearly follow.[46]

Of course, a fuller statement of this two-step argument requires an elaboration of the considerations that I have advanced in this paper. Nevertheless, I think that I have said enough to indicate how biocentrists can meet the three basic criticisms that have been raised against them by providing a set of environmental principles that (1) are clearly not biased in favor of human species, (2) can adjust to changes in ecological science, and (3) can reasonably distinguish what has intrinsic value from what doesn't. By showing how biocentrists can strike back and answer these criticisms, I think that I have also provided grounds for allowing biocentrists to justifiably appropriate the salutation, "Let the life force (or better the ethical demands of life) be with you."

Notes

1. See William French, "Against Biospherical Egalitarianism," *Environmental Ethics* 17 (1995): pp. 39–57.
2. Kristin Shrader-Frechette, "Individualism, Holism and Environmental Ethics," *Ethics and the Environment* 1 (1996): 55–69; Ned Hettinger and Bill Troop, "Refocusing Ecocentrism: Deemphasizing Stability and Defending Wildness," *Environmental Ethics,* forthcoming.
3. Frederik Kaufman, "Machines, Sentience and the Scope of Morality," *Environmental Ethics* 16 (1994): 57–70.
4. Arne Naess, *Ecology, Community and Lifestyle: An Outline of an Ecosophy,* trans. David Rothenberg (Cambridge: Cambridge University Press, 1989), pp. 167–68.
5. Ibid., p. 170.
6. Paul Taylor, *Respect for Life* (Princeton: Princeton University Press, 1986), p. 155.
7. Ibid., pp. 276–77.
8. "From Biocentric Individualism to Biocentric Pluralism," *Environmental Ethics* 17 (1995): 191–207; "Reconciling Anthropocentric and Nonanthropocentric Environmental Ethics," *Environmental Values* 3 (1994): 229–44.
9. Strictly speaking, not to treat humans as superior overall to other living beings is to treat them as either equal overall, or inferior overall, to other living beings, but I am using equal overall to include both of these possibilities since neither possibility involves the domination of nonhuman nature, and, moreover, the latter possibility is an unlikely course of action for humans to take.
10. The relevant actions here can be prohibited either by the principle of nondefense or by the principle of nonaggression which I discuss subsequently.
11. By human ethics, I simply mean those forms of ethics that assume, without argument, that only human beings count morally.
12. For a detailed discussion of this argument, see my article "From Liberty to Welfare," *Ethics* 104 (1994): 64–98.
13. The difference between a standard of a decent life and a standard of a healthy life is, however, only one of degree. A standard of a decent life emphasizes the cultural and social dimensions of basic needs while a standard of a healthy life emphasizes their physical and biological dimensions.
14. Moreover, this kind of fuzziness in the application of the distinction between basic and nonbasic needs is characteristic of the application of virtually all our classificatory concepts, and so is not an objection to its usefulness.
15. It is important to recognize here that we also have a strong obligation to prevent lifeboat cases from arising in the first place.
16. This is true not only of humans but also of other nonhuman species with which we are familar who are also capable of altruistic forbearance. I have added the qualification "normally" here because we know that, for example, that humans sometimes enter into a relationship of reciprocal altruism with the members of other species such as dogs and horses.
17. With respect to humans who lack the capacity for reciprocal altruism, the compassion of fellow humans and the difficulty of distinguishing them from other humans who have that capacity provide sufficient grounds for extending to them the same protections as are given to other humans. I owe this point to Mary Russo.

18. It should be pointed out that the principle of (aggression for) preservation must be implemented in a way that causes the least harm possible, which means that, other things being equal, basic needs should be met by aggressing against nonsentient living beings rather than against sentient living beings so as to avoid the pain and suffering that would otherwise be inflicted on sentient beings.

19. It should also be pointed out that the principle of (aggression for) preservation does not support an unlimited right of procreation. In fact, the theory of justice presupposed here gives priority to the basic needs of existing beings over the basic needs of future possible beings, and this priority should effectively limit (human) procreation. Nor does the principle of (aggression for) preservation allow humans to aggress against the basic needs of animals and plants even to meet their own basic needs when those needs could effectively be met by utilizing available human surplus resources.

20. Of course, libertarians have claimed that we can recognize that people have equal basic rights while, in fact, failing to meet, but not aggressing against, the basic needs of other human beings. However, I have argued in "From Liberty to Welfare" that this claim is mistaken.

21. It should be pointed out that although the principle of nonaggression prohibits aggressing against basic needs to serve nonbasic needs, the principle of defense permits defense of nonbasic needs against aggression of others. Thus, while one cannot legitimately aggress against others to meet nonbasic needs, one can legitimately defend nonbasic needs against the aggression of others.

22. Aldo Leopold, *A Sand County Almanac* (Oxford: Oxford University Press, 1949).

23. J. Baird Callicott, *In Defense of the Land Ethic* (Madison: University of Wisconsin Press, 1989), p. 58.

24. Holmes Rolston III, *Environmental Ethics* (Philadelphia: Temple University Press, 1988), p. 288.

25. Daniel Botkin, *Discordant Harmonies* (New York: Oxford University Press, 1990) and David Ehrenfeld, "Ecosystem Health and Ecological Theories," in Robert Costanza, Bryant Norton, and Benjamin Haskell, eds., *Ecosystem Health* (Washington, D.C.: Island Press, 1992); R. P. McIntosh, *The Background of Ecology: Concepts and Theory* (New York: Cambridge University Press, 1985).

26. Margaret Bryan Davis, "Climatic Instability, Time Lags, and Community Disequilibrium," in Jared Diamond and Ted J. Case, eds., *Community Ecology* (New York: Harper and Row, 1986), p. 269.

27. Donald Worster, "The Ecology of Order and Chaos," *Environmental History Review* 14 (1990): 13.

28. For the purposes of this paper, by *moral agent* I simply mean "agents that are capable of understanding and acting on principles like my environmental principles."

29. J. Baird Callicott, "Do Deconstructive Ecology and Sociobiology Undermine Leopold's Land Ethic?" *Environmental Ethics* 18 (1996): 369.

30. Ibid., p. 372.

31. To some extent, it was the difficulty ecologists had in specifying when ecosystems were in equilibrium that led them to endorse the ecology of disequilibrium.

32. There is no opposing sense of "instrumental value" here.

33. Taylor, *Respect for Nature*, pp. 68–71 and p. 17.

34. One might wonder whether, on Taylor's view, the theist's belief that human goodness has its source and exemplar in the goodness of God renders it impossible for the theist to reasonably hold that humans have a good of their own. Exploring this issue, however, would take us too far afield. Moreover, I hope to provide a characterization of what has intrinsic value that makes it easier to resolve this issue.

35. Laurence Johnson, *A Morally Deep World* (New York: Cambridge University Press, 1991), chap. 6. Johnson adapts this definition from Kenneth Sayre, *Cybernetics and the Philosophy of Mind* (New York: Humanities, 1996). See also Laurence Johnson, "Toward the Moral Considerability of Species and Ecosystems," *Environmental Ethics* 14 (1992): 147–57.

36. Gary Varner, "Biological Functions and Biological Interests," *Southern Journal of Philosophy* 27 (1990): 251–70.

37. Nicholas Agar, "Valuing Species and Valuing Individuals," *Environmental Ethics* 17 (1995): 397–415.

38. For this earlier argument, see "From Biocentric Individualism to Biocentric Pluralism."

39. I am not objecting here to all attempts to derive, or better ground "values" on "facts" but just to the arbitrariness that seems to characterize the one under consideration. For a discussion of what good derivations or groundings of values would look like, see Kurt Baier, *The Rational and the Moral Order* (Chicago: Open Court, 1995), chap. 1.

40. One notable exception to the requirement of independence are some species and subspecies of domesticated animals who have been made into beings who are dependent for their survival on humans. I contend that because of their historic interaction with these domesticated animals, humans have acquired a positive obligation to care for these animals provided certain mutually beneficial arrangements can be maintained. Such domestic animals also have intrinsic value (i.e., their good ought to constrain how others use them), but the reasons for their having this value derive from the way that they have been deprived of their independence by humans.

41. Moreover, to recognize a positive obligation to preserve living things, such as hearts and kidneys, also puts one in conflict with one's own good if it is the case that one's own heart or kidney is diseased or the good of other living beings if their hearts or kidneys are diseased. However, this line of thought

only shows that granting such a positive obligation leads to a *reducio ad absurdum* of the biocentrist's position. The qualification "as such" is added to allow for the possibility that one may have a obligation to preserve a particular heart or kidney if one should happen to have a obligation to preserve the person whose heart or kidney it is.

42. In the case of some species and subspecies of domesticated animals, however, there is a conditional obligation to provide positive support. See n. 41.

43. It would be interesting to explore how this moral framework applies to disputed moral problems like abortion and euthanasia. My hope is that all disputants would find this moral framework acceptable and that the framework will also provide additional resources for resolving these problems.

44. For further discussion, see Johnson, *A Morally Deep World,* p. 76.

45. Even the requirement that those who can be benefited or harmed in a nonderivative way must have a certain independence to their lives or a good of their own is, on my account, derived from what we can reasonably expect of moral agents.

46. For further discussion of these two fundamental characterizations of morality (1a) and (1b), see "From Liberty to Welfare."

19

◁ *From Heroic to Holistic Ethics:* ▷ *The Ecofeminist Challenge*

MARTI KHEEL

Marti Kheel is a writer and activist in the areas of ecofeminism and animal liberation. She has contributed to both Environmental Ethics *and* The Green Reader.

As the destruction of the natural world proceeds at breakneck speed, nature ethicists have found themselves in search of a theory that can serve to bring this destruction to a halt.[1] Just as the prototypical hero in patriarchal stories must rescue the proverbial "damsel in distress," so, too, the sought-after theory must demonstrate heroic qualities. It must, singlehandedly, rescue the ailing body of "Mother Nature" from the villains who have bound and subdued her. The theoretical underpinnings of environmental and animal liberation philosophies are seen by many ethical theorists as having the necessary "intellectual muscle" to perform this heroic feat. But is a heroic ethic a helpful response to the domination of nature, or is it another conqueror in a new disguise?

It is significant that ecofeminists have, by and large, declined to join the "hunt" for an environmental ethic or "savior theory." The writings within ecofeminism have largely ignored the heated debates engaged in by (predominantly) male philosophers over what should constitute the basis of an appropriate ethic for the natural world. A glance at the vast majority of ecofeminist writings reveals, instead, a tendency to concentrate on exposing the underlying mentality of exploitation that is directed against women and nature within the patriarchal world. Whereas nature ethicists have tended to concentrate on "rescuing" the "damsel in distress," ecofeminists have been more likely to ask how and why the "damsel" arrived at her present plight.

Clearly ecofeminists have taken a different approach to the current crisis in nature. No single theory is sought or expected to emerge, through reasoned competition with the others, as the most powerful or compelling one. In fact, no single ethical theory seems to be sought at all. What have been emerging, rather, are a number of theories or stories that, when woven together into a fabric or tapestry, help to provide a picture or "portrait" of the world in which we currently live. Whereas mainstream nature ethicists have based much of their analysis on abstract principles and universal rules, ecofeminists have tended to highlight the role of metaphors and images of nature. The emphasis has been not on developing razor-sharp theories that can be used to dictate future conduct, but rather on painting a "landscape" (or "mindscape") of the world.

This is not to say that ecofeminists have merely described our current problems, showing no interest in changing the world. On the contrary, ecofeminists have been deeply committed to social transformation. The method of transformation that ecofeminists have subscribed to, however, is premised on the insight that one cannot change what one does not understand. Understanding the inner workings of patriarchal society is emphasized precisely so that society might be transformed. The transformation that ecofeminists wish to bring about is, thus, often implicit in their critiques. If the images of women and nature under patriarchal society have facilitated the exploitation and abuse of both, then, clearly, new ways of perceiving the world must be sought. The natural world will be "saved" not by the sword of ethical theory, but rather through a transformed consciousness toward all of life.

The emphasis on developing new ways of perceiving the world is in keeping with much of the recent work in feminist moral theory. Feminist moral theorists have begun to show that ethics is not so much the imposition of obligations and rights, but rather a natural outgrowth of how one views the self, including one's relation to the rest of the world. Before one can change the current destructive relation to nature, we must, therefore, understand the world view upon which this relation rests. Just as a health-care practitioner would not attempt to treat an illness without understanding the nature and history of the disease, many feminists would argue that it is not possible to transform the current world view of patriarchy without understanding the disease that has infected the patriarchal mind. What, then, is the world view that patriarchy has bequeathed us?

THE CONQUEST OF NATURE:
THE DAMSEL IS DISTRESSED

The predominant image of nature throughout the Western, patriarchal world has been that of an alien force. Nature, which has been imaged as female, has been depicted as the "other," the raw material out of which culture and masculine self-identity are formed. Two major images have been used to achieve separation from nature. One of the most common images has been that of the Beast. The Beast is conceived as a symbol for all that is not human, for that which is evil, irrational, and wild. Civilization is thus achieved by driving out or killing the Beast. On an inward level, this involves driving out all vestiges of our own animality—the attempt to obliterate the knowledge that we are animals ourselves. Outwardly, the triumph over the Beast has been enacted through the conquest of wilderness, with its concomitant claim to the lives of millions of animals driven from their lands.

The triumph over the demonic Beast has been a recurring theme throughout the mythologies of the patriarchal world. Typically, the slain Beast is a former divinity from the earlier matriarchal world. The serpents, dragons, and horned gods, who were at one time worshiped as divine, are transformed in patriarchal mythology into devils and monsters that must be slain. Thus, Apollo slays Gaia's python; Perseus kills the three-headed Medusa (the triple goddess), who is described as having snakes writhing from her head; Hercules defeats the terrible multiheaded Hydra; and the pharaohs of later Egypt slay the dragon Apophys. In the Middle Ages, there were countless renditions of St. George's prowess in killing the dragon—again, to rescue the "damsel in distress."

Frequently the death of the Beast is said to herald the birth of light and order, either at the beginning or the end of time. Thus, in the Sumero-Babylonian *Epic of Gilgamesh,* Marduk kills his mother, the goddess Tiamat, the great whale-dragon or cosmic serpent, and from her body the universe is made. Both Judaism and Christianity continue the dragon-slaying tradition. According to St. John the Divine, at the world's end an angel with a key will subdue the dragon that is Satan. And in the Hebrew legend, the death of the serpentlike Leviathan is prophesied for the Day of Judgment. In Christianity, the task of killing the dragonlike monster was transferred from gods and heroes to saints and archangels. The archangel Michael was a notable dragon-slayer. Faith, prayer, and divine intervention came to be seen as the new dragon-slayers whose task it is to restore the world of order.

These myths of violence and conquest contrast sharply with the mythologies of prepatriarchal cultures. The cosmological stories of these societies typically depicted the beginning of life as emerging from a female-imaged goddess who embodied the earth. Thus, Gaia, in the earliest Greek myths, was thought to give birth to the universe by herself. And the snake, so much feared in our current culture, was worshiped in such societies as divine. By the time of the biblical story of the Garden of Eden, a totally new world view had emerged. Both a woman and an animal were by this time depicted as the source of all evil in the world. And "Man," above all other forms of life, was claimed to have a special relation to the divine.

Today, the heroic battle against unruly nature is reenacted as ritual drama in such masculine ventures as sport-hunting, bullfights, and rodeos. A similar mentality can be seen in the ritual degradation of women in pornography and rape. As Susan Griffin points out, pornography is ritual drama. It is the heroic struggle of the masculine ego to deny the knowledge of bodily feelings and one's dependence upon women and all of the natural world.

The second image of nature appears less heroic but is equally violent in its own way. It is the image of nature as mindless matter, which exists to serve the needs of superior, rational "Man." In this image, animals are depicted as having different, unequal natures rather than as wild or evil creatures that must be conquered and subdued. They are not so much irrational as nonrational beings. Along with women, they are viewed as mere "matter" (a word that, significantly, derives from the same root word as "mother").

Both Aristotelian and Platonic philosophy contributed to the conception of nature as inert or mindless matter. It was the Aristotelian notion of purpose and function, however, that especially helped to shape the Western world's instrumental treatment of women and nature. According to Aristotle, there was a natural hierarchical ordering to the world, within which each being moved toward fulfillment of its own particular end. Since the highest end of "Man" was the state of happiness achieved through rational contemplation, the rest of nature was conveniently ordered to free "Man" to attain this contemplative goal. Thus, plants existed to give subsistence to animals, and animals to give it to "Man"; and the specific function of women, animals, and slaves was to serve as instruments for the attainment of the highest happiness of free, adult men. There is no need to conquer nature in this conception, since nature has already been safely relegated to an inferior realm.

The Jewish-Christian tradition has also contributed to an instrumental and hierarchical conception of nature. The Genesis account of Creation must bear a large share of the guilt for this state of affairs. In the priestly account of the Genesis story of Creation, we are told that God gave "Man" "dominion over every living thing that moveth upon the earth" (Genesis 1:26). And in the Yahwist version, chronologically an earlier account, we are told that nonhuman animals were created by God to be helpers or companions for Adam, and when they were seen as unfit, Eve was created to fulfill this role (Genesis 2:22). Both stories, in their distinct ways, reinforce the notion that women and nature exist only for the purpose of serving "Man."

The conception of nature as an object for "Man's" use was carried to an ultimate extreme by Cartesian philosophy. According to Descartes, since animals were lacking in "consciousness" or "reason," they were mere machines that could feel no pain. Smashing the legs of a monkey, Descartes "reasoned," would hurt no more than removing the hands of a clock. With Cartesian philosophy, the wild, demonic aspect of nature was, thus, finally laid to rest, and the image of nature as a machine was born.

The image of nature (and women) as mindless objects is typically employed for more practical goals—profit, convenience, and knowledge. Division and control, not conquest, are the guiding motives; the rationality of the detached observer replaces the pleasure of conquest as the psychological mode. The use of animals in laboratories, factory farms, and fur ranches exemplifies this frame of mind, as does the image and use of women as "housewives" and "breeding machines." In the earlier (Beastly) image, nature is seen as a harlot; in this conception, nature is more like a slave or wife.

Although the two images of nature may seem unrelated, they merely represent different points along a single scale. In one image, nature is seen as a demonic being who must be conquered and subdued. In the other image, nature has been subdued to the point of death. Behind both images, however, lies a single theme—namely, the notion of nature as the "other," a mental construct in opposition to which a masculine, autonomous self is attained. In one, the violence appears to be perpetrated by an aggressive masculine will; in the other, through the use of reason. But the underlying theme remains the same—namely, the notion of the aggressive establishment of the masculine self through its opposition to all of the natural world.

Feminist psychoanalytic theory has helped to shed light on the psychological motives that lie behind the need men feel to separate violently from the female world. According to the object-relations theory, both the boy and the girl child's earliest experience is that of an undifferentiated oneness with the mother figure. Although both must come to see themselves as separate from the mother figure, the boy child, unlike the girl, must come to see himself as opposed to all that is female as well. Thus, the mother figure, and by extension all women, become not just an other, but the other—the object against which the boy child's identity is formed and defined.

Object-relations theorists, such as Dorothy Dinnerstein, have also argued that it is not just women who become an object against which men establish their sense of self, but that nature becomes objectified as well. Women and nature both come to represent the world of contingency and vulnerability that men must transcend. The twin need to separate from women and from nature can be discerned in typical male rituals of initiation into adulthood. A boy's entrance into manhood is typically marked by separation from women and often by violence toward the nonhuman world. In many tribal cultures a boy is initiated into manhood by being sent off to hunt and kill an animal. In other cultures, "baptisms of blood" occur when a young man goes to war or sexually penetrates a woman for the first time.

THE PROTECTION OF NATURE:
THE DAMSEL IS REDRESSED

If the cult of masculinity has been modeled on the image of predation, the field of nature ethics has been modeled on that of protection. Both animal liberation and environmental ethics spring from a common defensive reaction to the willful aggression perpetrated upon the natural world. Animal liberationists concentrate much of their energies on protecting those animals reduced to the status of inert matter or machines— that is, animals in laboratories and factory farms. Environmental ethicists, by contrast, devote themselves primarily to protecting those parts of nature that are still "wild." But the underlying motive remains the same—namely, the urge to defend and protect.

Various modalities have been proposed for how the defense of nature might best be waged. Typically, nature ethicists have felt compelled to arm themselves with the force of philosophical theory in coming to nature's defense. Whereas patriarchal society has sought to destroy the natural world, nature ethicists have sought to place it under the protective wing of ethical theory. However, as Sarah Hoagland points out, predation and protection are twin aspects of the same world view: "Protection objectifies just as much as predation."

In their attempt to forge iron-clad theories to defend the natural world, nature ethicists have come to rely on the power and strength of a reasoned defense. Reason is enlisted as the new hero to fight on nature's behalf. In the past, humans (primarily men) have conceived of themselves as proprietors of the object-laden natural world. Today, many nature ethicists conceive of themselves not as the owners of nature, but as the owners of value, which it is their prerogative to mete out with a theoretical sweep of their pens. Ethical deliberation on the value of nature is conceived more or less like a competitive sport. Thus, nature ethicists commonly view themselves as "judges" in a game that features competing values out of which a hierarchy must be formed. The outcome is that some must win and others must lose. If a part of nature is accorded high value (typically by being assigned a quality that human beings are said to possess, such as sentience, consciousness, rationality, autonomy), then it is allowed entrance into the world of "moral considerability." If, on the other hand, it scores low (typically by being judged devoid of human qualities), it is relegated to the realm of "objects" or "things," and seen as unworthy of "interests" or "rights." The conferral of value in ethical deliberation is conceived as the conferral of power. "Inherent value" or "inherent worth" (the highest values) accrue to nature to the extent that nature can be rescued from the object world. Much of the heated debate among nature ethicists occurs over what class of entities may rightfully be granted admittance to the subject realm. The presumption behind this conceptual scheme is that if an entity is not graced with the status of "subject," it will become the "object" of abuse.

Both animal liberationists and environmental ethicists seek to curb the willful destruction of the natural world through another act of human will. Reason is, once again, elevated above the natural instincts and asked to control our aggressive wills. The same reason that was used to take value out of nature (through objectification and the imposition of hierarchy) is now asked to give it value once again. A sound ethic, according to this view, must transcend the realm of contingency and particularity, grounding itself not in our untrustworthy instincts, but rather in rationally derived principles and abstract rules. It must stand on its own as an autonomous construct, distinct from our personal inclinations and desires, which it is designed to control. Ethics is intended to operate much like a machine. Feelings are considered, at best, as irrelevant, and at worst, as hazardous intrusions that clog the "ethical machinery." Basing an argument on love or compassion is tantamount to having no argument at all. As Peter Singer boasts in his well-known *Animal Liberation,* nowhere in his book will readers find an appeal to emotion where it cannot be substantiated by rational argument.[2]

In their attempt to forge iron-clad theories to defend the natural world, nature ethicists have, in many ways, come to replicate the aggressive or predatory conception of nature that they seek to oppose. They leave intact a Hobbesian world view in which nature is conceived as "red in tooth and claw," with self-interest as the only rule of human conduct. The presumption is that only reason compels people to submit to sovereign rule—in this case, not that of a king, but that of ethical theory. Ethics, according to this world view, comes to replicate the same instrumental mentality that has characterized our interaction with the natural world. It is reduced to the status of a tool, designed to restrain what is perceived as an inherently aggressive will.

Not all philosophers of nature have relied on axiological or value theory to rescue nature from her current plight. A number of writers, working in what some refer to as the field of ecophilosophy, have sought to ground their philosophy not in the rational calculation of value, but rather in a transformed consciousness toward all of life. Although they share with nature ethicists the urge to rescue nature from the object realm, they reject a "values in nature" philosophy in favor of grounding their philosophy in a particular phenomenological world view.

Often the search for this transformed consciousness is described in terminology that borrows freely from the field of resource development. For example, we read of the search for the "conceptual resources" or the "foundations" of an environmental consciousness. Although various religious and philosophical traditions have been proposed as suitable "resources" for the development of this consciousness, it is the images and metaphors of nature within these traditions that are the primary focus of concern. Some of the images and metaphors for nature that have been proffered as "fertile" grounds for the development of an environmental consciousness include that of an "interconnected web," "a community of living beings," an "organism," and an "expanded Self." The science of ecology has provided additional support for a world view that perceives all of life as an interconnected web or a single living being. The tendency of many ecophilosophers is to "mine" these conceptual systems for an ecological consciousness, rather than to examine their own feelings and emotions toward the natural world.

The underlying motive for the reconceptualization of the natural world is the urge to rescue nature from the aggression that is thought to ensue without these conceptual restraints. History has, in fact, shown that particular conceptions of nature have acted as a restraint against human aggression. As Carolyn Merchant points out:

> The image of the earth as a living organism and nurturing mother has historically served as a cultural constraint restricting the actions of human beings. One does not readily slay a mother, dig into her entrails for gold, or mutilate her body. . . . As long as the earth was considered to be alive and sensitive, it could be considered a breach of human ethical behavior to carry out destructive acts against it.

Many ecofeminists, inspired by the premodern conceptions of Gaia or "Mother Earth," have consciously sought to reclaim these images. For most ecofeminists, however, this attempt to revive the image of Gaia is grounded not in systematic phenomenology but, rather, in a feeling of spiritual connection with the natural world. A female image of the earth simply seems to have resonance for many ecofeminists as a contrast to the patriarchal notion of a male sky god.

Yet the image of the earth as a living being is insufficient in and of itself to bring a halt to the current destruction of the natural world. The attempt by many ecophilosophers to graft a new image onto our current conception of nature fails to challenge the underlying structures and attitudes that have produced the image they seek to supplant. The underlying tendencies toward aggression that exist under patriarchy are thus left intact.

The Gaia hypothesis, proposed by the scientist James Lovelock, illustrates this point. The hypothesis originally was hailed by ecophilosophers for reviving the notion of the earth as a living being. This initial enthusiasm, however, was subsequently tempered when Lovelock concluded that the earth, as a result of its self-regulating mechanisms, was perfectly capable of enduring humanity's insults. Lovelock boldly claimed, "It seems very unlikely that anything we do will threaten Gaia. . . . The damsel in distress [the environmentalist] expected to rescue appears as a buxom and robust man-eating mother." With Lovelock's theory, the earth was "revived," but the underlying structures and attitudes that promote aggression were left unchallenged. Thus, although ecophilosophers have avoided some of the pitfalls of nature ethics, with its attendant notion of obligations and rights, they have often left unchallenged the deeper problem entailed in the notion of ethics as a form of restraint.

The notion of ethical conduct as restraint of aggression is clearly illustrated in the writings of Aldo Leopold, considered by many to be the founder of ecophilosophy and the environmental movement. Deep ecologists have pointed to Leopold's "land ethic" as the embodiment of their ideal of the expanded Self. According to deep ecologists, when one expands one's identity to the "land" or to all of nature, nature will be protected, since to cause nature harm would be to harm oneself as well. Thus, the expanded Self, not axiological theory, is designed to defend the natural world from human abuse. However, if we examine Leopold's land ethic carefully, we find that what it most clearly conveys is the notion of ethics as a means of restraint. Far from eliminating the aggressive drives that are inherent in patriarchy, the expansion of identity merely contains the aggressive impulses so as not to exceed a specified limit, which might thus endanger the "land."

Leopold's land ethic maintains that a thing is right when it tends to preserve the "beauty, integrity, and stability of the biotic community." It is wrong when it does otherwise. This maxim, however, which has been widely quoted, gives an incomplete picture of Leopold's ideas. Not only are the "beauty, integrity and stability of the biotic community" in no way marred by the killing of individual animals for sport; they are actually *enhanced* by it, in Leopold's view: "The instinct that finds delight in the sight and pursuit of game is bred into the very fiber of the human race." He goes on to state that the desire to hunt lies deeper than the urge to participate in other outdoor sports: "Its source is a matter of instinct as well as competition. . . . A son of Robinson Crusoe, having never seen a racket, might get along nicely without one, but he would be pretty sure to hunt or fish whether or not he were taught to do so." In other words, for Leopold, a boy instinctively learns to shoot a gun, and, moreover, instinctively wants to hunt and kill. As he states: "A man may not care for gold and still be human but the man who does not like to see, hunt, photograph or otherwise outwit birds and animals is hardly normal. He is supercivilized, and I for one do not know how to deal with him."

According to Leopold, all boys and men have this aggressive instinct (interestingly, he had nothing to say about women and girls). Ethics, then, enters into the picture as the need to curb, *not eliminate,* this aggressive drive. The ability to exercise (and curb) this aggressive instinct, through such activities as hunting, is viewed by Leopold as an inalienable right:

Some can live without the opportunity for the *exercise and control* of the hunting instinct, just as I suppose some can live without work, play, love, business or other vital adventure. But in these days we regard such deprivation as unsocial. Opportunity for the exercise of all the normal instincts has come to be regarded more and more as an inalienable right. [Emphasis mine.]

Leopold goes on to complain that "the men who are destroying our wildlife are alienating one of these rights and doing a good job of it." In other words, wildlife should be preserved not because of the animal's inherent right to life, but because of the hunter's inherent right to kill! As he explains, "[The individual's] instincts prompt him to compete for his place in the community but his ethics prompt him also to cooperate (perhaps in order that there may be a *place to compete for*"). [Again the emphasis is mine.] As Leopold summarizes his ideas, "An ethic ecologically is a limitation on freedom of action in the struggle for existence. An ethic philosophically is a differentiation of social from antisocial conduct. These are two definitions of one thing. Good social conduct involves limitation of freedom."

Leopold's land ethic is, thus, inextricably tied to his ideas about proper hunting conduct. It involves what he calls "good sportsmanship." Much of Western ethics is based upon a similar idea of good sportsmanship, according to which you compete in the game but play by the rules.

The notion that ethical conduct involves restraining the errant or immoral passions can be found not only in Western philosophy but in Western religion as well. The Christian church changed the focus of morality from prudence to obedience. The sentiments of the Church fathers are aptly captured by Sarah Hoagland—namely, that "evil results when passion runs out of (their) [i.e., the Church fathers'] control." The Church was (and is) fond of buttressing this notion with appeals to biblical authority. We are told that in the biblical story of Genesis, Adam's sin is precisely a failure of will. Adam's failure to obey God's command is attributed to Eve, and Eve's lapse of obedience is in turn ascribed to the snake. Eve has gone down in history as the embodiment of evil for having trusted the word of an animal over God's command.

Obedience to a transcendent God or abstract concept has been one of the most common conceptions of ethics in the Western world. Behind this notion lies the even more fundamental notion of ethics as restraint. Indeed, the model of ethics as a form of restraint can be seen in the Jewish-Christian God Himself. Thus, feeling remorse for having destroyed most of the world, God forges a covenant with Noah after the flood to restrain Himself from further outbursts of this kind.

Frequently, aggressive conduct is not prohibited under patriarchy, merely restrained and controlled. Often aggression is explicitly condoned if it is properly channeled into ritualized form. In many cultures, killing a totem animal is customarily condemned, but honored on rare occasions when performed as a sacrifice to a god. Similarly, the laws of Kashrut sanction the killing of animals as long as it is done in a restrained and ritualized fashion, according to "God's command."

The institutionalization of violence in modern society serves a legitimating function similar to that of ritual violence. For example, it is illegal for someone to beat a dog wantonly on the street, but if an experimenter beats the same dog in the protective confines of a laboratory, while counting the number of times the dog "vocalizes," it is considered an honorable activity and called "science." The rules of the experiment operate, like the rules of ritual, to lend legitimacy to the violent act. Animal experimentation is accorded additional legitimation by borrowing the language of ritual. Animals are said to be "sacrificed" in laboratories, not killed. Behind this obfuscation of language lies the tragic belief that somehow, if animals are killed at the altars of science, human beings will be allowed to live.

Aggression is often condoned under patriarchy in the name of an abstract ideal, typically "the greater good." We are told that killing (whether in laboratories, in warfare, or in razing land) is necessary for the greater good of "Mankind." Again, the Christian God himself provides a perfect example of this conduct. Through the killing of his son, "God" is said to have sought the redemption of "Man," and hence the greater good.

Since the Enlightenment, ethical theory has tended to be based less on the Word of God and more on the god of Reason. The theme of controlling the unwieldy passions, however, has remained intact, receiving its most refined expression in the thought of Kant. While science and technology were mining nature for her riches, Kant, in analogous fashion, was attempting to strip human ethical conduct of its immersion in the natural world. As he writes, "To behold virtue in her proper shape is nothing other than to show morality stripped of all admixture with the sensuous and of all the spurious adornments of reward or self love." Moral individuals, according to Kant, rise above their personal inclinations or nature, and act out of duty. Duty is determined first by pure reason or logic, stripped of all feeling, and then by the exercise of the will.

The conception of morality as the rational control of irrational and aggressive desires contrasts sharply with the way in which many women have described their ethical behavior and thought. Research by Carol Gilligan suggests that women's ethical conduct and thought tend to derive more from a sense of connection with others and from the feelings of care and responsibility that such connection entails. Men's sense of morality, on the other hand, tends to derive more from an abstract sense of obligations and rights. According to one of Gilligan's respondents, Amy, "Responsibility signifies response, an extension rather than a limitation of action. Thus, it connotes an act of care, rather than restraint of aggression." For Jake, by contrast, responsibility "pertains to a limitation of action, a restraint of aggression."

For many women, what needs to be explained is not how and why people should be compelled to behave in moral ways, but how and why compassion and moral behavior fail to be sustained. As Alison Jaggar states, "Because we expect humans to be aggressive, we find the idea of cooperation puzzling. If, instead of focusing on antagonistic interactions, we focused on cooperative interaction, we would find the idea of competition puzzling."

TRUNCATED NARRATIVES

The founding of ethics on the twin pillars of human reason and human will is an act of violence in its own right. By denigrating instinctive and intuitive knowledge, it severs our ties to the natural world. But the violence of abstraction operates in other ways as well. Wrenching an ethical problem out of its embedded context severs the problem from its roots. Most nature ethicists debate the value of nature on an abstract or theoretical plane. Typically, they weigh the value of nature against the value of a human goal or plan. For example, we are asked to weigh the value of an animal used for research in a laboratory against the value of a human being who is ill. The problem is conventionally posed in a static, linear fashion, detached from the context in which it was formed. In a sense, we are given truncated stories and then asked what we think the ending should be. However, if we do not understand the world view that produced the dilemma that we are asked to consider, we have no way of evaluating the situation except on its own terms.

What, for example, is a mother to say when she is told that the only way that her child can be saved is through the "sacrifice" of animal life? The urgency of the situation leads the mother to believe what she is told and to feel that it is "right" that the animal should die to save her child's life. It is understandable that the mother would choose her daughter's life over that of an anonymous animal. It would also be understandable, however, if the mother chose the life of her daughter over that of an anonymous *child*. This, however, is not the ethical dilemma that she is asked to consider. No one has asked her to juxtapose the life of one human against that of another. Although it would clearly be more helpful to experiment on a human child to help save the life of another child, no one is proposing this. Animals, however, have been relegated to the status of objects or property. As such, their bodies can easily be conscripted into this tragic human story.

The mother of the ailing daughter consumes this story; she does not create it or even enact it. *She* is not the one who will be injecting poisons into animals and watching their bodies writhe in pain. *She* is not the one who will slice into their brains to see what bits of knowledge might lie therein. She is the consumer of a narrative or story from which these details have been conveniently excised.

Currently, ethics is conceived as a tool for making dramatic decisions at the point at which a crisis has occurred. Little if any thought is given to why the crisis or conflict arose to begin with. Just as Western allopathic medicine is designed to treat illness, rather than maintain health, Western ethical theory is designed to remedy crisis, not maintain peace. But the word "ethics" implies something far less dramatic and heroic—namely, an "ethos" or way of life.

According to Iris Murdoch, moral behavior is not a matter of weighing competing values and making the proper, rational choice. Rather, as she argues, what is crucial in the moral life is the act of attention *before* a moral choice is made. In her words, the moral life is "not something that is switched off in between the occurrence of explicit moral choices. What happens between such choices is indeed what is crucial." Murdoch contends: "If we consider what the work of attention is like, how continuously it goes on and how imperceptibly it builds up structures of values round about us, we shall not be surprised that at crucial moments of choice most of the business of choosing is already over." Morality, for Murdoch, is far from the notion of the rational control of an inherently aggressive will. When one directs a "patient, loving regard" upon "a person, a thing, a situation," according to Murdoch, the will is presented not as "unimpeded movement," but rather as "something very much more like obedience."

It is precisely this loving regard that patriarchal culture has failed to attain. Rather, in the patriarchal "look," nature has been reduced to a set of objects or symbols that are used to attain a sense of self that is detached from the rest of the natural world. Nature is imaged as wild and demonic, passive and inert, but never as a community of living beings with instincts, desires, and interests of their own.

The patriarchal mind has managed to look, but not see, act but not feel, think but not know. Claude Bernard, considered by many to be the founder of modern medicine and the widespread use of animals in research, embodies this failure of perception. According to Bernard: "The physiologist is not an ordinary man: he is a scientist, possessed and absorbed by the scientific idea that he pursues. He does not hear the cries of animals, he does not see their flowing blood, he sees nothing but his idea, and is aware of nothing but an organism that conceals from him the problem he is seeking to resolve.

It is this fixation on abstraction (God, Reason, ideas, or the "Word") that has hampered the patriarchal mind from perceiving other forms of life in caring ways. In order to disengage from this fixation on abstraction, it is necessary to engage in practice. If ecofeminists are serious about transforming the patriarchal world view, we must begin to take our own experiences and practices seriously. We might, for example, decide, on an abstract plane, that we are justified in eating meat. But if we are dedicated to an ecofeminist praxis, we must put our abstract beliefs to the practical test. We must ask ourselves how we would feel if we were to visit a slaughterhouse or factory farm. And how would we feel if we were to kill the animal ourselves? Ethics, according to this approach, begins with our own instinctive responses. It occurs in a holistic context in which we know the whole story within which our actions take place. It means rethinking the stories that we have come to believe under patriarchy, such as the belief that we must experiment on animals to save human life, or the belief that we must eat meat to lead healthy lives. As Carol Adams points out, we are brought up to accept that being eaten is the logical ending to the story of a farm animal's life. But stories such as these can only be conceived by a patriarchal mind that is unable to conceive of nature as important apart from human use.

Patriarchal society is adept at truncating stories and then adapting them to its own needs. It is true, for example, that *some* animals are predators; however, the vast majority are not. Most of the animals that humans eat are, in fact, vegetarian (cows, pigs, chickens). We are asked, under patriarchy, to model our behavior not after the vegetarian animals but after the predators. The narrative of predation thus becomes a convenient "pretext" to justify a wide range of violent acts. No other species of animal confines, enslaves, and breeds other animals to satisfy its taste for flesh. Yet, under patriarchy, *this* story remains untold. Nor are we told that predatory animals generally kill other animals only for survival reasons; that, unlike humans, these animals would not survive without eating meat. The story of predation is wrenched out of the larger context and served to us to consume.

Since we live in a fragmented world, we will need to stretch our imaginations to put it back together again. It is often difficult for us to conceive of the impact that our personal conduct has beyond our individual lives. Reason is easily divided from emotion when our emotions are divided from experience. Much of the violence that is perpetrated against the natural world occurs behind closed doors or out of our view. Most of us will never see a slaughterhouse, fur ranch, or animal research laboratory. If we are to engage in an ecofeminist praxis, the least we can do is inform ourselves of what transpires in these places. If we are to make holistic choices, the whole story must be known.

The story of meat eating must include not only the brutal treatment of animals on factory farms and in slaughterhouses, not only the devastating impact of meat eating on the ecology of the earth, on world hunger, and on human health—it must include *all* these and other details, which it must then weave together into a whole. Only when we have all the details of this and other stories will we be able to act holistically with our bodies, minds, and souls. It is the details that we need to live moral lives, not obedience to abstract principles and rules.

Holistic medicine provides a fitting paradigm for holistic ethics. Just as holistic medicine seeks to discover the whole story behind disease, so, too, holistic ethics seeks to discover the whole story behind ethical dilemmas. Western allopathic ethics, on the other hand, is designed to treat the symptoms of patriarchy (its dilemmas and conflicts), rather than the disease embodied in its total world view. Allopathic ethics like allopathic medicine operates on the notion of heroism. Just as Western heroic medicine spends most of its time, money, and resources on battling advanced stages of disease and emergency situations, so, too, Western heroic ethics is designed to treat problems at an advanced stage of their history—namely, at the point at which conflict has occurred.

It is not difficult to discern why allopathic medicine spends little to no research money on prevention. Prevention is simply not a very heroic undertaking. How can you fight a battle if the enemy does not yet exist? It is far more dramatic to allow disease and conflict to develop and then to call in the troops and declare war. The drama of illness is seen to lead ineluctably to the climax of a heroic, technological fix.

Heroic medicine, like heroic ethics, runs counter to one of the most basic principles in ecology—namely, that everything is interconnected. Ecology teaches us that no part of nature can be understood in isolation, apart from its context or ecological niche. So, too, I would argue, our moral conduct cannot be understood apart from the context (or moral soil) in which it grows. By uprooting ethical dilemmas from the environment that produced them, heroic ethics sees only random, isolated problems, rather than an entire diseased world view. But until the entire diseased world view is uprooted, we will always face moral crises of the same kind. There is an ecology to ethics, just as to every aspect of the natural world. If we do not care for our moral landscape, we cannot expect it to bear fruit.

WEAVING NEW STORIES

The "environmental crisis" is, above all, a crisis of perception. It is a crisis not only by virtue of what our culture sees, but by virtue of what it does not see. Adrienne Rich has shown how "lies, secrecy, and silence" have been used to perpetuate the exploitation of women.[3] The same may be said to apply to the exploitation of all of the natural world as well. If we are to transform the destructive consciousness that pervades our current culture, we must break through the lies, secrecy, and silence. This is not an individual endeavor. Holistic ethics is a collective undertaking, not a solitary task. It is a process of helping one another to piece together the wider stories of which our lives form a part. It means filling in the missing links. It may mean approaching a woman on the street who is wearing a fur coat and asking her if she is aware of how many animals died to make her coat, and if she is aware of how much suffering the animals had to endure. At the same time, it means understanding the cultural context that leads this woman to see glamour where others see death. She is the product of a society that robs women of their own self-image and then sells it back to them in distorted form. She thinks that she is "dressed to kill"; we must let her know that others have been killed for her to dress.

In order to engage in holistic ethics, we must also disengage from patriarchal discourse. Patriarchal discourse creates dilemmas that it then invites us to resolve. Thus, animal experimenters typically invite us to answer the question, "Who would we save if we had to choose between our drowning daughter and a drowning dog?" The crisis scenario is designed to lead us to believe that only one life can be saved, and only at the other's expense. Disengaging from patriarchal discourse means that we must refuse to dignify these dualistic questions with a response. Even to consider such questions is to give support and validity to the patriarchal world view. The best response to such questions is, perhaps, to pose a question of our own. We might ask why the child is ill to begin with. Was it due to the hormones found in the meat she was fed, or was it perhaps due to the consumption of drugs that had proved "safe" after testing on animals? And why was the proverbial dog touted by research scientists "drowning" to begin with? Had someone thrown the dog in the water (or, rather, the laboratory) in the pathetic belief that somehow, through the dog's death, a young child's life would be saved? And how and why did we develop a culture in which death is seen as a medical failure, rather than as a natural part of life?

As we disengage from patriarchal discourse, we begin to hear larger and fuller stories. Hearing these bigger stories means learning to listen to nature. The voice of women and the voice of nature have been muted under patriarchy. Women and nature are considered objects under patriarchy, and objects do not speak, objects do not feel, and objects have no needs. Objects exist only to serve the needs of others. But despite our society's refusal to listen, nature has been increasingly communicating her needs to us. Nature is telling us in myriad ways that we cannot continue to poison her rivers, forests, and streams, that she is not invulnerable, and that the violence and abuse must be stopped. Nature *is* speaking to us. The question is whether we are willing or able to hear.

The notion of obligations, responsibilities, and rights is one of the tools used by heroic ethics. But genuine responsibility for nature begins with the root meaning of the word—"our capacity for response." Learning to respond to nature in caring ways is not an abstract exercise in reasoning. It is, above all, a form of psychic and emotional health. Heroic ethics cannot manufacture health out of the void of abstraction. Psychic and emotional health cannot be manufactured at all. It can only be nurtured through the development of a favorable environment or context within which it can grow. The moral "climate" must be right.

Ecofeminists and other nature writers have often proclaimed the importance of a "holistic world view." By "holism" they refer to the notion of the "interdependence of all of life." But interdependence is hardly an ideal in and of itself. A master and slave may be said to be interconnected, but clearly that is not the kind of relation that ecofeminists wish to promote. The *quality* of relation is more important than the fact that a relation of some kind exists. If our society is to regain a sense of psychic health, we must learn to attend to the *quality* of relations and interactions, not just the *existence* of relations in themselves. Thus, when hunters claim to promote the well-being of the "whole" by killing individual animals, or to "love" the animals that they kill, we must challenge their story. Our own notion of holistic ethics must contain a respect for the "whole" *as well as* individual beings.

Respecting nature literally involves "looking again." We cannot attend to the quality of relations that we engage in unless we know the details that surround our actions and relations. If ecofeminists are sincere in their desire to live in a world of peace and nonviolence for all living beings, we must help each other through the painstaking process of piecing together the fragmented world view that we have inherited. But the pieces cannot simply be patched together. What is needed is a reweaving of all the old stories and narratives into a multifaceted tapestry.

As this tapestry begins to take shape, I stretch my imagination into the future and spin the following narrative. Many, many years from now, I am sitting by the fireside with my sister's grandchild. She turns to me and asks me to tell her a story of how things used to be, in the distant past. I turn to her and speak the following words:

"Once upon a time," I tell her, "there existed a period we now call the Age of Treason. During this time, men came to fear nature and revolted against the earlier matriarchal societies which had lived in harmony with the natural world as we do now. Many terrible things occurred during this time that will be difficult for you to understand. Women were raped and the earth was poisoned and warfare became routine.

"Animals were tortured throughout the land. They were trapped and clubbed so people could dress in their furs. They were enslaved in cages—in zoos, in laboratories, and on factory farms. People ate the flesh of animals and were frequently ill. Researchers told people that if they 'sacrificed' animals in laboratories they would be cured of disease. People no longer trusted in their own power to heal themselves and so they believed what they were told.

"The men had forgotten that they had formerly worshipped the animals they now reviled. Instead they worshipped a God that told them they had a special place in Creation, above all the other animals on earth. They found great comfort in this thought. And so they continued their cruel-hearted ways."

As I conclude my fantasy, I imagine my grandniece turning to me with a look of disbelief.

"Did they *really* used to eat animals?" she queries.

"Yes," I answer gently, "and much, much worse. But now that is all a matter of history. Like a very bad dream. Now, at long last, we can live in peace and harmony with all the creatures of the earth. The Age of Treason has passed."

NOTES

1. I have used the term "nature ethicists" to refer broadly to those writers working in the fields commonly referred to as "environmental ethics" and "animal liberation." I prefer the term "nature ethics" to that of "environmental ethics" since it more clearly implies the inclusion of humans within its parameters. The term "environmental ethics" tends to reinforce a dichotomous view of "humans" and "the rest of nature." For clarity, however, I sometimes use the term "environmental ethics" in order to distinguish this philosophical perspective from that of animal liberation. I also distinguish "nature ethics" from the field of "ecophilosophy." In contrast to nature ethicists, who seek to develop an *environmental ethic,* ecophilosophers, as referred to in this chapter, seek to develop *ecological consciousness* (see below).

2. There is considerable fluidity in the terminology of nature writers, and I am aware that not all writers employ the distinction I make between ecophilosophy and nature ethics. For alternate definitions of ecophilosophy, see Henrik Skolimowski, *Ecophilosophy: Designing New Tactics for Living* (Salem, N.H.: Marion Boyers, 1981); Arne Naess, "The Shallow and the Deep, Long-Range Ecology Movement: A Summary," *Inquiry* 16 (1973): 95–100.

   The term "ecosophy" has also been proposed to refer to "ecological wisdom," as opposed to the more abstract, philosophical approach implied by the term "ecophilosophy." This approach seems to bear the closest affinity to an ecofeminist consciousness or ethic; see, for example, Alan Drengson, *Beyond The Environmental Crisis: From Technocrat to Planetary Person* (New York: Peter Lang, 1989); Arne Naess, *Ecology Community and Lifestyle,* trans. and ed. David Rothenberg (Cambridge and New York: Cambridge University Press, 1990).

3. Stephan Lackner estimates that, disregarding the creatures slaughtered by humans, "only 5 percent of all animals are killed by other animals. Ninety-five percent of all animal lives are terminated without bloodshed: by old age, sickness and exhaustion, hunger and thirst, changing climates, and the like." *Peaceable Nature: An Optimistic View of Life on Earth* (San Francisco: Harper & Row, 1984), 12.

20

⊠ The Power and the Promise ⊠
of Ecological Feminism

KAREN J. WARREN

Karen Warren teaches philosophy at Macalester College. She edited several special issues on ecofeminism for Hypatia *and the* American Philosophical Association Newsletter on Feminism and Philosophy. *She is a co-editor of* Environmental Philosophy *and is completing a book with Jim Cheney entitled* Ecological Feminism.

INTRODUCTION

Ecological feminism (ecofeminism) has begun to receive a fair amount of attention lately as an alternative feminism and environmental ethic. Since Francoise d'Eaubonne introduced the term *ecofeminisme* in 1974 to bring attention to women's potential for bringing about an ecological revolution, the term has been used in a variety of ways. As I use the term in this paper, ecological feminism is the position that there are important connections—historical, experiential, symbolic, theoretical—between the domination of women and the domination of nature, an understanding of which is crucial to both feminism and environmental ethics. I argue that the promise and power of ecological feminism is that *it provides a distinctive framework both for reconceiving feminism and for developing an environmental ethic which takes seriously connections between the domination of women and the domination of nature.* I do so by discussing the nature of a feminist ethic and the ways in which ecofeminism provides a feminist and environmental ethic. I conclude that any feminist theory *and* any environmental ethic which fails to take seriously the twin and interconnected dominations of women and nature is at best incomplete and at worst simply inadequate.

FEMINISM, ECOLOGICAL FEMINISM,
AND CONCEPTUAL FRAMEWORKS

Whatever else it is, feminism is at least the movement to end sexist oppression. It involves the elimination of any and all factors that contribute to the continued and systematic domination or subordination of women. While feminists disagree about the nature of and solutions to the subordination of women, all feminists agree that sexist oppression exists, is wrong, and must be abolished.

A "feminist issue" is any issue that contributes in some way to understanding the oppression of women. Equal rights, comparable pay for comparable work, and food production are feminist issues wherever and whenever an understanding of them contributes to an understanding of the continued exploitation or subjugation of women. Carrying water and searching for firewood are feminist issues wherever and whenever women's primary responsibility for these tasks contributes to their lack of full participation in decision making, income producing, or high status positions engaged in by men. What counts as a feminist issue, then, depends largely on context, particularly the historical and material conditions of women's lives.

Environmental degradation and exploitation are feminist issues because an understanding of them contributes to an understanding of the oppression of women. In India, for example, both deforestation and reforestation through the introduction of a monoculture species tree (e.g., eucalyptus) intended for commercial production are feminist issues because the loss of indigenous forests and multiple species of trees has drastically affected rural Indian women's ability to maintain a subsistence household. Indigenous forests provide a variety of trees for food, fuel, fodder, household utensils, dyes, medicines, and income-generating uses, while monoculture-species forests do not. Although I do not argue for this claim here, a look at the global impact of environmental degradation on women's lives suggests important respects in which environmental degradation is a feminist issue.

Feminist philosophers claim that some of the most important feminist issues are *conceptual* ones: these issues concern how one conceptualizes such mainstay philosophical notions as reason and rationality, ethics, and what it is to be human. Ecofeminists extend this feminist philosophical concern to nature. They argue that, ultimately, some of the most important connections between the domination of women and the domination of nature are conceptual. To see this, consider the nature of conceptual frameworks.

A *conceptual framework* is a set of *basic* beliefs, values, attitudes, and assumptions which shape and reflect how one views oneself and one's world. It is a socially constructed lens through which we perceive ourselves and others. It is affected by such factors as gender, race, class, age, affectional orientation, nationality, and religious background.

Some conceptual frameworks are oppressive. An *oppressive conceptual framework* is one that explains, justifies, and maintains relationships of domination and subordination. When an oppressive conceptual framework is *patriarchal,* it explains, justifies, and maintains the subordination of women by men.

I have argued elsewhere that there are three significant features of oppressive conceptual frameworks: (1) value-hierarchical thinking, i.e., "up-down" thinking which places higher value, status, or prestige on what is "up" rather than on what is "down"; (2) value dualisms, i.e., disjunctive pairs in which the disjuncts are seen as oppositional (rather than as complementary) and exclusive (rather than as inclusive), and which place higher value (status, prestige) on one disjunct rather than the other (e.g., dualisms which give higher value or status to that which has historically been identified as "mind," "reason," and "male" than to that which has historically been identified as "body," "emotion," and "female"); and (3) logic of domination, i.e., a structure of argumentation which leads to a justification of subordination.

The third feature of oppressive conceptual frameworks is the most significant. A logic of domination is not *just* a logical structure. It also involves a substantive value system, since an ethical premise is needed to permit or sanction the "just" subordination of that which is subordinate. This justification typically is given on grounds of some alleged characteristic (e.g., rationality) which the dominant (e.g., men) have and the subordinate (e.g., women) lack.

Contrary to what many feminists and ecofeminists have said or suggested, there may be nothing *inherently* problematic about "hierarchical thinking" or even "value-hierarchical thinking" in contexts other than contexts of oppression. Hierarchical thinking is important in daily living for classifying data, comparing information, and organizing material. Taxonomies (e.g., plant taxonomies) and biological nomenclature seem to require *some* form of "hierarchical thinking." Even "value-hierarchical thinking" may be quite acceptable in certain contexts. (The same may be said of "value dualisms" in non-oppressive contexts.) For example, suppose it is true that what is unique about humans is our conscious capacity to radically reshape our social environments (or "societies"), as Murray Bookchin suggests. Then one could truthfully say that humans are better equipped to radically reshape their environments than are rocks or plants— a "value-hierarchical" way of speaking.

The problem is not simply *that* value-hierarchical thinking and value dualisms are used, but *the way* in which each has been used *in oppressive conceptual frameworks* to establish inferiority and to justify subordination.[1] It is the logic of domination, *coupled* with value-hierarchical thinking and value dualisms, which "justifies" subordination. What is explanatorily basic, then, about the nature of oppressive conceptual frameworks is the logic of domination.

For ecofeminism, that a logic of domination is explanatorily basic is important for at least three reasons. First, without a logic of domination, a description of similarities and differences would be just that—a description of similarities and differences. Consider the claim, "Humans are different from plants and rocks in that humans can (and plants and rocks cannot) consciously and radically reshape the communities in which they live; humans are similar to plants and rocks in that they are both members of an ecological community." Even if humans are "better" than plants and rocks with respect to the conscious ability of humans to radically transform communities, one does not *thereby* get any *morally* relevant distinction between humans and non-humans, or an argument for the domination of plants and rocks by humans. To get *those* conclusions one needs to add at least two powerful assumptions, viz., (A2) and (A4) in argument A below:

(A1) Humans do, and plants and rocks do not, have the capacity to consciously and radically change the community in which they live.

(A2) Whatever has the capacity to consciously and radically change the community in which it lives is morally superior to whatever lacks this capacity.

(A3) Thus, humans are morally superior to plants and rocks.

(A4) For any X and Y, if X is morally superior to Y, then X is morally justified in subordinating Y.

(A5) Thus, humans are morally justified in subordinating plants and rocks.

Without the two assumptions that *humans are morally superior* to (at least some) non-humans, (A2), and that *superiority justifies subordination,* (A4), all one has is some difference between humans and some nonhumans. This is true *even if* that difference is given in terms of superiority. Thus, it is the logic of domination, (A4), which is the bottom line in ecofeminist discussions of oppression.

Second, ecofeminists argue that, at least in Western societies, the oppressive conceptual framework which sanctions the twin dominations of women and nature is a patriarchal one characterized by all three features of an oppressive conceptual framework. Many ecofeminists claim that, historically, within at least the dominant Western culture, a patriarchal conceptual framework has sanctioned the following argument B:

(B1) Women are identified with nature and the realm of the physical; men are identified with the "human" and the realm of the mental.

(B2) Whatever is identified with nature and the realm of the physical is inferior to ("below") whatever is identified with the "human" and the realm of the mental; or, conversely, the latter is superior to ("above") the former.

(B3) Thus, women are inferior to ("below") men; or, conversely, men are superior to ("above") women.

(B4) For any X and Y, if X is superior to Y, then X is justified in subordinating Y.

(B5) Thus, men are justified in subordinating women.

If sound, argument B establishes *patriarchy,* i.e., the conclusion given at (B5) that the systematic domination of women by men is justified. But according to ecofeminists, (B5) is justified by just those three features of an oppressive conceptual framework identified earlier: value-hierarchical thinking, the assumption at (B2); value dualisms, the assumed dualism of the mental and the physical at (B1) and the assumed inferiority of the physical vis-à-vis the mental at (B2); and a logic of domination, the assumption at (B4), the same as the previous premise (A4). Hence, according to ecofeminists, insofar as an oppressive patriarchal conceptual framework has functioned historically (within at least dominant Western culture) to sanction the twin dominations of women and nature (argument B), both argument B and the patriarchal conceptual framework, from whence it comes, ought to be rejected.

Of course, the preceding does not identify which premises of B are false. What is the status of premises (B1) and (B2)? Most, if not all, feminists claim that (B1), and many ecofeminists claim that (B2), have been assumed or asserted within the dominant Western philosophical and intellectual tradition.[2] As such, these feminists assert, as a matter of historical fact, that the dominant Western philosophical tradition has assumed the truth of (B1) and (B2). Ecofeminists, however, either deny (B2) or do not affirm (B2). Furthermore, because some ecofeminists are anxious to deny any historical identification of women with nature, some ecofeminists deny (B1) when (B1) is used to support anything other than a strictly historical claim about what has been asserted or assumed to be true within patriarchal culture—e.g., when (B1) is used to assert that women properly are identified with the realm of nature and the physical.[3] Thus, from an ecofeminist perspective, (B1) and (B2) are properly viewed as problematic though historically sanctioned claims: they are problematic precisely because of the way they have functioned historically in a patriarchal conceptual framework and culture to sanction the dominations of women and nature.

What *all* ecofeminists agree about, then, is the way in which *the logic of domination* has functioned historically within patriarchy to sustain and justify the twin dominations of women and nature.[4] Since *all* feminists (and not just ecofeminists) oppose patriarchy, the conclusion given at (B5), all feminists (including ecofeminists) must oppose at least the logic of domination, premise (B4), on which argument B rests— whatever the truth-value status of (B1) and (B2) *outside* of a patriarchal context.

That *all* feminists must oppose the logic of domination shows the breadth and depth of the ecofeminist critique of B: it is a critique not only of the three assumptions on which this argument for the domination of women and nature rests, viz., the assumptions at (B1), (B2), and (B4); it is also a critique of patriarchal conceptual frameworks generally, i.e., of those oppressive conceptual frameworks which put men "up" and women "down," allege some way in which women are morally inferior to men, and use that alleged difference to justify the subordination of women by men. Therefore, ecofeminism is necessary to *any* feminist critique of patriarchy, and, hence, necessary to feminism (a point I discuss again later).

Third, ecofeminism clarifies why the logic of domination, and any conceptual framework which gives rise to it, must be abolished in order both to make possible a meaningful notion of difference which does not breed domination and to prevent feminism from becoming a "support" movement based primarily on shared experiences. In contemporary society, there is no one "woman's voice," no *woman* (or *human*) *simpliciter:* every woman (or human) is a woman (or human) of some race, class, age, affectional orientation, marital status, regional or national background, and so forth. Because there are no "monolithic experiences" that all women share, feminism must be a "solidarity movement" based on shared beliefs and interests rather than a "unity in sameness" movement based on shared experiences and shared victimization. In the words of Maria Lugones, "Unity—not to be confused with solidarity—is understood as conceptually tied to domination."

Ecofeminists insist that the sort of logic of domination used to justify the domination of humans by gender, racial or ethnic, or class status is also used to justify the domination of nature. Because eliminating a logic of domination is part of a feminist critique—whether a critique of patriarchy, white supremacist culture, or imperialism— ecofeminists insist that *naturism* is properly viewed as an integral part of any feminist solidarity movement to end sexist oppression and the logic of domination which conceptually grounds it.

ECOFEMINISM RECONCEIVES FEMINISM

The discussion so far has focused on some of the oppressive conceptual features of patriarchy. As I use the phrase, the "logic of traditional feminism" refers to the location of the conceptual roots of sexist oppression, at least in Western societies, in an oppressive patriarchal conceptual framework characterized by a logic of domination. Insofar as other systems of oppression (e.g., racism, classism, ageism, heterosexism) are also conceptually maintained by a logic of domination, appeal to the logic of traditional feminism ultimately locates the basic conceptual interconnections among *all* systems of oppression in the logic of domination. It thereby explains at a *conceptual* level why the eradication of sexist oppression requires the eradication of the other forms of oppression. It is by clarifying this conceptual connection between systems of oppression that a movement to end sexist oppression—traditionally the special turf of feminist theory and practice— leads to a reconceiving of feminism as *a movement to end all forms of oppression*.

Suppose one agrees that the logic of traditional feminism requires the expansion of feminism to include other social systems of domination (e.g., racism and classism). What warrants the inclusion of nature in these "social systems of domination"? Why must the logic of traditional feminism include the abolition of "naturism" (i.e., the domination or oppression of nonhuman nature) among the "isms" feminism must confront? The conceptual justification for expanding feminism to include ecofeminism is twofold. One basis has already been suggested: by showing that the conceptual connections between the dual dominations of women and nature are located in an oppressive and, at least in Western societies, patriarchal conceptual framework characterized by a logic of domination, ecofeminism explains how and why feminism, conceived as a movement to end sexist oppression, must be expanded and reconceived as also a movement to end naturism. This is made explicit by the following argument C:

(C1) Feminism is a movement to end sexism.

(C2) But Sexism is conceptually linked with naturism (through an oppressive conceptual framework characterized by a logic of domination).

(C3) Thus, Feminism is (also) a movement to end naturism.

Because, ultimately, these connections between sexism and naturism are conceptual—embedded in an oppressive conceptual framework—the logic of traditional feminism leads to the embracement of ecological feminism.

The other justification for reconceiving feminism to include ecofeminism has to do with the concepts of gender and nature. Just as conceptions of gender are socially constructed, so are conceptions of nature. Of course, the claim that women and nature are social constructions does not require anyone to deny that there are actual humans and actual trees, rivers, and plants. It simply implies that *how* women and nature are conceived is a matter of historical and social reality. These conceptions vary cross-culturally and by historical time period. As a result, any discussion of the "oppression or domination of nature" involves reference to historically specific forms of social domination of nonhuman nature by humans, just as discussion of the "domination of women" refers to historically specific forms of social domination of women by men. Although I do not argue for it here, an ecofeminist defense of the historical connections between the dominations of women and of nature, claims (B1) and (B2) in argument B, involves showing that within patriarchy the feminization of nature and the naturalization of women have been crucial to the historically successful subordinations of both.

If ecofeminism promises to reconceive traditional feminism in ways which include naturism as a legitimate feminist issue, does ecofeminism also promise to reconceive environmental ethics in ways which are feminist? I think so. This is the subject of the remainder of the paper.

CLIMBING FROM ECOFEMINISM TO ENVIRONMENTAL ETHICS

Many feminists and some environmental ethicists have begun to explore the use of first-person narrative as a way of raising philosophically germane issues in ethics often lost or underplayed in mainstream philosophical ethics. Why is this so? What is it about narrative which makes it a significant resource for theory and practice in feminism and environmental ethics? Even if appeal to first-person narrative is a helpful literary device for describing ineffable experience or a legitimate social science methodology for documenting personal and social history, how is first-person narrative a valuable vehicle of argumentation for ethical decision making and theory building? One fruitful way to begin answering these questions is to ask them of a particular first-person narrative.

Consider the following first-person narrative about rock climbing:

> For my very first rock climbing experience, I chose a somewhat private spot, away from other climbers and on-lookers. After studying "the chimney," I focused all my energy on making it to the top. I climbed with intense determination, using whatever strength and skills I had to accomplish this challenging feat. By midway I was exhausted and anxious. I couldn't see what to do next—where to put my hands or feet. Growing increasingly more weary as I clung somewhat desperately to the rock, I made a move. It didn't work. I fell. There I was, dangling midair above the rocky ground below, frightened but terribly relieved that the belay rope had held me. I knew I was safe. I took a look up at the climb that remained. I was determined to make it to the top. With renewed confidence and concentration, I finished the climb to the top.
>
> On my second day of climbing, I rappelled down about 200 feet from the top of the Palisades at Lake Superior to just a few feet above the water level. I could see no one—not my belayer, not the other climbers, no one. I unhooked slowly from the rappel rope and took a deep cleansing breath. I looked all around me— really looked—and listened. I heard a cacophony of voices—birds, trickles of water on the rock before me, waves lapping against the rocks below. I closed my eyes and began to feel the rock with my hands—the cracks and crannies, the raised lichen and mosses, the almost imperceptible nubs that might provide a resting place for my fingers and toes when I began to climb. At that moment I was bathed in serenity. I began to talk to the rock in an almost inaudible, child-like way, as if the rock were my friend. I felt an overwhelming sense of gratitude for what it offered me— a chance to know myself and the rock differently, to appreciate unforeseen miracles like the tiny flowers growing in the even tinier cracks in the rock's surface, and to come to know a sense of *being in relationship* with the natural environment. It felt as if the rock and I were silent conversational partners in a longstanding friendship. I realized then that I had come to care about this cliff which was so different from me, so unmovable and invincible, independent and seemingly indifferent my presence. I wanted to be with the rock as I climbed. Gone was the determination to conquer the rock, to forcefully impose my will on it; I wanted simply to work respectfully with the rock as I climbed. And as I climbed, that is what I felt. I felt myself *caring* for this rock and feeling thankful that climbing provided the opportunity for me to know it and myself in this new way.

There are at least four reasons why use of such a first-person narrative is important to feminism and environmental ethics. First, such a narrative gives voice to a felt sensitivity often lacking in traditional analytical ethical discourse, viz., sensitivity to conceiving of oneself as fundamentally "in relationship with" others, including the non-human environment. It is a modality which *takes relationships themselves seriously*. It thereby stands in contrast to a strictly reductionist modality that takes relationships seriously only or primarily because of the nature of the *relators* or parties to those relationships (e.g., relators conceived as moral agents, right holders, interest carriers, or sentient beings). In the rock-climbing narrative above, it is the climber's relationship with the rock she climbs which takes on special significance—which is itself a locus of value—in addition to whatever moral status or moral considerability she or the rock or any other parties to the relationship may also have.[5]

Second, such a first-person narrative gives expression to a variety of ethical attitudes and behaviors often overlooked or underplayed in mainstream Western ethics, e.g., the difference in attitudes and behaviors toward a rock when one is "making it to the top" and when one thinks of oneself as "friends with" or "caring about" the rock one climbs.[6] These different attitudes and behaviors suggest an ethically germane contrast between two different types of relationship humans or climbers may have toward a rock: an imposed conqueror-type relationship, and an emergent caring-type relationship. This contrast grows out of, and is faithful to, felt, lived experience.

The difference between conquering and caring attitudes and behaviors in relation to the natural environment provides a third reason why the use of first-person narrative is important to feminism and environmental ethics: it provides a way of conceiving of ethics and ethical meaning as *emerging out of* particular situations moral agents find themselves in, rather than as being *imposed on* those situations (e.g., as a derivation or instantiation of some predetermined abstract principle or rule). This emergent feature of narrative centralizes the importance of *voice*. When a multiplicity of cross-cultural *voices* are centralized, narrative is able to give expression to a range of attitudes, values, beliefs, and behaviors which may be overlooked or silenced by imposed ethical meaning and theory. As a reflection of and on felt, lived experiences, the use of narrative in ethics provides a stance from which ethical discourse can be held accountable to the historical, material, and social realities in which moral subjects find themselves.

Lastly, and for our purposes perhaps most importantly, the use of narrative has argumentative significance. Jim Cheney calls attention to this feature of narrative when he claims, "To contextualize ethical deliberation is, in some sense, to provide a narrative or story, from which the solution to the ethical dilemma emerges as the fitting conclusion." Narrative has argumentative force by suggesting *what counts* as an appropriate conclusion to an ethical situation. One ethical conclusion suggested by the climbing narrative is that what counts as a proper ethical attitude toward mountains and rocks is an attitude of respect and care (whatever that turns out to be or involve), not one of domination and conquest.

In an essay entitled "In and Out of Harm's Way: Arrogance and Love," feminist philosopher Marilyn Frye distinguishes between "arrogant" and "loving" perception as one way of getting at this difference in the ethical attitudes of care and conquest. Frye writes:

> The loving eye is a contrary of the arrogant eye.
> The loving eye knows the independence of the other. It is the eye of a seer who knows that nature is indifferent. It is the eye of one who knows that to know the seen, one must consult something other than one's own will and interests and fears and imagination. One must look at the thing. One must look and listen and check and question.
> The loving eye is one that pays a certain sort of attention. This attention can require a discipline but *not* a self-denial. The discipline is one of self-knowledge, knowledge of the scope and boundary of the self. . . . In particular, it is a matter of being able to tell one's own interests from those of others and of knowing where one's self leaves off and another begins. . . .
> The loving eye does not make the object of perception into something edible, does not try to assimilate it, does not reduce it to the size of the seer's desire, fear

and imagination, and hence does not have to simplify. It knows the complexity of the other as something which will forever present new things to be known. The science of the loving eye would favor The Complexity Theory of Truth [in contrast to The Simplicity Theory of Truth] and presuppose The Endless Interestingness of the Universe.

According to Frye, the loving eye is not an invasive, coercive eye which annexes others to itself, but one which "knows the complexity of the other as something which will forever present new things to be known."

When one climbs a rock as a conqueror, one climbs with an arrogant eye. When one climbs with a loving eye, one constantly "must look and listen and check and question." One recognizes the rock as something very different, something perhaps totally indifferent to one's own presence, and finds in that difference joyous occasion for celebration. One knows "the boundary of the self," where the self—the "I," the climber—leaves off and the rock begins. There is no fusion of two into one, but a complement of two entities _acknowledged_ as separate, different, independent, yet _in relationship;_ they are in relationship _if only_ because the loving eye is perceiving it, responding to it, noticing it, attending to it.

An ecofeminist perspective about both women and nature involves this shift in attitude from "arrogant perception" to "loving perception" of the nonhuman world. Arrogant perception of nonhumans by humans presupposes and maintains _sameness_ in such a way that it expands the moral community to those beings who are thought to resemble (be like, similar to, or the same as) humans in some morally significant way. Any environmental movement or ethic based on arrogant perception builds a moral hierarchy of beings and assumes some common denominator of moral considerability in virtue of which like beings deserve similar treatment or moral consideration and unlike beings do not. Such environmental ethics are or generate a "unity in sameness." In contrast, "loving perception" presupposes and maintains _difference_—a distinction between the self and other, between human and at least some nonhumans—in such a way that perception of the other as other _is_ an expression of love for one who/which is recognized at the outset as independent, dissimilar, different. As Maria Lugones says, in loving perception, "Love is seen not as fusion and erasure of difference but as incompatible with them." "Unity in sameness" alone is an _erasure of difference._

"Loving perception" of the nonhuman natural world is an attempt to understand what it means _for humans_ to care about the nonhuman world, a world _acknowledged_ as being independent, different, perhaps even indifferent to humans. Humans _are_ different from rocks in important ways, even if they are also both members of some ecological community. A moral community based on loving perception of oneself _in relationship with_ a rock, or with the natural environment as a whole, is one which acknowledges and respects difference, whatever "sameness" also exists. The limits of loving perception are determined only by the limits of one's (e.g., a person's, a community's) ability to respond lovingly (or with appropriate care, trust, or friendship)—whether it is to other humans or to the nonhuman world and elements of it.

If what I have said so far is correct, then there are very different ways to climb a mountain and _how_ one climbs it and _how_ one narrates the experience of climbing it matter ethically. If one climbs with "arrogant perception," with an attitude of "conquer and control," one keeps intact the very sorts of thinking that characterize a logic of domination and an oppressive conceptual framework. Since the oppressive conceptual framework which sanctions the domination of nature is a patriarchal one, one also thereby keeps intact, even if unwittingly, a patriarchal conceptual framework. Because the dismantling of patriarchal conceptual frameworks is a feminist issue, *how* one climbs a mountain and *how* one narrates—or tells the story—about the experience of climbing also are *feminist issues.* In this way, ecofeminism makes visible why, at a conceptual level, environmental ethics is a feminist issue.

CONCLUSION

I have argued in this paper that ecofeminism provides a framework for a distinctively feminist and environmental ethic. Ecofeminism grows out of the felt and theorized about connections between the domination of women and the domination of nature. As a contextualist ethic, ecofeminism refocuses environmental ethics on what nature might mean, morally speaking, *for* humans, and on how the relational attitudes of humans to others—humans as well as nonhumans—sculpt both what it is to be human and the nature and ground of human responsibilities to the nonhuman environment. Part of what this refocusing does is to take seriously the voices of women and other oppressed persons in the construction of that ethic.

A Sioux elder once told me a story about his son. He sent his seven-year-old son to live with the child's grandparents on a Sioux reservation so that he could "learn the Indian ways." Part of what the grandparents taught the son was how to hunt the four-leggeds of the forest. As I heard the story, the boy was taught, "to shoot your four-legged brother in his hind area, slowing it down but not killing it. Then, take the four legged's head in your hands, and look into his eyes. The eyes are where all the suffering is. Look into your brother's eyes and feel his pain. Then, take your knife and cut the four-legged under his chin, here, on his neck, so that he dies quickly. And as you do, ask your brother, the four-legged, for forgiveness for what you do. Offer also a prayer of thanks to your four-legged kin for offering his body to you just now, when you need food to eat and clothing to wear. And promise the four-legged that you will put yourself back into the earth when you die, to become nourishment for the earth, and for the sister flowers, and for the brother deer. It is appropriate that you should offer this blessing for the four-legged and, in due time, reciprocate in turn with your body in this way, as the four-legged gives life to you for your survival." As I reflect upon that story, I am struck by the power of the environmental ethic that grows out of and takes seriously narrative, context, and such values and relational attitudes as care, loving perception, and appropriate reciprocity, and doing what is appropriate in a given situation—however that notion of appropriateness eventually gets filled out. I am also struck by what one is able to see, once one begins to explore some of the historical and conceptual connections between the dominations of women and of nature. A *re-conceiving* and *re-visioning* of both feminism and environmental ethics, is, I think, the power and promise of ecofeminism.

NOTES

1. It may be that in contemporary Western society, which is so thoroughly structured by categories of gender, race, class, age, and affectional orientation, that there simply is no meaningful notion of "value-hierarchical thinking" which does not function in an oppressive context. For purposes of this paper, I leave that question open.
2. Many feminists who argue for the historical point that claims (B1) and (B2) have been asserted or assumed to be true within the dominant Western philosophical tradition do so by discussion of that tradition's conceptions of reason, rationality, and science. For a sampling of the sorts of claims made within that context, see "Reason, Rationality, and Gender," ed. Nancy Tuana and Karen J. Warren, a special issue of the American Philosophical Association's *Newsletter on Feminism and Philosophy* 88, no. 2 (March 1989): 17–71. Ecofeminists who claim that (B2) has been assumed to be true within the dom-

inant Western philosophical tradition include: Gray, *Green Paradise Lost;* Griffin, *Woman and Nature: The Roaring Inside Her;* Merchant, *The Death of Nature;* Ruether, *New Woman/New Earth.* For a discussion of some of these ecofeminist historical accounts, see Plumwood, "Ecofeminism." While I agree that the historical connections between the domination of women and the domination of nature is a crucial one, I do not argue for that claim here.

3. Ecofeminists who deny (B1) when (B1) is offered as anything other than a true, descriptive, historical claim about patriarchal culture often do so on grounds that an objectionable sort of biological determinism, or at least harmful female sex-gender stereotypes, underlie (B1). For a discussion of this "split" among those ecofeminists ("nature feminists") who assert and those ecofeminists ("social feminists") who deny (B1) as anything other than a true historical claim about how women are described in patriarchal culture, see Griscom, "On Healing the Nature/History Split."

4. I make no attempt here to defend the historically sanctioned truth of these premises.

5. Suppose, as I think is the case, that a necessary condition for the existence of a moral relationship is that at least one party to the relationship is a moral being (leaving open for our purposes what counts as a "moral being"). If this is so, then the Mona Lisa cannot properly be said to have or stand in a moral relationship with the wall on which she hangs, and a wolf cannot have or properly be said to have or stand in a moral relationship with a moose. Such a necessary-condition account leaves open the question whether *both* parties to the relationship must be moral beings. My point here is simply that however one resolves *that* question, recognition of the relationships themselves as a locus of value is a recognition of a source of value that is different from and not reducible to the values of the "moral beings" in those relationships.

6. It is interesting to note that the image of being friends with the Earth is one which cytogeneticist Barbara McClintock uses when she describes the importance of having "a feeling for the organism," "listening to the material [in this case the corn plant]," in one's work as a scientist. See Evelyn Fox Keller, "Women, Science, and Popular Mythology," in *Machina Ex Dea: Feminist Perspectives on Technology,* ed. Joan Rothschild (New York: Pergamon Press, 1983), and Evelyn Fox Keller, *A Feeling For the Organism: The Life and Work of Barbara McClintock* (San Francisco: W. H. Freeman, 1983).

21

⚏ *What Is Social Ecology?* ⚏

MURRAY BOOKCHIN

Murray Bookchin is cofounder and director emeritus of the Institute for Social Ecology. Some of his many books are Toward an Ecological Society, The Ecology of Freedom, The Rise of Urbanization and the Decline of Citizenship, *and* The Philosophy of Social Ecology.

What literally defines social ecology as "social" is its recognition of the often over-looked fact that nearly all our present ecological problems arise from deep-seated social problems. Conversely, present ecological problems cannot be clearly understood, much less resolved, without resolutely dealing with problems within society. To make this point more concrete: economic, ethnic, cultural, and gender conflicts, among many others, lie at the core of the most serious ecological dislocations we face today—apart, to be sure, from those that are produced by natural catastrophes.

If this approach seems a bit too "sociological" for those environmentalists who identify ecological problems with the preservation of wildlife, wilderness, or more broadly, with "Gaia" and planetary "Oneness," it might be sobering to consider certain recent facts. The massive oil spill by an Exxon tanker at Prince William Sound, the extensive deforestation of redwood trees by the Maxxam Corporation, and the proposed James Bay hydroelectric project that would flood vast areas of northern Quebec's forests, to cite only a few problems, should remind us that the real battleground on which the ecological future of the planet will be decided is clearly a social one.

Indeed, to separate ecological problems from social problems—or even to play down or give token recognition to this crucial relationship—would be to grossly misconstrue the sources of the growing environmental crisis. The way human beings deal with each other as social beings is crucial to addressing the ecological crisis. Unless we clearly recognize this, we will surely fail to see that the hierarchical mentality and class relationships that so thoroughly permeate society give rise to the very idea of dominating the natural world.

Unless we realize that the present market society, structured around the brutally competitive imperative of "grow or die," is a thoroughly impersonal, self-operating mechanism, we will falsely tend to blame technology as such or population growth as such for environmental problems. We will ignore their root causes, such as trade for profit, industrial expansion, and the identification of "progress" with corporate self-interest. In short, we will tend to focus on the symptoms of a grim social pathology rather than on the pathology itself, and our efforts will be directed toward limited goals whose attainment is more cosmetic than curative.

While some have questioned whether social ecology has dealt adequately with issues of spirituality, it was, in fact, among the earliest of contemporary ecologies to call for a sweeping change in existing spiritual values. Such a change would mean a far-reaching transformation of our prevailing mentality of domination into one of complementarity, in which we would see our role in the natural world as creative, supportive, and deeply appreciative of the needs of nonhuman life. In social ecology, a truly *natural* spirituality centers on the ability of an awakened humanity to function as moral agents in diminishing needless suffering, engaging in ecological restoration, and fostering an aesthetic appreciation of natural evolution in all its fecundity and diversity.

Thus social ecology has never eschewed the need for a radically new spirituality or mentality in its call for a collective effort to change society. Indeed, as early as 1965, the first public statement to advance the ideas of social ecology concluded with the injunction: "The cast of mind that today organizes differences among human and other life-forms along hierarchical lines of 'supremacy' or 'inferiority' will give way to an outlook that deals with diversity in an ecological manner—that is, according to an ethics of complementarity."[1] In such an ethics, human beings would complement nonhuman beings with their own capacities to produce a richer, creative, and developmental whole—not as a "dominant" species but as a supportive one. Although this idea, expressed at times as an appeal for the "respiritization of the natural world," recurs throughout the literature of social ecology, it should not be mistaken for a theology that raises a deity above the natural world or that seeks to discover one within it. The spirituality advanced by social ecology is definitely naturalistic (as one would expect, given its relation to ecology itself, which stems from the biological sciences), rather than supernaturalistic or pantheistic.

To prioritize any form of spirituality over the social factors that actually erode all forms of spirituality, raises serious questions about one's ability to come to grips with reality. At a time when a blind social mechanism, the market, is turning soil into sand, covering fertile land with concrete, poisoning air and water, and producing sweeping climatic and atmospheric changes, we cannot ignore the impact that a hierarchical and class society has on the natural world. We must earnestly deal with the fact that economic growth, gender oppressions, and ethnic domination—not to speak of corporate, state, and bureaucratic interests—are much more capable of shaping the future of the natural world than are privatistic forms of spiritual self-regeneration. These forms of domination must be confronted by collective action and major social movements that challenge the social sources of the ecological crisis, not simply by personalistic forms of consumption and investment that often go under the rubric of "green capitalism." We live in a highly cooptative society that is only too eager to find new areas of commercial aggrandizement and to add ecological verbiage to its advertising and customer relations.

NATURE AND SOCIETY

Let us begin, then, with basics—namely, by asking what we mean by nature and society. Among the many definitions of nature that have been formulated over time, one is rather elusive and often difficult to grasp because it requires a certain way of thinking—one that stands at odds with what we popularly call "linear thinking." This form of "nonlinear" or organic thinking is developmental rather than analytical, or, in more technical terms, dialectical rather than instrumental. Nature, conceived in terms of developmental thinking, is more than the beautiful vistas we see from a mountaintop or in the images that are fixed on the backs of picture postcards. Such vistas and images of nonhuman nature are basically static and immobile. Our attention, to be sure, may be arrested by the soaring flight of a hawk, or the bolting leap of a deer, or the low-slung shadowy loping of a coyote. But what we are really witnessing in such cases are the mere kinetics of physical motion, caught in the frame of an essentially static image of the scene before our eyes. It deceives us into believing in the "eternality" of a single moment in nature.

If we look with some care into nonhuman nature as more than a scenic view, we begin to sense that it is basically an evolving phenomenon, a richly fecund, even dramatic development that is forever changing. I mean to define nonhuman nature precisely as an evolving process, as the *totality,* in fact of its evolution. This encompasses the development from the inorganic into the organic, from the less differentiated and relatively limited world of unicellular organisms into that of multicellular ones equipped with simple, later complex, and presently fairly intelligent neural apparatuses that allow them to make innovative choices. Finally, the acquisition of warm-bloodedness gives to organisms the astonishing flexibility to exist in the most demanding climatic environments.

This vast drama of nonhuman nature is in every respect stunningly wondrous. It is marked by increasing subjectivity and flexibility and by increasing differentiation that makes an organism more adaptable to new environmental challenges and opportunities and renders a living being more equipped to alter its environment to meet its own needs. One may speculate that the potentiality of matter itself—the ceaseless interactivity of atoms in forming new chemical combinations to produce ever more complex molecules, amino acids, proteins, and, under suitable conditions, elementary life-forms—is inherent in inorganic nature. Or one may decide, quite matter-of-factly, that the "struggle for existence" or the "survival of the fittest" (to use popular Darwinian terms) explains why increasingly subjective and more flexible beings are capable of dealing with environmental changes more effectively than are less subjective and flexible beings. But the fact remains that the kind of evolutionary drama I have described did occur, and is carved in stone in the fossil record. That nature is this record, this history, this developmental or evolutionary process, is a very sobering fact.

Conceiving nonhuman nature as its own evolution rather than as a mere vista has profound implications—ethical as well as biological—for ecologically minded people. Human beings embody, at least potentially, attributes of nonhuman development that place them squarely within organic evolution. They are not "natural aliens," to use Neil Evernden's phrase, strange "exotics," phylogenetic "deformities" that, owing to their tool-making capacities, "cannot evolve *with* an ecosystem anywhere."[2] Nor are they "intelligent fleas," to use the language of Gaian theorists who believe that the earth ("Gaia") is one living organism. These untenable disjunctions between humanity and the evolutionary process are as superficial as they are potentially misanthropic. Humans are highly intelligent, indeed, very self-conscious primates, which is to say that they have emerged—not diverged—from a long evolution of vertebrate life-forms into mammalian, and finally, primate life-forms. They are a product of a significant evolutionary trend toward intellectuality, self-awareness, will, intentionality, and expressiveness, be it in oral or body language.

Human beings belong to a natural continuum, no less than their primate ancestors and mammals in general. To depict them as "aliens" that have no place or pedigree in natural evolution, or to see them essentially as an infestation that parasitizes a highly anthropomorphic version of the planet (Gaia) the way fleas parasitize dogs and cats, is bad thinking, not only bad ecology. Lacking any sense of process, this kind of thinking—regrettably so commonplace among ethicists—radically bifurcates the nonhuman from the human. Indeed, to the degree that nonhuman nature is romanticized as "wilderness," and seen presumably as more authentically "natural" than the works of humans, the natural world is frozen into a circumscribed domain in which human innovation, foresight, and creativity have no place and offer no possibilities.

The truth is that human beings not only belong in nature, they are products of a long, natural evolutionary process. Their seemingly "unnatural" activities—like the development of technology and science, the formation of mutable social institutions, of highly symbolic forms of communication, of aesthetic sensibilities, the creation of towns and cities—all would be impossible without the large array of physical attributes that have been eons in the making, be they large brains or the bipedal motion that frees their hands for tool making and carrying food. In many respects, human traits are enlargements of nonhuman traits that have been evolving over the ages. Increasing care for the young, cooperation, the substitution of mentally guided behavior for largely instinctive behavior—all are present more keenly in human behavior. The difference between the development of these traits among nonhuman beings is that among humans they reach a degree of elaboration and integration that yields cultures or, viewed institutionally in terms of families, bands, tribes, hierarchies, economic classes, and the state, highly mutable *societies* for which there is no precedent in the nonhuman world—unless the genetically programmed behavior of insects is to be regarded as "social." In fact, the emergence and development of human society is a shedding of instinctive behavioral traits, a continuing process of clearing a new terrain for potentially rational behavior.

Human beings always remain rooted in their biological evolutionary history, which we may call "first nature," but they produce a characteristically human social nature of their own, which we may call "second nature." And far from being "unnatural," human second nature is eminently a creation of organic evolution's first nature. To write the second nature created by human beings out of nature as a whole, or indeed, to minimize it, is to ignore the creativity of natural evolution itself and to view it onesidedly. If "true" evolution embodies itself simply in creatures like grizzly bears, wolves, and whales—generally, animals that *people* find aesthetically pleasing or relatively intelligent—then human beings are literally *de*-natured. In such views, whether seen as "aliens" or as "fleas," humans are essentially placed outside the self-organizing thrust of natural evolution toward increasing subjectivity and flexibility. The more enthusiastic proponents of this de-naturing of humanity may see human beings as existing apart from nonhuman evolution, thereby dealing with people as a "freaking," as Paul Shepard puts it, of the evolutionary process. Others simply avoid the problem of humanity's unique place in natural evolution by promiscuously putting human beings on a par with beetles in terms of their "intrinsic worth." In this "either/or" propositional thinking, the social is either separated from the organic, or flippantly reduced to the organic, resulting in an inexplicable dualism at one extreme or a naive reductionism at the other. The dualistic approach, with its quasi-theological premise that the world was "made" for human use is saddled with the name of "anthropocentricity," while the reductionist approach, with its almost meaningless notion of a "biocentric democracy," is saddled with the name of "biocentricity."

The bifurcation of the human from the nonhuman reveals a failure to think organically, and to approach evolutionary phenomena with an evolutionary way of thought. Needless to say, if we are content to regard nature as no more than a scenic vista, mere metaphoric and poetic description of it might suffice to replace systematic thinking about it. But if we regard nature as the history of nature, as an evolutionary process that is going on to one degree or another under our very eyes, we dishonor this process by thinking of it in anything but a processual way. That is to say, we require a way of thinking that recognizes that "what-is" as it seems to lie before our eyes is always developing into "what-it-is-not," that it is engaged in a continual self-organizing process in which past and present, seen as a richly differentiated but shared continuum, give rise to a new potentiality for a future, ever-richer degree of *wholeness*. Accordingly, the human and the nonhuman can be seen as aspects of an evolutionary continuum, and the emergence of the human can be located in the evolution of the nonhuman, without advancing naive claims that one is either "superior to" or "made for" the other.

By the same token, in a processual, organic, and dialectical way of thinking, we would have little difficulty in locating and explaining the emergence of the social out of the biological, of second nature out of first nature. It seems more fashionable these days to deal with ecologically significant social issues like a bookkeeper. One simply juxtaposes two columns—labeled "old paradigm" and "new paradigm"—as though one were dealing with debits and credits. Obviously distasteful terms like "centralization" are placed under "old paradigm," while more appealing ones like "decentralization" are regarded as "new paradigm." The result is an inventory of bumper-sticker slogans whose "bottom line" is patently a form of "absolute good versus absolute evil." All of this may be deliciously synoptic and easy for the eyes, but it is singularly lacking as food for the brain. To truly *know* and be able to give interpretative *meaning* to the social issues so arranged, we should want to know how each idea derived from others and is part of an overall development. What, in fact, do we mean by the notion of "decentralization," and how does it derive from or give rise in the history of human society to "centralization"? Again: processual thinking is needed to deal with processual realities so that we can gain some sense of *direction*—practical as well as theoretical—in dealing with our ecological problems.

Social ecology seems to stand alone, at present, in calling for the use of organic, developmental, and derivative ways of thinking out problems that are basically organic and developmental in character. The very definition of the natural world as a development indicates the need for an organic way of thinking, as does the derivation of human from nonhuman nature—a derivation that has the most far-reaching consequences for an ecological ethics that can offer serious guidelines for the solution of our ecological problems.

Social ecology calls upon us to see that nature and society are interlinked by evolution into one nature that consists of two differentiations: first or biotic nature, and second or human nature. Human nature and biotic nature share an evolutionary potential for greater subjectivity and flexibility. Second nature is the way in which human beings as flexible, highly intelligent primates *inhabit* the natural world. That is to say, people create an environment that is most suitable for their mode of existence. In this respect, second nature is no different from the environment that every animal, depending upon its abilities, creates as well as adapts to, the biophysical circumstances—or ecocommunity—in which it must live. On this very simple level, human beings are, in principle, doing nothing that differs from the survival activities of nonhuman beings—be it building beaver dams or gopher holes.

But the environmental changes that human beings produce are significantly different from those produced by nonhuman beings. Humans act upon their environments with considerable technical foresight, however lacking that foresight may be in ecological respects. Their cultures are rich in knowledge, experience, cooperation, and conceptual intellectuality; however, they may be sharply divided against themselves at certain points of their development, through conflicts between groups, classes, nation-states, and even city-states. Nonhuman beings generally live in ecological niches, their behavior guided primarily by instinctive drives and conditioned reflexes. Human societies are "bonded" together by institutions that change radically over centuries. Nonhuman communities are notable for their fixity in general terms or by clearly preset, often genetically imprinted, rhythms. Human communities are guided in part by ideological factors and are subject to changes conditioned by those factors.

Hence human beings, emerging from an organic evolutionary process, initiate, by the sheer force of their biology and survival needs, a social evolutionary development that profoundly involves their organic evolutionary process. Owing to their naturally endowed intelligence, powers of communication, capacity for institutional organization, and relative freedom from instinctive behavior, they refashion their environment—as do nonhuman beings—to the full extent of their biological equipment. This equipment now makes it possible for them to engage in social development. It is not so much that human beings, in principle, behave differently from animals or are inherently more problematical in a strictly ecological sense, but that the social development by which they grade out of their biological development often becomes more problematical for themselves and nonhuman life. How these problems emerge, the ideologies they produce, the extent to which they contribute to biotic evolution or abort it, and the damage they inflict on the planet as a whole lie at the very heart of the modern ecological crisis. Second nature, far from marking the fulfillment of human potentialities, is riddled by contradictions, antagonisms, and conflicting interests that have distorted humanity's unique capacities for development. It contains both the danger of tearing down the biosphere and, given a further development of humanity toward an ecological society, the capacity to provide an entirely new ecological dispensation.

SOCIAL HIERARCHY AND DOMINATION

How, then, did the social—eventually structured around status groups, class formations, and cultural phenomena—emerge from the biological? We have reason to speculate that as biological facts such as lineage, gender distribution, and age differences were slowly institutionalized, their uniquely social dimension was initially quite egalitarian. Later it acquired an oppressive hierarchical and then an exploitative class form. The lineage or blood tie in early prehistory obviously formed the organic basis of the family. Indeed, it joined together groups of families into bands, clans, and tribes, through either intermarriage or fictive forms of descent, thereby forming the earliest social horizon of our ancestors. More than in other mammals, the simple biological facts of human reproduction and protracted maternal care of the infant tended to knit siblings together and produced a strong sense of solidarity and group inwardness. Men, women, and their children were brought into a condition of a fairly stable family life, based on mutual obligation and an expressed sense of affinity that was often sanctified by marital vows of one kind or another.

Outside the family and all its elaborations into bands, clans, tribes and the like, other human beings were regarded as "strangers," who could alternatively be welcomed hospitably or enslaved or put to death. What mores existed were based on an unreflected body of *customs* that seemed to have been inherited from time immemorial. What we call *morality* began as the commandments of a deity, in that they required some kind of supernatural or mystical reinforcement to be accepted by the community. Only later, beginning with the ancient Greeks, did *ethical* behavior emerge, based on rational discourse and reflection. The shift from blind custom to a commanding morality, and finally, to a rational ethics occurred with the rise of cities and urban cosmopolitanism. Humanity, gradually disengaging itself from the biological facts of blood ties, began to admit the "stranger" and increasingly recognize itself as a shared community of human beings rather than an ethnic folk—a community of citizens rather than of kinsmen.

In the primordial and socially formative world that we must still explore, other of humanity's biological traits were to be reworked from the strictly natural to the social. One of these was the fact of age and its distinctions. In the emerging social groups that developed among early humans, the absence of a written language helped to confer on the elderly a high degree of status, for it was they who possessed the traditional wisdom of the community, the kinship lines that prescribed marital ties in obedience to extensive incest taboos, and techniques for survival that had to be acquired by both the young and the mature members of the group. In addition, the biological fact of gender distinctions were to be slowly reworked along social lines into what were initially complementary sororal and fraternal groups. Women formed their own food-gathering and care-taking groups with their own customs, belief systems, and values, while men formed their own hunting and warrior groups with their own behavioral characteristics, mores, and ideologies.

From everything we know about the socialization of the biological facts of kinship, age, and gender groups—their elaboration into early institutions—there is no reason to doubt that people existed in a complementary relationship with one another. Each, in effect, was needed by the other to form a relatively stable whole. No one "dominated" the others or tried to privilege itself in the normal course of things. Yet with the passing of time, even as the biological facts that underpin every human group were further reworked into social institutions, so the social institutions were slowly reworked at various periods and in various degrees, into hierarchical structures based on command and obedience. I speak here of a historical trend, in no way predetermined by any mystical force or deity, a trend that often did not go beyond a very limited development among many preliterate or aboriginal cultures, and even in certain fairly elaborate civilizations. Nor can we foretell how human history might have developed had certain feminine values associated with care and nurture not been overshadowed by masculine values associated with combative and aggressive behavior.

Hierarchy in its earliest forms was probably not marked by the harsh qualities it has acquired over history. Elders, at the very beginnings of gerontocracy, were not only respected for their wisdom but often beloved of the young, and their affection was often reciprocated in kind. We can probably account for the increasing stridency and harshness of later gerontocracies by supposing that the elderly, burdened by their failing powers and dependent upon the community's goodwill, were more vulnerable to abandonment in periods of material want than any other part of the population. In any case, that gerontocracies were the earliest forms of hierarchy is corroborated by their existence in communities as far removed from each other as the Australian Aborigines, tribal societies in East Africa, and Indian communities in the Americas. "Even in simple food-gathering cultures, individuals above fifty, let us say, apparently arrogated to themselves certain powers and privileges which benefitted themselves specifically," observes anthropologist Paul Radin, "and were not necessarily, if at all, dictated by considerations either of the rights of others or the welfare of the community."[3] Many tribal councils throughout the world were really councils of elders, an institution that never completely disappeared (as the word "alderman" suggests), even though they were overlaid by warrior societies, chiefdoms, and kingships.

Patricentricity, in which male values, institutions, and forms of behavior prevail over female ones, seems to have followed gerontocracy. Initially, this shift may have been fairly harmless, inasmuch as preliterate and early aboriginal societies were largely domestic communities in which the authentic center of material life was the home, not the "men's house" so widely present in tribal societies. Male rule, if such it can be strictly called, takes on its most severe and coercive form in patriarchy, an institution in which the eldest male of an extended family or clan has a life-and-death command over all members of the group. Women are by no means the exclusive or even the principal target of the patriarch's domination. The sons, like the daughters, may be ordered how to behave and whom to marry, and may be killed at the whim of the "old man." So far as patricentricity is concerned, however, the authority and prerogative of the male are the product of a slow, often subtly negotiated development in which the male fraternity tends to edge out the female sorority by virtue of the former's growing "civil" responsibilities. Increasing population, marauding bands of outsiders whose migrations may be induced by drought or other unfavorable conditions, and vendettas of one kind or another, to cite common causes of hostility or war, create a new "civil" sphere side by side with woman's domestic sphere, and the former gradually encroaches upon the latter. With the appearance of cattle-drawn plow agriculture, the male begins to invade the horticultural sphere of woman, who had used the simple digging stick, and her earlier economic predominance in the community's life is thereby diluted. Warrior societies and chiefs carry the momentum of male dominance to the level of a new material and cultural constellation. Male dominance becomes extremely active and ultimately yields a world that is managed by male elites who dominate not only women but also other men.

"Why" hierarchy emerges is transparent enough: the infirmities of age, increasing population, natural disasters, certain technological changes that privilege male activities of hunting and caring for animals over the horticultural functions of females, the growth of civil society, the spread of warfare. All serve to enhance the male's responsibilities at the expense of the female's. Marxist theorists tend to single out technological advances and the presumed material surpluses they produce to explain the emergence of elite strata—indeed, of exploiting ruling classes. However, this does not tell us why many societies whose environments were abundantly rich in food never produced such strata. That surpluses are necessary to support elites and classes is obvious, as Aristotle pointed out more than two millennia ago. But too many communities that had such resources at their disposal remained quite egalitarian and never "advanced" to hierarchical or class societies.

It is worth emphasizing that hierarchical domination, however coercive it may be, is not to be confused with class exploitation. Often the role of high-status individuals is very well-meaning, as in the case of commands given by caring parents to their children, of concerned husbands and wives to each other, or of elderly people to younger ones. In tribal societies, even where a considerable measure of authority accrues to a chief—and most chiefs are advisers rather than rulers—he usually must earn the esteem of the community by interacting with the people, and he can easily be ignored or removed from his position by them. Many chiefs earn their prestige, so essential to their authority, by disposing of gifts, and even by a considerable disaccumulation of their personal goods. The respect accorded to many chiefs is earned, not by hoarding surpluses as a means to power but by disposing of them as evidence of generosity.

Classes tend to operate along different lines. Power is usually gained by the acquisition of wealth, not by its disposal; rulership is guaranteed by outright physical coercion, not simply by persuasion; and the state is the ultimate guarantor of authority. That hierarchy is more entrenched than class can perhaps be verified by the fact that women have been dominated for millennia, despite sweeping changes in class societies. By the same token, the abolition of class rule and economic exploitation offers no guarantee whatever that elaborate hierarchies and systems of domination will disappear.

In nonhierarchical and even some hierarchical societies, certain customs guide human behavior along basically decent lines. Of primary importance in early customs was the "law of the irreducible minimum" (to use Radin's expression), the shared notion that all members of a community are entitled to the means of life, irrespective of the amount of work they perform. To deny anyone food, shelter, and the basic means of life because of infirmities or even frivolous behavior would have been seen as a heinous denial of the very right to live. Nor were the resources and things needed to sustain the community ever completely privately owned: overriding individualistic control was the broader principle of usufruct—the notion that the means of life that were not being used by one group could be used, as need be, by another. Thus unused land, orchards, and even tools and weapons, if left idle, were at the disposition of anyone in the community who needed them. Lastly, custom fostered the practice of mutual aid, the rather sensible cooperative behavior of sharing things and labor, so that an individual or family in fairly good circumstances could expect to be helped by others if their fortunes should change for the worse. Taken as a whole, these customs became so sedimented into society that they persisted long after hierarchy became oppressive and class society became predominant.

THE IDEA OF DOMINATING NATURE

"Nature," in the broad sense of a biotic environment from which humans take the simple things they need for survival, often has no meaning to preliterate peoples. Immersed in nature as the very universe of their lives, it has no special meaning, even when they celebrate animistic rituals and view the world around them as a nexus of life, often imputing their own social institutions to the behavior of various species, as in the case of "beaver lodges" and humanlike spirits. Words that express our conventional notions of nature are not easy to find, if they exist at all, in the languages of aboriginal peoples.

With the rise of hierarchy and human domination, however, the seeds are planted for a belief that nature not only exists as a world apart, but that it is hierarchically organized and can be dominated. The study of magic reveals this shift clearly. Early forms of magic did not view nature as a world apart. Its worldview tended to be such that a practitioner essentially pleaded with the "chief spirit" of the game to coax an animal in the direction of an arrow or a spear. Later, magic becomes almost entirely instrumental; the game is coerced by magical techniques to become the hunter's prey. While the earliest forms of magic may be regarded as the practices of a generally nonhierarchical and egalitarian community, the later forms of animistic beliefs betray a more or less hierarchical view of the natural world and of latent human powers of domination.

We must emphasize, here, that the *idea* of dominating nature has its primary source in the domination of human by human and the structuring of the natural world into a hierarchical Chain of Being (a static conception, incidentally, that has no relationship to the evolution of life into increasingly advanced forms of subjectivity and flexibility). The biblical injunction that gave to Adam and Noah command of the living world was above all an expression of a *social* dispensation. Its idea of dominating nature can be overcome only through the creation of a society without those class and hierarchical structures that make for rule and obedience in private as well as public life. That this new dispensation involves changes in attitudes and values should go without saying. But these attitudes and values remain vaporous if they are not given substance through objective institutions, the ways in which humans concretely interact with each other, and in the realities of everyday life from childrearing to work and play. Until human beings cease to live in societies that are structured around hierarchies as well as economic classes, we shall never be free of domination, however much we try to dispel it with rituals, incantations, ecotheologies, and the adoption of seemingly "natural" ways of life.

The idea of dominating nature has a history that is almost as old as that of hierarchy itself. Already in the Gilgamesh Epic of Mesopotamia, a drama that dates back some 7,000 years, the hero defies the deities and cuts down their sacred trees in his quest for immortality. The *Odyssey* is a vast travelogue of the Greek warrior, albeit a more canny than a heroic one, who essentially dispatches the nature deities that the Hellenic world inherited from its less well-known precursors. That elitist societies devastated much of the Mediterranean basin as well as the hillsides of China provides ample evidence that hierarchical and class societies had begun a sweeping remaking and despoliation of the planet long before the emergence of modern science, "linear" rationality, and "industrial society," to cite causal factors that are invoked so freely in the modern ecology movement. Second nature, to be sure, did not create a Garden of Eden in steadily absorbing and inflicting harm on first nature. More often than not, it despoiled much that was beautiful, creative, and dynamic in the biotic world, just as it ravaged human life itself in murderous wars, genocide, and acts of heartless oppression. Social ecology refuses to ignore the fact that the harm elitist society inflicted on the natural world was more than matched by the harm it inflicted on humanity; nor does it overlook the fact that the destiny of human life goes hand-in-hand with the destiny of the nonhuman world.

But the customs of the irreducible minimum, usufruct, and mutual aid cannot be ignored, however troubling the ills produced by second nature may seem. These customs persisted well into history and surfaced almost explosively in massive popular uprisings, from early revolts in ancient Sumer to the present time. Many of those demanded the recovery of caring and communitarian values when these were under the onslaught of elitist and class oppression. Indeed, despite the armies that roamed the landscape of warring areas, the taxgatherers who plundered ordinary village peoples, and the daily abuses that were inflicted by overseers on workers, community life still persisted and retained many of the cherished values of a more egalitarian past. Neither ancient despots nor feudal lords could fully obliterate them in peasant villages and in the towns with independent craft guilds. In ancient Greece, religions based on austerity and, more significantly, a rational philosophy that rejected the encumbering of thought and political life by extravagant wants, tended to scale down needs and delimit human appetites for material goods. They served to slow the pace of technological innovation to a point where new means of production could be sensitively integrated into a balanced society. Medieval markets were modest, usually local affairs, in which guilds exercised strict control over prices, competition, and the quality of the goods produced by their members.

"GROW OR DIE!"

But just as hierarchies and class structures tend to acquire a momentum of their own and permeate much of society, so too the market began to acquire a life of its own and extended its reach beyond limited regions into the depths of vast continents. Exchange ceased to be primarily a means to provide for modest needs, subverting the limits imposed upon it by guilds or by moral and religious restrictions. Not only did it place a high premium on techniques for increasing production; it also became the pro-creator of needs, many of which are simply useless, and gave an explosive impetus to consumption and technology. First in northern Italy and the European lowlands, later— and most effectively—in England during the seventeenth and eighteenth centuries, the production of goods exclusively for sale and profit (the capitalistic commodity) rapidly swept aside all cultural and social barriers to market growth.

By the late eighteenth and early nineteenth centuries, the new industrial capital-ist class with its factory system and commitment to limitless expansion began to colonize the entire world, and finally, most aspects of personal life. Unlike the feudal nobility, which had its cherished lands and castles, the bourgeoisie had no home but the mar-ketplace and its bank vaults. As a class, they turned more and more of the world into an ever-expanding domain of factories. Entrepreneurs of the ancient and medieval worlds had normally gathered their profits together to invest in land and live like country gen-try—given the prejudices of their times against "ill-gotten" gains from trade. On the other hand, the industrial capitalists of the modern world spawned a bitterly compet-itive marketplace that placed a high premium on industrial expansion and the commercial power it conferred, and functioned as though growth were an end in itself.

It is crucially important, in social ecology, to recognize that industrial growth does not result from a change in a cultural outlook alone—and least of all, from the impact of scientific rationality on society. It stems above all from *harshly objective factors* churned up by the expansion of the market itself, *factors that are largely impervious to moral consid-erations and efforts at ethical persuasion.* Indeed, despite the close association between capitalist development and technological innovation, the most driving imperative of the capitalist market, given the dehumanizing competition that defines it, is the need to grow, and to avoid dying at the hands of savage rivals. Important as greed or the power conferred by wealth may be, sheer survival requires that an entrepreneur must expand his or her productive apparatus to remain ahead of other entrepreneurs and try, in fact, to devour them. The key to this law of life—to survival—is expansion, and greater profit, to be invested in still further expansion. Indeed, the notion of progress, once identified by our ancestors as a faith in the evolution of greater human cooper-ation and care, is now identified with economic growth.

The effort by many well-intentioned ecology theorists and their admirers to reduce the ecological crisis to a cultural rather than a social problem can easily become obfus-catory. However ecologically concerned an entrepreneur may be, the harsh fact is that his or her very survival in the marketplace precludes a meaningful ecological orienta-tion. To engage in ecologically sound practices places a morally concerned entrepreneur at a striking, and indeed, fatal disadvantage in a competitive relationship with a rival— notably one who lacks any ecological concerns and thus produces at lower costs and reaps higher profits for further capital expansion.

Indeed, to the extent that environmental movements and ideologies merely mor-alize about the "wickedness" of our anti-ecological society, and emphasize change in personal life and attitudes, they obscure the need for social action. Corporations are skilled at manipulating this desire to be present as an ecological image. Mercedes-Benz, for example, declaims in a two-page ad, decorated with a bison painting from a Paleolithic cave wall, that "we must work to make more environmentally sustainable progress by including the theme of the environment in the planning of new products."[4] Such deceptive messages are commonplace in Germany, one of western Europe's worst polluters. Advertising is equally self-serving in the United States, where leading polluters piously declare that for them, "Every day is Earth Day."

The point social ecology emphasizes is not that moral and spiritual change is meaningless or unnecessary, but that modern capitalism is *structurally* amoral and hence impervious to any moral appeals. The modern marketplace has imperatives of its own, irrespective of who sits in the driver's seat or grabs on to its handlebars. The direction it follows depends not upon ethical factors but rather on the mindless "laws" of supply and demand, grow or die, eat or be eaten. Maxims like "business is business" explicitly tell us that ethical, religious, psychological, and emotional factors have absolutely no place in the impersonal world of production, profit, and growth. It is grossly misleading to think that we can divest this brutally materialistic, indeed, mechanistic, world of its objective character, that we can vaporize its hard facts rather than transforming it.

A society based on "grow or die" as its all-pervasive imperative must necessarily have a devastating ecological impact. Given the growth imperative generated by market competition, it would mean little or nothing if the present-day population were reduced to a fraction of what it is today. Insofar as entrepreneurs must always expand if they are to survive, the media that have fostered mindless consumption would be mobilized to increase the purchase of goods, irrespective of the need for them. Hence it would become "indispensable" in the public mind to own two or three of every appliance, motor vehicle, electronic gadget, or the like, where one would more than suffice. In addition, the military would continue to demand new, more lethal instruments of death, of which new models would be required annually.

Nor would "softer" technologies produced by a grow-or-die market fail to be used for destructive capitalistic ends. Two centuries ago, the forests of England were hacked into fuel for iron forges with axes that had not changed appreciably since the Bronze Age, and ordinary sails guided ships laden with commodities to all parts of the world well into the nineteenth century. Indeed, much of the United States was "cleared" of its forests, wildlife, soil, and aboriginal inhabitants with tools and weapons that would have been easily recognized, however much they were modified, by Renaissance people who had yet to encounter the Industrial Revolution. What modern technics did was to accelerate a process that was well under way at the close of the Middle Ages. It did not devastate the planet on its own; it abetted a phenomenon, the ever-expanding market system that had its roots in one of history's most fundamental social transformations: the elaboration of hierarchy and class into a system of distribution based on exchange rather than complementarity and mutual aid.

AN ECOLOGICAL SOCIETY

Social ecology is an appeal not only for moral regeneration but also, and above all, for social reconstruction along ecological lines. It emphasizes that an ethical appeal to the powers that be (that embody blind market forces and competitive relationships), taken by itself, is likely to be futile. Indeed, taken by itself, it often obscures the real power relationships that prevail today by making the attainment of an ecological society seem merely a matter of "attitude," of "spiritual change," or of quasi-religious redemption.

Although always mindful of the need for spiritual change, social ecology seeks to redress the ecological abuses that society has inflicted on the natural world by going to the structural as well as the subjective sources of notions like the "domination of nature." That is, it challenges the entire system of domination itself and seeks to eliminate the hierarchical and class edifice that has imposed itself on humanity and defined the relationship between nonhuman and human nature. It advances an ethics of complementarity in which human beings must play a supportive role in perpetuating the integrity of the biosphere, as potentially, at least, the most conscious products of natural evolution. Indeed humans are seen to have a moral responsibility to function creatively in the unfolding of that evolution. Social ecology thus stresses the need for embodying its ethics of complementarity in palpable social institutions that will give active meaning to its goal of wholeness, and of human involvement as conscious and moral agents in the interplay of species. It seeks the enrichment of the evolutionary process by diversification of life-forms. Notwithstanding romantic views, "Mother Nature" does not necessarily "know best." To oppose activities of the corporate world does not mean that one has to become naively romantic and "biocentric." By the same token, to applaud humanity's potential for foresight and rationality, and its technological achievements, does not mean that one is "anthropocentric." The loose usage of such buzzwords, so commonplace in the ecology movement, must be brought to an end by reflective discussion.

Social ecology, in effect, recognizes that—like it or not—the future of life on this planet pivots on the future of society. It contends that evolution, whether in first nature or in second, is not yet complete. Nor are the two realms so separated from each other that we must choose one or the other—either natural evolution with its "biocentric" halo, or social evolution, as we have known it up to now, with its "anthropocentric" halo—as the basis for a creative biosphere. We must go beyond both the natural and the social toward a new synthesis that contains the best of both. Such a synthesis will transcend them in the form of a creative, self-conscious, and therefore "free nature," in which human beings intervene in natural evolution with their best capacities—their moral sense, their unprecedented degree of conceptual thought, and their remarkable powers of communication.

But such a goal remains mere verbiage unless it can be given logistical and social tangibility. How are we to organize a "free nature" that goes beyond the rhetoric so plentiful in the ecology movement? Logistically, "free nature" is unattainable without the decentralization of cities into confederally united communities sensitively tailored to the natural areas in which they are located. It means the use of ecotechnologies, and of solar, wind, methane, and other sources of energy, the use of organic forms of agriculture, the design of humanly scaled, versatile industrial installations to meet regional needs of confederated municipalities. It means, too, an emphasis not only on recycling, but on the production of high-quality goods that can last for generations. It means the substitution of creative work for insensate labor and an emphasis on artful craftspersonship in preference to mechanized production. It means the leisure to be artful and engage in public affairs. One would hope that the sheer availability of goods and the freedom to choose one's material lifestyle would sooner or later influence people to adopt moderation in all aspects of life as a response to the "consumerism" that is promoted by the capitalist market.[5]

But no ethics or vision of an ecological society, however inspired, can be meaningful unless it is embodied in a living politics. By "politics" I do not mean the statecraft practiced by what we call "politicians"—namely, representatives elected or selected to formulate policies as guidelines for social life and to manage public affairs. To social ecology, politics means what it once meant in the democratic *polis* of Athens some two thousand years ago: the formation of policy by popular assemblies and their administration by mandated, carefully supervised boards of coordinators who could easily be recalled if they failed to abide by the decisions of the assembly's citizens. I am very mindful that Athenian politics, even in its most democratic periods, was marred by the existence of slavery, patriarchy, and the exclusion of the stranger from public life. In this respect, it differed very little from most of the Mediterranean civilizations—and Asian ones—of the time. What made Athenian politics unique, however, was that it produced institutions that were extraordinarily democratic—even directly so—by comparison with republican institutions in the so-called "democracies" of the Western world. Either directly or indirectly they inspired later, more all-encompassing democracies, such as certain medieval towns, the little-known "sections" of Paris (which were essentially forty-eight neighborhood assemblies) that propelled the French Revolution in a highly radical direction in 1793, New England town meetings, and more recent attempts at civic self-governance.[6]

Any community, however, risks the danger of becoming parochial, even racist, if it tries to live in isolation and develop a seeming self-sufficiency. Hence, the need to extend ecological politics into confederations of ecocommunities, and to foster a healthy interdependence, rather than an introverted, stultifying independence. Social ecology would embody its ethics in a politics of confederal municipalism, in which municipalities cojointly gain rights to self-governance through networks of confederal councils, to which towns and cities would send their mandated, recallable delegates to adjust differences. All decisions would have to be ratified by a majority of the popular assemblies of the confederated towns and cities. This institutional process could occur in the neighborhoods of giant cities as well as in networks of small towns. In fact, the formation of numerous "town halls" has already repeatedly been proposed in cities as large as New York and Paris, only to be defeated by well-organized elitist groups that sought to centralize power, rather than allow its decentralization.

Power will always belong to elite strata if it is not diffused, in face-to-face democracies, among the people, who are *empowered* as partly autonomous, partly social beings—that is to say, as free individuals, but as individuals responsible to popular institutions. Empowerment of the people in this sense will constitute a challenge to the nation-state—the principal source of nationalism, a regressive ideology, and of statism, the principal source of coercion. Diversity of cultures is obviously a desideratum, the source of cultural creativity, but never can it be celebrated in a nationalistic "apartness" from the general interests of humanity as a whole, without a regression into folkdom and tribalism.

The full reality of citizenship has begun to wane, and its disappearance would mark an irrevocable loss in human development. Citizenship, in the classical sense of the term, meant a lifelong, ethically oriented education to participation in public affairs, not the empty form of national legitimation that it so often indicates today. It meant the cultivation of an affiliation with the interests of the community, one in which the communal interest was placed above personal interest, or, more properly, in which the personal interest was congruent with and realized through the common.

Property, in this ethical constellation, would be shared and, in the best of circumstances, belong to the community as a whole, not to producers ("workers") or owners ("capitalists"). In an ecological society composed of a "Commune of communes," property would belong, ultimately, neither to private producers nor to a nation-state. The Soviet Union gave rise to an overbearing bureaucracy; the anarcho-syndicalist vision to competing "worker-controlled" factories that ultimately had to be knitted together by a labor bureaucracy. From the standpoint of social ecology, property "interests" would become generalized, not reconstituted in different conflicting or unmanageable forms. They would be *municipalized,* rather than nationalized or privatized. Workers, farmers, professionals, and the like would thus deal with municipalized property as citizens, not as members of a vocational or social group. Leaving aside any discussion of such visions as the rotation of work, the citizen who engages in both industrial and agricultural activity, and the professional who also does manual labor, the communal ideas advanced by social ecology would give rise to individuals for whom the collective interest is inseparable from the personal, the public interest from the private, the political interest from the social.

The step-by-step reorganization of municipalities, their confederation into ever-larger networks that form a dual power in opposition to the nation-state, the remaking of the constituents of republican representatives into citizens who participate in a direct democracy—all may take a considerable period of time to achieve. But in the end, they alone can potentially eliminate the domination of human by human and thereby deal with those ecological problems whose growing magnitude threatens the existence of a biosphere that can support advanced forms of life. To ignore the need for these sweeping but eminently practical changes would be to let our ecological problems fester and spread to a point where there would no longer be any opportunity to resolve them. Any attempt to ignore their impact on the biosphere or deal with them singly would be recipe for disaster, a guarantee that the anti-ecological society that prevails in most of the world today would blindly hurtle the biosphere as we know it to certain destruction.

NOTES

1. Murray Bookchin, "Ecology and Revolutionary Thought," initially published in the ecoanarchist journal *New Directions in Libertarian Thought* (Sept., 1964), and collected, together with all my major essays of the sixties in *Post-Scarcity Anarchism* (Berkeley: Ramparts Press, 1972; republished, Montreal: Black Rose Books, 1977). The expression "ethics of complementarity" is from *The Ecology of Freedom* (San Francisco: Cheshire Books, 1982; revised edition, Montreal: Black Rose Books, 1991).
2. Neil Evernden, *The Natural Alien* (Toronto: University of Toronto Press, 1986), p. 109.
3. Paul Radin, *The World of Primitive Man* (New York: Grove Press, 1960), p. 211.
4. See *Der Spiegel* (Sept. 16, 1991), pp. 144–45.
5. All of these views were spelled out in the essay "Ecology and Revolutionary Thought" by this writer in 1965, and were assimilated over time by subsequent ecology movements. Many of the technological views advanced a year later in "Toward a Liberatory Technology" were also assimilated and renamed "appropriate technology," a rather socially neutral expression in comparison with my original term "ecotechnology." Both of these essays can be found in *Post-Scarcity Anarchism.*
6. See the essay "The Forms of Freedom," in *Post-Scarcity Anarchism,* "The Legacy of Freedom," in *The Ecology of Freedom,* and "Patterns of Civic Freedom" in *The Rise of Urbanization and the Decline of Citizenship* (San Francisco: Sierra Club Books, 1987).

22

⊰ Overcoming Racism ⊱ in Environmental Decision Making

ROBERT D. BULLARD

Robert Bullard is a professor of philosophy at the University of California at Riverside. His books include Dumping in Dixie, Confronting Environmental Racism, *and* Unequal Protection.

Despite the recent attempts by federal agencies to reduce environmental and health threats in the United States, inequities persist.[1] If a community is poor or inhabited largely by people of color, there is a good chance that it receives less protection than a community that is affluent or white.[2] This situation is a result of the country's environmental policies, most of which "distribute the costs in a regressive pattern while providing disproportionate benefits for the educated and wealthy."[3] Even the Environmental Protection Agency (EPA) was not designed to address environmental policies and practices that result in unfair outcomes. The agency has yet to conduct a single piece of disparate impact research using primary data. In fact, the current environmental protection paradigm has institutionalized unequal enforcement, traded human health for profit, placed the burden of proof on the "victims" rather than on the polluting industry, legitimated human exposure to harmful substances, promoted "risky" technologies such as incinerators, exploited the vulnerability of economically and politically disenfranchised communities, subsidized ecological destruction, created an industry around risk assessment, delayed cleanup actions, and failed to develop pollution prevention as the overarching and dominant strategy. As a result, low-income and minority communities continue to bear greater health and environmental burdens, while the more affluent and white communities receive the bulk of the benefits.[4]

    The geographic distribution of both minorities and the poor has been found to be highly correlated to the distribution of air pollution, municipal landfills and incinerators, abandoned toxic waste dumps, lead poisoning in children, and contaminated fish consumption.[5] Virtually all studies of exposure to outdoor air pollution have found significant differences in exposure by income and race. Moreover, the race correlation is even stronger than the class correlation.[6] The National Wildlife Federation recently reviewed some sixty-four studies of environmental disparities; in all but one, disparities were found by either race or income, and disparities by race were more numerous than those by income. When race and income were compared for significance, race proved to be the more important factor in twenty-two out of thirty tests.[7] And researchers at Argonne National Laboratory recently found that

> in 1990, 437 of the 3,109 counties and independent cities failed to meet at least one of the EPA ambient air quality standards. . . . 57 percent of whites, 65 percent of African-Americans, and 80 percent of Hispanics live in 437 counties with substandard air quality. Out of the whole population, a total of 33 percent of whites, 50 percent of African-Americans, and 60 percent of Hispanics live in the 136 counties in which two or more air pollutants exceed standards. The percentage living in the 29 counties designated as nonattainment areas for three or more pollutants are 12 percent of whites, 20 percent of African-Americans, and 31 percent of Hispanics.[8]

The public health community has very little information on the magnitude of many air pollution-related health problems. For example, scientists are at a loss to explain the rising number of deaths from asthma in recent years. However, it is known that persons suffering from asthma are particularly sensitive to the effects of carbon monoxide, sulfur dioxide, particulate matter, ozone, and oxides of nitrogen.[9]

Current environmental decision making operates at the juncture of science, technology, economics, politics, special interests, and ethics and mirrors the larger social milieu where discrimination is institutionalized. Unequal environmental protection undermines three basic types of equity: procedural, geographic, and social.

PROCEDURAL EQUITY

Procedural equity refers to fairness—that is, to the extent that governing rules, regulations, evaluation criteria, and enforcement are applied in a nondiscriminatory way. Unequal protection results from nonscientific and undemocratic decisions, such as exclusionary practices, conflicts of interest, public hearings held in remote locations and at inconvenient times, and use of only English to communicate with and conduct hearings for non–English-speaking communities.

A 1992 study by staff writers from the *National Law Journal* uncovered glaring inequities in the way EPA enforces its Superfund laws: "There is a racial divide in the way the U.S. government cleans up toxic waste sites and punishes polluters. White communities see faster action, better results and stiffer penalties than communities where blacks, Hispanics and other minorities live. This unequal protection often occurs whether the community is wealthy or poor."[10]

After examining census data, civil court dockets, and EPA's own record of performance at 1,177 Superfund toxic waste sites, the authors of the *National Law Journal* reported the following:

- Penalties applied under hazardous waste laws at sites having the greatest white population were 500 percent higher than penalties at sites with the greatest minority population. Penalties averaged out at $335,566 at sites in white areas but just $55,318 at sites in minority areas.

- The disparity in penalties applied under the toxic waste law correlates with race alone, not income. The average penalty in areas with the lowest median income is $113,491—3 percent more than the average penalty in areas with the highest median income.
- For all the federal environmental laws aimed at protecting citizens from air, water, and waste pollution, penalties for non-compliance were 46 percent higher in white communities than in minority communities.
- Under the Superfund cleanup program, abandoned hazardous waste sites in minority areas take 20 percent longer to be placed on the National Priority List than do those in white areas.
- In more than half of the ten autonomous regions that administer EPA programs around the country, action on cleanup at Superfund sites begins from 12 to 42 percent later at minority sites than at white sites.
- For minority sites, EPA chooses "containment," the capping or walling off of a hazardous waste dump site, 7 percent more frequently than the cleanup method preferred under the law: permanent "treatment" to eliminate the waste or rid it of its toxins. For white sites, EPA orders permanent treatment 22 percent more often than containment.[11]

These findings suggest that unequal environmental protection is placing communities of color at risk. The *National Law Journal* study supplements the findings of several earlier studies and reinforces what grassroots activists have been saying all along: Not only are people of color differentially affected by industrial pollution but also they can expect different treatment from the government.[12]

GEOGRAPHIC EQUITY

Geographic equity refers to the location and spatial configuration of communities and their proximity to environmental hazards and locally unwanted land uses (LULUs), such as landfills, incinerators, sewage treatment plants, lead smelters, refineries, and other noxious facilities. Hazardous waste incinerators are not randomly scattered across the landscape. Communities with hazardous waste incinerators generally have large minority populations, low incomes, and low property values.[13]

A 1990 Greenpeace report (*Playing with Fire*) found that communities with existing incinerators have 89 percent more people of color than the national average; communities where incinerators are proposed for construction have minority populations that are 60 percent higher than the national average; the average income in communities with existing incinerators is 15 percent lower than the national average; property values in communities that host incinerators are 38 percent lower than the national average; and average property values are 35 percent lower in communities where incinerators have been proposed.[14]

The industrial encroachment into Chicago's Southside neighborhoods is a classic example of geographic inequity. Chicago is the nation's third largest city and one of the most racially segregated cities in the country. More than 92 percent of the city's 1.1 million African American residents live in racially segregated areas. The Altgeld Gardens housing project, located on the city's southeast side, is one of these segregated enclaves. The neighborhood is home to 150,000 residents, of whom 70 percent are African American and 11 percent are Latino.

Altgeld Gardens is encircled by municipal and hazardous waste landfills, toxic waste incinerators, grain elevators, sewage treatment facilities, smelters, steel mills, and a host of other polluting industries.[15] Because of its location, the area has been dubbed a "toxic doughnut" by Hazel Johnson, a community organizer in the neighborhood. There are 50 active or closed commercial hazardous waste landfills; 100 factories, including 7 chemical plants and 5 steel mills; and 103 abandoned toxic waste dumps.[16]

Currently, health and risk assessment data collected by the state of Illinois and the EPA for facility permitting have failed to take into account the cumulative and synergistic effects of having so many "layers" of poison in one community. Altgeld Gardens residents wonder when the government will declare a moratorium on permitting any new noxious facilities in their neighborhood and when the existing problems will be cleaned up. All of the polluting industries imperil the health of nearby residents and should be factored into future facility-permitting decisions.

In the Los Angeles air basin, 71 percent of African Americans and 50 percent of Latinos live in areas with the most polluted air, whereas only 34 percent of whites live in highly polluted areas.[17] The "dirtiest" zip code in California (90058) is sandwiched between South-Central Los Angeles and East Los Angeles.[18] The one-square-mile area is saturated with abandoned toxic waste sites, freeways, smokestacks, and wastewater pipes from polluting industries. Some eighteen industrial firms in 1989 discharged more than 33 million pounds of waste chemicals into the environment.

Unequal protection may result from land-use decisions that determine the location of residential amenities and disamenities. Unincorporated communities of poor African Americans suffer a "triple" vulnerability to noxious facility siting.[19] For example, Wallace, Louisiana, a small unincorporated African American community located on the Mississippi River, was rezoned from residential to industrial use by the mostly white officials of St. John the Baptist Parish to allow construction of a Formosa Plastics Corporation plant. The company's plants have been major sources of pollution in Baton Rouge, Louisiana; Point Comfort, Texas; Delaware City, Delaware; and its home country of Taiwan.[20] Wallace residents have filed a lawsuit challenging the rezoning action as racially motivated.

Environmental justice advocates have sought to persuade federal, state, and local governments to adopt policies that address distributive impacts, concentration, enforcement, and compliance concerns. Some states have tried to use a "fair share" approach to come closer to geographic equity. In 1990, New York City adopted a fair share legislative model designed to ensure that every borough and every community within each borough bears its fair share of noxious facilities. Public hearings have begun to address risk burdens in New York City's boroughs.

Testimony at a hearing on environmental disparities in the Bronx points to concerns raised by African Americans and Puerto Ricans who see their neighborhoods threatened by garbage transfer stations, salvage yards, and recycling centers.

On the Hunts Point peninsula alone there are at least thirty private transfer stations, a large-scale Department of Environmental Protection (DEP) sewage treatment plant and a sludge dewatering facility, two Department of Sanitation (DOS) marine transfer stations, a city-wide privately regulated medical waste incinerator, a proposed DOS resource recovery facility and three proposed DEP sludge processing facilities. That all of the facilities listed above are located immediately adjacent to the Hunts Point Food Center, the biggest wholesale food and meat distribution facility of its kind in the United States, and the largest source of employment in the South Bronx, is disconcerting. A policy whereby low-income and minority communities have become the "dumping grounds" for unwanted land uses, works to create an environment of disincentives to community-based development initiatives. It also undermines existing businesses.[21]

Some communities form a special case for environmental justice. For example, Native American reservations are geographic entities but are also quasi-sovereign nations. Because of less-stringent environmental regulations than those at the state and federal levels, Native American reservations from New York to California have become prime targets for risky technologies.[22] Indian natives do not fall under state jurisdiction. Similarly, reservations have been described as the "lands the feds forgot."[23] More than one hundred industries, ranging from solid waste landfills to hazardous waste incinerators and nuclear waste storage facilities, have targeted reservations.[24]

SOCIAL EQUITY

Social equity refers to the role of sociological factors, such as race, ethnicity, class, culture, lifestyles, and political power, in environmental decision making. Poor people and people of color often work in the most dangerous jobs and live in the most polluted neighborhoods, and their children are exposed to all kinds of environmental toxins on the playgrounds and in their homes and schools.

Some government actions have created and exacerbated environmental inequity. More stringent environmental regulations have driven noxious facilities to follow the path of least resistance toward poor, overburdened communities. Governments have even funded studies that justify targeting economically disenfranchised communities for noxious facilities. Cerrell Associates, Inc., a Los Angeles-based consulting firm, advised the state of California on facility siting and concluded that "ideally . . . officials and companies should look for lower socioeconomic neighborhoods that are also in a heavy industrial area with little, if any, commercial activity."[25]

The first state-of-the-art solid waste incinerator slated to be built in Los Angeles was proposed for the south-central Los Angeles neighborhood. The city-sponsored project was defeated by local residents.[26] The two permits granted by the California Department of Health Services for state-of-the-art toxic waste incinerators were proposed for mostly Latino communities: Vernon, near East Los Angeles, and Kettleman City, a farm-worker community in the agriculturally rich Central Valley. Kettleman City has 1,200 residents of which 95 percent are Latino. It is home to the largest hazardous waste incinerator west of the Mississippi River. The Vernon proposal was defeated, but the Kettleman City proposal is still pending.

PRINCIPLES OF ENVIRONMENTAL JUSTICE

To end unequal environmental protection, governments should adopt five principles of environmental justice: guaranteeing the right to environmental protection, preventing harm before it occurs, shifting the burden of proof to the polluters, obviating proof of intent to discriminate, and redressing existing inequities.

The Right to Protection

Every individual has a right to be protected from environmental degradation. Protecting this right will require enacting a federal "fair environmental protection act." The act could be modeled after the various federal civil rights acts that have promoted nondiscrimination—with the ultimate goal of achieving "zero tolerance"—in such areas as housing, education, and employment. The act ought to address both the intended and unintended effects of public policies and industrial practices that have a disparate impact on racial and ethnic minorities and other vulnerable groups. The precedents for this framework are the Civil Rights Act of 1964, which attempted to address both *de jure* and *de facto* school segregation, the Fair Housing Act of 1968, the same act as amended in 1988, and the Voting Rights Act of 1965.

For the first time in the agency's twenty-three-year history, EPA's Office of Civil Rights has begun investigating charges of environmental discrimination under Title VI of the 1964 Civil Rights Act. The cases involve waste facility siting disputes in Michigan, Alabama, Mississippi, and Louisiana. Similarly, in September 1993, the U.S. Civil Rights Commission issued a report entitled *The Battle for Environmental Justice in Louisiana: Government, Industry, and the People*. This report confirmed what most people who live in "Cancer Alley"—the 85-mile stretch along the Mississippi River from Baton Rouge to New Orleans—already knew: African American communities along the Mississippi River bear disproportionate health burdens from industrial pollution.[27]

A number of bills have been introduced into Congress that address some aspect of environmental justice:

- The Environmental Justice Act of 1993 (H.R. 2105) would provide the federal government with the statistical documentation and ranking of the top one hundred "environmental high impact areas" that warrant attention.
- The Environmental Equal Rights Act of 1993 (H.R. 1924) seeks to amend the Solid Waste Act and would prevent waste facilities from being sited in "environmentally disadvantaged communities."
- The Environmental Health Equity Information Act of 1993 (H.R. 1925) seeks to amend the Comprehensive Environmental Response, Compensation, and Liability Act of 1990 (CERCLA) to require the Agency for Toxic Substances and Disease Registry to collect and maintain information on the race, age, gender, ethnic origin, income level, and educational level of persons living in communities adjacent to toxic substance contamination.
- The Waste Export and Import Prohibition Act (H.R. 3706) banned waste exports as of 1 July 1994 to countries that are not members of the Organization for Economic Cooperation and Development (OECD); the bill would also ban waste exports to and imports from OECD countries as of 1 January 1999.

The states are also beginning to address environmental justice concerns. Arkansas and Louisiana were the first two to enact environmental justice laws. Virginia has passed a legislative resolution on environmental justice. California, Georgia, New York, North Carolina, and South Carolina have pending legislation to address environmental disparities.

Environmental justice groups have succeeded in getting President Clinton to act on the problem of unequal environmental protection, an issue that has been buried for more than three decades. On 11 February 1994, Clinton signed an executive order entitled "Federal Actions to Address Environmental Justice in Minority Populations and Low-Income Populations." This new executive order reinforces what has been law since the passage of the 1964 Civil Rights Act, which prohibits discriminatory practices in programs receiving federal financial assistance.

The executive order also refocuses attention on the National Environmental Policy Act of 1970 (NEPA), which established national policy goals for the protection, maintenance, and enhancement of the environment. The express goal of NEPA is to ensure for all U.S. citizens a safe, healthful, productive, and aesthetically and culturally pleasing environment. NEPA requires federal agencies to prepare detailed statements on the environmental effects of proposed federal actions significantly affecting the quality of human health. Environmental impact statements prepared under NEPA have routinely down-played the social impacts of federal projects on racial and ethnic minorities and low-income groups.

Under the new executive order, federal agencies and other institutions that receive federal monies have a year to implement an environmental justice strategy. For these strategies to be effective, agencies must move away from the "DAD" (decide, announce, and defend) modus operandi. EPA cannot address all of the environmental injustices alone but must work in concert with other stakeholders, such as state and local governments and private industry. A new interagency approach might include the following:

- Grassroots environmental justice groups and their networks must become full partners, not silent or junior partners, in planning the implementation of the new executive order.
- An advisory commission should include representatives of environmental justice, civil rights, legal, labor, and public health groups, as well as the relevant governmental agencies, to advise on the implementation of the executive order.
- State and regional education, training, and outreach forums and workshops on implementing the executive order should be organized.
- The executive order should become part of the agenda of national conferences and meetings of elected officials, civil rights and environmental groups, public health and medical groups, educators, and other professional organizations.

The executive order comes at an important juncture in this nation's history: Few communities are willing to welcome LULUs or to become dumping grounds for other people's garbage, toxic waste, or industrial pollution. In the real world, however, if a community happens to be poor and inhabited by persons of color, it is likely to suffer from a "double whammy" of unequal protection and elevated health threats. This is unjust and illegal.

The civil rights and environmental laws of the land must be enforced even if it means the loss of a few jobs. This argument was a sound one in the 1860s, when the Thirteenth Amendment to the Constitution, which freed the slaves in the United States, was passed over the opposition of proslavery advocates who posited that the new law would create unemployment (slaves had a zero unemployment rate), drive up wages, and inflict undue hardship on the plantation economy.

Prevention of Harm

Prevention, the elimination of the threat before harm occurs, should be the preferred strategy of governments. For example, to solve the lead problem, the primary focus should be shifted from treating children who have been poisoned to eliminating the threat by removing lead from houses.

Overwhelming scientific evidence exists on the ill effects of lead on the human body. However, very little action has been taken to rid the nation's housing of lead even though lead poising is a preventable disease tagged the "number one environmental health threat to children."[28]

Lead began to be phased out of gasoline in the 1970s. It is ironic that the "regulations were initially developed to protect the newly developed catalytic converter in automobiles, a pollution-control device that happens to be rendered inoperative by lead, rather than to safeguard human health."[29] In 1971, a child was not considered "at risk" unless he or she had 40 micrograms of lead per deciliter of blood (μg/dl). Since that time, the amount of lead that is considered safe has continually dropped. In 1991, the U.S. Public Health Service changed the official definition of an unsafe level to 10 μg/dl. Even at that level, a child's IQ can be slightly diminished and physical growth stunted.

Lead poisoning is correlated with both income and race. In 1988, the Agency for Toxic Substances and Disease Registry found that among families earning less than $6,000, 68 percent of African American children had lead poisoning, as opposed to 36 percent of white children.[30] In families with incomes exceeding $15,000, more than 38 percent of African American children suffered from lead poisoning, compared with 12 percent of white children. Thus, even when differences in income are taken into account, middle-class African American children are three times more likely to be poisoned with lead than are their middle-class white counterparts.

A 1990 report by the Environmental Defense Fund estimated that under the 1991 standard of 10 μg/dl, 96 percent of African American children and 80 percent of white children of poor families who live in inner cities have unsafe amounts of lead in their blood—amounts sufficient to reduce IQ somewhat, harm hearing, reduce the ability to concentrate, and stunt physical growth.[31] Even in families with annual incomes greater than $15,000, 85 percent of urban African American children have unsafe lead levels, compared to 47 percent of white children.

In the spring of 1991, the Bush administration announced an ambitious program to reduce lead exposure of children, including widespread testing of homes, certification of those who remove lead from homes, and medical treatment for affected children. Six months later, the Centers for Disease Control announced that the administration "does not see this as a necessary federal role to legislate or regulate the cleanup of lead poisoning, to require that homes be tested, to require home owners to disclose results once they are known, or to establish standards for those who test or clean up lead hazards."[32]

According to the *New York Times,* the National Association of Realtors pressured President Bush to drop his lead initiative because it feared that forcing homeowners to eliminate lead hazards would add from $5,000 to $10,000 to the price of those homes, further harming a real estate market already devastated by the aftershocks of Reaganomics.[33] The public debate has pitted real estate and housing interests against public health interests. Right now, the housing interests appear to be winning.

For more than two decades, Congress and the nation's medical and public health establishments have waffled, procrastinated, and shuffled papers while the lead problem steadily grows worse. During the years of President Reagan's "benign neglect," funding dropped very low. Even in the best years, when funding has risen to as much as $50 million per year, it has never reached levels that would make a real dent in the problem.

Much could be done to protect at-risk populations if the current laws were enforced. For example, a lead smelter operated for fifty years in a predominantly African American West Dallas neighborhood, where it caused extreme health problems for nearby residents. Dallas officials were informed as early as 1972 that lead from three lead smelters was finding its way into the bloodstreams of children who lived in two mostly African American and Latino neighborhoods: West Dallas and East Oak Cliff.[34]

Living near the RSR and Dixie Metals smelters was associated with a 36 percent increase in childhood blood lead levels. The city was urged to restrict the emissions of lead into the atmosphere and to undertake a large screening program to determine the extent of the public health problem. The city failed to take immediate action to protect the residents who lived near the smelters.

In 1980, EPA, informed about possible health risks associated with the Dallas lead smelters, commissioned another lead-screening study. This study confirmed what was already known a decade earlier: Children living near the Dallas smelters were likely to have greater lead concentrations in their blood than children who did not live near the smelters.[35]

The city only took action after the local newspapers published a series of head-line-grabbing stories in 1983 on the "potentially dangerous" lead levels discovered by EPA researchers in 1981.[36] The articles triggered widespread concern, public outrage, several class-action lawsuits, and legal action by the Texas attorney general.

Although EPA was armed with a wealth of scientific data on the West Dallas lead problem, the agency chose to play politics with the community by scrapping a voluntary plan offered by RSR to clean up the "hot spots" in the neighborhood. John Hernandez, EPA's deputy administrator, blocked the cleanup and called for yet another round of tests to be designed by the Centers for Disease Control with EPA and the Dallas Health Department. The results of the new study were released in February 1983. This study again established the smelter as the source of elevated lead levels in West Dallas children.[37] Hernandez's delay of cleanup actions in West Dallas was tantamount to waiting for a body count.[38]

After years of delay, the West Dallas plaintiffs negotiated an out-of-court settlement worth more than $45 million. The lawsuit was settled in June 1983 as RSR agreed to pay for cleaning up the soil in West Dallas, a blood-testing program for children and pregnant women, and the installation of new antipollution equipment. The settlement was made on behalf of 370 children—almost all of whom were poor black residents of the West Dallas public housing project—and forty property owners. The agreement was one of the largest community lead-contamination settlements ever awarded in the United States.[39] The settlement, however, did not require the smelter to close. Moreover, the pollution equipment for the smelter was never installed.

In May 1984, however, the Dallas Board of Adjustments, a city agency responsible for monitoring land-use violations, asked the city attorney to close the smelter permanently for violating the city's zoning code. The lead smelter had operated in the mostly African American West Dallas neighborhood for fifty years without having the necessary use permits. Just four months later, the West Dallas smelter was permanently closed. After repeated health citations, fines, and citizens' complaints against the smelter, one has to question the city's lax enforcement of health and land-use regulations in African American and Latino neighborhoods.

The smelter is now closed. Although an initial cleanup was carried out in 1984, the lead problem has not gone away.[40] On 31 December 1991, EPA crews began a cleanup of the West Dallas neighborhood. It is estimated that the crews will remove between 30,000 and 40,000 cubic yards of lead-contaminated soil from several West Dallas sites, including school property and about 140 private homes. The project will cost EPA from $3 million to $4 million. The lead content of the soil collected from dump sites in the neighborhood ranged from 8,060 to 21,000 parts per million.[41] Under federal standards, levels of 500 to 1,000 parts per million are considered hazardous. In April 1993, the entire West Dallas neighborhood was declared a Superfund site.

There have been a few other signs related to the lead issue that suggest a consensus on environmental justice is growing among coalitions of environmental, social justice, and civil libertarian groups. The Natural Resources Defense Council, the National Association for the Advancement of Colored People Legal Defense and Education Fund, the American Civil Liberties Union, and the Legal Aid Society of Alameda County joined forces and won an out-of-court settlement worth between $15 million and $20 million for a blood-testing program in California. The lawsuit (*Matthews v. Coye*) arose because the state of California was not performing the federally mandated testing of some 557,000 poor children who receive Medicaid. This historic agreement will likely trigger similar actions in other states that have failed to perform federally mandated screening.[42]

Lead screening is important but it is not the solution. New government-mandated lead abatement initiatives are needed. The nation needs a "Lead Superfund" clean-up program. Public health should not be sacrificed even in a sluggish housing market. Surely, if termite inspections (required in both booming and sluggish housing markets) can be mandated to protect individual home investment, a lead-free home can be mandated to protect human health. Ultimately, the lead debate—public health (who is affected) versus property rights (who pays for cleanup)—is a value conflict that will not be resolved by the scientific community.

Shift the Burden of Proof

Under the current system, individuals who challenge polluters must prove that they have been harmed, discriminated against, or disproportionately affected. Few poor or minority communities have the resources to hire the lawyers, expert witnesses, and doctors needed to sustain such a challenge. Thus, the burden of proof must be shifted to the polluters who do harm, discriminate, or do not give equal protection to minorities and other overburdened classes.

Environmental justice would require the entities that are applying for operating permits for landfills, incinerators, smelters, refineries, and chemical plants, for example, to prove that their operations are not harmful to human health, will not disproportionately affect minorities or the poor, and are nondiscriminatory.

A case in point is Louisiana Energy Services' proposal to build the nation's first privately owned uranium enrichment plant. The proposed plant would handle about 17 percent of the estimated U.S. requirement for enrichment services in the year 2000. Clearly, the burden of proof should be on Louisiana Energy Services, the state government, and the Nuclear Regulatory Commission to demonstrate that local residents' rights would not be violated in permitting the plant. At present, the burden of proof is on local residents to demonstrate that their health would be endangered and their community adversely affected by the plant.

According to the Nuclear Regulatory Commission's 1993 draft environmental impact statement, the proposed site for the facility is Claiborne Parish, Louisiana, which has a per capita income of only $5,800 per year—just 45 percent of the national average.[43] The enrichment plant would be just one-quarter mile from the almost wholly African American community of Center Springs, founded in 1910, and one and one-quarter miles from Forest Grove, which was founded by freed slaves. However, the draft statement describes the socioeconomic and community characteristics of Homer, a town that is five miles from the proposed site and whose population is more than 50 percent white, rather than those of Center Springs or Forest Grove. As far as the draft is concerned, the communities of Center Springs and Forest Grove do not exist; they are invisible.

The racial composition of Claiborne Parish is 53.43 percent white, 46.09 percent African American, 0.16 percent American Indian, 0.07 percent Asian, 0.23 percent Hispanic, and 0.01 percent "other."[44] Thus, the parish's percentage population of African Americans is nearly four times greater than that of the nation and nearly two and one-half times greater than that of Louisiana. (African Americans composed 12 percent of the U.S. population and 29 percent of Louisiana's population in 1990.)

Clearly, Claiborne Parish's current residents would receive fewer of the plant's potential benefits—high-paying jobs, home construction, and an increased tax base—than would those who moved into the area or commuted to it to work at the facility. An increasing number of migrants will take jobs at the higher end of the skill and pay scale. These workers are expected to buy homes outside of the parish. Residents of Claiborne Parish, on the other hand, are likely to get the jobs at the low end of the skill and pay scale.[45]

Ultimately, the plant's social costs would be borne by nearby residents, while the benefits would be more dispersed. The potential social costs include increased noise and traffic, threats to public safety and to mental and physical health, and LULUs.

The case of Richmond, California, provides more evidence of the need to shift the burden of proof. A 1989 study, *Richmond at Risk,* found that the African American residents of this city bear the brunt of toxic releases in Contra Costa County and the San Francisco Bay area.[46] At least, thirty-eight industrial sites in and around the city store up to ninety-four million pounds of forty-five different chemicals, including ammonia, chlorine, hydrogen fluoride, and nitric acid. However, the burden of proof is on Richmond residents to show that they are harmed by nearby toxic releases.

On 26 July 1993, sulfur trioxide escaped from the General Chemical plant in Richmond, where people of color make up a majority of the residents. More than twenty thousand citizens were sent to the hospital. A September 1993 report by the Bay Area Air Quality Management District confirmed that "the operation was conducted in a negligent manner without due regard to the potential consequences of a miscalculation or equipment malfunction, and without required permits from the District."[47]

When Richmond residents protested the planned expansion of a Chevron refinery, they were asked to prove that they had been harmed by Chevron's operation. Recently, public pressure has induced Chevron to set aside $4.2 million to establish a new health clinic and help the surrounding community.

A third case involves conditions surrounding the 1,900 *maquiladoras,* assembly plants operated by U.S., Japanese, and other countries' companies along the 2,000-mile U.S.-Mexican border.[48] A 1983 agreement between the United States and Mexico requires U.S. companies in Mexico to export their waste products to the United States, and plants must notify EPA when they are doing so. However, a 1986 survey of 772 *maquiladoras* revealed that only twenty of the plants informed EPA when they were exporting waste to the United States, even though 86 percent of the plants used toxic chemicals in their manufacturing processes. And in 1989, only ten waste-shipment notices were filed with EPA.[49]

Much of the waste from the *maquiladoras* is illegally dumped in sewers, ditches, and the desert. All along the Rio Grande, plants dump toxic wastes into the river, from which 95 percent of the region's residents get their drinking water. In the border cities of Brownsville, Texas, and Matamoros, Mexico, the rate of anencephaly—being born without a brain—is four times the U.S. national average.[50] Affected families have filed lawsuits against eighty-eight of the area's one hundred *maquiladoras* for exposing the community to xylene, a cleaning solvent that can cause brain hemorrhages and lung and kidney damage. However, as usual, the burden of proof rests with the victims. Unfortunately, Mexico's environmental regulatory agency is under-staffed and ill equipped to enforce the country's environmental laws adequately.

Obviate Proof of Intent

Laws must allow disparate impact and statistical weight—as opposed to "intent"—to infer discrimination because proving intentional or purposeful discrimination in a court of law is next to impossible. The first lawsuit to charge environmental discrimination in the placement of a waste facility, *Bean v. Southwestern Waste,* was filed in 1979. The case involved residents of Houston's Northwood Manor, an urban, middle-class neighborhood of homeowners, and Browning-Ferris Industries, a private disposal company based in Houston.

More than 83 percent of the residents in the subdivision owned their single-family, detached homes. Thus, the Northwood Manor neighborhood was an unlikely candidate for a municipal landfill except that, in 1978, it was more than 82 percent black. An earlier attempt had been made to locate a municipal landfill in the same general area in 1970, when the subdivision and local school district had a majority white population. The 1970 landfill proposal was killed by the Harris County Board of Supervisors as being an incompatible land use; the site was deemed to be too close to a residential area and a neighborhood school. In 1978, however, the controversial sanitary landfill was built only 1,400 feet from a high school, football stadium, track field, and the North Forest Independent School District's administration building.[51] Because Houston has been and continues to be highly segregated, few Houstonians are unaware of where the African American neighborhoods end and the white ones begin. In 1970, for example, more than 90 percent of the city's African American residents lived in mostly black areas. By 1980, 82 percent of Houston's African American population lived in mostly black areas.[52]

Houston is the only major U.S. city without zoning. In 1992, the city council voted to institute zoning, but the measure was defeated at the polls in 1993. The city's African American neighborhoods have paid a high price for the city's unrestrained growth and lack of a zoning policy. Black Houston was allowed to become the dumping ground for the city's garbage. In every case, the racial composition of Houston's African American neighborhoods had been established before the waste facilities were sited.[53]

From the early 1920s through the late 1970s, all five of the city-owned sanitary landfills and six out of eight of Houston's municipal solid-waste incinerators were located in mostly African American neighborhoods.[54] The other two incinerator sites were located in a Latino neighborhood and a white neighborhood. One of the oldest waste sites in Houston was located in Freedmen's Town, an African American neighborhood settled by former slaves in the 1860s. The site has been built over with a charity hospital and a low-income public housing project.

Private industry took its lead from the siting pattern established by the city government. From 1970 to 1978, three of the four privately owned landfills used to dispose of Houston's garbage were located in mostly African American neighborhoods. The fourth privately owned landfill, which was sited in 1971, was located in the mostly white Chattwood subdivision. A residential park, or "buffer zone," separates the white neighborhood from the landfill. Both government and industry responded to white neighborhood associations and their NIMBY (not in my backyard) organizations by siting LULUs according to the PIBBY (place in blacks backyards) strategy.[55]

The statistical evidence in *Bean v. Southwestern Waste* overwhelmingly supported the disproportionate impact argument. Overall, fourteen of the seventeen (82 percent) solid-waste facilities used to dispose of Houston's garbage were located in mostly African American neighborhoods. Considering that Houston's African American residents comprised only 28 percent of the city's total population, they clearly were forced to bear a disproportionate burden of the city's solid-waste facilities.[56] However, the federal judge ruled against the plaintiffs on the grounds that "purposeful discrimination" was not demonstrated.

Although the Northwood Manor residents lost their lawsuit, they did influence the way the Houston city government and the state of Texas addressed race and waste facility siting. Acting under intense pressure from the African American community, the Houston city council passed a resolution in 1980 that prohibited city-owned trucks from dumping at the controversial landfill. In 1981, the Houston city council passed an ordinance restricting the construction of solid-waste disposal sites near public facilities such as schools. And the Texas Department of Health updated its requirements of landfill permit applicants to include detailed land-use, economic, and sociodemographic data on areas where they proposed to site landfills. Black Houstonians had sent a clear signal to the Texas Department of Health, the city of Houston, and private disposal companies that they would fight any future attempts to place waste disposal facilities in their neighborhoods.

Since *Bean v. Southwestern Waste,* not a single landfill or incinerator has been sited in an African American neighborhood in Houston. Not until nearly a decade after that suit did environmental discrimination resurface in the courts. A number of recent cases have challenged siting decisions using the environmental discrimination argument: *East Bibb Twiggs Neighborhood Assocation v. Macon-Bibb County Planning and Zoning Commission* (1989), *Bordeaux Action Committee v. Metro Government of Nashville* (1990), *R.I.S.E. v. Kay* (1991), and *El Pueblo para El Aire y Agua Limpio v. County of Kings* (1991). Unfortunately, these legal challenges are also confronted with the test of demonstrating "purposeful" discrimination.

Redress Inequities

Disproportionate impacts must be redressed by targeting action and resources. Resources should be spent where environmental and health problems are greatest, as determined by some ranking scheme—but one not limited to risk assessment. The EPA already has geographic targeting that involves selecting a physical area, often a naturally defined area such as a watershed; assessing the condition of the natural resources and range of environmental threats, including risks to public health; formulating and implementing integrated, holistic strategies for restoring or protecting living resources and their habitats within that area; and evaluating the progress of those strategies toward their objectives.[57]

Relying solely on proof of a cause-and-effect relationship as defined by traditional epidemiology disguises the exploitative way the polluting industries have operated in some communities and condones a passive acceptance of the status quo.[58] Because it is difficult to establish causation, polluting industries have the upper hand. They can always hide behind "science" and demand "proof" that their activities are harmful to humans or the environment.

A 1992 EPA report, *Securing Our Legacy,* described the agency's geographic initiatives as "protecting what we love."[59] The strategy emphasized "pollution prevention, multimedia enforcement, research into causes and cures of environmental stress, stopping habitat loss, education, and constituency building."[60] Examples of geographic initiatives under way include the Chesapeake Bay, Great Lakes, Gulf of Mexico, and Mexican Border programs.

Such targeting should channel resources to the hot spots, communities that are burdened with more than their fair share of environmental problems. For example, EPA's Region VI has developed geographic information systems and comparative risk methodologies to evaluate environmental equity concerns in the region. The methodology combines susceptibility factors, such as age, pregnancy, race, income, preexisting disease, and lifestyle, with chemical release data from the Toxic Release inventory and monitoring information; state health department vital statistics data; and geographic and demographic data—especially from areas around hazardous waste sites—for its regional equity assessment.

Region VI's 1992 Gulf Coast Toxics Initiatives project is an outgrowth of its equity assessment. The project targets facilities on the Texas and Louisiana coast, a "sensitive . . . eco-region where most of the releases in the five-state region occur."[61] Inspectors will spend 38 percent of their time in this "multimedia enforcement effort."[62] It is not clear how this percentage was determined, but, for the project to move beyond the "first-step" phase and begin addressing real inequities, most of its resources (not just inspectors) must be channeled to the areas where most of the problems occur.

A 1993 EPA study of Toxic Release Inventory data from Louisiana's petrochemical corridor found that "populations within two miles of facilities releasing 90% of total industrial corridor air releases feature a higher proportion of minorities than the state average; facilities releasing 88% have a higher proportion than the Industrial Corridor parishes' average."[63]

To no one's surprise, communities in Corpus Christi, neighborhoods that run along the Houston Ship Channel and petrochemical corridor, and many unincorporated communities along the 85-mile stretch of the Mississippi River from Baton Rouge to New Orleans ranked at or near the top in terms of pollution discharges in EPA Region VI's Gulf Coast Toxics Initiatives equity assessment. It is very likely that similar rankings would be achieved using the environmental justice framework. However, the question that remains is one of resource allocation—the level of resources that Region VI will channel into solving the pollution problem in communities that have a disproportionately large share of poor people, working-class people, and people of color.

Health concerns raised by Louisiana's residents and grassroots activists in such communities as Alsen, St. Gabriel, Geismer, Morrisonville, and Lions—all of which are located in close proximity to polluting industries—have not been adequately addressed by local parish supervisors, state environmental and health officials, or the federal and regional offices of EPA.[64]

A few contaminated African American communities in southeast Louisiana have been bought out or are in the process of being bought out by industries under their "good neighbor" programs. Moving people away from the health threat is only a partial solution, however, as long as damage to the environment continues. For example, Dow Chemical, the state's largest chemical plant, is buying out residents of mostly African American Morrisonville.[65] The communities of Sun Rise and Reveilletown, which were founded by freed slaves, have already been bought out.

Many of the community buyout settlements are sealed. The secret nature of the agreements limits public scrutiny, community comparisons, and disclosure of harm or potential harm. Few of the recent settlement agreements allow for health monitoring or surveillance of affected residents once they are dispersed.[66] Some settlements have even required the "victims" to sign waivers that preclude them from bringing any further lawsuits against the polluting industry.

A FRAMEWORK FOR ENVIRONMENTAL JUSTICE

The solution to unequal protection lies in the realm of environmental justice for all people. No community—rich or poor, black or white—should be allowed to become a "sacrifice zone." The lessons from the civil rights struggles around housing, employment, education, and public accommodations over the past four decades suggest that environmental justice requires a legislative foundation. It is not enough to demonstrate the existence of unjust and unfair conditions; the practices that cause the conditions must be made illegal.

The five principles already described—the right to protection, prevention of harm, shifting the burden of proof, obviating proof of intent to discriminate, and targeting resources to redress inequities—constitute a framework for environmental justice. The framework incorporates a legislative strategy, modeled after landmark civil rights mandates, that would make environmental discrimination illegal and costly.

Although enforcing current laws in a nondiscriminatory way would help, a new legislative initiative is needed. Unequal protection must be attacked via a federal "fair environmental protection act" that redefines protection as a right rather than a privilege. Legislative initiatives must also be directed at states because many of the decisions and problems lie with state actions.

Noxious facility siting and cleanup decisions involve very little science and a lot of politics. Institutional discrimination exists in every social arena, including environmental decision making. Burdens and benefits are not randomly distributed. Reliance solely on "objective" science for environmental decision making—in a world shaped largely by power politics and special interests—often masks institutional racism. For example, the assignment of "acceptable" risk and use of "averages" often results from value judgments that serve to legitimate existing inequities. A national environmental justice framework that incorporates the five principles presented above is needed to begin addressing environmental inequities that result from procedural, geographic, and societal imbalances.

The antidiscrimination and enforcement measures called for here are no more regressive than the initiatives undertaken to eliminate slavery and segregation in the United States. Opponents argued at the time that such actions would hurt the slaves by creating unemployment and destroying black institutions, such as businesses and schools. Similar arguments were made in opposition to sanctions against the racist system of apartheid in South Africa. But people of color who live in environmental "sacrifice zones"—from migrant farm workers who are exposed to deadly pesticides to the parents of inner-city children threatened by lead poisoning—will welcome any new approaches that will reduce environmental disparities and eliminate the threats to their families' health.

NOTES

1. U.S. Environmental Protection Agency, *Environmental Equity: Reducing Risk for All Communities* (Washington, D.C., 1992); and K. Sexton and Y. Banks Anderson, eds., "Equity in Environmental Health: Research Issues and Needs," *Toxicology and Industrial Health 9* (September/October 1993).
2. R. D. Bullard, "Solid Waste Sites and the Black Houston Community," *Sociological Inquiry 53*, nos. 2 and 3 (1983): 273–88; idem., *Invisible Houston: The Black Experience in Boom and Bust* (College Station, Tex.:

Texas A&M University Press, 1987); idem., *Dumping in Dixie: Race, Class and Environmental Quality* (Boulder, Colo.: Westview Press, 1990); idem., *Confronting Environmental Racism: Voices from the Grass-roots* (Boston, Mass.: South End Press, forthcoming); D. Russell, "Environmental Racism," *Anncas Journal 11,* no. 2 (1989): 22–32; M. Lavelle and M. Coyle, "Unequal Protection," *National Law Journal,* 21 September 1992, 1–2; R. Austin and M. Schill, "Black, Brown, Poor, and Poisoned: Minority Grassroots Environmentalism and the Quest for Eco-Justice," *Kansas Journal of Law and Public Policy 1* (1991): 69–82; R. Godsil, "Remedying Environmental Racism," *Michigan Law Review 90* (1991):394–427; and B. Bryant and P. Mohai, eds., *Race and the Incidence of Environmental Hazards: A Time for Discourse* (Boulder, Colo.: Westview Press, 1992).

3. R. B. Stewart, "Paradoxes of Liberty, Integrity, and Fraternity: The Collective Nature of Environmental Quality and Judicial Review of Administration Action," *Environmental Law 7,* no. 3 (1977): 474–76; M. A. Freeman, "The Distribution of Environmental Quality," in *Environmental Quality Analysis,* ed. by A. V. Kneese and B. T. Bower (Baltimore, Md.: Johns Hopkins University Press for Resources for the Future, 1972); W. J. Kruvant, "People, Energy, and Pollution," in *American Energy Consumer,* ed. by D. K. Newman and D. Day (Cambridge, Mass.: Ballinger, 1975), 125–67; and L. Gianessi, H. M. Peskin, and E. Wolff, "The Distributional Effects of Uniform Air Pollution Policy in the U.S.," *Quarterly Journal of Economics 56,* no. 1 (1979): 281–301.

4. Freeman, note 3 above; Kruvant, note 3 above; Bullard, 1983 and 1990, note 2 above; P. Asch and J. J. Seneca, "Some Evidence on the Distribution of Air Quality," *Land Economics 54,* no. 3 (1978): 278–97; United Church of Christ Commission for Racial Justice, *Toxic Wastes and Race in the United States: A National Study of the Racial and Socioeconomic Characteristics of Communities with Hazardous Waste Sites* (New York: United Church of Christ, 1987); Russell, note 2 above; R. D. Bullard and B. H. Wright, "Environmentalism and the Politics of Equity: Emergent Trends in the Black Community," *Mid-American Review of Sociology 12,* no. 2 (1987): 21–37; idem, "The Quest for Environmental Equity: Mobilizing the African American Community for Social Change," *Society and Natural Resources 3,* no. 4 (1990): 301–11; M. Gelobter, "The Distribution of Air Pollution by Income and Race" (paper presented at the Second Symposium on Social Science in Resource Management, Urbana, Ill., June 1988); R. D. Bullard and J. R. Reagin, "Racism and the City," in *Urban Life in Transition,* ed. by M. Gottdiener and C. V. Pickvance (Newbury Park, Calif.; Sage, 1991): 55–76; R. D. Bullard, "Urban Infrastructure: Social, Environmental, and Health Risks to African Americans," in *The State of Black America 1992,* ed. by B. J. Tidwell (New York: National Urban League, 1992): 183–96; P. Ong and E. Blumenberg, "Race and Environmentalism" (paper prepared for the Graduate School of Architecture and Urban Planning, University of California at Los Angeles, 14 March 1990); and B. H. Wright and R. D. Bullard, "Hazards in the Workplace and Black Health," *National Journal of Sociology 4,* no. 1 (1990): 45–62.

5. Freeman, note 3 above; Gianessi, Peskin, and Wolff, note 3 above; Gelobter, note 4 above; D. R. Wernette and L. A. Nieves, "Breathing Polluted Air," *EPA Journal 18,* no. 1 (1992): 16–17; Bullard, 1983, 1987, and 1990, note 2 above; R. D. Bullard, "Environmental Racism," *Environmental Protection 2* (June 1991): 25–26; L. A. Nieves, "Not in Whose Backyard? Minority Population Concentrations and Noxious Facility Sites" (paper presented at the Annual Meeting of the American Association for the Advancement of Science, Chicago, 9 February 1992); United Church of Christ, note 4 above; Agency for Toxic Substances and Disease Registry, *The Nature and Extent of Lead Poisoning in Children in the United States: A Report to Congress* (Atlanta, Ga.: U.S. Department of Health and Human Services, 1988); K. Florini et al., *Legacy of Lead: America's Continuing Epidemic of Childhood Lead Poisoning* (Washington, D.C.: Environmental Defense Fund, 1990); and P. West, J. M. Fly, F. Larkin, and P. Marans, "Minority Anglers and Toxic Fish Consumption: Evidence of the State-Wide Survey of Michigan," in *The Proceedings of the Michigan Conference on Race and the Incidence of Environmental Hazards,* ed. by B. Bryant and P. Mohai (Ann Arbor, Mich.: University of Michigan School of Natural Resources, 1990): 108–22.

6. Gelobter, note 4 above; and M. Gelobter, "Toward a Model of Environmental Discrimination," in Bryant and Mohai, eds., note 5 above, 87–107.

7. B. Goldman, *Not Just Prosperity: Achieving Sustainability with Environmental Justice* (Washington, D.C.: National Wildlife Federation Corporate Conservation Council, 1994), 8.

8. Wernette and Nieves, note 5 above, 16–17.

9. H. P. Mak, P. Johnson, H. Abbey, and R. C. Talamo, "Prevalence of Asthma and Health Service Utilization of Asthmatic Children in an Inner City," *Journal of Allergy and Clinical Immunology 70* (1982): 367–72; I. F. Goldstein and A. L. Weinstein, "Air Pollution and Asthma: Effects of Exposure to Short-Term Sulfur Dioxide Peaks," *Environmental Research 40* (1986): 332–45; J. Schwartz et al., "Predictors of Asthma and Persistent Wheeze in a National Sample of Children in the United States," *American Review of Respiratory Disease 142* (1990): 555–62; U.S. Environmental Protection Agency, note 1 above; and E. Mann, *L.A.'s Lethal Air: New Strategies for Policy, Organizing and Action* (Los Angeles: Labor/Community Strategy Center, 1991).

10. Lavelle and Coyle, note 2 above, 1–2.

11. Ibid., 2.
12. Bullard, 1983 and 1990, note 2 above; Gelobter, note 4 above; and United Church of Christ, note 4 above.
13. Bullard, 1983 and 1990, note 2 above; P. Costner and J. Thornton, *Playing with Fire* (Washington, D.C.: Greenpeace, 1990); and United Church of Christ, note 4 above.
14. Costner and Thornton, note 13 above.
15. M. H. Brown, *The Toxic Cloud: The Poisoning of America's Air* (New York: Harper and Row, 1987); and J. Summerhays, *Estimation and Evaluation of Cancer Risks Attributable to Air Pollution in Southeast Chicago* (Washington, D.C.: U.S. Environmental Protection Agency, 1989).
16. "Home Street, USA: Living with Pollution," *Greenpeace Magazine,* October/November/December 1991, 8–13.
17. Mann, note 9 above; and Ong and Blumenberg, note 4 above.
18. Mann, note 9 above; and J. Kay, "Fighting Toxic Racism: L.A.'s Minority Neighborhood Is the 'Dirtiest' in the State," *San Francisco Examiner,* 7 April 1991, A1.
19. Bullard, 1990, note 2 above.
20. K. C. Colquette and E. A. Henry Robertson, "Environmental Racism: The Causes, Consequences, and Commendations," *Tulane Environmental Law Journal 5,* no. 1 (1991): 153–207.
21. F. Ferrer, "Testimony by the Office of Bronx Borough President," in *Proceedings from the Public Hearing on Minorities and the Environment: An Exploration into the Effects of Environmental Policies, Practices, and Conditions on Minority and Low-Income Communities* (Bronx, N.Y.: Bronx Planning Office, 20 September 1991).
22. B. Angel, *The Toxic Threat to Indian Lands: A Greenpeace Report* (San Francisco, Calif.: Greenpeace, 1992); J. Kay, "Indian Lands Targeted for Waste Disposal Sites," *San Francisco Examiner,* 10 April 1991, A1.
23. M. Ambler, "The Lands the Feds Forgot," *Sierra,* May/June 1989, 44.
24. Angel, note 22 above; C. Beasley, "Of Poverty and Pollution: Deadly Threat on Native Lands," *Buzzworm 2,* no. 5 (1990): 39–45; and R. Tomsho, "Dumping Grounds: Indian Tribes Contend with Some of the Worst of America's Pollution," *Wall Street Journal,* 29 November 1990, A1.
25. Cerrell Associates, Inc., *Political Difficulties Facing Waste-to-Energy Conversion Plant Siting* (Los Angeles: California Waste Management Board, 1984).
26. L. Blumberg and R. Gottlieb, *War on Waste: Can America Win Its Battle with Garbage?* (Washington, D.C.: Island Press, 1989).
27. U.S. Commission on Civil Rights, *The Battle for Environmental Justice in Louisiana: Government, Industry and the People* (Kansas City, Mo., 1993).
28. Agency for Toxic Substances and Diseases Registry, note 5 above.
29. P. Reich, *The Hour of Lead* (Washington, D.C.: Environmental Defense Fund, 1992).
30. Agency for Toxic Substances and Disease Registry, note 5 above.
31. Florini et al., note 5 above.
32. P. J. Hilts, "White House Shuns Key Role in Lead Exposure," *New York Times,* 24 August 1991, 14.
33. Ibid.
34. Dallas Alliance Environmental Task Force, *Alliance Final Report* (Dallas, Tex.: Dallas Alliance, 1983).
35. J. Lash, K. Gillman, and D. Sheridan, *A Season of Spoils: The Reagan Administration's Attack on the Environment* (New York: Pantheon Books, 1984), 131–39.
36. D. W. Nauss, "EPA Official: Dallas Lead Study Misleading," *Dallas Times Herald,* 20 March 1983, 1; idem, "The People vs. the Lead Smelter," *Dallas Times Herald,* 17 July 1983, 18; B. Lodge, "EPA Official Faults Dallas Lead Smelter," *Dallas Morning News,* 20 March 1983, A1; and Lash, Gillman, and Sheridan, note 35 above.
37. U.S. Environmental Protection Agency Region VI, *Report of the Dallas Area Lead Assessment Study* (Dallas, Tex., 1993).
38. Lash, Gillman, and Sheridan, note 35 above.
39. Bullard, 1990, note 2 above.
40. S. Scott and R. L. Loftis, "Slag Sites' Health Risks Still Unclear," *Dallas Morning News,* 23 July 1991, A1.
41. Ibid.
42. B. L. Lee, "Environmental Litigation on Behalf of Poor, Minority Children: *Matthews v. Coye: A Case Study*" (paper presented at the Annual Meeting of the American Association for the Advancement of Science, Chicago, 9 February 1992).
43. Nuclear Regulatory Commission, *Draft Environmental Impact Statement for the Construction and Operation of Claiborne Enrichment Centre, Homer, Louisiana* (Washington, D.C., 1993), 3–108.
44. See U.S. Census Bureau, *1990 Census of Population General Population Characteristics-Louisiana* (Washington, D.C.: U.S. Government Printing Office, May 1992).
45. Nuclear Regulatory Commission, note 43 above, pages 4–38.
46. Citizens for a Better Environment, *Richmond at Risk* (San Francisco, Calif., 1992).

47. Bay Area Air Quality Management District, *General Chemical Incident of July 26, 1993* (San Francisco, Calif., 15 September 1993), 1.
48. R. Sanchez, "Health and Environmental Risks of the Maquiladora in Mexicali," *National Resources Journal 30* (Winter 1990): 163–86.
49. Center for Investigative Reporting, *Global Dumping Grounds: The International Traffic in Hazardous Waste* (Washington, D.C.: Seven Locks Press, 1989), 59.
50. Working Group on Canada-Mexico Free Trade, "Que Pasa? A Canada-Mexico 'Free' Trade Deal," *New Solutions: A Journal of Environmental and Occupational Health Policy 2* (1991): 10–25.
51. Bullard, 1983, note 2 above.
52. Bullard, 1987, note 2 above.
53. Bullard, 1983, 1987, and 1990, note 2 above. The unit of analysis for the Houston waste study was the neighborhood, not the census tract. The concept of neighborhood predates census tract geography, which became available only in 1950. Neighborhood studies date back nearly a century. *Neighborhood* as used here is defined as "a social/spatial unit of social organization . . . larger than a household and smaller than a city." See A. Hunter, "Urban Neighborhoods: Its Analytical and Social Contexts," *Urban Affairs Quarterly 14* (1979): 270. The neighborhood is part of a city's geography, a place defined by specific physical boundaries and block groups. Similarly, the black neighborhood is a "highly diversified set of interrelated structures and aggregates of people who are held together by forces of white oppression and racism." See J. E. Blackwell, *The Black Community: Diversity and Unity* (New York: Harper & Row, 1985), xiii.
54. Bullard, 1983, 1987, and 1990, note 2 above.
55. Ibid.
56. Ibid.
57. U.S. Environmental Protection Agency, *Strategies and Framework for the Future: Final Report* (Washington, D.C., 1992), 12.
58. K. S. Shrader-Frechette, *Risk and Rationality: Philosophical Foundations for Populist Reform* (Berkeley, Calf.: University of California Press, 1992), 98.
59. U.S. Environmental Protection Agency, "Geographic Initiatives: Protecting What We Love," *Securing Our Legacy: An EPA Progress Report, 1989–1991* (Washington, D.C., 1992), 32.
60. Ibid.
61. U.S. Environmental Protection Agency, note 1 above, vol. 2, *Supporting Documents,* 60.
62. Ibid.
63. U.S. Environmental Protection Agency, *Toxic Release Inventory and Emission Reduction, 1987–1990, in the Lower Mississippi River Industrial Corridor* (Washington D.C., 1993), 25.
64. Bullard, 1990, note 2 above: C. Beasley, "Of Pollution and Poverty: Keeping Watch in Cancer Alley," *Buzzworm 2,* no. 4 (1990): 39–45; and S. Lewis, B. Keating, and D. Russell, *Inconclusive by Design: Waste, Fraud, and Abuse in Federal Environmental Health Research* (Boston, Mass.: National Toxics Campaign, 1992).
65. J. O'Byrne, "The Death of a Town," *Times Picayune,* 20 February 1991, A1.
66. Bullard, 1990, note 2 above; J. O'Byrne and M. Schleitstein, "Invisible Poisons," *Times Picayune,* 18 February 1991, A1; and Lewis, Keating, and Russell, note 64 above.

23

⊠ Ties That Bind: ⊠ Native American Beliefs as a Foundation for Environmental Consciousness

ANNIE L. BOOTH AND HARVEY M. JACOBS

Annie L. Booth and Harvey M. Jacobs are both associated with the Institute for Environmental Studies at the University of Wisconsin.

. . . Both deep ecologists and ecofeminists call for the development of a new human consciousness, one of humility, which recognizes the importance of all life, including the life of the organism Earth.[1] As radical activists and philosophers begin to articulate and implement their ideas for a truly ecological world, they find themselves drawn, again and again, to the beliefs and traditions of North America's Native Americans.[2] Native Americans are often portrayed as model ecological citizens, holding values and beliefs that industrialized humans have long since sacrificed in the pursuit of progress and comfort. This interest in Native American relationships with the natural world has an old history. As Cornell points out, influential members of the early American conservation movement were deeply impressed by Native Americans and their knowledge of and relations with the natural world.[3] Such interest is shared even by less radical elements in the environmental movement.[4]

Native American statements about the integrity and inherent importance of the natural world . . . stir many Western people, but there seems to be surprisingly little understanding of Native Americans' actual relationships with their environment. Even so, this does not keep elements of the environmental movement, mainstream and radical, recent and historical, from using Native Americans for their own ends. In this chapter we attempt to redress this situation by offering a synthetic, detailed discussion of Native American beliefs and relationships with the natural world as presented by Native Americans and by anthropologists and historians. As such, we take a broad approach to the nature of Native American culture, addressing it as a singular phenomenon. Although we are aware of the significant differences among Native American cultures, there is enough similarity in environmental views to warrant this type of cross-cutting approach. More detailed descriptions of the works used here are available in a related annotated bibliography.[5] It is our hope that this chapter will help the environmental movement develop an empathic and analytic understanding of traditions that they now use so loosely.

BELOVED MOTHER TO CONQUERED ENEMY

Although they varied significantly between different cultures, Native American relationships with the natural world tended to preserve biological integrity within natural communities, and did so over a significant period of historical time. These cultures engaged in relationships of mutual respect, reciprocity, and caring with an Earth and fellow beings as alive and self-conscious as human beings. Such relationships were reflected and perpetuated by cultural elements including religious belief and ceremonial ritual.[6]

We do not claim that natural communities remained unchanged by human activities, for they did change, considerably so, and in some instances, negatively so. However, the great majority of natural communities remained ecologically functional while supporting both Native American cultures and a great diversity of different plant and animal species.

In contrast, invading Europeans brought with them cultures that practiced relationships of subjugation and domination, even hatred, of European lands. They made little attempt to live *with* their natural communities, but rather altered them wholesale. The impoverishment of the ecological communities of sixteenth and seventeenth-century Europe was so great that, in contrast, early settlers of the New World found what they described as either a marvelous paradise or a horrendous wilderness, but certainly something completely outside their experience.[7]

Native American cultures had adapted their needs to the capacities of natural communities; the new inhabitants, freshly out of Europe, adapted natural communities to meet their needs. The differences between these two approaches have had profound impacts on the diversity and functioning of natural communities in North America.

NO SUCH THING AS EMPTINESS

In the songs and legends of different Native American cultures it is apparent that the land and her creatures are perceived as truly beautiful things. There is a sense of great wonder and of something which sparks a deep sensation of joyful celebration. Above all else, Native Americans were, and are, life-affirming; they respected and took pleasure in the life to be found around them, in all its diversity, inconsistency, or inconvenience. Everything had a place and a being, life and self-consciousness, and everything was treated accordingly. Hughes points out that only the newly arrived Europeans considered the land to be a "wilderness," barren and desolate.[8] To Native Americans, it was a bountiful community of living beings, of whom the humans were only one part. It was a place of great sacredness, in which the workings of the Great Spirit, or Great Mystery, could always be felt.

Hultkrantz argues that it is only because nature reflected the presence of the Great Mystery that it was considered to be sacred.[9] His interpretation suggests that the Indians' appreciation of nature, whether for its beauty or for its productivity, was influenced by the presence of other values. Hultkrantz felt that the Native American's relationship with nature reflected a dynamic tension, which was inherent in a relationship which both loves and exploits the natural world. This tension was reflected, in part, in the Native American's view of nature, which often included some quite terrifying aspects such as cannibalistic and malevolent spirits. Nature is both nurturing and attractive as well as destructive and dangerous.

In distinct contrast to Hultkrantz's interpretations, however, Native American writers focus on the wonders of the land. Standing Bear, a Lakota Sioux, wrote that Native Americans felt a special joy and wonder for all the elements and changes of season which characterized the land.[10] They felt that they held the spirit of the land within themselves, and so they met and experienced the elements and seasons rather than retreating from them. For Standing Bear and the Lakota, the Earth was so full of life and beings that they never actually felt alone.

[A] very central belief which seems consistent across many Native American cultures [is] that the Earth is a living, conscious being that must be treated with respect and loving care. The Earth may be referred to as Mother, or Grandmother, and these are quite literal terms, for the Earth is the source, the mother of all living beings, including human beings. Black Elk, a Lakota, asked, "Is not the sky a father and the earth a mother and are not all living things with feet and wings or roots their children?"[11] The Earth, and those who reside upon her, take their sacredness from that part of the Great Spirit which resides in all living beings. They are not the source of sacredness, but are no less sacred for that circumstance.

WE ARE THE LAND

The belief in a conscious, living nature is not simply an intellectual concept for Native American cultures. For most, perception of the landscape is important in determining perception of self. Vine Deloria, Jr., argues that Native Americans hold a perception of reality which is bound up in spatial references, references which refer to a physical place.[12] In Deloria's view, a spatial reference is important in establishing positive relationships with the natural world. Because of its basis in a particular land or place, a spatial orientation requires an intimate and respectful relationship with that land.

Not only do Native Americans see themselves as part of the land, they consider the land to be part of them. This goes beyond the romanticized love of nature that modern-day environmentalists are said to indulge in, for the Native American faced the best and worst of the land, and still found it to be sacred, a gift from the Great Mystery of great meaning and value: it offered them their very being. In a very organic sense, the roots of the Native American peoples were always, and still are, in the natural communities in which they have lived.[13]

This theme is echoed by Luther Standing Bear when he describes the elders of the Lakota Sioux as growing so fond of the Earth that they preferred to sit or lie directly upon it.[14] In this way, they felt that they approached more closely the great mysteries in life and saw more clearly their kinship with all life. Indeed, Standing Bear comments that the reason for the white culture's alienation from their adopted land is that they are not truly of it; they have no roots to anchor them for their stay has been too short.[15]

This interconnection between person and land is not merely a thing of historical significance. Present-day Native Americans continue to acknowledge their ties to their land. Utes in the Southwest faced with the question of mining on their lands are deeply troubled, for the land is more than mere resource;[16] . . .

RELATIVES IN FUR MASKS

Recognizing that they were part of the land meant that many Native American cultures did not intellectually or emotionally isolate themselves from the land and her other inhabitants, as did European-derived cultures.

> The idea which appears over and over is "kinship" with other living beings. In the Native American system, there is no idea that nature is somewhere over there while man is over here, nor that there is a great hierarchical ladder of being on which ground and trees occupy a very low rung, animals a slightly higher one, and man a very high one indeed—especially "civilized" man. All are seen to be brothers or relatives (and in tribal systems relationship is central), all are offspring of the Great Mystery, children of our mother, and necessary parts of an ordered, balanced and living whole.[17]

Brown comments that while humans serve as the intermediary between earth and sky, this does not lessen the importance of other beings, as they are the links between humans and the Great Mystery.[18] To realize the self, kinship with all beings must be realized. To gain knowledge, humans must humble themselves before all creation, down to and including the lowliest ant, and realize their own nothingness. Knowledge may come through vision quests, and this knowledge is transmitted and offered by animals. Nature is a mirror which reflects all things, including that which it is important to learn about, understand and value throughout life.

Standing Bear explains that all beings share in the life force which flows from Wakan Tanka, the Great Mystery, including "the flowers of the plains, the blowing winds, rocks, trees, birds, animals," as well as man. "Thus all things were kindred and brought together by the same Great Mystery."[19] The other animals had rights, the right to live and multiply, the right to freedom, and the right to man's indebtedness. The Lakota Sioux, says Standing Bear, respected those rights.

Most Native American legends speak of other species as beings who could shed their fur mask and look human, as beings who once shared a common language with humans, and who continued to understand humans after the humans had lost their ability to understand them. Callicott quotes the Sioux holy man Black Elk, who describes the world as sharing in spiritedness.[20] Because everything shares in this spiritedness, it is possible for humans to enter into social and kin relations with other beings.

Martin, discussing subarctic bands, also notes that Native Americans felt and acknowledged a spiritual kinship with the animals they dealt with.[21] A sympathy built up between the human person who hunted and the animal persons who were hunted, a sympathy which pervaded human life. Animals lived in a world that was spiritual, although they assumed a fleshy body in the physical world. Their connection with the spiritual world made them mediators in all things to do with the spiritual world, such as when humans attempted to enter that world.

According to Nelson, the Alaskan Koyukon sense that the world they live in is a world full of aware, sensate, personified, feeling beings, who can be offended and who at all times must be treated with the proper respect.[22] The animals with which the Koyukons interact are among these powerful, watchful beings. Legend states that they once were human, becoming animals when they died. Animals and humans are distinct beings, their souls being quite different, but the animals are powerful beings in their own right. They are not offended at being killed for use, but killing must be done humanely, and there should be no suggestion of waste. Nor can the body be mistreated:

it must be shown respect according to any number of taboos. Consequently a complex collection of rules, respectful activities, and taboos surround everyday life and assist humans in remaining within the moral code that binds all life. . . .

The practical consequences of such relationships with animals are profound. There is considerable archaeological evidence to suggest that the great prairies and the northeastern forests discovered by the Europeans were a product of modification. Hughes argues that the difference between these historical modifications and those made by the present-day inhabitants is demonstrated by the fact that the first Europeans found a forested and abundant country easily supporting the inhabitants, a country so different from fifteenth-century Europe that it was taken to be an unspoiled paradise.[23] Although animals were taken, sometimes in large numbers, rarely were species endangered or exterminated, for trying to exterminate a species would have meant trying to eliminate not only an essential of life, but a kindred being.

Hughes believes that the "ecological consciousness" of the Native American was in part due to their sense of kinship with the rest of the world, and in part made up of an extensive working knowledge and understanding of the world with which they lived. Much of this knowledge was codified and passed on through the medium of myths and legends handed down between generations. Such intimate knowledge permitted careful and judicious hunting, based on the knowledge of what animals resided in the area, how many there were, and how many were required to ensure a healthy population. Hunting territories were shared by families or bands, but misuse, such as excessive killing, might be grounds for war.

RECIPROCITY AND BALANCE IN ALL THINGS

Interactions with these important beings, these furcovered kin, required careful consideration. Reciprocity and balance were required from both sides in the relationships between humankind and other living beings. Balance was vital: the world exists as an intricate balance of parts, and it was important that humans recognized this balance and strove to maintain and stay within this balance. All hunting and gathering had to be done in such a way as to preserve the balance. Human populations had to fit within the balance. For everything that was taken, something had to be offered in return, and the permanent loss of something, such as in the destruction of a species, irreparably tore at the balance of the world. Thus, offerings were not so much sacrifices, as whites were inclined to interpret them, but rather a fair exchange for what had been taken, to maintain the balance. In this way, the idea of reciprocity emerges. From the Native American perspective, as Hughes puts it, "mankind depends on the other beings for life, and they depend on mankind to maintain the proper balance."[24] According to the Koyukons, for example, humans interact with natural things on the basis of a moral code, which, if properly attended to, contributes to a proper spiritual balance between humans and nonhumans.[25]

Momaday, a Kiowa writer and teacher, describes the necessary relationship as an act of reciprocal approbation, "approbations in which man invests himself in the landscape, and at the same time incorporates the landscape into his own most fundamental experience."[26] The respect and approval is two-way: humans both give and receive value and self-worth from the natural world. According to Momaday, this act of approbation is an act of the imagination, and it is a moral act. All of us are what we imagine ourselves to be, and the Native Americans imagine themselves specifically in terms of relationships with the physical world, among other things. Native Americans have been determining themselves in their imagination for many generations, and in the process, the landscape has become part of a particular reality. In a sense, for the Native American, the process is more intuitive and evolutionary than is the white Western rational linear process. The Native American has a personal investment in vision and imagination as a reality, or as part of a reality, whereas many whites believe such things have very little to do with what we call reality.

Toelken examines the idea of reciprocity between the Navaho people and what he describes as "the sacred *process* going on in the world."[27] Religion embodies a reciprocal relationship between the people and this process, and everything becomes a part of this circular, sacred give and take. Part of the idea of reciprocity is the necessity and importance of interaction. Participation in reciprocity is vital; a failure to interact, or a breakdown in interaction, leads to disease and calamity. Thus, everything that is used in everyday life is used for its part in that interaction; it becomes a symbol of sacred interaction and relationship between the people, the plants, the animals, and the land. Rituals such as those used for healing are not designed to ward off illness or directly cure the ill person. Rather, they are designed to remind the ill person of a frame of mind which is in proper relationship with the rest of the world, a frame of mind which is essential to the maintenance of good health. . . .

DEVELOPING AN ENVIRONMENTAL CONSCIOUSNESS

. . . For more than a century concerned Western environmentalists have held up Native Americans as one contemporary model of a way humans can learn to live in harmony with the natural world. Our detailed investigation of this assertion, cutting across Native American cultures, suggests that the basic premise of those holding this position is correct. However, it is likely that for many who hold this position, their conception of the Native American world view is limited in its appreciation of the depth and breadth of Native American integration with the land of which they are a part. For example, the extent to which Native Americans understand the Earth and all life upon it as fully alive and needing and deserving of a reciprocal, respectful relationship, and the thoroughly religious character of North American relationships with the natural world, demonstrate how far a construction of a Western environmental consciousness has to go to truly learn from and draw upon that which Native Americans have to teach.

Yet this is exactly the type of understanding which is reflected in the contemporary scholarship of environmental philosophy, particularly with regard to deep ecology and ecological feminism. Concerns and articulations of reciprocal respect for all life forms, a recognition of the Earth itself as a living being, and the recognition of the critical place of some form of spirituality in environmental consciousness permeate both strands of ecophilosophy. But these two approaches to a Western environmental consciousness have come to be characterized as oppositional, rather than integrative.[28] One lesson to be drawn from Native American beliefs is the unity of integrating these two approaches to ecophilosophy so they can work together in the construction of a Western environmental consciousness in which the Earth and all its beings, including humans, have a niche, and humans in particular have an awareness of the importance of all other life forms.

As we turn to Native American cultures for their wisdom, however, it is important to keep in mind that their cultures and relationship with the natural world will not provide any instantaneous solutions to the problems Western culture is presently facing. Cultures, or selected bits of one or two, cannot and should not be arbitrarily grafted onto one another.

Native American traditions, as in all cultures, are embedded in a particular context. The impact and meaning of a tradition stems from lifelong conditioning, preparation, and participation. It is built into the language, into the way day-to-day life is lived and experienced over time, and within a specific physical/social context. Attempts to borrow culture, whether it be wholesale or piecemeal, are doomed to failure.

If we ignore this fact, we risk harm not only to ourselves, but to Native Americans as well. There is a delicate line between respectful learning and intellectual plundering. Richard White questions our casual and constant habit of using the Native American as a symbol without reference or regard to real Native Americans or their attitudes and feelings.[29] In doing so, White argues, we are just as guilty of using and exploiting these cultures as we are when we steal their lands or their lives and spirits.

But there are less imperialistic approaches to Native American cultures. They can be studied as a contrast to our own destructive relationships with the natural world, and as a reminder that positive relationships can and do exist. An open-hearted and respectful investigation of Native American cultures, particularly when members of these cultures voluntarily share with us their understandings and perceptions, can help us discover new directions in which to travel to realize our own potentials.

Luther Standing Bear believed that it took generations of dying and being reborn within a land for that land to become a part of an individual and of a culture.[30] Deloria suggests that it is possible for peoples and lands to adapt and to relate to one another very powerfully, leading to a spiritual union which benefits both; a particular land determines and encourages the nature of a religion that will spring up upon it, and within a religion lies an entire way of life.[31] This is, in fact, exactly the premise of bioregionalists, who add a third strand to the deep ecology-ecofeminism discourse by stressing the need to become intimately aware of particular places, not just place in general.[32] The next step, then, in learning from Native Americans may be to move beyond general study to an examination of individual tribes and cultural groups to understand how the more universal themes addressed in this chapter were and are articulated in particular places.

All told, we may well be on the path to a sustainable Western environmental consciousness. At least in the case of Native Americans we appear to have encountered and long recognized enduring environmental wisdom, even if we have been unable to integrate it into the mainstream of Western culture. At present, the active discourse among deep ecologists, ecofeminists, and bioregionalists suggests serious work on the shaping of an environmental consciousness in a form appropriate to Western culture. We can and should look for assistance in this effort from Native Americans; they appear willing, even anxious, to aid, as long as in so doing we recognize the boundary between learning and exploiting.

NOTES

1. James E. Lovelock, *Gaia: A New Look at Life on Earth* (New York: Oxford University Press, 1979).
2. For one set of prominent examples see Devall, "The Deep Ecology Movement," and Green Party, *Politics For Life,* p. 13.
3. George L. Cornell, "The Influence of Native Americans on Modern Conservationists," *Environmental Review* 9 (1985): 105–17.
4. See for instance Stewart L. Udall, "Indians: First Americans, First Ecologists," in *Readings in American History–73/74* (Connecticut: Dushkin Publishing Group, 1973).
5. Annie L. Booth and Harvey M. Jacobs, *Environmental Consciousness: Native American Worldviews and Sustainable Natural Resource Management: An Annotated Bibliography,* CPL Bibliography no. 214 (Chicago: Council of Planning Librarians, 1988).

6. J. Donald Hughes, *American Indian Ecology* (El Paso: Texas University Press, 1983).

7. See William Cronan, *Changes in the Land: Indians, Colonists and the Ecology of New England* (New York: Hill and Wang, 1983); and Hughes, *American Indian Ecology.*

8. Hughes, *American Indian Ecology.*

9. Ake Hultkrantz, *Belief and Worship in Native North America* (Syracuse: Syracuse University Press, 1981).

10. Luther Standing Bear, *Land of the Spotted Eagle* (Lincoln: University of Nebraska Press, 1933).

11. John G. Neihardt, *Black Elk Speaks: Being the Life Story of a Holy Man of the Oglala Sioux* (New York: Pocket Books, 1975), p. 6.

12. Vine Deloria, Jr., *God Is Red* (New York: Grosset & Dunlap, 1973).

13. Paula Gunn Allen, *The Sacred Hoop: Recovering the Feminine in American Indian Traditions* (Boston: Beacon Press, 1986).

14. Standing Bear, *Land of the Spotted Eagle,* p. 192.

15. Ibid., p. 248.

16. Stephanie Romeo, "Concepts of Nature and Power: Environmental Ethics of the Northern Ute," *Environmental Review* 9 (1985): 160–61.

17. Paula Gunn Allen, "The Sacred Hoop: A Contemporary Indian Perspective on American Literature," in Geary Hobson (ed.), *The Remembered Earth* (Albuquerque: Red Earth Press, 1979), p. 225.

18. Joseph Epes Brown, *The Spiritual Legacy of the American Indian* (New York: Crossroad Publishing Co., 1985).

19. Standing Bear, *Land of the Spotted Eagle,* p. 193.

20. J. Baird Callicott, "Traditional American Indian and Traditional Western European Attitudes towards Nature: An Overview," in Robert Elliot and Arran Gare, eds., *Environmental Philosophy: A Collection of Readings* (University Park: Pennsylvania State University Press, 1983), pp. 231–59.

21. Calvin Martin, "Subarctic Indians and Wildlife," in C. Vecsey and R. W. Venables, eds., *American Indian Environments: Ecological Issues in Native American History* (Syracuse: Syracuse University Press, 1980), pp. 38–45.

22. Richard K. Nelson, *Make Prayers to the Raven* (Chicago: University of Chicago Press, 1983); Richard K. Nelson, "A Conservation Ethic and Environment: The Koyukon of Alaska," in Nancy M. Williams and Eugene S. Hunn, eds., *Resource Managers: North American and Australian Hunter Gatherers,* AAAS Selected Symposium no. 67 (Boulder: Westview Press, 1982), pp. 211–28.

23. J. Donald Hughes, "Forest Indians: The Holy Occupation," *Environmental Review* 2 (1977): 2–13.

24. Hughes, *American Indian Ecology,* p. 17.

25. Nelson, "A Conservation Ethic and Environment: The Koyukon of Alaska."

26. N. Scott Momaday, "Native American Attitudes towards the Environment," in Walter H. Capps, ed., *Seeing with a Native Eye* (New York: Harper & Row, 1976), p. 80.

27. Barre Toelken, "Seeing with a Native Eye: How Many Sheep Will It Hold?" in Walter H. Capps, ed., *Seeing with a Native Eye* (New York: Harper & Row, 1976), p. 14.

28. See for example Janet Biehl, "Ecofeminism and Deep Ecology: Unresolvable Conflict?" *Our Generation* 19 (1988): 19–31; and Warwick Fox, "The Deep Ecology-Ecofeminism Debate and Its Parallels," *Environmental Ethics* 11 (1989): 5–25.

29. Richard White, "Introduction" [to special issue on the American Indian and the environment], *Environmental Review* 9 (1985): 101–103.

30. Standing Bear, *Land of the Spotted Eagle,* p. 248.

31. Deloria, *God Is Red,* p. 294.

32. See for example, Peter Berg, ed., *Reinhabiting a Separate Country* (San Francisco: Planet Drum Foundation, 1978); Kirkpatrick Sale, *Dwellers in the Land: The Bioregional Vision* (San Francisco: Sierra Club Books, 1985); James J. Parsons, "On 'Bioregionalism' and 'Watershed Consciousness,'" *The Professional Geographer* 37 (1985): 1–6; Peter Berg, Beryl Magilavy, and Seth Zuckerman, *A Green City Program for San Francisco Bay Area Cities and Towns* (San Francisco: Planet Drum Books, 1989).

24

⚖ *African Biocommunitarianism* ⚖ *and Australian Dreamtime*

J. BAIRD CALLICOTT

J. Baird Callicott is Professor of Philosophy and Religious Studies at the University of North Texas. His works include Companion to "A Sand County Almanac," Nature in Asian Traditions of Thought, *and* Radical Environmental Philosophy.

THE AFRICAN SCENE

A Paradox

While less rich in sheer numbers of living species than tropical South America, tropical Africa is the richest place on earth for what conservation biologists call "charismatic megafauna."[1] Indeed, the mere mention of Africa conjures images in the mind's eye of wildebeests, springboks, hippopotami, rhinoceroses, zebras, giraffes, elephants, ostriches, flamingos, crocodiles, lions, leopards, cheetahs, monkeys, baboons, gorillas, chimpanzees, and many other kinds of animals. On the other hand, mention of African culture evokes no thoughts of indigenous African environmental ethics. Nor have contemporary scholars looked to African intellectual traditions, as they have to Zen Buddhism, Taoism, and American Indian thought, when casting about for conceptual resources from which to construct an exotic environmental philosophy.

This combination of circumstances is at once paradoxical and discomfiting. How could African peoples be blessed with such a wonderful complement of fellow voyagers in the odyssey of evolution and not have mirrored that singular environmental endowment in their several cultural worldviews? Perhaps they have, and both the popular new environmental movement and scholars in the even newer field of comparative environmental ethics have simply neglected African ecophilosophy.

Of course, all of us *Homo sapiens* are Africans. Our species is one among the indigenous charismatic megafauna incubated in Africa. We evolved shoulder to shoulder with our phylogenetic first cousins, the gorillas and chimpanzees. After our African genesis, we gradually dispersed throughout the world. Perhaps for those of us in the diaspora the reverence for the wildlife of Africa is like reverence for the things of home. It would be surprising to learn that our fellow Africans whose forebears remained at home during the past hundred thousand years did not share those feelings and incorporate them in their philosophies and religions.

Given these reflections, one may be stunned to discover that, generally speaking, indigenous African religions tend to be both monotheistic and anthropocentric. Most posit the existence of a high God, both literally and figuratively speaking, who created the world. And most hold that the world was created with all its creatures for the sake of humanity. Apparently reinforcing anthropocentrism is ancestor worship—the belief nearly ubiquitous in Africa that the spirits of dead relatives haunt the living and must be ritually honored, served, and propitiated.

According to the distinguished British student of African religions Geoffrey Parrinder, "most African peoples have clear beliefs in a supreme God."[2] The African philosopher J. S. Mbiti goes beyond generalization to universalization. He states categorically that "All African peoples believe in God."[3]

As to anthropocentrism, Noel Q. King makes the following claim:

> Having studied these systems [of African thought] in all of their diversity, a student is able to recognize their unity and can only then legitimately look for a paradigm, a pattern. . . . The point of departure is anthropocentric; the central and ultimate concern is with woman and man, their fullness of being and power, their health in the widest sense.[4]

. . . Even Africans who regularly hunt for a living take an anthropocentric stance toward the environment. The Lele are village dwellers and subsist primarily on the maize cultivated by the female members of the tribe, but the ritual and psychological life of the Lele centers on hunting. Yet, according to the British anthropologist Mary Douglas,

> they frequently dwell on the distinction between humans and animals, emphasizing the superiority of the former and their right to exploit the latter. . . . Of God, Njambi, they say that he has created men and animals, rivers and all things. The relation of God to men is like that of their owner to his slaves. He orders them, protects them, sets their affairs straight, and avenges injustice. Animals of the forest are also under God's power, though they have been given to the Lele for food.

This way of thinking, Douglas notes, has ominous consequences for wildlife conservation: "Game protection laws enforced by the Administration [of the Belgian Congo in the 1940s and 1950s] strike the Lele as an impious contravening of God's act, since he originally gave all the animals in the forest to their ancestors to hunt and kill."[5]

Apparently, therefore, Africa looms as a big blank spot on the world map of indigenous environmental ethics for a very good reason. African thought orbits, seemingly, around human interests. Hence one might expect to distill from it no more than a weak and indirect environmental ethic, similar to the type of ecologically enlightened utilitarianism, focused on long-range human welfare. Or perhaps one could develop a distinctly African stewardship environmental ethic grounded in African monotheism from the core belief—of Judaism, Christianity, and Islam—in God, the Creator of Heaven and Earth.

While Christianity and Islam, especially the latter, are well established in Africa, the monotheism described in the scholarly literature on indigenous African religions has a flavor all its own. And the anthropocentrism characteristic of Western utilitarianism drags in its train a lot of conceptual baggage that seems out of place in an African context. African peoples are traditionally tribal, and the typically African sense of self is bound up with family, clan, village, tribe, and, more recently, nation. To such folk, the individualistic moral ontology of utilitarianism and its associated concepts of enlightened rational self-interest, and the aggregate welfare of social atoms, each pursuing his or her own idiosyncratic "preference satisfaction," would seem foreign and incomprehensible. . . .

The Unity in Diversity of African Thought

For many centuries, the Africans north of the Sahara, from Morocco to Egypt, have been of predominantly Arab descent and predominantly Muslim in outlook. . . .

Like Christianity, Islam is an aggressive, intellectually colonizing worldview. On the continent of Africa, before the perfection of medieval transport (the camel caravan) and modern mechanized transport, the formidable Sahara Desert represented a natural barrier to human information exchange—both genetic and cultural—and the inroads of Islam were limited to Arabic centers of trade on equatorial Africa's east coast. As commerce across the Sahara was established in the eleventh and twelfth centuries, and North African Muslims increasingly frequented the Sahel, or sub-Saharan region of Africa (now including Senegal, Mali, Niger, Chad, and the Sudan), Islam predictably spread to the interior of tropical melanotic Africa.[6] Further south, as the savannah thickens to bush and the bush gives way to the forests of moist equatorial Africa, the influence and purity of Islam diminishes. Islam becomes more and more mixed with traditional African beliefs, rites, and customs. The belt of rain forest girdling central Africa constitutes a second natural barrier to human cultural diffusion, and has historically served to limit the spread of Islam to the southerly latitudes of the continent.

Christianity has enjoyed a longer but much weaker tenure in Africa. By the fourth century it had spread south into Ethiopia, but that's about as far as it got until the era of aggressive European colonialism. During the heyday of European empire in Africa, conversion to Christianity was a necessity for upward mobility in the native petite bourgeoisie created by the colonial regimes. Conversion to Christianity also meant conversion to the full spectrum—medical, educational, political—of Western beliefs, attitudes, and values. Living, so to speak, by European colonialism, the growth and vigor of Christianity stagnated with African independence. In post-colonial Africa, Christianity remains a minority family of religions, mixed with and enriched by native beliefs and rituals. Many of the new and often ephemeral cults and sects, the springing up of which has been a curious aspect of recent African religious experience, exhibit Christian foundations and motifs to one degree or another.[7]

When one turns from the relative simplicity and familiarity of North African and Sahelian Islam and Ethiopian Christianity to consider indigenous African worldviews, one is overwhelmed and bewildered by the diversity of African languages, cultures, and religions. The distinguished student of African religions E. Thomas Lawson points out that in the Niger-Congo language family alone there are over nine hundred distinct tongues, each having numerous dialects, and that traditional native African social structures range from small bands of gatherer-hunters to large kingdoms, and from small encampments and villages to ancient cities with thousands of inhabitants.[8]

On the other hand, many scholars, while keenly aware of Africa's cultural diversity, have insisted on a complementary unity. Putative unity in diversity has been approached in two ways. Geoffrey Parrinder and J. S. Mbiti both find lowest common denominators in African belief systems, as just illustrated (indeed, in the case of the latter, universal denominators). Another approach, more typical of the social sciences than the humanities, attempts to construct a cognitive taxonomy, or "typology," by means of which the myriad tribal mythologies of Africa can be categorized, abstracted, and organized by genera and species. This half of the chapter will note the authoritative claims that there are common themes in indigenous African belief systems and then pursue them in detail through reference to specific representatives.

Yoruba Anthropo-theology

The Yoruba are an agricultural people of equatorial West Africa, whose traditional tribal territory today lies mostly in Nigeria. They are well covered in the literature on African culture and belief and well represent their region of the continent intellectually. Warranting mention is the fact that elements of Yoruba belief may be found in Brazil, Jamaica, Haiti, Cuba, and the United States, having crossed the Atlantic with the slave trade.[9]

As noted, most African belief systems include a high God. The Yoruba name for the Supreme Being is *Olorun* or *Olodumaré,* the names meaning, in different dialects, "Owner-of-the-Sky."[10] The conceptual difference just hinted at between the typically African notion of God and the Judeo-Christian Jehovah and Muslim Allah can be understood by noting a manifest difference. So fundamental to Jewish, Christian, and Muslim religious practice is the locus of worship—the synagogue, temple, church, or mosque—that we scarcely pause to note its significance. In these related religions indigenous to the Middle East, the high God is the only God and the direct source of human blessing, grace, misfortune, and so on. God, by whatever name, is the central actor in history, from the initial creation of the universe to the vagaries of daily weather. Hence, God is the direct object of worship and prayer. But Olorun/Olodumaré has "no shrines . . . erected in his honor, no rituals . . . directed toward him, no sacrifices . . . made to placate him."[11] According to Parrinder, this is typical: "The general picture in Africa is that regular communal prayers to God are rare. Temples and priests are few, and found only among certain tribes."[12] Yoruba religious sites (shrines, temples, and the like) and religious practice (prayers, rituals, divination, and sacrifice) are far from rare, but center on a variety of subordinate spirits—called the *orisa*—instead of on the high God. According to Noel King, comparativists have thus been led to declare Olorun/Olodumaré "otiose, 'superfluous, out of circuit, supernumerary.'"[13]

Naturally, there has been scholarly speculation about this religious happenstance. According to one hypothesis, belief in a Supreme Being is not native to tropical Africa. It was gradually acquired from the literary religions of the Middle East over many centuries of incidental cultural contact and diffusion.[14] Eventually, belief in a Supreme Being was tacked onto—or, to shift metaphors, papered over—the many forms of polyspiritualism native to the region, or so this story goes. Therefore, lip service is paid to the (originally foreign) high God throughout Africa, while sincere, genuinely native ritual service to the indigenous gods proceeds as before, hardly affected by the intellectually alien accretion.

According to a hypothesis favored by J. S. Mbiti and also the African scholars Joseph B. Danqua and E. Bolaji Idowu, however, belief in a high God is as indigenous to Africa as it is widespread. Further, the cult spirits are not separate entities existing apart from the Supreme Being. They are, rather, Spinozistic modes and attributes of the one high God.[15] As Christians manage to believe in one God and three divine persons—Father, Son, and Holy Spirit—so the Yoruba believe in one divinity, Olorun/Olodumaré, who has multiple personalities and manifestations: the *orisa*. One or another of the *orisa* may have particular sites of worship, be addressed in prayer or sacrifice, and ritually served, depending on locale, season, and circumstance. Thus Olorun/ Olodumaré is, according to this hypothesis, hardly neglected in actual Yoruba religious practice. On the contrary, all prayers, services, sacrifices, and rites are ultimately addressed to him in his various guises. . . .

Fundamental to Yoruba cosmology is a division between sky (*orun*) and earth (*aiye*). Chief of the sky spirits is, of course, the remote and unapproachable Olorun, its "owner." The *orisa* and/or . . . departed ancestors are also residents of the sky. The number of *orisa* is large and indeterminate. Some are worshiped only by one clan in one village; others restrict their influence to but one region of Yoruba-land; still others are known to all Yoruba.

Myth, of course, is never entirely systematic or internally consistent, and one should not be exasperated if in addition to Olorun/Olodumaré the Yoruba should also speak of another spirit who had a hand in creation, *Orisa-nla,* also called *Obatala.* This being seems to be next in the hierarchy of sky dwellers, and in some quarters is particularly associated with the shaping of the human body.

Orunmila is the chief god of divination—though one may inquire of other spirits about things hidden from human ken, like the future, the cause of illness, lost objects, and so on.

Esu is a complex Yoruba spirit whom the Christian and Muslim missionaries identified with Satan. This unfortunate association seems to have arisen because Esu tries to trick people into misconduct, as does the Christian-Muslim devil. (Anthropologists draw a parallel of their own, to the "trickster" figures like Coyote and Nanabushu in American Indian narrative cycles.) Unlike the devil, however, Esu's intent is good, not evil; he provides people with the occasion to exercise self-restraint, or, if they succumb to temptation, to expiate their miscreancy through sacrifices to the gods. Esu also mediates between the people and the spirits on high. . . .

In *Shango,* one finally comes upon a being in the Yoruba pantheon who seems to be a bona fide nature spirit; he is the storm god, whose most powerful manifestation is thunder and lightning. Among his symbols are rams and the double-headed axe. The rivers are his wives.

Ogun is also plausibly interpreted as a nature spirit. He is associated with wild animals and the hunt and with iron. His personality is violent and impulsive.

The ecological alter ego of Ogun is *Orisa-oko,* the peaceful and benign god of farming and cultivation.

The Yoruba, it would seem significant for this study, also believe that the earth is a maternal goddess, *Ile.* For reasons that remain obscure, smallpox was (until eliminated) believed to be the "arm" or sanction imposed by Ile on those who did not respect her. . . .

In any case, even from the scant information recounted here, one can see that the representative Yoruba cannot be simply assimilated to Judeo-Christian-Islamic monotheism. Therefore—given the very un-Western hierarchical pantheon, headed by a remote high God—a corresponding stewardship environmental ethic would not seem fitting.

On the other hand, the *orisa* are on the whole not exactly nature spirits either, such as those encountered among native North Americans; thus an animist environmental ethic similar to that found in traditional Sioux or Ojibwa culture would appear no less forced and implausible.

Indeed, Yoruba belief does not fit into any of the three classic nineteenth-century religious categories just mentioned—monotheism, polytheism, and animism (or fetishism). The *orisa* seem more like deified ancestors than like "gods" or personified forms and forces of nature, even when they are linked with aspects of nature. Perhaps "ancestor worship" lies at the core of typically African systems of belief. . . .

Typical of the African outlook, the Yoruba worldview is this-worldly, not other-worldly. Since the dead are not packed off to another world, they remain concerned with and involved in the affairs of the living. (In this regard it is perhaps worth remembering that spirits reside in the sky, not in a realm beyond it.) Relations with socially important and influential relatives are maintained after they are deceased. The ritual nature of these relations has given rise to the common though somewhat misleading characterization of them as "ancestor worship."

But ancestor worship is a natural response to something in addition to the problem of what to do about the spirits of the dead when there is no Other World for them to go to. It is a natural response to a peculiar sense of personal identity or sense of self. Personal identity in Yoruba thinking is far more corporate than in modern Western atomic individualism. Mbiti has succinctly expressed the African view: "Whatever happens to the individual happens to the whole group, and whatever happens to the whole group happens to the individual."[16] Expressing the same thought more formally, the sociologist of religion Benjamin C. Ray writes, "African philosophy tends to define persons in terms of the social groups to which they belong. A person is thought of first of all as a *constituent* of a particular community, for it is the community that defines who he is and who he may become."[17]

An African's identity, nevertheless, is not confined to his or her role in the community. . . . Each individual is a distinct person, with his or her unique blend of personality, needs, desires, talents, and destiny. But, far more vividly than in the modern Western worldview, individuality is not only counterbalanced by community identity but one's unique individuality is defined in part by one's social relationships and expressed through social interaction.

This idea is especially reinforced by one aspect of Yoruba ancestor worship. The *ori* is the inner substance of an individual's essence—his or her soul, as it were. But the *ori* is also understood to be "the partial rebirth or reincarnation of a patrilineal ancestor."[18] Hence, what individuates one—one's *ori*—is drawn from a communal pool of personalities. Throughout one's life, one lives both as and for oneself and reexpresses the essence and destiny of a forebear. As Ray puts it, "Freedom and individuality are always balanced by destiny and community, and these in turn are balanced by natural and supernatural powers. Every person is a *nexus* of interacting elements of the self and the world which shape and are shaped by his behavior."[19] [Emphasis added.]

In this notion of embedded individuality—of individuality as a nexus of communal relationships—we may have the germ of an African environmental ethic. Add to the intense sense of social embeddedness an equally vivid sense of embeddedness in the *biotic* community, and anthropocentric African communitarianism might then be transformed into a nonanthropocentric African environmentalism. Indeed, traditional Africans may be better prepared to respond to contemporary ecology's story of a natural economy and social order than those of us who remain in the grip of the modern Western worldview. The traditional African is accustomed to think of personal identity and destiny as intimately bound up with community, while "the Western notion of individualism—the idea that men are essentially independent of their social and historical circumstances," as Ray characterizes it, may prevent unregenerately modern Westerners from internalizing the moral implications of ecology.[20]

A San Etiquette of Freedom

"San" is the preferred name of the south-central African people often called "bushmen," of which the Kalahari Desert !Kung are the best known. . . . Of all indigenous African peoples, the San may be an exception to the general nonassociation of traditional African cultures with responsible environmental attitudes and values.

Nonetheless, one looks in vain through the anthropological and ethnographic literature on the San for evidence of a sense of gratitude toward fellow members of the biotic community. . . .

The San seem to be no less matter-of-fact in their relations with supernatural entities. They believe in a creator high God who is, according to Lee, characteristically remote and inaccessible.[21] They also believe in a lower God who is something of a trickster. According to the folklorist Megan Biesele, this god began life as a human being and "later ascended to the sky and became divine." The stories of Kauha-the-trickster's tricks "are heard with anything but awed reverence. Instead, amused indignation greets the outrageous or bumbling adventures."[22]

Both Lee and Biesele report that according to San myth in the beginning all creatures were human beings, "persons of the early race."[23] In their originally human condition, moreover, the creatures who were eventually transformed into animals exhibited the personality traits that presently typify their species. One may immediately infer from this mythic particular that the San personify animal behavior. They regard the unusually diverse wildlife in their environment as a community of subjects—a community composed of beings animated by essentially the same consciousness enjoyed by a human being. This inference is confirmed by empirical studies of San beliefs about wildlife.[24] The San worldview puts human and nonhuman beings on the same metaphysical and psychological plane, the institution of insulting the meat notwithstanding. In some practical sense, therefore, the San regard themselves as "plain members and citizens" of the biotic community. . . .

For the San, success in hunting seems to be premised simply and squarely on skill and luck. As to skill, the San are perhaps most renowned for their ability to track and to read spoor. They are also very knowledgeable about animal behavior.[25] As to luck, that depends on the whereabouts of the game, which in turn depends on the moods, whims, and wiles of the beasts themselves, who are apparently believed to be no less interested in self-preservation than properly human beings are. In comparison with their North American counterparts, San hunter-gatherers seem to be members of a less enchanted, more everyday biotic community—though . . . one no less inwardly alive and shot through with subjectivity.

The difference may lie in the prehistoric human ecology of Africa and North America. In Africa, predatory *Homo sapiens* coevolved with the other fauna of the continent. In pre-Columbian North America, *Homo sapiens* were recent immigrants (by evolutionary measures of time), who encountered innocent, inexperienced populations of game. The encounter apparently led to tragedy—to the extinction of more than thirty genera of North American fauna and to a consequent post-Pleistocene New World human population explosion and crash.[26] The cultural evolution of explicit

North American environmental ethics, such as that of the Ojibwa, may have been a dialectical response to this debacle.

Despite enthusiastic hunting by indigenous *Homo sapiens,* Africa retained into the historical period its populations of elephants, zebras, and camels, while similar fauna were extirpated in North America. In Africa the animals may have taken care of themselves—may have evolved defensive measures adequate to ensure their species' survival. If so, there would have been no cause, as there was in North America, for the cultural evolution of explicit indigenous environmental ethics. In any case, according to Richard Lee, "Whatever the nature of their gods and ghosts, the !Kung do not spend their time in philosophical discourse (except when anthropologists prod them). They are more concerned with the concrete matters of life and death, health and illness in their daily lives."[27]

However little reflection the traditional San may give the matter, they behave as though they regarded themselves as plain members and citizens of the biotic community. A window into San biocommunitarianism is provided by Elizabeth Marshall Thomas in a 1990 essay in *The New Yorker.* She writes,

> What mattered to the integrity of the environment was that human hunter-gatherers had been there long enough to count as ecologically indigenous. . . . The ecosystem absorbed the impact of its people, who in vast areas of the Kalahari are the only primates, as it absorbed the impact of, say, its lions.[28]

A major—and beneficial—impact of its people on the Kalahari ecosystem was secondary but critical. The San set fires, and the fire regime in the Kalahari is a principal determinant of the structure of the floral community, favoring grasses and suppressing thornbushes.[29] Because the former are palatable and nutritious for the antelope and other grazers, the traditional human population was indeed the keystone species, in large measure responsible for a productive, diverse, and healthy biotic community. . . .

However little the San folkloric record may reflect their respect for fellow members of the biotic community, the ecological and ethological records testify to an accommodation both with the game and with other predators. The prey species remained abundant. They were not overhunted. The San venatic equipment was simple, fit only for securing enough meat to supplement a diet consisting mostly of vegetable foodstuffs.[30] Continued development even of Stone Age technology is certainly conceivable. Why was it not pursued? Nor did the San attempt to eradicate species such as lions, leopards, and hyenas, which competed with the San for game. Here again, a systematic campaign of removal is conceivable, even with Stone Age weapons. Again, why was it not pursued? One can only assume that the San, as suggested by their scanty cosmogony, regarded themselves as one with the other fauna and practiced a quiet policy of live and let live with their nonhuman neighbors. . . .

AUSTRALIAN ABORIGINAL CONSERVATORS

The aboriginal peoples of Australia are also sometimes referred to as bushmen. And indeed, they have more than a few things in common with the San. The Australian aborigines were (and some still are) traditional hunter-gatherers, with all that that implies economically and socially.[31] The majority still live in arid environments. Ancestors play a prominent role in their belief systems. And the beings in their native mythologies were at first human and later took on animal form.

From the perspective of this study, however, the bushmen of Africa and the bushmen of Australia differ profoundly in their verbally manifest environmental attitudes and values. While the San seem to have been well integrated into the interspecies community of the Kalahari Desert and to have remained in balance with their nonhuman neighbors, San mythology lacks elaborately articulated paradigms of interspecies relationships and—unlike San painting—does not celebrate or sanctify the landscape. In contrast, the Australian aborigines verbally as well as graphically express a very intimate and morally charged sense of relationship with other species and with the topography of their territories. Accordingly, Australian aboriginal thought is beginning to attract the same sort of attention from contemporary environmentalists that North American Indian thought has enjoyed. Most notably, perhaps, the nature-poet laureate of the United States, Gary Snyder, has touched on the ecophilosophical significance of Australian aboriginal attitudes toward nature in his book of beautiful essays, *The Practice of the Wild.*

At first glance, like Africa, Australia confronts the casual student with a bewildering diversity of native peoples—about five hundred tribes (defined as a group of people speaking a mutually intelligible language), according to the dean of Australian anthropology, A. P. Elkin.[32] But a closer look reveals an anthropological commonality greater than in Africa or, for that matter, in the Americas. All native Australians are of one racial stock. All were foragers, practicing no gardening or herding. Further, Australian languages and social structures have many similar features. . . .

One also finds an amazing unity in the cognitive culture of Australian aboriginals. . . . It would seem appropriate to sketch the Australian aboriginal worldview in profile, illustrating it by reference to this or that tribal detail, since in its general features it seems to have been virtually omnipresent on the continent. The environmental attitudes and values implicit in this composite native Australian belief system may then be spelled out.

Elements of an Australian Worldview

Australian aboriginal mythology is referred to as "The Dreaming" or "Dreamtime"— alternative translations of the Aranda word *alcheringa.*[33] The contemporary convention of capitalizing these terms indicates that they are better understood as proper names than as descriptive nouns. "The Dreaming," read literally, suggests that Australian aboriginal mythology originated in and was sustained by dreams. However, while dreams per se seem to play a vital part in the spiritual life of native Australia, their role is not as large as the name would suggest.[34] "Dreamtime" seems to be the less misleading term, since the reference is to a special sort of time—the familiar time of the mythic human mind, a time that is at once long past and existing alongside the present, perhaps as dreams exist parallel to waking experience. Elkin captures its dual sense of both long ago and right now, and its similarity to dreams: "the eternal dream-time—a time which is past and yet present, partaking of the nature of the dreamlife, unfettered by the limitations set by time and space."[35] Gary Snyder characterizes Dreamtime as "the mode of the eternal moment of creating, of being, as contrasted with the mode of cause and effect in time." And he has insightfully suggested further similarities between dreams proper and Dreamtime, "a time of fluidity, shape-shifting interspecies conversation and intersexuality." In this realm there occurred "radically creative moves, whole landscapes being altered."[36]

In the beginning, there was the sky and the land. But the land was featureless. "Culture heroes" or "ancestral beings" traveled the land along specific routes or "tracks." As they went, they transformed it, establishing hills here, ravines there, water holes yonder, and other topographical formations. The Australian religions scholar Nancy Munn reports that in Walbiri mythology "the ancestor first dreams his . . . travels—the country, the songs and everything he makes—inside his head before they are externalized."[37] The doings of these mythic beings at various sites along their travel routes also establish the rites and ceremonies for their human progeny to reenact on location, so to speak. How the ancestral beings did the things they did, like cooking animals in their skins and observing incest taboos, establishes "the Laws" (mores) of the tribes. Part of what it means to be an aboriginal person is to observe the Law.[38] . . .

The ancestral beings were human but also had the characteristics of various animals—such as the emu, kangaroo, bandicoot, or red flying fox—into which they would eventually transform themselves. When their walkabouts were complete, each ancestral being "went down" or "in" at a certain spot.[39]

Such spots are called "increase sites." There the spiritual power, essence, or life force of the ancestor permanently resides. From that site are born both the animals whose specific form the ancestral being assumed and the people who also happen to be its progeny. Since these culture heroes are the ancestors both of certain people and of certain animals, those people and those animals are of one kind, so to speak. Thus arises Australian aboriginal totemism. Some people are emus, some are kangaroos, others bandicoots, still others red flying foxes, and so on. . . .

It is necessary to stress the site and species particularity of the ancestral beings. Each mythic person in the Dreamtime is associated with its peculiar species and its particular increase site, though other sites may be associated with its wanderings and doings. David Bennett notes, "For example, if in Aranda country there is a water hole that is the [increase] site of Karora, the bandicoot, then that is the source for bandicoots and humans of the bandicoot totem. It is not a site, for example, of green parrots or red flying foxes."[40] In some instances, the particularity may extend to individual spirits. . . .

For the most part, the members of one group will all belong to the same local totem. And it falls to them to maintain the sacred sites marking the adventures along the tracks of the ancestral being who went down in their territory, even when these places happen to be in the vicinity of another ancestral being's increase site. They must also perform a cycle of rites and ceremonies, the patterns for which were set out by the actions of their ancestral being. Most important, at the increase site of their totemic ancestor, they must perform the annual "increase ceremony."

The purpose of an increase ceremony is to ensure the plentifulness of a species—the totem species of the group performing the ceremony. The object is not to bring about an occurrence contrary to the usual workings of nature but to assist and encourage the natural course of events.[41] The traditional Australian aboriginals believe that the neglect of increase ceremonies will result in abnormal declines in the respective species populations. Such declines, when they occur, are blamed on those totemites who must have been derelict in their duties. The efficacy of the increase ceremonies, the other ceremonies, and the Law manifest the same principle in Australian aboriginal thought—the rejuvenation by means of reenactment of the events of the past. Thus continuity of all life through time can be maintained, and both the order of human society and the order of nature, in which human society is embedded and on which it depends, can be preserved. . . .

In addition to maintaining the totemic species population, the persons whose totem the species is are forbidden at times to kill and eat members of that species, or may eat only ceremonial morsels on ritual occasions. "For most groups," according to Bennett, "the totem may not be eaten or harmed in certain seasons or at certain locations."[42]

And other taboos may restrict a person's activities in respect to his or her totem species, or in respect to the totems of certain classifications of kin.

As this brief sketch suggests, Australian aboriginal mythology is extremely rich, subtle, and complex. Indeed, Australian aborigines seem to have been at the opposite end of the spectrum of inclination to abstract speculation from their African counterparts. Aboriginal Australia evidently has consisted of a checkerboard of tribes and subgroups sharing a mythic worldview that is deeply rooted in the topography of the continent. Each local community provides a single tile, or small collection of tiles, in a single mosaic of ideas laid out on the landscape. . . .

The Dreamtime is also a map of the countryside. As the mythology celebrates the wanderings of the ancestral beings, the several cycles of songs coordinate the deeds of the heroes with landmarks. In journeying from place to place through the literally roadless outback, an aboriginal follows the tracks of an ancestral being, navigating from sacred site—distinguished by peculiar geographical features—to sacred site by means of the relevant song. Gary Snyder was particularly impressed with this aspect of the Dreamtime when he visited Australia. Each of the "special places" to which he was taken by his aboriginal guides was "out of the ordinary, fantastic even, and sometimes rich with life." Snyder mentions a place with "several unique boulders, each face and facet a surprise." He was charmed by "a sudden opening out of a hidden steep defile where two cliffs meet with just a little sandbed between, and some green bushes, some parrots calling, . . . [and by] a water hole you wouldn't guess was there, where a thirty-foot blade of rock stands on end, balancing."[43]

An Australian Environmental Ethic

If an environmental philosopher were to make up a "traditional" worldview from which environmental ethical implications would follow, he or she would find it hard to come up with anything more apt than what the Australian aboriginal peoples have actually articulated. Theirs is a worldview that at once unites human beings with the land and with the other forms of life on the land. . . .

The Australian aboriginal mind seems to have been deeply conservative—not, of course, in the contemporary political sense of the term but in its literal sense. In the Dreamtime, the past is in some way also the future, since the continued order of human life and of nature is perpetuated through the ritual reenactment of the heroic age. As Elkin succinctly puts it, "Sanctity, sanction, and life arise from the heroic and life-giving past. Conservatism and the maintenance of continuity with the past play an important part in the life . . . of the Aborigines."[44] Confirming Elkin, Berndt holds that "the 'deities' were not only creators but the stimulators of continuity: their power, released through human rituals, ensures the maintenance of the status quo."[45] Since natural features of the landscape are the enduring monuments to the deeds of the ancestral beings, then maintaining continuity with the past entails conserving the distinctive topography of Australia, be it forest, savannah, or desert.

One might therefore expect that contemporary Australian aboriginal groups would be at the forefront of resistance to land-defacing development in Australia. And according to Annette Hamilton, they are: From the aboriginal point of view, the acceptability of a development scheme

> depends on the nature of the development, where it is, and what level of local transformations may be expected. Is the proposed development going to affect a large

and significant sacred site or complex? Will it involve going under the ground in a limited way (oil wells) or in a large way (open-cut mining)? Will it involve roads that cut across traditional ritual pathways for carrying ceremonial objects from place to place? Will it involve towers that overlook vast areas including sacred sites and tracks? Will it cut across dreaming tracks in such a way as to "break" them?[46]

Hamilton raises the question of whether or not one can legitimately speak of "management" by traditional Australian aboriginal peoples as well as conservancy. Though they did not cultivate crops or herd animals, Australian aborigines judiciously employed fire to promote the kind of vegetation useful to themselves and to other animal species.[47] Moreover, there is considerable support for the view that the spectrum of behaviors and behavioral limitations surrounding totemism helped to prevent the overexploitation of native species. If by "management" one means the conscious adaptation of means to ends, then the Dreaming was not management. But like the social representation of nature among the Ojibwa and the seminal representation of energy flows among the Tukano, the Australian Dreamtime seems to have been a crucial element in the ecological adaptation of the people to the land.

More than anyone else, David Bennett has concerned himself with the specifically environmental attitudes and values implicit in Australian aboriginal thought. He thinks that indeed there existed a "conservation effect," especially in regard to native beliefs and associated practices, that prohibited the overuse of economically exploited species. As Bennett characterizes Australian aboriginal taboos concerning other species, they seem functionally equivalent to the game laws enacted by Europeans and their cultural progeny.

Bennett believes that the Aranda and other groups placed a severe restriction on eating one's own totem species not out of respect either for the species or its several specimens but out of respect for one's future spirit children, who may currently be inhabiting the bodies of one's totem, and for one's ancestors. (Only a token amount of totem meat, as in the Christian eucharist, he claims, may be consumed on ceremonial occasions—although during periods of protracted drought the taboo on nonritual consumption by totemites could be violated with impunity.) But he argues that the effect of this prohibition—whether or not it was consciously motivated—was conservation: "In a land with relatively few individuals of some species, prohibiting a segment of the human population from eating that species eases the pressure of human predation and promotes the continued existence of that species."[48]

Further, the increase site itself and its environs were "posted," so to speak, and no hunting or gathering of anything was allowed in the precinct of the sanctum sanctorum. It also had to be approached along the ritual track that the ancestral being had established, and sometimes, according to Bennett, "the proper approach extends to walking backwards." In any case, the conservation effect of this taboo was the creation of "game reserves."[49] On this point, Bennett has the support of the Australian anthropologist T. G. H. Strehlow, who comments that "many of the finest water holes . . . provided inviolable sanctuaries for kangaroo," and "while there is no evidence to show that the Aranda *pmara kutata* [increase sites] had intentionally been created as game reserves," that was in fact the result.[50]

In line with Strehlow's suggestion that there may have been a program of game management encoded in the geomancy of the Australian aborigines, the Australian zoologist A. E. Newsome found that "in Aranda mythology, the major totemic sites for the red kangaroo coincide with the most favorable habitat for the species."[51] Totemic sites in places where there is no habitat for the totem species are not likely to have been instituted in the mythology. One would hardly expect to find an increase site for, say, waterfowl miles from the nearest water. So a coincidence such as Newsome notes is not really noteworthy. Rather, what is notable is the prohibition of exploitation in the best habitat. . . .

Another basic technique of European and Euro-American "rational" or "scientific" game management is the establishment of "closed seasons," coinciding with the nesting of fowl, the suckling of mammals, and so on. David Bennett reports that among the aborigines of central Australia, "between the performance of an increase ceremony and the time when the ceremony is considered to have had its effect, eating the totemic species is normally restricted."[52] The time when the ceremony is considered to have had its effect presumably is the time when the young actually start to appear. . . .

The main reasons for formulating an interspecies ethic are to preserve species, which the world is losing at an abnormal rate, and more generally to abate practices destructive of other aspects of the environment. And these desiderata the Australian aboriginal worldview seems admirably adapted, if not actually designed, to achieve. Deborah Rose is more on target, in comparing an Australian aboriginal environmental ethic to the holistic Leopold land ethic rather than to an ethic primarily concerned with minimizing animal suffering.[53] Undeniably and unequivocally, Australian aboriginal totemism and associated increase ceremonies evidence a keen sense of kinship with and mutual dependency on other creatures, and express a concern for the flourishing of species populations. No less certainly, Australian aboriginal thought manifests a deep and abiding investment in place. The importance of "storied residence" for a "contextualized" environmental ethic has been stressed in the recent literature of environmental ethics and Deep Ecology.

For example, the American environmental philosopher Holmes Rolston, III, maintains that "an environmental ethic does not want merely to abstract out universals, if such there are, from all this drama of life, formulating some set of duties applicable across the whole." Then—without reference to (and almost certainly without a thought for) Australian aboriginal belief—he continues in terms that nevertheless evoke the mytho-geography of aboriginal Australia:

> An ethic is not just a theory but a track through the world. . . . If a holistic ethic is really to incorporate the whole story, it must systematically embed itself in historical eventfulness, or else it will not really be objective. It will not be appropriate, well-adapted to the way humans actually fit their niches. . . . An environmental ethic needs roots in locality and in specific appreciation of natural kinds—not always rooted in a single place, but moving through particular regions and tracks of nature so as to make a narrative career, a storied residence.[54]

And one might say without undue exaggeration that for Gary Snyder "a sense of place" lies at the foundation of any genuine and practical environmental ethic. Bennett writes, "Land gives Aborigines their identity. They are at home."[55] Snyder's warm and personal portrait of his aboriginal hosts and their historically eventful storied residence in their Australian homelands brings vividly to life Bennett's dry declaration. Snyder writes:

> Our place is part of what we are. Yet even a "place" has a kind of fluidity: it passes through space and time—"ceremonial time". . . . It is not enough just to "love nature" or to want to "be in harmony with Gaia." Our relation to our natural world takes place in a *place,* and it must be grounded in information and experience.[56]

Perhaps more clearly and vividly than any other peoples on the planet, the Australian aboriginals have articulated their sense of self in terms of place. According to the Australian environmental philosopher Val Plumwood,

> Aboriginal culture [is] a model of bioregionalism. Identity is not connected to nature as a general abstract category (as urged upon us by the proponents of Deep Ecology), but to particular areas of land, just as the connection one has to close relatives is highly particularistic and involves special attachments and obligations not held to humankind in general. And in complete contrast to Western views of land and nature as only accidentally related to self and as interchangeable means to human satisfaction, the land is conceptualized as just as essentially related to self as kin are, and its loss may be as deeply grieved for and felt as the death of kin.[57]

As this chapter ends, I pause to think of my own "place," my own spirit land. I find myself falling into a mode of consciousness that is human and natural, yet a mode of consciousness so unmodern and un-Western that imaginative immersion in a worldview from the other side of the earth is required to awaken it in me. I wonder what it would be like to stand in reverential silence in the fastness of a particular and familiar crane marsh and think to myself—and feel in my bones—that out of this watery wild both came I and the big birds trumpeting over the tamaracks. This place is the Crane, and I am a crane. Or so I dream.

NOTES

1. Brian J. Huntly, "Conserving and Monitoring Biotic Diversity: Some African Examples," in E. O. Wilson, ed., *Biodiversity* (Washington, D.C.: National Academy Press, 1988), pp. 248–60.
2. Geoffrey Parrinder, *African Traditional Religion* (New York: Harper & Row, 1976), p. 32.
3. J. S. Mbiti, *Introduction to African Religion* (London: Heinemann, 1975), p. 40.
4. Noel Q. King, *African Cosmos: An Introduction to Religion in Africa* (Belmont, CA: Wadsworth, 1986), p. 4.
5. Mary Douglas, "The Lele of Kasai," in Daryll Forde, ed., *African Worlds: Studies in the Cosmological Ideas and Social Values of African Peoples* (London: Oxford University Press, 1954), p. 9.
6. Benjamin C. Ray, *African Religions: Symbol, Ritual, and Community* (Upper Saddle River, NJ: Prentice Hall, 1976).
7. Ibid.
8. E. Thomas Lawson, *Religions of Africa: Traditions in Transformation* (San Francisco: Harper & Row, 1984), pp. 5–6.
9. King, *African Cosmos;* Lawson, *Religions of Africa.*
10. Lawson, *Religions of Africa,* p. 57.
11. Ibid., p. 58.
12. Parrinder, *African Traditional Religion,* p. 39.
13. King, *African Cosmos,* p. 9.
14. See C. G. Seligman, *Races of Africa* (London: Oxford University Press, 1930).
15. J. B. Danqua, *Akan Doctrine of God* (London: Frank Cass, 1968); E. B. Idowu, *Olodumaré: God in Yoruba Belief* (London: SCM Press, 1973); J. S. Mbiti, *African Religions and Philosophy* (New York: Anchor Books, 1970).
16. Mbiti, *African Religions,* p. 141.
17. Ray, *African Religions,* p. 132.
18. Ibid., p. 134.
19. Ibid., p. 132.
20. Ibid.
21. Laurens Van der Post, *The Lost World of the Kalahari* (New York: William Morrow, 1958), pp. 106–7.
22. Megan Biesele, "Aspects of !Kung Folklore," in Richard B. Lee and Irven DeVore, eds., *Kalahari Hunter-Gatherers: Studies of the !Kung San and Their Neighbors* (Cambridge: Harvard University Press, 1976), pp. 310, 308.
23. The quoted phrase is from Van der Post, *Lost World of the Kalahari,* p. 26.

24. Nicholas Blurton Jones and Melvin J. Conner, "!Kung Knowledge of Animal Behavior Study of Mankind Is Animals)," in Lee and DeVore, eds., *Kalahari Hunter-Gatherers*, pp. 32

25. Van der Post, *Lost World of the Kalahari*, p. 15.

26. See Paul S. Martin, "The Discovery of America," *Science* 179: 969–74.

27. Richard B. Lee, *The Dobe !Kung* (New York: Holt, Rinehart & Winston, 1984).

28. Elizabeth Marshall Thomas, "Reflections: The Old Way," *The New Yorker* (October 15, 1990), p. 80.

29. Thomas, "Reflections."

30. Lee, *The Dobe !Kung.*

31. See Richard B. Lee and Irven DeVore, eds., *Man the Hunter* (Chicago: Aldine, 1966).

32. A. P. Elkin, *The Australian Aborigines* (New York: Doubleday, 1964), p. 12.

33. See. W. E. H. Stanner, *The White Man Got No Dreaming: Essays 1938–1973* (Canberra: Australian National University Press, 1979), pp. 23–40.

34. Ibid.

35. Elkin, *Australian Aborigines,* p. 206.

36. Gary Snyder, *The Practice of the Wild* (San Francisco: North Point Press, 1990), p. 84.

37. Nancy D. Munn, "The Transformation of Subjects into Objects in Walbiri and Pitjantjara Myth," in M. Charlesworth, H. Morphy, D. Bell, and K. Maddock, eds., *Religion in Aboriginal Australia: An Anthology* (St. Lucia: University of Queensland Press, 1984), p. 61.

38. Annette Hamilton, "Culture Conflict and Resource Management in Central Australia," in Paul A. Olson, ed., *The Struggle for the Land: Indigenous Insight and Industrial Empire in the Semiarid World* (Lincoln: University of Nebraska Press, 1990).

39. See Munn, "The Transformation of Subjects into Objects," pp. 57–82, for a very thorough account of this process and its social and psychological implications.

40. David H. Bennett, *Inter-species Ethics: Australian Perspectives, A Cross-cultural Study of Attitudes Towards Non-human Animal Species* (Canberra: Preprint Series in Environmental Philosophy no. 14, Department of Philosophy, Australian National University, 1986), p. 103.

41. Bennett, *Inter-species Ethics;* and Elkin, *Australian Aborigines.*

42. Bennett, *Inter-species Ethics;* p. 108.

43. Snyder, *Practice,* p. 84.

44. Elkin, *Australian Aborigines,* p. 208.

45. R. M. Berndt, "Traditional Morality as Expressed through the Medium of an Australian Aboriginal Religion," in Charlesworth et al., eds., *Religion in Aboriginal Australia,* pp. 176–77.

46. Hamilton, "Culture Conflict," p. 221.

47. See Rhys Jones, "Fire-stick Farming," *Australian Natural History* 16 (1969): 224–28; and D. R. Horton, "The Burning Question: Aborigines, Fire, and Australian Ecosystems," *Mankind* 13 (1982): 237–51.

48. Bennett, "Inter-species Ethics," p. 137.

49. Ibid., p. 130.

50. T. G. H. Strehlow, "Culture, Social Structure, and Environment in Aboriginal Central Australia," in R. M. Berndt and C. H. Berndt, eds., *Aboriginal Man in Australia* (Sydney: Angus & Robertson, 1965), p. 144.

51. A. E. Newsome, "The Eco-mythology of the Red Kangaroo in Central Australia," *Mankind* 12 (1980): 327.

52. Bennett, "Inter-species Ethics," p. 133.

53. Rose, "Exploring an Aboriginal Land Ethic."

54. Holmes Rolston III, *Environmental Ethics: Duties to and Values in the Natural World* (Philadelphia: Temple University Press, 1988), pp. 349–52.

55. Bennett, "Inter-species Ethics," p. 157.

56. Snyder, *Practice,* pp. 27, 39.

57. Val Plumwood, "Plato and the Bush: Philosophy and Environment in Australia," *Meanjin* 49 (1990): 531.

25

✍ *The Buddhist Attitude* ✍ *toward Nature*

LILY DE SILVA

Lily de Silva is Professor of Buddhist Studies at the University of Peradeniya, Sri Lanka.

Buddhism strictly limits itself to the delineation of a way of life designed to eradicate human suffering. The Buddha refused to answer questions which did not directly or indirectly bear on the central problem of human suffering and its ending. Furthermore, environmental pollution is a problem of the modern age, unheard of and unsuspected during the time of the Buddha. Therefore it is difficult to find any specific discourse which deals with the topic we are interested in here. Nevertheless, as Buddhism is a full-fledged philosophy of life reflecting all aspects of experience, it is possible to find enough material in the Pali Canon to delineate the Buddhist attitude towards nature.

The word "nature" means everything in the world which is not organised and constructed by man. The Pali equivalents which come closest to "nature" are *loka* and *yathābhūta*. The former is usually translated as "world" while the latter literally means "things as they really are." The words *dhammatā* and *niyāma* are used in the Pali Canon to mean "natural law or way."

NATURE AS DYNAMIC

According to Buddhism changeability is one of the perennial principles of nature. Everything changes in nature and nothing remains static. This concept is expressed by the Pali term *anicca*. Everything formed is in a constant process of change (*sabbe sankhārā anicca*).[1] The world is therefore defined as that which disintegrates (*lujjatī ti loko*); the world is so called because it is dynamic and kinetic, it is constantly in a process of undergoing change.[2] In nature there are no static and stable "things"; there are only ever-changing, ever-moving processes.

MORALITY AND NATURE

The world passes through alternating cycles of evolution and dissolution, each of which endures for a long period of time. Though change is inherent in nature, Buddhism believes that natural processes are affected by the morals of man. . . . Buddhism believes that though change is a factor inherent in nature, man's moral deterioration accelerates the process of change and brings about changes which are adverse to human well being and happiness. . . .

[S]everal suttas from the Pali Canon show that early Buddhism believes there to be a close relationship between human morality and the natural environment. This idea has been systematised in the theory of the five natural laws (*pañca niyāmadhammā*) in the later commentaries.[3] According to this theory, in the cosmos there are five natural laws or forces at work, namely *utuniyāma* (lit. "season-law"), *bījaniyāma* (lit. "seed-law"), *cittaniyāma, kammaniyāma* and *dhammaniyāma*. They can be translated as physical laws, biological laws, psychological laws, moral laws and causal laws, respectively. While the first four laws operate within their respective spheres, the last-mentioned law of causality operates *within each of them as well as among* them.

This means that the physical environment of any given area conditions the growth and development of its biological component, i.e., flora and fauna. These in turn influence the thought pattern of the people interacting with them. Modes of thinking determine moral standards. The opposite process of interaction is also possible. The morals of man influence not only the psychological make-up of the people but the biological and physical environment of the area as well. Thus the five laws demonstrate that man and nature are bound together in a reciprocal causal relationship with changes in one necessarily bringing about changes in the other.

The commentary on the *Cakkavattisīhanāda Sutta* goes on to explain the pattern of mutual interaction further.[4] When mankind is demoralised through greed, famine is the natural outcome; when moral degeneration is due to ignorance, epidemic is the inevitable result; when hatred is the demoralising force, widespread violence is the ultimate outcome. If and when mankind realizes that large-scale devastation has taken place as a result of his moral degeneration, a change of heart takes place among the few surviving human beings. With gradual moral regeneration conditions improve through a long period of cause and effect and mankind again starts to enjoy gradually increasing prosperity and longer life. The world, including nature and mankind, stands or falls with the type of moral force at work. If immorality grips society, man and nature deteriorate; if morality reigns, the quality of human life and nature improves. Thus greed, hatred and delusion produce pollution within and without. Generosity, compassion and wisdom produce purity within and without. This is one reason the Buddha has pronounced that the world is led by the mind, *cittena niyata loko*.[5] Thus man and nature, according to the ideas expressed in early Buddhism, are interdependent.

HUMAN USE OF NATURAL RESOURCES

For survival mankind has to depend on nature for his food, clothing, shelter, medicine and other requisites. For optimum benefits man has to understand nature so that he can utilise natural resources and live harmoniously with nature. By understanding the working of nature—for example, the seasonal rainfall pattern, methods of conserving water by irrigation, the soil types, the physical conditions required for growth of various food crops, etc.—man can learn to get better returns from his agricultural pursuits. But this learning has to be accompanied by moral restraint if he is to enjoy the benefits of natural resources for a long time. Man must learn to satisfy his needs and not feed his greeds. The resources of the world are not unlimited whereas man's greed knows neither limit nor satiation. Modern man in his unbridled voracious greed for pleasure and acquisition of wealth has exploited nature to the point of near impoverishment.

Buddhism tirelessly advocates the virtues of non–greed, non–hatred and non–delusion in all human pursuits. Greed breeds sorrow and unhealthy consequences. Contentment (*santutthi*) is a much praised virtue in Buddhism.[6] The man leading a simple life with few wants easily satisfied is upheld and appreciated as an exemplary character.[7] Miserliness[8] and wastefulness[9] are equally deplored in Buddhism as two degenerate extremes. Wealth has only instrumental value; it is to be utilised for the satisfaction of man's needs. Hoarding is a senseless anti–social habit comparable to the attitude of the dog in the manger. The vast hoarding of wealth in some countries and the methodical destruction of large quantities of agricultural produce to keep the market prices from falling, while half the world is dying of hunger and starvation, is really a sad paradox of the present affluent age.

Buddhism commends frugality as a virtue in its own right. Once Ānanda explained to King Udena the thrifty economic use of robes by the monks in the following order. When new robes are received the old robes are used as coverlets, the old coverlets as mattress covers, the old mattress covers as rugs, the old rugs as dusters, and the old tattered dusters are kneaded with clay and used to repair cracked floors and walls.[10] Thus nothing usable is wasted. Those who waste are derided as "wood-apple eaters."[11] A man shakes the branch of a wood-apple tree and all the fruits, ripe as well as unripe, fall. The man would collect only what he wants and walk away leaving the rest to rot. Such a wasteful attitude is certainly deplored in Buddhism as not only anti–social but criminal. The excessive exploitation of nature as is done today would certainly be condemned by Buddhism in the strongest possible terms.

Buddhism advocates a gentle non–aggressive attitude towards nature. According to the *Sigālovāda Sutta* a householder should accumulate wealth as a bee collects pollen from a flower.[12] The bee harms neither the fragrance nor the beauty of the flower, but gathers pollen to turn it into sweet honey. Similarly, man is expected to make legitimate use of nature so that he can rise above nature and realise his innate spiritual potential.

ATTITUDE TOWARDS ANIMAL AND PLANT LIFE

The well-known Five Precepts (*pañca sīla*) form the minimum code of ethics that every lay Buddhist is expected to adhere to. Its first precept involves abstention from injury to life. It is explained as the casting aside of all forms of weapons, being conscientious about depriving a living being of life. In its positive sense it means the cultivation of compassion and sympathy for all living beings.[13] The Buddhist layman is expected to abstain from trading in meat too.[14]

The Buddhist monk has to abide by an even stricter code of ethics than the layman. He has to abstain from practices which would involve even unintentional injury to living creatures. For instance, the Buddha promulgated the rule against going on a journey during the rainy season because of possible injury to worms and insects that come to the surface in wet weather.[15] The same concern for non–violence prevents a monk from digging the ground.[16] Once a monk who was a potter prior to ordination built for himself a clay hut and set it on fire to give it a fine finish. The Buddha strongly objected to this as so many living creatures would have been burnt in the process. The hut was broken down on the Buddha's instructions to prevent it from creating a bad precedent for later generations.[17] The scrupulous non-violent attitude towards even the smallest living creatures prevents the monks from drinking unstrained water.[18] It is no doubt a sound hygienic habit, but what is noteworthy is the reason which prompts the practice, namely, sympathy for living creatures.

Buddhism also prescribes the practice of *mettā*, "loving-kindness" towards all creatures of all quarters without restriction. The *Karanīyamettā Sutta* enjoins the cultivation of loving-kindness towards all creatures, timid and steady, long and short, big and small, minute and great, visible and invisible, near and far, born and awaiting birth.[19] All quarters are to be suffused with this loving attitude. Just as one's own life is precious to oneself, so is the life of the other precious to himself. Therefore a reverential attitude must be cultivated towards all forms of life.

The understanding of kamma and rebirth, too, prepares the Buddhist to adopt a sympathetic attitude towards animals. According to this belief it is possible for human beings to be reborn in sub-human states among animals. The *Kukkuravatika Sutta* can be cited as a canonical reference which substantiates this view.[20] The Jātakas provide ample testimony to this view from commentarial literature. It is possible that our own close relatives have been reborn as animals. Therefore it is only right that we should treat animals with kindness and sympathy. The Buddhist notion of merit also engenders a gentle non-violent attitude towards living creatures. It is said that if one throws dish-washing water into a pool where there are insects and living creatures, intending that they feed on the tiny particles of food thus washed away, one accumulates merit even by such trivial generosity.[21] According to the *Macchuddāna Jātaka* the Bodhisatta threw his leftover food into a river in order to feed the fish, and by the power of that merit he was saved from an impending disaster.[22] Thus kindness to animals, be they big or small, is a source of merit—merit needed for human beings to improve their lot in the cycle of rebirths and to approach the final goal of Nibbāna.

Buddhism expresses a gentle non-violent attitude towards the vegetable kingdom as well. It is said that one should not even break the branch of a tree that has given one shelter.[23] Plants are so helpful to us in providing us with all necessities of life that we are expected not to adopt a callous attitude towards them. The more strict monastic rules prevent monks from injuring plant life.[24]

Prior to the rise of Buddhism people regarded natural phenomena such as mountains, forests, groves and trees with a sense of awe and reverence.[25] They considered them as the abode of powerful non-human beings who could assist human beings at times of need. Though Buddhism gave man a far superior Triple Refuge (*tisarana*) in the Buddha, Dhamma and Sangha, these places continued to enjoy public patronage at a popular level, as the acceptance of terrestrial non-human beings such as *devatās*[26] and *yakkhas*[27] did not violate the belief system of Buddhism. Therefore among the Buddhists there is a reverential attitude towards specially long-standing gigantic trees. They are called *vanaspati* in Pali, meaning "lords of the forests."[28] As huge trees such as the ironwood, the sāla and the fig are also recognised as the Bodhi trees of former Buddhas, the deferential attitude towards trees is further strengthened.[29] It is well known that the *ficus religiosa* is held as an object of great veneration in the Buddhist world today as the tree under which the Buddha attained Enlightenment.

The construction of parks and pleasure groves for public use is considered a great meritorious deed.[30] Sakka the lord of gods is said to have reached this status as a result of social services such as the construction of parks, pleasure groves, ponds, wells and roads.[31]

The open air, natural habitats and forest trees have a special fascination for the Eastern mind as symbols of spiritual freedom. The home life is regarded as a fetter (*sambādha*) that keeps man in bondage and misery. Renunciation is like the open air (*abbhokāsa*), nature unhampered by man's activity.[32] . . . (The Buddha's constant advice to his disciples also was to resort to natural habitats such as forest groves and glades. There, undisturbed by human activity, they could zealously engage themselves in meditation.[33]

ATTITUDE TOWARDS POLLUTION

Cleanliness was highly commended by the Buddhists both in the person and in the environment. They were much concerned about keeping water clean, be it in the river, pond or well. These sources of water were for public use and each individual had to use them with proper public-spirited caution so that others after him could use them with the same degree of cleanliness. Rules regarding the cleanliness of green grass were prompted by ethical and aesthetic considerations. Moreover, grass is food for most animals and it is man's duty to refrain from polluting it by his activities.

Noise is today recognised as a serious personal and environmental pollutant troubling everyone to some extent. The Buddha and his disciples revelled in the silent solitary natural habitats unencumbered by human activity. Even in the choice of monasteries the presence of undisturbed silence was an important quality they looked for.[34] Silence invigorates those who are pure at heart and raises their efficiency for meditation. But silence overawes those who are impure with ignoble impulses of greed, hatred and delusion.

The psychological training of the monks is so advanced that they are expected to cultivate a taste not only for external silence, but for inner silence of speech, desire and thought as well. The subvocal speech, the inner chatter that goes on constantly within us in our waking life, is expected to be silenced through meditation.[35] The sage who succeeds in quelling this inner speech completely is described as a *muni*, a silent one.[36] His inner silence is maintained even when he speaks! . . .

NATURE AS BEAUTIFUL

The Buddha and his disciples regarded natural beauty as a source of great joy and aesthetic satisfaction. The saints who purged themselves of sensuous worldly pleasures responded to natural beauty with a detached sense of appreciation. The average poet looks at nature and derives inspiration mostly by the sentiments it evokes in his own heart; he becomes emotionally involved with nature. For instance, he may compare the sun's rays passing over the mountain tops to the blush on a sensitive face, he may see a tear in a dew drop, the lips of his beloved in a rose petal, etc. But the appreciation of the saint is quite different. He appreciates nature's beauty for its own sake and derives joy unsullied by sensuous associations and self-projected ideas.

CONCLUSION

In the present ecocrisis man has to look for radical solutions. "Pollution cannot be dealt with in the long term on a remedial or cosmetic basis or by tackling symptoms: all measures should deal with basic causes. These are determined largely by our values, priorities and choices."[37] Man must reappraise his value system. The materialism that has guided his lifestyle has landed him in very severe problems. Buddhism teaches that mind is the forerunner of all things, mind is supreme. If one acts with an impure mind, i.e., a mind sullied with greed, hatred and delusion, suffering is the inevitable result. If one acts with a pure mind, i.e., with the opposite qualities of contentment, compassion and wisdom, happiness will follow like a shadow.[38] Man has to understand that pollution in the environment has been caused because there has been psychological pollution within himself. If he wants a clean environment he has to adopt a lifestyle that springs from a moral and spiritual dimension.

Buddhism offers man a simple moderate lifestyle eschewing both extremes of self-deprivation and self-indulgence. Satisfaction of basic human necessities, reduction of wants to the minimum, frugality and contentment are its important characteristics. Each man has to order his life on moral principles, exercise self-control in the enjoyment of the senses, discharge his duties in his various social roles, and conduct himself with wisdom and self-awareness in all activities. It is only when each man adopts a simple moderate lifestyle that mankind as a whole will stop polluting the environment. This seems to be the only way of overcoming the present ecocrisis and the problem of alienation. With such a lifestyle, man will adopt a non-exploitative, non-aggressive, gentle attitude towards nature. He can then live in harmony with nature, utilising its resources for the satisfaction of his basic needs. The Buddhist admonition is to utilise nature in the same way as a bee collects pollen from the flower, neither polluting its beauty nor depleting its fragrance. Just as the bee manufactures honey out of pollen, so man should be able to find happiness and fulfilment in life without harming the natural world in which he lives.

NOTES

All Pali texts referred to are editions of the Pali Text Society, London. Abbreviations used are as follows:

A.	Anguttara Nikāya
D.	Dīgha Nikāya
Dh.	Dhammapada
Dh.A.	Dhammapada Atthakathā
J.	Jātaka
M.	Majjhima Nikāya
S.	Samyutta Nikāya
Sn.	Sutta-nipāta
Thag.	Theragāthā
Vin.	Vinaya Pitaka

1. A. IV, 100.
2. S. IV, 52.
3. Atthasālini, 854.
4. D. A. III, 854.
5. S. I, 39.
6. Dh. v. 204.
7. A. IV, 2, 220, 229.
8. Dh. A. I, 20 ff.
9. Dh. A. III, 129 ff.
10. Vin. II, 291.
11. A. IV, 283.
12. D. III, 188.
13. D. I, 4.
14. A. III, 208.
15. Vin. I, 137.
16. Vin. IV, 125.
17. Vin. III, 42.
18. Vin. IV, 125.
19. Sn. vv. 143–152.
20. M. I, 387 f.
21. A. I, 161.

22. J. II, 423.
23. Petavatthu II, 9, 3.
24. Vin. IV, 34.
25. Dh. v. 188.
26. S. I, 1–45.
27. S. I, 206–215.
28. S. IV, 302; Dh. A. I, 3.
29. D. II, 4.
30. S. I, 33.
31. J. I, 199 f.
32. D. I, 63.
33. M. I, 118; S. IV, 373.
34. A.V, 15.
35. S. IV, 217, 293.
36. Sn: vv. 207–221; A. I, 273.
37. Robert Arvill, *Man and Environment* (Penguin Books, 1978), p. 170.
38. Dh. vv. 1, 2.

26

⊿ Taoism and the Foundation ⊾ of Environmental Ethics

PO-KEUNG IP

Po-Keung Ip has undergradatuate and graduate degrees from the Chinese University of Hong Kong and has done further graduate work at the University of Western Ontario.

INTRODUCTION

I take it that the major task of environmental ethics is the construction of a system of normative guidelines governing man's attitudes, behavior, and action toward his natural environment. The central question to be asked is: how *ought* man, either as an individual or as a group, to behave, to act, toward nature? By *nature* I mean the nonhuman environment man finds himself in. Surely, a question of this sort presupposes the appropriateness of the application of moral, ethical concepts to nature, viz., stones, fish, bears, trees, water, and so on. Questions about the legitimacy and meaningfulness of such an application automatically arise. However, in the present paper I presume such legitimacy without arguing for it.[1]

Any viable environmental ethics, it seems to me, should provide adequate answers to three questions: (1) What is the nature of nature? (2) What is man's relationship to nature? (3) How should man relate himself to nature? In this paper I show that Taoism gives reasonably good answers to these questions and I argue that Taoism, in this sense, is capable of providing a metaphysical foundation for environmental ethics.

SCIENCE AND ETHICS

Contemporary environmental crises, such as pollution of various sorts, overusage of natural resources, and extinction of rare species, force us to reconsider exactly what the relationships between man and nature are. At the same time they compel us to reflect once again on what sort of attitudes we ought to have toward nature. The kinds of questions raised here are both scientific and ethical. On the one hand, they are scientific because only recently has man come to realize how ignorant he is of the natural surrounding he is in. It is certainly an irony to twentieth-century man that even though modern science has made tremendous strides in probing both the very large and the very small, it has little to say about the middle, i.e., our surrounding ecosphere. The still immature state of the environmental sciences, nonetheless, sadly bears this out. On the other hand, the questions envisaged here are clearly ethical both in the descriptive and the normative senses. First, we need to understand how man actually conceives his relationship with nature. This is clearly an empirical problem that invites both sociological as well as historical studies. However, we also need to go beyond these empirical questions and ask ourselves whether such attitudes are morally justified. This inevitably involves us in the problems of moral criteria. . . .

THE TAOIST CONCEPTION OF NATURE

Recall the three questions posed at the beginning of the paper, viz., what is the nature of nature, of the man-nature relationship, of the right attitudes to nature? The first two questions are clearly metaphysical in nature and the last one ethical. Let us see how Taoism responds to these questions.

To understand the Taoist conception of nature, one must start with the notion of *Tao*. Using a mystical and poetical language, Lao Tzu in *Tao Té Ching* gives a rich but at times amorphous representation of how nature works. This is done by means of the notion of *Tao*. At the very beginning of *Tao Té Ching,* it is said:

> The Tao (Way) that can be told is not the eternal Tao,
> The name that can be named is not the eternal name,
> The nameless is the origin of Heaven and Earth. . . . (chap. 1)[2]

In other places, we are also told that "Tao is eternal and has no name" (chap. 32) and that

> There was something undifferentiated and yet complete, which existed before Heaven and Earth.
> Soundless and formless, It depends on nothing and does not change,
> It operates everywhere and is free from danger,
> It may be considered the mother of the Universe,
> I do not know its name; I call it Tao. (chap. 25)

From similar utterances in *Tao Té Ching,* we gather that Tao has the following attributes: it is nameless, intangible, empty, simple, all-pervasive, eternal, life-sustaining, nourishing.[3] Indeed, for Lao Tzu, *Tao* stands for the ultimate reality of nature. Unlike *Tien* (Heaven) and *Ti* (God),[4] *Tao* is not anything like a creator god. Rather it is a totally depersonalized concept of nature.

The namelessness of *Tao* is due to its infinite nature, since Lao Tzu believes that only finite things can be attached a name. To give a name to a thing is to individuate it and to give it a definite identity. However, *Tao* by virtue of its infinite nature certainly rejects all names. In other words, *Tao* cannot be exhaustively individuated in the domain of empirical beings, though the latter owe their existence to *Tao.* Hence, *Tao* is not characterizable in any finite manner. Therefore, although we can, in a sense, say we "know"

Tao by knowing this or that finite being, yet the knowledge thus arrived at is very incomplete. In this way, the nature of *Tao* is at best indeterminable insofar as human knowledge is concerned.

There is also a dynamic side of *Tao*. We are told that "reversion is the action of *Tao*" (chap. 40). *Tao* is also depicted as a process of change and transformation. In fact, everything in the universe is the result of self- and mutual-transformations which are governed by the dialectical interactions of *Tao*'s two cosmic principles—*Ying* and *Yang*[5]—which explain the rhythmic processes which constitute the natural world.

Since *Tao* nourishes, sustains, and transforms beings, a natural relationship is built between them. This relationship is best understood if we understand the meaning of the *Té* of *Tao*. *Té* signifies the potency, the power, of *Tao* that nourishes, sustains, and transforms beings. As a result, the nourishment, development, and fulfillment of beings are the consequence of *Té*. Because of the nature of *Té*, it is both a potency as well as a virtue, and by virtue of the possession of *Té*, *Tao* is itself virtuous as well. Since *Té* is internalized in all beings in the universe, there is no problem of relating beings in the world. Indeed, things are related to each other not only metaphysically but also morally. The *Té* of *Tao* provides the essential connections. Man, being a member of beings, is without exception internally linked to *Tao* as well as to everything else. Moreover, being endowed with *Té*, man is also endowed with the capacity of doing virtuous things toward his cosmic counterparts. Thus, a crucial metaphysical linkage between man and nature is established. In the Taoist world view, there is no unbridgeable chasm between man and nature, because everything is inherently connected to everything else. The *Tao* is not separated from the natural world of which it is the source. In Taoism, therefore, chaos is impossible.

The moral imperative to be virtuous toward nature is made possible by another feature of *Tao*, impartiality. According to Lao Tzu, *Tao* "being all embracing, is impartial" (chap. 16). *Tao* is impartial in the sense that everything is to be treated on an equal footing. To use a more apt term, everything is seen as being "ontologically equal."[6] Man receives no special attention or status from *Tao*. Homocentrism is simply an alien thing in the Taoist axiological ordering of beings. As a matter of fact, the Taoist holds that there is a kind of egalitarian axiology of beings. The notion of ontological and axiological equality of beings receives further elaborations in the hands of Chuang Tzu. For Chuang Tzu, beings are ontologically equal because they are formed as a result of a process of self- and mutual-transformations. The alleged individuality and uniqueness of beings can be determinable only in such process. Everything is related to everything else through these processes of self- and mutual-transformations.[7]

THE DOCTRINE OF WU WEI

Acknowledging the fact that man–nature is an inherently connected whole, and that man and other beings, animated or otherwise, are ontologically as well as axiologically equal, the question of how man should behave or act toward his natural surroundings is readily answerable, for the Taoist would take the doctrine of *Wu Wei* as the proper answer to this question.

Although the doctrine of *Wu Wei* is relatively well-known, care must be taken as to how one construes the meaning of *wu wei*. I am taking a position which is at variance with the classical rendition. A majority of writers, to my knowledge, translate the meaning of *wu wei* as inaction,[8] but I think there is a better way of translating it which is more coherent with the system of thought presented in *Tao Té Ching* and other representative Taoist texts. Perhaps the translation of *wu wei* as nonaction is the result of relying too heavily on the literal understanding of the meanings of the words *wu* and *wei*. Literally, *wu* means "not"; *wei*, on the hand, means "action" or "endeavor." However, the meaning of *wu wei* need not literally be translated as "inaction." The reasons are as follows. Although we are told that "*Tao* invariably takes no action [*wu wei*],[9] and yet there is nothing left undone" (chap. 37), given that Tao nourishes, sustains, and fulfills, *Tao* is invariably action-in-itself. To say *Tao wu wei* here is tantamount to saying that *Tao* acts in accordance with its own nature. Since *Tao* is action-in-itself, it certainly requires no additional action to act. To say *Tao* takes no action can best be understood as *Tao* taking no *exogenous* action to act, since such action would be redundant.

This construal of *wu wei* indeed has other textual support as well. For example, in characterizing the sage, Lao Tzu says that he

Deal[s] with things before they appear.
Put[s] things in order before disorder arises. . . .
A tower of nine storeys begins with a heap of earth.
The journey of a thousand *li* [1/3 mile] starts from where one stands,
He who takes an action fails.
He who grasps things loses them.
For this reason the sage takes no action and therefore does not fail. . . . (chap. 64)

To make sense of the above paragraph, *wu wei* should not be interpreted as non-action. To do otherwise would make it very difficult to make sense of the phrases, "Deal[s] with things before they appear. Put[s] things in order before disorder arises." Surely, not only are they not nonaction, they are indeed well-planned and deliberative actions. Moreover, when Lao Tzu says, "A tower of nine storeys begins with a heap of earth. The journey of a thousand *li* starts from where one stands," he seems to be saying that things simply work in accordance with the laws of nature. Anyone who tries to do things in violation of the laws of nature is doomed to failure. Therefore, the statements, "He who takes an action fails" and "the sage takes no action and therefore does not fail" are consistently [to] be interpreted as "he who takes action in violation of the laws of nature fails" and "the sage acts in accordance with the laws of nature and therefore does not fail." The sage, being the ideal Taoist man, surely understands the *Tao* well and is thus capable of not acting against nature.[10]

The moral to be drawn from the doctrine of *Wu Wei* is clear and straightforward, given our interpretation of the meaning of *wu wei*. That is, insofar as ecological action is concerned, the Taoist's recommendation is so simple that it almost amounts to a truism: act in accordance with nature. However, one should be reminded of the fact that such a proposal is well supported both by the metaphysical and axiological conceptions of the man-nature relation. It is exactly this kind of metaphysical grounding that an environmental ethic needs.

CONCLUSION—
THE TAOIST REVERSION

Western man inherited from the Enlightenment legacy a conception of nature which is patently antienvironmentalistic. The world is depicted, chiefly through the work of Descartes, as a big machine consisting only of extended matter. It has no life of its own and no value of its own. Its value can only be defined in terms of human needs and purposes. It does not have intrinsic value of any sort, but has only instrumental value defined in terms of human desires. Man, being the possessor of mind, can willfully

subject this allegedly lifeless world to his desires and purposes. The extreme consequence of such homocentrism is the ruthless and unlimited exploitation of the
environment.

Such an attitude assumes a clear dichotomy between subjectivity and objectivity.
On the subjective side, we find man with his feelings, desires, sentiments, passions, reasons, purposes, sensations, etc., all of these regarded as needing to be satisfied, fulfilled
or worthy of preserving and cultivating. On the objective side, we find the nonhuman
world totally devoid of any sentience, functioning blindly according to mechanical laws.
Such a machine-like world certainly cannot have any value and worth of its own except
as a means to the satisfaction and fulfillment of human needs and wants. Such human
needs and wants could range from the most notable to the most mean, from the purely
aesthetic to the cognitively epistemic and to the practically technological. The physical world is there for us to comprehend (Greek philosophers), to experiment with
(Francis Bacon), to transform into a humanized or human nature (Karl Marx), and to
exploit for material goods (Adam Smith and Milton Friedman).

Nevertheless, the man-nature relationship envisaged here is at best an external and
instrumental one. The world is simply something out there, ready to be subjected to
human control and use. It is simply an "otherness." As the Enlightenment teaches us:
there is no internal link between us and it. We do not feel that it is part of us, nor do
we feel that we are part of it. We are cast into a seemingly unsurpassable gap between
subject and object, between man and nature.

To transcend this human predicament, we need a philosophy which can break this
metaphysical barrier that separates man from his world, one which can reconnect the
essential link which has been mistakenly severed for so long between human and nonhuman counterparts. We need a philosophy which can attribute values to nonhuman
objects independently of human needs. That is, nonhuman beings should be regarded
as having intrinsic values of their own rather than having only extrinsic or instrumental values. Moreover, we also need a philosophy which can tell us that we are part of a
universe whose parts mutually nourish, support, and fulfill each other.

It seems to me that one philosophy which satisfies the above mentioned features
is the Taoist philosophy we have been discussing. Most important of all, one cannot find
in it the metaphysical schism that divides subject and object, for the supposed gap
between man and nature simply has no place in the Taoist conception of the man-nature
relationship. Subject and object, through self- and mutual-transformations, are metaphysically fused and unified. Moreover, the thesis of ontological equality of beings,
and hence the axiological equality of beings, completely annihilates the kind of homocentrism at the center of the Enlightenment world view. In addition, it also opens up
the possibility of ascribing values to nonhuman objects regardless of the latter's usefulness to human beings. Thus, a theory of intrinsic value for nature is indeed forthcoming
within the Taoist framework. These features are vitally important to the construction
of environmental ethics of any sort, and are, I believe, capable of providing the necessary metaphysical underpinnings upon which an environmental ethics has to rest.

Taoism, moreover, is compatible with science and is thus capable of providing a
minimally coherent ethics. First, it is not anti-scientific, for despite all its mystical over-
tones, Taoism is in fact a version of naturalism. The doctrine of *Wu Wei* implicitly entails
a notion of observation which is germane to science.[11] Second, ecology as a science
teaches us the interdependence of all life forms and nonliving things. It takes man as
only one part of the interdependent whole. Every member of this intricately integrated
complex is, in a very real sense, ecologically equal because each member depends on
all others for survival, sustenance, and fulfillment. Analogously, the Taoist concept of

ontological equality undoubtedly expresses the same idea, although in a more meta-physical way.

Note also that in the Taoist metaphysics, the notion of axiological equality comes together with the notion of ontological equality. This is due to the fact that in Taoist metaphysics fact and value are fused together, just as subject and object are. Such metaphysical unification of value and fact is crucial in giving us a foundation upon which we can bring science and ethics together. It also makes it possible and meaningful to say that science and ethics coheres in this metaphysical sense. Although it seems presumptuous to assert that the Taoist ideas anticipate cognate concepts in modern ecology, nevertheless, one certainly cannot deny that the insights of the Taoist are explicitly acknowledged and endorsed by the latter.

NOTES

1. Tom Regan recently has given a detailed discussion on this issue in "The Nature and Possibility of an Environmental Ethic," *Environmental Ethics* 3(1981):19–34.
2. All quotations from *Tao Té Ching* are from Chan Wing-Tsit, *A Source Book in Chinese Philosophy* (Princeton: Princeton University Press, 1963), pp. 139–73. They are identified in the text by chapter number.
3. See *Tao Té Ching,* chaps. 1, 74, 21, 35, 4, 6, 32.
4. The origins of the notions of *Ti* (God) and *Tien* (Heaven) were closely tied with ancestor worship in ancient China. *Ti* apparently represented a personal god and was supposed to be the perennial source of life. However, it was subsequently replaced by a less personalistic notion of *Tien*. The latter was a highly naturalistic notion which had no strong religious connotation, but was mainly used to stand for the physical sky. See Chang Chung-ying, "Chinese Philosophy: A Characterization," in A. Naess and A. Hannay, eds., *Introduction to Chinese Philosophy* (Oslo: Universitetsforlaget, 1972), pp. 141–65.
5. See Derk Bodde, "Harmony and Conflict in Chinese Philosophy," in A. F. Wright, ed., *Studies in Chinese Thought* (Chicago: University of Chicago Press, 1953), p. 121.
6. For more on the notion of ontological equality, see Chang, "Chinese Philosophy," p. 149.
7. For more on the self- and mutual-transformation of beings, see *Chuang Tzu,* chap. 2, in Chan, *Source Book*.
8. See Fung Yu-Lan, *A History of Chinese Philosophy,* vol. 1, trans. D. Bodde (Princeton: University Press, 1952), p. 187; Chan, *Source Book*.
9. I systematically replaced *wu wei* in all places in Chan's original translations.
10. For other textual evidence to support my interpretation, see *Haai Nan Tzu,* quoted in J. Needham, *Science and Civilization in China,* vol. 2 (Cambridge: Cambridge University Press, 1956), p. 51; and *Chuang Tzu* in Chan, *Source Book*.
11. Needham incidentally holds such a view; see Colin A. Ronan, *The Shorter Science and Civilization in China,* vol. 1 (Cambridge: Cambridge University Press, 1978), p. 98.

27

⊿ Global Warming: ⊾
How Serious Is the Threat?

G. TYLER MILLER

G. Tyler Miller is President of Earth Education and Research and Professor of Human Ecology at St. Andrews Presbyterian College.

What Is the Scientific Consensus about the Greenhouse Effect?

The greenhouse effect, first proposed by Swedish chemist Svante Arrhenius in 1896, has been confirmed by numerous laboratory experiments and atmospheric measurements. It is one of the most widely accepted theories in the atmospheric sciences. Indeed, without its current greenhouse gases (especially water vapor), the earth would be a cold and lifeless planet with an average surface temperature of $-18°C$ ($0°F$) instead of its current $15°C$ ($59°F$).

Between 1990 and 1995 the Intergovernmental Panel on Climate Change or IPCC (a network of more than 2,000 of the world's leading climate experts from 70 nations) published several reports evaluating the best available evidence concerning the greenhouse effect, past changes in global temperatures, and climate models projecting future changes in global temperatures and climate.

According to this global scientific consensus, the amount of heat trapped in the troposphere depends mainly on the concentrations of heat-trapping or *greenhouse gases* and the length of time they stay in the atmosphere. The major greenhouse gases are water vapor (H_2O), carbon dioxide (CO_2), ozone (O_3), methane (CH_4), nitrous oxide (N_2O), and chlorofluorocarbons (CFCs). Recently scientists have identified another greenhouse gas—perfluorocarbons (PFCs, such as CF_4)—emitted mostly from aluminum production. They remain in the atmosphere from 2,000 to 50,000 years.

The primary heat-trapping gas in the atmosphere is water vapor; because its concentration in the atmosphere is relatively high (1–5%), inputs of water vapor from human activities have little effect on this chemical's greenhouse effects. By contrast, the concentration of carbon dioxide in the atmosphere is so small (0.036%) that a fairly large input of CO_2 from human activities can significantly affect the amount of heat trapped in the atmosphere.

Measured atmospheric levels of certain greenhouse gases—CO_2, CFCs, methane, and nitrous oxide—have risen substantially in recent decades. Although molecules of CFCs, methane, and nitrous oxide trap much more heat per molecule than CO_2, the much larger input of CO_2 makes it the most important greenhouse gas produced by human activities. Most of the increased levels of these greenhouse gases since 1958 have been caused by human activities: burning fossil fuels, agriculture, deforestation, and use of CFCs.

Ice core analysis reveals that at the beginning of the industrial revolution the atmospheric concentration of CO_2 was about 280 parts per million (referred to as the *preindustrial level*). Between 1860 and 1995 the concentration of CO_2 in the atmosphere grew exponentially to 360 parts per million—higher than at any time during the past 150,000 years. The atmospheric concentrations of CO_2 and other greenhouse gases are projected to double from preindustrial (1860) levels sometime during the next century—probably by 2050—and then continue to rise.

What Is the Scientific Consensus about the Earth's Past Temperatures?

Analysis of the content of ancient ice in Antarctic glaciers and other data show that the earth's average surface temperature has fluctuated considerably over geologic time. These data show that during the past 800,000 years several ice ages have covered much of the planet with thick ice. Each glacial period lasted about 100,000 years and was followed by a warmer interglacial period of 10,000–12,500 years.

For the past 10,000 years we have enjoyed the warmth of the latest interglacial period. This climatic stability has prevented drastic changes in the nature of soils and vegetation patterns throughout the world, allowing large increases in food production and thus in population. However, even small temperature changes during this period have led to large migrations of peoples in response to changed agricultural and grazing conditions.

Analysis of gases in bubbles of air trapped in ancient ice show that over the past 160,000 years tropospheric water vapor levels (the dominant greenhouse gas) have remained fairly constant. During most of this period levels of CO_2 have fluctuated between 190 and 290 parts per million. Estimated changes in the levels of tropospheric CO_2 correlate fairly closely with estimated variations in the earth's mean surface temperature during the past 160,000 years.

Since 1860 (when measurements began), mean global temperature (after correcting for urban heat island effects;) has risen 0.3–0.6°C (0.5–1.1°F), with most of this rise occurring since 1946. Ten of the 15 years from 1980 to 1995 were among the hottest in the 114-year recorded history of land-surface temperature measurements; 1995 was the hottest of all, followed closely by 1990.

Many uncertainties remain. Some or even all of the roughly 0.5°C rise since 1860 could result from normal fluctuations in the mean global temperature. On balance, however, the Intergovernmental Panel on Climate Change concluded in its 1995 report that "the observed increase over the last century is unlikely to be entirely due to natural causes" and "the balance of evidence suggests that there is a discernible human influence on global climate."

What Is the Scientific Consensus about Future Global Warming and Its Effects?

To project the effects of increases in greenhouse gases on average global temperature and changes in the earth's climate, scientists develop *mathematical models* of such systems and run them on supercomputers. How well the results correspond to the real world depends on the design and assumptions of the model, the accuracy of the data used, factors in the earth's climate system that amplify or dampen changes in average global temperatures, and the effects of totally unexpected or unpredictable events (chaos).

Current models generally agree that global temperature will increase but generally disagree on the effects of such changes on individual regions. According to the latest climate models, the IPCC projects that the earth's mean surface temperature should rise 1–3.5°C (1.8–6.3°F) between 1990 and 2100; the most likely rise in temperature before 2100 would be about 2°C (3.6°F). This may not seem like much, but even at the lowest projected increase of 1.0°C, the earth would be warmer than it has been for 10,000 years. Current models project that climate change, once begun, will continue for hundreds of years.

According to the models, the Northern Hemisphere should warm more and faster than the Southern Hemisphere because the latter has more heat-absorbing ocean than land and because water cools more slowly than land. Current climate models project a more pronounced warming at the earth's poles. Measurements reveal that the surface temperatures at nine stations north of the Arctic circle have risen by about 5.5°C (9.9°F) since 1968. Since 1947 the average summer temperature at Antarctica has risen by almost 2°C (3.6°F), and the thick, massive ice shelves surrounding the continent are beginning to break up. In January 1995 an iceberg almost as big as Rhode Island or Luxembourg broke off, and ominous cracks are appearing in many parts of the ice shelf.

With a warmer climate global sea levels will rise, mainly because water expands slightly when heated. Satellite data indicate that ocean surface temperatures have been rising at a rate of about 0.1°C (0.18°F) per year since the 1980s. Between 1900 and 1990, global sea levels have risen by 9–18 centimeters (3.5–7 inches). Climate models estimate that two-thirds of this rise is the result of the expansion of the warmer water. Current climate models of global warming project that global sea levels will rise 15–95 centimeters (6–37 inches) between 1990 and 2100, with a best estimate of 48 centimeters (19 inches).

IPCC scientists warn that warming or cooling by more than 1°C (1.8°F) over a few decades (instead of over many centuries, as has been the pattern during the last 10,000 years) will cause serious disruptions of the current structure and functioning of the earth's ecosystems and of human economic and social systems.

Will the Earth Really Get Warmer?

There is much controversy over whether we are already experiencing global warming, how warm temperatures might be in the future, and the effects of such temperature increases. One problem is that many of the past measurements and estimates of the earth's average temperature are imprecise, and we have only about 100 years of accurate data. With such limited data, it is difficult to separate out the normal short-term ups and downs of global temperatures (called *climate noise*) from an overall rise in average global temperature.

What Factors Might Amplify or Dampen Global Warming?

Scientists have also identified a number of factors that might amplify or dampen a rise in average atmospheric temperature. These factors influence both how fast temperatures might climb and what the effects might be on various areas. Let's look more closely at the possible effects of such factors.

One factor is *changes in the amount of solar energy reaching the earth*. Solar output varies by about 0.1% over the 11–year and 22-year sunspot cycles, and over 80-year and other much longer cycles. These up-and-down changes in solar output can temporarily warm or cool the earth and thus affect the projections of climate models. Two 1992 studies concluded that the projected warming power of greenhouse gases should outweigh the climatic influence of the sun over at least the next 50 years.

Another problem is understanding the *effects of oceans on climate*. The world's oceans might amplify global warming by releasing more CO_2 into the atmosphere or might dampen it by absorbing more heat. We know that the oceans currently help moderate tropospheric temperature by removing about 29% of the excess CO_2 we pump into the atmosphere, but we don't know whether they can absorb more. If the oceans warm up enough, some of the dissolved CO_2 will bubble out into the atmosphere (just as in a glass of carbonated ginger ale left out in the sun), amplifying and accelerating global warming.

Global warming could be dampened if the oceans absorbed more heat, but this depends on how long the heat takes to reach deeper layers. Recent measurements indicate that deep vertical mixing in the ocean occurs extremely slowly (taking hundreds of years) in most places.

There is also the possibility that deep ocean currents could be disrupted. At present, these currents (driven largely by differences in water density and winds) act like a gigantic conveyor belt, transferring heat from one place to another and storing carbon dioxide in the deep sea. There is concern that global warming could halt this thermal conveyor belt by reducing the density and salinity of water. If this loop stalls out, evidence from past climate changes indicates that this could trigger atmosphere temperature changes of more than 5°C (9°F) over periods as short as 40 years.

Changes in the *water vapor content and the amount and types of cloud cover* also affect climate. Warmer temperatures would increase evaporation and the water-holding capacity of the air and create more clouds. Significant increases in water vapor, a potent greenhouse gas, could enhance warming.

However, it is difficult to predict the net effect of additional clouds on climate. They could have a warming or cooling effect depending on whether it is day or night and on their type (thin or thick) and altitude. Scientists don't know which of these factors might predominate or how cloud types and heights might vary in different parts of the world as a result of global warming.

Climate is also influenced by *changes in polar ice*. The light-colored Greenland and Antarctic ice sheets act like enormous mirrors, reflecting sunlight back into space without adding to the heating of the earth. If warmer temperatures melted some of this ice and exposed darker ground or ocean, more sunlight would be absorbed and warming would be accelerated. Then more ice would melt, further accelerating the rise in atmospheric temperature.

On the other hand, the early stages of global warming might increase the amount of the earth's water stored as ice. Warmer air would carry more water vapor, which could drop more snow on some polar glaciers, especially the gigantic Antarctic ice sheet. If snow accumulated faster than ice was lost, the ice sheet would grow, reflect more sunlight, and help cool the atmosphere, perhaps leading to a new ice age within a thousand years.

Climate can also be affected by *air pollution*. Projected global warming might be partially offset by *aerosols* (tiny droplets and solid particles of various pollutants) released or formed in the atmosphere from volcanic eruptions and human activities. This occurs because during daytime they reflect some of the incoming sunlight back into space. Nights, however, would be warmer because the clouds would still be there and prevent some of the heat stored in the earth's surface (land and water) during the day from being radiated back into space. These pollutants may explain why most recent warming in the Northern Hemisphere occurs at night.

However, these interactions are complex. Pollutants in the lower troposphere can either warm or cool the air and the surface below them, depending on the reflectivity of the underlying surface. These contradictory and patchy effects, plus improved air pollution control, make it unlikely that air pollutants will counteract projected global warming very much in the next half century. Aerosols also fall back to the earth or are washed out of the atmosphere within weeks or months, whereas CO_2 and other greenhouse gases remain in the atmosphere for decades to several hundred years.

We could maintain or increase levels of aerosol pollutants to offset possible global warming. However, because these air pollutants already kill hundreds of thousands of people a year and damage vegetation (including food crops), they must be reduced.

Another uncertainty is the *effect of increased CO_2 on photosynthesis*. Some studies suggest that more CO_2 in the atmosphere is likely to increase the rate of photosynthesis in areas with adequate amounts of water and other soil nutrients. This would remove more CO_2 from the atmosphere and help slow global warming.

However, other studies suggest that much of any increased plant growth could also be offset by plant-eating insects that breed more rapidly and year-round in warmer temperatures. Weeds may also grow more rapidly at the expense of food crops.

Another factor that can affect CO_2 levels is *forest turnover:* how fast trees grow and die in a forest. A 1994 study indicated that the turnover in tropical forests worldwide is accelerating. Besides reducing the biodiversity of tree species in tropical forests, this change could enhance global warming by reducing removal of CO_2 from the atmosphere because less dense, faster-growing trees require less CO_2 for growth.

Global warming could be accelerated by *increased release of methane, a potent greenhouse gas from wetlands*. A 1994 study indicated that increased uptake of CO_2 by wetland plants could boost emissions of methane by providing more organic matter for methane-producing anaerobic bacteria to decompose. Some scientists also speculate that in a warmer world huge amounts of methane now tied up in arctic tundra soils and in muds on the bottom of the Arctic Ocean might be released if the blanket of permafrost in tundra soils melts and the oceans warm considerably. Conversely, some scientists believe that bacteria in tundra soils would rapidly oxidize the escaping methane to CO_2, a less potent but still important greenhouse gas.

There is also concern over *how rapidly the earth's climate might change*. If moderate change takes place gradually over several hundred years, people in areas with unfavorable climate changes may be able to adapt to the new conditions. However, if the projected global temperature change takes place over several decades or all within the next century, we may not be able to switch food-growing regions and relocate the large portion of the world's population living near coastal areas fast enough. The result would be large numbers of premature deaths from lack of food, as well as social and economic chaos. Such rapid changes would also reduce the earth's biodiversity because many species couldn't move or adapt.

Recent data from analysis of ice cores suggest that the earth's climate has shifted often and more drastically and quickly than previously thought. This new evidence indicates that average temperatures during the warm interglacial period that began about 125,000 years ago varied as much as 10°C (18°F) in only a decade or two and that such warming and cooling periods each lasted 1,000 years or more.

If these findings are correct and also apply to the current interglacial period, fairly small changes in concentrations of greenhouse gases could trigger climate instability, with sharp and perhaps rapid up-and-down shifts in average global temperatures. Such rapid shifts would be disastrous for humans and many other forms of life on the earth.

As a result of the factors discussed in this section, climate scientists estimate that their projections about *global warming and rises in average sea levels during the next 50–100 years could be half the current projections (the best-case scenario) or double them (the worst-case scenario)*. In any event, possible climate change and its effects are likely to be erratic and mostly unpredictable.

SOME POSSIBLE EFFECTS OF A WARMER WORLD

Why Should We Worry if the Earth's Temperature Rises a Few Degrees?

So what's the big deal? Why should we worry about a possible rise of only a few degrees in the earth's average temperature? We often have that much change between May and July, or even between yesterday and today.

This is a common critical thinking trap that many people fall into. The key point is that we are not talking about normal swings in *local weather*, but about a projected *global* change in *climate*.

A warmer global climate could have a number of possible effects. One is *changes in food production,* which could increase in some areas and drop in others. Archaeological evidence and computer models indicate that climate belts would shift northward by 100–150 kilometers (60–90 miles) or upward 150 meters (500 feet) in altitude for each 1°C (1.8°F) rise in global temperature.

Whether such poleward shifts would actually lead to increased crop productivity in new crop-growing areas depends mainly on two factors: the fertility of the soil in such regions and the availability of enormous amounts of money to build a new agricultural infrastructure (for irrigation and food storage and distribution). In parts of Asia, food production in northern areas could increase because of favorable soils. However, in North America the northward expansion of crop-growing regions from the midwestern United States into Canada would be limited by the thinner and less fertile soils in this part of Canada.

Current climate models project declines in the global yield of key food crops ranging from 10% to 70%, and a loss in current cropland area of 10–50%, with most of the shortfalls confined to poorer countries. With current knowledge, we can't predict where changes in crop-growing capacity might occur or how long such changes might last. However, we do know that drops in global crop yields of only 10% would lead to large increases in hunger and starvation (especially in poor countries) and cause economic and social chaos.

Global warming would also *reduce water supplies* in some areas. Lakes, streams, and aquifers in some areas that have provided water to ecosystems, croplands, and cities for centuries could shrink or dry up altogether. This would force entire populations to migrate to areas with adequate water supplies—if they could. So far we can't say with much certainty where this might happen.

Global warming will also lead to a *change in the makeup and location of many of the world's forests.* Forests in temperate and subarctic regions would move toward the poles or to higher altitudes, leaving more grassland and shrubland in their wake.

Tree species, however, move slowly through the growth of new trees along forest edges—typically about 0.9 kilometer (0.5 mile) per year or 9 kilometers (5 miles) per decade. According to the 1995 report of the IPCC, midlatitude climate zones are projected to shift northward by 550 kilometers (340 miles) over the next century. At that rate some tree species such as beech might not be able to migrate fast enough and would die out. According to the IPCC, over the next century "entire forest types might disappear, including half of the world's dry tropical forests." Such forest diebacks would release carbon stored in their biomass and in surrounding soils and accelerate global warming.

Oregon State University scientists project that drying from global warming could cause massive *wildfires* in up to 90% of North American forests. If widespread fires occurred, large numbers of homes and large areas of wildlife habitats would be destroyed. In addition, huge amounts of CO_2 would be injected into the atmosphere, which would accelerate global warming.

Climate change would lead to *reductions in biodiversity* in many areas. Large-scale forest diebacks would cause mass extinction of plant and animal species that couldn't migrate to new areas. Fish would die as temperatures soared in streams and lakes and as lowered water levels concentrated pesticides. Any shifts in regional climate would threaten many parks, wildlife reserves, wilderness areas, wetlands, and coral reefs, wiping out many current efforts to stem the loss of biodiversity.

In a warmer world, water in the oceans would expand and lead to a *rise in sea level.* Even the best estimate of a 48-centimeter (19-inch) rise in sea level projected to occur by 2100 would flood coastal regions—where about one-third of the world's people and economic infrastructure are concentrated—as well as lowlands and deltas where crops are grown. It would also destroy most coral reefs, move barrier islands farther inland, accelerate coastal erosion, contaminate coastal aquifers with salt water, reduce already declining global fish catches, and flood tanks storing oil and other hazardous chemicals in coastal areas.

If warming at the poles caused ice sheets and glaciers to melt even partially, the global sea level would rise far more. One comedian jokes that he plans to buy land in Kansas because it will probably become valuable beach-front property; another boasts that she isn't worried because she lives in a houseboat—the "Noah strategy."

In a warmer world, *weather extremes* are expected to increase in number and severity. Prolonged heat waves and droughts could become the norm in many areas, taking a huge toll on many humans and ecosystems. As the upper layers of seawater warm, damaging hurricanes, typhoons, tornadoes, and violent storms will increase in intensity and occur more often.

Alarmed by an unprecedented series of hurricanes, floods, droughts, and wildfires in recent years, a growing number of the world's insurance companies are sharply raising their premiums for coverage of damages from such events and eliminating coverage in high-risk areas. Executives of some insurance companies are also pressuring government leaders to get more serious about slowing possible global warming and are spurring improvements in energy efficiency and increased use of renewable energy through their procurement and investment policies.

Global warming also poses *threats to human health*. According to the 1995 IPCC report, global warming would bring more heat waves. This would double or triple heat-related deaths among the elderly and people with heart disease.

A warmer world would also disrupt supplies of food and fresh water, displacing millions of people and altering disease patterns in unpredictable ways. The spread of warmer and wetter tropical climates from the equator would bring malaria, encephalitis, yellow fever, dengue fever, and other insect-borne diseases to formerly temperate zones.

Atmospheric warming also affects the respiratory tract by increasing air pollution in winter and increasing exposure to dusts, pollens, and smog in summer. Sea-level rise could spread infectious disease by flooding sewage and sanitation systems in coastal cities.

Climate changes would lead to *a growing number of environmental refugees*. According to environmental expert Norman Myers, by 2050 global warming could produce 50–150 million environmental refugees (compared to 7 million war refugees in Europe after World War II). Most of these refugees would illegally migrate to other countries, causing much social disorder and political instability. Thus, projected global warming has serious implications for the foreign, military, and economic security policies of nations.

SOLUTIONS: DEALING WITH POSSIBLE GLOBAL WARMING

Should We Do More Research or Act Now?

There are three schools of thought concerning global warming. A *very small* group of scientists (many of them not experts in climate research) contend that global warming is not a threat; some popular press commentators and writers even claim that it is a hoax. Widespread reporting of this *no-problem* minority view in the media has clouded the issue, cooled public support for action, and slowed international negotiations to deal with this threat.

A second group of scientists and economists believe we should wait until we have more information about the global climate system, possible global warming, and its effects before we take any action. Proponents of this *waiting strategy* question whether we should spend hundreds of billions of dollars phasing out fossil fuels and replacing deforestation with reforestation (and in the process risk disrupting national and global economies) to help ward off something that might not happen. They call for more research before making such far-reaching decisions.

A third group of scientists point out that greatly increased spending on research about the possibility and effects of global warming will not provide the certainty decision makers want because the global climate system is so incredibly complex. These scientists urge us to adopt a *precautionary strategy*. They believe that when dealing with risky and far-reaching environmental problems such as possible global warming, the safest course is to take informed action *before* there is overwhelming scientific knowledge to justify acting.

Those favoring doing nothing or waiting before acting point out that there is a 50% chance that we are *overestimating* the impact of rising greenhouse gases. However, those urging action now point out that there is also a 50% chance that we are *underestimating* such effects.

Some analysts say that we should take the actions needed to slow global warming even if there were no threat because of their important environmental and economic benefits. This so-called *no-regrets strategy* is an important part of the precautionary strategy.

How Can We Slow Possible Global Warming?

According to the 1994 IPCC report, stabilizing CO_2 levels at the current level would require reducing current global CO_2 emissions by 66–83%. This is a highly unlikely and politically charged change.

There are a variety of solutions analysts have suggested to slow possible global warming; currently, none of these solutions is being vigorously pursued. The quickest, cheapest, and most effective way to reduce emissions of CO_2 and other air pollutants over the next two to three decades is to use energy more efficiently.

Some analysts call for increased use of nuclear power because it produces only about one-sixth as much CO_2 per unit of electricity as coal. Other analysts argue that the danger of large-scale releases of highly radioactive materials from nuclear power-plant accidents and the very high cost of nuclear power make it a much less desirable option than improving energy efficiency and relying more on renewable energy resources.

Using natural gas could help us make the 40- to 50-year transition to an age of energy efficiency and renewable energy. When burned, natural gas emits only half as much CO_2 per unit of energy as coal, and it emits far smaller amounts of most other air pollutants. Because burning natural gas still emits CO_2, however, this approach would merely buy some time to increase energy efficiency and switch to renewable energy resources.

Reducing deforestation and switching to more sustainable food production would reduce CO_2 emissions and help preserve biodiversity and ecological integrity. According to most analysts, slowing population growth is also crucial. If we cut per capita greenhouse-gas emissions in half but world population doubles, we're back where we started.

Some call for a massive global reforestation program as a strategy for slowing global warming. However, studies suggest that such program (requiring each person in the world to plant and tend an average of 1,000 trees every year) would offset only about three years of our current CO_2 emissions from burning fossil fuels. However, a global program for planting and tending trees would help restore deforested and degraded land and reduce soil erosion and loss of biodiversity.

Some scientists have suggested various "technofixes" for dealing with possible global warming, including adding iron to the oceans to stimulate the growth of marine algae (which could remove more CO_2 through photosynthesis), unfurling gigantic foil-surfaced sun mirrors in space to reduce solar input, and injecting sunlight-reflecting sulfate particulates into the stratosphere to cool the earth's surface.

Many of these costly schemes might not work, and most would probably produce unpredictable short- and long-term harmful environmental effects. Moreover, once started, those that work could never be stopped without a renewed rise in CO_2 levels. Instead of spending huge sums of money on such schemes, many scientists believe it would be much more effective and cheaper to spend the money on improving energy efficiency and in shifting to renewable forms of energy that don't produce carbon dioxide.

What Has Been Done to Reduce Greenhouse Gas Emissions?

At the 1992 Earth Summit in Rio de Janeiro, 106 nations approved a Convention on Climate Change, in which developed countries committed themselves to voluntary reduction of their emissions of CO_2 and other greenhouse gases to 1990 levels by the year 2000. However, the convention does not *require* countries to reach this goal.

Environmentalists call the treaty, which officially went into effect in 1994, an important beginning. However, most environmentalists contend that it does not go far enough toward reaching the at least 60% cut in 1995 global emissions of greenhouse gases IPCC scientists say will be needed to reduce projected climate change to manageable levels. Instead of falling, energy-related CO_2 emissions are projected to rise by 30–93% by 2010. . . .

28

⊿ *The Ozone Backlash* ⊾

GARY TAUBES

Gary Taubes is a contributing editor of Discovery *and author of* Bad Science: the Short and Weird Times of Cold Fusion.

Last June, Mario Molina, an atmospheric chemist at the Massachusetts Institute of Technology, was scheduled to give a 30-minute presentation on ozone depletion at a scientific forum preceding the environmental summit in Rio de Janeiro. Molina had been at the forefront of ozone research since 1973, when he and chemist Sherwood Rowland of the University of California, Irvine, first put forward the theory that chlorofluorocarbons (CFCs) would break down in the stratosphere, releasing chlorine that in turn would destroy ozone molecules. Nonetheless, Molina was less than prepared for the talk that preceded his. A Brazilian meteorologist explained to the assembled scientists that the ozone depletion theory is a sham. So much chlorine is getting into the stratosphere from sea salt, volcanoes, and burning biomass, he said, that CFCs couldn't possibly have a noticeable effect on the ozone layer.

Molina was stunned. The meteorologist's arguments had been debated over the years by the scientific community, he says, and had been tested and found simply to be wrong. Nonetheless, says Molina, "it became clear to me that I was not going to be able to teach the audience in a half-hour presentation enough about the atmosphere to rebut what this fellow was saying in his half-hour. Given enough time I could have carefully rebutted his objections. They sounded reasonable, but they were only pseudoscientific."

Molina's experience has become a familiar one recently to researchers working on ozone depletion. Their understanding of the mechanisms of ozone destruction—especially the annual ozone hole that appears in the Antarctic—has grown stronger, yet everywhere they go these days, they seem to be confronted by critics attacking their theories as baseless. For instance, Rush Limbaugh, the conservative political talk-show host and now-best-selling author of *The Way Things Ought to Be,* regularly insists that the theory of ozone depletion by CFCs is a hoax: "balderdash" and "poppycock." Zoologist Dixy Lee Ray, former governor of the state of Washington and former head of the Atomic Energy Commission, makes the same argument in her book, *Trashing the Planet. The Wall Street Journal* and *National Review* have run commentaries by S. Fred Singer, a former chief scientist for the Department of Transportation, purporting to shoot holes in the theory of ozone depletion. Even the June issue of *Omni,* a magazine with a circulation of more than 1 million that publishes a mixture of science and science fiction, printed a feature article claiming to expose ozone research as a politically motivated scam.

These jabs may not have been sufficient to knock the world's leading atmospheric researchers off balance. But they have recently been hit with a flurry of new blows, as the critics have seized upon revisionist articles in the mainstream press to contend that the scientific community is retreating on the CFC-ozone connection. A recent *Washington Post* front-page article, for example, noted that, with the Montreal Protocol limiting global production of CFCs, "the problem appears to be heading toward solution before [researchers] can find any solid evidence that serious harm was or is being done." The otherwise balanced article played this point of view against what *Post* reporter Boyce Rensberger called "a decade of headlines and hand-wringing about erosion of the Earth's protective ozone layer." That was enough for *The Washington Times,* a conservative newspaper owned by Sun Myung Moon, to declare that the *Post, Science,* and other leading publications had joined "a growing chorus dismissing alarmist cries of ozone depletion."

Welcome back to the ozone wars, which many scientists believed were long settled. The backlash now being encountered by atmospheric researchers graphically demonstrates the problems of doing research on a politically charged issue when there are still many scientific uncertainties. The gap between the present danger of ozone depletion—little or none that can be attributed to rising ultraviolet radiation at Earth's surface—and the possible danger in the future, had not the Montreal Protocol been passed, provides plenty of room for a wide range of opinions as to how much concern is warranted. "The public tends to operate in one of two modes," says Harvard atmospheric chemist Jim Anderson, "either there's ozone loss, a hopeless disaster, and we panic and become dysfunctional, or it's no problem at all because there's no massive ozone loss. The truth, of course, is somewhere in between."

Atmospheric researchers have been forced to walk a political tight-rope: On the one hand are the dangers of reporting the situation as potentially disastrous and being called, in Limbaugh's words, "dunderhead alarmists and prophets of doom" (see box on p. 307). On the other are the dangers of presenting scientifically conservative scenarios and having their critics respond that there's no problem, and thus no reason for either further concern or further research.

ROOTS OF THE BACKLASH

Limbaugh, by virtue of his various talk-shows and his best-selling book, is the most visible and outspoken critic of the ozone depletion scenarios and the research community. He is quick to blame the ozone "scam" on self-interested scientists out to procure funding for their unnecessary research. "They always want more funding," he writes, "and today that means government funding. What could be more natural than for the National Aeronautics and Space Administration (NASA), with the space program winding down, to say

A Fateful Prediction

To critics of ozone-depletion science, researchers and their allies in the press and government showed their true colors at a 3 February 1992 press conference. These critics were already convinced that the scientific consensus, which holds that manmade chlorofluorocarbons (CFCs) are eroding the ozone layer, was based more on politics than science (see main text). The failure of the dire predictions aired at the press conference only sealed their conviction that atmospheric researchers are pursuing their own hidden agendas. For the researchers themselves, however, the event and its aftermath simply reflect the difficulties of making public pronouncements in areas where the science is uncertain.

The press conference was held by members of the Airborne Arctic Stratospheric Expedition and researchers working with the National Aeronautics and Space Administration's (NASA) Upper Atmosphere Research Satellite (UARS), which had been launched the previous September. Together, the high-altitude airplane flights of the arctic expedition and the instruments aboard UARS had detected unprecedented levels of chlorine and aerosols, two prerequisites for ozone depletion, in the stratosphere of the Northern Hemisphere. As a result, Harvard atmospheric chemist Jim Anderson told reporters, "the probability of significant ozone loss taking place in any given year is higher than we believed before." Worse, NASA officials added, this was no longer the remote Antarctic, but the atmosphere over "very populated regions."

The news conference sparked *New York Times* and *Washington Post* editorials calling for accelerated phase-out of CFCs. Then-Senator Al Gore made his memorable speech in Congress on the "ozone hole over Kennebunkport." The cover of *Time* declared "Vanishing Ozone: The Danger Moves Closer to Home." The Senate quickly voted unanimously to accelerate the CFC phase-out mandated by the Montreal Protocol, and the White House just as quickly went along with the speed-up.

The predictions of drastic ozone loss did not pan out, however. In April, NASA reported that the extreme cold in the Arctic required for ozone depletion didn't last; a sudden warming spell hit the Arctic in late January, causing ozone depletion to bottom out at only 10%.

The result was a slew of editorials and articles questioning the motives of the researchers, NASA officials, politicians, and the press. "Money, in part, may explain NASA's rush to get the 'evidence' of a likely ozone hole out 2 months before the arctic research project closed," said *The Washington Times,* for example. Talk-show host Rush Limbaugh called the press conference a "scam."

Anderson, for one, is convinced that NASA and the researchers took the right course. "The discovery of the extremely high chlorine monoxide levels over the Arctic was, from a scientific point of view, a very serious one. We felt it was a straightforward matter of releasing the information and discussing what we had seen," he said later.

Although researchers had pointed out at the press conference that drastic ozone loss was by no means certain, these caveats didn't always come across in the press that followed, which is often the case with reporting of complicated scientific issues. "At the time of the press conference," says Richard Stolarski of NASA, "they qualified everything properly. But the tone that came across was that this was an unmitigated disaster and we're all going to die, which in a sense just gives fuel to the Limbaughs, who think it's all hogwash."

—G.T.

that because we have this unusual amount of chlorine in the atmosphere we need funding? Obviously, we have to research this. But first we have to 'inform' the public."

Limbaugh gets his facts, he says in his book, from Ray's *Trashing the Planet*, which he calls "the most footnoted, documented book" he has ever read. Ray cites two other authors for most of her information on ozone depletion: Fred Singer and Rogelio Maduro. Maduro has a bachelor of science degree in geology and is an associate editor of *21st Century Science & Technology*, a magazine published by supporters of Lyndon LaRouche, an extremist politician currently serving 15 years in jail for conspiracy to evade taxes. Maduro is also co-author with Ralf Schauerhammer, a German writer, of *The Holes in the Ozone Scare: The Scientific Evidence That the Sky Isn't Falling*, which is also published by *21st Century*.

Maduro and Schauerhammer discuss at great length the source of chlorine in the stratosphere, arguing that natural sources dwarf any contributions from CFCs. As Limbaugh translates their case, the argument against the ozone depletion scenarios is simple: In one eruption, he says, Mount Pinatubo spewed forth "more than a thousand times the amount of ozone-depleting chemicals . . . than all the fluorocarbons manufactured by wicked, diabolical, and insensitive corporations in history." And the result was at best a minor depletion of ozone. Meanwhile, volcanoes have been spewing chlorine for billions of years, and yet the ozone is still there "in sufficient quantities to protect Democrats and environmentalist wackos alike from skin cancer." Atmospheric scientists counter that these claims have been intensively studied and found wanting (see box on page 309–311).

Although it's not common for a LaRouche publication to have an impact in mainstream thought, Maduro's arguments have not only percolated from Ray to Limbaugh, but are also the basis of much of the information in the *Omni* article, its author, novelist Jim Hogan, told *Science*. In addition, *21st Century* has circulated a petition around the scientific community citing Maduro's arguments and calling for the repeal of the Montreal Protocol. Among the dozen American researchers who have signed it are Derek Barton, a Nobel Prize–winning chemist at Texas A&M, and Petr Beckmann, a professor emeritus at the University of Colorado. Barton told *Science* that he signed because he's "one of these people who are opposed to getting scared about imaginary problems. I think the ozone hole and global heating are nonsense." Beckmann, who edits a newsletter called *Access to Energy*, told *Science* that he also got much of his information from Maduro's writings, describing them as "some very good material published, unfortunately, by not very reliable people."

Many of the atmospheric researchers interviewed by *Science* have read parts of *Holes in the Ozone Scare*. They often say they can see how readers who are not experts in the field might find the arguments compelling. "Part of the strategy in this backlash," says Anderson, "is to try to entrain apparently responsible scientists who clearly don't understand the problem and have not gone over the data before they've commented." And indeed, one National Science Foundation official commented, "I read that book, and found it made a lot of sense."

Those who are directly involved in the research, on the other hand, describe the work as based on a selective use of out-of-date scientific papers, and an equally discretionary choice of scientific results, often taken out of context. The end result may seem common-sensical, these researchers say, but along the way it loses touch with science. Retiring AAAS President Sherwood Rowland, who devoted part of his address to the AAAS annual meeting to the ozone backlash, for instance, calls the book "a good job of collecting all of the bad papers [in the field] in one place." Maduro responds that scientists like Rowland and his colleagues "have systematically ignored all the massive research which debunks elements of their theory."

Even Fred Singer, whose writings are cited by Ray, takes issue with Maduro and Schauerhammer's arguments about natural sources of chlorine, calling them "red herrings and completely false." Singer believes that the overall ozone depletion theory is still riddled with uncertainty but he describes himself as "somewhere in the middle" in the controversy. Many of the atmospheric researchers interviewed by *Science* say that he makes an effort to understand the data and speak to the scientists involved. Singer says he, too, once believed that natural sources of stratospheric chlorine overwhelm any manmade contribution, but the data have convinced him that CFCs are the major source.

Nevertheless, researchers who try to debate the critics quickly find themselves in a no-win situation. The reason: Maduro and Limbaugh say the researchers are part of what is in essence a massive conspiracy to ignore or bury any findings at odds with the accepted theory. In their book, Maduro and Schauerhammer, for example, accuse the proponents of the ozone depletion theory of having "deliberately obfuscated the facts about ozone research" and add that these researchers are now "in top posts with command power over scientific journals and associations and, ultimately, public opinion." That the great majority of atmospheric researchers agree on the basic findings of ozone depletion by CFCs is only considered evidence of how widespread is the conspiracy. Says Maduro: "What I am most concerned with is that scientists who have been presenting an opposing view have a public forum, the ability to present their work to the public."

Stratospheric Chlorine: Blaming It on Nature

Much of the bitter public debate over ozone depletion has centered on the claim that chlorofluorocarbons (CFCs) pale into insignificance alongside natural sources of chlorine in the stratosphere. If so, goes the argument, chlorine could not be depleting ozone as atmospheric scientists claim, because the natural sources have been around since time immemorial, and the ozone layer is still there.

The claim, put forward in a book by Rogelio Maduro and Ralf Schauerhammer, has since been touted by former Atomic Energy Commissioner Dixy Lee Ray and talk-show host Rush Limbaugh, and it forms the basis of much of the backlash now being felt by atmospheric scientists (see main text). The argument is simple: Maduro and Schauerhammer calculate that 600 million tons of chlorine enters the atmosphere annually from seawater, 36 million tons from volcanoes, 8.4 million tons from biomass burning, and 5 million tons from ocean biota. In contrast, CFCs account for a mere 750,000 tons of atmospheric chlorine a year. Besides disputing the numbers, scientists have both theoretical and observational bases for doubting that much of this chlorine is getting into the stratosphere, where it could affect the ozone layer.

Linwood Callis of the National Aeronautics and Space Administration's (NASA) Langley Research Center points out one crucial problem with the argument: Chlorine from natural sources is soluble, and so it gets rained out of the lower atmosphere. CFCs, in contrast, are insoluble and inert and thus make it to the stratosphere to release their chlorine. What's more, observations of stratospheric chemistry don't support the idea that natural sources are contributing much to the chlorine there.

If sea salt were making it up to the stratosphere, argues Richard Turco, an atmospheric chemist at the University of California, Los Angeles, then there should be evidence of sodium from the salt in the lower stratosphere. "It's just not there," says Turco. Chlorine from biomass burning should also have a distinctive signature: the chlorine-containing compound methylchloride. Maduro and Schauerhammer quote a 1979 *Nature* article by atmospheric chemist Paul Crutzen and his colleagues, estimating that biomass burning releases at least 420,000 metric tons of chlorine a year in the form of methylchloride; then they multiply that figure by 20 based on much higher estimates of biomass burning than Crutzen used. But that chlorine isn't making it to the stratosphere, Crutzen says; satellite data reveal that only 20% of the chlorine in the stratosphere is bound up in methylchloride. What's more, says Jurgen Lobert of the National Oceanic and Atmospheric Administration, who has worked with Crutzen, the most accurate estimates of global biomass burning today suggest that this source can account for only one-fourth of the total methylchloride in the stratosphere, or 5% of the total chlorine budget. "Very significant," Lobert says, but not as significant as chlorine from CFCs.

Even if seawater and biomass don't hold up as major sources of stratospheric chlorine, Limbaugh, Ray, Maduro, and Schauerhammer point to a source that they believe is sufficient on its own to render CFCs irrelevant: volcanoes in general, and Mount Erebus—a volcano in Antarctica that has been erupting constantly since 1973—in particular.

The volcano theory begins with a 1980 *Science* paper by the late David Johnston, a volcanologist with the U.S. Geological Survey. Johnston estimated the chlorine emitted by a 1976 eruption of Mount Augustine in Alaska, and concluded that it pumped 175,000 tons of hydrogen chloride (HCl) into the stratosphere. Johnston then suggested that the "eruption of the Bishop Tuff from Long Valley Caldera, California, 700,000 years ago . . . may have injected 289 million tons of HCl into the stratosphere, equivalent to about 570 times the 1975 world industrial production of chlorine in fluorocarbons."

In her book *Trashing the Planet,* Ray takes this speculation and incorrectly attributes Johnston's numbers for the gargantuan Bishop Tuff volcano to the 1976 Mount St. Augustine eruption, and Limbaugh picks up on Ray's misstatement and goes further, applying similar numbers to the eruption of Mt. Pinatubo.

As for Mt. Erebus, Maduro and Schauerhammer cite a 1985 *Nature* paper by William Rose of Michigan Technological University and his colleagues estimating that Erebus emits more than 1000 tons of chlorine a day. "In short," write Maduro and Schauerhammer, "the chlorine measured in Antarctica should be no mystery. Mt. Erebus is constantly blowing out a huge cloud of chlorine and other volcanic gases."

Atmospheric researchers counter that Erebus, although 14,000 feet high, is still several kilometers below the base of the stratosphere in Antarctica. And Erebus does not erupt explosively, which is a necessary condition to lift chlorine from volcanoes into the stratosphere. "The highest they've ever seen the plume rise [from Erebus]," says NASA's Rich Stolarski, "is half a kilometer above the mountain. Most of the time it doesn't even make it that far, it's usually oozing over the side." What's more, Philip Kyle, a co-author of the 1985 *Nature* paper, now reports that Erebus emits only 15,000 metric tons of chlorine per *year,* only 1/24 what was originally reported.

Even Fred Singer, whose own skepticism about some aspects of the ozone depletion theory has been cited by the critics to bolster their case, refers to the argument over volcanoes as "polemics." The volcano issue, he says, "has to be decided on the basis of data." And so far, expeditions that have brought back direct experimental data on volcanic emissions into the stratosphere suggest that volcanoes play a relatively minor role.

Bill Mankin and Michael Coffey, both of the National Center for Atmospheric Research, sampled emissions from El Chichón after its 1982 eruption. According to

Mankin, they saw a "significant increase in HCl [in the stratospheric cloud], roughly 40% above the background level." This represented a 10% increase in global stratospheric chlorine at a time when the stratospheric HCl budget was increasing by 5% each year. Thus, says Mankin, El Chichón seems to have advanced chlorine buildup in the stratosphere by just 2 years. Similar measurements were attempted after Mount Pinatubo erupted in April 1991, but according to Mankin, the nature of the cloud from Pinatubo made the measurements more difficult than those from El Chichon. Nonetheless, he says, Pinatubo appeared to have emitted an amount of HCl, "perhaps less than, perhaps comparable to, El Chichón."

For the global picture, atmospheric researchers point to measurements from the ATMOS instrument, which flew on the space shuttle in 1985. The instrument precisely determined the total chlorine budget in the stratosphere by making measurements of 30 molecular signatures, including the major CFCs, as well as their sinks and sources. According to Curtis Rinsland of NASA Langley, the measurements showed that chlorine is bound up in CFCs at lower levels of the stratosphere and in the predicted by-products of CFC breakdown, HCl and hydrogen fluoride (HF), at higher levels—just as the ozone theory predicts.

Further studies done from the Kitt Peak Observatory, by Rinsland and his colleagues, and from a base in the Swiss Alps by Rodolphe Zander, an atmospheric physicist with the University of Liège, and his colleagues, document the rise in HCl and HF over the past 20 years for Kitt Peak, and 40 years for the Swiss station. Both show a steady atmospheric increase of the two molecules, with HF rising at a consistently higher rate than HCl. Whereas HCl does have some natural sources, HF is produced almost entirely by photo-disassociation of CFCs. "When you monitor the increase," says Zander, "and see the ratio of HF and HCl have a kind of constancy, you can say that HCl and fluorine in the stratosphere are coming from the same source, namely the [CFCs]."

Singer agrees now that Zander, Rinsland, and colleagues have done "a very careful job of tracing the amount of chlorine and fluorine in the stratosphere." He adds that this seems to settle at least one point: "I'm now reasonably convinced," Singer told *Science,* "that CFCs make the major contribution to stratospheric chlorine, and what has convinced me is the published data." And that leaves the critics with little basis for claiming that the ozone layer has long withstood high levels of chlorine without harm.

—G.T.

THE REMAINING QUESTIONS

In such a polarized and political environment, researchers say it is difficult at best to do science and make sensible public policy recommendations. Stephen Schneider, an atmospheric modeler at Stanford University, describes the problem as being "caught between the exaggerations of the advocates, the exploitations of political interests, the media's penchant to turn everything into a boxing match, and your own colleagues saying we should be above this dirty business and stick to the bench."

What is perhaps most ironic, or frustrating, to the research community is that their most vocal critics focus on the least uncertain aspect of ozone depletion science. It is well established, they note, that levels of CFCs are increasing in the stratosphere and that chlorine levels are rising in tandem. And the evidence that the Antarctic ozone hole is caused by chemical reactions, in which chlorine plays a key role, is equally robust.

Yet atmospheric scientists freely admit that, as a January 1993 review of the Department of Energy's (DOE) Atmospheric Chemistry Program's Ozone Project put it, current understanding of global ozone behavior is "fraught with uncertainty." Among these uncertainties are whether ozone depletion in the Northern Hemisphere is due to natural variation and changes in atmospheric circulation, chlorine from CFCs, or some combination of both. Another crucial unknown is whether ozone depletion has led to a measurable increase in the flux of ultraviolet light at Earth's surface. The only existing study, by Joseph Scotto, then of the National Cancer Institute, published in *Science* in 1988, showed no increase in ultraviolet light in eight locations in the United States, and perhaps a slight decrease. Scotto, however, used data obtained from instruments that were not built for measuring yearly trends.

What everyone seems to agree on is that more research is needed. For now, what to do is a question of scientific politics: What constitutes enough certainty to require action and regulation? The dilemma was aptly described in the DOE's Ozone Project review: "On the one hand, recent evaluations of stratospheric and global tropospheric ozone trends indicate substantial anthropogenic impacts that, if allowed to continue, could result in widespread and unacceptable damage. On the other hand, current and proposed remediation efforts have resulted and will result in severe and potentially unacceptable, socioeconomic impacts."

From there, opinions will naturally vary on what action is necessary. Singer, for instance, argues that the Montreal Protocol was passed prematurely, while the state of the science was still far too uncertain and the possible deleterious effects of ozone depletion unknown as well. Ari Patrinos, director of the DOE program, like many of the researchers *Science* spoke to, argues the opposite—for the necessity of taking action. "There's only one atmosphere," says Patrinos, "and sometimes we have to be very conservative in the actions we take."

29

☀ *International Convention* ☀
on Climate Change

The Parties to this Convention.

Acknowledging that change in the Earth's climate and its adverse effects are a common concern of humankind,

Concerned that human activities have been substantially increasing the atmospheric concentrations of greenhouse gases, that these increases enhance the natural greenhouse effect, and that this will result on average in an additional warming of the Earth's surface and atmosphere and may adversely affect natural ecosystems and humankind,

Noting that the largest share of historical and current global emissions of greenhouse gases has originated in developed countries, that per capita emissions in developing countries are still relatively low and that the share of global emissions originating in developing countries will grow to meet their social and development needs,

Aware of the role and importance in terrestrial and marine ecosystems of sinks and reservoirs of greenhouse gases,

Noting that there are many uncertainties in predictions of climate change, particularly with regard to the timing, magnitude and regional patterns thereof,

Acknowledging that the global nature of climate change calls for the widest possible cooperation by all countries and their participation in an effective and appropriate international response, in accordance with their common but differentiated responsibilities and respective capabilities and their social and economic conditions,

Recalling the pertinent provisions of the Declaration of the United Nations Conference on the Human Environment, adopted at Stockholm on 16 June 1972,

Recalling also that States have, in accordance with the Charter of the United Nations and the principles of international law, the sovereign right to exploit their own resources pursuant to their own environmental and developmental policies, and the responsibility to ensure that activities within their jurisdiction or control do not cause damage to the environment of other States or of areas beyond the limits of national jurisdiction,

Reaffirming the principle of sovereignty of States in international cooperation to address climate change,

Recognizing that States should enact effective environmental legislation, that environmental standards, management objectives and priorities should reflect the environmental and developmental context to which they apply, and that standards applied by some countries may be inappropriate and of unwarranted economic and social cost to other countries, in particular developing countries,

Recalling the provisions of General Assembly resolution 44/228 of 22 December 1989 on the United Nations Conference on Environment and Development, and resolutions 43/53 of 6 December 1988, 44/207 of 22 December 1989, 45/212 of 21 December 1990 and 46/169 of 19 December 1991 on protection of global climate for present and future generations of mankind,

Recalling also the provisions of General Assembly resolution 44/206 of 22 December 1989 on the possible adverse effects of sea level rise on islands and coastal areas, particularly low-lying coastal areas and the pertinent provisions of General Assembly resolution 44/172 of 19 December 1989 on the implementation of the Plan of Action to Combat Desertification,

Recalling further the Vienna Convention for the Protection of the Ozone Layer, 1985, and the Montreal Protocol on Substances that Deplete the Ozone Layer, 1987, as adjusted and amended on 29 June 1990,

Noting the Ministerial Declaration of the Second World Climate Conference adopted on 7 November 1990,

Conscious of the valuable analytical work being conducted by many States on climate change and of the important contributions of the World Meteorological Organization, the United Nations Environment Programme and other organs, organizations and bodies of the United Nations system, as well as other international and intergovernmental bodies, to the exchange of results of scientific research and the coordination of research,

Recognizing that steps required to understand and address climate change will be environmentally, socially and economically most effective if they are based on relevant scientific, technical and economic considerations and continually re-evaluated in the light of new findings in these areas,

Recognizing that various actions to address climate change can be justified economically in their own right and can also help in solving other environmental problems,

Recognizing also the need for developed countries to take immediate action in a flexible manner on the basis of clear priorities, as a first step towards comprehensive response strategies at the global, national and, where agreed, regional levels that take into account all greenhouse gases, with due consideration of their relative contributions to the enhancement of the greenhouse effect,

Recognizing further that low-lying and other small island countries, countries with low-lying coastal, arid and semi-arid areas or areas liable to floods, drought and desertification, and developing countries with fragile mountainous ecosystems are particularly vulnerable to the adverse effects of climate change,

Recognizing the special difficulties of those countries, especially developing countries, whose economies are particularly dependent on fossil fuel production, use and exportation, as a consequence of action taken on limiting greenhouse gas emissions,

Affirming that responses to climate change should be coordinated with social and economic development in an integrated manner with a view to avoiding adverse impacts on the latter, taking into full account the legitimate priority needs of developing countries for the achievement of sustained economic growth and the eradication of poverty,

Recognizing that all countries, especially developing countries, need access to resources required to achieve sustainable social and economic development and that, in order for developing countries to progress towards that goal, their energy consumption will need to grow taking into account the possibilities for achieving greater energy efficiency and for controlling greenhouse gas emissions in general, including through the application of new technologies on terms which make such an application economically and socially beneficial,

Determined to protect the climate system for present and future generations,

Have agreed as follows:

ARTICLE 2. OBJECTIVE

The ultimate objective of this Convention and any related legal instruments that the Conference of the Parties may adopt is to achieve, in accordance with the relevant provisions of the Convention, stabilization of greenhouse gas concentrations in the atmosphere at a level that would prevent dangerous anthropogenic interference with the climate system. Such a level should be achieved within a time frame sufficient to allow ecosystems to adapt naturally to climate change, to ensure that food production is not threatened and to enable economic development to proceed in a sustainable manner.

ARTICLE 3. PRINCIPLES

In their actions to achieve the objective of the Convention and to implement its provisions, the Parties shall be guided, *inter alia,* by the following:

1. The Parties should protect the climate system for the benefit of present and future generations of humankind, on the basis of equity and in accordance with their common but differentiated responsibilities and respective capabilities. Accordingly, the developed country Parties should take the lead in combating climate change and the adverse effects thereof.

2. The specific needs and special circumstances of developing country Parties, especially those that are particularly vulnerable to the adverse effect of climate change, and of those Parties, especially developing country Parties, that would have to bear a disproportionate or abnormal burden under the Convention, should be given full consideration.

3. The Parties should take precautionary measures to anticipate, prevent or minimize the causes of climate change and mitigate its adverse effects. Where there are threats of serious or irreversible damage, lack of full scientific certainty should not be used as a reason for postponing such measures, taking into account that policies and measures to deal with climate change should be cost-effective so as to ensure global benefits at the lowest possible cost. To achieve this, such policies and measures should take into account different socio-economic contexts, be comprehensive, cover all relevant sources, sinks and reservoirs of greenhouse gases and adaptation, and comprise all economic sectors. Efforts to address climate change may be carried out cooperatively by interested Parties.

4. The Parties have a right to, and should, promote sustainable development. Policies and measures to protect the climate system against human-induced change should be appropriate for the specific conditions of each Party and should be integrated with national development programmes, taking into account that economic development is essential for adopting measures to address climate change.

5. The Parties should cooperate to promote a supportive and open international economic system that would lead to sustainable economic growth and development in all Parties, particularly developing country Parties, thus enabling them better to address the problems of climate change. Measures taken to combat climate change, including unilateral ones, should not constitute a means of arbitrary or unjustifiable discrimination or a disguised restriction on international trade.

ARTICLE 4. COMMITMENTS

1. All Parties, taking into account their common but differentiated responsibilities and their specific national and regional development priorities, objectives and circumstances, shall:

(a) Develop, periodically update, publish and make available to the Conference of the Parties, in accordance with Article 12, national inventories of anthropogenic emissions by sources and removals by sinks of all greenhouse gases not controlled by the Montreal Protocol, using comparable methodologies to be agreed upon by the Conference of the Parties;

(b) Formulate, implement, publish and regularly update national and, where appropriate, regional programmes containing measures to mitigate climate change by addressing anthropogenic emissions by sources and removals by sinks of all greenhouse gases not controlled by the Montreal Protocol, and measures to facilitate adequate adaptation to climate change;

(c) Promote and cooperate in the development, application and diffusion, including transfer, of technologies, practices and processes that control, reduce or prevent anthropogenic emissions of greenhouse gases not controlled by the Montreal Protocol in all relevant sectors, including the energy, transport, industry, agriculture, forestry and waste management sectors;

(d) Promote sustainable management, and promote and cooperate in the conservation and enhancement, as appropriate, of sinks and reservoirs of all greenhouse gases not controlled by the Montreal Protocol, including biomass, forests and oceans as well as other terrestrial, coastal and marine ecosystems;

(e) Cooperate in preparing for adaptation to the impacts of climate change; develop and elaborate appropriate and integrated plans for coastal zone management, water resources and agriculture, and for the protection and rehabilitation of areas, particularly in Africa, affected by drought and desertification, as well as floods;

(f) Take climate considerations into account, to the extent feasible, in their relevant social, economic and environmental policies and actions, and employ appropriate methods, for example impact assessments, formulated and determined nationally, with a view to minimizing adverse effects on the economy, on public health and on the quality of the environment, of projects or measures undertaken by them to mitigate or adapt to climate change;

(g) Promote and cooperate in scientific, technological, technical, socio-economic and other research, systematic observation and development of data archives related to the climate system and intended to further the understanding and to reduce or eliminate the remaining uncertainties regarding the causes, effects, magnitude and timing of climate change and the economic and social consequences of various response strategies;

(h) Promote and cooperate in the full, open and prompt exchange of relevant scientific, technological, technical, socio-economic and legal information related to the climate system and climate change, and to the economic and social consequences of various response strategies;

(i) Promote and cooperate in education, training and public awareness related to climate change and encourage the widest participation in this process, including that of non-governmental organizations; and

(j) Communicate to the Conference of the Parties information related to implementation.

30

⊿ Duties to Endangered Species ⊾

HOLMES ROLSTON III

Holmes Rolston III is Professor of Philosophy at Colorado State University and is Past President of the International Society for Environmental Ethics. He is author of Philosophy Gone Wild *and* Environmental Ethics.

In the Endangered Species Act, Congress has lamented the lack of "adequate concern [for] and conservation [of]" species (US Congress 1973). But neither scientists nor ethicists have fully realized how developing this concern requires an unprecedented mix of biology and ethics. What logic underlies duties involving forms of life? Looking to the past for help, one searches in vain through 3000 years of philosophy (back at least to Noah!) for any serious reference to endangered species. Among present theories of justice, Harvard philosopher John Rawls (1971, p. 512) asserts, "The destruction of a whole species can be a great evil," but also admits that in his theory "no account is given of right conduct in regard to animals and the rest of nature." Meanwhile, there is an urgency to the issue. The *Global 2000 Report* (1980–1981) projects a massive loss of species, up to 20% within a few decades.

DUTIES TO PERSONS CONCERNING SPECIES

The usual way to approach a concern for species is to say that there are no duties directly to endangered species, only duties to other persons concerning species. From a utilitarian standpoint (Hampshire 1972, pp. 3–4), the protection of nature and "the preservation of species are to be aimed at and commended only in so far as human beings are, or will be, emotionally and sentimentally interested." In an account based on rights, Feinberg (1974, p. 56) reaches a similar conclusion. "We do have duties to protect threatened species, not duties to the species themselves as such, but rather duties to future human beings." Using traditional ethics to confront the novel threat of extinctions, we can reapply familiar duties to persons and see whether this is convincing. This line of argument can be impressive but seems to leave deeper obligations untouched.

Persons have a strong duty not to harm others and a weaker, though important, duty to help others. Arguing the threat of harm, the Ehrlichs (1981) maintain, in a blunt metaphor, that species are rivets in the Earthship in which humans are flying. Extinctions are maleficent rivet popping. In this model, nonrivet species, if there are any, would have no value; humans desire only the diversity that prevents a crash. The care is not for particular species but, in a variant metaphor, for the sinking ark (Myers 1979a). To worry about a sinking ark seems a strange twist on the Noah story. Noah built the ark to preserve each species. In the Ehrlich/Myers account, the species-rivets are preserved to keep the ark from sinking! The reversed justification is revealing.

On the benefits side, species that are not rivets may prove to be resources. Thomas Eisner testified to Congress that only two percent of the flowering plants have been tested for alkaloids, which often have medical value (US Congress 1982, p. 296). A National Science Foundation report (1977) advocated saving the Devil's Hole pupfish, *Cyprinodon diabolis,* because it thrives in extremes and "can serve as useful biological models for future research on the human kidney—and on survival in a seemingly hostile environment." Myers (1979b) further urges "conserving our global stock." At first, this advice seems wise, yet later somewhat demeaning for humans to regard all other species as *stock.*

Destroying species is like tearing pages out of an unread book, written in a language humans hardly know how to read, about the place where they live. No sensible person would destroy the Rosetta Stone, and no self-respecting persons will destroy the mouse lemur, endangered in Madagascar and thought to be the nearest modern animal to the relatively unspecialized primates from which the human line evolved. Still, following this logic, humans do not have duties to the book, the stone, or the species but to ourselves, duties of prudence and education. Humans need insight into the full text of ecosystem evolution. It is not endangered species but an endangered human future that is of concern. Such reasons are pragmatic and impressive. They are also moral, since persons are benefited or hurt. But are they exhaustive?

One problem is that pragmatic reasons get overstated. Peter H. Raven testified before Congress that a dozen dependent species of insects, animals, or other plants typically become extinct with each plant that goes extinct (US Congress 1982, p. 293). But Raven knows that such cascading, disastrous extinction is true only on statistical average, since a plant named for him, Raven's manzanita, *Arctostaphylos hookeri* ssp. *ravenii,* is known from a single wild specimen, and its extinction is unlikely to trigger others. Rare species add some backup resilience. Still, if all 79 plants on the endangered species list disappeared, it is doubtful that the regional ecosystems involved would measurably shift their stability. Few cases can be cited where the removal of a rare species damaged an ecosystem.

Let's be frank. A substantial number of endangered species have no resource value. Beggar's ticks, *Bidens* spp., with their stick–tight seeds, are a common nuisance through much of the United States. One species, tidal shore beggar's tick, *B. bidentoides,* which differs little in appearance from the others, is endangered. It seems unlikely to be a potential resource. As far as humans are concerned, its extinction might be good riddance.

We might say that humans ought to preserve for themselves an environment adequate to match their capacity to wonder. But this is to value the *experience* of wonder, rather than the *objects* of wonder. Valuing merely the experience seems to commit a fallacy of misplaced wonder, for speciation is itself among the wonderful things on Earth. Valuing speciation directly, however, seems to attach value to the evolutionary process, not merely to subjective experiences that arise when humans reflect over it.

We might say that humans of decent character will refrain from needless destruction of all kinds, including destruction of species. Vandals destroying art objects do not so much hurt statues as cheapen their own character. But is the American shame at destroying the passenger pigeon only a matter of self-respect? Or is it shame at our ignorant insensitivity to a form of life that (unlike a statue) had an intrinsic value that placed some claim on us?

The deeper problem with the anthropocentric rationale, beyond overstatement, is that its justifications are submoral and fundamentally exploitive, even if subtly. This is not true intraspecifically among humans, when out of a sense of duty an individual defers to the values of fellows. But it is true interspecifically, since *Homo sapiens* treats all other species as rivets, resources, study materials, or entertainments. Ethics has always been about partners with entwined destinies. But it has never been very convincing when pleaded as enlightened self-interest (that one ought always to do what is one's intelligent self-interest), including class self-interest, even though in practice genuinely altruistic ethics often needs to be reinforced by self-interest. To value all other species only for human interests is like a nation's arguing all its foreign policy in terms of national interest. Neither seems fully moral.

Perhaps an exploiting attitude, and the tendency to justify it ethically, has been naturally selected in *Homo sapiens,* at least in the population that has become dominant in the West. But humans—scientists who have learned to be disinterested and ethicists who have learned to consider the interests of others—ought to be able to see further. Humans have learned some intraspecific altruism. The challenge now is to learn interspecific altruism. Utilitarian reasons for saving species may be good ones, necessary for policy. But can we not also discover the best reasons, the full extent of human duties? Dealing with a problem correctly requires an appropriate way of thinking about it. What is offensive in the impending extinctions is not merely the loss of rivets and resources, but the maelstrom of killing and insensitivity to forms of life and the forces producing them. What is required is not prudence but principled responsibility to the biospheric Earth.

SPECIFIC FORMS OF LIFE

There are many barriers to thinking of duties to species, however, and scientific ones precede ethical ones. It is difficult enough to argue from the fact that a species exists to the value judgment that a species ought to exist—what philosophers call an argument from *is* to *ought*. Matters grow worse if the concept of species is rotten to begin with. Perhaps the concept is arbitrary and conventional, a mapping device that is only theoretical. Perhaps it is unsatisfactory theoretically in an evolutionary ecosystem. Perhaps species do not exist. Duties to them would be as imaginary as duties to contour lines or to lines of latitude and longitude. Is there enough factual reality in species to base duty there?

Betula lenta uber, round-leaf birch, is known from only two locations on nearby Virginia creeks and differs from the common *B. lenta* only in having rounded leaf tips. For 30 years it was described as a subspecies or merely a mutation. But M. L. Fernald pronounced it a species, *B. uber,* and for 40 years it has been considered one. High fences have been built around all known specimens. If a greater botanist were to redesignate it a subspecies, would this change in alleged facts affect our alleged duties? Ornithologists recently reassessed an endangered species, the Mexican duck, *Anas diazi,* and lumped it with the common mallard, *A. platyrhynchos,* as subspecies *diazi,* US Fish and Wildlife authorities took it off the endangered species list partly as a result. Did a duty cease? Was there never one at all?

If a species is only a category, or class, boundary lines may be arbitrarily drawn. Darwin (1968 [1859], p. 108) wrote, "I look at the term species, as one arbitrarily given for the sake of convenience to a set of individuals closely resembling each other." Some natural properties are used to delimit species—reproductive structures, bones, teeth. But which properties are selected and where the lines are drawn vary with taxonomists. When A. J. Shaw (1981) recently "discovered" a new species of moss, *Pohlia tundrae,* in the alpine Rocky Mountains, he did not find any hitherto unknown plants; he just regrouped herbarium material that had been known for decades under other names. Indeed, biologists routinely put after a species the name of the "author" who, they say, "erected" the taxon.

Individual organisms exist, but if species are merely classes, they are inventions. A. B. Shaw (1969) claims, "The species concept is entirely subjective," and, concluding a presidential address to paleontologists, even exclaims, "Help stamp out species!" He refers, of course, to the artifacts of taxonomists, not to living organisms. But if species do not exist except embedded in a theory in the minds of classifiers, it is hard to see how there can be duties to save them. No one proposes duties to genera, families, orders, or phyla; everyone concedes that these do not exist in nature.

But a biological species is not just a class. A species is a living historical form (Latin *species*), propagated in individual organisms, that flows dynamically over generations. Simpson (1961, p. 153) concludes, "An evolutionary species is a lineage (an ancestral-descendant sequence of populations) evolving separately from others and with its own unitary evolutionary role and tendencies." Mayr (1969a, p. 26) holds, "Species are groups of interbreeding natural populations that are reproductively isolated from other such groups." He (1969b) can even emphasize, though many biologists today would deny this, that "*species are the real units of evolution,* they are the entities which specialize, which become adapted, or which shift their adaptation." Recently, Mayr (1982) has sympathized with Ghiselin (1974) and Hull (1976), who hold that species are integrated individuals, and species names proper names, with organisms related to their species as part is to whole. Eldredge and Cracraft (1980, p. 92) find that "a species is a diagnosable cluster of individuals within which there is a parental pattern of ancestry and descent, beyond which there is not, and which exhibits a pattern of phylogenetic ancestry and descent among units of like kind." Species, they insist, are "*discrete entities in time as well as space.*"

It is admittedly difficult to pinpoint precisely what a species is, and there may be no single, quintessential way to define species; a polythetic or polytypic gestalt of features may be required. All we need for this discussion, however, is that species be objectively there as living processes in the evolutionary ecosystem; the varied criteria for defining them (descent, reproductive isolation, morphology, gene pool) come together at least in providing evidence that species are really there. In this sense, species are dynamic natural kinds, if not corporate individuals. A species is a coherent, ongoing form of life expressed in organisms, encoded in gene flow, and shaped by the environment.

The claim that there are specific forms of life historically maintained in their environments over time does not seem arbitrary or fictitious at all but, rather, as certain as anything else we believe about the empirical world, even though at times scientists revise the theories and taxa with which they map these forms. Species are not so much like lines of latitude and longitude as like mountains and rivers, phenomena objectively there to be mapped. The edges of all these natural kinds will sometimes be fuzzy, to some extent discretionary. We can expect that one species will slide into another over evolutionary time. But it does not follow from the fact that speciation is sometimes in progress that species are merely made up, instead of found as evolutionary lines articulated into diverse forms, each with its more or less distinct integrity, breeding population, gene pool, and role in its ecosystem.

At this point, we can anticipate how there can be duties to species. What humans ought to respect are dynamic life forms preserved in historical lines, vital informational processes that persist genetically over millions of years, overleaping short-lived individuals. It is not *form* (species) as mere morphology, but the *formative* (speciating) process that humans ought to preserve, although the process cannot be preserved without its products. Neither should humans want to protect the labels they use, but the living process in the environment. Endangered "species" is a convenient and realistic way of tagging this process, but protection can be interpreted (as the Endangered Species Act permits) in terms of subspecies, variety, or other taxa or categories that point out the diverse forms of life.

DUTIES TO SPECIES

The easiest conclusion to reach from prevailing theories of justice, which involve tacit or explicit "contracts" between persons, is that duties and rights are reciprocal. But reciprocally claiming, recognizing, exercising, and enjoying rights and duties can only be done by reflective rational agents. Humans have entered no contract with other species; certainly they have not with us. There is no ecological contract parallel to the social contract; all the capacities for deliberate interaction so common in culture vanish in nature. Individual animals and plants, to say nothing of species, cannot be reasoned with, blamed, or educated into the prevailing contract.

But to make rights and duties reciprocal supposes that only moral agents count in the ethical calculus. Duties exist as well to those persons who cannot argue back—to the mute and powerless—and perhaps this principle extends to other forms of life. Morality is needed wherever the vulnerable must be protected from the powerful.

The next easiest conclusion to reach, either from rights-based or utilitarian theories, is that humans have duties wherever there are psychological interests involving the capacity for experience. That moves a minimal criterion for duty past rational moral agency to sentience. The question is not whether animals can reciprocate the contract but whether they can suffer. Singer (1979) thinks that the only reason to be concerned about endangered species is the interests of humans and other sentient animals at stake in their loss. Only they can enjoy benefits or suffer harm, so only they can be treated justly or unjustly.

But species, not sentience, generate some duties. On San Clemente Island, the US Fish and Wildlife Service and the California Department of Fish and Game asked the Navy to shoot 2000 feral goats to save three endangered plant species, *Malacothamnus clementinus, Castilleja grisea,* and *Delphinium kinkiense.* That would kill several goats for each known surviving plant. (Happily, the Fund for Animals rescued most of the goats; unhappily, they could not trap them all and the issue is unresolved.) The National Park Service did kill hundreds of rabbits on Santa Barbara Island to protect a few plants of *Dudleya traskiae,* once thought extinct and curiously called the Santa Barbara live-for-ever. Hundreds of elk starve in Yellowstone National Park each year, and the Park Service is not alarmed, but the starving of an equal number of grizzly bears, which would involve about the same suffering in psychological experience, would be of great concern.

A rather difficult claim to make under contemporary ethical theory is that duty can arise toward any living organism. Such duties, if they exist, could be easy to override, but by this account humans would have at least a minimal duty not to disrupt living beings without justification.

Here the question about species, beyond individuals, is both revealing and challenging because it offers a biologically based counterexample to the focus on individuals—typically sentient and usually persons—so characteristic in Western ethics. In an evolutionary ecosystem, it is not mere individuality that counts, but the species is also significant because it is a dynamic life form maintained over time by an informed genetic flow. The individual represents (re-presents) a species in each new generation. It is a token of a type, and the type is more important than the token.

It is as logical to say that the individual is the species' way of propagating itself as to say that the embryo or egg is the individual's way of propagating itself. We can think of the cognitive processing as taking place not merely in the individual but in the gene pool. Genetically, though not neurally, a species over generations "learns" (discovers) pathways previously unknown. A form of life reforms itself, tracks its environment, and sometimes passes over to a new species. There is a specific groping for a valued *ought*-to-be beyond what now *is* in any individual. Though species are not moral agents, a biological identity—a kind of value—is here defended. The dignity resides in the dynamic form; the individual inherits this, instantiates it, and passes it on. To borrow a metaphor from physics, life is both a particle (the individual) and a wave (the specific form).

A species lacks moral agency, reflective self-awareness, sentience, or organic individuality. So we may be tempted to say that specific-level processes cannot count morally. But each ongoing species defends a form of life, and these are on the whole good things, arising in a process out of which humans have evolved. All ethicists say that in *Homo sapiens* one species has appeared that not only exists but ought to exist. But why say this exclusively of a late-coming, highly developed form? Why not extend this duty more broadly to the other species (though perhaps not with equal intensity over them all, in view of varied levels of development)? These kinds defend their forms of life, too. Only the human species contains moral agents, but perhaps conscience *ought not* be used to exempt every other form of life from consideration, with the resulting paradox that the single moral species acts only in its collective self-interest toward all the rest.

Extinction shuts down the generative processes. The wrong that humans are doing, or allowing to happen through carelessness, is stopping the historical flow in which the vitality of life is laid. Every extinction is an incremental decay in stopping life processes—no small thing. Every extinction is a kind of superkilling. It kills forms (*species*), beyond individuals. It kills "essences" beyond "existences," the "soul" as well as the "body." It kills collectively, not just distributively. It is not merely the loss of potential human information that is tragic, but the loss of biological information, present independently of instrumental human uses for it.

"Ought species *x* to exist?" is a single increment in the collective question, "Ought life on Earth to exist?" The answer to the question about one species is not always the same as the answer to the bigger question, but since life on Earth is an aggregate of many species, the two are sufficiently related that the burden of proof lies with those who wish deliberately to extinguish a species and simultaneously to care for life on Earth. To kill a species is to shut down a unique story; and, although all specific stories must eventually end, we seldom want unnatural ends. Humans ought not to play the role of murderers. The duty to species can be overridden, for example with pests or disease organisms. But a prima facie duty stands nevertheless.

One form of life has never endangered so many others. Never before has this level of question—superkilling by a superkiller—been faced. Humans have more understanding than ever of the speciating processes, more predictive power to foresee the intended and unintended results of their actions, and more power to reverse the undesirable consequences. The duties that such power and vision generate no longer attach simply to individuals or persons but are emerging duties to specific forms of life. If, in this world of uncertain moral convictions, it makes any sense to claim that one ought not to kill individuals without justification, it makes more sense to claim that one ought not to superkill the species, without superjustification.

INDIVIDUALS AND SPECIES

Many will be uncomfortable with this claim because their ethical theory does not allow duty to a collection. Feinberg (1974, p. 55) writes, "A whole collection, as such, cannot have beliefs, expectations, wants, or desires. . . . Individual elephants can have interests, but the species elephant cannot." Singer (1979, p. 203) asserts, "Species as such are not conscious entities and so do not have interests above and beyond the interests of the individual animals that are members of the species." Regan (1983, p. 359) maintains, "The rights view is a view about the moral rights of individuals. Species are not individuals, and the rights view does not recognize the moral rights of species to anything, including survival." Rescher (1980, p. 83) says, "Moral obligation is thus always interest-oriented. But only individuals can be said to have interests; one only has moral obligations to particular individuals or particular groups thereof. Accordingly, the duty to save a species is not a matter of moral duty toward it, because moral duties are only oriented to individuals. A species as such is the wrong sort of target for a moral obligation."

Even those who recognize that organisms, nonsentient as well as sentient, can be benefited or harmed may see the good of a species as the sum of and reducible to the goods of individuals. The species is well off when and because its members are; species well-being is just aggregated individual well-being. The "interests of a species" constitute only a convenient device, something like a center of gravity in physics, for speaking of an aggregated focus of many contributing individual member units.

But duties to a species are not duties to a class or category, not to an aggregation of sentient interests, but to a lifeline. An ethic about species needs to see how the species *is* a bigger event than individual interests or sentience. Making this clearer can support the conviction that a species *ought* to continue.

Events can be good for the well-being of the species, considered collectively, although they are harmful if considered as distributed to individuals. This is one way to interpret what is often called genetic load (Fraser 1962), genes that somewhat reduce health, efficiency, or fertility in most individuals but introduce enough variation to permit improving the specific form. Less variation and better repetition in reproduction would, on average, benefit more individuals in any one next generation, since individuals would have less "load." But on a longer view, variation can confer stability in a changing world. A greater experimenting with individuals, although this typically makes individuals less fit and is a disadvantage from that perspective, benefits rare, lucky individuals selected in each generation, with a resulting improvement in the species. Most individuals in any particular generation carry some (usually slightly) detrimental genes, but the variation is good for the species. Note that this does not imply species selection; selection perhaps operates only on individuals. But it does mean that we can distinguish between the goods of individuals and the larger good of the species.

Predation on individual elk conserves and improves the species *Cervus canadensis.* A forest fire harms individual aspen trees, but it helps *Populus tremuloides* because fire restarts forest succession, without which the species would go extinct. Even the individuals that escape demise from external sources die of old age; their deaths, always to the disadvantage of those individuals, are a necessity for the species. A finite lifespan makes room for those replacements that enable development to occur, allowing the population to improve in fitness or adapt to a shifting environment. Without the "flawed" reproduction that permits variation, without a surplus of young or predation and death, which all harm individuals, the species would soon go extinct in a changing environment, as all environments eventually are. The individual is a receptacle of the form, and the receptacles are broken while the form survives; but the form cannot otherwise survive.

When a biologist remarks that a breeding population of a rare species is dangerously low, what is the danger to? Individual members? Rather, the remark seems to imply a specific-level, point-of-no-return threat to the continuing of that form of life. No individual crosses the extinction threshold; the species does.

Reproduction is typically assumed to be a need of individuals, but since any particular individual can flourish somatically without reproducing at all, indeed may be put through duress and risk or spend much energy reproducing, by another logic we can interpret reproduction as the species keeping up its own kind by reenacting itself again and again, individual after individual. In this sense a female grizzly does not bear cubs to be healthy herself, any more than a woman needs children to be healthy. Rather, her cubs are *Ursus arctos,* threatened by nonbeing, recreating itself by continuous performance. A species in reproduction defends its own kind from other species, and this seems to be some form of "caring."

Biologists have often and understandably focused on individuals, and some recent trends interpret biological processes from the perspective of genes. A consideration of species reminds us that many events can be interpreted at this level too. An organism runs a directed course through the environment, taking in materials, using them resourcefully, discharging wastes. But this single, directed course is part of a bigger picture in which a species via individuals maintains its course over longer spans of time. Thinking this way, the life the individual has is something passing through the individual as much as something it intrinsically possesses. The individual is subordinate to the species, not the other way around. The genetic set, in which is coded the *telos,* is as evidently a "property" of the species as of the individual.

Biologists and linguists have learned to accept the concept of information in the genetic set without any subject who speaks or understands. Can ethicists learn to accept value in, and duty to, an informed process in which centered individuality or sentience is absent? Here events can be significant at the specific level, an additional consideration to whether they are beneficial to individuals. The species-in-environment is an interactive complex, a selective system where individuals are pawns on a chessboard. When human conduct endangers these specific games of life, duties may appear.

A species has no self. It is not a bounded singular. Each organism has its own centeredness, but there is no specific analogue to the nervous hookups or circulatory flows that characterize the organism. But, like the market in economics, an organized system does not have to have a controlling center to have identity. Having a biological identity reasserted genetically over time is as true of the species as of the individual. Individuals come and go; the marks of the species collectively remain much longer.

A consideration of species strains any ethic focused on individuals, much less on sentience or persons. But the result can be a biologically sounder ethic, though it revises what was formerly thought logically permissible or ethically binding. The species line is fundamental. It is more important to protect this integrity than to protect individuals. Defending a form of life, resisting death, regeneration that maintains a normative identity over time—all this is as true of species as of individuals. So what prevents duties arising at that level? The appropriate survival unit is the appropriate level of moral concern.

SPECIES AND ECOSYSTEM

A species is what it is inseparably from its environment. The species defends its kind against the world, but at the same time interacts with its environment, functions in the ecosystem, and is supported and shaped by it. The species and the community are complementary processes in synthesis, somewhat parallel to but a level above the way the species and the individual have distinguishable but entwined identities. Neither the individual nor the species stands alone; both are embedded in a system. It is not preservation of *species* but of *species in the system* that we desire. It is not just what they are but where they are that we must value correctly.

The species *can* only be preserved in situ; the species *ought* to be preserved in situ. Zoos and botanical gardens can lock up a collection of individuals, but they cannot begin to simulate the ongoing dynamism of gene flow under the selection pressures in a wild biome. The full integrity of the species must be integrated into the ecosystem. Ex situ preservation, while it may save resources and souvenirs, does not preserve the generative process intact. Again, the appropriate survival unit is the appropriate level of moral concern.

It might seem that ending the history of a species now and again is not far out of line with the routines of the universe. But artificial extinction, caused by human encroachments, is radically different from natural extinction. Relevant differences make the two as morally distinct as death by natural causes is from murder. Though harmful to a species, extinction in nature is no evil in the system; it is rather the key to tomorrow. Such extinction is a normal turnover in ongoing speciation.

Anthropogenic extinction has nothing to do with evolutionary speciation. Hundreds of thousands of species will perish because of culturally altered environments radically differing from the spontaneous environments in which such species were naturally selected and in which they sometimes go extinct. In natural extinctions, nature takes away life when it has become unfit in habitat, or when the habitat alters, and supplies other life in its place. Artificial extinction shuts down tomorrow because it shuts down speciation. Natural extinction typically occurs with transformation, either of the extinct line or related or competing lines. Artificial extinction is without issue. One opens doors; the other closes them. Humans generate and regenerate nothing; they only dead-end these lines.

From this perspective, humans have no duty to preserve rare species from natural extinctions, although they might have a duty to other humans to save such species as resources or museum pieces. Humans cannot and need not save the product without the process.

Through evolutionary time, nature has provided new species at a higher rate than the extinction rate; hence, the accumulated diversity. In one of the best documented studies of the marine fossil record, Raup and Sepkoski (1982) summarize a general increase in standing diversity (Figure 30–1). Regardless of differing details on land or

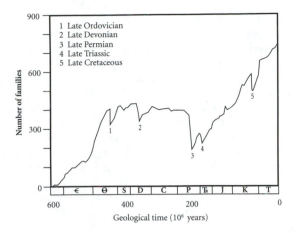

Figure 30–1. Standing diversity through time for families of marine vertebrates and invertebrates; numbers refer to catastrophic extinctions. Source: Raup and Sepkoski (1982). ©1982 by AAAS; reprinted with permission.

biases in the fossil record, a graph of the increase of diversity on Earth must look something like this.

There have been four or five catastrophic extinctions, each succeeded by a recovery of previous diversity. These anomalies so deviate from the trends that many paleontologists look for extraterrestrial causes. If due to supernovae, collisions with asteroids, or oscillations of the solar system above and below the plane of the galaxy, such events are accidental to the evolutionary ecosystem. Thousands of species perished at the impingement of otherwise unrelated events. The disasters were irrelevant to the kinds of ecosystems in which such species had been selected. If the causes were more terrestrial—cyclic changes in climates or continental drift—the biological processes are still to be admired for their powers of recovery. Even interrupted by accident, they maintain and increase the numbers of species. Raup and Sepkoski further find that the normal extinction rate declines from 4.6 families per million years in the Early Cambrian to 2.0 families in recent times, even though the number of families (and species) enormously increases. This seems to mean that optimization of fitness increases through evolutionary time.

An ethicist has to be circumspect. An argument might commit what logicians call the genetic fallacy to suppose that present value depended on origins. Species judged today to have intrinsic value might have arisen anciently and anomalously from a valueless context, akin to the way life arose mysteriously from nonliving materials. But in a historical ecosystem, what a thing is differentiates poorly from the generating and sustaining matrix. The individual and the species have what value they have, to some extent, in the context of the forces that beget them.

Imagine that Figure 30–1 is the graph of the performance of a 600-million-year-old business. Is it not a healthy one? But this is the record of the business of life, and the long-term performance deserves ethical respect. There is something awesome about an Earth that begins with zero and runs up toward 5 to 10 million species in several billion years, setbacks notwithstanding.

What is valuable about species is not to be isolated in them for what they are in themselves. Rather, the dynamic account evaluates species as process, product, and instrument in the larger drama toward which humans have duties, reflected in duties to species. Whittaker (1972) finds that on continental scales and for most groups, "increase of species diversity . . . is a self-augmenting evolutionary process without any evident limit." There is a tendency toward "species packing." Nature seems to produce as many species as it can, not merely enough to stabilize an ecosystem or only species that can directly or indirectly serve human needs. Humans ought not to inhibit this exuberant lust for kinds. That process, along with its product, is about as near to ultimacy as humans can come in their relationship with the natural world.

Several billion years worth of creative toil, several million species of teeming life, have been handed over to the care of this late-coming species in which mind has flowered and morals have emerged. Ought not those of this sole moral species do something less self-interested than count all the produce of an evolutionary ecosystem as rivets in their spaceship, resources in their larder, laboratory materials, recreation for their ride? Such an attitude hardly seems biologically informed, much less ethically adequate. Its logic is too provincial for moral humanity. Or, in a biologist's term, it is ridiculously territorial. If true to their species epithet, ought not *Homo sapiens* value this host of species as something with a claim to care in its own right?

AN ENDANGERED ETHIC?

Contemporary ethical systems seem misfits in the role most recently demanded of them. There is something overspecialized about an ethic, held by the dominant class of *Homo sapiens,* that regards the welfare of only one of several million species as an object of duty. If this requires a paradigm change about the sorts of things to which duty can attach, so much the worse for those ethics no longer functioning in, or suited to, their changing environment. The anthropocentrism associated with them was fiction anyway. There is something Newtonian, not yet Einsteinian, besides something morally naive, about living in a reference frame where one species takes itself as absolute and values everything else relative to its utility.

REFERENCES

Darwin, C. 1968 [1859]. *The Origin of Species.* Penguin Books, Harmondsworth, UK.

Ehrlich, P. R., and A. H. Ehrlich. 1981. *Extinction.* Random House, New York.

Eldredge, N., and J. Cracraft. 1980. *Phylogenetic Patterns and the Evolutionary Process.* Columbia University Press, New York.

Feinberg, J. 1974. The rights of animals and unborn generations. Pages 43–68 in W. T. Blackstone, ed. *Philosophy and Environmental Crisis.* University of Georgia Press, Athens.

Fraser, G. R. 1962. Our genetical "load": a review of some aspects of genetical variation. *Ann. Hum. Genet.* 25: pp. 387–415.

Ghiselin, M. T. 1974. A radical solution to the species problem. *Syst. Zool.* 23: pp. 536–544.

The Global 2000 Report to the President: Entering the Twenty-first Century. 1980–1981. Council on Environmental Quality and the Department of State. US Government Printing Office, Washington, DC.

Hampshire, S. 1972. *Morality and Pessimism.* Cambridge University Press, Cambridge, UK.

Hull, D. L. 1976. Are species really individuals? *Syst. Zool.* 25: pp. 174–191.

Mayr, E. 1969a. *Principles of Systematic Zoology.* McGraw-Hill, New York.

———. 1969b. The biological meaning of species. *Biol. J. Linn. Soc.* 1: pp. 311–320.

———. 1982. *The Growth of Biological Thought.* Harvard University Press, Cambridge, MA.

Myers, N. 1979a. *The Sinking Ark.* Pergamon Press, Oxford, UK.

————. 1979b. Conserving our global stock. *Environment* 21(9): pp. 25–33.

National Science Foundation (NSF). 1977. The biology of aridity. *Mosaic* 8(1): pp. 28–35.

Raup, D. M., and J. J. Sepkoski, Jr. 1982. Mass extinctions in the marine fossil record. *Science* 215: pp. 1501–1503.

Rawls, J. 1971. *A Theory of Justice.* Harvard University Press, Cambridge, MA.

Regan, T. 1983. *The Case for Animal Rights.* University of California Press, Berkeley.

Rescher, N. 1980. *Unpopular Essays on Technological Progress.* University of Pittsburgh, Pittsburgh, PA.

Shaw, A. B. 1969. Adam and Eve, paleontology, and the non-objective arts. *J. Paleontol.* 43: pp. 1085–1098.

Shaw, A. J. 1981. *Pohlia andrewsii* and *P. tundrae,* two new arctic-alpine propaguliferous species from North America. *Bryologist* 84: pp. 65–74.

Simpson, G. G. 1961. *Principles of Animal Taxonomy.* Columbia University Press, New York.

Singer, P. 1979. Not for humans only. Pages 191–206 in K. E. Goodpaster and K. M. Sayre, eds. *Ethics and Problems of the 21st Century.* University of Notre Dame, Notre Dame, IN.

Whittaker, R. H. 1972. Evolution and measurement of species diversity. *Taxon* 21: pp. 213–251.

US Congress, 1973. Sec. 2(a)(1) in *Endangered Species Act,* 87 STAT. 884 (Public Law 93–205).

————. 1982. *Endangered Species Act Oversight.* Hearings before the US Senate, 97th Cong., 1st sess., 8 and 10 December. 97–H34. US Government Printing Office, Washington, DC.

31

⚞ *Seeking Global Solutions* ⚟

JOHN TUXILL

John Tuxill is a Research Fellow with the Worldwatch Institute. He is a co-author of the Institute's 1998 reports State of the World *and* Vital Signs.

At its root, the accelerating loss of vertebrate species and other strands in the fabric of life is driven by the unprecedented expansion of humanity and its material demands in the last century. Unless we can develop a new balance between human needs and those of the natural world, no conservation areas or parks, no matter how well supported, will be able to head off further deterioration of biodiversity. We must come to terms with population growth, inequitable social systems, and short-sighted economic practices if we are to restore the ecological health of our planet, particularly in the landscapes and ecosystems we depend upon for food, water, fiber, energy, and our other material needs. In a sense, this is conserving habitat not so much by establishing specific zones or regions for conservation, as by developing more ecologically and socially sustainable ways of managing wildlife populations, raising crops and livestock, securing energy supplies, procuring, processing, and using timber and fibers, and guiding national economies and international investment. Local, national, and international efforts must all be linked in this effort to deal effectively with the underlying pressures on the landscapes and ecosystems that support biological diversity.

According to United Nations population experts, human numbers are likely to climb from their 1995 total of 5.7 billion to between 7.7 and 11.2 billion by the middle of the next century. The population total that prevails will depend especially upon the availability and effectiveness of family planning programs, women's access to education, and other social factors. Many developing countries, where most of the new people on Earth will be born—and which shelter most of our planet's biodiversity as well as most currently threatened species—already experience the strains a steadily expanding population places on land, natural resources, and social systems. At the same time that regional chiefs and chieftainesses in Zambia, for example, are regaining their traditional role in managing wildlife, they are facing the effects of a rural population boom. They are not able to allocate as much fallow farmland to needy families as is customary—most good land is already taken, and people are having to cultivate smaller and more marginal plots. As a result, the local ecology suffers along with the local people. Extending the reach of national family planning programs in Zambia and other African countries could play a decisive role in determining whether the continent in the year 2050 will hold 1.7 billion people (the low-fertility scenario), 2.0 billion (the medium-fertility scenario), or 2.4 billion (the high-fertility scenario). If Africa is able to stabilize its population near the bottom of this wide range, the challenge of meeting the peoples' basic needs, as well as protecting the continent's biological wealth, will be less daunting.[1]

The fact that most population expansion will take place in those countries least able to cope with it highlights the importance of developing more ecologically sound approaches to meeting human needs. The challenge is particularly urgent in rural regions worldwide where natural systems remain the most intact. Sometimes the foundations for ecologically sound development are already present in rural traditions and customs—as witness the advancements made in Nepal once authority for forest and wildlife management was returned to village committees. However, virtually all areas today are in the midst of tremendous change—including greater integration into national economies and a corresponding desire for cash income, rising human population densities, and abandonment of customary beliefs and knowledge systems by younger generations. Few land management traditions or local political institutions will be able to confront such trends and avoid environmental degradation all on their own.[2]

Although managing biological resources wisely and creating a sustainable society will continue to be the work of communities and nations, such activities are bolstered by an international legal process that began to develop early in this century and has accelerated greatly in the last two decades. One of the most successful international environmental treaties is the Convention on International Trade in Endangered Species (1973), which provides a powerful legal tool for controlling international trade in wildlife and plants. The CITES secretariat can request information from governments about species they are trading, and also can demand reports from countries that appear to be following questionable practices. CITES also provides clear guidelines for customs agents and inspectors who monitor wildlife shipments and pursue illegal smuggling rings. CITES was the mechanism through which countries agreed in 1989 to ban international trade in African elephant ivory, which for two decades had fueled heavy poaching that reduced elephant numbers from several million to 500,000 or less. Immediately following the ban, African elephant poaching appeared to drop substantially in many areas.[3]

But CITES and other international agreements are only part of the puzzle when it comes to reforming networks as complex and entrenched as the ivory trade. International demand for ivory, particularly in East Asia, has remained strong this decade, while a number of elephant range countries, such as the Democratic Republic of Congo (formerly Zaire) have experienced political instability and declines in government antipoaching efforts. As a result, poaching intensity has crept gradually back upward, and illegal elephant kills are again being reported regularly. The real test in nations' commitments to ensuring a sound future for African elephants will come in 1999, when elephant ivory may once again be legally traded on a limited basis. Delegates at the 1997

CITES conference of the parties agreed that three southern African nations with robust elephant populations—Namibia, Botswana, and Zimbabwe—would be able to trade limited volumes of ivory with Japan starting in 1999, provided they establish an independently verifiable system to closely track the entire trade process. Since the three African countries involved have pledged to reinvest the funds generated by the ivory sales back into wildlife conservation, limited trade could benefit elephants—but only if the monitoring system is rigorous enough to keep illegally harvested ivory out of the trade pipeline.[4]

CITES has on occasion been backed up by sanctions and trade restrictions. In 1994, for instance, the United States, acting under a domestic law called the Pelly Amendment, banned the import of fish and wildlife products from Taiwan because of that nation's continuing trade in tiger body parts and rhino horn—both illegal under CITES. Subsequently, Taiwan stepped up the implementation of its wildlife conservation laws, retrained officers responsible for wildlife enforcement, and developed a new education and public outreach campaign on the endangered status of species used medicinally. As a result, the frequency of rhino and tiger parts in Taiwanese shops fell markedly, and the volume of illegal wildlife shipments seized by customs officials increased. In response, U.S. officials lifted trade sanctions against Taiwan in 1996.[5]

While such unilateral enforcement of wildlife protection laws has gotten results, most countries do not have the political and economic clout to implement unilateral sanctions and standards effectively. These actions are also extremely controversial and are opposed vigorously in many international quarters. The World Trade Organization (WTO), for one, deems trade measures implemented to protect threatened species to be illegal under the General Agreement on Tariffs and Trades (GATT). During the early 1990s, the United States restricted yellowfin tuna imports from countries whose fleets did not take steps to eliminate tuna-fishing practices known to kill large numbers of dolphins. (Spotted dolphins, the species that swims most often with yellowfin tuna, were estimated in 1993 to have suffered population declines of nearly 75 percent). The U.S. restrictions were appealed by Mexico to a GATT panel, which ruled in Mexico's favor. Subsequently, Mexico agreed to suspend its appeal and entered into direct negotiations with the United States, producing in the end a resolution that allowed the U.S. trade standards promoting dolphin-safe tuna to stand. Nevertheless, in other rulings, the WTO has remained hostile to environmental standards that restrict trade—most recently in April 1998 when it ruled against a U.S. ban on shrimp imports from Asian nations that do not require fishermen to equip their shrimping gear with turtle excluder devices.[6]

Since unilateral sanctions inevitably generate controversy, governments will probably remain reluctant to implement them for environmental reasons unless pushed hard to do so by domestic constituencies. Multilateral sanctions are more difficult to negotiate, but once in place they tend to be harder for countries to avoid through appeals or other means. CITES has the power to call for limited multilateral sanctions, and did so in 1991 on Thailand because of that country's role as a regional center for illegal trade in endangered wildlife. The Thai government did not attempt to fight the sanctions and began enforcing wildlife laws more vigorously.[7]

One area where institutions concerned with international trade could make a positive contribution to biodiversity conservation is in establishing guidelines to control the inadvertent spread of invasive species. Many exotics get to a new place by stowing away in the cargo holds of planes, boats, or trucks, or hitching a ride in the bilge water that ships take in at the start of a voyage and discharge at the end. Some countries already recognize the threat that invasives pose to native species and communities, and monitor incoming ships, planes, and other vessels in an attempt to catch intruders before they become established. The United States since 1991 has required by law close scrutiny of ships and planes that arrive in Hawaii from Guam, the goal being to detect brown tree snakes—which have stowed away in the cargo holds of planes on more than one occasion. Should the snake become established on Hawaii—which like Guam has no equivalent predators—it could similarly devastate the archipelago's remaining native birds.[8]

The most thorough test to date of the international community's will to face up to the biodiversity crisis is the Convention on Biological Diversity (CBD), which came out of the 1992 Earth Summit in Rio de Janeiro. Now ratified by 172 countries, the CBD is a legally binding agreement that commits national governments to reversing the ongoing global decline in biological diversity. Under the convention, countries are supposed to accomplish this feat by actively conserving biodiversity, for instance in systems of national parks, forest reserves, and other protected areas; by making sure biological resources—timber, fisheries, forage for livestock—are used in ecologically sound ways; and by ensuring that the benefits of genetic resources—such as traditional crop varieties used in breeding new lines—are shared fairly and equitably. To implement this approach, governments are required to take a number of steps forward. (See Table 31–1.)[9]

The CBD is far more comprehensive than other environmental treaties, and the report card on governments' compliance so far has been barely passing. The United States, for one, has not even ratified the convention. The CBD requires each signatory government to prepare a national strategy for conserving their country's biological endowment; the first round of these reports was due in January 1998, but less than half the signatory governments met that deadline. Between 1991 and 1997, donor countries pledged over $3.3 billion in funding to the Global Environment Facility (GEF), which was established in 1991 as a joint initiative of the United Nations Development Programme (UNDP), United Nations Environment Programme (UNEP), and the World Bank to address global environment problems, and was subsequently designated the interim funding mechanism for the CBD. Thirty-eight percent of the GEF's funding to date has been allocated in support of biodiversity conservation, in 156 separate projects. But even with the GEF, wealthy countries have still failed to meet their treaty-specified responsibility to provide "new and additional" financing for conservation. Total annual international aid for programs related to biodiversity conservation (including programs for reducing population growth, combatting deforestation, and promoting women's role in development, sustainable agriculture, and wildlands management) actually fell 11 percent, from $6.4 billion in 1987 to $5.7 billion in 1994.[10]

TABLE 31–1 Requirements for Signatory Nations to the Convention on Biological Diversity

- Adopt national biodiversity strategies and action plans.
- Establish nation-wide systems of protected areas.
- Adopt measures that provide incentives to promote conservation and sustainable use of biological resources.
- Restore degraded habitats.
- Conserve threatened species and ecosystems.
- Minimize or avoid adverse impacts on biodiversity from the use of biological resources.
- Respect, preserve, and maintain knowledge, innovations, and practices of local and indigenous communities.
- Ensure the safe use and application of biotechnology products.

Source: See endnote 9.

There is also reason to question the effectiveness of conservation funds spent by the GEF. The institution was restructured in 1994 following an independent evaluation that concluded the GEF spent much of its money on hap-hazard, poorly executed projects that likely made only a "marginal contribution" to biodiversity conservation. Interestingly, the area of the GEF that appears most promising is the one with the least money to offer—the small-grants program, which provides grants up to $50,000. The program has funded such projects as coastal zone management in Turkey, and a gene bank in the Philippines that preserves native plants with medicinal value; it has been successful enough to receive additional aid from Denmark, Canada, and other countries.[11]

Although the slow pace of implementation reflects the ambivalence of governments about how strong they want the CBD to be, it nonetheless holds promise as an international mechanism for self-policing. If fully implemented, the CBD could also serve as an important forum for minimizing the impacts on biodiversity caused by an an equally international phenomenon—the rapid growth and globalization of economies everywhere. Increasingly long economic chains link natural resources in remote and often biodiversity-rich regions of countries to consumer demands in distant cities and other nations. In some cases, these external economic relationships trigger environmental degradation far more severe than that produced by internal trends like regional population growth.

Some of the most ecologically harmful activities of this kind involve businesses and individuals—both unscrupulous operators and legitimate business ventures—that seek quick exploitation of timber, fish stocks, minerals, and other elements of our planet's natural wealth without regard for the environmental and social damage they inflict. There is often a fundamental imbalance between the political power of rural communities and that of outsiders who have other plans for their lands and resources. Instances where heedless exploitation is occurring are legion: foreign boats rake in fish and lobsters off Nicaragua's Caribbean coast; Indonesian, Malaysian, and French timber companies cruise the rainforests of Gabon and Cameroon; commercial shrimp farms pollute coastal waters and destroy local fisheries in India and Honduras; miners lace Amazonian river beds with toxic mercury compounds to precipitate out gold deposits. Some of these undertakings are sponsored by multinational corporations, which in recent years have found an increasingly friendly international climate in which to operate as countries relax trade restrictions and open their borders. Others primarily benefit developing-country elites who own resource extraction companies—which often garner subsidies and other incentives from their governments.[12]

One reason natural resource extraction continues apace is that the developing countries shoulder heavy loads of international debt. The quick foreign currency generation promised by logging operations, mining companies, or factory fishing fleets is understandably enticing, and financially pressed governments commonly respond with generous concessions to forests, mineral deposits, and fish stocks. All too often, these concessions are granted on remaining natural resource frontiers, where intact or less-disturbed landscapes still hold a wealth of biological diversity.[13]

The onerous debt burdens of developing countries reduce opportunities for conservation in other ways too. Governments that seek to restructure their obligations with international creditors are invariably required to adopt the "structural adjustment" programs of the International Monetary Fund (IMF). While the IMF's intent is to put countries' financial houses in order, the restrictions it insists upon can severely constrain the ability of governments to fund and implement the public policy structure—from environmental lawyers to forest guards—necessary for sound natural resource management at the national level.[14]

Other means of addressing the debt crisis have been more environmentally beneficial. Since the 1980s, a number of debt forgiveness programs have involved "debt for nature" swaps, where governments or conservation groups buy back or forgive a portion of a country's debt (usually at a discounted market price) in exchange for the country government's commitment to fund conservation programs at a specified level in local currency. Debt-for-nature swaps have been concluded in 16 countries and have generated nearly $130 million in local conservation funds. In some cases, these monies have been used to establish conservation endowments, which then provide a steady source of funds to bolster natural areas management or other programs.

Overall, however, neither debt-for-nature swaps nor other reduction approaches have made a dent in the total indebtedness of developing countries, which has continued to grow steadily, surpassing $2 trillion in 1995. Clearly, debt relief must be undertaken on a much larger scale if affected governments are to dig out from under their overall debt burdens.[15]

Another approach to stemming biodiversity-depleting resource exploitation is to support the development of alternative, more environmentally benign ways for people to make their livelihoods. Ecotourism—or travel oriented around natural sites, native species, and traditional cultural practices—is one commonly proffered alternative economic activity that can extract value from ecological landscapes with minimal harm. Ecotourism has helped spur communities to protect coral reefs near Phuket Island in Thailand and around the Caribbean island of Bonaire. It is also the leading foreign exchange earner in Costa Rica, and helps support that country's protected areas system. "Biodiversity prospecting"—the search for species that might yield new chemicals, drug precursors, or genes—is another commonly touted alternative, particularly as an incentive for protecting species-rich natural communities like coral reefs and tropical forests. A number of bioprospecting agreements between pharmaceutical companies and species-rich tropical countries have been signed in recent years: Merck is working with Costa Rica's National Biodiversity Institute (INBIO), Glaxo with Ghana, Novo is active in Nigeria, and Bristol Myers Squibb is collaborating in Suriname with a consortium of conservationists, indigenous healers, and a Surinamese pharmaceutical company.[16]

Ecotourism, and bioprospecting agreements to a lesser degree, have been effective at generating foreign currency for developing countries, and they also influence national-level environmental policies. The benefits provided to local communities and to actual conservation projects, however, have been much more limited. Realizing these latter benefits depends on how ecotourist and bioprospecting ventures are structured and administered, and who participates in them. If bioprospectors are to make use of flora or fauna from lands traditionally managed by indigenous cultures, they should negotiate agreements with indigenous representatives as well as national government agencies. Clear guidelines need to be in place to ensure that the companies benefitting from bioprospecting provide fair compensation for the right to review samples of species with pharmaceutical potential, as well as royalties on any commercial products that result. Receipts from tourist visits should go to local conservation or community development funds, and not just to tour operators or national treasuries. Local residents should also have a say (as many aboriginal communities in Australia now do) in determining when, where, and how many tourists can visit protected areas—say, for instance, a national park that also contains sites sacred to residents' religious beliefs.[17]

Unfortunately, it is all too easy for governments and economic elites to support efforts like ecotourism with one hand, but continue encouraging shortsighted natural resource management with the other. This situation will only change with fundamental government policy reform in many areas—for instance in eliminating subsidies for cattle ranching that involves clearing native forests (as Brazil did in the late 1980s), and rewriting national land and marine tenure laws to uphold the claims of indigenous peoples with strong traditional ties to land and sea resources. While increased funding for sound natural resource management to complement such reforms is certainly needed, this is more likely to make a difference when coupled with reductions in existing subsidies to frontier-style economic activities that damage biodiversity. During the Convention on Biological Diversity's first three years of implementation, for example, donor countries provided about $18 billion in international aid for conservation-related purposes. Yet during that same time period, global subsidies to biodiversity-damaging activities such as fisheries overexploitation, road building, and excessive fossil fuel burning totaled approximately $1.8 trillion—100 times as much.[18]

It is also important to realize that national resource exploiters are doing the bidding of consumers—especially those of us in developed countries and the rapidly industrializing nations of the Pacific Rim. Take the massive fires that swept across vast areas of the Indonesian islands of Kalimantan and Sumatra during 1997, destroying over 100,000 hectares of primary tropical forest and peat swamp forest—critical habitat for endangered creatures like Asian elephants and orangutans—and enfolding 70 million people in a smoky, sickening haze. These fires were started deliberately, mostly by 176 companies and concessionaires who took advantage of the unusually dry El Niño conditions to clear land for industrial pulpwood and oil palm plantations. Oil palm, which yields an edible vegetable oil, has been heavily promoted as a plantation cash crop by the Indonesian government—the country's palm oil exports rose 162 percent between 1987 and 1997, from 986,000 tons to 2.58 million tons. Recently, the Suharto government has seen agribusiness development as a primary way for Indonesia to dig itself out of its current economic crisis, and oil palm plantations are scheduled to expand even more frenetically, from 2 million hectares to over 3 million within the next two years.[19]

Part of Indonesia's increased pulpwood production will be destined for industrialized countries such as Japan and the United States, while the world's fastest-growing major market for Indonesia's palm oil is China. China's annual consumption of oilseeds (of which oil palm is one kind) has risen steadily from 31.6 million tons in 1987 to 43 million tons in 1997, the result of population increases as well as economic growth permitting more people to eat higher on the food chain. China cannot meet its increased demand for vegetable oil with domestic production alone, and thus has turned to international markets. Annual Chinese imports of palm oil have risen 316 percent during the last 10 years and now top 1.5 million tons. This chain of events illustrates how the ecological price for growth in today's global economy—whether in North America, Europe, Asia, or other emerging markets—is often not paid by those who reap its benefits. And it is not just biodiversity that suffers; replacing native forests with plantations in Indonesia has meant that local subsistence farmers now have fewer sources of the wild forest foods they traditionally rely upon during lean harvest years—and this year's El Niño-afflicted rice crop in Kalimantan is expected to be very poor indeed.[20]

One route for inserting more ecological and social considerations into the national and international chains that supply consumer goods is programs that certify products which meet high environmental and social standards. Environmental certification programs have been implemented most extensively for sustainably harvested timber, primarily through the efforts of the Forest Stewardship Council, a body established in 1993 by environmental groups, indigenous peoples representatives, and progressive foresters and businesses to establish uniform guidelines for certification. By 1997, more than 6 million hectares of forest land had been certified as being under ecologically sound timber management. This is still only a small fraction of the world's forest estate, but the number of certified timber-harvesting operations is growing rapidly. A consortium of the World Bank and environmental and business representatives recently endorsed a resolution to increase the forest area under certified management to 200 million hectares within 10 years. Most of the demand for certified timber has come from the United States and Europe—in Great Britain, for instance, a buyer's group of 75 companies comprising 25 percent of the nation's wood demand has pledged to phase out all purchases of non-certified wood products. So far, little demand for certified timber has materialized in Asia, although the concept has been introduced to Japan, the world's largest importer of whole logs.[21]

Certification programs can also provide specific benefits for conservation of our planet's biodiversity endowment. In the Americas, many migratory songbirds that breed in North America spend part of their winters in coffee plantations from Mexico to Colombia, where coffee bushes have traditionally been grown under a canopy of native forest trees. Unfortunately this habitat is disappearing as plantations intensify and replant with higher-yielding, sun-tolerant coffee varieties that do not require shade—leaving neotropical migrants to search ever harder for suitable wintering territory. Recognition of the importance of traditional shaded coffee plantations for migratory birds and other wildlife has led the Rainforest Alliance to establish a certifiation program for Latin American shade coffee plantations. Participating farms must maintain forest cover over coffee plants and meet a series of environmental and social criteria for sound management, such as limiting agrochemical applications, controlling soil erosion, and providing their workers with fair wages and environmental education training. Certified shade-grown coffee from Guatemala is now available in the United States through 11 coffee distributors and mail-order retailers, and vendors who sell it emphasize its environmental advantages over standard coffee.[22]

All of these approaches demonstrate that in today's increasingly crowded and interconnected world, the most important steps we can all take to conserve biodiversity may be the least direct ones. The fate of birds, mammals, frogs, fish, and all the rest of biodiversity depends not so much on what happens in parks but what happens where we live, work, and obtain the wherewithal for our daily lives. To give biodiversity and wildlands breathing space, we must reduce the size of our own imprint on the planet. That means stabilizing the human population. It means far greater efficiency in our materials and energy use, and careful consideration of the social and ecological side effects of our international trading links. It means intelligently designed communities. And it means educational standards that build an awareness of our responsibility in managing 3.2 billion years' worth of biological wealth. Ultimately it means creating a less materialist, more environmentally literate way of life.[23]

Humans, after all, are not dinosaurs. We can change. Even in the midst of the current mass extinction, we still largely control our destiny, but we are unwise to delay taking action. The fate of untold numbers of species depends on it. And so does the fate of our children, in ways we can barely begin to conceive.

NOTES

1. Population figures from U.N. Population Division, *World Population Projections to 2150* (New York: United Nations Secretariat, 1998); future population projection is using low and high fertility scenarios.
2. Katrina Brandon, "Policy and Practical Considerations in Land-Use Strategies for Biodiversity Conservation," in Kramer et al.
3. William J. Snape III, "International Protection: Beyond Human Boundaries," in William J. Snape III, ed., *Biodiversity and the Law* (Washington, DC: Island Press/Defenders of Wildlife, 1996); African elephant information from Robin Sharp, "The African Elephant: Conservation and CITES," *Oryx,* April 1997.

4. Sharp, op. cit. note 3; Susan L. Crowley, "Saving Africa's Elephants: No Easy Answers," *African Wildlife News,* May–June 1997; World Wildlife Fund, "Summary Report on the 1997 CITES Conference," *TRAFFIC USA Bulletin,* August 1997.
5. WWF, "Taiwan Certification Officially Lifted," *TRAFFIC USA Bulletin,* December 1996.
6. Leesteffy Jenkins, "Using Trade Measures to Protect Biodiversity," in Snape, op. cit. note 3; Adam Entous, "WTO Rules Against U.S. on Sea Turtle Protection Law," *Reuters,* 6 April 1998.
7. "International Ban Imposed on Thai Wildlife Trade," *The Nation* (Bangkok), 16 April 1991; "Government Will Not Oppose U.S. Ban on Thai Wildlife Imports," *The Nation* (Bangkok), 5 July 1991.
8. Snape, op. cit. note 3; brown tree snake information from Mark Jaffe, *And No Birds Sing* (New York: Simon & Schuster, 1994).
9. Convention on Biological Diversity Secretariat, <http://www.biodiv. org>, viewed 22 April 1998; IUCN-World Conservation Union, *The Global Environment Facility-From Rio to New Delhi: A Guide for NGOs* (Gland, Switzerland and Cambridge, U.K.: IUCN, 1997); Anatole F. Krattiger et al., eds., *Widening Perspectives on Biodiversity* (Gland, Switzerland: IUCN-World Conservation Union and International Academy of the Environment, 1994).
10. CBD country report numbers from "National Reports," 15 March 1998, <http://www.biodiv.org/natrepo.html>; IUCN-World Conservation Union, op. cit. note 9; amounts pledged to GEF from Hilary F. French, *Partnership for the Planet: An Environmental Agenda for the United Nations,* Worldwatch Paper 126 (Washington, DC: Worldwatch Institute, July 1995); donor country aid shortfalls from BirdLife International, *New and Additional? Financial Resources for Biodiversity Conservation in Developing Countries 1987–1994* (Bedfordshire, U.K.: Royal Society for the Protection of Birds, 1996).
11. IUCN-World Conservation Union, op. cit. note 3; Scott Hajost and Curtis Fish, "Biodiversity Conservation and International Instruments," in Snape, op. cit. note 3.
12. Neitschmann, op. cit. note 88; Janet N. Abramovitz, "Sustaining the World's Forests," in Lester R. Brown et al., op. cit. note 58; Susan C. Stonich, "Reclaiming the Commons: Grassroots Resistance and Retaliation in Honduras," *Cultural Survival Quarterly,* spring 1996; Hilary F. French, *Investing In the Future: Harnessing Private Capital Flows for Environmentally Sustainable Development,* Worldwatch Paper 139 (Washington, DC: Worldwatch Institute, February 1998).
13. French, op. cit. note 10.
14. French, op. cit. note 10.
15. Ibid.
16. Hinrichsen, op. cit. note 57; French op. cit. note 10; Pimbert and Pretty, op. cit. note 92.
17. Douglas W. Yu, Thomas Hendrickson, and Ada Castillo, "Ecotourism and Conservation in Amazonian Peru: Short-term and Long-term Challenges," *Environmental Conservation,* June 1997; Terry de Lacy and Bruce Lawson, "The Uluru/Kakadu Model: Joint Management of Aboriginal-Owned National Parks in Australia," in Stevens, op. cit. note 88.
18. Brazil policy change from Ronald A. Foresta, *Amazonian Conservation in the Age of Development* (Gainesville, FL: University of Florida Press, 1991); examples of other needed reforms from Colchester and Nietschmann, both op. cit. note 88; and from Peter Herlihy, "Indigenous Peoples and Biosphere Reserve Conservation in the Mosquitia Rainforest Corridor, Honduras," in Stevens, ed., op. cit. note 88; conservation funding from BirdLife International, op, cit. note 10; David Malin Roodman, *Paying the Piper: Subsidies, Politics and the Environment,* Worldwatch Paper 133 (Washington, DC: Worldwatch Institute, December 1996); Hajost and Fish, op. cit. note 11.
19. The Indonesian government claims that the total area (primary forest, secondary forest, and scrubland) engulfed by fires was 300,000 hectares, while non-governmental organizations estimate between 750,000 and 2 million hectares were affected. Todd Crowell and Peter Morgan, "The Year the Sky Turned Yellow," *Asiaweek,* 26 December 1997; Nick Brown, "Out of Control: Fires and Forestry in Indonesia," *Trends in Ecology and Evolution,* January 1998; Bruno Manser-Fonds, "Why Are the Forests Burning?" *The Ecologist,* January/February 1998; Nigel Dudley, *The Year the World Caught Fire* (Godalming, U.K.: World Wide Fund for Nature, 1997); U.S. Department of Agriculture (USDA), *Production, Supply and Distribution,* electronic database, Washington, DC, updated March 1998; Center for International Forestry Research, "Indonesian Forests and the Financial Crisis," <http://www.cgiar.org/cifor>, viewed 15 March 1998.
20. USDA, op. cit.; Carol Pierce Colfer, "El Niño's Human Face," *CIFOR News,* September 1997.
21. Abramovitz, op. cit. note 12.
22. Ivette Perfecto, Robert Rice, Russell Greenberg, and Martha Van der Voort, "Shade Coffee: A Disappearing Refuge for Biodiversity," *Bioscience,* September 1996; Rainforest Alliance, "Eco-OK Roasters," *The Canopy,* September/October 1997; Eco-OK Coffee Program news release, <http: //www.rainforest-alliance.org/pr_okun.html>, viewed 10 March 1998.
23. Niles Eldredge, *The Miner's Canary: Unraveling the Mysteries of Extinction* (New York: Prentice Hall Press, 1991).

32

⩔ International Convention ⩓ on Biological Diversity

The Contracting Parties,

Conscious of the intrinsic value of biological diversity and of the ecological, genetic, social, economic, scientific, educational, cultural, recreational and aesthetic values of biological diversity and its components,

Conscious also of the importance of biological diversity for evolution and for maintaining life sustaining systems of the biosphere,

Affirming that the conservation of biological diversity is a common concern of humankind,

Reaffirming that States have sovereign rights over their own biological resources,

Reaffirming also that States are responsible for conserving their biological diversity and for using their biological resources in a sustainable manner,

Concerned that biological diversity is being significantly reduced by certain human activities,

Aware of the general lack of information and knowledge regarding biological diversity and of the urgent need to develop scientific, technical and institutional capacities to provide the basic understanding upon which to plan and implement appropriate measures,

Noting that it is vital to anticipate, prevent and attack the causes of significant reduction or loss of biological diversity at source.

Noting also that where there is a threat of significant reduction or loss of biological diversity, lack of full scientific certainty should not be used as a reason for postponing measures to avoid or minimize such a threat,

Noting further that the fundamental requirement for the conservation of biological diversity is the *in-situ* conservation of ecosystems and natural habitats and the maintenance and recovery of viable populations of species in their natural surroundings,

Noting further that *in-situ* measures, preferably in the country of origin, also have an important role to play,

Have agreed as follows:

ARTICLE 1. OBJECTIVES

The objectives of this Convention, to be pursued in accordance with its relevant provisions, are the conservation of biological diversity, the sustainable use of its components and the fair and equitable sharing of the benefits arising out of the utilization of genetic resources, including by appropriate access to genetic resources and by appropriate transfer of relevant technologies, taking into account all rights over those resources and to technologies, and by appropriate funding.

ARTICLE 3. PRINCIPLE

States have, in accordance with the Charter of the United Nations and the principles of international law, the sovereign right to exploit their own resources pursuant to their own environmental policies, and the responsibility to ensure that activities within their jurisdiction or control do not cause damage to the environment of other States or of areas beyond the limits of national jurisdiction.

ARTICLE 4. JURISDICTIONAL SCOPE

Subject to the rights of other States, and except as otherwise expressly provided in this Convention, the provisions of this Convention apply, in relation to each Contracting Party:

(a) In the case of components of biological diversity, in areas within the limits of its national jurisdiction; and

(b) In the case of processes and activities, regardless of where their effects occur, carried out under its jurisdiction or control, within the area of its national jurisdiction or beyond the limits of national jurisdiction.

ARTICLE 5. COOPERATION

Each Contracting Party shall, as far as possible and as appropriate, cooperate with other Contracting Parties, directly or, where appropriate, through competent international organizations, in respect of areas beyond national jurisdiction and on other matters of mutual interest, for the conservation and sustainable use of biological diversity.

ARTICLE 6. GENERAL MEASURES FOR CONSERVATION AND SUSTAINABLE USE

Each Contracting Party shall, in accordance with its particular conditions and capabilities:

(a) Develop national strategies, plans or programmes for the conservation and sustainable use of biological diversity or adapt for this purpose existing strategies, plans or programmes which shall reflect, *inter alia,* the measures set out in this Convention relevant to the Contracting Party concerned; and

(b) Integrate, as far as possible and as appropriate, the conservation and sustainable use of biological diversity into relevant sectoral or cross-sectoral plans, programmes and policies.

33

◿ *Tora! Tora! Tora!* ◺

PAUL WATSON

Paul Watson was a leading activist in Greenpeace, but he was later expelled from the group because he rejected a completely nonviolent approach. Later, Watson founded the Sea Shepherd Society and is the author of Sea Shepherd: My Fight for Whales and Seals.

On December 7, 1941, the Imperial Japanese First Naval Air fleet launched a surprise attack against the US Naval base at Pearl Harbor on the Hawaiian island of Oahu.

As the Japanese planes swooped in low, their wing commander gave his orders. The Japanese words "tora, tora, tora" crackled through the cockpits of the torpedo bombers.

"Attack, attack, attack." Such was the battle cry of a people who had mastered the martial strategies of Asia. The attack was swift, surprising, ruthless, and effective.

As an ecological strategist, I have faced the Japanese as adversaries on numerous occasions. For this reason, I have studied Japanese martial strategy, especially the classic work entitled *A Book of Five Rings* written by Miyamoto Musashi in 1648. Musashi advocated the "twofold way of pen and sword," which I interpret to mean that one's actions must be both effective and educational.

In March 1982, the Sea Shepherd Conservation Society successfully negotiated a halt to the slaughter of dolphins at Iki Island in Japan. Contributing to this success was our ability to quote Musashi and talk to the Japanese fishermen in a language they could understand—the language of no compromise confrontation.

During our discussion, a fisherman asked me, "What is of more value, the life of a dolphin or the life of a human?"

I answered that, in my opinion, the life of a dolphin was equal in value to the life of a human.

The fisherman then asked, "If a Japanese fisherman and a dolphin were both caught in a net and you could save the life of one, which would you save?"

341

All the fishermen in the room smirked. They had me pegged a liberal and felt confident that I would say that I would save the fisherman, thus making a mockery of my declaration that humans and dolphins are equal.

I looked about the room and smiled. "I did not come to Japan to save fishermen; I am here to save dolphins."

They were surprised but not shocked by my answer. All the fishermen treated me with respect thereafter.

Why? Because the Japanese understand duty and responsibility. Saving dolphins was both my chosen duty and my responsibility.

Sea Shepherd had already established a reputation in Japan as the "Samurai protector of whales." This came in an editorial that appeared in the Tokyo daily *Asahi Shimbun* in July 1979, a few days after we rammed and disabled the Japanese owned pirate whaler, the *Sierra,* off the coast of Portugal.

That incident ended the career of the most notorious outlaw whaler. In February of 1980, we had the *Sierra* sunk in Lisbon harbor. A few months later, in April, our agents sank two outlaw Spanish registered whalers, the *Isba I* and the *Isba II,* in Vigo Harbor in northern Spain.

We then gave attention to two other Japanese pirate whalers, the *Susan* and the *Theresa.* Given the controversy of the *Sierra,* and the fact that the *Susan* and the *Theresa* were owned by the same Japanese interests, the South Africans, who had just publicly denounced whaling did not want the stigma of harboring illegal whaling ships. The South African Navy confiscated and sank the *Susan* and *Theresa* for target practise after we publicly appealed to them to do so, in 1980.

The last of the Atlantic pirate whalers, the *Astrid* was shut down after I sent an agent to the Spanish Canary Islands with a reward offer of $25,000 US to any person who would sink her. The owners saw the writing on the wall and voluntarily retired the whaler.

Because of these actions many have labeled us pirates ourselves. Yet we have never been convicted of a criminal charge nor have we ever caused injury or death to a human. Nor have we attempted to avoid charges. On the contrary, we have always invited our enemies to continue the fight in the courts. Most times they have refused and the few times that they complied, they lost.

Vigilante buccaneers we may well be but we are policing the seas where no policing authority exists. We are protecting whales, dolphins, seals, birds, and fish by enforcing existing regulations, treaties and laws that heretofore have had no enforcement.

In November 1986, when two Sea Shepherd agents, Rod Coronado and David Howitt, attacked the Icelandic whaling industry, they were enforcing the law. The International Whaling Commission (IWC) had banned commercial whaling, yet Iceland continued to whale without a permit. We did not wish to debate the issue of legality with the Icelanders. We acted instead. Coronado and Howitt destroyed the whaling station and scuttled half the Icelandic whaling fleet.

Iceland refused to press charges. I traveled to Reykjavik to insist that they press charges. They refused and deported me without a hearing. The only legal case to result from the incident is my suit against Iceland for illegal deportation.

In March of 1983, the crew of the *Sea Shepherd II* were arrested under the Canadian Seal Protection Regulations, an Orwellian set of rules which actually protected the sealing industry. The only way to challenge these unjust rules was to break them. We did and at the same time we chased the sealing fleet out of the nursery grounds of the Harp Seals. We beat the charges and in the process helped the Supreme Court of Canada in its decision to dismiss the Seal Protection Act as unconstitutional.

In the years since, we have intervened against the Danish Faeroese fishermen in the North Atlantic to save the Pilot Whales they kill for sport. We have shut down seal hunts in Scotland, England and Ireland. We have confronted Central American tuna seiners off the coast of Costa Rica in an effort to rescue dolphins.

In 1987, we launched our first campaign to expose drift net operations in the North Pacific. Our ship the *Divine Wind* voyaged along the Aleutian chain documenting the damage of the drift nets and ghost nets (abandoned nets). We helped convince Canada to abandon plans to build a drift net industry.

For new supporters who do not know what drift nets are, I will briefly explain. Drift nets are to the Pacific Ocean what clearcuts are to the Amazon Rainforest or the Pacific Northwest Temperate Rainforest. Drift-netting is strip-mine fishing.

From May until late October, some 1800 ships each set a net measuring from 10 to 40 miles in length! These monofilament nylon gill nets drift freely upon the surface of the sea, hanging like curtains of death to a depth of 26 or 34 feet. Each night, the combined fleet sets between 28,000 and 35,000 miles of nets. The nets radiate across the breadth of the North Pacific like fences marking off property. The nets are efficient. Few squid and fish escape the perilous clutches of the nylon. Whales and dolphins, seals and sea lions, sea turtles, and sea birds are routinely entangled. The death is an agonizing ordeal of strangulation and suffocation.

Drifts nets take an annual incidental kill of more than one million sea birds and a quarter of a million marine mammals each year, plus hundreds of millions of tons of fish and squid. A few short years ago, the North Pacific fairly teemed with dolphins, turtles, fur seals, sea lions, dozens of species of birds and uncountable schools of fish. Today it is a biological wasteland.

The Japanese say their nets are taking fewer incidental kills now than a few years ago. This is true, but the reason the kills are down is simply that there are now fewer animals to kill.

For many years, governments and environmental groups have talked about the problem. Nobody actually did anything about it. Sick of talk, the Sea Shepherd Conservation Society decided to take action.

The *Sea Shepherd II* moved to Seattle, Washington, in September 1989 to prepare for an expedition to intercept the Japanese North Pacific drift net fleet. We set our departure date for June 1990. Overhauls and refitting were completed by May to meet the targeted date.

We were unable to leave Seattle. One of our crew was a paid infiltrator working, we believe, for the Japanese fishing industry. He successfully sabotaged our engine by pouring crushed glass into our oil, destroying our turbo-charger, and destroying electrical motors. Although we discovered the damage and identified the saboteur, we faced extensive repairs.

The saboteur fled to Britain. We asked Scotland Yard to track him down and investigate the incident. However, the damage was done and we were hardly in a position to cry foul. After all, we had already been responsible for destroying six whaling ships ourselves. The enemy had succeeded in striking a blow—it was as simple as that. We were down, but not for long.

We immediately set to work to repair the damage. Thanks to an appeal to Sea Shepherd Society members, funds were raised to purchase a replacement turbo-charger.

The *Sea Shepherd II* was prepared for departure again on August 5. We left Seattle and stopped briefly in Port Angeles on the Olympic Peninsula. Port Angeles resident and Sea Shepherd veteran David Howitt stopped by to visit us. He could not bring himself to leave. The ship departed with David on board. He had left his job and an understanding wife on the spur of the moment. We needed him and he knew it and that was reason enough to return to the eco-battles. He took the position of 1st Engineer.

It was with confidence that I took the helm of our ship and headed out the Strait of Juan de Fuca for the open Pacific beyond. I had a good crew, including many veterans.

Myra Finkelstein was 2nd Engineer. A graduate zoologist, Myra had worked for weeks in the bowels of the engine room to repair the damage to the engine. She was a veteran of the 1987 drift net campaign and the 1989 tuna dolphin campaign. In addition she had been a leader of the Friends of the Wolf campaign in northern British Columbia where she had parachuted into the frigid and remote wilderness to interfere with a government sponsored wolf kill.

Sea Shepherd Director Peter Brown was on board with the camera gear to document the voyage. Peter was also helmsman and my deputy coordinator for the expedition.

Marc Gaede, who had sailed with us a year ago on the campaign off the coast of Costa Rica, returned as our photographer. Trevor Van Der Gulik, my nephew, a lad of only 15 from Toronto, Canada, became—by virtue of his skills—our 3rd Engineer. Trevor had helped to deliver the *Sea Shepherd* from Holland to Florida in 1989.

Also sailing with us this summer was Robert Hunter. Bob and I had both been founders of Greenpeace and he had been the first President of the Greenpeace Foundation. Both had been the dynamic force behind the organization and ultimate success of Greenpeace. Like myself, he had been forced out of Greenpeace by the marauding bureaucrats who in the late 1970s ousted the original activists and replaced us with fundraisers and public relations people.

With Bob on board, I felt a little of the old spirit which got us moving in the early 70s. We had no doubts: we would find the drift net fleets.

Five days out to sea, we saw a military ship on the horizon, moving rapidly toward us. We identified her as a large Soviet frigate. The frigate hailed us and asked us what we were about. I replied that we were searching for the Japanese drift net fleet and asked if they had seen any Japanese fishing vessels.

The Russians said they thought the Japanese were a few days to the west. Then, surprisingly, the Soviet officer, who spoke impeccable English, said, "Good luck, it is a noble cause that you follow. We are with you in spirit."

Eco-glasnost? Only a few years ago we battled the Russian whalers. In 1975 Bob Hunter and I had survived a Russian harpoon fired over our heads by a Soviet whaler we had confronted. In 1981, we had invaded Siberia to capture evidence on illegal whaling by the Russians. We had narrowly escaped capture. Now, here we were being hailed by the Soviets with a statement of support. We have indeed made progress.

In fact, the Soviets were allies in more than just words. On 29 May 1990, the Russians had seized a fleet of North Korean fishing boats with drift nets in Soviet waters. Japan was diplomatically embarrassed when it was discovered that the 140 supposedly North Korean fishermen in Soviet custody were in fact Japanese.

On the eighth day out from Seattle, I put the *Sea Shepherd II* on a course of due west and decided not to correct the drift. I felt that the drift would take us to the outlaws. Slowly we began to drift north on the course line. Forty-eight hours later, my intuition proved itself right. The sea herself had taken us directly to a drift net fleet.

At 2030 Hours on August 12, we sailed into the midst of six Japanese drift netters. The fleet had just completed laying their nets—more than 200 miles of net in the water. The Japanese ships were each about 200 feet long, equal in size to our own.

As we approached, the Japanese fishermen warned us off, angrily telling us to avoid their nets. Our ship is a large 657 ton North Atlantic trawler with an ice strengthened bow and a fully enclosed protected prop. We were able to cruise harmlessly over the lines of floating nets. We made close runs on the vessels to inspect them closely.

With darkness rapidly closing in, we decided to wait until morning before taking action against the ships. The Japanese vessels had shut down for the night. They drifted quietly. We waited out the night with them.

An hour before dawn they began to move. We moved with them. For three hours, we filmed the hauling in of mile after mile of net from the vessel *Shunyo Maru #8*. We watched the catch of two foot long squids being hauled into the boat along with incidental kills of sharks, sea-birds and dolphins. The catching of the sea birds violated the Convention for the Protection of Migratory Birds, a treaty signed between the US and Japan in March 1972. The nets impact more than 22 species of birds, 13 of which are protected by the treaty. It was to enforce this treaty that our ship and crew had made this voyage.

The fishing boats were brilliantly illuminated and the work on the deck could be adequately filmed. As the power blocks pulled in the nets, the bodies of squid, fish and birds fell from the nets to the deck or back into the sea.

We had the evidence we needed. We had seen the bodies of protected species in the net. For the next step we needed more light. It was painful to continue watching but it was imperative that we wait for dawn and the light we needed to properly film events.

At 0540 Hours, there was enough light. We prepared the deck and the engine room for confrontation. We positioned our cameramen and photographers. I took the wheel. We brought the engine up to full power and charged across the swells toward the *Shunyo Maru #8* whose crew were still hauling in nets. Our objective was to destroy the net retrieval gear. To do so, we had to hit her on an angle on her port mid-side.

We sounded a blast on our horn to warn the Japanese crew that we were coming in. I piloted the *Sea Shepherd II* into position. We struck where intended. The ships ground their hulls together in a fountain of sparks amidst a screeching cacophony of tearing and crushing steel. The net was severed, the power blocks smashed. We broke away as the Japanese stood dumbfounded on their decks.

One fisherman, however, hurtled his knife at photographer Marc Gaede. The knife missed Marc and hit the sea. The same fisherman grabbed a second knife and sent it flying at cameraman Peter Brown. Peter's camera followed it as it came toward the lens. It fell at Peter's feet.

As we pulled away, I looked with satisfaction on the damage we had inflicted. One ship down for the season. On board our own ship, a damage control party reported back that we had suffered minimal injury. The Japanese ships were no match for our ice-strengthened steel reinforced hull.

We immediately targeted a second ship, the *Ryoun Maru #6*. The Japanese were attempting to cut a large shark out of the net. Looking up, they saw us bearing down at full speed upon them. Eyes wide, they ran toward the far deck.

We struck where intended. Again to the roaring crescendo of tortured metal, the power blocks and gear were crushed; the deck and gunnels buckled. The net was severed.

We broke off and immediately set out for the third ship. By now, the Japanese realized what was happening. The first and second ships had been successfully Pearl Harbored. The third was not to be surprised. As we approached, she dropped her net and fled. We pursued.

We then turned and targeted a fourth ship. She also fled, dropping her net in panic. We stopped and pulled up alongside the radio beacon marking the abandoned net. We confiscated the beacon. We then grappled the net, secured a ton of weight to one end and dropped it, sending the killer net to the bottom, two miles beneath us. We watched the cork line drop beneath the surface, the floats disappearing in lines radiating out from our ship toward the horizon.

On the bottom the net would be rendered harmless. Small benthic creatures would literally cement it to the ocean floor over a short period of time.

We cleaned up the remaining nets and then returned to the chase. For the next twenty hours, we chased the six ships completely out of the fishing area.

The next morning, we could look at what we had achieved with pleasure. Two ships completely disabled from further fishing, a million dollars worth of net sunk and destroyed and all six ships prevented from continued fishing and running scared.

We had delivered our message to the Japanese fishing industry. Our tactics had been both effective and educational. Effective in that we directly saved lives by shutting down a fleet, and educational in that we informed the Japanese fishing industry that their greed will no longer be tolerated.

Our ship was only slightly damaged. Most importantly, there were no injuries on any of the ships involved.

I turned the bow of our ship southward to Honolulu to deliver the documentation to the media and to begin again the tedious task of fund-raising which will allow us to mount further attacks against these mindless thugs slaughtering our oceans.

As we headed south, we stopped repeatedly to retrieve drifting remnants of nets. In one we found 54 rotting fish. In another a large dead mahi-mahi. In another a dead albatross. These "ghost nets" present an additional problem for life in the sea. Each day the large fleets lose an average of six miles of net. At present an estimated 10,000 plus miles of ghost nets are floating the seas. These non-biodegradable nets kill millions of fish and sea creatures each year. Decaying fish attract more fish and birds . . . a vicious cycle of death and waste.

Arriving in Honolulu, we berthed at pier eleven, ironically just in front of two fishery patrol vessels, one from Japan, the other from Taiwan. The crew of each scowled at us.

We were prepared for the Japanese to attempt to lay charges against us or failing that to publicly denounce us. Instead, they refused to even recognize that an incident took place.

We contacted the Japanese Consulate and declared that we had attacked their ships and had destroyed Japanese property. We informed the Consulate that we were ready to contest charges, be they in the International Court at the Hague or in Tokyo itself. The Consulate told us he had no idea of what we were talking about.

The Japanese realize they have nothing to gain by taking us to court and much to lose. Which means that we must return to the oceans and must escalate the battle.

The Taiwanese drift netters are beginning to move into the Caribbean Sea. We must head them off. We must continue to confront the Japanese fleets, and we must take on the Koreans.

Each net we sink will cost the industry a million dollars. Each vessel we damage will buy time for the sea animals. Each confrontation we mount will embarrass the drift net industry.

This summer, we won a battle. However, the war to end high seas drift netting continues.

The Japanese, Taiwanese, and Korean drift net fleets can be driven from the oceans. We need only the will, the courage, and the financial support to do so.

34

✒ *Earth First!* ✒

DAVE FOREMAN

Dave Foreman is a founder of the Earth First! Movement and the author of Eco-defense: A Field Guide to Monkey Wrenching.

Maybe—some of us began to feel, even before Reagan's election—it was time for a new joker in the deck: a militant, uncompromising group unafraid to say what needed to be said or to back it up with stronger actions than the established organizations were willing to take. This idea had been kicking around for a couple of years; finally last year several of us (including, among others, Susan Morgan, formerly educational director for the Wilderness Society: Howie Wolke, former Wyoming representative for Friends of the Earth: Bart Koehler, former Wyoming representative for the Wilderness Society, and myself) decided that the time for talk was past. We formed a new national group: EARTH FIRST! We set out to be radical in style, positions, philosophy, and organization in order to be effective and to avoid the pitfalls of co-option and moderation which we had already experienced.

What, we asked ourselves as we sat around a campfire in the Wyoming mountains, were the advantages, the reasons for environmental radicalism?

- To state honestly the views held by many conservationists.
- To demonstrate that the Sierra Club and its allies were raging moderates, believers in the system, and to refute the Reagan/Watt contention that they were "extremist environmentalists."
- To balance such anti-environmental radicals as the Grand County commission and provide a broader spectrum of viewpoints.

- To return some vigor, joy, and enthusiasm to the allegedly tired environmental movement.
- To keep the established groups honest. By stating a pure, noncompromise pro-Earth position, we felt EARTH FIRST! could help keep the other groups from straying too far from their philosophical base.
- To give an outlet to many hard-line conservationists who were no longer active because of disenchantment with compromise politics and the co-option of environmental organizations.
- To provide a productive fringe since it seems that ideas, creativity, and energy spring up on the fringe and later spread into the middle.
- To inspire others to carry out activities straight from the pages of *The Monkey Wrench Gang* even though EARTH FIRST!, we agreed, would itself be ostensibly law-abiding.
- To question the system; to help develop a new world view, a biocentric paradigm, an Earth philosophy. To fight, with uncompromising passion, for Mother Earth.

The name—EARTH FIRST!—was chosen deliberately because it succinctly summed up the one thing on which we could all agree: That in *any* decision, consideration for the health of the Earth must come first, or, as Aldo Leopold said, "A thing is right when it tends to preserve the integrity, stability, and beauty of the biotic community. It is wrong when it tends otherwise."

In a true Earth-radical group, concern for wilderness preservation must be the keystone. The idea of wilderness, after all, is the most radical in human thought—more radical than Paine, than Marx, than Mao. Wilderness says: Human beings are not dominant, Earth is not for *Homo sapiens* alone, human life is but one life form on the planet and has no right to take exclusive possession. Yes, wilderness for its own sake, without any need to justify it for human benefit. Wilderness for wilderness. For grizzlies and whales and titmice and rattlesnakes and stink bugs. And . . . wilderness for human beings. Because it is the laboratory of three million years of human evolution—and because it is home.

It is not enough to protect our few remaining bits of wilderness. The only hope for Earth (and humanity for that matter) is to withdraw huge areas as inviolate natural sanctuaries from the depredations of modern industry and technology. Keep Cleveland, Los Angeles. Contain them. Try to make them habitable. But identify areas—big areas—that can be restored to a semblance of natural conditions, reintroduce the griz and wolf and prairie grasses, and declare them off limits to modern civilization.

In the United States pick an area for each of our major ecosystems and recreate the American wilderness—not in little pieces of a thousand acres but in chunks of a million or ten million. Move out the people and cars. Reclaim the roads and plowed land. It is not enough any longer to say no more dams on our wild rivers. We must begin tearing down some dams already built—beginning with Glen Canyon, Hetch Hetchy, Tellico, and New Melones—and freeing shackled rivers.

This emphasis on wilderness is not to ignore other environmental issues or to abandon the people who suffer because of them. In the United States blacks and Chicanos of the inner cities are the ones most affected by air and water pollution, the ones most trapped by the unnatural confines of urbanity. So we decided that not only should eco-militants be concerned with these human environmental problems; we should also make common ground with other progressive elements of society whenever possible.

Obviously, for a group more committed to Gila monsters and mountain lions than to people, there will not be a total alliance with the other social movements. But there are issues where Earth radicals can cooperate with feminist, Indian rights, anti-nuke, peace, civil rights, and civil liberties groups. The inherent conservatism of the conservation community has made it wary of snuggling too close to these questionable (in their minds) leftist organizations. We hoped that the way might be paved for better cooperation from the entire conservation movement.

We believed that new tactics were needed—something more than commenting on dreary environmental impact statements and writing letters to members of Congress. Politics in the streets. Civil disobedience. Media stunts. Holding the villains up to ridicule. Using music to charge the cause.

Action is the key. Action is more important than philosophical hairsplitting or endless refining of dogma (for which radicals are so well known). Let our actions set the finer points of our philosophy. And let us recognize that diversity is not only the spice of life, it is also the strength. All that would be required to join us, we decided, was a belief in Earth first. Apart from that, EARTH FIRST! would be big enough to contain street poets and cowboy bar bouncers, agnostics and pagans, vegetarians and raw steak eaters, pacifists and those who think that turning the other cheek is a good way to get a sore face.

Radicals frequently verge toward a righteous seriousness. But we felt that if we couldn't laugh at ourselves we would be merely another bunch of dangerous fanatics who should be locked up (like the oil companies). Not only does humor preserve individual and group sanity, it retards hubris, a major cause of environmental rape, and it is also an effective weapon. Additionally, fire, passion, courage, and emotionalism are called for. We have been too reasonable, too calm, too understanding. It's time to get angry, to cry, to let rage flow at what the human cancer is doing to Mother Earth, to be uncompromising. For EARTH FIRST! it is all or nothing. Win or lose. No truce or cease fire. No surrender. No partitioning of the territory.

Ever since the Earth goddesses of ancient Greece were supplanted by the macho Olympians, repression of women and Earth has gone hand in hand with imperial organization. EARTH FIRST! decided to be nonorganizational: no officers, no bylaws or constitution, no incorporation, no tax status; just a collection of women and men committed to the Earth. At the turn of the century William Graham Sumner wrote a famous essay entitled "The Conquest of the United States by Spain." His thesis was that Spain had ultimately won the Spanish-American War because the United States took on the imperialism and totalitarianism of Spain as a result. We felt that if we took on the organization of the industrial state, we would soon accept their anthropocentric paradigm (much as Audubon and the Sierra Club already had).

In keeping with that view, EARTH FIRST! took the shape of a circle, a group of thirteen women and men around the country who more or less direct the movement, and a collection of regional contacts. We also have local affiliates (so far in Alaska, Montana, Wyoming, Colorado, Arizona, New Mexico, Utah, Arkansas, Maine, and Virginia). We publish a newsletter eight times a year and are developing position papers on a range of issues from automobiles to overgrazing. We also send out press releases. Membership is free, although we do encourage members to kick in ten bucks or more, if they can afford it, to help with expenses. We have not sought any grants or funding with strings attached, nor do we plan to have paid staff (although we hope to have field organizers receiving expenses in the tradition of the Wobblies).

And, when we are inspired, _we act._

Massive, powerful, like some creation of Darth Vader's. Glen Canyon Dam squats in the canyon of the Colorado River on the Arizona-Utah border and backs the cold dead waters of Lake Powell some 180 miles upstream, drowning the most awesome and magical canyon on Earth. More than any other single entity, Glen Canyon Dam is the symbol of the destruction of wilderness, of the technological rape of the West. The finest fantasy of *eco*-warriors in the West is the destruction of the dam and the liberation of the Colorado. So it was only proper that on March 21, 1981—on the Spring Equinox, the traditional time of rebirth—EARTH FIRST! held its first national gathering at Glen Canyon Dam.

On that morning, seventy-five members of EARTH FIRST! lined the walkway of the Colorado River Bridge 700 feet above the once free river and watched five compatriots busy at work with an awkward black bundle on the massive dam just upstream. Those on the bridge carried placards reading "Damn Watt, Not Rivers," "Free the Colorado," and "Let It Flow." The four men and one woman on the dam attached ropes to a grill on the dam, shouted out "Earth first!" and let 300 feet of black plastic unfurl down the side of the dam, creating the impression of a growing crack. Those on the bridge returned the cheer.

A few minutes later, Edward Abbey, author of *The Monkey Wrench Gang,* a novel of environmental sabotage in the Southwest, told the protesters of the "green and living wilderness" that was Glen Canyon only nineteen years ago:

"And they took it away from us. The politicians of Arizona, Utah, New Mexico, and Colorado, in cahoots with the land developers, city developers, industrial developers of the Southwest, stole this treasure from us in order to pursue and promote their crackpot ideology of growth, profit, and power—growth for the sake of power, power for the sake of growth."

Speaking toward the future, Abbey offered this advice: "Oppose. Oppose the destruction of our homeland by these alien forces from Houston, Tokyo, Manhattan, Washington, D.C., and the Pentagon. And if opposition is not enough, we must resist. And if resistance is not enough, then subvert."

Abbey then launched a nationwide petition campaign demanding the dismantling of Glen Canyon Dam. Hardly had he finished speaking when Park Service police and Coconino County sheriff's deputies arrived on the scene. While they questioned the organizers of the illegal assembly and tried to disperse it, outlaw country singer Johnny Sagebrush led the demonstrators in song for another twenty minutes.

The Glen Canyon Dam caper brought EARTH FIRST! an unexpected degree of media attention. Membership in our group has spiraled to more than a thousand with members from Maine to Hawaii. Even the Government is interested—according to reliable reports, the FBI dusted the entire Glen Canyon Dam crack for fingerprints!

Last Fourth of July more than 200 EARTH FIRST!ers gathered in Moab, Utah, for the first Sagebrush Patriot Rally to express support for Federal public lands and to send a message to anti-Earth fanatics that there are Americans who are patriotic about *their* wilderness.

When a few of us kicked off EARTH FIRST! we sensed a growing environmental radicalism in the country but we did not expect the response we have received. Maybe EARTH FIRST! is in the right place at the right time. Tom Turner, editor of Friends of the Earth's *Not Man Apart,* recently wrote to us to say:

"Russ Train once said, 'Thank God for Dave Brower—he makes it so easy for the rest of us to appear reasonable.' Youze guys are about to make Dave Brower look reasonable, and more power to you!"

The cynical may smirk. "But what can you really accomplish? How can you fight Exxon, Coors, David Rockefeller, Japan, and the other great corporate giants of the Earth? How, indeed, can you fight the dominant dogmas of Western Civilization?"

Perhaps it _is_ a hopeless quest. But is that relevant? Is that important? No, what is important is that one who loves Earth can do no less. Maybe a species will be saved or a forest will go uncut or a dam will be torn down. Maybe not. A monkey wrench thrown into the gears of the machine may not stop it. But it might delay it. Make it cost more. And it feels good to put it there.

35

⊰ Take Back the Earth ⊱

CHAIA HELLER

Chaia Heller is an ecofeminist from the Burlington Ecofeminist Network in Vermont.

For thousands of years the patriarchy has waged a war against women; a war in which it controls and violates our bodies with rape, battering, forced motherhood, and conditioned self-hatred. As well as assigning women the exclusive sexual functions of reproduction and providing men pleasure, the patriarchy reduces women to instruments of labour: Currently women do two-thirds of the world's agricultural and industrial work while owning less than 1% of the world's land and property.

There is another war on the planet; a war against nature. Industrial capitalism, in both its state and corporate forms, has emerged as an economic system which reduces human labor and all of nature into lifeless objects, cashing them in for the profit of a few elite, white men. Western industrial society treats nature with the same condescending and paternalistic attitude historically reserved for women. Patriarchal thought defines women as irrational, passive and in need of men's control. According to this view, men's protection of women is "traded" generously for complete access to women's bodies and labour. In the same way, nature is also defined as a passive, irrational "thing" to be protected and plundered according to men's needs. The justification for the domination of nature flows smoothly out of the justification for the domination of women. Within Western society, all forms of human and natural life are defined as a mere "resource" to be controlled and squandered for the enhancement of "civilization."

Ecofeminism is a movement of women who understand the connection between the war against women and the war against nature. It is women working together to fight all forms of social and ecological exploitation in order to increase our chance of survival. Ecofeminists see the oppression of women, people of color, children, lesbians and gays and the destruction of nature as linked and mutually reinforcing in a system of domination which is legitimized and perpetuated by various institutions such as the state, the military, religion, the patriarchal family, and industrial capitalism. We fight for the freedom and self-determination of all oppressed peoples as well as for a harmonious relationship with nature: We realize that until we are all free from social and ecological exploitation, no one is free.

Women feel directly the destruction of the planet: In so called "developing countries," lands are confiscated and poisoned, making it impossible for women to feed their children. All over the world women are subject to forced sterilization, literally worked to death in factories, and poisoned by toxic chemicals. Everywhere, the toxics that are dumped into water, dumped into backyards, impair women's reproductive systems, poisoning their breast-milk, their food and their children.

Inheriting thousands of years of compulsory motherhood and caretaking activities, women have been socialized to care only for others, never for themselves. Understandably then, some feminists fear that ecofeminism could be yet another setup for women, compelling them, in the name of ecology, to take on the house-cleaning chores of the world. However, ecofeminists need not fall into the trap of janitorial martyrdom: Fighting oppressive and ecologically destructive institutions saves *women's* lives. We choose to fight for our *own* survival, as well as for the survival of others. Fighting for our own liberation as women is inextricably linked to the survival of the planet.

In addition, ecofeminism demands more than ecological survival. We fight so that we may flourish. We will be free from the shackles of the state and the church who want to deny women the choice to parent when and *if* we choose and to love *whomever* we choose. We demand to be free from constant threats and acts of violence: We will be free from rape and battering in our homes, in the streets, and harrassment on the job. We will fight for our passions, our pleasures, creating democratic communities in which work, art and ethics are both mutually and ecologically enhancing.

Already, women all over the world are striking out against the devastation of women and nature. In the Chipko movement in India, women are saving entire forests through direct action. Women in the South Pacific are speaking out against the poisoning of their bodies and their land from the nuclear testings of the 1950s. In Israel, Jewish and Palestinian women are speaking out for the right to peaceful cooperation between their peoples and for an end to violence, poverty and oppression perpetuated by the Israeli, Arab and American governments. The ecofeminist movement in the U.S. is lagging way behind in the ecological and land reform movements of women all over the world. We must respond.

It is time to take it to Wall Street. Last time we were there was in 1984 for the "Not In Our Name" action; the demonstration in which over 1000 women took to the streets of New York City. We were there to inform the world that the U.S. corporations could no longer wage war against people all over the world in the name of American women. In that action, we swarmed the headquarters of the corporations and banks that manufacture and finance everything from nuclear weapons to apartheid in South Africa.

This year, in 1990, we will return to Wall Street with others in the ecology, labour, peace and human liberation movements to shut down the headquarters of the perpetrators of the war against women and nature; the perpetrators of the war against the planet itself.

We will disrupt the lethal flow of the day-to-day activity of the corporate elite who whimsically murder the wills and bodies of women all over the world, stripping the earth of its creativity and diversity.

The patriarchy has determined the fates of women's bodies. Now capitalism seeks to determine the fate of the earth. We will not have our fate determined by a few corporate and governmental elite whose only aspirations are to increase their own personal power and wealth. Women from all over the country will gather at Wall Street to throw a wrench into the gears of their deadly machine, saying "No More. We will take back our lives! We will take back the Earth."

36

⋈ Ecological Sabotage: ⋈ Pranks or Terrorism?

EUGENE HARGROVE

In 1975 Edward Abbey wrote a novel called *The Monkey Wrench Gang* which recounts the adventures of three men and one woman filled with "healthy hatred" who decide to sabotage construction projects which they find environmentally distasteful. Meeting accidentally near the Glen Canyon Dam, casual conversation about the possibility of blowing up the dam turns to serious plans for ecological sabotage on a smaller scale. Passing reference is made to the Luddite movement of the nineteenth century and *sabotage* is defined as the destruction of machinery using wooden shoes. No underlying philosophy, set of principles, or ideology is developed, however, then or at any time later in the book:

"Do we know what we are doing and why?"

"No."

"Do we care?"

"We'll work it out as we go along. Let our practice form our doctrine, thus assuring precise theoretical coherence."

The group agrees to stop short of murdering people—planning to murder machines instead—but such niceties fall by the wayside as the police close in after an abortive attempt to blow up a bridge. Two surrender. One is captured without a fight. The fourth, the Vietnam veteran, chooses to fight it out to the end, an end in which his "riddled body hung on the rimrock for a final moment before the impact of the hail of steel, like hammer blows, literally pushed it over the edge," and it "fell like a sack of garbage into the foaming gulf of the canyon, vanishing forever from men's eyes."

Now, seven years later, this book is the inspiration for a new environmental group, Earth First! which, according to *Newsweek* (19 July 1982, pp. 26–27), is "pledged to 'ecological sabotage' and other forms of civil disobedience," and is endorsed by Abbey himself who is quoted as telling the organization: "Oppose, resist and if necessary subvert. Of course, I never advocate illegal action at any time. Except at night. . . ."

Perhaps if the group is really able to engage in civil disobedience (pranks, according to *Newsweek*), there will be no cause for alarm—but the activities in Abbey's book, as acknowledged by the characters themselves, are criminal, not civil, in nature, and it is hard to imagine a group of people enthusiastically inspired by Abbey's book foregoing the acts described in it indefinitely. Indeed, it seems hard to imagine the ecological sabotage of the book having anything to do with civil disobedience at all. Persons who engage in civil disobedience normally participate in some legally unacceptable activity in order to get arrested and thereby publicize their cause. The book, however, is filled with paramilitary operations for the purpose of destroying equipment and bridges. The participants try to keep their identities a secret and avoid capture. These activities seem closer to terrorism than civil disobedience, and seem to differ from them only in the preference for killing machines, rather than humans, a preference abandoned easily by the most militant member of the gang once the police arrive.

Although presumably the organization, like the book, has no clear philosophy, there does seem to be something there implicitly and it is more radical than any position put forward in the field of environmental ethics to date. In the past, environmental ethicists have talked about *extending* moral considerability in some way to include nature (Leopold and his followers, for example), but here nature, rather than being included, is given priority. This nature chauvinism is a nonhumanistic, indeed an antihumanistic, position, and probably has much to do with Abbey's earlier attitudes in *Desert Solitaire:* "I'm a humanist; I'd rather kill a *man* than a snake."

I would doubt that many members of Earth First! would be ready at this time to put Abbey's sentiments into action; however, as their practice forms their doctrine, who knows where their theory will lead them? We live in a society socially and politically dedicated to the protection of property (including construction equipment and bridges). As Locke put it long ago, a man who destroys property declares a state of war with society and in that state, society has the right to destroy the offender "as a *Lyon* or a *Tyger,* one with whom Men can have no Society nor Security." This right was invoked when the Vietnam veteran took his stand in the book, and it is what will inevitably happen in real life if authentic ecological sabotage begins. From there, it should be a small step for the surviving and uncaptured saboteurs to begin protecting the snake by killing the man.

In the twentieth century, terrorism (the use of force as a political weapon to demoralize, intimidate, and subjugate) has been the last resort when normal political action was frustrated and improvement through peaceful means was absolutely impossible. The environmental movement, however, with its beginnings in the nineteenth century with Yosemite and Yellowstone and culminating in the 1960s and 1970s with the wilderness, endangered species, and clean air and water acts, to name a few, has been an immensely successful political movement. In this context, what could be the practical, ethical, or political justification for acts which could easily create a terrible backlash undoing all the good that has been done and preventing future accomplishments?

37

⚜ *Do We Consume Too Much?* ⚜

MARK SAGOFF

Mark Sagoff is Director of the Center for Philosophy and Public Policy at the University of Maryland. His most recent book is The Economy of the Earth.

In 1994, when delegates from around the world gathered in Cairo for the International Conference on Population and Development, representatives from developing countries protested that a baby born in the United States will consume during its lifetime twenty times as much of the world's resources as an African or an Indian baby. The problem for the world's environment, they argued, is overconsumption in the North, not overpopulation in the South.

Consumption in industrialized nations "has led to overexploitation of the resources of developing countries," a speaker from Kenya declared. A delegate from Antigua reproached the wealthiest 20 percent of the world's population for consuming 80 percent of the goods and services produced from the earth's resources.

Do we consume too much? To some, the answer is self-evident. If there is only so much food, timber, petroleum, and other material to go around, the more we consume, the less must be available for others. The global economy cannot grow indefinitely on a finite planet. As populations increase and economies expand, natural resources must be depleted; prices will rise, and humanity—especially the poor and future generations at all income levels—will suffer as a result.

Other reasons to suppose we consume too much are less often stated though also widely believed. Of these the simplest—a lesson we learn from our parents and from literature since the Old Testament—may be the best: although we must satisfy basic needs, a good life is not one devoted to amassing material possessions; what we own comes to own us, keeping us from fulfilling commitments that give meaning to life, such as those to family, friends, and faith. The appreciation of nature also deepens our lives. As we consume more, however, we are more likely to transform the natural world, so that less of it will remain for us to appreciate.

The reasons for protecting nature are often religious or moral. As the philosopher Ronald Dworkin points out, many Americans believe that we have an obligation to protect species which goes beyond our own well-being: we "think we should admire and protect them because they are important in themselves, and not just if or because we or others want or enjoy them." In a recent survey Americans from various walks of life agreed by large majorities with the statement "Because God created the natural world, it is wrong to abuse it." The anthropologist who conducted this survey concluded that "divine creation is the closest concept American culture provides to express the sacredness of nature."

During the nineteenth century preservationists forthrightly gave ethical and spiritual reasons for protecting the natural world. John Muir condemned the "temple destroyers, devotees of ravaging commercialism" who "instead of lifting their eyes to the God of the mountains, lift them to the Almighty dollar." This was not a call for better cost-benefit analysis: Muir described nature not as a commodity but as a companion. Nature is sacred, Muir held, whether or not resources are scarce.

Philosophers such as Emerson and Thoreau thought of nature as full of divinity. Walt Whitman celebrated a leaf of grass as no less than the journeywork of the stars: "After you have exhausted what there is in business, politics, conviviality, love, and so on," he wrote in *Specimen Days,* and found that none of these finally satisfy, or permanently wear—what remains? Nature remains." These philosophers thought of nature as a refuge from economic activity, not as a resource for it.

Today those who wish to protect the natural environment rarely offer ethical or spiritual reasons for the policies they favor. Instead they say we are running out of resources or causing the collapse of ecosystems on which we depend. Predictions of resource scarcity appear objective and scientific, whereas pronouncements that nature is sacred or that greed is bad appear judgmental or even embarassing in a secular society. Prudential and economic arguments, moreover, have succeeded better than moral or spiritual ones in swaying public policy.

These prudential and economic arguments are not likely to succeed much longer. It is simply wrong to believe that nature sets physical limits to economic growth— that is, to prosperity and the production and consumption of goods and services on which it is based. The idea that increasing consumption will inevitably lead to depletion and scarcity, as plausible as it may seem, is mistaken both in principle and in fact. It is based on four misconceptions.

MISCONCEPTION NO. 1:
WE ARE RUNNING OUT OF RAW MATERIALS

In the 1970s Paul Ehrlich, a biologist at Stanford University, predicted that global shortages would soon send prices for food, fresh water, energy, metals, paper, and other materials sharply higher. "It seems certain," Paul and Anne Ehrlich wrote in *The End of Affluence* (1974), "that energy shortages will be with us for the rest of the century, and that before 1985 mankind will enter a genuine age of scarcity in which many things besides energy will be in short supply." Crucial materials would near depletion during the 1980s, Ehrlich predicted, pushing prices out of reach. "Starvation among people will be accompanied by starvation of industries for the materials they require."

Things have not turned out as Ehrlich expected. In the early 1990s real prices for food overall fell. Raw materials—including energy resources—are generally more abundant and less expensive today than they were twenty years ago. When Ehrlich wrote, economically recoverable world reserves of petroleum stood at 640 billion barrels. Since that time reserves have *increased* by more than 50 percent, reaching more than 1,000 billion barrels in 1989. They have held steady in spite of rising consumption. The pre-tax real price of gasoline was lower during this decade than at any other time since 1947. The World Energy Council announced in 1992 that "fears of imminent [resource] exhaustion that were widely held 20 years ago are now considered to have been unfounded."

The World Resources Institute, in a 1994–1995 report, referred to "the frequently expressed concern that high levels of consumption will lead to resource depletion and to physical shortages that might limit growth or development opportunity." Examining the evidence, however, the institute said that "the world is not yet running out of most nonrenewable resources and is not likely to, at least in the next few decades." A 1988 report from the Office of Technology Assessment concluded, "The nation's future has probably never been less constrained by the cost of natural resources."

It is reasonable to expect that as raw materials become less expensive; they will be more rapidly depleted. This expectation is also mistaken. From 1980 to 1990, for example, while the prices of resource-based commodities declined (the price of rubber by 40 percent, cement by 40 percent, and coal by almost 50 percent), reserves of most raw materials increased. Economists offer three explanations.

First, with regard to subsoil resources, the world becomes ever more adept at discovering new reserves and exploiting old ones. Exploring for oil, for example, used to be a hit-or-miss proposition, resulting in a lot of dry holes. Today oil companies can use seismic waves to help them create precise computer images of the earth. New methods of extraction—for example, using bacteria to leach metals from low-grade ores—greatly increase resource recovery. Reserves of resources "are actually functions of technology," one analyst has written. "The more advanced the technology, the more reserves become known and recoverable."

Second, plentiful resources can be used in place of those that become scarce. Analysts speak of an Age of Substitutability and point, for example, to nanotubes, tiny cylinders of carbon whose molecular structure forms fibers: a hundred times as strong as steel, at one sixth the weight. As technologies that use more-abundant resources substitute for those needing less-abundant ones—for example, ceramics in place of tungsten, fiber optics in place of copper wire, aluminum cans in place of tin ones—the demand for and the price of the less-abundant resources decline.

One can easily find earlier instances of substitution. During the early nineteenth century whale oil was the preferred fuel for household illumination. A dwindling supply prompted innovations in the lighting industry, including the invention of gas and kerosene lamps and Edison's carbon-filament electric bulb. Whale oil has substitutes, such as electricity and petroleum-based lubricants. Whales are irreplaceable.

Third, the more we learn about materials, the more efficiently we use them. The progress from candles to carbon-filament to tungsten incandescent lamps, for example, decreased the energy required for and the cost of a unit of household lighting by many times. Compact fluorescent lights are four times as efficient as today's incandescent bulbs and last ten to twenty times as long. Comparable energy savings are available in other appliances: for example, refrigerators sold in 1993 were 23 percent more efficient than those sold in 1990 and 65 percent more efficient than those sold in 1980, saving consumers billions in electric bills.

Amory Lovins, the director of the Rocky Mountain Institute, has described in these pages a new generation of ultralight automobiles that could deliver the safety and muscle of today's cars but with far better mileage—four times as much in prototypes and ten times as much in projected models (see "Reinventing the Wheels," January, 1995, *Atlantic*). Since in today's cars only 15 to 20 percent of the fuel's energy reaches the wheels (the rest is lost in the engine and the transmission), and since materials lighter and stronger than steel are available or on the way, no expert questions the feasibility of the high-mileage vehicles Lovins describes.

Computers and cameras are examples of consumer goods getting lighter and smaller as they get better. The game-maker Sega is marketing a hand-held children's game, called Saturn, that has more computing power than the 1976 Cray supercomputer, which the United States tried to keep out of the hands of the Soviets. Improvements that extend the useful life of objects also save resources. Platinum spark plugs in today's cars last for 100,000 miles, as do "fill-for-life" transmission fluids. On average, cars bought in 1993 have a useful life more than 40 percent longer than those bought in 1970.

As lighter materials replace heavier ones, the U.S. economy continues to shed weight. Our per capita consumption of raw materials such as forestry products and metals has, measured by weight, declined steadily over the past twenty years. A recent World Resources Institute study measured the "materials intensity" of our economy—that is, "the total material input and the hidden or indirect material flows, including deliberate landscape alterations" required for each dollar's worth of economic output. "The result shows a clearly declining pattern of materials intensity, supporting the conclusion that economic activity is growing somewhat more rapidly than natural resource use." Of course, we should do better. The Organization for Economic Cooperation and Development, an association of the world's industrialized nations, has proposed that its members strive as a long-range goal to decrease their materials intensity by a factor of ten.

Communications also illustrates the trend toward lighter, smaller, less materials-intensive technology. Just as telegraph cables replaced frigates in transmitting messages across the Atlantic and carried more information faster, glass fibers and microwaves have replaced cables—each new technology using less materials but providing greater capacity for sending and receiving information. Areas not yet wired for telephones (in the former Soviet Union, for example) are expected to leapfrog directly into cellular communications. Robert Solow, a Nobel laureate in economics, says that if the future is like the past, "there will be prolonged and substantial reductions in natural-resource requirements per unit of real output." He asks, "Why shouldn't the productivity of most natural resources rise more or less steadily through time, like the productivity of labor?"

MISCONCEPTION NO. 2:
WE ARE RUNNING OUT OF FOOD AND TIMBER

The United Nations projects that the global population, currently 5.7 billion, will peak at about 10 billion in the next century and then stabilize or even decline. Can the earth feed that many people? Even if food crops increase sufficiently, other renewable resources, including many fisheries and forests, are already under pressure. Should we expect fish stocks to collapse or forests to disappear?

The world already produces enough cereals and oilseeds to feed 10 billion people a vegetarian diet adequate in protein and calories. If, however, the idea is to feed 10 billion people not healthful vegetarian diets but the kind of meat-laden meals that Americans eat, the production of grains and oilseeds may have to triple—primarily to feed livestock. Is anything like this kind of productivity in the cards?

Maybe. From 1961 to 1994 global production of food doubled. Global output of grain rose from about 630 million tons in 1950 to about 1.8 billion tons in 1992, largely as a result of greater yields. Developing countries from 1974 to 1994 increased wheat yields per acre by almost 100 percent, corn yields by 72 percent, and rice yields by 52 percent. "The generation of farmers on the land in 1950 was the first in history to double the production of food," the Worldwatch Institute has reported. "By 1984, they had outstripped population growth enough to raise per capita grain output an unprecedented 40 percent." From a two-year period ending in 1981 to a two-year period ending in 1990 the real prices of basic foods fell 38 percent on world markets, according to a 1992 United Nations report. Prices for food have continually decreased since the end of the eighteenth century, when Thomas Malthus argued that rapid population growth must lead to mass starvation by exceeding the carrying capacity of the earth.

Farmers worldwide could double the acreage in production, but this should not be necessary. Better seeds, more irrigation, multi-cropping, and additional use of fertilizer could greatly increase agricultural yields in the developing world, which are now generally only half those in the industrialized countries. It is biologically possible to raise yields of rice to about seven tons per acre—about four times the current average in the developing world. Super strains of cassava, a potato-like root crop eaten by millions of Africans, promise to increase yields tenfold. American farmers can also do better. In a good year, such as 1994, Iowa corn growers average about 3.5 tons per acre, but farmers more than double that yield in National Corn Growers Association competitions.

In drier parts of the world the scarcity of fresh water presents the greatest challenge to agriculture. But the problem is regional, not global. Fortunately, as Lester Brown, of the Worldwatch Institute, points out, "there are vast opportunities for increasing water efficiency" in arid regions, ranging from installing better water-delivery systems to planting drought-resistant crops. He adds, "Scientists can help push back the physical frontiers of cropping by developing varieties that are more drought resistant, salt tolerant, and early maturing. The payoff on the first two could be particularly high."

As if in response, Novartis Seeds has announced a program to develop water-efficient and salt-tolerant crops, including genetically engineered varieties of wheat. Researchers in Mexico have announced the development of drought-resistant corn that can boost yields by a third. Biotechnologists are converting annual crops into perennial ones, eliminating the need for yearly planting. They also hope to enable cereal crops to fix their own nitrogen, as legumes do, minimizing the need for fertilizer (genetically engineered nitrogen-fixing bacteria have already been test-marketed to farmers). Commercial varieties of crops such as corn, tomatoes, and potatoes which have been genetically engineered to be resistant to pests and diseases have been approved for field testing in the United States; several are now being sold and planted. A new breed of rice, 25 percent more productive than any currently in use, suggests that the Gene Revolution can take over where the Green Revolution left off. Biotechnology, as the historian Paul Kennedy has written, introduces "an entirely new stage in humankind's attempts to produce more crops and plants."

Biotechnology cannot, however, address the major causes of famine: poverty, trade barriers, corruption, mismanagement, ethnic antagonism, anarchy, war, and male-dominated societies that deprive women of food. Local land depletion, itself a consequence of poverty and institutional failure, is also a factor. Those who are too poor to use sound farming practices are compelled to overexploit the resources on which they depend. As the economist Partha Dasgupta has written, "Population growth, poverty and degradation of local resources often fuel one another." The amount of food in world trade is constrained less by the resource base than by the maldistribution of wealth.

Analysts who believe that the world is running out of resources often argue that famines occur not as a result of political or economic conditions but because there are "too many people." Unfortunately, as the economist Amartya Sen has pointed out, public officials who think in Malthusian terms assume that when absolute levels of food supplies are adequate, famine will not occur. This conviction diverts attention from the actual causes of famine, which has occurred in places where food output kept pace with population growth but people were too destitute to buy it.

We would have run out of food long ago had we tried to supply ourselves entirely by hunting and gathering. Likewise, if we depend on nature's gifts, we will exhaust many of the world's important fisheries. Fortunately, we are learning to cultivate fish as we do other crops. Genetic engineers have designed fish for better flavor and color as well as for faster growth, improved disease resistance, and other traits. Two farmed species— silver carp and grass carp—already rank among the ten most-consumed fish worldwide. A specially bred tilapia, known as the "aquatic chicken," takes six months to grow to a harvestable size of about one and a half pounds.

Aquaculture produced more than 16 million tons of fish in 1993; capacity has expanded over the past decade at an annual rate of 10 percent by quantity and 14 percent by value. In 1993 fish farms produced 22 percent of all food fish consumed in the world and 90 percent of all oysters sold. The World Bank reports that aquaculture could provide 40 percent of all fish consumed and more than half the value of fish harvested within the next fifteen years.

Salmon ranching and farming provide examples of the growing efficiency of aquacultural production. Norwegian salmon farms alone produce 400 million pounds a year. A biotech firm in Waltham, Massachusetts, has applied for government approval to commercialize salmon genetically engineered to grow four to six times as fast as their naturally occurring cousins. As a 1994 article in *Sierra* magazine noted. "There is so much salmon currently available that the supply exceeds demand, and prices to fishermen have fallen dramatically."

For those who lament the decline of natural fisheries and the human communities that grew up with them, the successes of aquaculture may offer no consolation. In the Pacific Northwest, for example, overfishing in combination with dams and habitat destruction has reduced the wild salmon population by 80 percent. Wild salmon—but not their bio-engineered aquacultural cousins—contribute to the cultural identity and sense of place of the Northwest. When wild salmon disappear, so will some of the region's history, character, and pride. What is true of wild salmon is also true of whales, dolphins, and other magnificent creatures—as they lose their economic importance, their aesthetic and moral worth becomes all the more evident. Economic considerations pull in one direction, moral considerations in the other. This conflict colors all our battles over the environment.

The transition from hunting and gathering to farming, which is changing the fishing industry, has taken place more slowly in forestry. Still there is no sign of a timber famine. In the United States forests now provide the largest harvests in history, and there is more forested U.S. area today than there was in 1920. Bill McKibben has observed in these pages that the eastern United States, which loggers and farmers in the eighteenth and nineteenth centuries nearly denuded of trees, has become reforested during this century (see "An Explosion of Green," April, 1995, *Atlantic*). One reason is that farms reverted to woods. Another is that machinery replaced animals; each draft animal required two or three cleared acres for pasture.

Natural reforestation is likely to continue as biotechnology makes areas used for logging more productive. According to Roger Sedjo, a respected forestry expert, advances in tree farming, if implemented widely, would permit the world to meet its entire demand for industrial wood using just 200 million acres of plantations—an area equal to only five percent of current forest land. As less land is required for commercial tree production, more natural forests may be protected—as they should be, for aesthetic, ethical, and spiritual reasons.

Often natural resources are so plentiful and therefore inexpensive that they undercut the necessary transition to technological alternatives. If the U.S. government did not protect wild forests from commercial exploitation, the timber industry would have little incentive to invest in tree plantations, where it can multiply yields by a factor of ten and take advantage of the results of genetic research. Only by investing in plantation silviculture can North American forestry fend off price competition from rapidly developing tree plantations in the Southern Hemisphere. Biotechnology-based silviculture can in the near future be expected to underprice "extractive" forestry worldwide. In this decade China will plant about 150 million acres of trees; India now plants four times the area it harvests commercially.

The expansion of fish and tree farming confirms the belief held by Peter Drucker and other management experts that our economy depends far more on the progress of technology than on the exploitation of nature. Although raw materials will always be necessary, knowledge has become the essential factor in the production of goods and services. "Where there is effective management," Drucker has written, "that is, application of knowledge to knowledge, we can always obtain the other resources." If we assume, along with Drucker and others, that resource scarcities do not exist or are easily averted, it is hard to see how economic theory, which after all concerns scarcity, provides the conceptual basis for valuing the environment. The reasons to preserve nature are ethical more often than they are economic.

MISCONCEPTION NO. 3:
WE ARE RUNNING OUT OF ENERGY

Probably the most persistent worries about resource scarcity concern energy. "The supply of fuels and other natural resources is becoming the limiting factor constraining the rate of economic growth," a group of experts proclaimed in 1986. They predicted the exhaustion of domestic oil and gas supplies by 2020 and, within a few decades, "major energy shortages as well as food shortages in the world."

Contrary to these expectations, no global shortages of hydrocarbon fuels are in sight. "One sees no immediate danger of 'running out' of energy in a global sense," writes John P. Holdren, a professor of environmental policy at Harvard University. According to Holdren, reserves of oil and natural gas will last seventy to a hundred years if exploited at 1990 rates. (This does not take into account huge deposits of oil shale, heavy oils, and gas from unconventional sources.) He concludes that "running out of energy resources in any global sense is not what the energy problem is all about."

The global energy problem has less to do with depleting resources than with controlling pollutants. Scientists generally agree that gases, principally carbon dioxide, emitted in the combustion of hydrocarbon fuels can build up in and warm the atmosphere by trapping sunlight. Since carbon dioxide enhances photosynthetic activity, plants to some extent absorb the carbon dioxide we produce. In 1995 researchers reported in *Science* that vegetation in the Northern Hemisphere in 1992 and 1993 converted into trees and other plant tissue 3.5 billion tons of carbon—more than half the carbon produced by the burning of hydrocarbon fuels worldwide.

However successful this and other feedback mechanisms may be in slowing the processes of global warming, a broad scientific consensus, reflected in a 1992 international treaty, has emerged for stabilizing and then decreasing emissions of carbon dioxide and other "greenhouse" gases. This goal is well within the technological reach of the United States and other industrialized countries. Amory Lovins, among others, has described commercially available technologies that can "support present or greatly expanded worldwide economic activity while stabilizing global climate—and saving money." He observes that "even very large expansions in population and industrial activity need not be energy-constrained."

Lovins and other environmentalists contend that pollution-free energy from largely untapped sources is available in amounts exceeding our needs. Geothermal energy—which makes use of heat from the earth's core—is theoretically accessible through drilling technology in the United States in amounts thousands of times as great as the amount of energy contained in domestic coal reserves. Tidal energy is also promising. Analysts who study solar power generally agree with Lester Brown of the Worldwatch Institute, that "technologies are ready to begin building a world energy system largely powered by solar resources." In the future these and other renewable energy sources may be harnessed to the nation's system of storing and delivering electricity.

Last year Joseph Romm and Charles Curtis described in these pages advances in photovoltaic cells (which convert sunlight into electricity), fuel cells (which convert the hydrogen in fuels directly to electricity and heat, producing virtually no pollution), and wind power ("Mideast Oil Forever?" April, 1996, *Atlantic*). According to these authors, genetically engineered organisms used to ferment organic matter could, with further research and development, bring down the costs of ethanol and other environmentally friendly "biofuels" to make them competitive with gasoline.

Environmentalists who, like Amory Lovins, believe that our economy can grow and still reduce greenhouse gases emphasize not only that we should be able to move to renewable forms of energy but also that we can use fossil fuels more efficiently. Some improvements are already evident. In developed countries the energy intensity of production—the amount of fuel burned per dollar of economic output—has been decreasing by about two percent a year.

From 1973 to 1986, for example, energy consumption in the United States remained virtually flat while economic production grew by almost 40 percent. Compared with Germany or Japan, this is a poor showing. The Japanese, who tax fuel more heavily than we do, use only half as much energy as the United States per unit of economic output. (Japanese environmental regulations are also generally stricter than ours; if anything, this has improved the competitiveness of Japanese industry.) The United States still wastes hundreds of billions of dollars annually in energy inefficiency. By becoming as energy-efficient as Japan, the United States could expand its economy and become more competitive internationally.

If so many opportunities exist for saving energy and curtailing pollution, why have we not seized them? One reason is that low fossil-fuel prices remove incentives for fuel efficiency and for converting to other energy sources. Another reason is that government subsidies for fossil fuels and nuclear energy amounted to many billions of dollars a year during the 1980s, whereas support for renewables dwindled to $114 million in 1989, a time when it had been proposed for near elimination. "Lemon socialism," a vast array of subsidies and barriers to trade, protects politically favored technologies, however inefficient, dangerous, filthy, or obsolete. "At heart, the major obstacles standing in the way [of a renewable-energy economy] are not technical in nature," the energy consultant Michael Brower has written, "but concern the laws, regulations, incentives, public attitudes, and other factors that make up the energy market."

In response to problems of climate change, the World Bank and other international organizations have recognized the importance of transferring advanced energy technologies to the developing world. Plainly, this will take a large investment of capital, particularly in education. Yet the "alternative for developing countries," according to José Goldemberg, a former Environment Minister of Brazil, "would be to remain at a dismally low level of development which . . . would aggravate the problems of sustainability."

Technology transfer can hasten sound economic development worldwide. Many environmentalists, however, argue that economies cannot expand without exceeding the physical limits nature sets—for example, with respect to energy. These environmentalists, who regard increasing affluence as a principal cause of environmental degradation, call for economic retrenchment and retraction—a small economy for a small earth. With Paul Ehrlich, they reject "the hope that development can greatly increase the size of the economic pie and pull many more people out of poverty." This hope is "basically a humane idea," Ehrlich has written, "made insane by the constraints nature places on human activity."

In developing countries, however, a no-growth economy "will deprive entire populations of access to better living conditions and lead to even more deforestation and land degradation," as Goldemberg warns. Moreover, citizens of developed countries are likely to resist an energy policy that they associate with poverty, discomfort, sacrifice, and pain. Technological pessimism, then, may not be the best option for environmentalists. It is certainly not the only one.

MISCONCEPTION NO. 4:
THE NORTH EXPLOITS THE SOUTH

William Reilly, when he served as administrator of the Environmental Protection Agency in the Bush Administration, encountered a persistent criticism at international meetings on the environment. "The problem for the world's environment is your consumption, not our population," delegates from the developing world told him. Some of these delegates later took Reilly aside. "The North buys too little from the South," they confided. "The real problem is too little demand for our exports."

The delegates who told Reilly that the North consumes too little of what the South produces have a point, "With a few exceptions (notably petroleum)," a report from the World Resources Institute observes, "most of the natural resources consumed in the United States are from domestic sources." Throughout the 1980s the United States and Canada were the world's leading exporters of raw materials. The United States consistently leads the world in farm exports, running huge agricultural trade surpluses. The share of raw materials used in the North that it buys from the South stands at a thirty-year low and continues to decline; industrialized nations trade largely among themselves. The World Resources Institute recently reported that "the United States is largely self-sufficient in natural resources." Again, excepting petroleum, bauxite (from which aluminum is made), "and a few other industrial minerals; its material flows are almost entirely internal."

Sugar provides an instructive example of how the North excludes—rather than exploits—the resources of the South. Since 1796 the United States has protected domestic sugar against imports. American sugar growers, in part as a reward for large contributions to political campaigns, have long enjoyed a system of quotas and prohibitive tariffs against foreign competition. American consumers paid about three times world prices for sugar in the 1980s, enriching a small cartel of U.S. growers. *Forbes* magazine has estimated that a single family, the Fanjuls, of Palm Beach, reaps more than $65 million a year as a result of quotas for sugar.

The sugar industry in Florida, which is larger than that in any other state, makes even less sense environmentally than economically. It depends on a publicly built system of canals, levees, and pumping stations. Fertilizer from the sugarcane fields chokes the Everglades. Sugar growers, under a special exemption from labor laws, import Caribbean laborers to do the grueling and poorly paid work of cutting cane.

As the United States tightened sugar quotas (imports fell from 6.2 to 1.5 million tons annually from 1977 to 1987), the Dominican Republic and other nations with climates ideal for growing cane experienced political turmoil and economic collapse. Many farmers in Latin America, however, did well by switching from sugar to coca, which is processed into cocaine—perhaps the only high-value imported crop for which the United States is not developing a domestic substitute.

Before the Second World War the United States bought 40 percent of its vegetable oils from developing countries. After the war the United States protected its oilseed markets—for example, by establishing price supports for soybeans. Today the United States is one of the world's leading exporters of oil and oilseeds, although it still imports palm and coconut oils to obtain laurate, an ingredient in soap, shampoo, and detergents. Even this form of "exploitation" will soon cease. In 1994 farmers in Georgia planted the first commercial acreage of a high-laurate canola, genetically engineered by Calgene, a biotechnology firm.

About 100,000 Kenyans make a living on small plots of land growing pyrethrum flowers, the source of a comparatively environmentally safe insecticide of which the United States has been the largest importer. The U.S. Department of Commerce, however, awarded $1.2 million to a biotechnology firm to engineer pyrethrum genetically. Industrial countries will soon be able to synthesize all the pyrethrum they need and undersell Kenyan farmers.

An article in *Foreign Policy* in December of 1995 observed that the biotechnological innovations that create "substitutes for everything from vanilla to cocoa and coffee threaten to eliminate the livelihood of millions of Third World agricultural workers." Vanilla cultured in laboratories costs a fifth as much as vanilla extracted from beans, and thus jeopardizes the livelihood of tens of thousands of vanilla farmers in Madagascar. In the past, farms produced agricultural commodities and factories processed them. In the future, factories may "grow" as well as process many of the most valuable commodities—or the two functions will become one. As one plant scientist has said, "We have to stop thinking of these things as plant cells, and start thinking of them as new microorganisms, with all the potential that implies"—meaning, for instance, that the cells could be made to grow in commercially feasible quantities in laboratories, not fields.

The North not only balks at buying sugar and other crops from developing countries; it also dumps its excess agricultural commodities, especially grain, on them. After the Second World War, American farmers, using price supports left over from the New Deal, produced vast wheat surpluses, which the United States exported at concessionary prices to Europe and then the Third World. These enormous transfers of cereals to the South, institutionalized during the 1950s and 1960s by U.S. food aid, continued during the 1970s and 1980s, as the United States and the European Community vied for markets, each outdoing the other in subsidizing agricultural exports.

Grain imports from the United States "created food dependence within two decades in countries which had been mostly self-sufficient in food at the end of World War II," the sociologist Harriet Friedmann has written. Tropical countries soon matched the grain gluts of the North with their own surpluses of cocoa, coffee, tea, bananas, and other export commodities. Accordingly, prices for these commodities collapsed as early as 1970, catching developing nations in a scissors. As Friedmann describes it, "One blade was food import dependency. The other blade was declining revenues for traditional exports of tropical crops."

It might be better for the environment if the North exchanged the crops for which it is ecologically suited—wheat, for example—for crops easily grown in the South, such as coffee, cocoa, palm oil, and tea. Contrary to common belief, these tropical export crops—which grow on trees and bushes, providing canopy and continuous root structures to protect the soil—are less damaging to the soil than are traditional staples such as cereals and root crops. Better markets for tropical crops could help developing nations to employ their rural populations and to protect their natural resources. Allen Hammond, of the World Resources Institute, points out that "if poor nations cannot export anything else, they will export their misery—in the form of drugs, diseases, terrorism, migration, and environmental degradation."

Peasants in less-developed nations often confront intractable poverty, an entrenched land-tenure system, and a lack of infrastructure; they have little access to markets, education, or employment. Many of the rural poor, according to the environmental consultant Norman Myers, "have no option but to over-exploit environmental resource stocks in order to survive"—for example, by "increasingly encroaching onto tropical forests among other low-potential lands." These poorest of the poor "are causing as much natural-resource depletion as the other three billion developing-world people put together."

Myers observes that traditional indigenous farmers in tropical forests moved from place to place without seriously damaging the ecosystem. The principal agents of tropical deforestation are refugees from civil war and rural poverty, who are forced to eke out a living on marginal lands. Activities such as road building, logging, and commercial agriculture have barely increased in tropical forests since the early 1980s, according to Myers; slash-and-burn farming by displaced peasants accounts for far more deforestation—roughly three fifths of the total. Its impact is fast expanding. Most of the wood from trees harvested in tropical forests—that is, those not cleared for farms—is used locally for fuel. The likeliest path to protecting the rain forest is through economic development that enables peasants to farm efficiently, on land better suited to farming than to forest.

Many have argued that economic activity, affluence, and growth automatically lead to resource depletion, environmental deterioration, and ecological collapse. Yet greater productivity and prosperity—which is what economists mean by growth—have become prerequisite for controlling urban pollution and protecting sensitive ecological systems such as rain forests. Otherwise, destitute people who are unable to acquire food and fuel will create pollution and destroy forests. Without economic growth, which also correlates with lower fertility, the environmental and population problems of the South will only get worse. For impoverished countries facing environmental disaster, economic growth may be the one thing that is sustainable.

WHAT IS WRONG WITH CONSUMPTION?

Many of us who attended college in the 1960s and 1970s took pride in how little we owned. We celebrated our freedom when we could fit all our possessions—mostly a stereo—into the back of a Beetle. Decades later, middle-aged and middle-class, many of us have accumulated an appalling amount of stuff. Piled high with gas grills, lawn mowers, excess furniture, bicycles, children's toys, garden implements, lumber, cinder blocks, ladders, lawn and leaf bags stuffed with memorabilia, and boxes yet to be unpacked from the last move, the two-car garages beside our suburban homes are too full to accommodate the family minivan. The quantity of resources, particularly energy, we waste and the quantity of trash we throw away (recycling somewhat eases our conscience) add to our consternation.

Even if predictions of resource depletion and ecological collapse are mistaken, it seems that they *should* be true, to punish us for our sins. We are distressed by the suffering of others, the erosion of the ties of community, family, and friendship, and the loss of the beauty and spontaneity of the natural world. These concerns reflect the most traditional and fundamental of American religious and cultural values.

Simple compassion instructs us to give to relieve the misery of others. There is a lot of misery worldwide to relieve. But as bad as the situation is, it is improving. In 1960 nearly 70 percent of the people in the world lived at or below the subsistence level. Today less than a third do, and the number enjoying fairly satisfactory conditions (as measured by the United Nations Human Development Index) rose from 25 percent in 1960 to 60 percent in 1992. Over the twenty-five years before 1992 average per capita consumption in developing countries increased 75 percent in real terms. The pace of improvements is also increasing. In developing countries in that period, for example, power generation and the number of telephone lines per capita doubled, while the number of households with access to clean water grew by half.

What is worsening is the discrepancy in income between the wealthy and the poor. Although world income measured in real terms has increased by 700 percent since the Second World War, the wealthiest people have absorbed most of the gains. Since 1960 the richest fifth of the world's people have seen their share of the world's income increase from 70 to 85 percent. Thus one fifth of the world's population possesses much more than four fifths of the world's wealth, while the share held by all others has correspondingly fallen; that of the world's poorest 20 percent has declined from 2.3 to 1.4 percent.

Writing in these pages, Benjamin Barber ("Jihad vs. McWorld," March, 1992, *Atlantic*) described market forces that "mesmerize the world with fast music, fast computers, and fast food—with MTV, Macintosh, and McDonald's, pressing nations into one commercially homogeneous global network: one McWorld tied together by technology, ecology, communications, and commerce." Affluent citizens of South Korea, Thailand, India, Brazil, Mexico, and many other rapidly developing nations have joined with Americans, Europeans, Japanese, and others to form an urban and cosmopolitan international society. Those who participate in this global network are less and less beholden to local customs and traditions. Meanwhile, ethnic, tribal, and other cultural groups that do not dissolve into McWorld often define themselves in opposition to it—fiercely asserting their ethnic, religious, and territorial identities.

The imposition of a market economy on traditional cultures in the name of development—for example, the insistence that everyone produce and consume more—can dissolve the ties to family, land, community, and place on which indigenous peoples traditionally rely for their security. Thus development projects intended to relieve the poverty of indigenous peoples may, by causing the loss of cultural identity, engender the very powerlessness they aim to remedy. Pope Paul VI, in the encyclical *Populorum Progressio* (1967), described the tragic dilemma confronting indigenous peoples: "either to preserve traditional beliefs and structures and reject social progress; or to embrace foreign technology and foreign culture, and reject ancestral traditions with their wealth of humanism."

The idea that everything is for sale and nothing is sacred—that all values are subjective—undercuts our own moral and cultural commitments, not just those of tribal and traditional communities. No one has written a better critique of the assault that commerce makes on the quality of our lives than Thoreau provides in *Walden*. The cost of a thing, according to Thoreau, is not what the market will bear but what the individual must bear because of it: it is "the amount of what I will call life which is required to be exchanged for it, immediately or in the long run."

Many observers point out that as we work harder and consume more, we seem to enjoy our lives less. We are always in a rush—a "Saint Vitus' dance," as Thoreau called it. Idleness is suspect. Americans today spend less time with their families, neighbors, and friends than they did in the 1950s. Juliet B. Schor, an economist at Harvard University, argues that "Americans are literally working themselves to death." A fancy car, video equipment, or a complex computer program can exact a painful cost in the form of maintenance, upgrading, and repair. We are possessed by our possessions; they are often harder to get rid of than to acquire.

That money does not make us happier, once our basic needs are met is a common place overwhelmingly confirmed by sociological evidence. Paul Wachtel, who teaches social psychology at the City University of New York, has concluded that bigger incomes "do not yield an increase in feelings of satisfaction or well-being, at least for populations who are above a poverty or subsistence level." This cannot be explained simply by the fact that people have to work harder to earn more money: even those who hit jackpots in lotteries often report that their lives are not substantially happier as a result. Well-being depends upon health, membership in a community in which one feels secure, friends, faith, family, love, and virtues that money cannot buy. Robert Lane, a political scientist at Yale University, using the concepts of economics, has written, "If 'utility' has anything to do with happiness, above the poverty line the long-term marginal utility of money is almost zero."

Economists in earlier times predicted that wealth would not matter to people once they attained a comfortable standard of living. "In ease of body and peace of mind, all the different ranks of life are nearly upon a level," wrote Adam Smith, the eighteenth-century English advocate of the free market. In the 1930s the British economist John Maynard Keynes argued that after a period of great expansion further accumulation of wealth would no longer improve personal well-being. Subsequent economists, however, found that even after much of the industrial world had attained the levels of wealth Keynes thought were sufficient, people still wanted more. From this they inferred that wants are insatiable.

Perhaps this is true. But the insatiability of wants and desires poses a difficulty for standard economic theory, which posits that humanity's single goal is to increase or maximize wealth. If wants increase as fast as income grows, what purpose can wealth serve?

Critics often attack standard economic theory on the ground that economic growth is "unsustainable." We are running out of resources, they say: we court ecological disaster. Whether or not growth is sustainable, there is little reason to think that once people attain a decent standard of living, continued growth is desirable. The economist Robert H. Nelson recently wrote in the journal *Ecological Economics* that it is no longer possible for most people to believe that economic progress will "solve all the problems of mankind, spiritual as well as material." As long as the debate over sustainability is framed in terms of the physical limits to growth rather than the moral purpose of it, mainstream economic theory will have the better of the argument. If the debate were framed in moral or social terms, the result might well be otherwise.

MAKING A PLACE FOR NATURE

According to Thoreau, "a man's relation to Nature must come very near to a personal one." For environmentalists in the tradition of Thoreau and John Muir, stewardship is a form of fellowship; although we must use nature, we do not value it primarily for the economic purposes it serves. We take our bearings from the natural world—our sense of time from its days and seasons, our sense of place from the character of a landscape and the particular plants and animals native to it. An intimacy with nature ends our isolation in the world. We know where we belong, and we can find the way home.

In defending old-growth forests, wetlands, or species we make our best arguments when we think of nature chiefly in aesthetic and moral terms. Rather than having the courage of our moral and cultural convictions, however, we too often rely on economic arguments for protecting nature, in the process attributing to natural objects more instrumental value than they have. By claiming that a threatened species may harbor lifesaving drugs, for example, we impute to that species an economic value or a price much greater than it fetches in a market. When we make the prices come out right, we rescue economic theory but not necessarily the environment.

There is no credible argument, moreover, that all or even most of the species we are concerned to protect are essential to the functioning of the ecological systems on which we depend. (If whales went extinct, for example, the seas would not fill up with krill.) David Ehrenfeld, a biologist at Rutgers University, makes this point in relation to the vast ecological changes we have already survived. "Even a mighty dominant like the American chestnut," Ehrenfeld has written, "extending over half a continent, all but disappeared without bringing the eastern deciduous forest down with it." Ehrenfeld points out that the species most likely to be endangered are those the biosphere is least likely to miss. "Many of these species were never common or ecologically influential; by no stretch of the imagination can we make them out to be vital cogs in the ecological machine."

Species may be profoundly important for cultural and spiritual reasons, however. Consider again the example of the wild salmon, whose habitat is being destroyed by hydroelectric dams along the Columbia River. Although this loss is unimportant to the economy overall (there is no shortage of salmon), it is of the greatest significance to the Amerindian tribes that have traditionally subsisted on wild salmon, and to the region as a whole. By viewing local flora and fauna as a sacred heritage—by recognizing their intrinsic value—we discover who we are rather than what we want. On moral and cultural grounds society might be justified in making great economic sacrifices—removing hydroelectric dams, for example—to protect remnant populations of the Snake River sockeye, even if, as critics complain, hundreds or thousands of dollars are spent for every fish that is saved.

Even those plants and animals that do not define places possess enormous intrinsic value and are worth preserving for their own sake. What gives these creatures value lies in their histories, wonderful in themselves, rather than in any use to which they can be put. The biologist E. O. Wilson elegantly takes up this theme: "Every kind of organism has reached this moment in time by threading one needle after another, throwing up brilliant artifices to survive and reproduce against nearly impossible odds." Every plant or animal evokes not just sympathy but also reverence and wonder in those who know it.

In *Earth in the Balance* (1992) Al Gore, then a senator, wrote, "We have become so successful at controlling nature that we have lost our connection to it." It is all too easy Gore wrote, "to regard the earth as a collection of 'resources' having an intrinsic value no larger than their usefulness at the moment." The question before us is not whether we are going to run out of resources. It is whether economics is the appropriate context for thinking about environmental policy.

Even John Stuart Mill, one of the principal authors of utilitarian philosophy, recognized that the natural world has great intrinsic and not just instrumental value. More than a century ago, as England lost its last truly wild places, Mill condemned a world

> with nothing left to the spontaneous activity of nature; with every rood of land brought into cultivation, which is capable of growing food for human beings; every flowery waste or natural pasture ploughed up; all quadrupeds or birds which are not domesticated for man's use exterminated as his rivals for food, every hedgerow or superfluous tree rooted out, and scarcely a place left where a wild shrub or flower could grow without being eradicated as a weed in the name of improved agriculture.

The world has the wealth and the resources to provide everyone the opportunity to live a decent life. We consume too much when market relationships displace the bonds of community, compassion, culture, and place. We consume too much when consumption becomes an end in itself and makes us lose affection and reverence for the natural world.

38

⋈ No Middle Way ⋈ on the Environment: A Response to Sagoff

PAUL R. EHRLICH, GRETCHEN C. DAILY, SCOTT C. DAILY, NORMAN MYERS, AND JAMES SALZMAN

Paul R. Ehrlich, Gretchen C. Daily, Scott C. Daily, Norman Myers, and James Salzman are all environmental scientists.

Laypeople frequently assume that in a political dispute the truth must lie somewhere in the middle, and they are often right. In a scientific dispute, though, such an assumption is usually wrong. Copernicus, in *De Revolutionibus Orbium Coelestium* (1543), showed (to the distress of the establishment) that the earth both rotated on its axis and, along with the other planets, revolved around the sun. The controversy about what revolved where was not resolved by a compromise that had the earth stationary on its axis but circling the sun. Pasteur put an end to the debate over whether some organisms could be produced by "spontaneous generation" by showing that bacteria descended from other bacteria. The answer wasn't a compromise in which mice couldn't be spontaneously generated whereas flies and microbes could.

There has long been a dispute between "cornucopians" and scientists over whether too much consumption in rich countries poses a serious threat to the global environment. In his recent article regarding the state of our planet, "Do We Consume Too Much?" (June *Atlantic*), Mark Sagoff fell headlong into the truth-in-the-middle trap by asserting that "neither side has it right." He has done a disservice to the public by promoting once again the dangerous idea that technological fixes will solve the human predicament.

But the debate goes well beyond Sagoff. In challenging his views, we are also challenging a whole current of opinion based on a sophistic application of a political model (in which split-the-difference outcomes are the rule) to the environment.

Sagoff argues that concern over the depletion of natural resources and the impact of their current levels of use is misplaced, and that technological innovation will remedy any problems that do arise. This view certainly is not shared by the scientific community. For example, the 1992 "World Scientists' Warning to Humanity" (signed by more than 1,500 leading scientists, including more than half of all living Nobel laureates in the sciences) stated that "human beings and the natural world are on a collision course" and that people in developed nations "must greatly reduce their over-consumption, if we are to reduce pressures on resources and the global environment."

A 1993 statement on world population issued by fifty-eight scientific academies dealt with consumption in a similar vein. The academies, which include the U.S. National Academy, the British Royal Society, the French, German, Swedish, Russian, and Indian Academies, and the Third World Academy, represent the global scientific community. They concluded,

> If all people of the world consumed fossil fuels and other natural resources at the rate now characteristic of developed countries (and with current technologies), this would greatly intensify our already unsustainable demands on the bios-phere. . . . As scientists cognizant of the history of scientific progress and aware of the potential of science for contributing to human welfare, it is our collective judg-ment that continuing population growth poses a great risk to humanity. Furthermore, it is not prudent to rely on science and technology alone to solve problems created by rapid population growth, wasteful resource consumption, and poverty.

Thus the very people who would produce the technological fixes in which Sagoff places such faith do not share his complacency.

Sagoff's thesis rests on a series of basic misconceptions.

MISCONCEPTION NO. 1:
OVERCONSUMPTION IS ONLY A MORAL ISSUE

"It is simply wrong to believe that nature sets physical limits to economic growth." Or, as Sagoff put it at another point, "The idea that increasing consumption will inevitably lead to depletion and scarcity, as plausible as it may seem, is mistaken both in principle and in fact."

This statement, Sagoff's core message, misses the point. Since natural resources are finite, increasing consumption obviously *must* "inevitably lead to depletion and scarcity." Currently there are very large supplies of many mineral resources, including iron and coal. But when they become "depleted" or "scarce" will depend not simply on how much is in the ground but also on the rate at which they can be produced and the amount societies can afford to pay, in standard economic or environmental terms, for their extraction and use.

For most resources, economic and environmental constraints will limit consump-tion while substantial quantities remain. Long before coal disappears, coal production will probably be limited by the lack of atmospheric capacity to absorb safely more carbon dioxide, the greenhouse gas of which coal burning is an especially prolific source. For others, however, global "depletion"—that is, decline to a point where worldwide demand can no longer be met economically—is already on the horizon. Petroleum is a textbook example of such a resource. Ironically, Sagoff cites it as a resource that is increasing in abundance, asserting,

> Raw materials—including energy resources—are generally more abundant and less expensive today than they were twenty years ago. [In the 1970s] economi-cally recoverable world reserves of petroleum stood at 640 billion barrels. Since

that time reserves have *increased* by more than 50 percent, reaching more than 1,000 billion barrels in 1989.

These impressive figures are, unfortunately, figments of the bureaucratic imagination. In an unpublished report Amos Nur, an earth scientist at Stanford University, wrote,

> In 1987 . . . there was a sudden boost of reported crude-oil reserves. It turns out that all of this came from Middle Eastern governments: Iraq, Iran, and a few other countries increased their proven reserves by 250 percent overnight! It was not improved technology or new discoveries that led to this; the governments of those countries simply recalculated the volume of recoverable oil in the fields. So 'proven reserves' are completely unreliable. What *is* reliable in this business is actual production—and in that regard the United States is well over the peak, and the world as a whole is at the peak right now.

Steps can and should be taken to stretch oil supplies; conservation and improved secondary recovery (extracting oil that remains after standard pumping operations) are the most promising. But conservation is often politically difficult to sell (especially when prices are kept low), and secondary recovery is expensive and can require large amounts of water, another resource in short supply. In China water is already being forcibly withheld from farmers along the Yellow River in order to flush residual oil from the wells of the Shingle Oil Field Company. But, as Nur emphasizes, even though the last drops of petroleum will never be extracted from the earth, "the supply of oil is truly finite."

That finitude may actually be a good thing, because—as Sagoff observes, quoting our colleague John Holdren, a professor of environmental policy at Harvard University—the overall problem with energy is not mobilizing enough of it but containing the environmental consequences of its use. Sagoff is right that solar and other technologies hold great promise as replacements for the fossil fuels that may (or, if we're lucky, may not) be pushing the world toward catastrophically rapid climatic change. But he seems oblivious of the timetable for the large-scale replacement of energy technologies. Even if a widespread deployment of new technologies began today, society's dangerous dependence on fossil fuels could not be significantly reduced for many decades; and there is no sign of such deployment. Furthermore, no way of mobilizing energy is free of environmentally damaging side effects, and the uses to which energy from any source is put usually have negative environmental side effects as well. Bulldozers that ran on hydrogen generated by solar power could still destroy wetlands and old-growth forests.

MISCONCEPTION NO. 2: "IN DEFENDING OLD-GROWTH FORESTS, WETLANDS, OR SPECIES WE MAKE OUR BEST ARGUMENTS WHEN WE THINK OF NATURE CHIEFLY IN AESTHETIC AND MORAL TERMS"

Few environmental scientists would dispute the importance of aesthetic and moral arguments in defense of biodiversity—the plants, animals, and microorganisms with which we share the earth. But few indeed would assert that these are the "best" arguments, in light of the materialistic, growth-oriented philosophy that now dominates the planet.

The idea that technology can fully substitute for natural life-support systems recently underwent a damning test in the first Biosphere 2 "mission." Eight people moved into a 3.15-acre closed ecosystem, intending to stay for two years. The $200-million–plus habitat featured agricultural land, "wetlands," "rain forest," "desert," "savanna," and even a mini-ocean with coral reefs. A sample of biodiversity thought adequate to keep the system functioning was included, and the system was designed to supply the "biospherians" with all basic material needs and more. But comfort was short-lived, and the experiment ended early in failure: atmospheric oxygen concentration had dropped to 14 percent (a level typical of elevations of 17,500 feet); carbon dioxide spiked erratically; nitrous-oxide concentrations rose to levels that can impair brain function; nineteen of twenty-five vertebrate species went extinct; all pollinators went extinct, thereby dooming to eventual extinction most of the plant species; aggressive vines and algal mats overgrew other vegetation and polluted the water; crazy ants, cockroaches, and katydids ran rampant. Not even heroic efforts on the part of the system's desperate inhabitants could suffice to make the system viable.

What went wrong? Evidently more was involved than aesthetic or moral arguments for having the right components of nature in the closed system of Biosphere 2. This is also true in the closed system of the earth as a whole. The biospherians learned a basic lesson the hard way: humanity derives a wide array of crucial economic and life-support benefits from biodiversity and the natural ecosystems in which it exists. Many of these benefits are captured in the term "ecosystem services," which refers to the wide range of conditions and processes through which natural ecosystems, and the species that are a part of them, sustain and fulfill human life. These services yield ecosystem goods, such as seafood, wild game, forage, timber, biomass fuels, and natural fibers. They also underpin agricultural productivity, the pharmaceutical industry (nine of the top ten pharmaceuticals in the United States are derived from natural sources), and many other aspects of industrial production.

Natural ecosystems perform critical life-support services that make consumption possible and upon which the prosperity of all societies depends. These include the purification of air and water; the mitigation of droughts and floods; the generation and preservation of soils and renewal of their fertility; the detoxification and decomposition of wastes; the pollination of crops and natural vegetation; control of the vast majority of potential agricultural pests; and partial control of climate. This array of services is generated by a complex interplay of natural cycles powered by solar energy and operating across a wide range of space and time scales.

These services operate on such a grand scale, and in such intricate and little-explored ways, that most of them could not be replaced by technology—even if no expense were spared, as Biosphere 2 showed. Ecosystem services are worth trillions of dollars annually, but since they are not traded in economic markets, they do not carry prices. If they did, changes in those prices might serve to alert society to reductions in their supply or to deterioration of the underlying ecological systems that generate them. Moreover, humanity came into being after the underlying systems had been in operation for hundreds of millions to billions of years. Thus it is easy to take ecosystem services for granted and hard to imagine their disruption beyond repair. No one knows precisely which, or approximately how many, species are required to sustain human life; but to say, as Sagoff does, that "there is no credible argument . . . that . . . all or even most of the species we are concerned to protect are essential to the functioning of the ecological systems on which we depend" is dangerously absurd. Until science can say *which* species are essential in the long term, we exterminate *any* at our peril.

Today human activities are driving species extinction at a rate of several species per hour—thousands of times as fast as the rate of evolution of new species. This is akin to popping the rivets out of the airplane your children must fly in. We are entering the first episode of mass extinction in 65 million years—the first ever since human beings came into existence. The consequences for the ecosystem services on which humanity depends could be severe. Recovery from previous mass extinctions—caused by, for example, giant asteroid impacts—took tens of millions of years. Today's mass extinction is driven primarily by the overconsumption of natural habitat and resources, and the toxic by-products of this consumption. The earth could not avoid the path of an asteroid. We can change our consumption patterns.

MISCONCEPTION NO. 3:
PRICE SIGNALS WILL GIVE WARNING OF DISASTERS

Part of Sagoff's complacency stems from his implicit assumption that price is the same thing as cost, and that price signals will therefore warn of any impending problems. This is a confusion that some ecologists, including Paul Ehrlich, shared a quarter century ago, and one that increasing interactions between ecologists and leading economists have long since dispelled. The price of raw materials often declines as, for example, giant corporations push external costs off onto consumers or indigenous peoples who have little choice but to accept them. The tropical hardwood used in an expensive home does not include in its price the loss of biodiversity in a tropical forest or the carbon dioxide added to the atmosphere as waste wood decayed or was burned and as fossil fuels were used to cut, transport, and process the wood. Also absent from the price are the costs incurred by tropical-forest peoples when their environments and ways of life are destroyed.

External costs are a major reason that price signals are unreliable. A good example is the price of gasoline, which carries a social cost of *at least* $4.00 a gallon but is sold to Americans for $1.20. Another source of unreliable price signals is perverse government subsidies. In Mexico City the real cost of water may be as high as a dollar per cubic meter, but the government charges only a tenth of that—simultaneously creating an annual deficit for water services of about $1 billion and hiding the catastrophic state of the city's water supplies. Three separate analyses have estimated that such subsidies cost the global economy some $500–$600 billion annually—as much as the Rio Earth Summit's proposed budget for sustainable development. In other words, if subsidies were eliminated, saving the earth would not need to cost the earth.

MISCONCEPTION NO. 4: SIMPLE EXTRAPOLATION
OF PAST TRENDS PROVIDES A CLEAR VIEW
OF THE FUTURE

Today's situation is wholly unprecedented. Whereas it took our species hundreds of thousands of years to reach a population of 10 million, we are now adding (net) 10 million people to the planet every six weeks. Whereas in the past human impacts on the environment were local, reversible, and escapable through migration, they are now typically global, irreversible, and inescapable.

- Human-induced land degradation inflicted since the end of the Second World War affects about 40 percent of the planet's vegetated land surface, and the rate of degradation is accelerating nearly everywhere, reducing crop yields and posing a serious threat to agriculture.

- Humanity is overpumping (at rates higher than recharge) groundwater stored during the last glacial period by some trillions of gallons a year. Another ice age will be required to refill some depleted aquifers.

- Humanity is using about 50 percent of accessible freshwater runoff globally. New dam construction could increase this accessible runoff by about 10 percent over the next thirty years, but it won't do so fast enough to keep up with population growth. The number of people is projected to increase by more than 30 percent during that period.

- The burning of fossil fuels, deforestation, paddy rice production, nitrogen-based fertilization, and other routine human activities have possibly changed the composition of the atmosphere enough to induce a devastating pace and magnitude of climate change.

Our generation is supporting itself on a one-time depletion of natural capital. In his optimistic assessment of future food-production possibilities, Sagoff conveniently ignores the depletion of these critical capital inputs into agriculture: biodiversity, ecosystem services, productive land, irrigation water, and favorable weather.

MISCONCEPTION NO. 5: WHAT'S BIOLOGICALLY, PHYSICALLY, ECONOMICALLY, OR POLITICALLY POSSIBLE AT ONE PLACE OR SCALE IS PROBABLE AT OTHER PLACES AND SCALES

Sagoff holds out a few technological advances from around the globe, such as genetically engineered fish, as environmental silver bullets. Although advances in biotechnology are important, proposed dietary or technological fixes for the *world* food problem have proved to be chimeras. We are not feeding the world on plankton, algae farmed on sewage ponds, single-cell proteins from microorganisms grown on petroleum, or meat from whales raised in atolls. The world as a whole has not approached the agricultural productivity of Iowa—nor will it, because the necessary soil quality, climate, and expertise, among other prerequisites, are not universally available.

Technological fixes for environmental problems have a mixed record, just as do fixes for food problems. They often work locally or temporarily but prove unworkable on regional or global scales or over the long term. Dumping pollutants in the Mississippi River can solve the disposal problems of those people who are living upstream while creating an impossible mess for the residents of New Orleans. Air-pollution "control" devices have also often turned out to be a means of shifting pollution to some other place or population. Tall smokestacks tend to convert local air pollution into regional acid rain. Smokestack scrubbers produce cleaner air in exchange for toxic sludge. Can technology reduce the environmental impacts of modern society? Absolutely—but to regard it as the answer to the threats detailed above ignores the record to date. Remember that the target is moving. If the level of consumption in the developing world should rise to that of North America—which is the trend—under current technologies we would require two additional earths to meet everyone's food and timber needs.

Above all, one must recognize that what is technically and economically feasible is often sociopolitically impossible. People consider many technological "solutions" (the widespread use of nuclear power, for example) to be unacceptable, often because they do not trust the political entities that propose to manage the technologies safely for the benefit of all. Many ordinary citizens have come to the same conclusion that the distinguished demographer Nathan Keyfitz claimed as a finding of the social sciences: "If we have one piece of empirically backed knowledge, it is that bad policies are widespread and persistent."

MISCONCEPTION NO. 6: THE NORTH DOESN'T EXPLOIT THE SOUTH AND ECONOMIC GROWTH SAVES THE ENVIRONMENT

There is much more to exploitation than is subsumed under trade in natural resources. Exploitation is a complex subject, but in a world in which huge international disparities in wealth and power persist, the rich-poor gap is increasing. In 1960 the ratio of the income of the richest 20 percent of humanity to that of the poorest 20 percent was 30:1; according to the United Nations *Human Development Report 1997,* it was nearly 80:1 in 1994. And the rich show pathetically little interest in closing that gap. Since 1950 the richest fifth of humankind has doubled its per capita consumption of energy, meat, timber, steel, and copper, and quadrupled its car ownership, greatly increasing global emissions of CFCs and greenhouse gases, accelerating tropical deforestation, and intensifying other environmental impacts. The poorest fifth of humankind has increased its per capita consumption hardly at all. Indeed, those in the poorest fifth average a cash income of less than a dollar a day, and those in the next fifth average only three dollars a day. This means that 40 percent of humankind accounts for a mere 6.5 percent of the world's income.

With only 4.5 percent of the world's population, the United States uses about 25 percent of the earth's resources and contributes more than 20 percent of global emissions of carbon dioxide—the atmospheric pollutant that accounts for about half of global warming. In 1996 the United States contributed one fifth more carbon to everybody's atmosphere than did China, which is 4.5 times as populous. The poor will be affected by global warming whether they are major or minor sources of carbon dioxide. The winds carry no passports.

Promoting intensive cash-crop industrial farming techniques, in which the overuse of fertilizers and the broadcast use of pesticides replace more ecologically sound food-crop agriculture, is another form of exploitation—and one of the chief generators of the displaced peasants that Sagoff cites as a major cause of deforestation. But in Indonesia and Malaysia, the two most forested countries of Southeast Asia, where forests are disappearing fastest, logging by large corporations and clearing to create oil-palm plantations are the prime causes of deforestation. The logging is pursued in no small part to meet rich-world demand for specialty hardwoods at prices that are very far from reflecting the costs entailed. Recently the independent London-based Environmental Investigation Agency asserted that the $100 billion timber industry is "out of control," threatening "the extermination of most of the world's species and massive social and economic disturbance." Similarly, fish farming, which Sagoff sees as the solution to the decline of oceanic fisheries, is fine for supplying salmon or shrimp to the rich. But those salmon and shrimp, at $7–$15 a pound, are far out of reach for poor people making less than $2,000 a year, who once depended on indigenous fisheries for the protein in their diets.

The claim that economic growth and prosperity are a cure for environmental degradation is arguable. It is based largely on the "Kuznets curves" observed in some forms of pollution. When the amount of pollution is plotted against per capita GNP, an inverted U curve is produced. As economic activity grows, pollution first increases. Then, presumably because an increased concern for environmental amenities appears when basic needs are satisfied, pollution control is implemented and pollution decreases. Prosperity thus saves the environment. Unfortunately, such Kuznets curves are of limited application. Economic growth has helped to mitigate some kinds of air and water pollution, but production of many of the most important pollutants, among them carbon dioxide, keeps right on rising with prosperity.

WHY WORRY ABOUT THE MUDDLED MIDDLE?

"Middle ground" pronouncements on the debate between cornucopians and the environmental scientists who understand the deteriorating state of our life-support systems are counterproductive in solving the human predicament. They obviously encourage those who wish to continue humanity's current trajectory, for whatever motives. For our part, until a systematic analysis shows the Nobel laureate economist James Meade to be wrong, we'll continue to agree with his assessment:

> Pollution and the exhaustion of natural resources depend and will depend in the future on the absolute level of total economic activity. This means that it is necessary to restrain both the rate of growth of population and, at least in the developed countries, the rate of growth of consumption per head.

Restraining the growth of consumption does not mean going back to living in caves and cooking over buffalo chip fires. For decades in the rich nations increased consumption has not been correlated with increased satisfaction, and perpetuating Third World poverty is a luxury that the prosperous can no longer afford. Greatly enhanced efficiency, reduced consumption among today's superconsumers, more-sensible choices of energy technologies, and a halt to population growth followed by a gradual decline might, as John Holdren and others have clearly shown, lead to a closing of the rich-poor gap without an ecological collapse. Over the next century, with careful planning, mutual trust, and cooperation, humanity could create a sustainable global society with a higher quality of life for everyone.

39

✍ Reply to My Critics ✍

MARK SAGOFF

In their reply to my essay "Do We Consume Too Much?" Paul Ehrlich and his co-authors ("No Middle Way on the Environment," December *Atlantic*) cite the economist James Meade's assessment that "pollution and the exhaustion of natural resources depend and will depend in the future on the absolute level of total economic activity" in the world. The principle that economic growth or prosperity must lead to resource depletion and ecological degradation, an article of faith for Ehrlich, is simply false. The evidence overwhelmingly shows that people in poor societies who hunt and gather for resources can denude the landscape, while wealthy nations can deploy technologies that produce food sustainably, control pollution, and preserve nature. The "World Scientists' Warning to Humanity," which my critics invoke, does not say that the world must produce and consume less overall, only that it must produce and consume differently. It declares, "We must, for example, move away from fossil fuels to more benign, inexhaustible energy sources to cut greenhouse gas emissions and the pollution of our air and water."

I did not argue, as my critics charge, that "concern over the depletion of natural resources and the impact of their current levels of use is misplaced." Rather, like the "World Scientists," I proposed that society should respond to this concern by adopting technologies now available or plainly in view that can sustain greater global economic activity without imperiling natural systems or depleting natural resources.

Ehrlich and his colleagues argue that a series of misconceptions underlies my thesis. First, they say, I fail to understand that since natural resources are finite, the expansion of the global economy must inevitably lead to depletion and scarcity. In their view, pollution and depletion vary directly with the absolute level of global economic activity. In other writings Ehrlich expresses this assumption in a formula that measures adverse environmental impact as a function of population, affluence, and technology. Because technology appears in the numerator of Ehrlich's equation, it can only increase the bad impacts of population and affluence. Yet smart and environment-friendly technology should appear in the denominator, since it diminishes these impacts. If the world adopts cleaner and smarter technologies, for example, more-efficient cars, it does not have to use more resources to produce more of the things people want. The enormous gains in economic activity associated with the software industry, to take another example, did not create a lot of pollution or exhaust resources.

My second "misconception" is to believe that aesthetic and moral arguments, such as those associated with the preservationist John Muir, provide the most persuasive reasons for protecting old-growth forests, wetlands, and endangered species. Of course, no one believes that we conserve raw materials, such as copper ore, for aesthetic reasons. I argued that many of nature's most beautiful and expressive objects—an ancient stand of redwoods, for instance, or a rare and magnificent species of bird—possess far greater intrinsic value than economic or instrumental value. We are more likely to protect these objects if we value them for their own sake rather than for the ways we use them.

Ehrlich and colleagues, while acknowledging aesthetic, religious, and moral concerns, believe that I misconceive how nature works. Referring to Biosphere 2—a failed attempt to replicate natural cycles artificially—these scientists point out how much better-designed are the "conditions and processes through which natural ecosystems, and the species that are a part of them, sustain and fulfill human life." Apparently my critics would rule out virtually everything human beings have done to feed, clothe, and shelter themselves—not just farming but even hunting and gathering—since any change may alter nature's delicate and unknown "conditions and processes" and therefore may rend its "intricate and little-explored" design. Ehrlich and colleagues analogize the extinction of a rare gopher, butterfly, or lousewort, no matter how little it affects surroundings, to "popping the rivets out of the airplane your children must fly in." They caution, "Until science can say which species are essential in the long term, we exterminate any at our peril." We need more than vague references to nature's equilibrious and beneficent design, however, to argue against particular proposals that make apparent economic sense—for example, to convert the habitat of an endangered beetle or badger to a university, day-care center, or hospital.

Third, Ehrlich and his co-authors call to my attention political and social obstacles a quick transition to efficient technologies and renewable resources. But like my critics, I deplored what my essay calls "lemon socialism." "A vast array of subsidies and barriers to trade," I wrote, "protects politically favored technologies, however inefficient, dangerous, filthy, or obsolete." I also quoted the environmental consultant Michael Brower: "At heart, the major obstacles standing in the way are not technical in nature, but concern the laws, regulations, incentives, public attitudes, and other factors that make up the energy market." Rather than overlooking such factors, my essay tried to show that it is precisely these obstacles—and not the purported existence of absolute limits to the earth's "carrying capacity"—that ought to be the focus of environmental policy.

Fourth, to refute my "misconception" that the North doesn't exploit the resources of the South, Ehrlich and colleagues note that "the rich-poor gap" is increasing. I wrote, "What is worsening is the discrepancy in income between the wealthy and the poor." The income gap between Silicon Valley billionaires and starving Hutu warriors, however, did not arise because one group exploited the natural resources of the other. I intended to refute the persistent idea that the world works on the colonial system in which rich countries import raw materials from poor ones and ship back finished goods. Today rich nations exclude and displace from world trade the commodities that poor countries offer for sale.

How does Ehrlich propose to rectify the "rich-poor" gap? He rules out "the hope that development can greatly increase the size of the economic pie and pull many more people out of poverty." This "basically ... humane idea," he has written, is "made insane by the constraints nature places on human activity." If the global economy has reached its limit—if nature shuts the door on economic growth—then any gain the poor make must come at the expense of the rich. In this zero-sum game we must lop off the peaks to fill in the valleys. It may be a hard political sell to get the rich countries to adopt the policy I favor, which is to transfer to poor countries efficient and nonpolluting technologies. It would be an even harder sell, however, to get the rich nations to divide their wealth equally with poorer ones.

40

⚘ *Consuming the Earth:* ⚘ *The Biophysics of Sustainability*

WILLIAM E. REES

William Rees is Professor and Director of the School of Community and Regional Planning at the University of British Columbia and co-author of Our Ecological Footprint.

PREMISE AND PURPOSE

The underlying premise of this paper is that much of economics is, or should be, human ecology (Rees and Wackernagel 1994). The economy is that set of activities and relationships by which human beings acquire, process, and distribute the material necessities and wants of life. It therefore includes that subset of activities by which humankind interacts with the rest of the ecosphere. If we were dealing with any other species, these relationships would indisputably fall within the realm of "ecology." To this extent then, economists are arguably human ecologists.

However, there is a problem. Ecologists study non-human species and the ecosystems that sustain them by measuring and analyzing the physical flows of energy, material, and information essential to the continuous restructuring and self-organization of those systems. By contrast, most economic analyses are money-based and totally ignore both physical reality and the behavioral dynamics of ecosystems. Economics as presently structured is therefore seriously flawed as (human) ecology. In the context of sustainability, its analytic blindness generates a false sense of societal well-being and leads to potentially disastrous economic prescriptions. To make matters worse, ecologists have themselves spent little effort on the study of humans. With neither discipline properly focused, it is little wonder that we still have such a poor understanding of the biophysical dimensions of the sustainability problem.

In this light, a major goal of ecological economics is to reconstruct economics on a firm foundation of theory governing physical relationships and material transformations in nature. Thus, the specific purpose of this paper is to illustrate the critical role of such biophysical analyses in assessing progress toward ecologically/economically sustainable development.

LINES OF CONVERGENCE AND DIVERGENCE

One thing that both economists and ecologists agree upon is that human beings are consumer organisms. In fact, in today's increasingly market-based society people are as likely to be called "consumers" as they are citizens, even when the context is a non-economic one. The designated role of people in the economy is to consume the goods and services produced by businesses, which are deemed to constitute the only other major component of the economy.

Ecologists would actually refer to humans as *macro*-consumers. In general, macro-consumers are large organisms, mainly animals, that depend on other organisms, either green plants or other animals, which they consume directly to satisfy their metabolic needs. However, a complete human ecology would also have to consider the consumption demands of our manufactured capital. Indeed, the major ecological difference between humans and other species is that in addition to our biological metabolism, the human enterprise is characterised by an industrial metabolism. All our toys and tools, factories and infrastructure, are "the exosomatic equivalent of organs" (Sterrer 1993) and, like bodily organs, require continuous flows of energy and material from and to "the environment" for their production, maintenance, and operation.

Economists and ecologists also both see humans as producers. We can only marvel at the enormous quantity of goods and services, both essential and frivolous, that advanced economies have spewed into a willing marketplace. However, there is a fundamental difference between production in nature and production in the economy. In nature, green plants are the factories. Using the simplest of low-grade inorganic chemicals (mainly water, carbon dioxide and a few mineral nutrients) and an extra-terrestrial source of relatively low-grade energy, light from the sun, plants assemble the high-grade fats, carbohydrates, proteins, and nucleic acids upon which most other life forms and the functioning of the ecosphere are dependent. Because they are essentially self-feeding and use only dispersed (high entropy) substances for their growth and maintenance, green plants are called *primary* producers.

By contrast, human beings and their economies are strictly *secondary* producers. The production and maintenance of our bodies and all the products of human factories require enormous inputs of high-grade energy and material resources from the rest of the ecosphere. That is, all production by the human enterprise, from the increase in population to the accumulation of manufactured capital, requires the consumption of a vastly larger quantity of available energy and material *first produced by nature* (typically at least ten times more). This last point is critical when we consider that people and their economies are part of nature. Indeed, humans have become the major consumer organism in virtually all the significant ecosystems types on earth - in structural terms, the expanding human enterprise is positioned to consume the ecosphere from within.

THE HIDDEN DIMENSIONS OF CONSUMPTION

Since the beginning of the industrial revolution, human populations have been growing, material standards have been rising, and increasingly sophisticated methods have been developed for resource extraction and "harvesting." Globally, ever greater quantities of energy and material are used for the manufacture and maintenance of productive capital and for the production of goods and services. On this basis, one might argue *a priori* that the rate of resource consumption by industrial economies will routinely exceed the rate of production by local ecosystems. In the absence of trade, such economies are fundamentally unsustainable.

Growing the Economy, Dissipating Nature

A recent study of human impacts on the carbon cycle in the Lower Fraser Basin of British Columbia, Canada, from the beginning of European settlement in the 1820s to 1990, provides ample support for this hypothesis (Boyle and Lavkulich 1997). The Lower Fraser Basin is in temperate rainforest zone of coastal western North America, one of the most productive terrestrial ecosystems on Earth. With an area of approximately 8300 km^2, the study region had a 1990 population of 1.7 million. Its early formal economy was based on furs and fish, evolving rapidly through timber and agriculture, to light manufacturing and, most recently, high-end services. The region has always been heavily engaged in trade. This economic progression has been marked by intense resource exploitation, steady population growth, and rising incomes. Indeed, the Lower Fraser basin is today one of the most economically privileged regions on the planet.

The expansion of the human economy has, however, been at the expense of the economy of nature. Boyle and Lavkulich (1997) found that the human "development" of the Lower Fraser has resulted in a net release of 231 million tonnes of biomass carbon into the atmosphere from exploited terrestrial ecosystems. Forty-three percent of the carbon has come from soils, 42 % from logged forests, and 14% from degraded wetlands. This is a carbon release rate of more than 130 tonnes per person increase in population, or an average of 278 tonnes per hectare. For comparison, extrapolating from Houghton and Skole (1990), we can estimate a net carbon loss from terrestrial habitats worldwide of 160 billion tonnes since 1800, during which time the human population increased by about 4.3 billion (to 1990). This is a carbon release rate of 37 tonnes per person increase or 11 tonnes per terrestrial hectare. Lower Fraser Basin carbon releases are therefore 3.6 times global releases per person increase since 1800, and more than 25 times the global contribution per hectare (Table 40–1).

These data highlight the physical dimensions of (industrial) economic reality that are completely hidden from conventional monetary analysis. We have already noted that

TABLE 40–1 Biomass Carbon Dissipated from Lower Fraser Basin Ecosystems Compared to Global Averages

	Total	Net Carbon Releases Since 1800			
		Releases per capita *increase in* population (tonnes)	Per hectare (tonnes)	Fraser Basin to global ratio	
				P.cap	Per ha
Lower Fraser Basin[1]	231 million tonnes	135	278	3.6	25
Worldwide[2]	160 billion tonnes	37	11		

[1] Source: Boyle, C. and L. Lavkulich. 1997 [11] Carbon Pool Dynamics in the Lower Fraser Basin from 1827 to 1990. *Environmental Management* 21:443–445.

[2] Houghton, R.A. and D.L. Skole. 1990. Carbon. In: *The Earth as Transformed by Human Action* (pp. 393–408). (L. B. Turner II, *et al.* eds.) Cambridge: Cambridge University Press.

secondary production necessarily consumes large quantities of high-grade energy and biomass. Only a small portion of this is converted to human population growth and the accumulation of manufactured capital. The rest is dissipated widely as low grade waste (e.g., carbon dioxide in the present example). Modern interpretations of the second law of thermodynamics suggest that such behaviour is an invariable characteristic of all highly-ordered complex systems. The economy can grow and maintain its internal structure in a dynamic non-equilibrium state only through the continuous dissipation of available energy/matter "imported" from its host environment. Thus, the material demands of our growth-addicted urban-industrial economies must inevitably exceed the fixed productive and waste assimilation capacities of regional ecosystems. The observed "dissipation" of carbon from the ecosystems of the Lower Fraser Basin symbolizes both the depletion of the region's natural capital stocks and the overtaxing of local waste sinks (at the expense of rising global CO_2 levels and potential climate change).

The Invisible Foot of the Economy

But the story does not end there. While Boyle and Lavkulich (1997) show that the rate of carbon release from the Lower Fraser has been declining since the 1930s, the regional population and economy are among the most rapidly growing in North America. These opposing trends are possible only because consumption in the region is now sustained largely by production outside its boundaries. A new tool I have developed with my students, ecological footprint analysis, shows that the average resident of the Lower Fraser currently appropriates through trade and natural flows the biophysical goods and services of about five hectares of productive land and water (adjusted from Rees and Wackernagel 1994, Rees 1996, Wackernagel and Rees 1996). Thus, the 472,000 residents of the City of Vancouver, sitting on just 11,400 hectares, actually use the ecological output of 2.3 million hectares. Similarly, the two million inhabitants (1997) of the basin as a whole require about 10 million hectares of productive ecosystem to support their consumer lifestyles. In short, the true but invisible "ecological footprint" of the region's population is 12 times the geographic area of its home territory (Table 40–2). Having overused or drawn down their own natural capital stocks, the people of the Lower Fraser are now nearly wholly dependent on temporary surpluses elsewhere.

CONCLUSIONS: THE ECONOMY AS PARASITE

Our technological prowess feeds the common belief that humans and their economies have become increasingly independent of nature. Indeed, the dollar contribution of the primary sector to many service- and knowledge-based economies is so small that economists now routinely omit land/resources from their production functions in accounting for economic growth. This presumed economy-environment decoupling is pure illusion sustained by abstract monetary models of economic process. The foregoing biophysical analysis shows that modern high income economies are actually becoming

TABLE 40–2 Ecological Footprints of Vancouver and the Lower Fraser Basin

Geographic Unit	Population	Land Area (ha)	Ecological Ftprnt (ha)	Overshoot Factor
Vancouver City	472,000	11,400	2,360,600	207
L. Fraser Basin	2,000,000	830,000	10,000,000	12

increasingly *indebted* to nature. Most are running massive unsustainable ecological deficits with the rest of the world (Rees 1996, Wackernagel and Rees 1996, Wackernagel *et al.* 1997). Technology and trade have merely obscured this relational truth by displacing the negative consequences of growth to distant ecosystems and the future. Rising productivity and incomes produce overweening confidence in human ingenuity while imposing ever-larger ecological footprints on the earth. The latter goes unnoticed by policy advisors and ordinary citizens alike.

Meanwhile, the trophic relationship of industrial economies to their host environments remains that of parasite to host—the former gains vitality at the expense of the vitality and regenerative capacity of the latter (see Peacock 1995, Rees 1998). Temporarily shielded from the negative consequences of material profligacy, high-income countries continue blindly to consume the earth while actively encouraging the developing world to adopt the same driving values and lifestyles. This virtually guarantees that the entropic degradation of the environment will be raised to the level of the ecosphere, eventually affecting everyone more or less simultaneously (as is happening with ozone depletion).

From this perspective, the prognosis for sustainability may seem bleak indeed. While the mainstream approach to sustainability requires a five to ten-fold expansion of world industrial activity, the present analysis shows that throughput growth on anything like this scale is physically impossible. One can hardly imagine more diametrically opposed positions on humanity's—and the ecosphere's—future prospects. However, a clear understanding of the sustainability problem is a prerequisite for any effective solution. To the extent that the biophysically-based ecological economics advocated here approximates reality better than prevailing expansionist models, it may help to break the stalemate. In any event, it shows that economists can never become true human ecologists until they embrace the need for integrated biophysical analyses.

LITERATURE CITED

Boyle, C. and L. Lavkulich, 1997. "Carbon Pool Dynamics in the Lower Fraser Basin from 1827 to 1990." *Environmental Management* 21:443–445.

Houghton, R.A. and D.L. Skole. 1990. "Carbon." In: *The Earth as Transformed by Human Action* (pp. 393–408).(L. B. Turner II, *et al.* eds.) Cambridge: Cambridge University Press.

Peacock, K. A. 1995. "Sustainability as Symbiosis." *Alternatives* 21:4:16–22.

Rees, W. 1996. "Revisiting Carrying Capacity: Area-based Indicators of Sustainability." *Population and Environment* 17:3:195–215.

Rees, W. E. and M. Wackernagel. 1994. "Ecological Footprints and Appropriated Carrying Capacity: Measuring the Natural Capital Requirements of the Human Economy." In *Investing in Natural Capital: The Ecological Economics Approach to Sustainability* (pp.362–390). (A-M. Jansson, M. Hammer, C. Folke, and R. Costanza, eds.) Washington: Island Press.

Rees, W.E. 1998. "How Should a Parasite Value its Host?" *Ecological Economics* 25: 49–52.

Sterrer, W. 1993. "Human Economics: A Non-human Perspective." *Ecological Economics* 7: 183–202.

Wackernagel, M. and W. E. Rees. 1996. *Our Ecological Footprint: Reducing the Human Impact on the Earth.* Gabriola Island, BC and Stony Creek, CT: New Society Publishers.

Wackernagel, M., et al. 1997. *Ecological Footprints of Nations.* Report to the Earth Council, Costa Rica.

INTERNET RESOURCES

International Society for Environmental Ethics Newsletter

An invaluable resource listing conferences, videos and films, articles, summaries of books and Ph.D. and Masters theses, and brief notes about current environmental issues. Subscriptions and information from Professor Laura Westra, Department of Philosophy, University of Windsor, Windsor, Ontario N9B 3P4 Canada:
<westra@uwindsor.ca>

Graduate Work in Environmental Philosophy

These sites are at the University of North Texas and are maintained by Environmental Philosophy, Inc. They have valuable links.
http:www.cep.unt.edu
http://www.cep.unt.edu/gradstudents/html

The Master Bibliography in Environmental Ethics

Compiled by Holmes Rolston III: <rolston@lamar.colostgate.edu> or
<http://www.cep.unt.edu/ISEE/html>

Natural Resources Information and Environmental networks

Fisheries: http://golgi.harvard.edu/biopages/biodiversity.html
http:www.actwin.com/wwwyl-Fish.html
Fish and Wildlife Information Exchange: http://www.fw.vt.edu/fishex/
EcoNet: http://www.econet.apc.org/econet
EcoWeb: http://ecosys.drdr.virginia.edu./EcoWeb.html
EnviroLink Network: http://envirolink.org/
Department of the Interior's Natural Resources Library, contains general collection and the law collection: http://www.ios.doi.gov/nrl/
U.S. Fish and Wildlife Service Home Page
http://www.fws.gov/
International information, including biodiversity, ecotourism climate change: Panos Institute (London): http://www.oneworld.org/panos/index.html
Biopolitics International Organization. A nonprofit, private organization founded in Athens in 1985, promoting a shift to biocentric values:
http://www.hol.gr/bio/web/html/biopolit.htm
Information on the conservation and sustainable use of the world's living resources:
http://www.wcmc.org.uk/

Environmental Organizations

Sierra Club: http://www.sierraclub.org
Natural Resources Defense Council: http://www.nrdc.org
Association of Forest Service Employees for Environmental Ethics:
http://www.afseee.org

Attfield, Robin. *The Ethics of Environmental Concern*. New York: Columbia University Press, 1983.

Birch, Charles, and John B. Cobb, Jr. *The Liberation of Life: From the Cell to the Community*. Cambridge: Cambridge University Press, 1981; 2d ed., Denton, Tex.: Environmental Ethics Books, 1990.

Blackstone, William T., ed. *Philosophy and Environmental Crisis*. Athens: University of Georgia Press, 1972.

Booth, Douglas. *Valuing Nature: The Decline and Preservation of Old Growth Forests*. Lanham, Md.: Rowman and Littlefield, 1993.

Bratton, Suan Power. *Six Billion & More: Human Population Regulation and Christian Ethics*. Louisville, Ky.: Westminster/John Knox Press, 1992.

Brennan, Andrew. *Thinking about Nature: An Investigation of Nature, Value and Ecology*. Athens: University of Georgia Press, 1989.

Callicott, J. Baird, ed. *Companion to the Sand Country Almanac*. Madison: University of Wisconsin Press, 1987.

Callicott, J. Baird. *In Defense of the Land Ethic*. Albany, N.Y.: SUNY Press, 1989.

Coleborn, Theo, Dianne Dumanoski, and John Myers. *Our Stolen Future*. New York: Dutton, 1996.

Davis, Donald Edward. *Ecophilosophy: A Field Guide to the Literature*. San Pedro, Calif.: R. and E. Miles, 1989.

DeGrazia, David. *Taking Animals Seriously*. New York: Cambridge University Press, 1996.

Devall, Bill, and George Sessions. *Deep Ecology: Living as if Nature Mattered*. Salt Lake City: Peregrine Smith Books, 1985.

Eskersley, Robyn. *Environmentalism and Political Theory: Toward an Ecocentric Approach*. Albany, N.Y.: SUNY Press, 1992.

Flader, Susan L. *Thinking Like A Mountain: Aldo Leopold and the Evolution of an Ecological Attitude Toward Deer, Wolves and Forests*. Lincoln: University of Nebraska Press, 1978.

Fox, Warwick. *Toward a Transpersonal Ecology: Developing New Foundations for Environmentalism*. Boston and London: Shambhala, 1990.

Gaard, Greta, ed. *Ecofeminism: Women, Animals, Nature*. Philadelphia: Temple University Press, 1993.

Goodpaster, K. E., and K. M. Sayre, eds. *Ethics and Problems of the 21st Century*. Notre Dame, Ind.: University of Notre Dame Press, 1979.

Hardin, Garrett. *Living Within Limits: Ecology, Economics, and Population Taboos*. New York: Oxford University Press, 1993.

Hargrove, Eugene C. *Foundations of Environmental Ethics*. Upper Saddle River, N.J.: Prentice Hall, 1989.

Hargrove, Eugene C., ed. *Beyond Spaceship Earth: Environmental Ethics and the Solar System*. San Francisco: Sierra Club Books, 1986.

Hargrove, Eugene C., ed. *Religion and Environmental Crisis*. Athens: University of Georgia Press, 1986.

Hargrove, Eugene C., ed. *The Animal Rights/Environmental Ethics Debate: The Environmental Perspective*. Albany, N.Y.: SUNY Press, 1993.

Johnston, Lawrence E. *A Morally Deep World: An Essay on Moral Significance and Environmental Ethics*. New York: Cambridge University Press, 1991.

Katz, Eric. *Nature as Subject*. Lanham, Md.: Rowman and Littlfield, 1997.

Leopold, Aldo. *A Sand County Almanac: With Essays on Conservation from Round River*. New York: Ballantine Books, 1970.

List, Peter. ed. *Radical Environmentalism*. Belmont, Calif.: Wadsworth Publishing Co. 1993.

Meine, Curt. *Aldo Leopold: His Life and Work*. Madison: University of Wisconsin Press, 1989.

Merchant, Carolyn. *Radical Ecology: The Search for a Liveable World*. London and New York: Routledge, 1993.

Midgley, Mary. *Animals and Why They Matter*. Athens: University of Georgia Press, 1983.

Naess, Arne. *Ecology, Community and Lifestyle: Outline of an Ecosophy*. New York: Cambridge University Press, 1989.

Nash, Roderick Frazier. *The Rights of Nature: A History of Environmental Ethics*. Madison: University of Wisconsin Press, 1989.

Norton, Bryan G. *Toward Unity Among Environmentalists*. New York: Oxford University Press, 1991.

Norton, Bryan G. *Why Preserve Natural Diversity?* Princeton, N.J.: Princeton University Press, 1988.

Norton, Bryan G., ed. *The Preservation of Species: The Value of Biological Diversity*. Princeton, N.J.: Princeton University Press, 1986.

Oelschlaeger, Max, ed. *After Earthday: Continuing the Conservation Effort*. Denton, Tex.: University of North Texas Press, 1992.

Oelschlaeger, Max, ed. *The Wilderness Condition: Essays on Wilderness and Civilization*. San Francisco: Sierra Club Books, 1992.

Oelschlaeger, Max. *The Idea of Wilderness from Prehistory to the Present*. New Haven, Conn.: Yale University Press, 1991.

Passmore, John. *Man's Responsibility for Nature: Ecological Problems and Western Traditions*. New York: Scribner's, 1974; 2d ed., London: Duckworth, 1980.

Pojman, Louis. *Global Environmental Ethics*. Mountain View, Calif.: Mayfield, 1999.

Ramakrishna, Kilaparti, and George M. Woodwell, eds. *World Forests for the Future*. New Haven, Conn.: Yale University Press, 1993.

Regan, Tom, and Peter Singer, eds. *Animal Rights and Human Obligations*. Upper Saddle River, N.J.: Prentice Hall, 1976; 2d ed., 1989.

Regan, Tom, ed. *Matters of Life and Death: New Introductory Essays in Moral Philosophy* 2nd ed. New York: Random House, 1980, 1986.

Regan, Tom. *Earthbound: New Introductory Essays in Environmental Ethics*. New York: Random House, 1984.

Regan, Tom. *The Case for Animal Rights*. Berkeley and Los Angeles: University of California Press, 1983.

Rolston, Holmes, III. *Environmental Ethics*. Philadelphia: Temple University Press, 1988.

Rolston, Holmes, III. *Philosophy Gone Wild: Essays in Environmental Ethics*. Buffalo, N.Y.: Prometheus Books, 1986.

Sagoff, Mark. *The Economy of the Earth: Philosophy, Law, and the Environment*. Cambridge: Cambridge University Press, 1988.

Shrader-Frechette, K. S. *Nuclear Power and Public Policy*. Dordrecht/Boston: D. Reidel, 1980.

Shrader-Frechette, Kristin S. *Burying Uncertainty: Risk and the Case Against Geological Disposal of Nuclear Waste*. Berkeley: University of California Press, 1993.

Singer, Peter. *Animal Liberation: A New Ethics for Our Treatment of Animals*. New York: Avon Books, 1992.

Stone, Christopher. *Earth and Other Ethics: The Case for Moral Pluralism*. New York: Harper and Row, 1987.

Stone, Christopher. *Should Trees Have Standing? Toward Legal Rights for Natural Objects*. Los Altos, Calif.: William Kaufmann, 1974.

Taylor, Paul W. *Respect for Nature: A Theory of Environmental Ethics*. Princeton, N.J.: Princeton University Press, 1986.

Tobias, Michael, ed. *Deep Ecology.* San Diego: Avant Books, 1985.

Torrance, John, ed. *The Concept of Nature*. New York: Oxford University Press, 1993.

VanDeVeer, Donald, and Christine Pierce, eds. *The Environmental Ethics and Policy Book*. Belmont, Calif.: Wadsworth, 1993.

Wenz, Peter. *Environmental Justice*. Albany, N.Y.: SUNY Press, 1988.

Western, David, and Mary Pearl, eds. *Conservation for the 21st Century*. New York: Oxford University Press, 1989.

Weston, Anthony. *Toward Better Problems: New Perspectives on Abortion, Animal Rights, the Environment, and Justice*. Philadelphia: Temple University Press, 1992.

Westra, Laura. *An Environmental Proposal for Ethics: The Principle of Integrity*. Lanham, Md.: Rowman and Littlefield, 1993.

Westra, Laura, and Peter Wenz, eds. *The Faces of Environmental Racism*. Lanham, Md.: Rowman and Littlefield, 1995

Westra, Laura. *Living with Integrity*. Lanham, Md.: Rowman and Littlefield, 1998

White, Rodney, R. *North, South, and the Environmental Crisis*. Toronto: University of Toronto Press, 1993.

Zimmerman, Michael et al., eds. *Environmental Philosophy*. Upper Saddle River, N.J.: Prentice Hall, 1993.